Compiler Construction Using
Java, JavaCC, and Yacc

Compiler Construction Using Java, JavaCC, and Yacc

ANTHONY J. DOS REIS

State University of New York at New Paltz

A JOHN WILEY & SONS, INC., PUBLICATION

Library of Congress Cataloging-in-Publication Data:

Dos Reis, Anthony J.
  Compiler construction using Java, JavaCC, and Yacc / Anthony J. Dos Reis.
    p. cm.
  ISBN 978-0-470-94959-7 (hardback)
  1. Compilers (Computer programs) 2. Java (Computer program language) I. Title.
  QA76.76.C65D67 2011
  005.4'53—dc23   2011013211

oBook ISBN: 978-1-118-11276-2
ePDF ISBN: 978-1-118-11287-8
ePub ISBN: 978-1-118-11277-9
eMobi ISBN: 978-1-118-11288-5

10 9 8 7 6 5 4 3 2 1

To little sister

CONTENTS

Preface   **xv**

Chapter 1   Strings, Languages, and Compilers   **1**

1.1   Introduction   1
1.2   Basic Language Concepts   1
1.3   Basic Compiler Concepts   3
1.4   Basic Set Theory   4
1.5   Null String   6
1.6   Concatenation   7
1.7   Exponent Notation   7
1.8   Star Operator   8
1.9   Concatenation of Sets of Strings   9
1.10   Plus Operator   11
1.11   Question Mark Operator   11
1.12   Shorthand Notation for a Set Containing a Single String   12
1.13   Operator Precedence   12
1.14   Regular Expressions   13
1.15   Limitations of Regular Expressions   15
       Problems   16

Chapter 2   Context-Free Grammars, Part 1   **19**

2.1   Introduction   19
2.2   What is a Context-Free Grammar?   20
2.3   Derivations Using a Context-Free Grammar   21
2.4   Language Defined by a Context-Free Grammar   23
2.5   Different Ways of Representing Contet-Free Grammars   25
2.6   Some Simple Grammars   26
2.7   Techniques for Generating Languages with Context-Free Grammars   29
2.8   Regular and Right Linear Grammars   35

2.9	Counting with Regular Grammars	37
2.0	Grammars for Lists	39
2.10	An Important Language that is Not Context Free	44
	Problems	45

Chapter 3   Context-Free Grammars, Part 2   **49**

3.1	Introduction	49
3.2	Parse Trees	49
3.3	Leftmost and Rightmost Derivations	51
3.4	Substitution	52
3.5	Ambiguous Grammars	54
3.6	Determining Nullable Nonterminals	59
3.7	Eliminating Lambda Productions	60
3.8	Eliminating Unit Productions	64
3.9	Eliminating Useless Nonterminals	66
3.10	Recursion Conversions	71
3.11	Adding the Null String to a Language	76
	Problems	77

Chapter 4   Context-Free Grammars, Part 3   **83**

4.1	Introduction	83
4.2	Grammars for Arithmetic Expressions	83
4.3	Specifying Associativity and Precedence in Grammars	90
4.4	Backus–Naur Form	92
4.5	Syntax Diagrams	94
4.6	Abstract Syntax Trees and Three-Address Code	96
4.7	Noncontracting Grammars	97
4.8	Essentially Noncontracting Grammars	97
4.9	Converting a Context-Free Grammar to an Essentially Noncontracting Grammar	98
4.10	Pumping Property of Context-Free Languages	101
	Problems	104

Chapter 5   Chomsky's Hierarchy   **107**

5.1	Introduction	107
5.2	Context-Sensitive Productions	107
5.3	Context-Sensitive Grammars	110
5.4	Unrestricted Grammars	111
	Problems	112

Chapter 6   Top-Down Parsing   **115**

6.1	Introduction	115
6.2	Top-Down Construction of a Parse Tree	115
6.3	Parses that Fail	117
6.4	A Bad Grammar for Top-Down Parsing	118
6.5	Deterministic Parsers	119
6.6	A Parser that Uses a Stack	120
6.7	Table Representation of a Stack Parser	124
6.8	Handling Productions with Nonleading Terminal	126

6.9   Writing a Stack Parser in Java   127
       Problems   134

Chapter 7   LL(1) Grammars   137

7.1   Introduction   137
7.2   FIRST Set of the Right Side of a Production   137
7.3   Determining Operation Sequences   140
7.4   Determining Selection Sets of Lambda Productions   142
7.5   Whatever-Follows-Left-Follows-Rightmost Rule   145
7.6   Selection Sets for Productions with Nullable Right Sides   147
7.7   Selection Sets Containing End-of-Input Symbol   149
7.8   A Stack Parser for a Grammar with Lambda Productions   152
7.9   Converting a Non-LL(1) Grammar to an LL(1) Grammar   153
7.10   Parsing with an Ambiguous Grammar   160
7.11   Computing FIRST and FOLLOW Sets   163
       Problems   165

Chapter 8   Table-Driven Stack Parser   171

8.1   Introduction   171
8.2   Unifying the Operations of a Stack Parser   172
8.3   Implementing a Table-Driven Stack Parser   175
8.4   Improving Our Table-Driven Stack Parser   180
8.5   Parsers that are Not Deterministic—A Digression on Theory   181
       Problems   183

Chapter 9   Recursive-Descent Parsing   185

9.1   Introduction   185
9.2   Simple Recursive-Descent Parser   185
9.3   Handling Lambda Productions   192
9.4   A Common Error   197
9.5   Java Code for Productions   198
9.6   Left Factoring in a Recursive-Descent Parser   199
9.7   Eliminating Tail Recursion   204
9.8   Translating the Star, Plus, and Question Mark Operators   108
9.9   Doing Things Backward   210
       Problems   211

Chapter 10   Recursive-Descent Translation   215

10.1   Introduction   215
10.2   A Simple Translation Grammar   215
10.3   Converting a Translation Grammar to Java Code   217
10.4   Specifications for a Translation Grammar   218
10.5   Passing Information During a Parse   231
10.6   L-Attributed Grammars   236
10.7   New Token Manager   238
10.8   Solving the Token Lookahead Problem   241
10.9   Code for the New Token Manager   241
10.10 Translation Grammar for Prefix Expression Compiler   253

10.11   An Interesting Use of Recursion   257
        Problems   261

Chapter 11   Assembly Language   **265**

11.1   Introduction   265
11.2   Structure of the J1 Computer   265
11.3   Machine Language Instructions   266
11.4   Assembly Language Instructions   268
11.5   Pushing Characters   269
11.6   aout Instruction   270
11.7   Using Labels   270
11.8   Using the Assembler   272
11.9   stav Instruction   275
11.10   Compiling an Assignment Statement   277
11.11   Compiling print and println   280
11.12   Outputting Strings   281
11.13   Inputting Decimal Numbers   283
11.14   Entry Directive   284
11.15   More Assembly Language   285
        Problems   285

Chapter 12   S1—A Simple Compiler   **289**

12.1   Introduction   289
12.2   The Source Language   289
12.3   Grammar for Source Language   290
12.4   The Target Language   291
12.5   Symbol Table   292
12.6   Code Generator   293
12.7   Token Class   293
12.8   Writing the Translation Grammar   294
12.9   Implementing the S1 Compiler   299
12.10   Trying Out S1   315
12.11   Advice on Extending the S1 Compiler   318
12.12   Specifications for S2   320
        Problems   324

Chapter 13   JavaCC   **331**

13.1   Introduction   331
13.2   JavaCC Extended Regular Expressions   333
13.3   JavaCC Input File   337
13.4   Specifying Actions for Regular Expressions   344
13.5   JavaCC Input File for S1j   348
13.6   Files Produced by JavaCC   355
13.7   Using the Star and Plus Operators   359
13.8   Choice Points and the Lookahead Directive   362
13.9   JavaCC's Choice Algorithm   367
13.10   Syntactic and Semantic Lookahead   371
13.11   Using JavaCC to Create a Token Manager Only   372
13.12   Using the Token Chain   373
13.13   Suppressing Warning Messages   377
        Problems   387

Chapter 14   Building on S2   **383**

14.1   Introduction   383
14.2   Extending `println` and `print`   383
14.3   Cascaded Assignment Statement   388
14.4   Unary Plus and Minus   313
14.5   `readint` Statement   393
14.6   Controlling the Token Trace from the Command Line   395
14.7   Specifications for S3   396
        Problems   396

Chapter 15   Compiling Control Structures   **399**

15.1   Introduction   399
15.2   `while` Statement   399
15.3   `if` Statement   403
15.4   `do-while` Statement   407
15.5   Range Checking of Numerical Constants   408
15.6   Handling Backslash-Quote in a String   410
15.7   Handling Backslash-Quote with JavaCC   411
15.8   Universal Blocks in JavaCC   416
15.9   Handling Strings that Span Lines   418
15.10   Handling Strings that Span Lines Using JavaCC   419
15.11   `SPECIAL_TOKEN` Block in JavaCC   422
15.12   Error Recovery   424
15.13   Error Recovery in JavaCC   429
15.14   Specifications for S4   430
        Problems   431

Chapter 16   Compiling Programs in Functional Form   **435**

16.1   Introduction   435
16.2   Separate Assembly and Linking   435
16.3   Calling and Returning from Fuctions   439
16.4   Source Language for S5   443
16.5   Symbol Table for S5   445
16.6   Code Generator for S5   446
16.7   Translation Grammar for S5   447
16.8   Linking with a Library   457
16.9   Specifications for S5   458
16.10   Extending S5   458
        Problems   461

Chapter 17   Finite Automata   **465**

17.1   Introduction   465
17.2   Deterministic Finite Automata   466
17.3   Converting a DFA to a Regular Expression   468
17.4   Java Code for a DFA   472
17.5   Nondeterministic Finite Automata   474
17.6   Using an NFA as an Algorithm   476
17.7   Converting an NFA to a DFA with the Subset Algorithm   478
17.8   Converting a DFA to a Regular Grammar   479
17.9   Converting a Regular Grammar to an NFA   482

17.10 Converting a Regular Expression to an NFA   484
17.11 Finding the Minimal DFA   488
17.12 Pumping Property of Regular Languages   493
        Problems   495

Chapter 18   Capstone Project: Implementing Grep Using Compiler   **499**
                Technology

18.1   Introduction   499
18.2   Regular Expressions for Our Grep Program   501
18.3   Token Manager for Regular Expression   501
18.4   Grammar for Regular Expressions   503
18.5   Target Language for Our Regular Expression Compiler   503
18.6   Using an NFA for Pattern Matching   508
        Problems   513

Chapter 19   Compiling to a Register-Oriented Architecture   **515**

19.1   Introduction   515
19.2   Using the Register Instruction Set   516
19.3   Modifications to the Symbol Table for R1   517
19.4   Parser and Code Generator for R1   518
        Problems   526

Chapter 20   Optimization   **529**

20.1   Introduction   529
20.2   Using the `ldc` Instruction   531
20.3   Reusing Temporary Variables   532
20.4   Constant Folding   535
20.5   Register Allocation   537
20.6   Peephole Optimization   540
        Problems   543

Chapter 21   Interpreters   **547**

21.1   Introduction   547
21.2   Converting S1 to I1   549
21.3   Interpreting Statements that Transfer Control   552
21.4   Implementing the Compiler-Interpreter CI1   553
21.5   Advantages of Interpreters   558
        Problems   559

Chapter 22   Bottom-Up Parsing   **561**

22.1   Introduction   561
22.2   Principles of Bottom-Up Parsing   561
22.3   Parsing with Right- versus Left-Recursive Grammars   565
22.4   Bottom-Up Parsing with an Ambiguous Grammar   566
22.5   Do-Not-Reduce Rule   569
22.6   SLR(1) Parsing   570
22.7   Shift/Reduce Conflicts   577
22.8   Reduce/Reduce Conflicts   579
22.9   LR(1) Parsing   579
        Problems   584

Chapter 23   yacc   **587**

23.1   Introduction   587
23.2   yacc Input and Output Files   587
23.3   A Simple yacc-Generated Parser   588
23.4   Passing Values Using the Value Stack   596
23.5   Using yacc With an Ambiguous Grammar   602
23.6   Passing Values down the Parse Tree   604
23.7   Implementing S1y   606
23.8   jflex   612
          Problems   618

Appendix A   Stack Instruction Set   **621**

Appendix B   Register Instruction Set   **625**

References   **629**

Index   **631**

PREFACE

My principal goal in writing this book is to provide the reader with a clear exposition of the theory of compiler design and implementation along with plenty of opportunities to put that theory into practice. The theory, of course, is essential, but so is the practice.

NOTABLE FEATURES

- Provides numerous, well-defined projects along with test cases. These projects ensure that students not only know the theory but also know how to apply it. Instructors are relieved of the burden of designing projects that integrate well with the text.

- Project work starts early in the book so that students can apply the theory as they are learning it.

- The compiler tools (JavaCC, Yacc, and Lex) are optional topics.

- The entire book is Java oriented. The implementation language is Java. The principal target language is similar to Java's bytecode. The compiler tools generate Java code. The form of attributed grammar used has a Java-like syntax.

- The target languages (one is stack oriented like Java's bytecode; the other is register oriented) are very easy to learn but are sufficiently powerful to support advanced compiler projects.

- The software package is a dream come true for both students and instructors. It automatically evaluates a student's compiler projects with respect to correctness, run time, and size. It is great for students: they get immediate feedback on their projects. It is great for instructors: they can easily and accurately evaluate a student's work. With a single command, an instructor can generate a report for an entire class. The software runs on three platforms: Microsoft Windows, Linux, and the Macintosh OS X.

- Demonstrates how compiler technology is not just for compilers. In a capstone project, students design and implement grep using compiler technology.

- Includes a chapter on interpreters that fits in with the rest of the book.

- Includes a chapter on optimization that is just right for an introductory course. Students do not simply read about optimization techniques—they implement a variety of techniques, such as constant folding, peephole optimization, and register allocation.

- The book uses a Java-like form of grammars that students can easily understand and use. This is the same form that JavaCC uses. Thus, students can make transition to JavaCC quickly and easily.

- Provides enough theory that the book can be used for a combined compiler/automata/formal languages course. The book covers most of the topics covered in an automata/formal languages course: finite automata, stack parsers, regular expressions, regular grammars, context-free grammars, context-sensitive grammars, unrestricted grammars, Chomsky's hierarchy, and the pumping lemmas. Pushdown automata, Turing machines, computability, and complexity are discussed in supplements in the software package. The software package also includes a pushdown automaton simulator and Turing machine simulator.

- Covers every topic that should be in a first course or in an only course on compilers. Students will learn not only the theory and practice of compiler design but also important system concepts.

SOFTWARE PACKAGE

The software package for the textbook has some unusual features. When students run one of their compiler-generated programs, the software produces a log file. The log file contains a time stamp, the student's name, the output produced by the compiler-generated program, and an evaluation of the compiler-generated program with respect to correctness, program size, and execution time. If the output is not correct (indicating that the student's compiler is generating incorrect code), the log file is marked with NOT CORRECT. If the compiled program is too big or the execution time too long, the log file is marked with OVER LIMIT.

The name of a log file contains the student's name. For example, the log file for the S3 project of a student whose last name is Dos Reis would be S3.dosreis.log. Because each log file name is unique, an instructor can store all the log files for a class in a single directory. A single command will then produce a report for the entire class.

The software supports two instruction sets: the stack instruction set and the register instruction set. The stack instruction set is the default instruction set. To use the register instruction set, a single directive is placed in the assembly language source program. The software then automatically reconfigures itself to use the register instruction set.

The three principal programs in the software package are **a** (the assembler/linker), **e** (the executor), and **l** (the library maker). The software package also includes **p** (a pushdown automaton simulator) and **t** (a Turing machine simulator).

The software package for this book is available from the publisher. The compiler tools are available on the Web. At the time of this writing, JavaCC is at http://java.net/downloads/javacc, Byacc/j is at http://byaccj.sourceforge.net/, and Jflex is at http://jflex.de/.

PROJECTS

This textbook specifies many well-defined projects. The source language has six levels of increasing complexity. A student can write a compiler for each level that translates to the stack instruction set. A student can also write a compiler for each level that translates to the register instruction set, or incorporates optimization techniques. For each level, a student can write a pure interpreter or an interpreter that uses an intermediate code. A student can implement several variations of grep using compiler technology. A student can write the code for any of these projects by hand or by using JavaCC or Yacc. Many of the chapter problems provide additional projects. In short, there are plenty of projects.

For each project, the textbook provides substantial support. Moreover, many of the projects are incremental enhancements of a previous project. This incremental approach works well; each project is challenging but not so challenging that students cannot do it.

Most projects can be completed in a week's time. Thus, students should be able to do ten or even more projects in a single semester.

USEFUL REFERENCES

For background material, the reader is referred to the author's *An Introductions to Programming Using Java* (Jones & Bartlett, 2010) and *Assembly Language and Computer Architecture Using C++ and Java* (Course Technology, 2004). Also recommended is JFLAP (available at http://www.jflap.org), an interactive program that permits experimentation with various types of automata and grammars.

ACKNOWLEDGMENTS

I would like to thank Professors Robert McNaughton and Dean Arden who years ago at RPI taught me the beauty of formal language theory, my students who used preliminary versions of the book and provided valuable feedback, Katherine Guillemette for her support of this project, my daughter Laura for her suggestions on the content and structure of the book, and my wife for her encouragement.

ANTHONY J. DOS REIS

New Paltz, New York
October 2011

1

STRINGS, LANGUAGES, AND COMPILERS

1.1 INTRODUCTION

Compiler construction is truly an engineering science. With this science, we can methodically—almost routinely—design and implement fast, reliable, and powerful compilers.

You should study compiler construction for several reasons:

- Compiler construction techniques have very broad applicability. The usefulness of these techniques is not limited to compilers.
- To program most effectively, you need to understand the compiling process.
- Language and language translation are at the very heart of computing. You should be familiar with their theory and practice.
- Unlike some areas of computer science, you do not typically pick up compiler construction techniques "on the job." Thus, the formal study of these techniques is essential.

To be fair, you should also consider reasons for *not* studying compiler construction. Only one comes to mind: Your doctor has ordered you to avoid excitement.

1.2 BASIC LANGUAGE CONCEPTS

In our study of compiler design theory, we begin with several important definitions. An *alphabet* is the finite set of characters used in the writing of a language. For example, the alphabet of the Java programming language consists of all the characters that can appear in a program: the upper- and lower-case letters, the digits, whitespace (space, tab, newline, and carriage return), and all the special symbols, such as =, +, and {. For most of the examples in this book, we will use very small alphabets, such as {b, c} and {b, c, d}. We will avoid using the letter "a" in our alphabets because of the potential confusion with the English article "a".

A *string over an alphabet* is a finite sequence of characters selected from that alphabet. For example, suppose our alphabet is {b, c, d}. Then

```
cbd
cbcc
c
```

are examples of strings over our alphabet. Notice that in a string over an alphabet, each character in the alphabet can appear any number of times (including zero times) and in any order. For example, in the string cbcc (a string over the three-letter alphabet {b, c, d}), the character b appears once, c appears three times, and d does not appear.

The *length of a string* is the number of characters the string contains. We will enclose a string with vertical bars to designate its length. For example, |cbcc| designates the length of the string cbcc. Thus, |cbcc| = 4.

A *language* is a set of strings over some alphabet. For example, the set containing just the three strings cbd, cbcc, and c is a language. This set is not a very interesting language, but it is, nevertheless, a language according to our definition.

Let us see how our definitions apply to a "real" language—the programming language Java. Consider a Java program all written on a single line:

```
class C { public static void main(String[] args) {} }
```

Clearly, such a program is a single string over the alphabet of Java. We can also view a multiple-line program as a single string—namely, the string that is formed by connecting successive lines with a line separator, such as a newline character or a carriage return/newline sequence. Indeed, a multiline program stored in a computer file is represented by just such a string. Thus, the multiple-line program

```
class C
{
  public static void main(String[] args)
  {
  }
}
```

is the single string

```
class C□{ □  public static void main(String[] args)□  {□  }□}
```

where □ represents the line separator. The *Java language* is the set of all strings over the Java alphabet that are valid Java programs.

A language can be either finite or infinite and may or may not have a meaning associated with each string. The Java language is infinite and has a meaning associated with each string. The meaning of each string in the Java language is what it tells the computer to do. In contrast, the language {cbd, cbcc, c} is finite and has no meaning associated with each string. Nevertheless, we still consider it a language. A language is simply a set, finite or infinite, of strings, each of which may or may not have an associated meaning.

Syntax rules are rules that define the form of the language, that is, they specify which strings are in a language. *Semantic rules* are rules that associate a meaning to each string in a language, and are optional under our definition of language.

Occasionally, we will want to represent a string with a single symbol very much like x is used to represent a number in algebra. For this purpose, we will use the small letters at the end of the English alphabet. For example, we might use x to represent the string cbd and y to represent the string cbcc.

1.3 BASIC COMPILER CONCEPTS

A *compiler* is a translator. It typically translates a program (the *source program*) written in one language to an equivalent program (the *target program*) written in another language (see Figure 1.1). We call the languages in which the source and target programs are written the *source* and *target languages*, respectively.

Typically, the source language is a high-level language in which humans can program comfortably (such as Java or C++), whereas the target language is the language the computer hardware can directly handle (*machine language*) or a symbolic form of it (*assembly language*).

If the source program violates a syntax rule of the source language, we say it has a *syntax error*. For example, the following Java method has one syntax error (a right brace instead of a left brace on the second line):

```
public void greetings()
}                                    // syntax error
   System.out.println("hello");
}
```

A *logic error* is an error that does not violate a syntax rule but results in the computer performing incorrectly when we run the program. For example, suppose we write the following Java method to compute and return the sum of 2 and 3:

```
public int sum()
{
   return 2 + 30;     // logic error
}
```

This method is a valid Java method but it tells the computer to do the wrong thing—to compute 2 + 30 instead 2 + 3. Thus, the error here is a logic error.

A compiler in its simplest form consists of three parts: the token manager, the parser, and the code generator (see Fig. 1.2).

The source program that the compiler inputs is a stream of characters. The *token manager* breaks up this stream into meaningful units, called *tokens*. For example, if a token manager reads

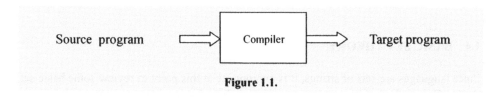

Figure 1.1.

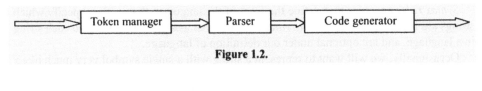

Figure 1.2.

```
int x;          // important example
x = 55;
```

it would output the following sequence of tokens:

```
int
x
;
x
=
55
;
```

The token manager does not produce tokens for white space (i.e., space, tab, newline, and carriage return) and comments because the parser does need these components of the source program. A token manager is sometimes called a *lexical analyzer, lexer, scanner,* or *tokenizer.*

A *parser* in its simplest form has three functions:

1. It analyzes the structure of the token sequence produced by the token manager. If it detects a syntax error, it takes the appropriate action (such as generating an error message and terminating the compile).
2. It derives and accumulates information from the token sequence that will be needed by the code generator.
3. It invokes the code generator, passing it the information it has accumulated.

The *code generator,* the last module of a compiler, outputs the target program based on the information provided by the parser.

In the compilers we will build, the parser acts as the controller. As it executes, it calls the token manager whenever it needs a token, and it calls the code generator at various points during the parse, passing the code generator the information the code generator needs. Thus, the three parts of the compiler operate concurrently. An alternate approach is to organize the compiling process into a sequence of *passes.* Each pass reads an input file and creates an output file that becomes the input file for the next pass. For example, we can organize our simple compiler into three passes. In the first pass, the token manager reads the source program and creates a file containing the tokens corresponding to the source program. In the second pass, the parser reads the file of tokens and outputs a file containing information required by the code generator. In the third pass, the code generator reads this file and outputs a file containing the target program.

1.4 BASIC SET THEORY

Since languages are sets of strings, it is appropriate at this point to review some basic set theory. One method of representing a set is simply to list its elements in any order. Typically, we use the left and right braces, "{" and "}", to delimit the beginning and end, respectively, of the list of elements. For example, we represent the set consisting of the integers 3 and 421 with

$\{3, 421\}$ or $\{421, 3\}$

Similarly, we represent the set consisting of the two strings b and bc with

{b, bc} or { bc, b}

This approach cannot work for an infinite set because it is, of course, impossible to list all the elements of an infinite set. If, however, the elements of an infinite set follow some obvious pattern, we can represent the set by listing just the first few elements, followed by the ellipsis (. . .). For example, the set

{b, bb, bbb, . . .}

represents the infinite set of strings containing one or more b's and no other characters. Representing infinite sets this way, however, is somewhat imprecise because it requires the reader to figure out the pattern represented by the first few elements.

Another method for representing a set—one that works for both finite and infinite sets—is to give a rule for determining its elements. In this method, a set definition has the form

$\{E : defining\ rule\}$

where E is an expression containing one or more variables, and the defining rule generally specifies the allowable ranges of the variables in E. The colon means "such that." We call this representation the *set-builder notation*. For example, we can represent the set containing the integers 1 to 100 with

$\{x : x$ is an integer and $1 \leq x \leq 100\}$

Read this definition as "the set of all x such that x is an integer and x is greater than or equal to 1 and less than or equal to 100." A slightly more complicated example is

$\{n^2 : n$ is an integer and $n \geq 1\}$

Notice that the expression preceding the colon is not a single variable as in the preceding example. The defining rule indicates that n can be 1, 2, 3, 4, and so on. The corresponding values of n^2 are the elements of the set—namely, 1, 4, 9, 16, etc. Thus, this is the infinite set of integer squares:

$\{1, 4, 9, 16, . . .\}$

In set notation, the mathematical symbol $\in$ means "is an element of." A superimposed slash on a symbol negates the condition represented. Thus, $\notin$ means "is not a element of." For example, if $P = \{2, 3, 4\}$, then $3 \in P$, but $5 \notin P$.

The *empty set* [denoted by either {} or ϕ] is the set that contains no elements. The *universal set* (denoted by U) is the set of all elements under consideration. For example, if we are working with sets of integers, then the set of all integers is our universe. If we are working with strings over the alphabet {b, c}, then the set of all strings over {b, c} is our universe.

The set operations *union, intersection,* and *complement,* form new sets from given sets. The union operator is most often denoted by the special symbol ∪. We, however, use the vertical bar | to denote the union operator. The advantage of | is that it is available on standard keyboards. We will use ∩ and ~ to denote the intersection and complement operators, respectively. ∩, the standard symbol for set intersection, unfortunately is not available on keyboards. However, we will use set intersection so infrequently that it will not be necessary to substitute a keyboard character for ∩.

Set union, intersection, and complement are defined as follows:

Union of P and Q: $P \mid Q = \{x : x \in P \text{ or } x \in Q\}$
Intersection of P and Q: $P \cap Q = \{x : x \in P \text{ and } x \in Q\}$
Complement of P: $\sim P = \{x : x \in U \text{ and } x \notin P\}$

Here are the definitions in words of these operators:

$P \mid Q$ is the set of all elements that are in either P or Q or both.

$P \cap Q$ is the set of elements that are in both P and Q.

$\sim P$ is the set of all elements in the universe U that are not in P.

For example, if $P = \{b, bb\}$, $Q = \{bb, bbb\}$, and our universe $U = \{b, bb, bbb, \ldots\}$, then

$P \mid Q$ $= \{b, bb, bbb\}$
$P \cap Q$ $= \{bb\}$
$\sim P$ $= \{bbb, bbbb, bbbbb, \ldots\}$
$\sim Q$ $= \{b, bbbb, bbbbb, \ldots\}$

A collection of sets is *disjoint* if the intersection of every pair of sets from the collection is the empty set (i.e., they have no elements in common). For example, the sets {b}, {bb, bbb}, and {bbbb} are disjoint since no two have any elements in common.

The set P is a subset of Q (denoted $P \subseteq Q$) if every element of P is also in Q. The set P is a proper subset of the set Q (denoted $P \subset Q$) if P is a subset of Q, and Q has at least one element not in P. For example, if $P = \{b, bb\}$, $Q = \{b, bb, bbb\}$, and $R = \{b, bb\}$, then P is proper subset of Q, but P is not a proper subset of R. However, P is a subset of R. Two sets are equal if each is the subset of the other. With P and R given as above, $P \subseteq R$ and $R \subseteq P$. So we can conclude that $P = R$. Note that the empty set is a subset of any set; that is, $\{\} \subseteq S$ for any set S.

We can apply the set operations union, intersection, and complement to any sets. We will soon see some additional set operations specifically for sets of strings.

1.5 NULL STRING

When prehistoric humans started using numbers, they used the natural numbers 1, 2, 3, ... It was easy to grasp the idea of oneness, twoness, threeness, and so on. Therefore, it was natural to have symbols designating these concepts. In contrast, the number 0 is hardly a natural concept. After all, how could something (the symbol 0) designate nothing? Today, of course, we are all quite comfortable with the number 0 and put it to good use every day. A similar situation applies to strings. It is natural to think of a string as a sequence of one or more characters. But, just as the concept zero is useful to arithmetic, so is the concept of a *null string*—the string whose length is zero—useful to language theory. The null string is the string that does not contain any characters.

How do we designate the null string? Normally, we designate strings by writing them down on a piece of paper. For example, to designate a string consisting of the first three small letters of the English alphabet, we write abc. A null string, however, does not have any characters, so there is nothing to write down. We need some symbol, preferably one that does not appear in the alphabets we use, to represent the null string. Some writers of compiler books use the Greek letter ϵ for the null string. However, since ϵ is easily confused with the symbol for set membership, we will use the small Greek letter λ (lambda) to represent the null string.

One common misconception about the null string is that a string consisting of a single space is the null string. A space is a character whose length is one; the null string has length zero. They are not the same. Another misconception has to do with the empty set. The null string is a string. Thus, the set $\{\lambda\}$ contains exactly one string—namely the null string. The empty set $\{\}$, on the other hand, does not contain any string.

1.6 CONCATENATION

We call the operation of taking one string and placing it next to another string in the order given to form a new string *concatenation*. For example, if we concatenate bcd and efg, we get the string bcdefg. Note that the concatenation of any string x with the null string λ yields x. That is,

$$x\lambda = \lambda x = x$$

1.7 EXPONENT NOTATION

A nonnegative exponent applied to a character or a sequence of characters in a string specifies the replication of that character or sequence of characters. For example b^4 is a shorthand representation of bbbb. We use parentheses if the scope of the replication is more than one character. Hence, $b(cd)^2e$ represents bcdcde. A string replicated zero times is by definition the null string; that is, for any string x, $x^0 = \lambda$.

We can use exponent notation along with set-builder notation to define sets of strings. For example, the set

$$\{b^i : 1 \leq i \leq 3\}$$

is the set

$$\{b^1, b^2, b^3\} = \{b, bb, bbb\}$$

The exponent in exponent notation can never be less than zero. If we do not specify its lower bound in a set definition, assume it is zero. For example, the set

$$\{b^i : i \leq 3\}$$

should be interpreted as

$$\{b^i : 0 \le i \le 3\} = \{b^0, b^1, b^2, b^3\} = \{\lambda, b, bb, bbb\}$$

Exercise 1.1

Describe in English the language defined by $\{b^i c^{2i} : i \ge 0\}$.

Answer:

The set of all strings consisting of b's followed by c's in which the number of c's is twice the number of b's. This set is $\{\lambda, bcc, bbcccc, bbbcccccc, \ldots\}$. ∎

1.8 STAR OPERATOR (ALSO KNOWN AS THE ZERO-OR-MORE OPERATOR)

We have just seen that an exponent following a character represents a single string (for example, b^3 represents bbb). In contrast, the star operator, *, following a character (for example, b*) represents a set of strings. The set contains every possible replication (including zero replications) of the starred character. For example,

$$b^* = \{b^0, b^1, b^2, b^3, \ldots\} = \{b^n : n \ge 0\} = \{\lambda, b, bb, bbb, \ldots\}$$

Think of the star operator as meaning "zero or more."

The star operator always applies to the item immediately preceding it. If a parenthesized expression precedes the star operator, then the star applies to whatever is inside the parentheses. For example, in (bcd)*, the parentheses indicate that the star operation applies to the entire string bcd. That is,

$$(bcd)^* = \{\lambda, bcd, bcdbcd, bcdbcdbcd, \ldots \}$$

The star operator can also be applied to sets of strings. If A is a set of strings, then A^* is the set of strings that can be formed from the strings of A using concatenation, allowing any string in A to be replicated any number of times (including zero times) and used in any order. By definition, the null string is always in A^*.

Here are several examples of starred sets:

$$\{b\}^* = \{\lambda, b, bb, bbb, \ldots\} = b^*$$
$$\{b, c\}^* = \{\lambda, b, c, bb, bc, cb, cc, bbb, \ldots\}$$
$$\{\lambda\}^* = \{\lambda\}$$
$$\{\}^* = \{\lambda\}$$
$$\{bb, cc\}^* = \{\lambda, bb, cc, bbbb, bbcc, ccbb, cccc, \ldots\}$$
$$\{b, cc\}^* = \{\lambda, b, bb, cc, bbb, bcc, ccb, bbbb \ldots\}$$

Notice that $\{b\}^* = b^*$. That is, starring a set that contains just one string yields the same set as starring just that string.

Here is how to determine if a given string is in A^*, where A is an arbitrary set of strings: If the given string is the null string, then it is in A^* by definition. If the given string is nonnull, and it can be divided into substrings such that each substring is in A, then the given string is in $A*$. Otherwise, the string is not in $A*$. For example, suppose $A = \{b, cc\}$. We can divide the string bccbb into four parts: b, cc, b, and b, each of which is in A. Therefore, bccbb $\in A*$. On the other hand, for the string bccc the required subdivision is impossible. If we divide bccc into b, cc, and c, the first two strings are in A but the last is not. All other subdivisions of bccc similarly fail. Therefore, bccc $\notin A*$.

We call the set that results from the application of the star operator to a string or set of strings the *Kleene closure,* in honor of Stephen C. Kleene, a pioneer in theoretical computer science.

Let us now use the star operator to restate two important definitions that we gave earlier. Let the capital Greek letter Σ (sigma) represent an arbitrary alphabet. A *string over the alphabet* Σ is any string in $\Sigma*$. For example, suppose $\Sigma = \{b, c\}$. Then

$$\Sigma* = \{\lambda, b, c, bb, bc, cb, cc, bbb, \ldots\}$$

Thus, λ, b, c, bb, bc, cb, cc, bbb,. . . are strings over Σ. It may appear strange to view λ as a string over the alphabet $\Sigma = \{b, c\}$. Actually, this view is quite reasonable since λ has no characters *not* in $\{b, c\}$. λ is always a string over Σ regardless of the content of Σ because, by definition, λ is always in $\Sigma*$. A *language over the alphabet* Σ is any subset of $\Sigma*$. For example $\{\lambda\}$, $\{b\}$, and $\{b, cc\}$ are each languages over $\Sigma = \{b, c\}$. Even the empty set is a language over Σ because it is a subset of $\Sigma*$.

Exercise 1.2

a) List all the strings of length 3 in $\{b, cc\}*$.

b) Is ccbcc $\in \{b, cc\}*$?

Answer:

a) bbb, bcc, ccb.

b) Yes. To confirm this, subdivide ccbcc into cc, b, and cc, all of which are elements of (b, cc).

1.9 CONCATENATION OF SETS OF STRINGS

Concatenation can be applied to sets of strings as well as individual strings. If we let A and B be two sets of strings, then AB, the *concatenation of the sets A and B,* is

$$\{xy : x \in A \text{ and } y \in B\}$$

That is, AB is the set of all strings that can be formed by concatenating a string A with a string B. For example, if $A = \{b, cc\}$ and $B = \{d, dd\}$, then

$AB = \{bd, bdd, ccd, ccdd\}$
$BA = \{db, dcc, ddb, ddcc\}$

As an example of concatenation, consider the set b*c*, the concatenation of the sets b* and c*. Each string in b*c* consists of some string from b* concatenated to some string in c*. That is, each string consists of zero or more b's followed by zero or more c's. The number of b's does not have to equal the number of c's, but all b's must precede all c's. Thus, b*c* = {λ, b, c, bb, bc, cc, bbb, bbc, bcc, ccc, ...}. In exponent notation, b*c* = {$b^i c^j : i \geq 0$ and $j \geq 0$}.

A string can also be concatenated with a set. If x is a string and A is a set of strings, then xA, the concatenation of x with A is

$$\{xy : y \in A\}$$

Similarly, Ax is

$$\{yx : y \in A\}$$

For example, bbc*, the concatenation of the string bb and the set c*, is the set of all strings consisting of bb followed by a string in c*. Thus,

$$bbc^* = \{bb\lambda = bb, bbc, bbcc, bbccc, ...\}$$

Notice that it follows from our definitions that $xA = \{x\}A$, where x is an arbitrary string and A is a set of strings. That is, we get the same result whether we concatenate x (the string) or $\{x\}$ (the set containing just x) to a set A.

Exercise 1.3

a) List all strings in b*cb* of length less than 3.
b) Write an expression using the star operator which defines the same set as {$b^p c^q d^r : p \geq 0, q \geq 1, r \geq 2$}.

Answer:

a) c, bc, cb.
b) b*cc*ddd*.

■

The union operator implies a choice with respect to the makeup of the strings in the language specified. For example, we can interpret

$$\{b\} (\{c\} \mid \{d\})$$

as the set of strings consisting of a b followed by a choice of c or d. That is, the set consists of the strings bc and bd.

Exercise 1.4

Describe in English the set defined by b*({c} | {d})e*.

Answer:

The set of all strings consisting of zero or more b's, followed by either c or d, followed by zero or more e's.

■

1.10   PLUS OPERATOR (ALSO KNOWN AS THE ONE-OR-MORE OPERATOR)

The *plus operator* is like the star operator, except that the former means "one or more" instead of "zero or more." We can apply it either to an individual string or a set of strings. It appears as a + following the item to which it applies. For example,

$$b+ \quad = \{b^1, b^2, b^3, \ldots\} = \{b^i : i \geq 1\}$$
$$\{b, c\}+ = \{b, c, bb, bc, cb, cc, bbb, \ldots\}$$

$A+$, where A is a set of strings, contains the null string only if the set A itself contains the null string. $A*$, on the other hand, always contains the null string for any set A.

Consider the set bb*. Each string in bb* consists of a single b followed a string in b*. Because the shortest string in b* is λ, the shortest string in bb* is bλ = b. Thus, every string in bb* contains one or more b's. That is, bb* = b+. In general, for a string x and a set of strings A,

$$xx* = x*x = x+$$

and

$$AA* = A*A = A+$$

We call the set that results from the application of the plus operator to a string or a set of strings the *positive closure*.

Exercise 1.5

Show that $\{\lambda\} \mid b+ = b*$.

Answer:

$$\{\lambda\} \mid b+ = \{\lambda\} \mid \{b, bb, bbb, \ldots\} = \{\lambda, b, bb, bbb, \ldots\} = b*.$$

∎

1.11   QUESTION MARK OPERATOR (ALSO KNOWN AS ZERO-OR-ONE OPERATOR)

The question mark operator specifies an optional item. We can apply it to either an individual string or a set of strings. It appears as a ? following the item to which it applies. For example, bc? specifies a b followed by an optional c—that is, a b followed by zero or one c. Thus bc? is the set $\{b, bc\}$. Think of c? as representing the set $\{\lambda\} \mid \{c\} = \{\lambda, c\}$. Thus, bc? = b$\{\lambda, c\}$ = $\{b, bc\}$.

If A is a set of strings, then bA? specifies a b optionally followed by any single string in A, which is the set $\{b\} \mid bA$. For example, b$\{b, c\}$? is the set $\{b, bb, bc\}$.

Exercise 1.6

Show that $(b+)? = b*$.

Answer:

$(b+)? = \{\lambda\} \mid b+ = \{\lambda\} \mid \{b, bb, bbb, \ldots\} = \{\lambda, b, bb, bbb, \ldots\} = b^*$.

■

1.12   SHORTHAND NOTATION FOR A SET CONTAINING A SINGLE STRING

$\{b\}$ and b are not the same. The former is a set containing one string; the latter is a string—not a set containing a string. In spite of this distinction, it is common practice to represent the former (the set) by writing the latter (the string). We follow this practice only when the context clearly implies the correct interpretation, or where it does not make a difference. For example, instead of writing $\{c\} \mid bd^*$, we can write $c \mid bd^*$ (recall we are using $\mid$ to represent the set union). The union operator clearly implies that the c to its left must represent the set $\{c\}$ and not the string c. In some expressions, it does not matter which interpretation we use. For example, whether we interpret b as a string or as a set makes no difference in the Kleene closure b^*. Similarly, in $b+$ and bA, our interpretation makes no difference.

1.13   OPERATOR PRECEDENCE

If an expression contains more than one kind of operator, then the operations are performed in an order determined by their *precedence*. Specifically, operations with higher precedence are performed before operations with lower precedence. Our string operations, ordered from highest to lowest precedence, with equal precedence operations listed on the same line, are

Complementation
Star, Plus, Question Mark
Concatenation
Intersection
Union

For example, in $c \mid bd^*$, we first apply the star to the d, then we concatenate b and d^*, and last, we take the union of c and bd^*. We can override this order by using parentheses. For example, in $((c \mid b)d)^*$, we perform the union first, then the concatenation, and the star operation last.

If the star, plus, or question mark operators appear consecutively, we perform their corresponding operations left to right. For example, in $(bb)?+$, we perform the question mark operation first, then the plus operation. Thus, $(bb)?+ = \{\lambda, bb\}+ = (bb)^*$.

Exercise 1.7

Write an expression without using $\sim$ that defines the same set as $\sim(b^*)$. Assume complementation is with respect to the set Σ^*, where $\Sigma = \{b, c\}$.

Answer:

b^* is the set of all strings over the alphabet with no c's. Therefore, its complement is the set of strings that have at least one c. Thus, every string in $\sim(b^*)$ must be of the form xcy, where x and y are arbitrary strings over {b, c}. Thus, $\sim(b^*) = (b \mid c)^* c (b \mid c)^*$. Another expression that defines the same set is $b^* c (b \mid c)^*$.

■

1.14   REGULAR EXPRESSIONS

Let us use our convention of designating a set containing a single string by writing just the string. For example, let us write b to represent the set {b} . Then each of these following expressions designates a set of strings:

ϕ
λ
b
c
λ|b
bbc
b^*c^*
b|(cc)*
$(b \mid c)^*$

For example, ϕ, λ, b, c, and λ|b designate, respectively, the sets {}, {λ}, {b} , {c}, and {λ, b}. In every expression above, the only operations that appear, if any, are union, concatenation, and star. We call such expressions *regular expressions.* We can use regular expressions to define languages—that is, to define sets of strings.

Let us look at a precise definition of a regular expression: A *regular expression over the alphabet Σ* is any of the following:

ϕ
λ
any single symbol in Σ

These expressions are the *base regular expressions.* In addition, we can construct additional regular expressions using the following *construction rule:*

If r and s are arbitrary regular expressions, then the following expressions are also regular:

(r)
$r|s$
rs
r^*

Our construction rule allows us to construct new regular expressions, using union, concatenation, star, and parenthesis, from our base regular expressions or expressions previously constructed using the construction rule. For example, since b and c are regular expressions, so are (b), b | c, bc, and b^* by our construction rule. We can continue applying our construction rule, producing ever more complex regular expressions. For example, using our previously constructed regular expressions bc and b*, we can now, in turn, construct bc | b* with our construction rule. We are not allowed to apply our construction rule an infinite number of times when building a regular expression. This restriction implies that any regular expression must be of finite length.

Every regular expression defines (i.e., represents) a language. For example, b | c defines the language {b, c}. We call any language that can be defined with a regular expression a *regular language*.

Every regular language has more than one regular expression that defines it. For example, bb*, λbb*, and b*b all define the language consisting of one or more b's.

An assumption we have made about regular expressions over an alphabet Σ is that Σ does not contain |, *, (, or). Thus, when we see b | c, we know the vertical bar is the union operator. However, if the vertical bar were in Σ, then b | c would be ambiguous. It could represent either the set {b, c} (if we regard | as the union operator) or the set containing the single string "b | c" (if we regard | as a symbol from Σ). A simple way to disambiguate an expression like b | c is to quote the symbols in a regular expression that come from Σ. Accordingly, we would write "b | c" or "b" "|" "c" to represent the single string "b | c". Here, the vertical bar is a symbol from Σ. We know this because the vertical bar is in quotes. But we would write "b" | "c" to represent the set {b, c}. Here, the vertical bar is the union operator. We know this because here the vertical bar is not in quotes.

Exercise 1.8

Give the strings in the set specified by "b" | "c" "|" "d".

Answer:

Two strings: "b" and "c | d".   ■

Let us look at some expressions that are not regular expressions:

bb | bbb | bbbb | . . .	(the ellipsis ". . . " is not allowed)
(cc)+	(the plus operator is not allowed)
(cc)?	(the question mark operator is not allowed)
{$b^i : i \geq 0$}	(exponent and set-builder notation is not allowed)

Because we do not allow the ellipsis, the plus operator, the exponent notation, or the set builder notation in regular expressions, the expressions above are not regular expressions. The languages they represent, however, are regular because we can represent them with regular expressions, namely bbb*, cc(cc)*, λ|cc, and b*, respectively.

When we analyze regular expressions, it is often helpful to think of the union operator as indicating a choice. For example, we can think of the regular expression (b | c) d as representing the set of strings consisting of the choice b or c followed by d—that is, as the set consisting of bd and cd.

If we allow our regular expressions to include the ~, +, and ? operators in addition to |, *, and concatenation, we get the class of expressions called *extended regular expressions*. Any language defined by an extended regular language can also be defined by a nonextended regular language. In other words, extended regular expressions are no more powerful than nonextended regular expressions in defining languages. Thus, every extended regular expression necessarily has a nonextended equivalent. For example, the extended regular expression (b | c)? has the nonextended equivalent λ|b | c.

Although extended regular expressions are no more powerful than nonextended regular expressions, they are, nevertheless, useful because they are often easier to use and understand than their nonextended equivalents.

1.15 LIMITATIONS OF REGULAR EXPRESSIONS

Regular expressions have limitations. They cannot represent every language. For example, consider the following language that we call *PAIRED*:

$$PAIRED = \{b^i c^i : i \geq 0\} = \{\lambda, bc, bbcc, bbbccc, bbbbcccc, \ldots\}$$

Each string in *PAIRED* consists of some number of b's followed by the *same* number of c's. With a regular expression, it is possible to capture the condition that all b's precede all c's (as in b*c*). But there is no way to capture the condition that the number of b's equals the number of c's unless we limit the length of the string (we give a proof for this in Chapter 17). The language represented by b*c* includes strings in which the number of b's is equal to the number of c's (for example, bbcc). But it also includes strings in which the number of b's is not equal to the number of c's (for example, bcc). *PAIRED*, on the other hand, contains only strings in which the number of b's is equal to the number of c's. *PAIRED* is not equal to b*c* but is, in fact, a proper subset of it.

Another attempt at a regular expression for *PAIRED* is the infinite-length expression

$\lambda|bc\,|\,bbcc\,|\,bbbccc\,|\,bbbbcccc\,|\ldots$

Although this expression does represent *PAIRED*, it is not a regular expression because regular expressions cannot be of infinite length.

Let us place an upper bound on the exponent i in the preceding definition of *PAIRED*. We then get a new language that is, in fact, regular. For example,

$\{b^i c^i : 0 \leq i \leq 2\}$

is a regular language represented by the regular expression

$\lambda|bc\,|\,bbcc$

That a regular expression cannot represent the language *PAIRED* is a serious limitation since similar constructs frequently appear in programming languages. For example, in Java, arithmetic expressions may be nested with parentheses to an arbitrary depth:

$(\,(\,(\,.\quad.\,)\,)\,)$

Similarly, blocks of code may be nested to an arbitrary depth with braces:

$\{\,\{\,\{\,.\quad.\,\}\,\}\,\}$

We cannot describe either of these constructs with regular expressions unless we place an upper limit on the depth of nesting.

When we assert that the two regular expressions are equal, we are asserting that the languages defined by those regular expressions are equal. For example, when we write

$\lambda|bb^* = b^*$

we are asserting that the language defined by $\lambda|bb^*$ is equal to the language defined by b^*.

Although regular expressions are too limited to fully describe the typical programming language, they are still quite useful to the compiler designer. Their usefulness appears in the design of the token manager. In particular, we can use regular expressions to describe the various tokens that the token manager provides to the parser. For example, if we let D represent any digit 0 through 9, then the regular expression DD^* represents an unsigned integer token. We will see in Chapter 13 how regular expressions in conjunction with the software tool JavaCC can automate the implementation of the token manager.

PROBLEMS

1. How long is the shortest possible Java program?
2. What is the advantage of organizing a compiler into a sequence of passes?
3. Describe in words the set $\{b, c\}^*$.
4. What does the set $\{\}^*$ contain?
5. Is it true that $x^* = \{x\}^*$ for any string x?
6. Under what circumstances are P and $\sim P$ disjoint?
7. What does $P \mid Q = P$ imply?
8. What does $P \cap Q = P$ imply?
9. If $P = \{b\}$ and $Q = \{bb, c\}$, then what does $P^* \cap Q^*$ equal?
10. If $A = \{\lambda, b\}$, how many distinct strings are in AA? List them.
11. Is x^* always an infinite set? If not, give an example for which it is not infinite.
12. Does $b^*c^* = \{b, c\}^*$? Justify your answer.
13. Represent the set $\phi|\{\lambda\}|bbbc(bbbc)^*$ with a regular expression that does not use the | operator.
14. Using exponent notation, represent the set $b^*c^*b^*$.
15. Write a regular expression for the set of all strings over the alphabet $\{b, c\}$ containing exactly one b.
16. Write a regular expression for the set of all strings over the alphabet $\{b, c\}$ containing at least one b.
17. Write an expression using exponent notation for the set $(b^ic^id^j : i \geq 0, j \geq 0\} \cap \{b^pc^qd^q : p \geq 0 \text{ and } q \geq 0\}$ without using the $\cap$ operator.
18. Is $(b^*c^*)^* = \{b, c\}^*$? If not, provide a counterexample.
19. List all the strings in $\{b, cc\}^*$ that are of length 3.
20. Does $(b^*|b^*ccc)^* = \{b, ccc\}^*$? Justify your answer.
21. Is concatenation distributive over a union. That is, for all sets of strings A, B, C, does $A(B \mid C) = AB \mid AC$?
22. Is the star operation distributive over a union. That is, for all sets of strings A, B, does $(A|B)^* = A^*|B^*$?
23. Suppose $X, A,$ and B are sets of strings, $\lambda \notin B$, and $X = A|XB$. What can be concluded about X? Hint: does X contain AB?
24. Does xA always equal $\{x\}A$, where x is a string and A is a set of strings?

25. The parser in a compiler does not need the tokens corresponding to white space and comments. Yet, syntax errors may occur if white space and comments are removed from the source program. Explain this apparent contradiction.

26. Write a regular expression that defines the same language as b*c* ∩ c*d*.

27. Write a regular expression that defines the same language as {b, cc}* ∩ c*.

28. Write a regular expression that defines the same language as (bb)* ∩ (bbb)*.

29. Write a regular expression for the set of all strings over the alphabet {b, c} containing an even number of b's.

30. Write a nonextended regular expression that defines the same language as (~b)*, where the universe is (b | c | d)*.

31. Write a nonextended regular expression that defines the same language as ~({b, c}*), where the universe is (b | c | d)*.

32. Prove that any finite language is regular.

33. Describe in English the strings in (bb | cc|((bc | cb)(bb | cc)*(bc | cb)))*.

34. Is (((b))) a regular expression over the alphabet {b, c}?

35. Is () a regular expression over the alphabet {b, c}?

36. Give three regular expressions that define the empty set.

37. Suppose the alphabet for regular expressions consists of the symbols b, c, the backslash, the vertical bar, the single quote, and the double quote. Give an unambiguous regular expression that specifies the set consisting of b, c, the backslash, the vertical bar, the single quote, and the double quote.

38. Convert (b | c?)+ to an equivalent nonextended regular expression.

39. Show that extended regular expressions are not more powerful than regular expressions. That is, show that any language that can be defined by an extended regular expression can also be defined by a nonextended regular expression.

2

CONTEXT-FREE GRAMMARS, PART 1

2.1 INTRODUCTION

One of the jobs of a compiler is to determine if the source program is indeed one of the strings that make up the source language. If it is not, we say that the source program has a *syntax error*. For example, in the following Java program,

```
public class Bug
{
    public static void main(String[] args)
    {
        System.out.println("hello")  // missing semicolon
    }
}
```

the missing semicolon at the end of the `println` statement is a syntax error. The compiler should detect this error and generate an appropriate error message.

To detect every possible syntax error, the compiler obviously must have complete knowledge of the syntax of the source language. This knowledge should be embedded in the compiler in a form that is

1. Concise, otherwise the compiler would be too big
2. Precise, otherwise the compiler could not accurately check syntax
3. Sufficiently powerful to completely describe the syntax
4. Suitable for an efficient syntax-checking algorithm

Let us consider how well a very common representation of syntax—the introductory programming textbook—meets these four requirements:

1. Suppose our programming textbook has 1000 pages, half of which is devoted to syntax, with 2000 characters per page. In that case, the textbook uses a total of one million characters for syntax specification. Hardly concise.

2. Precise? No way. English descriptions of syntax always leave many fine points open to question.

3. Powerful? Most textbooks for programming languages do not fully describe the syntax of the language they are presenting. For example, how many Java textbooks let you know if a field and a method in a class can have the same name? Normally, you would always want to use distinct names so this detail of Java syntax is not important from a programming perspective. However, it is a detail that is essential for the compiler to know.

4. Does an algorithm exist that can read and correctly interpret a textbook? Maybe we will develop one by the year 2100. But even if we had such an algorithm, requirements 2 and 3 would still be problems.

Clearly, embedding syntax knowledge in the form of a textbook into a compiler is not the way to go. We will now study context-free grammars, representations of syntax that are almost perfect on all four of our requirements.

2.2   WHAT IS A CONTEXT-FREE GRAMMAR?

A *context-free grammar* consists of four parts:

1. A finite set N of symbols called the *nonterminal alphabet*
2. A finite set T of symbols called the *terminal alphabet*
3. A finite set of *productions*
4. A *start symbol* from the set N

Let us consider an example of a context-free grammar that we will call G2.1 ("G2.1" designates grammar 1 of Chapter 2). The four parts of G2.1 are

1. A nonterminal alphabet $N = \{S, B, C\}$
2. A terminal alphabet $T = \{b, c\}$
3. A finite set of productions:
    1. $S \rightarrow BC$
    2. $B \rightarrow bB$
    3. $B \rightarrow \lambda$
    4. $C \rightarrow ccc$
4. The start symbol S

The nonterminal alphabet N and the terminal alphabet T should not have any elements in common. We can state this requirement mathematically with

$$N \cap T = \phi$$

We call the symbols in N and T *nonterminals* and *terminals,* respectively. We call a string over the terminal alphabet—that is, a string in T^*—a *terminal string*. Note that λ (i.e., the null string) is always a terminal string since it is always in T^*, regardless of the elements in T. However, λ is not a terminal symbol because it is never an element of T. We call $N \mid T$, the union of the nonterminal and terminal alphabets, the *total alphabet*.

Productions are string replacement rules. Each production consists of two strings separated by the symbol →. The symbol → means "can be replaced by." For example, production 1 in G2.1, S → BC, says that S can be replaced by BC. Because the phrase "can be replaced by" is a mouthful, we will often use the shorter but less descriptive phrase "goes to." For example, we read the production S → BC as "S goes to BC."

The left side of every production must be a single symbol from N. Thus, *only nonterminal symbols can be replaced.* The right side, on the other hand, can be any string over N | T; that is, it consists of zero or more symbols from N and/or T. For example, in G2.1, each left side is a single symbol from N (either S, B, or C). Each right side is either

- A string of symbols from N (as in production 1)
- A string of symbols from N and T (as in production 2)
- A string of symbols from T (as in production 4)
- The null string (as in production 3)

Using the string notation we developed in Chapter 1, we can describe the properties of a production very concisely:

Each production in a context-free grammar has the form

$x \rightarrow y$

where $x \in N$ and $y \in (N \mid T)*$

The fourth part of a context-free grammar, the start symbol, must always be a symbol from the nonterminal alphabet N. That is,

Start Symbol $\in N$

2.3 DERIVATIONS USING A CONTEXT-FREE GRAMMAR

Production 1 (S → BC) in G2.1 says that we can replace S with BC. We can then, in turn, replace either the B (using either production 2 or 3) or the C (using production 4) in BC. Let us replace the C using production 4. We can show the resulting transformations by writing

```
S  ⇒  BC  ⇒  Bccc
1        4
```

The symbol ⇒ means "directly derives." That is, the string on its left is transformed to the string on its right by a *single* application of a production in the grammar. Thus, S directly derives BC, and BC in turn directly derives Bccc. We may indicate the production we use to make a replacement by writing its number under the nonterminal replaced by that production. Thus, we write 1 under S because we used production 1 to replace this S, and we write 4 under C because we used production 4 to replace this C. Continuing, by replacing B using production 2, we get

```
S  ⇒  BC  ⇒  Bccc  ⇒  bBccc
1        4        2
```

Finally, let us replace the B using production 3:

$$S \Rightarrow BC \Rightarrow Bccc \Rightarrow bBccc \Rightarrow bccc$$
$$1 \quad\quad 4 \quad\quad 2 \quad\quad\quad 3$$

In this last step, the application of production 3 yields bλccc, but this string is simply bccc because λ is the null string. We call the preceding sequence of strings, which shows the step-by-step transformation of S into bccc, a *derivation* of bccc from S. Productions replace only nonterminal symbols. Thus, once we derive bccc (a string with no nonterminals) in the preceding derivation, the derivation must terminate.

When we apply a production whose right side is λ in a derivation, we delete a nonterminal. For example, in the derivation above, applying production 3 has the effect of deleting B. We call a production whose right side is λ a *lambda production*.

There are numerous ways in common use of asserting that we can obtain bccc from S using the productions in the grammar. We can use any of the following:

S derives bccc.

$$S \overset{*}{\Rightarrow} bccc$$

$$S \overset{+}{\Rightarrow} bccc$$

In the second approach, the symbol ⇒ (which by itself means "derives in one step") is modified by the asterisk on top to mean "derives in zero or more steps." Similarly, the plus symbol in the last approach modifies ⇒ to mean "derives in one or more steps." Since S derives bccc in three steps, we can use ⇒ with either an asterisk or a plus sign on top.

You may be wondering what deriving a string in zero steps means. It means to take a string and do nothing to it. Obviously, every string derives itself in zero steps. That is, it is always the case that

$$x \overset{*}{\Rightarrow} x$$

for any string x in the total alphabet regardless of the productions in the grammar. However, it is true that

$$x \overset{+}{\Rightarrow} x$$

only if x can be derived from itself though the application of one or more productions in the grammar. For example, if a grammar contains the productions

$$S \rightarrow A$$
$$A \rightarrow S$$

then it would be correct to assert that $S \overset{+}{\Rightarrow} S$ because we can derive S from S in one or more steps, as the following derivation demonstrates

$$S \Rightarrow A \Rightarrow S$$

Of course, it is not always the case that $S \overset{+}{\Rightarrow} S$. For example, it does not hold for G2.1.

Exercise 2.1

a. Show that S derives ccc in G2.1.

b. Show that B derives bb in G2.1.

Answers:

a. S $\Rightarrow$ BC $\Rightarrow$ C $\Rightarrow$ ccc
    1   3   4

b. B $\Rightarrow$ bB $\Rightarrow$ bbB $\Rightarrow$ bb
    2   2   3

                                                   ■

If a derivation starts with the start symbol, then we call each string in the derivation a *sentential form* (see Fig. 2.1).

If we think of the final terminal string as a "sentence", then each string in the derivation in Figure 2.1 is a form of this final sentence; hence, the name "sentential form" for each of these strings.

2.4   LANGUAGE DEFINED BY A CONTEXT-FREE GRAMMAR

It is easy to see that S in G2.1 derives many terminal strings. For example, S derives bbbccc, as the following derivation demonstrates:

  S $\Rightarrow$ BC $\Rightarrow$ bBC $\Rightarrow$ bbBC $\Rightarrow$ bbbBC $\Rightarrow$ bbbC $\Rightarrow$ bbbccc
  1   2   2   2   3   4

Note that each time we use production 2, we get another b. In the preceding derivation, we use production 2 three times. Thus, we get three b's. If we do not use production 2 at all, that is, if we use production 3 without first using production 2, then we get no b's:

  S $\Rightarrow$ BC $\Rightarrow$ C $\Rightarrow$ ccc
  1   3   4

Thus, production 2 in combination with production 3 can produce any number (including zero) of b's.

What exactly is the language defined by a context-free grammar? Let us take G2.1 as an example. As we have seen, the terminal strings bccc and bbbccc are derivable from the start symbol S in G2.1. The set of all such strings—that is, *terminal strings derivable from the start symbol*—is the language that G2.1 defines.

Using the notation we have developed, we can concisely describe L(G), the *language defined by a context-free grammar G:*

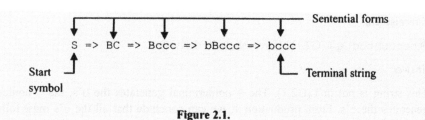

Figure 2.1.

L(G), the language defined by a context-free grammar G with start symbol S and terminal alphabet T is

$$\{x : S \overset{*}{\Rightarrow} x \text{ and } x \in T^*\}$$

That is, L(G) is the set of all strings x such that $S \overset{*}{\Rightarrow} x$ (i.e., x is derivable from S) and $x \in T^*$ (i.e., x is a terminal string). We call any language that can be defined by some context-free grammar a *context-free language*.

Let us determine a regular expression that defines the same language as G2.1. First consider the effect of production 2. We can use production 2 zero or more times. Each time we use it, it produces a b. To derive a terminal string, we ultimately have to use production 3 to delete B. Thus, from B we can get zero or more b's. That is, we can get any string in b*. From C with can get only one string: ccc. From production 1, we can see that S derives BC. Thus, S can derive any string in b*ccc. L(G2.1) is b*ccc.

By now you can probably guess why the four parts of a context-free grammar—the productions, the nonterminal alphabet, the terminal alphabet, and the start symbol—are so-called. Consider:

- A production *produces* the string on its right side.
- Terminals are *terminating* symbols. That is, once they are generated, we cannot replace them because the left side of a production in a context-free grammar is always a nonterminal.
- Nonterminals are *nonterminating* symbols. That is, they allow the derivation process to continue.
- The derivations that determine the language defined by a grammar all *start* from the start symbol.

A term that we will use frequently when discussing grammars is "generates." This term has slightly different meanings depending on its context. Roughly, it means "can produce." For example, we might say

G2.1 generates b*ccc.
Meaning: L(G2.1) = b*ccc

G2.1 generates ccc.
Meaning: ccc $\in$ L(G2.1)

B $\rightarrow$ bB generates a b.
Meaning: B $\rightarrow$ bB allows B to be replaced by a string that contains b.

B generates b*
Meaning: The set of strings derivable from B is b*.

Exercise 2.2

Is bcccbbccc $\in$ L(G2.1)? If yes, show its derivation.

Answer:

This string is not in L(G2.1). The B nonterminal generates the b's; the C nonterminal generates the c's. From production 1, we can conclude that all the c's must follow all the b's. Thus, this string—with b's following c's— cannot be in the language defined by G2.1.

■

A production in a grammar can be applied to a string whenever the nonterminal on the left side of that production appears in the string. Thus, the order in which the productions are listed is purely arbitrary. Changing the order in which the productions are listed *does not affect how those productions can be used,* nor does it affect the language defined by the grammar.

2.5   DIFFERENT WAYS OF REPRESENTING CONTEXT-FREE GRAMMARS

A common way of representing a group of productions with the same left side is to write the common left side once, followed by →, followed by the several right sides, each separated by the vertical bar |. You should interpret the vertical bar as meaning "or." Using this approach, G2.1 becomes

G2.2
```
S  →  BC
B  →  bB  |  λ
C  →  ccc
```

We call the special characters, such as the vertical bar, that we sometimes use in grammars *metasymbols.* "meta" here means "beyond." Metasymbols are symbols beyond (i.e., in addition to) the terminal and nonterminal symbols.

For the next several chapters in this textbook, we will use uppercase letters exclusively for nonterminals, lowercase letters exclusively for terminals, and S for the start symbol. A more versatile approach, which we will use when we write complex grammars, is to quote terminal symbols. Distinguishing terminals from nonterminals by quoting the terminal symbols allows us to use any character as a terminal and any character except a metasymbol for a nonterminal. Moreover, if we require a space between successive terminal and nonterminal symbols on the right side of each production, we can use multiple-character names for nonterminals. For example, consider the following production:

```
expr  →  term  "|"  term
```

The vertical bar is a terminal symbol in this production—not the "or" operator. It cannot be a metasymbol because it is in quotes. term must be a nonterminal. It cannot be a terminal because it is not quoted. Nor can it be the four consecutive nonterminals—t, e, r, m—because we require a space between successive components of the right side of a production. If we wanted four nonterminals—t, e, r, and m—we would have to write the production this way:

```
expr → t  e  r  m  "|"  t  e  r  m
```

The spaces on the right side of the preceding production are there to separate successive terminal and nonterminal symbols. They are not part of the strings the production generates. If, however, we wanted to specify a space as a terminal symbol, we can simply enclose the space in quotes. For example, the right side of the production

```
expr → term " " term
```

consists of the two occurrences of the nonterminal `term` surrounding the terminal symbol " " (the space character).

2.6 SOME SIMPLE GRAMMARS

To reinforce your understanding of context-free grammars, we now will look at several simple examples. For each grammar, we will analyze the specific mechanisms it uses to generate strings. You should study these examples thoroughly.

Our first grammar generates b*, the set of strings containing zero or more b's:

G2.3
  1. S → bS
  2. S → λ

Here is how G2.3 works: Each time we use production 1, it generates b. Therefore, to generate a string of n b's, we use production 1 n times followed by a single use of production 2 to delete S. For example, the derivation of bbbb is

```
S ⇒ bS ⇒ bbS ⇒ bbbS ⇒ bbbbS ⇒ bbbb
1     1      1       1        2
```

We can generate the null string with G2.3 by using production 2 first in the derivation:

```
S ⇒ λ
2
```

This derivation illustrates an important feature of context-free grammars: You do not have to use productions in the order listed. The order in which the productions in a grammar are listed has no effect on the language defined by that grammar.

Another grammar that generates b* is

G2.4
  1. S → Sb
  2. S → λ

The derivation of bbbb using G2.4 illustrates the difference between G2.3 and G2.4: G2.3 generates b's left to right but G2.4 generates b's right to left:

```
S ⇒ Sb ⇒ Sbb ⇒ Sbbb ⇒ Sbbbb ⇒ bbbb
1     1      1       1        2
```

Grammars are like computer programs in that grammars that do the same thing (i.e, define the same language) may differ substantially in size (i.e., the number of productions), efficiency (i.e., the number of steps needed to generate terminal strings), or in their basic approach to generating strings. We call grammars that define the same language, like G2.3 and G2.4, *equivalent grammars*.

Exercise 2.3

Write a grammar that defines (bb)*.

Answer:

1. S → bbS
2. S → λ

∎

Let us now write a grammar for b*|c*. We might try adding the production

S → cS

to G2.3. Since G2.3 generates b* and our new production generates zero or more c's, perhaps our new grammar will generate b* | c* :

G2.5

$\left.\begin{array}{l}1.\ \text{S} \rightarrow \text{bS} \\ 2.\ \text{S} \rightarrow \lambda\end{array}\right\}$ G2.3

3. S → cS added

Productions 1 and 2 generate b*. Similarly, productions 2 and 3 generate c*. Thus, G2.5 can certainly generate every string in b*|c*. But, unfortunately, it can also generate many strings (an infinite number, in fact) that are not in b*|c*. Here is why: Every string in b*|c* is exclusively b's or exclusively c's or the null string, but G2.5 can generate strings containing both b's and c's. For example:

S ⇒ bS ⇒ bcS ⇒ bc
1   3   2

G2.5, in fact, can generate any string of b's and c's left to right by using production 1 whenever a b is needed, production 3 whenever a c is needed, or production 2 when the string ends. That is, G2.5 generates (b|c)*. Note that b*|c* is not equal to (b|c)*. Rather, b*|c* is a proper subset of (b|c)*.

A grammar that defines b*|c* must be able to generate both b's and c's. But once a b is generated in a string, then it should be impossible to generate any c's in that string, and vice versa. A grammar that does this is

G2.6

1. S → λ
2. S → B
3. S → C
4. B → bB
5. B → b
6. C → cC
7. C → c

Notice that B generates only b's and C generates only c's. Thus, if we use production 2 first, then only b's are generated; if we use production 3 first, then only c's are generated; if we use production 1 first, then the null string is generated.

Our next grammar also defines b*|c*:

G2.7

    1. S → λ
    2. S → bB
    3. S → cC
    4. B → bB
    5. B → λ
    6. C → cC
    7. C → λ

Productions 2 and 3 determine if b's or if c's are generated. These productions, unlike the corresponding productions in G2.6, generate a terminal symbol. Notice that to derive the terminal string b, we must use the lambda production B → λ:

    S ⇒ bB ⇒ b
    2   5

We have a similar situation for the string c. We need the lambda productions for B and C because, otherwise, B and C could not produce a string of length 0 and, thus, S—by virtue of productions 2 and 3—could not produce a string of length 1.

Exercise 2.4

Modify G2.7 by replacing productions 5 and 7 with B → b and C → c, respectively. Give a regular expression that defines the same language as the modified grammar.

Answer:

λ|bbb*|ccc*

■

The next language we will consider is b*cd*. We can easily construct a grammar for this language by allowing the start symbol to generate BcD and then using B and D to generate b* and d*, respectively:

G2.8

    1. S → BcD
    2. B → bB
    3. B → λ
    4. D → dD
    5. D → λ

Alternatively, we can generate b*cd* strictly left to right with

G2.9

    1. S → bS
    2. S → cD
    3. D → dD
    4. D → λ

Production 1, used repeatedly, generates strings in b*, production 2 generate c, and productions 3 and 4 generates strings in d*. The number of times productions 1 and 3 in G2.10 are used determines the number of b's and d's, respectively, in the generated string. For example, we generate the string $b^i c d^j$ by using

> production 1 i times
> production 2 once
> production 3 j times
> production 4 once

For our final example we will consider two grammars that both define bb*. Note that every string in bb* has at least one b. The two grammars use different ways to force at least one b in every generated string. G2.10 forces a b at the end of a derivation; G2.11 forces a b at the beginning of a derivation:

G2.10
> 1. S → bS
> 2. S → b forces b at end of derivation

G2.11
> 1. S → bB forces b at beginning of derivation
> 2. B → bB
> 3. B → λ

For G2.10, every derivation of a terminal string must end with production 2. Thus, every terminal string must have at least one b. For G2.11, every derivation must start with production 1. Thus, in this grammar as well, every terminal string derivable from S must have at least one b.

Exercise 2.5

Indicate the order and the number of times each production in G2.11 is used to generate b^n, where $n \geq 1$.

Answer:

Production 1 once

Production 2 (n-1) times

Production 3 once

■

2.7 TECHNIQUES FOR GENERATING LANGUAGES WITH CONTEXT-FREE GRAMMARS

One way to become skillful at analyzing and writing context-free grammars is to observe and catalog the various techniques that you can use to generate strings. You probably have already started doing this in your study of the examples in the preceding section. In this section, we describe and catalog five important techniques:

1. Direct right recursion
2. Direct left recursion
3. Direct interior recursion
4. Indirect recursion
5. In parts

Each technique is characterized by the application of a production of a particular form. In presenting these production forms, we will use capital letters to represent arbitrary nonterminal symbols and the lower-case letters x and y to represent arbitrary nonnull strings over the total alphabet (i.e., strings of terminals and/or nonterminals).

Direct right recursion corresponds to a production of the form

$$A \rightarrow xA$$

Notice that the nonterminal on the left side also appears rightmost on the right side. We call productions of this form *directly right recursive*. Each application of a production of this form generates an occurrence of an x. Repeated applications create a list of x's, generated in left-to-right order. For example, if we use the directly right recursive production

$$S \rightarrow dS$$

three times, we get three d's:

$$S \Rightarrow dS \Rightarrow ddS \Rightarrow dddS$$

The d's are generated left to right. Thus, the leftmost d is the first d generated; the rightmost, the last generated. Since there is no limit on the number of applications of the production $S \rightarrow dS$, the list of d's generated can be any size. The list is terminated when some other S production is used that eliminates the S nonterminal. We have already seen several grammars that use this technique. For example, G2.3 uses the $S \rightarrow bS$ to generate a list of zero or more b's, and $S \rightarrow \lambda$ to terminate the list.

Direct right recursion generates a list left to right.

Direct left recursion is like direct right recursion, except that it generates a list right to left instead of left to right. It corresponds to a production of the form

$$A \rightarrow Ax$$

We call productions of this form *directly left recursive*. For example, in

G2.12
1. $S \rightarrow Sbc$
2. $S \rightarrow d$

production 1 is directly left recursive. It generates the list (bc)* from right to left. Production 1 terminates the list by generating a leading d. It, therefore, generates the language d(bc)*. Here is the derivation of dbcbcbc:

$$S \Rightarrow Sbc \Rightarrow Sbcbc \Rightarrow Sbcbcbc \Rightarrow dbcbcbc$$

Notice that the three occurrences of bc are generated right to left.

Direct left recursion generates lists right to left.

Sometimes a language that contains lists cannot be generated using either direct left or right recursion. For example, let us consider two similar languages, b*c* = $\{b^i c^j : i, j \geq 0\}$ and *PAIRED* = $\{b^i c^i : i \geq 0\}$. In b*c*, unlike *PAIRED*, the number of b's does not have to equal the number of c's. We will see that b*c* can be generated using either the directly left or right recursive techniques, but *PAIRED* cannot.

b*c* consists of a list of zero or more b's followed by a list of zero or more c's. A grammar that generates this language using direct right recursion is

G2.13
1. S → λ
2. S → bS
3. S → cC
4. C → cC
5. C → λ

Productions 2 and 4 are directly right recursive productions that generate, respectively, a list of b's and c's.

Now consider the *PAIRED* language. For this language, an arbitrary number of b's must be generated followed by the *same* number of c's. Direct right recursion can certainly generate the list of b's but it has no way of keeping count of the number generated so that it can subsequently generate the same number of c's.

We, however, can generate *PAIRED* by our third technique, *direct interior recursion*. Corresponding to this technique is the production form

A → xAy

Each application of a production of this form generates an x to the left of the A and a y to the right. Repeated applications, of course, produce the same number of x's and y's. We call productions of this form *directly interior recursive*. Using such a production, we can easily write a grammar that generates the language *PAIRED*:

G2.14
1. S → bSc
2. S → λ

In the derivation of bbbccc in G2.14, we can see how the nonterminal S sits in the interior of each intermediate string and generates b's to the left and c's to the right:

```
S⇒ bSc  ⇒ bbScc ⇒ bbbSccc ⇒ bbbccc
1     1          1             2
```

G2.14 ensures that the number of b's and c's are equal by always generating b's and c's in pairs. Thus, the grammar does not have to keep count of the number of b's (which would be impossible) and then subsequently generate the same number of c's.

Programming languages frequently have constructs that are similar in structure to the language *PAIRED*. These constructs can be generated by direct interior recursion but not direct left or right recursion. For example, consider the use of nested braces in Java and C++. The grammar for this construct must be able to generate exactly one right brace for each left brace. Another example of the *PAIRED* structure is the nesting of parentheses in arithmetic expressions. For example, consider

    (a + ((b + c) + d)))

Each right parenthesis must be matched by exactly one left parenthesis.

Exercise 2.6

Write a grammar that generates $\{b^i c^i : i \geq 1\}$.

Answer:

Note that $\{b^i c^i : i \geq 1\}$ is the language *PAIRED* less the null string. Two grammars for this language are

1. S → bSc	1) S → bAc
2. S → bc	2) A → bAc
	3) A → λ

The two grammars differ in how they force at least one bc pair in every terminal string. The grammar on the left does it at the end of a derivation using production 2. The grammar on the right does it at the beginning of a derivation using production 1.

∎

As a final example of direct interior recursion, let's write a grammar for the language $\{b^{j+k} c^j d^k : j, k \geq 0\}$. Since $b^{j+k} = b^j b^k = b^k b^j$, we can write this language as $\{b^k b^j c^j d^k : j, k \geq 0\}$. In this form, we see that the number of d's on the right is matched by the same number of b's on the left. Nested within these exterior strings are strings that have an equal number of b's and c's. A grammar that generates this language is

G2.15
  1. S → bSd
  2. S → λ
  3. S → bAc
  4. A → bAc
  5. A → λ

Production 1 generates the exterior b's and matching d's. Productions 3 and 4 generate the interior b's and matching c's.

Exercise 2.7

Write a grammar that generates $\{b^{j+k} c^j d^k : j, k \geq 1\}$.

Answer:

This language is a subset of L(G2.15)—it does not include the strings corresponding to $j = 0$ or $k = 0$.

  1. S → bSd
  2. S → bAd

3. A → bAc

4. A → bc

To generate $b^{j+k}c^jd^k$, use

production 1 $(k - 1)$ times

production 2 once

production 3 $(j - 1)$ times

production 4 once

Since both production 2 and 4 must be used once, at least one exterior b-d pair and interior b-c pair are always generated.

■

Direct interior recursion can generate two lists with the same number of elements. However, it cannot generate more than two lists with the same number of elements. Consider the language *TRIPLED* = $\{b^ic^id^i : i \geq 0\}$ which consists of strings made up of three lists: a list of b's, a list of c's, and a list of d's. The three lists have equal lengths. Direct interior recursion can generate any two of the three lists. It, however, cannot generate all three lists. *TRIPLED*, in fact, cannot be generated by any context-free grammar (we give a proof for this in Chapter 4). Fortunately, programming languages rarely have constructs like *TRIPLED*, so this limitation of context-free grammars is not a problem for the compiler designer.

In all of the variations of direct recursion—right, left, or interior—we use a production in which the nonterminal on the left side also appears on the right side. Thus, an application of such a production causes the left-side nonterminal to immediately regenerate itself. *Indirect recursion* also causes a nonterminal to regenerate but the regeneration takes at least two derivation steps. Let us look at an example of a grammar with indirect recursion:

G2.16

1. S → bAc

2. S → e

3. A → cSd

None of the productions in G2.16 are directly recursive. However, S can generate an A (by production 1) which can, in turn, regenerate S (by production 3):

S ⇒ bAc ⇒ bcSdc
1   3

Since the regeneration takes more than one derivation step, this recursion, by definition, is indirect.

It is not hard to determine L(G2.16). Here is our analysis: Any derivation of a terminal string from S requires n applications of productions 1 and 3 where $n \geq 0$, followed by a single application of production 2. Each application of production 1 and 3 produces a bc on the left and a dc on the right. The application of production 2 at the end of a derivation generates an e in the middle of the terminal string. Thus, L(G2.16) = $\{(bc)^ie(dc)^i : i \geq 0\}$.

We can convert the indirect recursion in G2.16 to direct recursion by allowing S to generate bcSdc immediately. The equivalent grammar that results is

G2.17
1. S → bcSdc
2. S → e

We can characterize indirect recursion, like direct recursion, as right, left, or interior, depending on where the regenerated nonterminal appears in the string it generates. G2.16 is an example of indirect interior recursion since

$$S \stackrel{*}{\Rightarrow} bcSdc$$

Some conversions on recursive grammars are not possible. For example, the language *PAIRED* requires a grammar with interior recursion (direct or indirect). Thus, any grammar for *PAIRED* cannot be converted to an equivalent grammar without interior recursion. There are, however, some conversions on recursive grammars that are always possible. For example, we can always convert an indirectly recursive grammar to a directly recursive grammar, and a left recursive grammar to a right recursive grammar, and vice versa. In Chapter 3, we study procedures for performing these recursion conversions.

Exercise 2.8

Write an indirectly right recursive grammar that generates (bc)*.

Answer:

1. S → bA
2. S → λ
3. A → cS

■

Our final technique for generating strings with context-free grammars is the *in-parts technique*. The corresponding production form is

$$A \rightarrow A_1 A_2 \ldots A_p$$

where $p \geq 2$. With this technique, the strings generated by A are generated in p parts. These component parts are generated by $A_1, A_2 \ldots, A_p$ using one of our five basic techniques. For example, we generate the language bb*c*dd* in three parts, bb*, c*, and dd*, with the nonterminals B, C, and D, respectively, in

G2.18
1. S → BCD
2. B → bB
3. B → b
4. C → cC
5. C → λ
6. D → dD
7. D → d

2.8   REGULAR AND RIGHT LINEAR GRAMMARS

A *regular grammar* is a context-free grammar in which each production must be of one of the following forms:

1. A → bB
2. A → b
3. A → λ

where A and B are any nonterminal symbols (not necessarily different), and b is any single terminal symbol. For example, a regular grammar that generates bd* is

G2.19
1. S → bD
2. D → dD
3. D → λ

Of the three production forms allowed in a regular grammar, only the first form has a nonterminal on its right side. Since this nonterminal is rightmost on the right side, regular grammars can be right recursive but never left or interior recursive. Thus, languages whose generation requires interior recursion (for example, *PAIRED* in Section 2.7) cannot be generated by any regular grammar. In spite of their limitations, regular grammars are quite useful to the compiler designer.

Now let us consider two more production forms:

4. A → zB
5. A → z

where z is a sequence of two or more terminals and A and B are arbitrary nonterminal symbols, not necessarily distinct. Neither of these forms is allowed in a regular grammar. However, we can always convert productions in either form to an equivalent set of regular productions. For example, consider the production A → bcdB. We can achieve the effect of this nonregular production with three regular productions, the first generating b, the second generating c, and the third generating dB:

A → bP
P → cQ
Q → dB

where P and Q are new nonterminals that are not already in the grammar. Clearly, these three productions have the same effect as the single production A → bcdB, as demonstrated by the following derivation:

A ⇒ bP ⇒ bcQ ⇒ bcdB

We call a grammar all of whose productions are of form 1–5 a *right linear grammar*. We can always convert a right linear grammar to an equivalent regular grammar (just replace its nonregular productions with their regular equivalents). Thus, right linear grammars can never generate a language that regular grammars cannot. Right linear grammars, however, can often generate a language in a more obvious, straightforward way than can a regular grammar. For example, consider the right linear grammar for the language (bcd)*e:

G2.20
    1. S → bcdS
    2. S → e

Rewritten as a regular grammar, the grammar becomes considerably more obtuse:

G2.21
    1. S → bC.
    2. S → e
    3. C → cD
    4. D → dS

Exercise 2.9

a. Write a right linear grammar that generates (bbb)+.

b. Write a regular grammar that generates (bbb)+.

c. Write two grammars that generate b*c*—one regular, the other using direct left recursion

Answers:

a. 1. S → bbbS
    2. S → bbb

b. 1. S → bA
    2. A → bB
    3. B → bS
    4. B → b

c. Regular   Directly Left Recursive

Regular	Directly Left Recursive
1. S → bS	1. S → Sc
2. S → λ	2. S → λ
3. S → cC	3. S → Bb
4. C → cC	4. B → Bb
5. C → λ	5. B → λ

A *regular language* is any language that can be defined with a regular grammar. Recall from Chapter 1 that we defined a regular language as any language that can be defined with a regular expression. This dual use of "regular language" is permitted since regular expressions and regular grammars have exactly the same power to define languages. That is, any language that we can define with a regular expression, we can also define with a regular grammar, and vice versa (we prove this in Chapter 17). Thus, the two definitions of regular languages are equivalent.

Since every regular grammar is also a context-free grammar, every regular language is also a context-free language. However, not every context-free language is regular (*PAIRED* is one such language). Thus, context-free grammars are more powerful than regular expressions and regular grammars. To define the syntax of the typical programming languages, we need the superior power of context-free grammars.

Although most programming languages are not regular, the various categories of tokens into which the token manager decomposes the source program are almost always regular. For example, we can nicely describe an identifier that starts with a letter followed by zero or more letters and/or digits with the regular expression

L(L|D)*

where L represents any letter and D any digit.

2.9 COUNTING WITH REGULAR GRAMMARS

In our discussion of the language *PAIRED* = $\{b^i c^i : i \geq 0\}$ in Section 2.7, we observed that we cannot use a right-recursive grammar because the grammar would have to do something it cannot, namely, keep count of the number of b's it generates. We will see that regular grammars can, in fact, count, but their counting ability is not sufficient to handle the language *PAIRED*.

A grammar can count by using distinct nonterminal symbols to represent distinct counts. For example, in G2.22, which generates bbb, the nonterminals S, A, B, and C represent the count of the number of b's generated so far.

G2.22

1. S → bA
2. A → bB
3. B → bC
4. C → λ

As the derivation of bbb shows, each nonterminal appears in a sentential form when its corresponding count (S = 0, A = 1, B = 2, C = 3) equals the number of b's generated:

S ⇒ bA ⇒ bbB ⇒ bbbC ⇒ bbb

Since distinct nonterminals are used to count, the number of nonterminals in a grammar determines an upper limit on how high the grammar can count. Since the number of nonterminals in a grammar must be finite, any counting grammar necessarily has an upper limit on how high it can count.

A more complex type of counting is illustrated by G2.23, which generates *PAIRED3* = $\{b^i c^i : i \leq 3\}$ = $\{\lambda, bc, bbcc, bbbccc\}$:

G2.23

1. S → λ
2. S → bA
3. S → bE
4. A → bB
5. A → bD
6. B → bC
7. C → cD

8. D → cE
9. E → c

Here, S, A, B, and C count the number of b's generated so far in a derivation. C, D, and E count the c's. However, instead of counting the number c's generated so far, C, D, and E count the number of c's needed for the derivation to terminate. C means three more c's are needed; D means two more c's are needed; E means one more c is needed. S, A , B, and C are used to count up. C, D, and E are used to count down. For example, whenever a D appears in an intermediate string, exactly two more c's must be generated to yield a terminal string. As the four derivations in this grammar (only four derivations of terminal strings are possible) illustrate, a derivation can terminate whenever the count is zero—that is, whenever the number of c's equals the number of b's:

$$S \Rightarrow \lambda$$
$$S \Rightarrow bE \Rightarrow bc$$
$$S \Rightarrow bA \Rightarrow bbD \Rightarrow bbcE \Rightarrow bbcc$$
$$S \Rightarrow bA \Rightarrow bbB \Rightarrow bbbC \Rightarrow bbbcD \Rightarrow bbbccE \Rightarrow bbbccc$$

With the up–down counting we used in G2.23, we can easily construct a similar grammar for $PAIRED4 = \{b^i c^i : i \leq 4\} = \{\lambda, bc, bbcc, bbbccc, bbbbcccc\}$. In fact, with this approach we can construct a grammar for every language $PAIREDn = \{b^i c^i : i \leq n\}$, where n is fixed positive integer. For large values of n, the corresponding grammar must count high and, therefore, have many nonterminal symbols. We cannot, however, extend this technique to produce a grammar for $PAIRED = \{b^i c^i : i \geq 0\}$ since this language has no upper bound on the number of b's and c's and would, therefore, require an infinite number of nonterminals. Grammars are not allowed to have an infinite number of nonterminals. Thus, no matter how high a given grammar can count, there are always strings in $PAIRED$ that would exceed that grammar's counting capability.

Exercise 2.10

Write a regular grammar that generates {b, bb, bbb} by counting the number of b's generated.

Answer:

1. S → bA
2. A → bB
3. A → λ
4. B → bC
5. B → λ
6. C → λ

The counting ability of a context-free grammar is limited, just like the counting ability of regular grammars, by the number of nonterminals in the grammar. Thus, context-free grammars are no better at counting than regular grammars. However, context-free grammars can do something regular grammars cannot: generate any number of symbols or groups of symbols in pairs using the interior recursive technique. With this technique, we can generate a language like *PAIRED*. The context-free grammar that generates *PAIRED* is not counting b's and c's. It is simply generating b's and c's in pairs.

2.10 GRAMMARS FOR LISTS

Lists occur very frequently in programming languages. Let us look at several examples. For each list, we will see if it uses a separator character (a character to separate successive elements) and if the null list (the list without any elements) is permitted.

Our first example is a variable list that appears in a Java or C++ declaration:

```
int w,x,y,z;
```

Following the keyword `int` is a list of identifiers with the comma used as the separator. A null list in this context, believe it or not, is permitted in C++ but not Java. That is, in C++ the statement,

```
int  ;
```

is legal (but useless) code.

Our next example is a compound statement in Java or C++:

```
{
    x = 1;
    y = 2;
}
```

The list here, consisting of the two assignment statements, uses no separator character. The semicolons are terminators rather than separators (we will clarify the distinction between a terminator and a separator later when we examine grammars for compound statements). Like our first example, this list may also be null. That is,

```
{
}
```

is legal.

Our third example is an arithmetic expression:

```
w + x - y + z
```

Here, we have a list of operands, w, x, y, and z, separated by the operators + and −. Expressions may or may not be null depending on where they are used in a program.

Our last example is a positive integer constant consisting of a list of digits:

```
4523
```

Here, the list has no separators and must be nonnull.

Now let us write grammars for the following four categories of lists:

1. Lists that do not use a separator and may be null
2. Lists that do not use a separator and are always nonnull
3. Lists that use a separator and are always nonnull
4. Lists that use a separator and may be null

To keep things simple, we will consider lists in which each element is a single b and the separator, if used, is the comma.

We can view lists in category 1 as strings in the language b*, for which we have the simple grammar

G2.24
   1. S → bS   no separator, may be null
   2. S → λ

Category 2 corresponds to the language bb*. The simplest grammar for this language is

G2.25
   1. S → bS
   2. S → b

Another grammar is

G2.26
   1. S → bL   generates a leading b   no separator, nonnull
   2. L → bL⎫
           ⎬ generates zero or more additional b's
   3. L → λ ⎭

In G2.26, production 1 generates a leading b. Then L generates a list of zero or more additional b's. Alternatively, we can have L generate only nonnull lists of b's. Then S must be allowed to generate the initial b without an L list following it:

G2.27
   1. S → b   generates an initial b
   2. S → bL   generates an initial b followed by an L list
   3. L → bL   L generates one or more b's
   4. L → b

Thus, if we use production 2, any string generated will have at least two b's. Production 1 allows G2.27 to generate a string with only one b.

Let us look at the three shortest strings in category 3:

   b
   b,b
   b,b,b

We can view each string in this category as a member of b(,b)*—that is, as a single b followed by a list of zero or more occurrences of ",b". For example, b,b,b,b consists of b followed by three occurrences of ",b":

   b   ,b   ,b   ,b

With this interpretation, we can easily write the grammar:

G2.28

1. S → bL   forces an initial b   separator, non-null
2. L → ,bL   generates the rest of the list
3. L → λ

Production 1 forces the generation of the initial b. L generates the zero or more occurrences of ", b". Another approach is to have L generate only nonnull lists. Then S must be allowed to generate the initial b without an L list following it:

G2.29

1. S → b   generates an initial b without list
2. S → bL   generates an initial b with list
3. L → ,bL   generates a nonnull list
4. L → ,b

A third approach is to view each string as a member of (b,)*b. This gives rise to:

G2.30

1. S → b,S   generates (b,)*
2. S → b   generates the last b

All of the grammars above generate strings left to right. For each, there is the "mirror-image" grammar that generates the same language right to left.

Exercise 2.11

Write a grammar that defines the language consisting of strings of one or more b's, with successive b's separated by exactly one space. Use meaningful names for your nonterminal symbols. Enclose terminal symbols with quotes.

Answer:

```
bList → "b" blistTail
blistTail → " " "b" blistTail
blistTail → λ
```

Category 4 is the same as category 3 except for the addition of the null string. Can our category 3 grammars, G2.28, G2.29, and G2.30, be converted to grammars for category 4 lists simply by adding the production S → λ? This modification does, in fact, work for G2.28 and G2.29 but not for G2.30. The category 4 grammar obtained from G2.28 by adding S → λ is

G2.31

1. S → bL   forces an initial b   separator, may be null
2. S → λ   allows S to generate the null string
3. L → ,bL   generates the rest of the list
4. L → λ

The category 4 grammar obtained from G2.29 by adding S → λ is

G2.32

1. S → b   generates b
2. S → bL   generates an initial b when there is more than one b

3. $S \rightarrow \lambda$ allows S to generate the null string
4. $L \rightarrow , bL$ generates the rest of list
5. $L \rightarrow , b$

What about G2.30? Why can we not simply add $S \rightarrow \lambda$ to it to create a category 4 grammar? Unfortunately, in G2.30, adding $S \rightarrow \lambda$ adds more than the null string to the language generated. The problem with G2.30 is that S appears on the right side of production 1. Thus, $S \rightarrow \lambda$ can be used to eliminate this S, allowing the grammar to generate new strings. For example, with $S \rightarrow \lambda$, it can generate b followed by a comma:

$$S \Rightarrow b, S \Rightarrow b,$$

To modify G2.30 so it can generate category 4 lists, we first create a new start symbol S' (S then is no longer the start symbol) and add the production $S' \rightarrow S$. In our modified grammar, S' generates S, which, in turn, can generate anything G2.30 can. Thus, we have not changed the language generated by adding this production. Next, we add the production $S' \rightarrow \lambda$, which adds the null string and only the null string because our new start symbol S' never appears on the right of any production. Our new grammar is

G2.33   1. $S' \rightarrow S$ new start symbol S'
        2. $S' \rightarrow \lambda$ allows S' to generate the null string
        3. $S \rightarrow b, S$ generates (b,)*
        4. $S \rightarrow b$ generates the last b

Exercise 2.12

List the three shortest strings in each of the following languages. Write a grammar for each language.

1. (b,)*
2. (b,)+
3. b(,b)*;

Answers:

1. λ $S \rightarrow b, S$
   b, $S \rightarrow \lambda$
   b, b,

2. b, $S \rightarrow b, S$ or $S \rightarrow b, L$
   b, b, $S \rightarrow b,$ $L \rightarrow b, L$
   b, b, b, $L \rightarrow \lambda$

3. b; $S \rightarrow bL$
   b, b; $L \rightarrow , bL$
   b, b, b; $L \rightarrow ;$

Now let us write a grammar for a compound statement of the form

{
         statement

```
        statement
          ...
        statement
    }
```

in which the statements within the braces use the semicolon as a terminator (as in Java and C+). To keep our grammar simple, we will restrict a statement to an assignment statement. In this grammar, we will use descriptive names for nonterminals and enclose terminals in quotes:

G2.34

```
  1. compoundStatement    → "{ " statementList "} "
  2. statementList        → statement statementList
  3. statementList        → λ
  4. statement            → assignStatement
  5. assignStatement      → identifier "=" expression ";"
```

Productions 2 and 3 produce a category 1 list; they generate a list of zero or more `statement` nonterminals within the braces that delimit a compound statement (notice the parallel between these productions and the productions in G2.24). Production 4 generates an `assignStatement` for each `statement`. `assignstatement`, in turn, generates an assignment statement. Production 5 clearly shows that the semicolon is both part of and terminates an assignment statement. Thus, we call the semicolon a *terminator* as it is used here.

Now suppose we use a different grammar for a compound statement:

G2.35

```
  1. compoundStatement    → "{ " statementList "} "
  2. statementList        → statement statementListTail
  3. statementList        → λ
  4. statementListTail    → ";" statement statementListTail
  5. statementListTail    → λ
  6. statement            → assignStatement
  7. assignStatement      → identifier "=" expression
```

Productions 4 and 7 in this grammar show that the semicolon functions as a *separator* of successive statements rather than as a terminator. Thus, the last assignment statement in a sequence will not be terminated by a semicolon. For example, in the following compound statement, which G2.35 can generate, a semicolon is not at the end of the second assignment statement:

```
  {
    x = 1;   // this semicolon separates this statement from the next
    y = 2    // no semicolon at the end of this statement
  }
```

Notice the parallel between productions 2, 3, 4, and 5 in G2.35 and the productions in G2.31. Production 7 shows that the semicolon is not part of the assignment statement.

2.11 AN IMPORTANT LANGUAGE THAT IS NOT CONTEXT-FREE

Let us write a grammar that generates a list of one or more elements separated by commas. Each element of the list should be an arbitrary string in (b|c)+. Here are some examples of lists that the grammar should generate:

```
b,c,bb
b,c,bc
c,b,c
b
```

Notice that the same string can appear more than once in a list. For example, in the third list above, the element c appears twice. Each list can have an arbitrarily large number of elements and each element can be an arbitrarily long string of b's and/or c's.

One straightforward grammar that generates these lists is

G2.36

1. S → Q
2. S → Q,S
3. Q → bQ
4. Q → cQ
5. Q → b
6. Q → c

Productions 1 and 2 generate a list of one or more Q' s separated by commas. Productions 3 through 6 allow each Q to generate a nonnull string of b's and/or c's.

Now let us consider lists in which each element must be distinct. Can we write a grammar that will generate just these nonrepeating lists? Our grammar would have to remember which elements it has already generated to avoid repeating them. Thus, to generate nonrepeating lists of arbitrary length would require a context-free grammar that has unlimited memory. Unfortunately, just as a regular grammar's counting ability is limited by the number of nonterminals it contains, so is the memory of a context-free grammar. Thus, a context-free grammar cannot generate nonrepeating lists if the lists can be arbitrarily long. Take a few minutes to try to write a grammar for our nonrepeating lists. You will not be able to find a grammar that works.

We now have seen two languages that are not context-free: the *TRIPLED* language in Section 2.7 and nonrepeating lists. That *TRIPLED* is not context-free is of little concern to compiler designers since constructs similar to *TRIPLED* rarely appear in programming languages. Nonrepeating lists, on the other hand, commonly appear in programming languages. For example, consider this variable declaration in Java:

```
int b, c, bb;    // three distinct identifiers
```

The variable list that follows int should be a nonrepeating list. A compiler has to detect and flag any declaration in which a variable identifier repeats, as in, for example,

```
int b, c, b;    // syntax error—b repeats
```

Obviously, in order for a compiler to perform complete syntax checking, it must have at its disposal complete syntax information. But a context-free grammar alone cannot provide this complete information since it cannot represent nonrepeating lists. Thus, a compiler based on a context-free grammar must be provided with additional information. Otherwise, it would not be able to completely check the source program. Later on, when we design and implement a simple compiler, you will see the exact form that this additional information takes.

Context-free grammars are not perfect—they cannot describe some features of common programming languages. However, they can describe most features, and whatever remains we can relatively easily describe by some other means.

PROBLEMS

1. Write a grammar that generates the language { }.
2. Write a grammar that generates the language {λ}.
3. Write a grammar that generates bbb* cc* that uses directly left recursive productions.
4. Write a regular grammar that generates bbb* c* .
5. Write a regular grammar that generates b* | c* | d* .
6. Write a grammar that generates the language consisting of all strings of b's in which successive b's are separated by at least one comma. Successive commas are allowed. For example, b, b, , , b, b, , b.
7. Write a regular grammar equivalent to
   1. S → Sb
   2. S → c
   3. S → d
   4. S → e
8. Write a regular grammar equivalent to
   1. S → bcdS
   2. S → cbaS
   3. S → bbA
   4. A → bbc
9. Write a grammar that generates a list in which each element is either b, c, or d, and in which successive elements are separated by exactly one comma. Your grammar should also generate the null string. Sample strings:

   λ

   b

   b, b, b, c, d, b
10. Write a grammar that generates {$b^{2i}c^i : i \geq 0$}.
11. Given arbitrary grammars G1 and G2, show how to construct grammars G3 and G4 such that L(G3) = L(G1)|L(G2) and L(G4) = L(G1)L(G2).
12. Describe the language generated by
    1. S → SS
    2. S → bSc
    3. S → cSb
    4. S → λ
13. Write a regular grammar that generates (bcd)* eee.

14. Write a right linear grammar that generates (bcd) * eee.

15. Prove that a finite language is always regular.

16. Convert the following grammar to a right linear grammar:
    1. S $\rightarrow$ Sbcd
    2. S $\rightarrow$ fg

17. Write a grammar that generates $\{b^i c^{i+j} d^j : i \geq 1, j \geq 2\}$.

18. Describe the language generated by
    1. S $\rightarrow$ bB
    2. B $\rightarrow$ cC
    3. C $\rightarrow$ dS
    4. C $\rightarrow$ d

19. How many distinct derivations of bcde are possible using
    1. S $\rightarrow$ BCDE
    2. B $\rightarrow$ b
    3. C $\rightarrow$ c
    4. D $\rightarrow$ d
    5. E $\rightarrow$ e

20. Write a grammar that generates all properly nested parenthesized strings. Some examples of strings in the language are

    ( )

    ( ) ( ) ( )

    (( ) ( ))

    ((( ))) ( ) ( ) (( ) ( ))

21. Write a grammar that generates $\{b^i c^j : i > 2, j \geq 3\}$.

22. How many times (in terms of i, j, and k) and in what order must the productions below be used to generate the string $b^i c^j d^k$?
    1. S $\rightarrow$ bSd
    2. S $\rightarrow$ bA
    3. A $\rightarrow$ bAc
    4. A $\rightarrow$ c

23. Write a grammar that generates (bc*)+.

24. Prove that any grammar that generates the language $\{b^i c^i : i \geq 0\}$ cannot contain the production S $\rightarrow$ bS, where S is the start symbol.

25. Write a regular grammar that generates $\{b^i c^i : i \leq 4\}$ by counting.

26. Write a regular grammar equivalent to G2.36.

27. Let L denote the language defined by the following grammar:
    1. S $\rightarrow$ bcS
    2. S $\rightarrow$ d

    Modify this grammar so that it generates the language $L \mid \{\lambda\}$.

28. Give a summary of the proof that the language *PAIRED* in Section 2.7 is not regular (see Section 17.12).

29. Give a regular expression for the language defined by G2.30 to which S $\rightarrow$ λ has been added.

30. Give a summary of the proof that the language *TRIPLED* in Section 2.7 is not context-free (see Section 4.10).

31. Prove that the language consisting of arbitrarily long nonrepeating lists is not context-free.

32. Convert the following grammar to a regular grammar:

    1. S → bcdeS
    2. S → edcb

33. If you make no assumptions about the terminal alphabet for the grammar below, can you determine how many strings are in the language it generates?

    S → b | c

    If you know the terminal alphabet is {b, c}, how many strings are in the language?

34. Give a regular expression that defines the same language as the following grammar:

    1. b → "b" b
    2. b → "b"

35. Is production 1 in G2.32 necessary?

3

CONTEXT-FREE GRAMMARS, PART 2

3.1 INTRODUCTION

Although the notion of a context-free grammar is straightforward, there is, nevertheless, much about context-free grammars for the compiler designer to learn. In this chapter, we continue our study of context-free grammars. We start by introducing parse trees. A parse tree is a graphical representation of the replacements that occur during a derivation. We then describe several language-preserving transformations on context-free grammars, that is, transformations that do not affect the language generated.

3.2 PARSE TREES

We can represent the replacements that occur during a derivation of a string graphically with a parse tree. In a parse tree, the root is the start symbol of the grammar. Each nonterminal in the tree has immediately below it the symbols—each as a separate node—used to replace it in the derivation. For example, if B is replaced by bcD in a derivation, the corresponding portion of the parse tree would look like this:

```
      B
     /|\
    b c D
```

Let us look at an example of a derivation and its corresponding parse tree. Consider the following grammar:

G3.1
1. S → BD
2. B → bc

3. D → dD
4. D → λ

A derivation of the string bcdd in this grammar is

S ⇒ BD ⇒ bcD ⇒ bcdD ⇒ bcddD ⇒ bcdd
1   2   3   3   4

The corresponding parse tree is given in Figure 3.1. The leaf nodes (i.e., the nodes with no children) spell out left to right the symbols in the generated string.

A parse tree may be constructed in step with a derivation. Each intermediate string has a corresponding intermediate tree. For example, the first two steps in the derivation above produces the intermediate string bcD. The corresponding intermediate parse tree is given in Figure 3.2.

Notice that the leaf nodes in this tree spell out the intermediate string bcD.

A derivation tree makes it easy to see the replacements made in the derivation of a string. However, it does not completely specify the order in which replacements are made. For example, the tree in Figure 3.1 does not tell us if the replacement of B occurred before, after, or in between the replacements of the three D nonterminals. There are, in fact, four distinct derivations of bcdd using G3.1, all of which have the parse tree in Figure 3.1. They are

1. S ⇒ BD ⇒ bcD ⇒ bcdD ⇒ bcddD ⇒ bcdd
   1   2   3   3   4
2. S ⇒ BD ⇒ BdD ⇒ bcdD ⇒ bcddD ⇒ bcdd
   1   3   2   3   4
3. S ⇒ BD ⇒ BdD ⇒ BddD ⇒ bcddD ⇒ bcdd
   1   3   3   2   4
4. S ⇒ BD ⇒ BdD ⇒ BddD ⇒ Bdd ⇒ bcdd
   1   3   3   4   2

Unlike the tree in Figure 3.1, some parse trees have only one corresponding derivation. Such trees have the following property: all the nonterminals must lie on a single path starting with the start symbol. For such a tree, nonterminals must be replaced in the order in which they lie on this path. There is never any choice. Thus, only one derivation is possible. For example, in a derivation corresponding to the tree in Figure 3.3, the nonterminals S, D, and B must be replaced in that order.

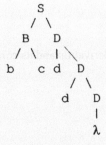

Figure 3.1.

Figure 3.1.

3.3   LEFTMOST AND RIGHTMOST DERIVATIONS

Among the possibly many derivations corresponding to a parse tree, two are particularly important to the compiler designer. We call one the leftmost derivation and the other the rightmost derivation. In a *leftmost derivation,* we replace the leftmost nonterminal at every step; in a *rightmost derivation,* we replace the rightmost nonterminal at every step. For example, consider:

G3.2

1. S → AB
2. A → CD
3. B → EF
4. C → c
5. D → d
6. E → e
7. F → f

In this grammar the leftmost derivation of cdef is

S ⇒ AB ⇒ CDB ⇒ cDB ⇒ cdB ⇒ cdEF ⇒ cdeF ⇒ cdef
1   2   4   5   3   6   7

In Figure 3.4, we subscript the nonterminals in the corresponding parse tree according to the order in which we replace them in the leftmost derivation. We can see that the nonterminals are replaced in *depth-first order* with preference given to the leftmost. That is, we always replace the nonterminal at the greatest depth from the root. When there is more than one nonterminal at the greatest depth, we replace the leftmost. For example, after we replace S in Figure 3.4, A and B are of equal depth. So we replace A next because it is leftmost. We then replace C because it is the leftmost nonterminal at the greatest depth.

A rightmost derivation corresponds to an order in which we replace the nonterminal at the greatest depth at every step, with preference given to the rightmost. Thus, a rightmost

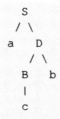

Figure 3.3.

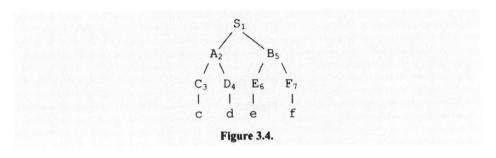

Figure 3.4.

derivation, like a leftmost derivation, corresponds to a depth-first order, but with preference given to the rightmost nonterminal when there is more than one nonterminal at the greatest depth. In Figure 3.5, we have subscripted the nonterminals of the parse tree according to the order in which we replace them in a rightmost derivation.

The first step in the design of a compiler is the writing of a grammar that defines the source language (i.e., the language the compiler must translate). We then write a parser for this grammar. We generally construct a parser to determine a particular derivation, usually either the leftmost or rightmost.

Parsers can be written either by hand or automatically by a computer program called a *parser generator*. A parser generator (see Figure 3.6) inputs a grammar and outputs the parser for that grammar. The parser that is generated can then be "plugged into" a compiler. A parser generator can substantially cut the amount of time needed to program a compiler. In Chapters 13 and 23, we will study parser generators.

Starting with the next section, we begin our study of *language-preserving transformations* of context-free languages. Such transformations modify grammars in a way that does not affect the language generated; hence, the name "language-preserving." Why would a compiler designer need to transform a grammar if the new grammar is going to generate the same language as the old grammar? The answer is that parsing algorithms generally require grammars in a very specific form. If a given grammar is not in the required form, one of these transformations may be able to convert it to the required form. Why doesn't the compiler designer write a grammar in the required form to begin with? Sometimes it is easier to write a grammar in the wrong form and then convert it to the required form than to write a grammar directly in the required form.

3.4   SUBSTITUTION

Substitution is a language-preserving transformation. Let us look at an example using the following grammar:

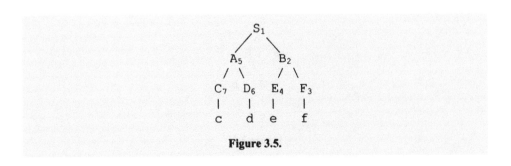

Figure 3.5.

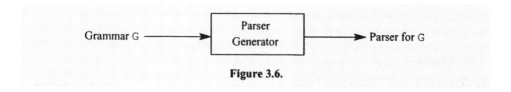

Figure 3.6.

G3.3
1. S → BC
2. B → bB
3. B → d
4. C → c

In this grammar, S generates BC. We can then replace the B in BC using productions 2 or 3, yielding bBC or dC. An alternative approach is to allow S to generate bBC and dC directly by adding the following productions:

1a. S → bBC
1b. S → dC

Then we do not need production 1. Our new grammar, equivalent to G3.3, is

G3.4
1a. S → bBC
1b. S → dC
2. B → bB
3. B → d
4. C → c

In this example, we obtain our two new productions by substituting the right sides of the B productions for B in production 1. The transformed grammar is equivalent to the original grammar.

We may generalize what we have done with G3.3 with the following rule: Suppose a grammar contains p productions for some nonterminal N:

$N → z_1$
$N → z_2$
.
.
.
$N → z_p$

Suppose the grammar also contains the A production

$A → xNy$

where x and y are arbitrary strings over the total alphabet. We can then eliminate this A production from the grammar if we add the following new productions:

$A → xz_1y$
$A → xz_2y$

.
.
.

$$A \rightarrow xz_py$$

We obtain each new A production from the original A production, $A \rightarrow xNy$, by substituting for N. The resulting grammar generates the same language as the original. We call this procedure *substitution*.

Let us do another example of substitution. If we wish to replace production 1 in the following grammar using substitution,

G3.5

1. S → dB
2. B → bB
3. B → d
4. B → cccS

we must add three new S productions, one for each B production. We obtain each new S production by replacing the B on the right side of production 1 with the right side of an B production. The equivalent grammar that results is

G3.6

1a. S → dbB
1b. S → dd
1c. S → dcccS
2. B → bB
3. B → d
4. B → cccS

Exercise 3.1

Replace production 1 in the following grammar using substitution. Give the equivalent grammar that results.

1. S → bS
2. S → b

Answers:

We must substitute the S on the right side of production 1 with bS (from production 1) and with b (from production 2, yielding two new productions. These two production replace production 1. The new grammar is

1a. S → bbS   (from production 1)
1b. S → bb   (from production 1)
2. S → b   (original production 2)

■

3.5 AMBIGUOUS GRAMMARS

Let us consider the parse trees for the strings b, bb, and bbb in the following grammar:

G3.7
  1. S → SS
  2. S → b

The parse tree for b is

    S
    |
    b

to which there corresponds exactly one derivation. The parse tree for bb is

      S
     / \
    S   S
    | |
    b   b

This tree corresponds to two distinct derivations:

    S ⇒ SS ⇒ bS ⇒ bb
    1   2   2

    S ⇒ SS ⇒ Sb ⇒ bb
    1   2   2

That more than one derivation corresponds to a single tree is no surprise. This is true for most parse trees. Note that both derivations correspond to the same parse tree. For the string bbb, however, we have quite a different situation: There is more than one parse tree (see Figure 3.7).

Although the two trees are similar (one is "left-handed"; the other, "right-handed"), they are nevertheless distinct. We call a grammar like G3.7 that generates at least one string that has more than one parse tree an *ambiguous grammar*. G3.7, in fact, generates an infinite number of strings with more than one parse tree (bbb, bbbb, bbbbb, ...). It takes only one string, however, with more than one parse tree to make a grammar ambiguous. For example, consider

G3.8
  1. S → b
  2. S → B

Figure 3.7.

3. S → cC
4. B → b
5. C → cC
6. C → λ

This ambiguous grammar generates an infinite number of strings of which only one—the string b—has more than one parse tree.

Exercise 3.2

a. What language is generated by G3.8?

b. Draw the two parse trees for b using G3.8.

Answers:

a. b | c+

b.

We can almost always convert an ambiguous grammar to an equivalent grammar (i.e., one generating the same language) that is not ambiguous. Let us see if we can develop some general techniques for converting ambiguous grammars to unambiguous equivalents.

One useful technique is to study the ambiguous grammar to determine the language it defines. Then it is usually easy to write a completely new grammar for the language that, hopefully, is unambiguous. Let us consider an example. Refer back to the ambiguous grammar G3.7, which generates the language b+. We can easily write a grammar that generates b+ in strict left-to-right order. Since grammars which generate strictly left-to-right or right-to-left are rarely ambiguous, we can be reasonably confident we will get an unambiguous grammar. Our result is, indeed, an unambiguous equivalent grammar:

G3.9
1. S → bS
2. S → b

Exercise 3.3

For each of the following grammars, determine the language defined and write an equivalent unambiguous grammar:

a. 1. S → bS
   2. S → Sb
   3. S → c

b. 1. S → BSD
   2. S → λ
   3. B → bB
   4. B → b

    5. D → dD
    6. D → d

Answers:

a. b* cb*
    1. S → bS
    2. S → cA
    3. A → bA
    4. A → λ
b. λ|b+d+
    1. S → λ
    2. S → bB
    3. B → bB
    4. B → dD
    5. D → dD
    6. D → λ

■

Another useful technique in converting ambiguous grammars is to use a type of production that we aptly call a *one-way street*. Consider the following grammar:

G3.10
    1. S → bSd   (generates b's and d's)
    2. S → bS   (generates excess b's)
    3. S → λ   (eliminates S)

The language defined by G3.10 is $\{b^i d^j : i \geq j\}$. To derive the string $b^i d^j$, the productions in G3.10 should be used as follows:

1. production 1 j times (to generate j b's and d's).
2. production 2 $(i - j)$ times (to generate the b's that are in excess of the d's).
3. production 3 once (to eliminate the nonterminal S).

We must use production 3 (which terminates the derivation) last. However, until we use production 3, we may use productions 1 and 2 in any order, and therein lies the ambiguity of the grammar. For example, we can generate the string bbd by applying productions 1, 2, and 3, in 1–2–3 order or in 2–1–3 order. These two derivations correspond to different parse trees (see Figure 3.8).

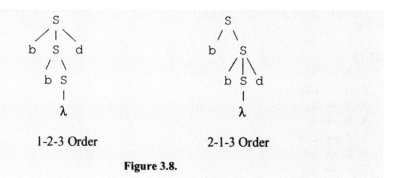

1-2-3 Order   2-1-3 Order

Figure 3.8.

The trick in converting G3.10 to an unambiguous grammar is to force a particular order in which the productions may be used. The following grammar is equivalent to G3.10 but is not ambiguous. It forces the generation of the b's and d's first, then the excess b's.

G3.11

    1. S $\rightarrow$ bSd   (generate b's and d's)
    2. S $\rightarrow$ B   (take one-way street)
    3. B $\rightarrow$ bB   (generate excess b's)
    4. B $\rightarrow$ λ (eliminate B)

Production 1 generates b's and matching d's to the right. However, once we use production 2 in G3.11, we eliminate the S nonterminal. We can, therefore, no longer use production 1. We can think of production 2 as a "one-way street" away from production 1. Once we use it, there is no going back. Thus, the generation of excess b's, if any, by production 3 in G3.11 must follow the generation of b–d pairs by production 1. For G3.11, there is only one order that generates the string $b^i d^j$:

    1. production 1 j times
    2. production 2 once
    3. production 3 $(i - j)$ times
    4. production 4 once

Exercise 3.4

Eliminate the ambiguity in G3.10 by forcing the generation of excess b's before the b-d pairs, rather than in the reverse order as we did in G3.11. Again use a one-way street.

Answer:

    1. S $\rightarrow$ bS   (generate excess b's)
    2. S $\rightarrow$ C   (one-way street)
    3. C $\rightarrow$ bCd   (generate b's and d's)
    4. C $\rightarrow$ λ (eliminate C)

                                                 ■

Here is one more technique for eliminating ambiguity. Sometimes a grammar has two or more productions that do, in effect, the same thing and thereby cause the ambiguity. By deleting all but one of these productions, we sometimes get an equivalent unambiguous grammar. You should use this technique with care—deleting productions usually results in a nonequivalent grammar. However, in the following grammar, this deletion technique works:

G3.12

    1. S $\rightarrow$ BC
    2. B $\rightarrow$ bBc
    3. B $\rightarrow$ Bc
    4. B $\rightarrow$ λ
    5. C $\rightarrow$ cCd
    6. C $\rightarrow$ cC
    7. C $\rightarrow$ λ

G3.12 defines the language $\{b^n c^p d^m : p \geq n + m\}$. In this language, there must be at least as many c's as there are b's and d's combined. The middle c's that are not balanced either by b's on the left or d's on the right (i.e., those in excess of $n + m$) can be generated by either production 3 or 6. We can eliminate this ambiguity by deleting either production 3 or 6.

You might be wondering why we are making all the fuss about ambiguous grammars. The problem is that ambiguity can result in multiple meanings. A famous example of multiple meanings in the English language is the sentence, "Time flies like an arrow." This single sentence has three quite distinct meanings. These three meanings correspond to the three possible verbs in the sentence: "Time", "flies", or "like." If "Time" is the verb, then you should use your stop watch to time the insects the same way you time arrows; if "flies" is the verb, then you are commenting on how quickly the years go by; if "like" is the verb, you are asserting that the insects called "time flies" have an affection for an arrow. In a similar fashion, if a grammar for a programming language is ambiguous, then a single program could have more than one "meaning" (a program's meaning is what it tells to computer to do). How then is a compiler supposed to translate such a program? Although ambiguous grammars are problematical, a compiler designer can sometimes put them to good use. We will see how to use them in Chapter 7.

We have just seen several language-preserving techniques that eliminate ambiguity from a context-free grammar. Unfortunately, these techniques work only in very specific circumstances. In fact, there are some context-free languages for which no unambiguous context-free grammar exists. In other words, it is *impossible* to write an unambiguous context-free grammar for these languages. We call such languages *inherently ambiguous*. Thus, there can be no general algorithm for eliminating ambiguity that will work for every grammar. In fact, even if we consider only languages that are not inherently ambiguous, there still is no general procedure for eliminating ambiguity. It is impossible for such an algorithm to exist! The problem of eliminating ambiguity in an arbitrary context-free grammar has a subtle complexity that makes it unsolvable in the general case.

3.6 DETERMINING NULLABLE NONTERMINALS

A nonterminal is *nullable* if it can generate the null string. For example, consider

G3.13

   1. S $\rightarrow$ AB
   2. S $\rightarrow$ a
   3. A $\rightarrow$ aA
   4. A $\rightarrow$ λ
   5. B $\rightarrow$ bB
   6. B $\rightarrow$ λ

The nonterminals A and B are obviously nullable since they appear on the left sides of lambda productions. It follows that AB, the right side of production 1, is nullable, which, in turn, implies that S is nullable.

Here is an algorithm that marks a nonterminal if and only if it is nullable:

1. If a nonterminal appears on the left side of a lambda production, then mark every occurrence of this nonterminal.

2. If an unmarked nonterminal appears on the left side of a production whose right side has every symbol marked, then mark every occurrence of this nonterminal.
3. Continue marking according to step 2 until no more marking is possible.

Let us apply this algorithm to the grammar in Figure 3.9. We will mark a symbol by placing an x above it. In step 1 of our algorithm, every occurrence of A and B is marked because the grammar has A and B lambda productions (see Figure 3.9a). Now the right side of production 1 is completely marked. Thus, in step 2, we mark every occurrence of S (see Figure 3.9b). The algorithm then terminates because no more marking is possible. The nullable terminals are those that are marked, namely, S, A, and B. The nonnullable nonterminals are those that are not marked, namely, C.

3.7 ELIMINATING LAMBDA PRODUCTIONS

We generally view a production in a context-free grammar as a replacement rule. An occurrence of the left side of a production in a string can be replaced by the right side of the production. A lambda production, on the other hand, is more correctly viewed as a deletion rule whose application deletes an occurrence of the lambda production's left side.

Now consider this: If a nonterminal in a derivation is to be deleted, why generate it in the first place? If we do not generate the nonterminal, then we do not have to delete it. If we do not have to delete it, then do not need the lambda production, in which case we can eliminate the lambda production from the grammar without affecting the language defined. For example, suppose we would like to convert the following grammar to an equivalent grammar that does not have any lambda productions:

G3.14

1. S → dBC
2. B → bB
3. B → λ

(a)

```
       xx
1) S → AB

2) S → aCS
   x    x
3) A → aA
   x
4) A → λ
   x    x
5) B → bB
   x
6) B → λ

7) C → c
```

(b)

```
   x   xx
1) S → AB
   x     x
2) S → aCS
   x    x
3) A → aA
   x
4) A → λ
   x    x
5) B → bB
   x
6) B → λ

7) C → c
```

Figure 3.9.

4. C → cC
5. C → λ

When we use production 3, a lambda production, it deletes a B that comes from the right side of either production 1 or 2 (see Figure 3.10a). But if we add the productions

S → dC
B → b

to our grammar, we can use them in place of productions 1 and 2 whenever we want to generate dC or b, respectively, from S or B. These new productions do not generate the B's that productions 1 and 2 generate. So after using them, there are no B's that we have to delete (see Figure 3.10b). We can then throw away production 3 without affecting the language defined. Of course, we need to keep productions 1 and 2 to generate the B's that are not eventually deleted but, instead, expanded into nonnull strings by production 2. Similarly, since production 5 is a lambda production, we add

S → dB
C → c

to our grammar and use them in place of productions 1 and 4 to generate dB and c, respectively. Because these productions do not generate C's that have to be deleted, we can throw away production 5 without affecting the language defined.

There is one more possibility to consider. What if we delete both B and C in production 1 with the lambda productions? Then S effectively generates a single d. To accomplish the same effect without using lambda productions, we need the production

S → d

By adding the five productions above to G3.14, we make the lambda productions unnecessary. Whatever we can generate with lambda productions we can now generate without them. Thus, our new grammar with the lambda productions deleted is equivalent to our original grammar, G3.14. Our new grammar is

G3.15
1. S → dBC
2. S → dC

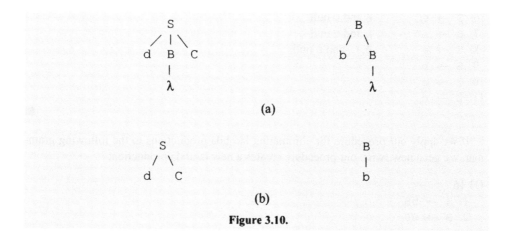

Figure 3.10.

3. S → dB
4. S → d
5. B → bB
6. B → b
7. C → cC
8. C → c

Comparing G3.15 with G3.14, we see an obvious advantage of using lambda productions: there are fewer productions. G3.15, however, has the advantage of having shorter derivations than G3.14 since it does not have the overhead associated with the generation and subsequent deletion of nonterminals. This "space" (i.e., the number of productions) versus "time" (i.e., the length of the derivation) trade-off is characteristic of the elimination of lambda productions.

Exercise 3.5

Convert the following grammar to an equivalent grammar without lambda productions:

1. S → eBCD
2. B → b
3. B → λ
4. C → c
5. C → λ
6. D → d
7. D → λ

Answers:

In the first production of this grammar, we may or may not delete each of its three nonterminals. That is, there are two possibilities for B, two for C, and two for D. We, therefore, have 2 × 2 × 2 = 8 variations (see productions 1 to 8 in the following grammar). Our new grammar, therefore, has the original S production plus seven new ones, one for every possible variation. The new grammar is

1. S → eBCD	B, C, and D all nonnull
2. S → eBC	Only D null
3. S → eBD	Only C null
4. S → eCD	Only B null
5. S → eB	C and D null
6. S → eC	B and D null
7. S → eD	B and C null
8. S → e	B, C, and D null
9. B → b	
10. C → c	
11. D → d	

■

If we apply our procedure for eliminating lambda productions to the following grammar, we get a new twist: our procedure creates a new lambda production:

G3.16
1. S → bB
2. B → CD

3. C → c
4. C → λ
5. D → d
6. D → λ

To make the two lambda productions in G3.16 unnecessary, we add productions to the grammar for any production that has C or D on its right side. Thus, for production 2, we must add

B → D   (production 2 with C deleted)
B → C   (production 2 with D deleted)
B → λ   (production 2 with both C and D deleted)

In adding productions to make the lambda productions unnecessary, we have introduced a new lambda production. We must now make the new lambda production unnecessary by adding the appropriate productions. The only production with B on the right side is production 1. If we add the production

S → b

then the new lambda production is also unnecessary. Our general procedure, then, is to continue adding productions until all lambda productions—original and new—are unnecessary, which we, therefore, can delete. Our final grammar equivalent to G3.16 but without lambda productions is

G3.17
1. S → bB
2. S → b
3. B → CD
4. B → C
5. B → D
6. C → c
7. D → d

Our procedure for eliminating lambda productions breaks down for one case: if the grammar generates the null string. Such a grammar must contain at least one lambda production, or else it could not generate the null string. Thus, our procedure applied to such a grammar must fail. Let us try an example and see what happens:

G3.18
1. S → AB
2. A → dS
3. A → λ
4. B → b
5. B → λ

Since we have lambda productions for nonterminals A and B, we must add the following productions, derived from production 1, to make these lambda productions unnecessary:

S → A
S → B
S → λ

Now, however, we have a new lambda production, S → λ. To make this new lambda production unnecessary, we must add the production A → d (derived from production 2). Then, instead of using production 2 to generate dS and subsequently deleting the S with the production S → λ, we can generate d by itself with our new production A → d. There is, however, one use of S → λ that remains necessary: using it in the first step of a derivation to generate the null string. Thus, if we now eliminate all the lambda productions including S → λ, our new grammar can do anything G3.18 can do except generate the null string. We get

G3.19

1. S → AB
2. S → A
3. S → B
4. A → dS
5. A → d
6. B → b

G3.19 and G3.18 are almost equivalent; G3.19 generates everything G3.18 generates except for the null string.

Our procedure for eliminating lambda productions is not language preserving if the language for the original grammar contains the null string. The new grammar produced by our procedure will generate everything the original grammar does except for the null string.

The procedure we have described for eliminating lambda productions may create new lambda productions, as illustrated by G3.16 above. We then have to eliminate these new lambda productions. It is, however, easy to avoid creating any new lambda productions. We simply use the algorithm described in Section 3.6 to determine the nullable nonterminals. We then add productions depending on which nonterminals are nullable. For example, in G3.16, production 1, S → bB can ultimately generate b by itself since B is nullable. Once we remove all the lambda productions, B will no longer be nullable. Thus, we should add the production S → b so that S can generate a b by itself without the aid of lambda productions. Because C and D are nullable, production 3, B → CD, requires that we add the productions B → C and B → D. But now we do not have to add the production B → λ because we have already identified B as a nullable and have transformed the grammmar accordingly.

3.8   ELIMINATING UNIT PRODUCTIONS

A unit production is a production whose left and right sides consist of a single nonterminal. For example, in the following grammar, the unit productions are productions 2 and 4:

G3.20

1. S → bBDE
2. B → D
3. D → d
4. D → E
5. E → e

Productions 3 and 5 are not unit productions because their right sides are not nonterminals.

Unit production elimination uses the same basic approach that we used in lambda production elimination: add productions that make the production to be eliminated unnecessary. However, unlike lambda production elimination, our unit production elimination procedure is always language preserving. Let us consider an example. Consider production 2 in G3.20. If we allow B to generate directly anything that D can generate directly, then this unit production becomes unnecessary. In G3.20, D can generate d (see Figure 3.11a). So we add the production B → d so B can generate d directly (see Figure 3.11b).

Because D can also generate E, we add B → E. Another unit production! We can, however, make this new unit production unnecessary by adding the appropriate productions. In particular, we have to allow B to generate directly anything E can generate directly. Checking with G3.20, we see that the only E production is E → e. Therefore, we have to add B → e to our grammar. Next, we work on production 4. We allow D to generate directly anything E can generate directly. We have to add only D → e. We now have made all our unit productions unnecessary. We can, therefore, delete them all and get a grammar without any unit productions equivalent to G3.20:

G3.21

   1. S → bBDE
   2. B → d
   3. B → e
   4. D → d
   5. D → e
   6. E → e

Our general procedure to eliminate unit productions is like our procedure to eliminate lambda productions: we keep adding productions until all unit productions—original and new—are unnecessary. We then can delete all the unit productions. For a variation of this procedure, see Problem 3.14. It describes a procedure that eliminates unit productions without ever producing new ones.

Exercise 3.6

Transform the following grammar to an equivalent one that does not contain any unit productions:

   1. S → B
   2. B → S
   3. B → b

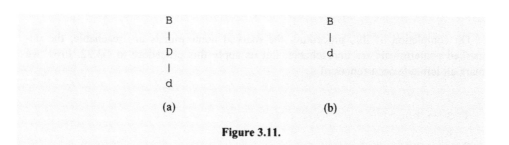

(a)   (b)

Figure 3.11.

Answer:

For the unit production S → B, we should add the productions S → S (because of B → S) and S → b (because of B → b). We can delete the "do nothing" production S → S immediately without affecting the language generated by the grammar. For the other unit production B → S, we should add the B → B (because of S → B). But we can also delete this production immediately. Our final grammar consists of S → b and B → b. ∎

3.9 ELIMINATING USELESS NONTERMINALS

A *useless nonterminal* is a nonterminal that can never be used in a "successful" derivation; that is, a derivation that starts with the start symbol and ends with a terminal string. Therefore, we can delete all productions that contain any useless nonterminals without changing the language generated by the grammar. There are two types of useless nonterminals: unreachable and dead.

An *unreachable nonterminal* is one that can never appear in a derivation that starts with the start symbol. Consider the nonterminals B, C, D, and U in

G3.22

    1. S → bSc
    2. S → bBc
    3. B → bB
    4. B → λ
    5. B → BC
    6. C → c
    7. U → dU
    8. U → d

The start symbol S can produce a B (by production 2), which, in turn, can produce a C (by production 5). The nonterminals B and C, therefore, are reachable from S. However, S cannot produce U, either directly through a single production or indirectly through multiple productions. Thus, U is unreachable. Productions containing unreachable nonterminals are useless, that is, they can never participate in the derivation of a terminal string from the start symbol. Thus, in G3.22, we can delete productions 7 and 8 without affecting the language generated.

Here is a simple algorithm that marks a nonterminal if and only if it is reachable. Note that this algorithm marks only the left sides of productions.

1. Mark every left-side occurrence of the start symbol.
2. Mark every left-side occurrence of any nonterminal not already marked that appears on the right side of a production whose left side is marked.
3. Continue the marking according to step 2 until no more marking is possible.

On completion of this procedure, the marked nonterminals are reachable; the unmarked nonterminals are unreachable. Let us apply this procedure to G3.22. First, we mark all left-side occurrences of S:

    x
1. S → bSc
    x
2. S → bBc

3. B → bB
4. B → λ
5. B → BC
6. C → c
7. U → dU
8. U → d

Because B is on the right side of a production whose left side is marked (production 2), we now mark all left-side occurrences of B:

```
    x
1.  S → bSc
    x
2.  S → bBc
    x
3.  B → bB
    x
4.  B → λ
    x
5.  B → BC
6.  C → c
7.  U → dU
8.  U → d
```

Because C is on the right side of a production whose left side is marked (production 5), we now mark all left-side occurrences of C:

```
    x
1.  S → bSc
    x
2.  S → bBc
    x
3.  B → bB
    x
4.  B → λ
    x
5.  B → BC
    x
6.  C → c
7.  U → dU
8.  U → d
```

At this point we cannot mark any more productions. Only U remains unmarked, and is, therefore, the only unreachable nonterminal.

Exercise 3.7

Determine the unreachable nonterminals in

1. S → fB
2. B → b
3. B → cC

4. C → c
5. C → dD
6. D → d
7. E → e

Answer:

   x
1. S → fB
   x
2. B → b
   x
3. B → cC
   x
4. C → c
   x
5. C → dD
   x
6. D → d
7. E → e

E is the only unreachable nonterminal.

■

The second kind of useless nonterminal, a *dead nonterminal*, is one from which a terminal string cannot be derived. For example, consider the following grammar:

G3.23
    1. S → bBC
    2. S → D
    3. B → bB
    4. B → λ
    5. C → c
    6. D → dE
    7. E → dD

D and E are reachable from the start symbol. But notice that the only D production replaces a D with a string that contains an E, and the only E production replaces an E with a string that contains a D. Thus, once a D appears in an intermediate string, all subsequent intermediate strings must have either a D or an E. D and E can never derive a terminal string. Thus, D and E are dead nonterminals. We can, therefore, delete any productions containing a D or E, without changing the language generated by the grammar.

Here is an algorithm that marks a nonterminal if and only if it is not dead:

1. Mark every occurrence of a nonterminal that appears on the left side of a production whose right side is a terminal string (including the null string).

2. Mark every occurrence of a nonterminal not already marked that appears on the left side of a production whose right side contains no unmarked nonterminals.

3. Continue marking according to step 2 until no more marking is possible.

On completion of this procedure, all the nondead nonterminals are marked; all the dead nonterminals are not marked.

Let us apply this procedure to G3.23. In step 1, we mark every occurrence of B (because of production 4) and C (because of production 5):

```
          xx
1. S  →  bBC
2. S  →  D
       x    x
3. B  →  bB
       x
4. B  →  λ
       x
5. C  →  c
6. D  →  dE
7. E  →  dD
```

Now production 1 has no unmarked nonterminals on its right side. Therefore, in step 2, we mark every occurrence of S:

```
     x     xx
1. S  →  bBC
     x
2. S  →  D
     x       x
3. B  →  bB
     x
4. B  →  λ
     x
5. C  →  c
6. D  →  dE
7. E  →  dD
```

At this point, we cannot mark any more nonterminals. Only D and E are unmarked and, therefore, are the only dead nonterminals.

Exercise 3.8

Give a grammar in which a nonterminal occurs that is both unreachable and dead.

Answer:

```
1. S  →  b
2. B  →  bB
```

B is both unreachable and dead.

■

When we eliminate dead nonterminals from a grammar, we can create new unreachable nonterminals, but not vice versa. For example, consider the following grammar:

G3.24
```
1. S  →  e
2. S  →  BD
```

   3. B → b
   4. D → dD
   5. U → c

In this grammar, D is dead and U is unreachable. When we eliminate all productions containing D, we get

G3.25
   1. S → e
   2. B → b
   3. U → c

Now, in G3.25, B, as well as U, is unreachable. If we now eliminate our unreachable nonterminals, we are left with a single production:

G3.26
   1. S → e

Since eliminating dead nonterminals can produce new unreachable nonterminals but not vice versa, we should always eliminate useless nonterminals in the following order:

   1. Dead
   2. Unreachable

We call this the "duh rule" (the "du" in "duh" indicates proper order: "d" (i.e., dead) first, then "u" (unreachable). If we eliminate dead nonterminals first, any unreachable nonterminals created will then be eliminated when, in step 2, we eliminate unreachable nonterminals. If, on the other hand, we eliminate unreachable nonterminals first, we may be left with new unreachable nonterminals after we eliminate the dead nonterminals. For example, if we first eliminate unreachable nonterminals from G3.24, we get

G3.27
   1. S → e
   2. S → BD
   3. B → b
   4. D → dD

If we now eliminate the dead nonterminals, we get

G3.28
   1. S → e
   2. B → b

The nonterminal B is a new unreachable nonterminal.

    An important check to perform on any grammar is to determine if it has any useless nonterminals. Useless productions generally mean that the creator of the grammar made a mistake when writing it, and, thus, the grammar does not correctly define the intended language. In this case, the proper course of action is to correct the grammar rather than transform it to an equivalent (and also incorrect) grammar without useless nonterminals.

3.10 RECURSION CONVERSIONS

Recall from Chapter 2 that direct left recursion refers to a production whose left-hand side starts its right side, that is, a production of the form

A → A*x*

where *x* is any nonnull string. Directly left recursive productions generate lists from right to left. For example, the following grammar generates a list of d's and e's preceded by b or cc:

G3.29
   1. S → Sd   (generates a d on the right)
   2. S → Se   (generates an e on the right)
   3. S → b   (generates an initial b)
   4. S → cc   (generates an initial cc)

We can use productions 1 and 2 any number of times and in any order. Thus, these two productions generate the list (d|e)*. Then production 3 or 4 terminates the derivation by generating a leading b or cc. Thus, G3.29 defines the language (b|cc)(d|e)*. Here is the derivation bdde in this grammar:

S ⇒ Se ⇒ Sde ⇒ Sdde ⇒ bdde

Notice the derivation starts by generating a string in (d|e)* in right-to-left order using productions 1 and 2. It then terminates by generating a b with production 3.

It is generally a simple matter to eliminate direct left recursion; simply generate the list from left to right rather than from right to left. For example, a grammar equivalent to G3.29 that generates the list left to right is

G3.30
   1. S → bL   (generate an initial b)
   2. S → ccL   (generate an initial cc)
   3. L → dL   (L generates a list of d's and/or e's left to right)
   4. L → eL
   5. L → λ

Note that the resulting grammar, G3.30, is directly right recursive. We eliminate direct left recursion by converting it to direct right recursion. Similarly, if we start with a grammar with direct right recursion, we can eliminate it by converting it to direct left recursion.

In G3.30, the list generated by L can be null. Alternatively, we can have L generate only nonnull lists. But then we have to add the productions S → b and S → cc so S can generate a b or cc (we cannot use S → bL and S → ccL because L now cannot generate λ) The grammar then is

G3.31
   1. S → bL   (L generates a nonnull list)
   2. S → ccL   (L generates a nonnull list)
   3. S → b   (allows generation of just b)

4. S → cc   (allows generation of just cc)
5. L → dL
6. L → eL
7. L → d
8. L → e

Observe that if we eliminate the lambda production in G3.30 using our procedure from Section 3.7, the result is G3.31.

Exercise 3.9

Eliminate the direct left recursion in the following grammar:

1. S → Sc
2. S → SBBB
3. S → ScB
4. S → B
5. S → c
6. B → b

Answer:

Notice that the grammar generates a leading B, c, or b followed by a list consisting of zero or more occurrences of c, BBB, and cB. Two equivalent grammars, one with lambda productions and one without, are:

1. S → BL	1. S → BL
2. S → cL	2. S → cL
3. S → bL	3. S → bL
4. L → cL	4. S → B
5. L → BBBL	5. S → c
6. L → cBL	6. S → b
7. L → λ	7. L → cL
	8. L → BBBL
	9. L → cBL
	10. L → c
	11. L → BBB
	12. L → cB
	13. B → b

Another type of recursion, called *indirect recursion,* is illustrated by

G3.32

1. S → ABC
2. A → Bd
3. B → Ce   three nonterminal cycle
4. B → b
5. C → Ac

Although none of the productions in G3.32 are directly recursive, it is possible to get the same effect by using multiple productions. For example, we can derive the string of Acbd from A using productions 2, 3, and 4:

```
A ⇒ Bd ⇒ Ced ⇒ Aced
2      3       4
```

We have a three nonterminal cycle in G3.32: A to B, B to C, and C back to A. We categorize indirect recursion as left, right, or interior, depending on where the regenerated nonterminal appears in the string it generates. If the regenerated nonterminal reappears in the leftmost, rightmost, or interior position, we call the recursion left, right, or interior, respectively. Since A reappears leftmost in the derivation above, we categorize the recursion in G3.32 as indirect left recursion.

We can eliminate indirect recursion—left, right, and interior—by converting it to direct recursion. We do this by progressively reducing the size of the recursive cycle until it is equal to one. We do this conversion by using the substitution technique (see Section 3.4) on the nonterminals in the recursive cycle. For example, in G3.32, if we substitute Bd for A in production 5 (as allowed by production 2), we reduce our recursive cycle by one:

G3.33

1. S → ABC
2. A → Bd
3. B → Ce ⟵
4. B → b   ⟧ two nonterminal cycle
5. C → Bdc ⟶

Our cycle is now from B to C (production 3) and from C back to B (production 5). Our next step is to again reduce the size of the cycle. This time we substitute Ce and b for B in production 5 (as allowed by productions 3 and 4). Since there are two B productions in G3.33, we get two new productions, one by substituting Ce for B, the other by substituting b for B:

G3.34

1. S → ABC
2. A → Bd
3. B → Ce
4. B → b
5. C → Cedc   (direct left recursion)
6. C → bdc

In G3.34, the recursive cycle size is now one—that is, we have direct left recursion. Notice that productions 5 and 6 generate right to left the strings in bdc(edc)*. We can easily eliminate the direct left recursion by replacing production 5 and 6 with productions that generate bdc(edc)* from left to right:

```
C → bdcL
L → edcL
L → λ
```

Our final grammar has no left recursion, either direct or indirect:

G3.35

1. S → ABC
2. A → Bd
3. B → Ce

4. B → b
5. C → bdcL
6. L → edcL
7. L → λ

Exercise 3.10

Convert the following grammar to an equivalent grammar that contains no left recursion:

1. S → Be
2. S → d
3. B → Sc
4. B → b

Answer:

First, convert the indirect left recursion to direct left recursion:

1. S → Be
2. S → d
3. B → Bec
4. B → dc
5. B → b

Now eliminate the direct left recursion:

1. S → Be
2. S → d
3. B → dcL
4. B → bL
5. L → ecL
6. L → λ

                                                  ■

A slightly more complicated example of left recursion is

G3.36
    1. S → Af
    2. A → Sb
    3. A → Ac
    4. A → Bd
    5. B → e

G3.36 contains both indirect left recursion (productions 1 and 2) and direct left recursion (production 3). To eliminate both recursions, we first reduce the size of the indirect recursive cycle to one using the substitution technique: Substitute the right side of production 1 for S in production 2. We get

G3.37
    1. S → Af
    2. A → Afb
    3. A → Ac

4. A → Bd
5. B → e

We now have two directly left recursive productions, which we can eliminate easily. We get

G3.38
1. S → Af
2. A → BdL
3. L → fbL
4. L → cL
5. L → λ
6. B → e

When eliminating left recursion, it is helpful to think of each production whose right side starts with a nonterminal as "pointing" to that nonterminal. For example, production 1 in G3.36, S → Af, points to the A nonterminal. Furthermore, since the A productions are listed after the S production in G3.36, we can say this production "points forward." Similarly, production 4 points forward. Production 2 "points backward" (since the S production precedes the A production). Production 3 is "self-pointing" (i.e., it is directly left recursive). Production 5 is "nonpointing" since its right side does not start with a nonterminal. In terms of this terminology, we can summarize the general technique for eliminating left recursion:

1. Group productions by their left sides.
2. Process each group in order. For each group,
3. First eliminate any backward pointing productions using the substitution technique.
4. Then eliminate any self-pointing productions using the technique for eliminating direct left recursion.

After we apply this procedure, each group of productions can contain only forward pointing and nonpointing productions (since we have eliminated all the backward pointing and self-pointing productions). The grammar, therefore, contains no left recursion, direct or indirect. Furthermore, the very last group of productions processed—because it has no successor group—must contain only nonpointing productions (for example, the B-production in G3.38). The technique works regardless of the order in which the groups of productions are placed for processing.

Exercise 3.11

Eliminate left recursion in the following grammar by

a. processing the S-production first;

b. processing the A-productions first.
1. S → Ag
2. A → Sb
3. A → Sc
4. A → Ad
5. A → Ae
6. A → f

Answers:

a. 1. S → Ag
   2. A → fL
   3. L → gbL
   4. L → gcL
   5. L → dL
   6. L → eL
   7. L → λ

b. 1. S → fLgM
   2. M → bLgM
   3. M → cLgM
   4. M → λ
   5. A → SbL
   6. A → ScL
   7. A → fL
   8. L → dL
   9. L → ˙eL
   10. L → λ

3.11   ADDING THE NULL STRING TO A LANGUAGE

With the exception of lambda production elimination, the context-free grammar transformations we have discussed so far are language preserving (recall that lambda production elimination is language preserving only if the language does not contain the null string). We now look at another transformation that is not language preserving. It adds the null string and only the null string to a language that does not already contain the null string.

To add the null string to the language defined by a grammar, can we simply add the production S → λ? Unfortunately, this transformation does not always work. If S appears on the right side of some production, then the added production may allow nonnull strings to be derivable that were not previously derivable. For example, suppose we add the production S → λ to the following grammar:

G3.39
   1. S → bS
   2. S → c

The new production now allows the new grammar to generate not only the null string but any string containing b's exclusively, none of which can be generated by the original grammar. For example, with the addition of S → λ to G3.39 we can generate b:

   S ⇒ bS ⇒ b

G3.39 defines is b*c but the new language is b*|b*c. We want a grammar that generates b*c|λ. To correctly transform G3.39, we first create a new start symbol S′ and add the production S′ → S. Since S′ generates S, and S generates the original language, the new grammar still generates the original language. Now, however, the start symbol, S′, does not appear on the right side on any production. Thus, if we add S′ → λ, we add the null string and only the null string to the language. The final grammar is

G3.40

   1. $S' \rightarrow \lambda$
   2. $S' \rightarrow S$
   3. $S \rightarrow bS$
   4. $S \rightarrow c$

We can now, of course, eliminate the unit production $S' \rightarrow S$ if we want, using the procedure in Section 3.8, yielding

G3.41

   1. $S' \rightarrow \lambda$
   2. $S' \rightarrow bS$
   3. $S' \rightarrow c$
   4. $S \rightarrow bS$
   5. $S \rightarrow c$

Exercise 3.12

Transform the following grammar so that it defines the null string plus the original language.

1. $S \rightarrow SS$
2. $S \rightarrow d$

Answers:

Using the new start symbol approach, we get:

1. $S' \rightarrow \lambda$
2. $S' \rightarrow S$
3. $S \rightarrow SS$
4. $S \rightarrow d$

Alternatively, we can write a completely new grammar. Since the original language is $d+$, we need a grammar for $d*$:

1. $S \rightarrow dS$
2. $S \rightarrow \lambda$

                                               ■

PROBLEMS

1. How many different parse trees does bbbbb have in grammar G3.7?

2. How many different words can be generated by the following grammar? Show the parse tree for each word.

    1. $S \rightarrow CBADE$
    2. $A \rightarrow N$
    3. $B \rightarrow R$
    4. $C \rightarrow E$
    5. $D \rightarrow I$
    6. $E \rightarrow b$

    7. E → λ

    8. I → t

    9. N → r

    10. R → e

3. Convert the following grammar to an equivalent grammar that contains no left recursion:

    1. S → Sb

    2. S → Sc

    3. S → Sd

    4. S → b

    5. S → c

    6. S → d

4. Convert the following grammar to an equivalent unambiguous grammar:

    1. S → SbS

    2. S → e

5. Using a "one-way street" production, convert the following grammar to an equivalent unambiguous grammar:

    1. S → bS

    2. S → Sbe

    3. S → d

6. Show that the deletion of all productions in a grammar containing unreachable nonterminals never creates new dead nonterminals.

7. Convert the following grammar to an equivalent grammar that contains no left recursion:

    1. S → Ad

    2. S → d

    3. A → Bb

    4. A → b

    5. B → Sc

    6. B → c

8. Convert the following grammar to an equivalent grammar with no lambda productions:

    1. S → BD

    2. B → bBBBDd

    3. B → λ

    4. D → e

9. Convert the following grammar to an equivalent grammar that contains no left recursion:

    1. S → Af

    2. S → fA

    3. A → Bb

    4. A → bB

    5. B → Cc

    6. B → cC

7. C → dS

8. C → Sd

9. C → e

10. Convert G3.8 to an equivalent grammar with no unit productions.

11. Convert the following grammar to an equivalent grammar that has no lambda productions:

    1. S → BcD

    2. B → BB

    3. B → b

    4. B → λ

    5. D → DdD

    6. D → dD

    7. D → λ

12. Can a string have more than one leftmost derivation in a grammar but only one rightmost derivation? Justify your answer.

13. Eliminate the useless nonterminals in the following grammar:

    1. S → AB

    2. A → CD

    3. C → CC

    4. C → λ

    5. D → DdD

    6. D → eE

    7. E → ee

14. Does the following procedure correctly eliminate unit productions:

    > For every pair of nonterminals A and Z such that Z can be derived from A using only unit productions, add the production A → x for every nonunit production Z → x. After adding all such productions, delete all unit productions.

    Note that this procedure never creates new unit productions.

15. Another technique for eliminating unit productions can be based on the following observation: Suppose a grammar contains the production A → B, which replaces A with B. Instead of generating A and then replacing it with B, why not generate B directly? Then the unit production would not be needed. Eliminate the unit productions in G3.20 using this technique. Does the technique ever fail?

16. Find an algorithm that for every pair of nonterminals A, B in a context-free grammar determines if

    $$A \overset{+}{\Rightarrow} B$$

    How could such an algorithm be used in eliminating unit productions from a grammar?

17. Convert the following grammar to an equivalent grammar that has only five productions:

    1. S → d

    2. S → bB

    3. S → Be

4. S → cc

5. B → bB

6. B → Be

7. B → cc

18. Convert the following grammar to an equivalent grammar that has only seven productions:

    1. S → BCD

    2. S → BC

    3. S → BD

    4. S → CD

    5. S → B

    6. S → C

    7. S → D

    8. S → λ

    9. B → bBBb

    10. B → bBb

    11. B → bb

    12. C → cC

    13. C → c

    14. D → Dd

    15. D → d

19. Is the following grammar ambiguous?

    1. S → bbbS

    2. S → Sa

    3. S → d

20. Convert the following grammar to an equivalent unambiguous grammar:

    1. S → bSd

    2. S → bS

    3. S → Sd

    4. S → c

21. Prove that any context-free grammar can be converted to an equivalent grammar that has at most one lambda production.

22. Convert the following grammar to an equivalent grammar that contains no left recursion. Process productions both in the order given and in the reverse order.

    1. S → Ag

    2. S → g

    3. A → Sb

    4. A → Bd

    5. A → b

    6. B → Sd

    7. B → Ae

    8. B → f

23. When eliminating left recursion, in what order should the groups of productions be processed to minimize the total number of productions in the final grammar?

24. Write a program that determines the useless nonterminals in a context-free grammar.

25. Write an ambiguous grammar that defines

$$\{a^i b^i c^j : i, j \geq 0 \} \mid \{a^p b^q c^q : p, q \geq 0\}$$

Try writing an unambiguous grammar for the language. Warning: this language is an inherently ambiguous context-free language. That is, no unambiguous context-free grammar exists for it.

26. Consider the procedures described in Sections 3.7 and 3.8 for eliminating lambda and unit productions. Is it possible that adding productions to make one production unnecessary may make another production previously made unnecessary once again necessary? Justify your answer.

27. Is the following grammar ambiguous:

   1. S → SS
   2. S → dA
   3. A → bB
   4. B → cS

28. Can we use the procedure in Section 3.7 for eliminating lambda productions to determine the nullable nonterminals in a grammar?

29. Convert the following grammar to an equivalent grammar that has no unit productions:

   1. S → Bd
   2. B → C
   3. B → b
   4. C → D
   5. C → c
   6. D → E
   7. D → d
   8. E → e

Do this conversion two ways: Use the approach described in Problem 3.14, and use the approach described in Section 3.8.

30. Convert the following grammar to an equivalent grammar that is not ambiguous:

   1. S → bS
   2. S → cS
   3. S → Sd
   4. S → Se
   5. S → f

4

CONTEXT-FREE GRAMMARS, PART 3

4.1 INTRODUCTION

In this chapter, we finish our general investigation of context-free grammars. First, we give several important grammars for a "real" language—the language of arithmetic expressions. These grammars are extremely important to the compiler designer. Next, we present two alternative methods of representing context-grammars: the Backus–Naur form (which is similar to the representation we have been using so far) and syntax diagrams (which resemble railroad track diagrams). Next, we introduce essentially noncontracting grammars, a grammar type to which every context-free grammar can be converted. Finally, we present a property that every infinite context-free language has—the pumping property. Since every infinite context-free language has the pumping property, any infinite language that does not have this property cannot be context-free. We will use the pumping property to show that some languages are not context-free.

4.2 GRAMMARS FOR ARITHMETIC EXPRESSIONS

We now depart from our study of languages from an abstract point of view and consider several grammars for a "real" language—namely, the language of arithmetic expressions. To keep our discussion simple, we will limit our language to the operations of addition denoted by +, multiplication denoted by * , and the operands b, c, and d. Let us list several strings in our language to get some sense of its syntax:

1. b
2. b+b+b
3. b+c
4. b*c+d
5. (b+c+d)*b
6. b+(c+d)

Compiler Construction Using Java, JavaCC, and Yacc, First Edition. Anthony J. Dos Reis
© 2012 the IEEE Computer Society, Inc. Published 2012 by John Wiley & Sons, Inc.

    7. (b)
    8. ((b))

An arithmetic expression can consist of a single operand (string 1) or several operands separated by either the + or * operators (strings 2, 3, and 4). We can use parentheses to indicate a specific order of evaluation (strings 5 and 6). For example, in string 5, the parentheses indicate that the two addition operations should occur before the multiplication operation. An arithmetic expression that is enclosed in parentheses is also an arithmetic expression, even if the parentheses are not needed to indicate a specific order of evaluation (strings 7 and 8).

The following strings are *not* arithmetic expressions:

    9. bc
   10. ()
   11. b++c
   12. b*)c+d(

Multiplication cannot be specified simply by juxtaposing (i.e., placing next to each other) two operands, as we commonly do in conventional mathematical notation (string 9). Parentheses cannot be used without enclosing an expression (string 10). Operators cannot be juxtaposed (string 11). A left parenthesis cannot be used without a balancing right parenthesis to its right, and a right parenthesis cannot be used without a balancing left parenthesis to its left (string 12).

Now that we have a sense of its syntax, let us write a grammar that generates the language of arithmetic expressions. In this grammar, we distinguish terminals from nonterminals by quoting terminals. We also place a space between successive terminals and nonterminals, and use descriptive names for nonterminals.

G4.1

```
1. expr → expr "+" expr
2. expr → expr "*" expr
3. expr → "b"
4. expr → "c"
5. expr → "d"
6. expr → "(" expr ")"
```

Let us consider the parse tree for the string b+c*d in this grammar. There are, in fact, two parse trees (see Figure 4.1). The first parse tree (Figure 4.1a) suggests that we perform the addition operation first since the substring b+c corresponds to a subtree. This interpretation is inconsistent with the mathematical convention that multiplication has precedence over addition. The second parse tree (Figure 4.1b), on the other hand, is consistent with mathematical convention; that is, it implies that the multiplication operation is performed first. Clearly, G4.1 is ambiguous with respect to operator precedence.

Let us devise a grammar that does not have the multiplication–addition precedence ambiguity of G4.1. We will use the "one-way street" technique (see Section 3.5) to force an ordering on the use of the productions, thereby eliminating this ambiguity. We get

G4.2

```
1. expr → expr "+" expr
2. expr → term      (one-way street)
```

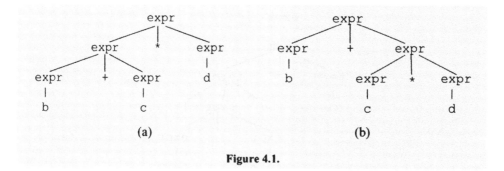

Figure 4.1.

3. term → term "*" term
4. term → "b"
5. term → "c"
6. term → "d"
7. term → "(" expr ")"

Production 2, the "one-way street," forces multiplication below addition in the parse tree, thereby giving multiplication higher precedence. Now, only one parse tree exists for b+c*d (see Figure 4.2).

Parentheses in an arithmetic expression can change the order of operation. For example, consider the string b*(c+d), whose parse tree using G4.2 is in Figure 4.3.

Because the parenthesized expression is a term in the multiplication operation, it must be evaluated before the multiplication operation. Note that the parentheses in Fig. 4.3 force the addition operation to occur lower than multiplication in the parse tree.

Although G4.2 does not have the addition–multiplication ambiguity that is in G4.1, it, along with G4.1, has an ambiguity regarding the evaluation order of like operations (for example, successive additions or successive multiplications). There are, for example, two parse trees for the string b+c+d (see Figure 4.4).

In Figure 4.4a, b+c corresponds to a subtree, suggesting, therefore, that the addition operations in b+c+d are performed in left-to-right order. The second parse tree (Figure 4.4b), however, has c+d as a subtree, suggesting a right-to-left order.

Let us now convert G4.2 to a grammar that implies that left associativity, that is, equal precedence operations (which, of course, includes like operations), are performed in left-to-right order unless parentheses override that order. We will do this by forcing the generation of the addition operators and associated terms in right-to-left order. Because we

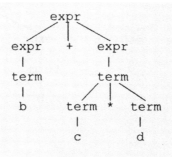

Figure 4.2.

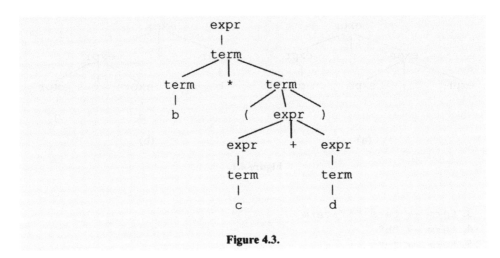

Figure 4.3.

generate the leftmost operator last, it ends up lowest in the parse tree. Thus, the resulting parse tree implies the leftmost addition is performed first. Our new grammar is

G4.3

1.	expr	→	expr "+" term
2.	expr	→	term
3.	term	→	term "*" factor
4.	term	→	factor
5.	factor	→	"b"
6.	factor	→	"c"
7.	factor	→	"d"
8.	factor	→	"(" expr ")"

This grammar is good
for bottom-up parsers.

The use of production 1 zero or more times generates a list of of zero or more occurrences of

```
"+" term
```

from right to left. Production 2 then generates a single `term` that precedes this list. Similarly, production 3 generates a list of zero or more occurrences of

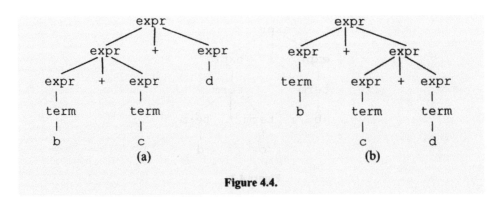

Figure 4.4.

from right to left. Production 4 then generates a single `factor` that precedes this list. Figure 4.5 shows the parse tree for b+c+d in G4.3. Note that the left addition operator is lower in the tree than the right addition operator, thereby implying left associativity.

We obtained G4.3 from G4.2 by eliminating the remaining ambiguity in G4.2. G4.3 captures both the desired precedence and the desired associativity rules for addition and multiplication, in addition to specifying the language of arithmetic expressions.

Exercise 4.1

Construct the parse tree for b+c+d* b* c* d using G4.3.

Answer:

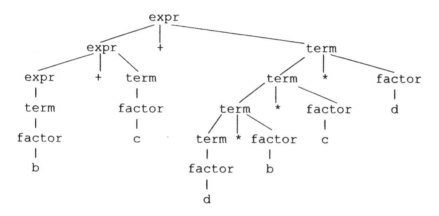

Notice that the subtree corresponding to b+c is the left operand for the right addition operator. This configuration implies left associativity for addition. The multiplication operators are similarly configured, implying left associativity for multiplication as well. Notice also that the subtree corresponding to d* b* c* d is the right operand for the right addition operator. This configuration implies the higher precedence of multiplication relative to addition.

■

Figure 4.5.

Although G4.1 and G4.3 are equivalent grammars, G4.3 provides more information, namely, operator precedence and associativity. If we design a compiler based on G4.3, the proper precedence and associativity are specified by the grammar. However, if we use G4.1, then we would have to specify precedence and associativity information elsewhere, since it is not provided by the grammar.

Grammar G4.3 has two left recursions, one in production 1 and one in production 3. Each of these left recursions generates a list right to left. Production 1, along with production 2, generates a list of terms, separated by +:

```
term + term + ... + term
```

Production 3, along with production 4, generates a list of factors, separated by *:

```
factor * factor * ... * factor
```

Some parsing techniques are incompatible with grammars that have left recursion, so let us eliminate the left recursions in G4.3 by converting them to right recursions using the technique that we studied in Section 3.10. To generate the list of terms, we can use

```
expr      → term termList
termList → "+" term termList
termList → λ
```

Here the `expr` production generates the initial `term`. `termList` then generates zero or more occurrences of

```
"+" term
```

to the right. To generate the list of factors, we can use

```
term        → factor factorList
factorList → "*" factor factorList
factorList → λ
```

Here the `term` production generates the initial `factor`. `factorList` then generates zero or more occurrences of

```
"*" factor
```

to the right. Our new grammar is

G4.4   This grammar is good
   1. expr   → term termList   for top-down parsers.
   2. termList   → "+" term termList
   3. termList   → λ
   4. term   → factor factorList
   5. factorList → "*" factor factorList
   6. factorList → λ

7. factor   → "b"
8. factor   → "c"
9. factor   → "d"
10. factor   → "(" expr ")"

G4.4 creates rather unusual parse trees. Let us look at the parse trees for b+c*d and b+c+d given in Figure 4.6. From Figure 4.6, it is not clear what associativity or precedence, if any, G4.4 implies. However, in Chapter 7 we will see that G4.4 does, indeed, imply the desired associativity and precedence for addition and multiplication.

G4.3 and G4.4 are two important grammars for the compiler designer. Both specify the language of arithmetic expressions and, in addition, capture the desired associativity and precedence.

Parsers fall into one of two categories: *top-down* or *bottom-up*. Grammars with left recursion are good for bottom-up parsers but not for top-down parsers; grammars with right recursion are good for top-down parsers but not bottom-up parsers. Thus, G4.3 is well suited for bottom-up parsers, and G4.4 is well-suited for top-down parsers. We will see both of these grammars again when we study top-down parsers (in Chapter 7) and bottom-up parsers (in Chapter 22).

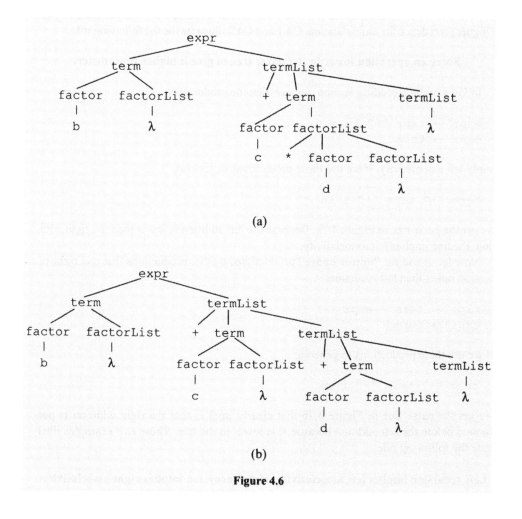

(a)

(b)

Figure 4.6

Exercise 4.1

What is the effect of changing production 1 in G4.3 to

```
expr → term "+" expr
```

and production 3 to

```
term → factor "*" term
```

Answer:

The modified grammar generates the same language but implies right associativity for addition and multiplication. Because the modified grammar does not capture the associativity we want for addition and multiplication, it is not a good grammar for either top-down or bottom-up parsing.

■

4.3   SPECIFYING ASSOCIATIVITY AND PRECEDENCE IN GRAMMARS

G4.1 in the preceding section has an ambiguity with respect to operator precedence. We eliminated this ambiguity with a "one-way street" (production 2 in G4.2). The effect of the one-way street is to position multiplication below addition in the parse tree. This structure implies a higher precedence for multiplication. G4.1 and G4.2 illustrate the the following rule:

Force an operation lower in the parse tree to give it higher precedence.

In G4.3 in the preceding section, we saw that the productions

```
expr → expr "+" term
expr → term
```

imply left associativity. If we use these productions to generate

```
term "+" term "+" term
```

we get the parse tree in Figure 4.7a. Because the left addition is lower than the right addition, the tree implies left associativity.

Now let us use the "mirror-image" productions, that is, productions that use right-recursion rather than left recursion:

```
expr → term + expr
expr → term
```

If we use these productions to generate

```
term "+" term "+" term
```

we get the parse tree in Figure 4.7b that clearly implies that the right addition is performed before the left addition because it is lower in the tree. These two examples illustrate the following rule:

Left recursion implies left associativity; right recursion implies right associativity.

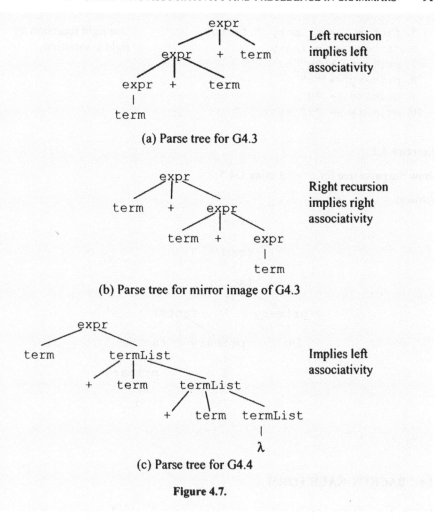

(a) Parse tree for G4.3

(b) Parse tree for mirror image of G4.3

(c) Parse tree for G4.4

Figure 4.7.

However, this rule applies only to situations in which operators, along with their operands, constitute subtrees of operands higher in the tree (as we have in Figure 4.7a and 4.7b). Notice we do not have this situation for G4.4 (see Figure 4.7c). G4.4 uses right recursion (see productions 2 and 5) but, in fact, implies left associativity for both addition and multiplication (we will show this in Chapter 7 where we revisit G4.4).

Let us now augment G4.3 with the exponentiation operator (denoted with "^"). Mathematical convention gives exponentiation right associativity and higher precedence than multiplication. To get higher precedence, we simply have the multiplication operands (i.e., the `factor` nonterminal) generate the exponentiation expressions. Exponentiation operations will, therefore, appear lower than multiplication operations in a parse tree. To get right associativity, we use right recursion. Our new grammar is

G4.5

1.	expr	→ expr "+" term	Use left recursion for
2.	expr	→ term	left associativity
3.	term	→ term "*" factor	
4.	term	→ factor	

```
 5. factor  → primary ^ factor          Use right recursion for
 6. factor  → primary                    right associativity
 7. primary → "b"
 8. primary → "c"
 9. primary → "d"
10. primary → "(" expr ")"
```

Exercise 4.2

Draw the parse tree for b^c^d using G4.5.

Answer:

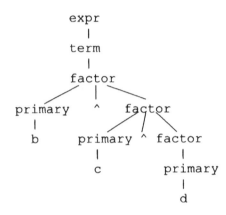

4.4 BACKUS–NAUR FORM

Jim Backus and Peter Naur are two pioneers in programming languages and compiler design, after whom the Backus–Naur form is named. *Backus–Naur form* (BNF) is a particular form in which we can represent context-free grammars. Actually, there are a number of variants of BNF. In the one we will use:

- "∶" is used instead of "→ " to separate the left side of a production from its right side.
- Productions with the same left side are written together, with the left side appearing once and the right sides separated by "|".
- Terminal symbols are surrounded by quotes.
- Spaces separate successive symbols on the right side of productions.

For example, G4.4 in BNF is

G4.6
```
expr       : term termList
termList   : "+" term termList | λ
term       : factor factorList
factorList : "*" factor factorList | λ
factor     : "b" | "c" | "d" | "(" expr ")"
```

Since lists and optional items occur so frequently in programming languages, BNF is usually extended to allow the direct specification of lists and optional items. In *extended BNF*:

- An asterisk indicates that the preceding item is repeated zero or more times.
- A plus indicates that the preceding item is repeated one or more times.
- A question mark indicates that the preceding item is optional.
- The vertical bar can not only separate the right sides of productions with the same left side but also separate choices within the right side of one production.
- Parentheses specify the scope of the vertical bar, asterisk, plus, and question mark symbols.

Let us rewrite G4.6 in extended BNF. We get:

G4.7
```
expr   : term  ("+" term)*
term   : factor ("*" factor)*
factor : "b" | "c" | "d" | "(" expr ")"
```

The `expr` production indicates that an expression consists of a leading term followed by zero or more occurrences of

```
"+" term
```

Similarly, the `term` production indicates that a term consists of a leading factor followed by zero or more occurrences of

```
"*" factor
```

The `factor` production above is actually four separate productions, one for each alternative listed. Here, the vertical bar separates the right sides of these four productions. The vertical bar can also separate choices within the right side of a production. For example, in the production

```
B : "c" ("d" | "e")
```

the vertical bar indicates there is a choice between "d" and "e" after a "c." The parentheses show the scope of the vertical bar operator. Thus, this BNF production represents two productions:

```
B → cd
B → ce
```

Suppose we omit the parentheses in the BNF production above to get

```
B : "c" "d" | "e"
```

Then the left alternative includes both "c" and "d." Thus, this BNF production represents the following two productions:

```
B → cd
B → e
```

If we want the symbols |, ?, (,), *, +, or the blank in extended BNF to be part of the language (i.e., to be treated as terminal symbols of the grammar), we simply enclose them in quotes. For example, "b" "*" represents b followed by the terminal symbol *; but ("b")* represents zero or more b's.

4.5 SYNTAX DIAGRAMS

Another way to represent a context-free grammar is to use a *syntax diagram,* a graphical structure that represents the grammar's productions. Every group of productions in a grammar with the same left side can be represented by one syntax diagram. Every path through a syntax diagram for some nonterminal "spells out" an allowable sequence of symbols for that nonterminal. Nonterminals are enclosed in rectangles. Let us start with a simple example. The grammar

G4.8

   1. S → AAd
   2. A → e
   3. A → f
   4. A → ec
   5. A → ed
   6. A → fc
   7. A → fd

represented by syntax diagrams is

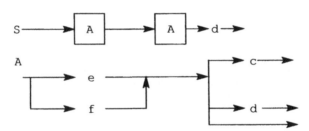

The first diagram spells out AAd, indicating that S generates AAd. The second diagram spells out the various strings that A generates. It shows that A generates either an initial e or f (since every path through the diagram starts with either e or f) optionally followed by c or d. We know c and d are optional because there is a path along the bottom arrow on the right that is unlabeled. Thus, we can exit to the right without spelling out c or d. This diagram illustrates how a syntax diagram represents choice (by a fork in the diagram) and an optional item (by a fork with one arrow unlabeled).

    Lists in a syntax diagram are represented with a loop. Consider

G4.9

   1. S → bS
   2. S → c

Every string generated by this grammar consists of a list of zero or more b's followed by a single c. Its syntax diagram is

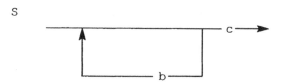

We can also represent G4.9 with

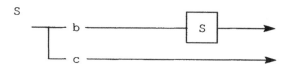

However, this syntax diagram simply reflects the recursion in the grammar. Thus, the language it defines is somewhat obscure compared to the previous syntax diagram.

Exercise 4.3:

Represent G4.4 using syntax diagrams.

Answer:

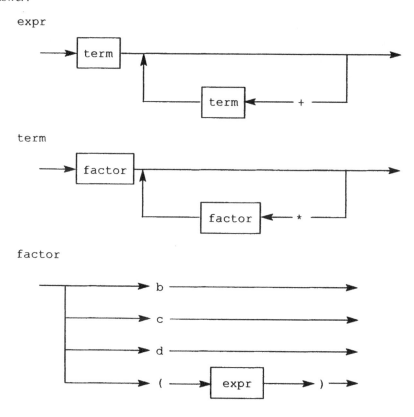

A disadvantage of syntax diagrams is that they take up a lot of space. Their advantage is that they are essentially "pictures" of the grammatical structure of a language and are, therefore, easy for us to comprehend.

4.6   ABSTRACT SYNTAX TREES AND THREE-ADDRESS CODE

To translate a source program, a compiler has to determine its structure. The structure of a program can be represented by its parse tree. However, a more efficient and easier-to-work-with representation of the structure of a program is its *abstract syntax tree*. In an abstract syntax tree, each nonleaf contains an operator. An operator can be an arithmetic operator, such and + or *. It can also be a symbol that represents a more complex action such as that performed by an `if` statement. For example, Figure 4.8a shows the parse tree for b+c+d corresponding to G4.3. Figure 4.8b shows its corresponding abstract syntax tree. Figure 4.8c shows the abstract syntax tree for the `if` statement

```
if (x) y = 2;
```

Notice that the abstract syntax trees specify only the essentials: the operator and the operands on which it operates.

Parsers in compilers often translate the source code to an abstract syntax tree. Other components of the compiler then operate on the abstract syntax tree. For example, the *semantic analyzer* can add attributes to the tree, such as data types, and perform type checking. The *optimizer* can modify the tree so that the target code that is ultimately generated from it by the code generator is more efficient (see Figure 4.9).

An abstract syntax tree is one type of internal representation that a compiler can use. Another type of internal representation is *three-address code*. Three-address code consists of instructions each containing an operation and up to three addresses—one address for up to two operands, and one address for the result. For example, the three-address code for the abstract syntax tree in Fig. 4.8b is

```
(+, @t1, b, c)      // add b and c and assign to @t1
(+, @t2,@t1,d)      // add @t1 and d and assign to @t2
```

where @t1 and @t2 are compiler-generated temporaries. For Figure 4.8c, the three-address code is

```
(if_false, x, @L0, null)    // if x is false, goto @L0
(=, y, 2, null)             // assign 2 to y
@L0:
```

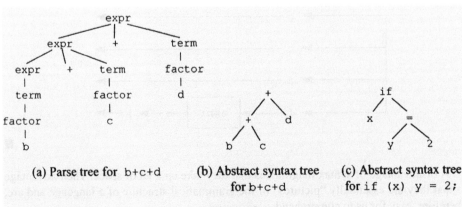

(a) Parse tree for b+c+d   (b) Abstract syntax tree
for b+c+d

(c) Abstract syntax tree
for if (x) y = 2;

Figure 4.8.

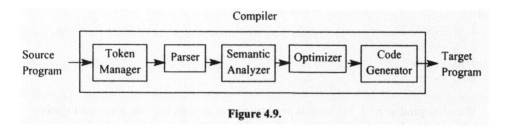

Figure 4.9.

For the compilers we will develop in this book, we will stick with the simple approach shown in Figure 1.2. That is, the principal components of our compilers will be the token manager, the parser, and the code generator. In our compilers, we will incorporate the functions of the semantic analyzer and the optimizer into the parser and code generator. Thus, we will not need separate components for these functions.

4.7 NONCONTRACTING GRAMMARS

A *noncontracting grammar* is a grammar in which the right side of each production is at least as long as its left side. We call such productions *noncontracting productions*. Obviously, in a noncontracting grammar, the application of a production in a derivation results in a string at least as long as the one to which it is applied. Thus, noncontracting grammars yield derivations in which every sentential form is at least as long as its preceding one. For example, consider the following noncontracting grammar:

G4.10
  1. S → bS
  2. S → b

In the derivation,

  S ⇒ bS ⇒ bbS ⇒ bbb

the first sentential form (S) is length one, the second (bS) is length two, the third (bbS) is length three, and the fourth (bbb) is length three. Each sentential form is at least as long as the preceding one.

In context-free grammars, all productions except for lambda productions are noncontracting. Lambda productions, however, are contracting because the left side of a lambda production has length one and its right side has length zero.

4.8 ESSENTIALLY NONCONTRACTING GRAMMARS

An essentially noncontracting grammar is either

  1. A noncontracting grammar.
  2. A grammar in which the start symbol does not appear on the right side of any production, and whose only contracting production is a lambda production whose left side is the start symbol.

The word "essentially" here means "in all cases except for one minor exception." For example, the following grammar is essentially noncontracting:

G4.11
    1. $S \rightarrow \lambda$
    2. $S \rightarrow BC$
    3. $B \rightarrow bb$
    4. $C \rightarrow c$

We allow production 1, the lambda production, because its left side is the start symbol, and the start symbol does not appear on the right side of any production. Production 1 is, of course, a contracting production. However, this production can be used only once and only at the very beginning of a derivation. Observe that any derivation that does not start with the application of production 1 must start with production 2 (the other S production). Since production 2 eliminates S, we can never use production 1 later on in the derivation. If we use production 1 at all, we must use it in the first step of a derivation. If a contraction can occur in an essentially noncontracting grammar, it can occur only in the first step of a derivation. Thus, the impact of the lambda production is limited: *it can only add the null string to the language.*

The following grammar is *not* essentially noncontracting because the start symbol, S, appears on the right side of the first production:

G4.12
    1. $S \rightarrow bS$
    2. $S \rightarrow \lambda$

Its lambda production can produce a contraction in any step of a derivation, at which point the derivation ends. For example, in

$$S \Rightarrow bS \Rightarrow \underbrace{bbS \Rightarrow bb}_{\text{contraction}}$$

a contraction occurs in the third step of the derivation.

4.9   CONVERTING A CONTEXT-FREE GRAMMAR TO AN ESSENTIALLY NONCONTRACTING GRAMMAR

As we have seen in the preceding section, some context-free grammars are essentially noncontracting and some are not. We will now see that every context-free grammar that is not essentially noncontracting can be converted to an equivalent context-free grammar that is essentially noncontracting. Thus, we can define every context-free language with an essentially noncontracting grammar.

We need to consider two cases when converting a context-free grammar to an essentially noncontracting grammar:

1. The grammar does not generate the null string.
2. The grammar generates the null string.

In the first case, we simply eliminate all lambda productions using the transformation described in Section 3.7. For example, consider

G4.13
    1. S → dB
    2. B → bB
    3. B → λ

Since production 1 is the only S production and, therefore, has to be used in the first step of any derivation, we can conclude that every string generated by G4.13 must start with the d that appears on the right side of production 1. Thus, G4.13 does not generate the null string. To convert it to a noncontracting grammar, we eliminate the lambda productions to get a grammar that is noncontracting and, therefore, by definition, essentially noncontracting:

G4.14
    1. S → dB
    2. S → d
    3. B → bB
    4. B → b

    Now consider an example of the second case (a grammar that can generate the null string):

G4.15
    S → bcS
    S → λ

For this case, our conversion involves a two step procedure. First, like case 1, we eliminate all lambda productions. We then get a grammar that generates everything G4.15 does, except the null string:

G4.16
    1. S → bcS
    2. S → bc

Next, we modify the grammar so it can also generate the null string by

    1. Creating a new start symbol, say S′ (then S is no longer the start symbol)
    2. Adding the productions
        S′ → λ
        S′ → S

We get

G4.17
    1. S′ → λ
    2. S′ → S
    3. S → bcS
    4. S → bc

G4.17 can generate every nonnull string that G4.16 can generate. Simply use production 2 to generate the old start symbol S, and then use the productions from G4.16 (all of which are in G4.17) to generate whatever G4.16 can generate. For example, a derivation of bcbc in G4.17 is

$$S' \Rightarrow S \Rightarrow bcS \Rightarrow bcbc$$

G4.17, however, can also generate the null string, by virtue of production 1. Thus, G4.17 is equivalent to our original grammar G4.15, and, moreover, it is essentially noncontracting since the only lambda production it contains has the start symbol on its left side, and the start symbol does not appear on the right side of any production.

If an essentially noncontracting grammar has any unit productions, we can eliminate the unit productions using the technique given in Section 3.8. Note that the equivalent grammar without unit productions that results remains essentially noncontracting. For example, if we eliminate the unit production (production 2) from G4.17, we get a new grammar that is also essentially a noncontracting grammar:

G4.18
  1. $S' \to \lambda$
  2. $S' \to bcS$
  3. $S' \to bc$
  4. $S \to bcS$
  5. $S \to bc$

We can conclude that

Any context-free grammar can be converted to an equivalent essentially noncontracting context-free grammar that contains no unit productions.

Exercise 4.4:

Convert

$S \to BC$
$B \to bB$
$B \to \lambda$
$C \to cC$
$C \to \lambda$

to an equivalent essentially noncontracting grammar.

Answer:

$S' \to \lambda$
$S' \to S$
$S \to BC$
$S \to B$
$S \to C$
$B \to bB$
$B \to b$
$C \to cC$
$C \to c$

4.10   PUMPING PROPERTY OF CONTEXT-FREE LANGUAGES (OPTIONAL)

Finite languages are always context-free. To see this, consider an arbitrary finite language F consisting of n strings:

$$F = \{x_1, x_2, \ldots, x_n\}$$

A context free grammar that defines F consists of n S productions with right sides x_1, x_2, $\ldots$, x_n:

G4.21
1. S $\rightarrow x_1$
2. S $\rightarrow x_2$

   .

   .

   .

n. S $\rightarrow x_n$

We can even make a stronger assertion about finite languages: they are all regular. To establish this assertion, all we have to do is give a regular expression that defines F:

$$x_1|x_2| \ldots |x_n$$

Of course, the actual regular expression would list all the strings rather than using the ellipsis "...".

Infinite languages, unlike finite languages, are not always context-free. Some like *PAIRED* = $\{b^ic^i : i \geq 0\}$ are context-free and some like *TRIPLED* = $\{b^ic^id^i : i \geq 0\}$ are not (we have yet to prove this).

We now wish to describe a property called the pumping property that all infinite context-free languages have. But before we do, we need to make a few observations about infinite context-free languages and their parse trees.

Suppose all strings in a language L have lengths less than or equal to some number n. We say that n is an *upper bound* on the length of strings in the language. An upper bound on string length implies that L is finite. For example, suppose that $n = 2$ and our language's alphabet is $\Sigma = \{b, c\}$. Then Σ^* has only seven strings whose length is less than or equal to 2 (λ, b, c, bb, bc, cb, cc). Thus, any language over Σ with 2 as an upper bound on string length can have at most seven strings. With larger alphabets and upper bounds, the number of strings is larger but still finite.

If an upper bound on string length implies that a language is *finite,* it follows that an *infinite* language has no upper bound on string length. Thus, for any number n, an infinite language must have strings whose length is greater than n. Longer strings, in general, require taller parse trees. Because there is no upper bound on the length of strings in an infinite context-free language, there similarly cannot be an upper bound on the height of parse trees. All infinite context-free languages, therefore, have the following property:

For any number m, we can always find a string in an infinite context-free language that is long enough that the height of its parse tree has to be greater than m.

Suppose L is an infinite context-free language. From Section 4.9, we know that there must exist an essentially noncontracting grammar G with no unit productions that defines L. Suppose G has k nonterminals. Let us select a string z in L that is long enough that the height of its parse tree is at least $k + 2$, that is, the tree has at least $k + 2$ levels. $k + 2$ or more levels implies that there must exist at least one path from the bottom of the tree to the top that contains at least $k + 1$ nonterminal symbols plus one terminal symbol at the bottom (see Figure 4.10). Now here is a critical observation: Since there are only k *distinct* nonterminals in the grammar, there must be at least one repetition of a nonterminal along this path. Let us say this repeated nonterminal is R. Let us examine a derivation in which the nonterminal R repeats as in Figure 4.10. Consider the grammar

G4.22
1. S $\rightarrow$ bbbRccc
2. R $\rightarrow$ dddReee
3. R $\rightarrow$ fff

The derivation of bbbdddfffeeeccc is

$$S \Rightarrow bbb\ R\ ccc \Rightarrow bbb\ ddd\ R\ eee\ ccc \Rightarrow bbb\ ddd\ fff\ eee\ ccc$$

$$\begin{array}{cccccccccc} & u & \uparrow & y & & u & v & \uparrow & x & y & & u & v & w & x & y \\ & & \text{upper R} & & & & & \text{lower R} \end{array}$$

We have designated various substrings in the derivation above with the letters u, v, w, x, and y. We have also inserted spaces to set off these substrings. We can see that as the derivation proceeds from S to the upper occurrence of R, the substrings u and y appear to the left and right, respectively, of the upper R. Then, as the derivation continues to the lower R, two additional substrings, v and x, appear to the left and right, respectively, of the lower R. Finally, the lower R generates the substring w. Let us summarize the essential features of this derivation.

Whenever we have a nonterminal repetition as in Figure 4.10, the derivation structure shown in Figure 4.11 necessarily exists. This derivation structure produces five substrings—u, v, w, x, y—as described above, of the generated string z such that $uvwxy = z$. Figure 4.12 shows the form of its corresponding parse tree.

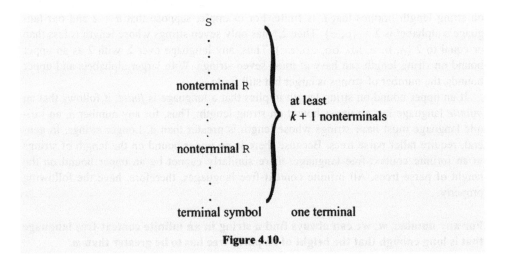

Figure 4.10.

$$S \overset{*}{\Rightarrow} uRy \overset{*}{\Rightarrow} uvRxy \overset{*}{\Rightarrow} uvwxy = z$$

— a second R appears below the first R

— an R appears

Figure 4.11.

The substrings u, w, w, x, and y in Figure 4.12 have some very interesting properties. Let us see what they are. Because our grammar is essentially noncontracting and has no unit productions, v and x cannot both be null. If both v and x were null, then the portion of the parse tree from the upper to lower R would have to have nothing sprouting off to the left and right. This feature, in turn, would imply that only unit productions were used from the upper R to the lower R. But our grammar has no unit productions. Thus, v and x cannot both be null. Mathematically stated, we have that $|vx| > 0$.

In the path from the terminal symbol up to the start symbol in Figure 4.8, we know there has to be at least one repetition of a nonterminal symbol. Assume the upper R in Figure 4.10 is the *first* nonterminal repeated as we proceed up from the terminal symbol at the bottom (there may be more than one repetition). We can then conclude that the subtree rooted at the upper R has at most $k + 2$ levels (k distinct nonterminals plus one terminal symbol at the bottom plus one repeated nonterminal). That is, the subtree rooted at the upper R has an upper bound on its height, namely, $k + 2$. But this implies that there is an upper bound on the length of substring the upper R ultimately generates. That is, there is an upper bound on the length of vwx. Moreover, this upper bound does not depend of the particular string z we pick. It depends only on the grammar. In other words, there is a single upper bound that applies to any z we might pick. Mathematically stated, we have that $|vwx| < p$, for some constant p that does not depend of z.

Consider the tail end of the derivation in Figure 4.11:

$$uvRxy \overset{*}{\Rightarrow} uvwxy$$

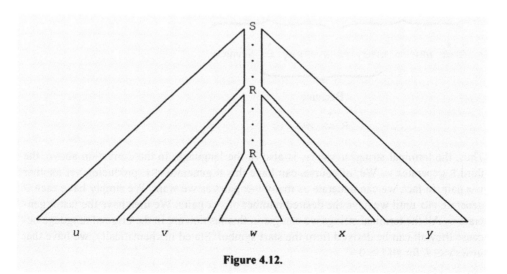

Figure 4.12.

It tells us that

$$R \stackrel{*}{\Rightarrow} w$$

But then that implies the following derivation—a new derivation—is possible:

The first
part of the
original
derivation

$$S \stackrel{*}{\Rightarrow} u\mathrm{R}y \stackrel{*}{\Rightarrow} uwy$$

Because

$$R \stackrel{*}{\Rightarrow} w$$

Thus, *uwy* is also a string in the language because we have a derivation of it from S. Now consider the middle portion of the derivation in Figure 4.9:

$$u\mathrm{R}y \stackrel{*}{\Rightarrow} uv\mathrm{R}xy$$

It tells us that

$$R \stackrel{*}{\Rightarrow} v\mathrm{R}x$$

But this means that the following derivation is also possible:

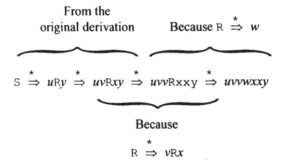

From the
original derivation   Because $R \stackrel{*}{\Rightarrow} w$

$$S \stackrel{*}{\Rightarrow} u\mathrm{R}y \stackrel{*}{\Rightarrow} uv\mathrm{R}xy \stackrel{*}{\Rightarrow} uvv\mathrm{R}xxy \stackrel{*}{\Rightarrow} uvvwxxy$$

Because

$$R \stackrel{*}{\Rightarrow} v\mathrm{R}x$$

Thus, the terminal string, *uvvwxxy*, is also in the language. In the derivation above, the third R generates *w*. We, of course, can have this R generate *v*R*x*, producing yet another *v*–*x* pair. In fact, we can generate as many *v*–*x* pairs as we want. We simply have each R generate *v*R*x* until we have the desired number of *v*–*x* pairs. We then have the last R generate *w*. All the terminal strings we can get in this fashion are in the original language because they all can be derived from the start symbol. Stated mathematically, we have that $uv^iwx^iy \in L$ for all $i \geq 0$.

We now can state the *pumping property* of infinite context-free languages:

Let L be an infinite context-free language. If z is in L and is long enough, then there exists a u, v, w, x, and y such that

$$z = uvwxy$$

where

1. $|vx| > 0$
2. $|vwx| < p$ for some constant p that does not depend on z
3. $uv^iwx^iy \in L$ for all $i \geq 0$

∎

Keep in mind that the pumping property does not assert that properties 1–3 above hold for *every* decomposition of z into five substrings u, v, w, x, and y. It asserts only that there must be *at least one* decomposition for which 1–3 hold.

Since every infinite context-free language has the pumping property, any infinite language that does not have the pumping property cannot be context-free. Thus, if we show that an infinite language does not have the pumping property, we have proven that the language is not context-free. Let us prove that $TRIPLED = \{b^ic^id^i : i \geq 0\}$ is not context-free using this approach.

Take the string $z = b^nc^nd^n$ in *TRIPLED*. Select n big enough so that z is long enough for the pumping property to apply. If *TRIPLED* is context-free, then, according to the pumping property, $z = b^nc^nd^n$ must be decomposable in at least one way into $uvwxy$ such that $uv^iwx^iy \in TRIPLED$ for $i \geq 0$. Let us try to find one decomposition that works. Suppose v spans a b–c boundary in z. For example, suppose $v = $ bbccc. Then $vv = $ bbcccbbccc. Since c's precede b's in vv, any string that contains vv cannot be in *TRIPLED*. Thus, $uvvwxxy$ cannot be in *TRIPLED* so this decomposition does not work. Similarly, any decomposition in which v spans a c–d boundary or x spans a b–c or c–d boundary does not work. The only remaining possible decompositions is to have v and x each entirely in the b, c, or d regions. But then at least one region—b, c, or d—has neither v nor x. But then $uvvwxxy$ cannot be in *TRIPLED* because the region without v or x will not be affected by the replication of v and x in $uvvwxxy$. $uvvwxxy$ will not have an equal number of b's, c's, and d's. As we "pump up" z (i.e., increase the exponent i in uv^iwx^iy) or "pump down" z (by setting i in uv^iwx^iy to 0), we get strings that are not in the given language *TRIPLED*.

Regardless of how we decompose z into $uvwxy$, the set $\{uv^iwx^iy : i \geq 0\}$ has strings not in *TRIPLED*. Thus, *TRIPLED* does not have the pumping property, proving that *TRIPLED* is not a context-free language.

PROBLEMS

1. Add the operations subtraction and division to grammars G4.1, G4.2, G4.3, and G4.4.
2. Draw the parse tree for b+ (((b+c))) using grammar G4.4.
3. Convert G4.3 to a grammar that implies a right-to-left evaluation of like operations.
4. Write a grammar that generates all the strings over the alphabet {b, c} in which the number of b's equals the number of c's. (Hint: You need only four productions.)
5. Draw the parse tree of b★ c★ d+c★ d+d using G4.3, G4.4, and G4.5.

6. Write a grammar that generates arithmetic expresions in postfix notation (i.e., the operator appears after the two operands). Use left recursion. Parentheses are never needed in postfix notation. Why? How are operator precedence and associativity handled in postfix notation?

7. Rewrite G4.1 in BNF and extended BNF.

8. Rewrite G4.2 in BNF and extended BNF.

9. Represent G4.5 using syntax diagrams.

10. Represent G4.10 using syntax diagrams.

11. Draw the parse tree for b+c* d^b using G4.5.

12. Convert the following grammar to an equivalent essentially noncontracting grammar:

    1. S → BCD
    2. S → bS
    3. B → bBB
    4. B → λ
    5. C → c
    6. D → D·
    7. D → λ

13. Convert the following grammar to an equivalent essentially noncontracting grammar:

    1. S → A
    2. A → B
    3. B → C
    4. C → λ
    5. C → c

14. Suppose G is a grammar that does not generate the null string. Does adding S → λ to G (where S is the start symbol) add the null string and only the null string to L(G)? Explain.

15. Prove that the language $\{b^ic^id^ie^i : i \geq 0\}$ is not context-free.

16. Prove that the set of all strings over the alphabet $\{b, c, d\}$ in which the number of b's is equal to the number of c's, and the number of c's is equal to the number of d's, is not context-free. Note that the b's, c's, and d's can appear in any order in this language.

17. Prove that the language of nonrepeating lists in Section 2.11 is not context-free.

18. Prove that the language $\{ww : w \in (b \mid c)^*\}$ is not context-free.

19. Prove that the language $\{b^ic^jd^k : i > j > k\}$ is not context-free. Hint: use $z = b^{n+2}c^{n+1}d^n$ and pump both up and down.

20. Prove that the language $\{b^ic^jd^ie^j : i, j \geq 0\}$ is not context-free.

21. Can a language that is not context-free have the pumping property?

22. Does it follow from our discussion in Section 4.10 that if an infinite language has the pumping property, it is necessarily a context-free language?

23. Show that the context-free languages are closed under union. That is, let L_1 and L_2 be arbitrary context-free languages. Show that $L_1 \mid L_2$ is also a context-free language.

24. Let $L_1 = \{b^ic^jd^j : i, j \geq 0\}$ and $L_2 = \{b^ic^id^j : i, j \geq 0\}$. What is the language $L_1 \cap L_2$? Are the context-free languages closed under intersection? That is, does the intersection of two context-free languages always yield a context-free language?

5

CHOMSKY'S HIERARCHY (OPTIONAL)

5.1 INTRODUCTION

In Section 2.9, we saw that context-free grammars are more powerful than regular grammars. That is, every language that can be defined with a regular grammar can also be defined by a context-free grammar, but not every language that can be defined by a context-free grammar can be defined by a regular grammar. In this chapter, we study context-sensitive grammars and unrestricted grammars, two new types of grammars. Context-sensitive grammars are more powerful than context-free grammars. Unrestricted grammars, in turn, are more powerful than context-sensitive grammars. Thus, our four types of grammars—regular, context-free, context-sensitive, and unrestricted—define languages that form a hierarchy; each language type in this hierarchy includes all the languages in the preceding language type: All regular languages are context-free, all context-free languages are context-sensitive, and all context-sensitive languages are unrestricted (see Figure 5.1). We call this hierarchy of languages *Chomsky's hierarchy*, named after Noam Chomsky, a pioneer in formal language theory.

Although context-sensitive and unrestricted grammars are more powerful than context-free grammars, we do not use them in compiler design for two reasons:

1. Context-free grammars are powerful enough.
2. Processing a language based on a context-sensitive or unrestricted grammar is more complex than processing a language based on a context-free grammar.

Although we do not use context-sensitive and unrestricted grammars in compiler design, we should, nevertheless, familiarize ourselves with them. They provide a valuable insight into grammars.

5.2 CONTEXT-SENSITIVE PRODUCTIONS

The substrings that immediately precede and immediately follow a symbol in a string are called, respectively, the *left and right contexts* of that symbol. For example, in the string

Compiler Construction Using Java, JavaCC, and Yacc, First Edition. Anthony J. Dos Reis.
© 2012 the IEEE Computer Society, Inc. Published 2012 by John Wiley & Sons, Inc.

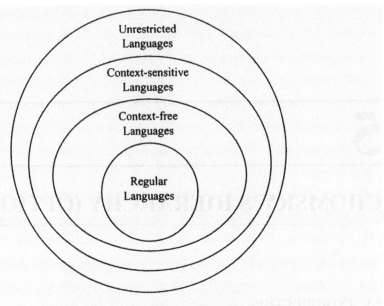

Figure 5.1. Chomsky's hierarchy.

bBcAdC, the left contexts of A are the substrings that extend up to A, namely, bBc, Bc, and c. The right contexts of A are those substrings that start with d, namely, dC and d. We call the entire substring that precedes A (i.e., bBc) and the entire substring that follows A (i.e., dC) the *full left context* of A and the *full right context* of A, respectively (Figure 5.2).

All the productions in a context-free grammar are rules that specify a replacement without regard to context (hence, the name "context-free"). For example, we can use the production A → db to replace A anywhere A appears, regardless of its left and right contexts. A *context-sensitive production,* on the other hand, can specify both a replacement and the required context in which the replacement can occur. For example, the production A → db *together with* the requirement that A must be preceded by c and followed by d is a context sensitive production. With this production, we can replace the A in bBcAdC with db. But we cannot replace the A in eAe since the context requirements are not met by eAe.

A simple way to represent a context-sensitive production is to have the left side of the production specify the required context. For example, we can represent the preceding context-sensitive production with cAd → cdbd. This production is really specifying a replacement for A only, in the context of c__d. The initial c and trailing d on the left side of the production—the required contexts—are carried over to the right-hand side. We can also use this technique to specify just a left context or just a right context. For example, the production cA → cdb specifies that A can be replaced by db whenever its left context is c. In this case, we do not require a particular right context.

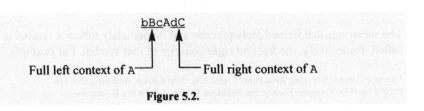

Figure 5.2.

Now consider the production that commutes A and B:

AB → BA

It is certainly not context-free since its left side is not a single nonterminal. Neither is it a context-sensitive production (if A is a left context, then A should be leftmost on the right side; if B is a right context, then B should be rightmost on the right side).

Now suppose we start with the string AB and apply the following productions, all of which are context-sensitive, in the order given:

AB → AQ	A is the left context
AQ → BQ	Q is the right context
BQ → BA	B is the left context

Using these productions, we can get the derivation

AB ⇒ AQ ⇒ BQ ⇒ BA

Notice that the effect of these three context-sensitive productions is the same as the effect of AB → BA, namely, to commute AB. Because we can realize the effect of a production like AB → BA with a set of context-sensitive productions, we classify such productions as context-sensitive, although in a strict sense, they are not.

For a grammar with nonterminal set N and terminal set T, we can show that any production of the form $x \to y$ where $x \in (N|T)+$ and $y \in (N|T)*$ is either context-sensitive already or can be converted to an equivalent set of context-sensitive productions using the technique we applied to AB → BA. Thus, it is quite reasonable to classify all such productions as context-sensitive.

Observe that a context-sensitive production can contract (i.e., have a right side shorter than its left side). For example, cAc → cc and ABA → cD are both contracting productions, neither of which is a lambda production. Thus, a grammar with no lambda productions is not necessarily noncontracting (unless, of course, it is a context-free grammar).

An example of a grammar with context-sensitive productions is

G5.1

1. S   → bSc
2. bS   → beA
3. Ac   → Aec
4. Ae   → Aee
5. eAe → ede

The derivation of bedeec in this grammar is:

$$\underline{S} \Rightarrow \underline{bS}c \Rightarrow be\underline{Ac} \Rightarrow be\underline{Ae}c \Rightarrow be\underline{Aee}c \Rightarrow bedeec$$
$$1 \quad\quad 2 \quad\quad\quad 3 \quad\quad\quad 4 \quad\quad\quad 5$$

In each intermediate string above, we give the number of the production used and underline the substring replaced. On inspection of this grammar, we can see that we must use the productions in the following order:

production 1 i times ($i \ge 1$)	which generates $b^i Sc^i$
production 2 once	which generates $b^i eAc^i$
production 3 once	which generates $b^i eAec^i$

production 4 j times ($j \geq 0$)   which generates $b^i e A e^{j+1} c^i$
production 5 once   which generates $b^i e d e^{j+1} c^i$

The language generated, therefore, is $\{b^i e d e^{j+1} c^i : i \geq 1, j \geq 0\}$. This language can also be generated by a context-free grammar (see Problem 5.2). Providing an equivalent context-free grammar for a grammar that uses context-sensitive productions, however, is not always possible. That is, languages exist that can be generated by grammars containing context-sensitive productions that cannot be generated by any context-free grammar.

5.3   CONTEXT-SENSITIVE GRAMMARS

A *context-sensitive grammar* is any essentially noncontracting grammar (see Section 4.8). Thus, a context-sensitive grammar can include context-sensitive productions but not contracting productions (such as $ABC \rightarrow aC$ or $A \rightarrow \lambda$) with one exception: It can contain a lambda production for the start symbol as long as the start symbol does not appear on the right side of any production. The only restriction on the left side of a production is that it must be nonnull. A *context-sensitive language* is any language that can be defined by a context-sensitive grammar.

Not all context-free grammars are context-sensitive grammars—only those context-free grammars that are essentially noncontracting. However, we can always convert a context-free grammar that is not a context-sensitive grammar to an equivalent context-sensitive grammar. We simply convert it to an essentially noncontracting grammar using the technique in Section 4.9. For example, consider the following context-free grammar:

G5.2
  1. S → bS
  2. S → λ

G5.2 is not essentially noncontracting, and, therefore, not a context-sensitive grammar. Converting G5.2 to an essentially noncontracting grammar using the technique in Section 4.9, we get:

G5.3
  1. S′ → S
  2. S′ → λ
  3. S   → bS
  4. S   → b

G5.3 is equivalent to G5.2 and is both a context-free grammar and a context-sensitive grammar. Since we can define every context-free language with a context-sensitive grammar, we can conclude that

All context-free languages are also context-sensitive languages.

Recall from Section 4.10 that the language *TRIPLED* = $\{b^i c^i d^i : i \geq 0\}$ cannot be generated by any context-free grammar. Let us now examine a context-sensitive grammar that can generate this language:

G5.4
1. S → λ
2. S → Q
3. Q → bCQd
4. Q → bcd
5. Cb → bC
6. Cc → cc

The heart of this grammar is production 3 which allows Q to generate b's and C's to its left and d's to its right.

The number of b's, C's, and d's produced by the repeated use of production 3 are always equal (since each single application of production 3 produces an equal number of b's, C's, and d's—exactly one). Because each C will ultimately generate c, the b's and C's produced by production 3 are not in the proper order to generate a string in *TRIPLED*. All the b's should precede all the C's. Production 5, however, allows any Cb pair to be commuted. With its repeated use, production 5 can rearrange the b's and C's so that all the b's precede all the the C's, and all the C's precede all the d's. Repeated use of production 6 can then convert the C's to c's. Here is the complete derivation of bbccdd:

$$\underline{S} \Rightarrow Q \Rightarrow bCQd \Rightarrow b\underline{Cb}cdd \Rightarrow bb\underline{Cc}cdd \Rightarrow bbccdd$$
$$\quad 2 \quad\quad 3 \quad\quad\quad 4 \quad\quad\quad 5 \quad\quad\quad\quad 6$$

It is not hard to see that G5.4 can generate every string in *TRIPLED*. We must also make sure G5.4 can generate only strings in *TRIPLED*. For example, G5.4 should not be able to generate bcbcdd. Let us try to derive bcbcdd and see what happens:

$$\underline{S} \Rightarrow Q \Rightarrow bCQd \Rightarrow bCbcdd$$
$$\quad 2 \quad\quad 3 \quad\quad\quad 4$$

When we reach bCbcdd, we are stuck. We cannot change C to c unless it has c to its right. Thus, we have to commute C and b using production 5 and then use production 6. But then we get bbccdd, not bcbcdd.

From G5.4, we can conclude that

Not all context-sensitive languages are context-free languages.

5.4 UNRESTRICTED GRAMMARS

An *unrestricted grammar* is a grammar in which no restrictions are placed on the form of productions, except for the requirement that the left side of a production be nonnull. The difference between context-sensitive and unrestricted grammars is that the latter allow contracting productions. Contracting productions provide unrestricted grammars with additional power relative to context-sensitive grammars. That is, there are languages that can be defined by an unrestricted grammar but not by a context-sensitive grammar.

Since every type of production allowed in a context-sensitive grammar is also allowed in an unrestricted grammar, every context-sensitive grammar is also an unrestricted grammar. The reverse, however, is not always true. For example, G5.5 is unrestricted but not context-sensitive because it can contract (remember that in a context-sensitive grammar we allow the production $S \rightarrow \lambda$ only if S does not appear on the right side of any production):

G5.5

    1. S $\rightarrow$ bCSd
    2. S $\rightarrow \lambda$
    3. S $\rightarrow$ bcd
    4. Cb $\rightarrow$ bC
    5. Cc $\rightarrow$ cc

G5.5 also generates *TRIPLED* but with fewer productions than in G5.4.

One interesting property of unrestricted grammars is that they have the same power to define languages as computer programs running on general-purpose computers. That is, if a computer program exists that can recognize all the strings in a given language, then that language can also be defined by an unrestricted grammar, and vice versa. A *Turing machine* is an abstract model of a general-purpose computer. It has the same power to define languages as a general-purpose computer. Thus, a Turing machine also has the same power to define languages as unrestricted grammars. For more information on Turing machines, see the files `turing.txt` and `t.txt` in the J1 Software Package.

PROBLEMS

1. Describe the language defined by

    1. S $\rightarrow$ dB
    2. B $\rightarrow$ bB
    3. bB $\rightarrow$ AB
    4. AB $\rightarrow$ Ab
    5. Ab $\rightarrow$ Ba
    6. dA $\rightarrow$ dc

2. Write a context-free grammar equivalent to G5.1.
3. Write a context-sensitive grammar that defines $\{b^i c^i d^i : i \geq 1\}$.
4. Write a context-sensitive grammar that defines $\{ww : i \in (b|c)^*\}$.
5. Write a context-sensitive grammar that defines $\{b^i c^j d^k : i < j < k\}$.
6. Write a context-senstive grammar that defines $QUADRUPLED = \{b^i c^i d^i e^i : i \geq 1\}$.
7. Devise an algorithm that will work with any essentially noncontracting grammar that will determine if an arbitrary string is generated by the grammar. Does your algorithm also work for unrestricted grammars?
8. Try using the same technique we used to convert a contracting context-free grammar to a noncontracting grammar on contracting unrestricted grammars. Why does this technique fail?
9. Convert the production WXYZ $\rightarrow$ ZYXW to an equivalent set of genuine context-sensitive productions (i.e., productions that specify a left and/or right context).
10. Contracting productions increase the power of a grammar to generate languages. In a context-free grammar, contracting productions increases power minimally; they allow the grammar to generate the null string. On the other hand, in an unrestricted

grammar, contracting productions substantially increase the power of the grammar. Why this difference?

11. Describe an unrestricted language that is not a context-sensitive language. You will probably have to consult a textbook on formal languages to answer this question (look under the topic of Turing machines or recursive languages).

6

TOP-DOWN PARSING

6.1 INTRODUCTION

To *parse* a string means to determine its parse tree. Parsing techniques can be divided into two categories: top-down and bottom-up. These two terms refer to the order in which we determine the parse tree. In *top-down parsing*, we determine the parse tree starting from the root (i.e., the start symbol), working down to the terminals. In *bottom-up parsing*, we determine the parse tree starting from the terminals at the bottom, working up to the root (i.e., the start symbol).

This chapter is devoted to the basic techniques used in top-down parsing. We will restrict ourselves to grammars whose productions have right sides that start with a terminal. In the next chapter we will consider more general grammars. In Chapter 22, we consider bottom-up parsing.

6.2 TOP-DOWN CONSTRUCTION OF A PARSE TREE

Let us see how the parse tree for a string can be constructed top down. Our construction will follows these three rules:

1. At any point in the construction, always expand the leftmost nonterminal that has not already been expanded.

2. If the nonterminal to be expanded has more than one production, then use the current token—that is, the leftmost token in the input string not yet generated—to determine which production to use.

3. Whenever the current token is generated, advance to the next input symbol.

An example should make this approach clear. Consider the grammar

G6.1
1. S →   dBC
2. B →   dC

Compiler Construction Using Java, JavaCC, and Yacc, First Edition. Anthony J. Dos Reis.
© 2012 the IEEE Computer Society, Inc. Published 2012 by John Wiley & Sons, Inc.

3. B → b
4. C → bB
5. C → c

Let us construct the parse tree for the string ddcbb. We will call this string the *input string*. We call each character of the input string a *token*. Figure 6.1 shows the parse tree in its successive stages of construction. In each picture, the current token is marked with the caret symbol, "^".

Initially, the current token is the leftmost symbol of the input string. The root of the tree is S, the start symbol of the grammar (Figure 6.1a). To expand the S node, we must use production 1 since it is the only S production. Figure 6.1b shows its effect: The first token of the input string and the nonterminals B and C are generated. In addition, we advance to the next token in the input string because production 1 generates the current token.

From Figure 6.1b, it is clear that the remainder of the input string (dcbb) must come from the nonterminals B and C. In particular, B must generate the current token d.

Our next step is to expand the leftmost nonterminal node (the B node). Suppose we wanted to expand the C node instead. How would we determine which C production to use? We would need to know which tokens in the remaining input C generates. But we do not know where these tokens start since that depends on what B generates. Moreover, even if we did know the location of the tokens generated by C, we would have to pay a penalty to examine them: We would have to *look ahead* (i.e., look beyond the current token) in the input string—an operation that would add to the complexity of the parsing process. If, on the other hand, we expand the B node, then the current token immediately tells us which B production to use. We do not have to look ahead in the input string. Because the current token is d, we must use production 2. Production 2 is the only B production that generates a leading d.

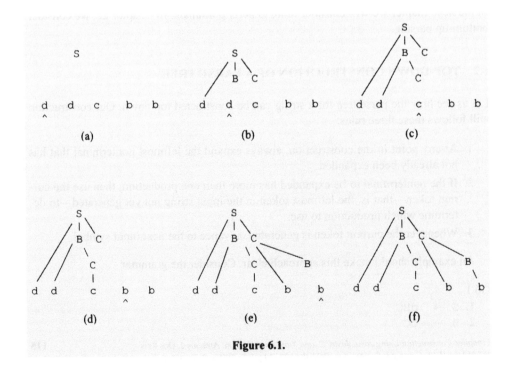

Figure 6.1.

The remainder of Figure 6.1 shows the rest of the construction of the parse tree. At each step, we use the current token to determine which B production to use when we have to expand B, and, similarly, which C production to use when we have to expand C.

Now compare the leftmost derivation of ddcbb,

$$S \Rightarrow dBC \Rightarrow ddCC \Rightarrow ddcC \Rightarrow ddcbB \Rightarrow ddcbb$$

with the trees in Figure 6.1. Observe that the leaf nodes read left to right in the successive trees in Figure 6.1 spell out the successive strings in the leftmost derivation. This correspondence, of course, is no surprise since we construct the tree by replacing the leftmost nonterminal at every step. Our parsing technique determines the leftmost derivation of the input string and constructs the parse tree in step with this derivation. Moreover, as we already know from Section 3.2, a parse tree constructed in step with a leftmost derivation is constructed in depth-first order with preference given to the leftmost node. That is, the node at the greatest depth is always expanded next. If there is more than one node at the greatest depth, the leftmost is expanded next. Let's summarize these important points:

The top-down parsing technique determines the leftmost derivation of the input string and constructs the derivation tree in depth-first order with preference given to the leftmost node.

"Top-down" is a somewhat imprecise description of a top-down parse. Although a top-down parse starts at the top and ends at the bottom, there is usually up-and-down movement in between. For example, in Figure 6.1c, we expand the first C. But next we expand the second C (Figure 6.1d), which is above the first C in the parse tree. That is, we move up in the parse tree at this point in the top-down parse.

6.3 PARSES THAT FAIL

If the string to be parsed is not in the language defined by the grammar, then the parse will fail at some point. For example, a parse using G6.1 would fail immediately on any input string that starts with b since the S production cannot generate it. A parse would also fail if there are too many or too few nonterminals. For example, consider the parse in Figure 6.2 of dbb using G6.1. After the last step (Figure 6.2d), the entire input string has been generated, but the nonterminal B remains. There are too many nonterminals, and, therefore, the parse fails.

The opposite situation—too few nonterminals—is illustrated by the parse of dbcc given in Figure 6.3. After the last step (Figure 6.3d), one input token remains. But there are

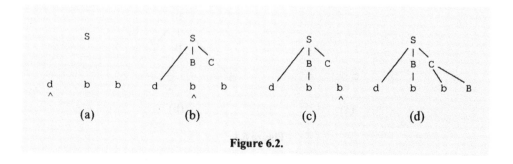

Figure 6.2.

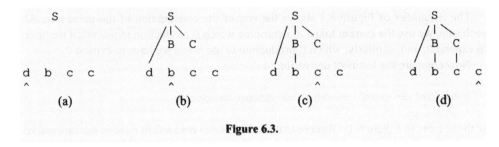

Figure 6.3.

no more nonterminals to generate it. There are too few nonterminals, and, therefore, the parse fails.

A parse can also fail if the nonterminal to be expanded next cannot generate the current token. In Figure 6.4, the parse fails when we have to expand B. The current token is c, but B can generate only a leading d or b (see productions 2 and 3 in G6.1).

6.4   A BAD GRAMMAR FOR TOP-DOWN PARSING

The success of our parsing technique depends on selecting at each step the correct production to use. Unfortunately, this is not possible for some grammars. For example, consider

G6.2
   1. S →   dBC
   2. B →   dC
   3. B →   d
   4. C →   bB
   5. C →   c

Whenever B has to be expanded and the current token is d, the parser will not be able to determine which B production to use because both B productions generate a leading d. Our parser would have to either

- Look at the tokens following the current token to determine the correct B production to use
- Take a guess at the correct B production and continue the parse. If it succeeds, then all is well. If not, *backtrack* (i.e., return) to this point in the parse, try the other the B production, and continue the parse.

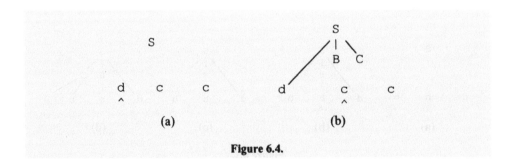

Figure 6.4.

Both of these approaches are undesirable. They result in a more complex and time-consuming parse.

6.5 DETERMINISTIC PARSERS

We call a parser that never has to guess at the correct production to use a *deterministic parser*. The term "deterministic" means that every step is completely determined. That is, there never is any choice. Deterministic parsers never have to guess and backtrack. At each step, they determine the production to use from the nonterminal to be expanded next and the remaining input. The most desirable type of deterministic parser is one that never has to look beyond the current token at any point. Such a parser, in general, is less complex and more efficient than parsers that have to look beyond the current token to determine the production to use.

We call grammars like G6.1, which allow deterministc top-down parsing without looking beyond the current token, *LL(1) grammars*. This rather strange name is derived from the characteristics of our parsing technique. The first "L" in "LL(1)" is for "Left" and indicates that the parser scans the input string from left to right. The second "L" is for "Leftmost" and indicates that the parser determines the leftmost derivation. The "1" indicates that at every step of the parse, the parser never needs to look at more than one input token—the current token—from the input string.

Note that G6.1 has more than one production whose right side starts with d (productions 1 and 2). However, these productions have distinct left sides (S and B). G6.2, also has more than one production whose right side starts with d. However, two of these productions (the B productions) have the same left side, making G6.2 a non-LL(1) grammar.

At every step of a parse with an LL(2) grammar, we never need to look at more than two tokens from the input string—the current token and the token that follows it. By definition, an LL(1) grammar is also LL(2) (if one input token suffices then, of course, two tokens would also suffice). However, an LL(2) grammar is not necessarily LL(1). For example, consider

G6.3
1. S $\rightarrow$ bS
2. S $\rightarrow$ b

Suppose the current token is b in a top-down parse. From this current token alone we cannot determine which production to use because both productions generate a leading b. Thus, G6.3 is not LL(1). However, if we inspect both the current token and the following token, we can always select the correct production using the following criteria:

- If the current token and the token that follows the current token are both b, then use production 1. Production 2 would not work here since it generates only a single b and eliminates S, terminating the derivation.
- If the current token is b and the end-of-input marker follows it (i.e., the b is the last token in the input string), then use production 2. Production 1 would not work here since its right side ultimately generates at least two b's.
- For all other cases, the input string is not in the language defined by the grammar.

Since two tokens—the current token and the token that follows it—are sufficient to select the correct production, G6.3 is LL(2). G6.3 requires a *lookahead* of 2: the current token and the token that follows it.

Parsing with an LL(2) grammar is more complex than parsing with an LL(1) grammar. With an LL(2) grammar, we must do more work to determine the correct production to use. At each step in the parse, we have to look at two input tokens to determine the next production to use. Grammars that require even longer lookaheads [LL(3), LL(4), and so on] are even worse. For top-down parsing, an LL(1) grammar is the best kind of grammar.

Exercise 6.1:

Give a grammar that is LL(3) but not LL(2).

Answer:

1. S →   bS
2. S →   bb

6.6   A PARSER THAT USES A STACK

The parsing technique that we described in Section 6.1 constructs the parse tree corresponding to the input string. The construction of the actual parse tree, however, is not a necessary part of the parsing process. One alternative to the construction of the parse tree is to use a stack in place of the actual parse tree.

Before we learn how to use a stack in a parser, let us see what information the parsing process needs. Consider the partially constructed parse tree in Figure 6.1b, reproduced here:

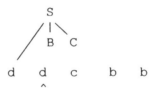

This tree provides information that determines what happens next in the parse. Here, the tree indicates that we should expand the B node next. Then, after we expand every nonterminal node below the B node, we should expand the C node. The parse tree at every step of its construction tells us which nonterminals still need to be expanded and in what order. A stack can easily provide the same information. When applying the production S → dBC, the parser simply pushes B and C in reverse order (i.e., C first, then B) onto a stack:

Stack

The stack then contains those nonterminals that need to be processed. The nonterminal symbols on the right side of S → dBC are pushed in reverse order so that the symbol to be processed next is on top. When we use a stack, it is easy to determine each step in the parse: the top of the stack provides the next nonterminal to expand; the current token, along with the nonterminal on the top of the stack, determines the production to use. We call a parser that uses a stack in this way a *stack parser*.

Let us parse the string ddcbb using G6.1 and a stack parser. We will show the input string and the stack at each step in the parse. To save space, we will show the stack horizontally, with its top to the left. We will use the caret (^), the pound sign (#), and the dollar sign ($) to indicate, respectively, the current token, the end of the input string, and the bottom of the stack. We call the operation in which we move to the next token in the input string an *advance operation*.

Here is the initial configuration of the input string and stack:

Input string   Stack

ddcbb#   S$
   ^

The current token initially is the leftmost symbol of the input string; the stack contains only the start symbol and the bottom-of-stack marker.

The successive configurations in the parse have a direct correspondence to successive trees shown in Figure 6.1. In fact, to understand the operations of our stack parser, it is very helpful to compare each configuration with its corresponding tree in Figure 6.1.

At each step in the parse, the parser must determine the appropriate production to use. In our initial configuration, S is on top of the stack. Thus, we need an S production. Because there is only one S production in G6.1, the parser does not need the current token to determine which S production to use. However, it should make a check on the current token to confirm that it is d, since any other input symbol would indicate an invalid string, in which case the parse would fail.

If S ultimately generates the input string ddcbb, and S → dBC is used to expand S, then BC must ultimately generate dcbb, which is the input string less its initial d (see Figure 6.1b). Therefore, our next configuration should be

ddcbb#   BC$
   ^

The operations necessary to reach this configuration from the preceding one are

pop, push(C), push(B), advance

These operations makes perfect sense. The production S → dBC generates two nonterminals, B and C, that ultimately have to be expanded. So the parser should push them onto to the stack in C, B order after popping the S. Because the production S → dBC generates the current token, the parser should also advance to the next token.

After the parser performs these operations, the top of the stack is B, and the current token is d. Thus, the next production to use is B → dC. To get the next configuration, we reason as follows: if the parser uses B → dC to expand B, BC becomes dCC. Thus, if BC ultimately generates dcbb, dCC must also ultimately generates dcbb, which, in turn, implies that CC must ultimately generate cbb (see Figure 6.1c). Therefore, the next configuration is

ddcbb#   CC$
   ^

The operations necessary to reach this configuration are

pop, push(C), advance

The parse continues until the *accept configuration* occurs—that is, until the top of the stack is $ (i.e., the stack is empty) and the current token is # (i.e., there is no more input). Figure 6.5 shows the complete parse.

Associated with each production is a sequence of operations that the parser performs when it uses that production. If we assume each production in our grammar starts with a terminal, these operations are

1. Pop.
2. Push *in reverse order* everything to the right of the leading terminal. If the right side contains only a single terminal, then do not push anything.
3. Advance.

For example, the operations for S → dBC are pop, push(C), push(B), and advance:

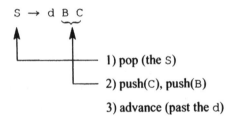

For B → b, the operations are pop and advance.

Input	Stack	Operations	Production Used
ddcbb# ^	S$	pop, push(C), push(B), advance	S → dBC
ddcbb# ^	BC$	pop, push(C), advance	B → dC
ddcbb# ^	CC$	pop, advance	C → c
ddcbb# ^	C$	pop, push(B), advance	C → bB
ddcbb# ^	B$	pop, advance	B → b
ddcbb# ^	$	accept	

Figure 6.5.

We do not have to do the advance operation last. It does not affect the pop and push operations, so we can do it at any time. However, the pop must precede the push operations. Moreover, the pushes must be performed in the correct order.

Here is one case for which the stack operations can be optimized. Suppose a grammar contains the following production:

C → cABC

For this production, the operations specified by 1, 2, and 3 above are pop, push(C), push(B), push(A), and advance. But the pop, which pops C, and the push(C) cancel each other out. Therefore, the parser should omit both, resulting in the more efficient sequence push(B), push(A), and advance. The parser should use this optimization whenever the symbol on the left side of a production matches the rightmost symbol on the right side.

With this special case incorporated, the operation sequence for a production that starts with a terminal symbol becomes

1. Pop if the left side is different from the rightmost symbol on the right side.
2. Push in reverse order everything to the right of the leading terminal, except for the rightmost symbol if it also appears on the left side of the production. If the right side contains only a single terminal, then do not push anything.
3. Advance.

Look again at Figure 6.5. For each configuration, let us concatenate the input generated so far with the symbols on the stack. For example, for the second configuration, we concatenate d with BC to get dBC. Here are the results for the six configurations in Figure 6.5:

1. S
2. dBC
3. ddCC
4. ddcC
5. ddcbB
6. ddcbb

Now compare this sequence with the leftmost derivation of ddcbb:

S ⇒ dBC ⇒ ddĊC ⇒ ddcC ⇒ ddcbB ⇒ ddcbb

We see that they are the same. We, of course, expect this correspondence because the stack parser determines the leftmost derivation. At each step, it replaces the leftmost nonterminal.

One aspect of our stack parser that may be hard to understand is the *accept configuration* (i.e., an empty stack together with the end of input). How can we convince ourselves that a parse ending in this configuration implies that the input string is in the language generated by the grammar? Here's our reasoning: An empty stack implies that the parse tree constructed is complete, that is, all its nonterminals have been expanded. End of input implies that the entire input string has been generated by whatever portion of the parse tree has been constructed so far. Thus, the two together imply that the constructed parse tree generates precisely the input string.

The string ddcbb is in L(G6.1) so the parse in Figure 6.5 ends in the accept configuration. If, on the other hand, the input string were not in L(G6.1), then sooner or later the parse would get stuck—it would not be able to apply any production and it would not be in an accept configuration. We describe this situation as a *reject configuration*. If a parser enters a reject configuration, it should take the appropriate action. For example, it might generate an error message and terminate.

Figure 6.6 shows the parse for an input string not in the language defined by G6.1, and its final parse tree.

In the last configuration in Figure 6.6, the parser has reached the end of input. But the stack is not empty, indicating that the corresponding parse tree is not complete.

Figure 6.7 shows another parse that ends in the reject configuration, and its final parse tree. This time, the stack is empty but end of input has not been reached, indicating that the parse tree generates only an initial substring of the input string.

The third possibility for a reject configuration is shown in Figure 6.8. When this parse ends, both the stack is not empty and the end of input has not occurred, indicating, respectively, that the tree is incomplete and only an initial substring of the input has been generated.

We sometimes refer to a stack parser as a *pushdown automaton,* particularly in textbooks that treat languages and language processing from a theoretical point of view. The term "pushdown" refers to the action of a stack. An *automaton* is a computing model whose operations are precisely specified and, therefore, can theoretically operate automatically, that is, without human intervention.

6.7 TABLE REPRESENTATION OF A STACK PARSER

The operations of a stack parser can be specified compactly in table form. We call such a table a *parse table.* Each row of a parse table corresponds to a stack symbol or the bottom-of-stack marker $. Each column corresponds to an input token or the end-of-input marker #. Each entry in the table contains the parser operations appropriate for its row and column. Blank entries in the table correspond to reject configurations.

Input	Stack	Operations	Production Used
dbb# ^	S$	pop, push(C), push(B), advance	S → dBC
dbb# ^	BC$	pop, advance	B → b
dbb# ^	C$	pop, push(B), advance	C → bB
dbb# ^	B$	reject	

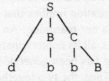

Figure 6.6.

Input	Stack	Operations	Production Used
dbcc# ^	S$	pop, push(C), push(B), advance	S → dBC
dbcc# ^	BC$	pop, advance	B → b
dbcc# ^	C$	pop, advance	C → c
dbcc# ^	$	reject	

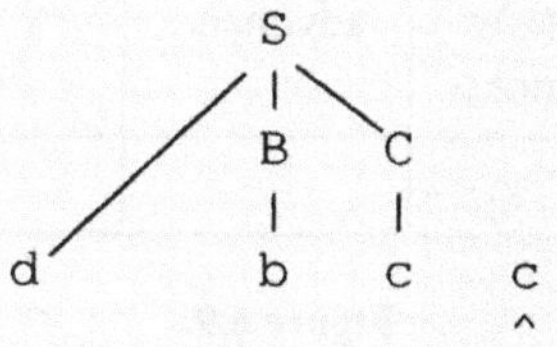

```
              S
            / |  \
          /   B    C
        /     |    |
      d       b    c     c
                        ^
```

Figure 6.7.

Take a look at the parse table given in Figure 6.9 of the stack parser for G6.1. Suppose S is on top of the stack and the current token is d. The operations the parser would take are given in the entry at row S column d [pop, push(C), push(B), advance]. Now suppose S is on top of the stack but the current token is b. Then the entry at row S column b gives the appropriate operations. This entry is blank, indicating a reject configuration.

Exercise 6.2:

Construct the parse table for the stack parser for

1. S → bS
2. S → c

Input	Stack	Operations	Production Used
dcc# ^	S$	pop, push(C), push(B), advance	S → dBC
dcc# ^	BC$	reject	

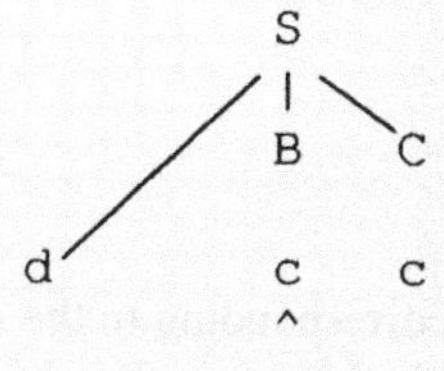

```
              S
            / |  \
          /   B    C
        /     |    |
      d       c    c
             ^
```

Figure 6.8.

Current token

	b	c	d	#
S			pop push(C) push(B) advance	
B	pop advance		pop push(C) advance	
C	pop push(B) advance	pop advance		
$				accept

Symbol on top of stack

Figure 6.9.

Answer:

	b	c	#
S	advance	pop advance	
$			accept

6.8   HANDLING PRODUCTIONS WITH NONLEADING TERMINALS

One form of a production we have yet to consider is a production that has one or more nonleading terminals in addition to a leading terminal. For example, in the production, S → bSc, b is the leading terminal and c is a nonleading terminal. With a little thought, you should be able to convince yourself that the operation sequence given in Section 6.6—pop, push in reverse order everything to the right of the leading terminal, and advance—also applies to this production. Notice that c now becomes a stack symbol as well as an input symbol. The c that is pushed on the stack should match a c somewhere in the remaining input. When the c on the stack reaches the top, the matching c in the input should then be the current token. When this occurs, the appropriate operation is to get rid of both c's, that is, to pop and advance.

Let us look at the parse table in Figure 6.10 for the following grammar:

G6.4
  1. S → bSc
  2. S → c

Notice that the table contains a row corresponding to the stack symbol c. The operations in the c column of this row—pop and advance—get rid of both the c on top of the stack and the matching c in the current token.

	b	c	#
S	pop push(c) push(S) advance	pop advance	
c		pop advance	
$			accept

Figure 6.10.

Exercise 6.3:

Construct the parse table for the stack parser for

1. S → bcSbSS
2. S → c

Answer:

	b	c	#
S	push(S) push(b) push(S) push(c) advance	pop advance	
b	pop advance		
c		pop advance	
$			accept

■

6.9   WRITING A STACK PARSER IN JAVA

So far in this chapter, we have learned how to convert a grammar to a parse table that defines the operation of the grammar's stack parser. We now will learn how to go from the parse table to a Java program. Actually, there is very little to learn. We can convert the operations specified by the parse table in an obvious way to `if` and `switch` statements in Java. What is remarkable is how little creative work is necessary to produce a parser in Java, given the grammar. Each step in the design and implementation process follows almost trivially from its preceding step. Let us go through a complete example for the following grammar:

G6.5
   1. S → bScA
   2. S → cbd

3. A → bcA
4. A → d

First, we construct the parser's parse table using our rules for determining operation sequences. The table is in Figure 6.11. Next, we design the Java program based on this table. Let us start by determining the overall structure of the program. The program contains a loop, each iteration of which will perform one step of the parse. The code inside the loop must inspect the top of the stack and the current token and then perform the appropriate operations. There are two conditions under which our loop should terminate:

1. The stack is empty. Then the stack parser accepts the input string if the current token is #, and rejects otherwise.
2. The top of the stack and the current token correspond to a blank (i.e., reject) entry in the parse table. Then, of course, the stack parser rejects.

If either of these conditions occurs, the code within the loop sets a boolean variable done to true, which, in turn, causes the loop to terminate.

We provide the program for the string it is to process via the command line. For example, to process the string cbd, we run the program (which is in the class Fig0612) with

```
java Fig0612 cbd
```

Because cbd is in the language defined by G6.5, the program responds with

```
input = cbd
accept
```

The complete program is given in Figure 6.12.

			Current token		
		b	c	d	#
Symbol on top of stack	S	pop push(A) push(c) push(S) advance	pop push(d) push(b) advance		
	A	push(c) advance		pop advance	
	b	pop advance			
	c		pop advance		
	d			pop advance	
	$				accept

Figure 6.11.

```
1  /* Figure 6.12: Top-down stack parser for
2
3       1) S -> bScA
4       2) S -> cbd
5       3) A -> bcA
6       4) A -> d
7  */
8  import java.util.*;  // import Stack and Scanner classes
9  //=========================================================
10 class Fig0612
11 {
12   public static void main(String[] args)
13   {
14     // construct token manager
15     ArgsTokenMgr tm = new ArgsTokenMgr(args);
16
17     // construct parser, pass it the token manager
18     Fig0612Parser parser = new Fig0612Parser(tm);
19
20     parser.parse();                      // do parse
21   }
22 }                                        // end of Fig0612
23 //=========================================================
24 class ArgsTokenMgr
25 {
26   private int index;
27   String input;
28   //---------------------
29   public ArgsTokenMgr(String[] args)
30   {
31     if (args.length > 0)
32       input = args[0];
33     else  // treat no command line arg as null string
34       input = "";
35     index = 0;
36     System.out.println("input = " + input);
37   }
38   //---------------------
39   public char getNextToken()
40   {
41     if (index < input.length())
42       return input.charAt(index++); // return next char
43     else
44       return '#';                   // # signals end of input
45   }
46 }                                   // end of ArgsTokenMgr
47 //=========================================================
48 class Fig0612Parser
49 {
```

Figure 6.12. *(Continues on next page.)*

```
50    private ArgsTokenMgr tm;               // token manager
51    private Stack<Character> stk;           // stack for parser
52    private char currentToken;             // current token
53    //----------------------
54    public Fig0612Parser(ArgsTokenMgr tm)
55    {
56      this.tm = tm;                        // save tm
57      advance();                           // prime currentToken
58      stk = new Stack<Character>();         // create stack
59      stk.push('$');                       // mark stack bottom
60      stk.push('S');                       // push start symbol
61    }
62    //----------------------
63    private void advance()
64    {
65      // get next token and save in currentToken
66      currentToken = tm.getNextToken();
67    }
68    //----------------------
69    public void parse()
70    {
71      boolean done = false;                // controls loop exit
72
73      while (!done)
74      {
75        switch(stk.peek())
76        {
77          case 'S':
78            if (currentToken == 'b')
79            {
80              stk.pop();                   // apply production 1
81              stk.push('A');
82              stk.push('c');
83              stk.push('S');
84              advance();
85            }
86            else
87            if (currentToken == 'c')
88            {
89              stk.pop();                   // apply production 2
90              stk.push('d');
91              stk.push('b');
92              advance();
93            }
94            else
95              done = true;                 // exit on reject config
96            break;
97
98          case 'A':
```

Figure 6.12. *Continued.*

```
 99            if (currentToken == 'b')
100            {
101              stk.push('c');      // apply production 3
102              advance();
103            }
104            else
105            if (currentToken == 'd')
106            {
107              stk.pop();          // apply production 4
108              advance();
109            }
110            else
111              done = true;        // exit on reject config
112            break;
113
114          case 'b':
115          case 'c':
116          case 'd':
117            if (stk.peek().charValue() == currentToken)
118            {
119              stk.pop();     // discard terminal on stack
120              advance();     // discard matching input
121            }
122            else
123              done = true;   // exit on reject config
124            break;
125
126          case '$':          // exit on empty stack
127            done = true;
128            break;
129        }                        // end of switch
130      }                          // end of while
131
132      // test if in accept configuration
133      if (currentToken == '#' && stk.peek() == '$')
134        System.out.println("accept");
135      else
136        System.out.println("reject");
137    }
138 }
```

Figure 6.12. *Continued.*

The program in Figure 6.12 starts by creating a token manager and a parser (the line numbers on the following Java code are the line numbers from Figure 6.12):

```
14      // create token manager
15      ArgsTokenMgr tm = new ArgsTokenMgr(args);
16
17      // create parser, pass it the token manager
18      Fig0612Parser parser = new Fig0612Parser(tm);
```

On line 15, args is passed to the constructor for the token manager. On line 18, tm, the reference to the token manager, is passed to the constructor for the parser.

Each time the parser calls its advance() method, advance() in turn calls get-NextToken() in the token manager. getNextToken() returns the next token (i.e., the next character) from the command line argument. advance() then places this token in the instance variable currentToken:

```
63    private void advance()
64    {
65      // get next token and save in currentToken
66      currentToken = tm.getNextToken();
67    }
```

Thus, at any time during the parse, the parser has access to the current token in the variable currentToken. To advance in the input, the parser simply calls advance().

The getNexttoken() method in the token manager returns the next character in the input string unless all the characters have been processed, in which case it returns #:

```
39    public char getNextToken()
40    {
41      if (index < input.length())
42        return input.charAt(index++); // return next char
43      else
44        return '#';                    // # signals end of input
45    }
```

The call of the parse() method in the parser starts the parse:

```
20       parser.parse();                        // do parse
```

On line 56, the constructor Fig0612Parser for the parser saves the tm reference it is passed in an identically named instance variable tm, "primes" the input by calling advance() on line 57, and creates and initializes the stack on lines 58 to 60:

```
54    public Fig0612Parser(ArgsTokenMgr tm)
55    {
56      this.tm = tm;                    // save tm
57      advance();                       // prime currentToken
58      stk = new Stack<Character>();    // create stack
59      stk.push('$');                   // mark stack bottom
60      stk.push('S');                   // push start symbol
61    }
```

The stack is initialized with $ (the bottom-of-stack marker) and S (the start symbol in the grammar). We use the Stack class is in the java.util package so we do not have to define our own. We use its push(), pop(), and peek() methods. peek() returns the top of the stack without popping it.

The while loop that starts on line 73 performs the parsing operations. The switch statement starting on line 75 implements the parse table:

```
75       switch(stk.peek())
```

The `switch` statement passes control to the appropriate sequence of operations based on the character `peek()` returns. For example, if `peek()` returns `S` (i.e., `S` is on top of the stack), then control goes to the statements that implement the `S` row of the parse table:

```
77        case 'S':
78          if (currentToken == 'b')
79          {
80            stk.pop();          // apply production 1
81            stk.push('A');
82            stk.push('c');
83            stk.push('S');
84            advance();
85          }
86          else
87          if (currentToken == 'c')
88          {
89            stk.pop();          // apply production 2
90            stk.push('d');
91            stk.push('b');
92            advance();
93          }
94          else
95            done = true;        // exit on reject config
96          break;
```

Following the `while` loop is the code that tests the final configuration:

```
133     if (currentToken == '#' && stk.peek() == '$')
134       System.out.println("accept");
135     else
136       System.out.println("reject");
```

If the input is completely consumed and the stack is empty, `accept` is displayed Otherwise, `reject` is displayed.

Notice that we specify an argument of type `char` when we call the `push()` method. For example in

```
81                stk.push('A');
```

the argument is `'A'` (whose type is the primitive type `char`), but the stack consists of `Character` objects. This type mismatch, however, is not an error because the character we specify is automatically converted to a `Character` object which is then pushed onto the stack. The Java terminology for this automatic conversion is *autoboxing*. Because of autoboxing, the statement above has the same effect as

```
stk.push(new Character('A'));              // convert to Character
```

Here, we are explicitly specifying the conversion of `'A'` to an object whose type—`Character`—is the wrapper class for the argument `'A'`. An automatic conversion also occurs on line 75:

75   `switch(stk.peek())`

Here, the `Character` object returned by `peek()` is automatically *unboxed*—that is, the character it contains is extracted. This character is then used by the `switch` statement.

PROBLEMS

1. Rewrite the program in Figure 6.12, using the `empty()` method in the `Stack` class in place of the bottom-of-stack marker `$`. Test your program with cbd and cbb.
2. Rewrite the program in Figure 6.12 so that it uses the `int` 0 instead of `'#'` to signal the end of input. Why is using 0 better?
3. Using a regular expression, specify the language specified by G6.1.
4. Imitating Figure 6.1, construct step-by-step the parse tree for dbbdc using G6.1.
5. Imitating Figure 6.5, show the parse of dbbdc using G6.1.
6. Construct the parse table for

   1. S → bSb
   2. S → cAc
   3. A → bAA
   4. A → cASAb
   5. A → dcb

7. Implement the stack parser for the grammar in Problem 6.6. Test your parser with the strings cdcbc, bcdcbcb, cbdcbdcbc, ccdcbcdcbcdcbbcr, cdcbbb, cdcb, and λ.
8. Construct the parse table for the following grammar:

   1. S → bSc
   2. S → d

9. Implement the stack parser for the grammar in problem 6.8. Test your parser with the strings d, bdc, bbdcc, b, c, bbcd, and bcdd.
10. Implement the stack parser for the following grammar:

    1. S → bcdefg

11. What should you do to a grammar before using it to construct a parser? Consider, for example,

    1. S → bABCD
    2. S → c
    3. A → bA
    4. B → bB
    5. C → bC
    6. D → d

12. Show that the following grammar is LL(2):

    1. S → bbbS
    2. S → b

13. Give an example of a grammar that is LL(4) but not LL(3).

14. Show that the following grammar is not LL(k) for any k:

    1. S → Ab
    2. S → Ac
    3. A → bA
    4. A → λ

15. What operations should a top-down parser take when it is using a production whose right side starts with a nonterminal. Consider, for example, D → ABC.

16. Give the grammar that corresponds to the following table:

	b	c	#
S	pop push(B) push(B) advance	advance	
B		pop advance	
$			accept

17. Give an example of a RR(1) grammar (for those of us who like to read backward).

18. Write a parser for G6.2 that uses the backtracking technique. Test your program with ddc, cdbdbdc, ddd, and bcc.

19. Write a parser for G6.2 that uses the lookahead technique. Test your program with ddc, cdbdbdc, ddd, and bcc.

20. Write a Java method that traverses a binary tree in depth-first order using the same general technique that we used in a stack parser.

21. Write a grammar for b*c*d*, design a stack parser based on your grammar, and write a program that implements your parser. Test your parser with b, c, d, bc, bd, cd, bcd, λ, bcdb, cb, and db.

22. An alternative approach a stack parser can take is to push the entire right side of production in reverse order (rather than everything up to but not including the leading terminal symbol). In what way, would our stack parser have to be modified to handle this alternative approach? Give the parse table for G6.1 using this alternative approach.

23. Modify the program in Fig 6.12 so that it constructs the parse tree as it parses the input string. When the parse is completed, the program should display every node of the constructed parse tree by traversing it in depth-first order.

24. Is this statement true: An LL(1) grammar is LL(k) for all $k \geq 1$.

25. Is the following grammar LL(k) for some k? Justify your answer.

    1. S → bB
    2. S → bC
    3. B → bB
    4. B → d
    5. C → bC
    6. C → e

7

LL(1) GRAMMARS

7.1 INTRODUCTION

Recall from the last chapter that an LL(1) grammar is a grammar that permits top-down parsing without backtracking or looking beyond the current token. In our investigation so far of top-down parsing and LL(1) grammars, we have limited ourselves to grammars whose productions all have right sides that start with a terminal symbol. In this chapter, we do away with this restriction. We will learn how to determine if an arbitrary context-free grammar is LL(1), and, if it is, how to construct its corresponding top-down parser.

7.2 FIRST SET OF THE RIGHT SIDE OF A PRODUCTION

Let us construct the parse tree for bde in parallel with a top-down parse using the following grammar (for now, ignore the sets shown to the right of each production).

G7.1   FIRST set of right side
  1. S → BC   {b, d}
  2. S → CB   {c, e}
  3. B → bB   {b}
  4. B → d   {d}
  5. C → cC   {c}
  6. C → e   {e}

Figure 7.1 shows the tree in its successive stages of construction. At each stage, the symbol ^ marks the current token. Initially, b, the leftmost symbol in the input string, is the current token, and S is the nonterminal to expand. The first step in the construction of the parse tree is to determine which S production to use (see Figure 7.1a). Neither S production has a right side that starts with a terminal symbol. Thus, we must examine the right side of each S production to determine which one can ultimately generate the current token. Notice that the right side of production 1 starts with B. B can generate either a lead-

Compiler Construction Using Java, JavaCC, and Yacc. First Edition. Anthony J. Dos Reis
© 2012 the IEEE Computer Society, Inc. Published 2012 by John Wiley & Sons, Inc.

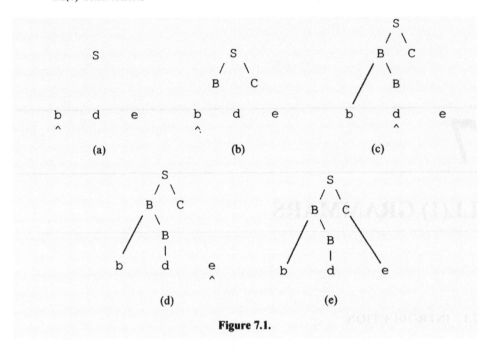

Figure 7.1.

ing b (by production 3) or a leading d (by production 4). Thus, the right side of production 1 can ultimately generate a leading b or d as demonstrated by

S ⇒ BC ⇒ bBC
S ⇒ BC ⇒ dC

Now consider the right side of production 2. It can generate either a leading c or e as demonstrated by

S ⇒ CB ⇒ cCB
S ⇒ CB ⇒ eB

Since production 1 can ultimately generate a leading b (the current token), but production 2 cannot, production 1 must be the one to use in the parse of the input string bde. Figure 7.1b shows its effect. Notice that the current token marker does *not* advance because production 1 does not directly generate it.

In the next step of our construction, we must expand the B node. Since the current token is still b, we must use the B production that ultimately generates a leading b. Clearly, production 3 is our only choice. Because production 3 generates the current token b (production 3 has a leading b on its right side), we advance to the next token (see Figure 7.1c). Next, we use production 4 because it generates d, the current token at this point. In Figure 7.1d, we use production 6 because it generates e, the current token at this point. At each step in the parse, we use the current token to determine which production to use.

It is helpful at this point to introduce an important definition: Suppose *x* is a string over the total alphabet of a grammar. Then, FIRST(*x*) is the set of leading terminals that *x* can generate. FIRST(*x*) is sometimes defined to include λ if *x* can generate λ. There are some notational advantages in doing so. But it is illogical: Every string can be viewed as starting with λ so why should λ be in FIRST(*x*) only if *x* can generate λ? In this book, we define FIRST(x) as the set of leading *terminals* x can generate. Thus, FIRST(x) never contains λ because λ is not a terminal.

If x starts with a terminal, then every string derived from x has to start with that terminal. Thus, FIRST(x) is the set that contains just that terminal. For example, FIRST(bA) = {b}.

Let us restate the technique we used in the construction of the parse tree in Figure 7.1 in terms of FIRST sets. When we expanded the S node, we selected the S production whose right side has a FIRST set that contains the current token. That is, we selected the S production whose right side could ultimately generate the current token as a leading terminal. We similarly used FIRST sets to select the B or C production when expanding B or C, respectively.

In G7.1 above, we show the FIRST set of the right side of each production to the right of each production. Since these sets determine which productions we select during a top-down parse, we call them *selection sets*.

A selection set is an important concept so let us formally define it: The selection set of a production is the set of current tokens for which that production should be used in a top-down parse. Thus, in G7.1, when S must be expanded and the current token is either b or d, we should use production 1; if the current token is c or e, we should use production 2; if the current token is other than b, c, d, or e, then the input string is not in the language defined by the grammar.

In G7.1, the selection set of each production is just the FIRST set of its right side. Is the selection set of a production always the FIRST set of its right side? The answer is yes if the grammar does not contain any lambda productions. We shall consider the selection sets for grammars with lambda productions in Section 7.4.

G7.1 has an important property: Each group of productions with the same left side has disjoint selection sets (i.e., has no members in common). For example, the selection sets, {b, d} and {c, e}, for the two S productions have no members in common. Similarly, the two B productions and the two C productions have disjoint selection sets. There is, therefore, never more than one possible production to use during a top-down parse. Whenever we have to expand an S, B, or C, the current token determines which production to use. Thus, during a top-down parse, it is never necessary to guess or look beyond the current token. In other words, G7.1 is an LL(1) grammar.

Now consider

G7.2   FIRST set of right side

1.	S	→ BC	{b, c}
2.	S	→ CB	{c, e}
3.	B	→ bB	{b}
4.	B	→ c	{c}
5.	C	→ cC	{c}
6.	C	→ e	{e}

Notice that the selection sets for the two S productions are not disjoint—they have c in common. Therefore, when we must expand S in a top-down parse and the current token is c, we cannot determine from the current token alone which S production is the correct one to use. We would have to either arbitrarily choose one (and later backtrack if it did not yield a successful parse) or look beyond the current token to determine the correct one to use. In other words, G7.2 is not LL(1).

In the preceding chapter, we defined an LL(1) grammar as a grammar that allows top-down parsing without backtracking and without looking beyond the current token. Clearly, any LL(1) grammar must have the property that any group of productions with the same left side has disjoint selection sets. Conversely, any grammar with this property must be LL(1). In fact, an LL(1) grammar is usually defined as any grammar with this property. Let us state the formal definition of an LL(1) grammar: An *LL(1) grammar* is a grammar without any useless nonterminals in which each group of productions with the same left side have disjoint selection sets.

Exercise 7.1

If the input string starts with c, how can you determine which S production in G7.2 to use in a top-down parse?

Answer:

If the input string ends with e, use production 1; if it ends with c, use production 2. Notice that we have to look beyond the current token.

∎

7.3   DETERMINING OPERATION SEQUENCES

In the preceding chapter, we learned the operations that a top-down stack parser must perform corresponding to various types of productions. As a review, consider the following productions and their operation sequences:

Production	Operation Sequence
A → bAcB	pop, push(B), push(c), push(A), advance
A → b	pop, advance
A → cBA	push(B), advance
A → dA	advance

Do you understand why each one of these operation sequences is required by its corresponding production? If not, you should carefully reread Chapter 6 before continuing in this chapter.

Now let us determine the appropriate operation sequence for a production that starts with a nonterminal. Consider Figure 7.1a. The corresponding configuration in a stack parser is

```
bde#          S$
^
```

The first step in the top-down parse is to replace S with BC, yielding the tree in Figure 7.1b. If S can generate bde and we replace S with BC, then BC should be able to generate bde. Clearly, the next configuration should be

```
bde#          BC$
^
```

Notice that we have *not* advanced to the next token because production 1 does not directly generate the current token. To go from the first configuration above to the second, we must pop the stack and then push the entire right side of production 1 in reverse order. That is, the operation sequence is pop, push(C), and push(B). Our rules for determining stack operations, amended to handle productions whose right sides start with nonterminals, are

1. Pop if the left side is different from the rightmost symbol on the right side.
2. Push in reverse order the right side of the production, except for the leftmost symbol if it is a terminal, and the rightmost symbol if it also appears on the left side.
3. Advance if the production starts with a terminal.

The parse table for G7.1 is

Current token

		b	c	d	e	#
	S	pop push(C) push(B)	pop push(B) push(C)	pop push(C) push(B)	pop push(B) push(C)	
Symbol on top of stack	B	advance		pop advance		
	C		advance		pop advance	
	$					accept

Since the selection set for production 1 is {b, d}, its operation sequence appears in the b and d columns of the S row. Similarly, the operation sequences for the other productions appear in the columns corresponding to their selection sets.

Exercise 7.2

Determine the selection sets for each production and construct the parse table for

1. S → bS
2. S → CS
3. S → c
4. C → d

Answer:

The selection set of each production is the FIRST set of its right side since the grammar has no lambda productions. The selection sets, in order, are {b}, {d}, {c}, and {d}. Since the three S productions have mutually disjoint selection sets, the grammar is LL(1). The parse table is

	b	c	d	#
S	advance	pop advance	push(C)	
C			pop advance	
$				accept

7.4   DETERMINING SELECTION SETS OF LAMBDA PRODUCTIONS

The selection set for a production in a grammar that has no lambda productions is easy to determine, it is simply the FIRST set of the right side of the production. In a grammar with lambda productions, however, the selection sets are more difficult to determine. Consider the following grammar:

G7.3   Selection Set
   1. S → BC   {b, c}
   2. B → bB   {b}
   3. B → λ   {c}
   4. C → c   {c}

Suppose we wish to construct the parse tree for the input string bc. We start by using the only S production, production 1, after which the current token is still the leading b in the input string (see Figure 7.2a). In the next step of the construction, we must select one of the two B productions. If we use production 3, the lambda production, we eliminate the B nonterminal. Thus, the current token *must be generated by the symbol that*

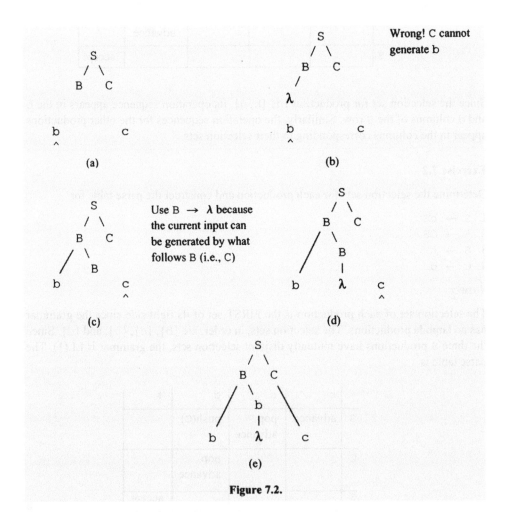

Figure 7.2.

follows B, namely, C (see Figure 7.2b). But C cannot generate a leading b. Thus, we cannot use production 3. If, on the other hand, we use production 2, we directly generate the current token. The current token marker then advances to c, and we must again expand B (see Figure 7.2c). At this point, we cannot use production 2 because it generates a leading b. We can, however, use production 3 to eliminate B. Then we can generate the current token, c, with C, the symbol that *follows* B in the parse tree (see Figures 7.3d and 7.3e).

Based of the preceding example, we can formulate the following rule for lambda productions: Use a lambda production whenever the current token can be generated by a symbol that can follow the symbol on left side of the lambda production. For example, in G7.3, we should use B $\rightarrow$ λ whenever the current token can be generated by a symbol that can follow B. We can see from production 1 that C can follow B and, from production 4, that C can generate a leading c. Thus, we should use the production B $\rightarrow$ λ whenever the current token is c. For productions 1, 2, and 4 in G7.3, their selection sets are the FIRST sets of their right sides. For production 3, the lambda production, its selection set is the set of inputs that can follow the symbol on its left side.

Let us introduce some new terminology:

> **The *FOLLOW set of a nonterminal N* [denoted by FOLLOW(N)] is the set of inputs that can immediately follow N in some derivation (not necessarily leftmost) that starts with the start symbol. The FOLLOW set of the start symbol always contains the end-of-input marker #.**

We will explain in Section 7.7 why # is always in the FOLLOW set of the start symbol. The selection set of a lambda production is the FOLLOW set of the symbol on its left side. For example, in G7.3, the selection set of production 3 is FOLLOW(B).

The determination of FIRST sets is made somewhat more complicated by lambda productions. If x is a nonnull string over the total alphabet of a grammar without lambda productions, then FIRST(xy) is always equal to FIRST(x). However, in a grammar with lambda productions, x could be nullable, in which case FIRST(xy) is FIRST(x)|FIRST(y), because any leading terminal that y can generate can also be generated by xy by nulling out x. For example, in G7.3, C can generate a leading c:

$$C \Rightarrow c$$

Therefore, BC can also generate a leading c by taking B to λ:

$$BC \Rightarrow C \Rightarrow c$$

Thus, FIRST(BC) = FIRST(B)|FIRST(C) = {b}|{c} = {b, c}. Accordingly, the selection set for production 1 is {b, c}.

Notice that the selection sets for the two B productions in G7.3 are disjoint. Therefore, G7.3 is LL(1). Now consider the grammar obtained from G7.3 by changing production 4:

G7.4   Selection Set

   1. S $\rightarrow$ BC   {b}
   2. B $\rightarrow$ bB   {b}
   3. B $\rightarrow$ λ {b}
   4. C $\rightarrow$ b   {b}

C still follows B but C now generates b. Therefore, the selection set for production 3 is {b}. Now, whenever we must expand B in a top-down parse and the current token is b, we have to choose between productions 2 and 3, both of whose selection sets contain b. To determine the correct choice, we have to look beyond the current token. If the current token is a b and is followed by another b, then we should use production 2 (see Figure 7.3a). If, on the other hand, the current token is b and is followed by the end-of-input marker, then we should use production 3 (see Figure 7.3b) followed by production 4 (see Figure 7.3c).

Because we must look beyond the current token to determine which production to use, G7.4 is not LL(1). It is, however, LL(2).

Let us consider a second example of a grammar with lambda productions:

G7.5			Selection Set
1.	S	→ BCd	{b, c, d}
2.	B	→ bb	{b}
3.	B	→ λ	{c, d}
4.	C	→ cc	{c}
5.	C	→ λ	{d}

Let us start by computing the selection set, FIRST(BCd), of production1. Since B is nullable, FIRST(BCd) = FIRST(B)|FIRST(Cd). But C is also nullable so FIRST(Cd) = FIRST(C)|FIRST(d). Thus, FIRST(BCd) = FIRST(B)|FIRST(C)|FIRST(d) = {b}|{c}|{d} = {b, c, d}.

The selection sets for productions 2 and 4 are obvious—each contains just the leading terminal. The selection set for production 5 is FOLLOW(C). By examining the right side of every production, we find only one case of something following C: d in production 1. Thus, FOLLOW(C) = {d}.

The selection set for production 3 is FOLLOW(B). We see in production 1 that Cd follows B. Thus, FOLLOW(B) = FIRST(Cd). Since C is nullable, FIRST(Cd) = FIRST(C)|FIRST(d). Thus, FOLLOW(B) ={c}|{d} = {c, d}.

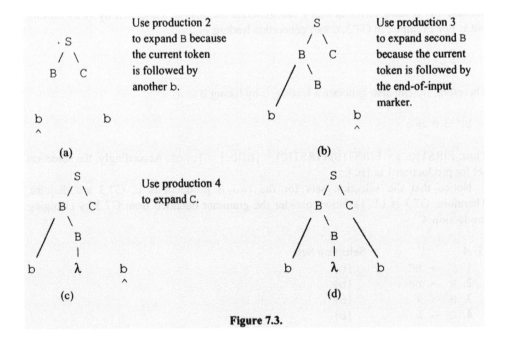

Figure 7.3.

From the preceding example, it is obvious that we need to know which nonterminals are nullable when computing both FIRST and FOLLOW sets. In a simple grammar such as G7.5, the nullable nonterminals are obvious. However, for a more complex grammar, we should use the algorithm to identify nullables given in Section 3.6.

7.5 WHATEVER-FOLLOWS-LEFT-FOLLOWS-RIGHTMOST RULE

The next grammar illustrates some additional points to consider when we are computing FOLLOW sets:

G7.6	Selection Set
1. S → Bd	{b}
2. B → bC	{b}
3. C → cC	{c}
4. C → λ	{d}

The selection set for production 4 is FOLLOW(C). But, in G7.6, nothing appears to follow C: In each production in which C appears on the right side, C occupies the rightmost position. However, consider the partial parse tree that appears in Figure 7.4a corresponding to production 1.

If we expand B using production 2, as in Figure 7.4b, then d follows C, since C is rightmost in production 2. Thus, *any symbol that follows* B *also follows* C. We can arrive at the same conclusion by considering derivations instead of parse trees: Suppose d follows B. Then, by definition, there must exist a derivation in which d immediately follows B:

$$S \overset{\star}{\Rightarrow} xBdy$$

where x and y are strings over the total alphabet. But if we now replace B with bC according to production 2, we get

$$S \overset{\star}{\Rightarrow} xBdy \Rightarrow xbCdy$$

Thus, d also follows C. Our conclusion: Anything that can follow B can also follow C or, mathematically stated, FOLLOW(B) ⊆ FOLLOW(C). Figure 7.4 shows that *whatever follows the nonterminal on the left side of a production also follows the rightmost symbol on its right side*. In G7.6, since d follows B, it also follows C by virtue of the production B → bC. Thus, the selection set for production 4 is {d}.

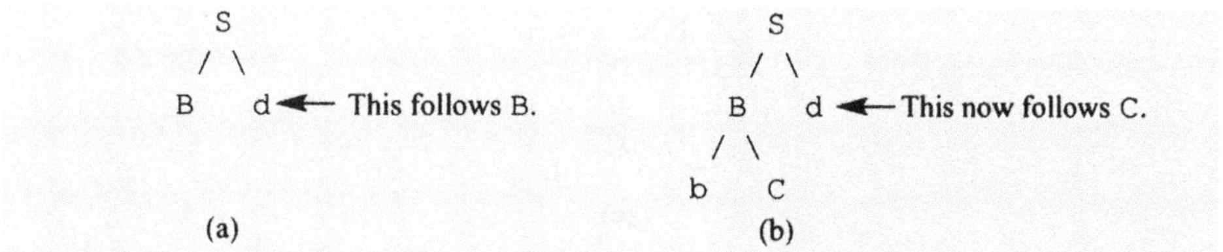

Figure 7.4.

Let us apply the same sort of reasoning that we used with G7.6 to our next grammar:

G7.7   Selection Set
  1. S → Be   {b}
  2. B → bCD   {b}
  3. C → cC   {c}
  4. C → λ   {d, e}
  5. D → dD   {d}
  6. D → λ   {e}

First, note that FOLLOW(B) = {e}. Since D is the rightmost symbol in production 2, whatever follows B also follows D. Moreover, because D is nullable, the C on the right side of production 2 can effectively be the rightmost symbol (by taking D to the null string). Thus, whatever follows B follows not only D but also C (see Figure 7.5).

In light of these observations, we need to generalize our rule on FOLLOW sets:

> **Whatever follows the non-terminal on the left side of a production also follows the rightmost symbol on the right side. It also follows any symbol on the right side that has exclusively nullable nonterminal symbols to its right.**

Since we will use this rule frequently, we need to give it a name. Let us call it the *whatever-follows-left-follows-rightmost rule.*

Exercise 7.3

Determine the nullable nonterminals; the FIRST and FOLLOW sets for S, A, B, C, and D; and the selection set for each production:

  1. S → Ae
  2. A → fBCD
  3. B → b

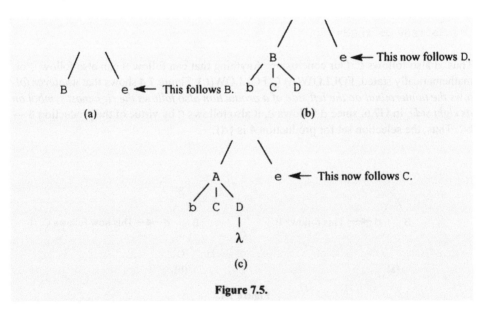

Figure 7.5.

4. B → λ
5. C → c
6. C → λ
7. D → d
8. D → λ

Answers:

Nullable nonterminals: B, C, **and** D

	FIRST Set	FOLLOW Set
S	{f}	{#}
A	{f}	{e}
B	{b}	{c, d, e}
C	{c}	{d, e}
D	{d}	{e}

Selection Set

1. S → Ae   FIRST(Ae)   = {f}
2. A → fBCD   FIRST(fBCD) = {f}
3. B → b   FIRST(b)   = {b}
4. B → λ   FOLLOW(B) = {c, d, e}
5. C → c   FIRST(c)   = {c}
6. C → λ   FOLLOW(C) = {d, e}
7. D → d   FIRST(d)   = {d}
8. D → λ   FOLLOW(D) = {e}

7.6 SELECTION SETS FOR PRODUCTIONS WITH NULLABLE RIGHT SIDES

We have seen two rules for determining selection sets for the grammars we have seen so far: for a lambda production, the selection set is the FOLLOW set of its left side; for any other production, the selection set is the FIRST set of its right side. There is, however, one type of production we have yet to consider whose selection set contains *both* the FIRST set of its right side and the FOLLOW set of its left side. Consider:

G7.8		Selection Set
1. S → AD	FIRST(AD) =	{b, c, d}
2. A → BC	FIRST(BC) | FOLLOW(A) =	{b, c} | {d} = {b, c, d}
3. B → b	FIRST(b) =	{b}
4. B → λ	FOLLOW(B) =	{c, d}
5. C → c	FIRST(c) =	{c}
6. C → λ	FOLLOW(C) =	{d}
7. D → d	FIRST(d) =	{d}

Notice that both B and C are nullable. Therefore, BC, the right side of production 2 is also nullable. The selection set for production 2 is the union of the FIRST set of its right side and the FOLLOW set of its left side. Thus, the selection set for production 2 is FIRST(BC) | FOLLOW(A) = {b, c, d}.

Let us try to understand why this new rule makes sense. Consider the construction of the parse tree for bd at the point illustrated in Figure 7.6a. The current token is b and we must expand A. Since b is in the FIRST set of the right side of production 2, this production can ultimately generate the current token. Thus, it makes sense to expand A with production 2 and then to expand the B in production 2 with production 3 (see Figure 7.6b).

Now let us consider another scenario. Suppose the current token is d, and we must expand A (see Figure 7.7a). Since d is in the FOLLOW set of A, the current token can be generated by the symbol that follows A. Thus, it makes sense to use production 2 because we can null out its right side, and let D, the symbol that follows A, generate the current token d (see Figure 7.7b). These two possible scenarios imply that the selection set for production 2 in G7.8 includes both FIRST(BC) and FOLLOW(A).

Our rule for determining a selection set for a production with a nullable right side actually applies to lambda productions as well. For example, let us apply this rule to production 4 [whose selection set is FOLLOW(B) in G7.8]. Our rule tells us its selection set is FIRST(λ) | FOLLOW(B). But the FIRST set of λ is {}. Thus, FIRST(λ) | FOLLOW(B) = {} | FOLLOW(B) = FOLLOW(B). We, therefore, have only two rules for selection sets. These two rules apply to all types of productions. The rules are

1. The selection set of a production with a nonnullable right side is the FIRST set of its right side.
2. The selection set of a production with a nullable right side (which, of course, includes lambda productions) is the union of the FIRST set of its right side and the FOLLOW set of its left side.

Exercise 7.4

Determine the selection sets for

1. S → Ad
2. A → B
3. B → C
4. C → c
5. C → λ

Answers:

1. S → Ad   FIRST(Ad) = {c, d}
2. A → B   FIRST(B) | FOLLOW(A) = {c} | {d} = {c, d}
3. B → C   FIRST(C) | FOLLOW(B) = {c} | {d} = {c, d}

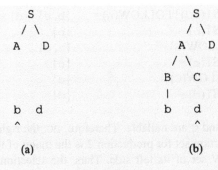

Figure 7.6.

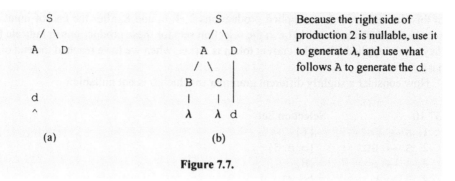

Figure 7.7.

4. C → c	FIRST(C) = {c}
5. C → λ	FIRST(λ) | FOLLOW(C) = {} | {d} = {d}

■

7.7 SELECTION SETS CONTAINING THE END-OF-INPUT MARKER

Suppose we wish to determine the leftmost derivation of a terminal string z in an LL(1) grammar. Suppose at some point during the derivation, the sentential form zBCD appears. What should we do? We have generated the desired terminal string z, but we have extra non-terminals, B, C, and D, on the right. Obviously, we need to get rid of B, C, and D, leaving just z, our desired terminal string. To do this, we need to apply a B production whose right side is nullable, and then proceed to null it out. We should then similarly null out C and then D.

Now consider a different scenario. Suppose we produce zBCD in our derivation, and B and C are nullable but D is not. What should we do? There is no point in nulling out B and C since the derivation is doomed to fail—the derivation cannot generate just z since D will generate at least one terminal symbol to the right of z. Thus, in this case, we should terminate the parse and reject the input string.

Let us consider examples of these two cases. Suppose we wish to generate fefe using G7.9:

G7.9	Selection Set
1. S → feS	{f}
2. S → BCD	{b, c, d, #}
3. B → b	{b}
4. B → λ	{c, d, #}
5. C → c	{c}
6. C → λ	{d, #}
7. D → d	{d}
8. D → λ	{#}

Let us start the derivation of fefe:

    S ⇒ feS ⇒ fefeS ⇒ fefeBCD

At this point, we have generated our desired string fefe. Now we eliminate B, C, and D using productions 4, 6, and 8, respectively. The complete derivation is

    S ⇒ feS ⇒ fefeS ⇒ fefeBCD ⇒ fefeCD ⇒ fefeD ⇒ fefe

In this derivation we have applied productions 2, 4, 6, and 8, after the end-of-input has been reached. Thus, # should be in the selection sets for these productions to indicate that they can be applied when the current token is # (i.e., when we have reached the end of input).

Now consider a slightly different grammar in which D is not nullable:

G7.10	Selection Set
1. S → feS	{f}
2. S → BCD	{b, c, d}
3. B → b	{b}
4. B → λ	{c, d}
5. C → c	{c}
6. C → λ	{d}
7. D → d	{d}

If we attempt to derive fefe using G7.10, we get

$$S \Rightarrow feS \Rightarrow fefeS \Rightarrow fefeBCD$$

At this point, we have generated the complete input string, so we now need to get rid of B, C, and D (the current token at this point is #). Should we, therefore, delete B and C using productions 4 and 6, respectively? No, we should not because the derivation is doomed to fail. To get a successful derivation, we have to eliminate B, C, and D. But D is not nullable. For G7.10, we should not apply any of its productions once we have reached the end of input. Thus, # should not be any of its selection sets.

Clearly, it does not make sense to use a production whose right side is not nullable when the current token is # (because the production will ultimately generate a nonnull string for which there is no corresponding input). But it *also* does not make sense to use a production (like production 4 in G7.10) whose left side can never appear rightmost in a leftmost derivation, or have only nullables to its right because the symbols to its right will necessarily generate a nonnull string for which there is no corresponding input. These two observations lead to the following rule: Include # in a selection set if and only if

1. The production's right side is nullable
2. The symbol on the production's left side can appear in a leftmost derivation either as the rightmost symbol or with only nullable nonterminal symbols to its right

Applying this rule to G7.9, we find that # should be in the selections sets for productions 2, 4, 6, and 8.

Let us call any symbol that satisfies requirement 2 above a *righty*. Using our new term righty, we can restate our "#-rule" very simply:

> **Include # in a selection for any production whose left side is a righty and whose right side is nullable.**

In G7.9, productions 2, 4, 6, and 8 all have nullable right sides and righty left sides. These productions, therefore, have # in their selection sets. In G7.10, however, only S and D are righties. But there is no S or D production with a nullable right side. Thus, none of the selection sets for G7.10 contain #.

Let us determine the selection sets for the following grammar:

G7.11			Selection Set
1.	S	→ dA	{d}
2.	A	→ BC	{b, c, #}
3.	B	→ b	{b}
4.	B	→ λ	{c, #}
5.	C	→ c	{c}
6.	C	→ λ	{#}

We first determine which nonterminals are righties. Obviously, S always qualifies since S appears alone (and, therefore, rightmost) in the first line of any derivation. If S is rightmost, then by replacing S with dA (according to production 1), A becomes rightmost. Then by replacing A with BC (according to production 2), C becomes rightmost. Furthermore, B will then have only C (which is nullable) to its right. Thus, B is also a righty. For G7.11, S, A, B, and C are all righties. Accordingly, the selection sets for productions 2, 4, and 6 (the productions with nullable right sides and righty left sides) include #.

By definition, # is in FOLLOW(S). Let us now use the whatever-follows-left-follows-rightmost rule to determine which FOLLOW sets for G7.11 contain #. From production 1, we know that whatever follows S also follows A. Thus # is in FOLLOW(A). By production 2, we know that whatever follows A follows C. Moreover, C is nullable. Thus, production 2 also implies that whatever follows A also follows B. Because # is in FOLLOW(A), # is also in FOLLOW(B) and FOLLOW(C). Notice that to determine which FOLLOW sets contain #, we do precisely what we do to determine which nonterminals are righties. We can conclude that

A nonterminal is a righty if and only if its FOLLOW set contains #.

To determine the righties in a grammar, we simply place # in FOLLOW(S) and use the whatever-follows-left-follows-right rule to compute FOLLOW sets. # will end up in the FOLLOW set of every righty. But this means that if we use our standard rules for computing selection sets, # will end up in the selection set of any production whose left side is a righty and whose right side is nullable, that is, in precisely the selection sets in which # belongs. For example, consider the following production:

A → BCD

Suppose # belongs in its selection set (i.e., A is a righty and BCD is nullable). Because BCD is nullable, our rules for computing selection sets tell us that the selection set for this production is FIRST(BCD) | FOLLOW(A). But FOLLOW(A) necessarily includes # because A is a righty. Thus, our rules for computing selection sets correctly places # in the selection set for this production.

In summary, handling the end-of-input marker is easy: we simply place # in the FOLLOW set of the start symbol, and then compute selection sets as we normally do. # will then end up in the appropriate selection sets.

Exercise 7.5

Determine the selection sets for

1. S → ABC
2. A → dSd

3. A → λ
4. B → bBe
5. B → λ
6. C → c
7. C → λ

Answer:

FOLLOW(S) contains d (by production 2) and # (by definition). By the what-follows-left-follows-rightmost rule and production 1, FOLLOW(A), FOLLOW(B), and FOLLOW(C) all contain FOLLOW(S). FOLLOW(A) also contains FIRST(BC) (by production 1). FOL-LOW(B) also contains FIRST(C) (by production 1) and e (by production 4). FIRST(ABC) = {d, b, c}, FIRST(BC) = {b, c}, and FIRST(C) = {c}.

1. S → ABC   FIRST(ABC) | FOLLOW(S) =   {d, b, **c**} | {d, #}
2. A → dSd   FIRST(dSd) =   {d}
3. A → λ   FIRST(λ}| FOLLOW(A) =   {} | {b, c, d, #}
4. B → bBe   FIRST(bBe) =   {b}
5. B → λ   FIRST(λ}| FOLLOW(B) =   {} | {c, d, e, #}
6. C → c   FIRST(c) =   {c}
7. C → λ   FIRST(λ) | FOLLOW(C) =   {} | {d, #}

7.8 A STACK PARSER FOR A GRAMMAR WITH LAMBDA PRODUCTIONS

When we use a lambda production during a top-down parse, we eliminate the nonterminal to which we apply the lambda production. For example, suppose our input-stack configuration is

    bc#   BC$
    ^

If we now apply a lambda production to B, we eliminate B to get

    bc#   C$
    ^

The operation sequence we need to transform the first configuration above to the second is simply a pop operation. Notice that the steps we listed in Section 7.3 for determining stack operation sequences already correctly indicate the operation for a lambda production: Step 1 says to pop. Step 2 says to push λ (the right side of the production in reverse order). But pushing λ is, in effect, concatenating λ to the top of the stack, the effect of which is to leave the stack unchanged. Step 3 does not apply.

Let us construct the parse table for the following grammar:

G7.12   Selection Set
    1. S → BC   {b, c, #}
    2. B → bB   {b}
    3. B → λ   {c, #}
    4. C → cCb   {c}
    5. C → λ   {b, #}

The selection set for each production determines in which columns its corresponding operation sequence appears. For example, since the selection set for production 5 is {b, #}, its operation sequence (pop) appears in row C, columns b and #. The parse table appears in Figure 7.8.

7.9 CONVERTING A NON-LL(1) GRAMMAR TO AN LL(1) GRAMMAR

There are several useful techniques for converting a non-LL(1) grammar to an equivalent LL(1) grammar. These techniques are usually successful in producing the desired LL(1) equivalent grammar. If, however, these techniques fail to produce an LL(1) grammar, the compiler designer should study the given grammar to "understand" the language defined, and then write a completely new grammar. Hopefully, the new grammar will be LL(1) or can be converted to an LL(1) grammar by these techniques. Beware, however, that some context-free languages cannot be defined by any LL(1) grammar. For such languages, any conversion technique is doomed to fail.

We have already learned two of these techniques in Chapter 3, namely, the elimination of ambiguity and the elimination of left recursion. A grammar that is ambiguous or contains left recursion (direct or indirect) is never LL(1). Let us convince ourselves that this assertion is true.

If a grammar is ambiguous, then the corresponding top-down parser must somewhere exhibit a choice in its operation, reflecting the multiple parse trees that are possible for at least one input string. But a top-down parser based on an LL(1) grammar is deterministic—there is never any choice in its operations. Thus, an ambiguous grammar is never LL(1). Let us consider an example:

G7.13   Selection Set
  1. S → bS   {b}
  2. S → B   {b}
  3. B → bB   {b}
  4. B → b   {b}

Two parse trees exist for bb in this grammar (see Figure 7.9).

	b	c	#
S	pop push(C) push(B)	pop push(C) push(B)	pop push(C) push(B)
B	advance	pop	pop
C	pop	pop push(b) push(C) advance	pop
b	pop advance		
$			accept

Figure 7.8.

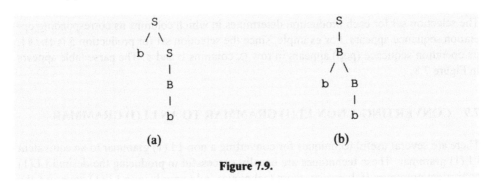

Figure 7.9.

The parse trees in Figures 7.9a and 7.9b initially use production 1 and production 2, respectively. A top-down parser should be able parse according to either of these trees, and, therefore, must allow a choice in the production to use first in a derivation. This choice is reflected in the selection sets for productions 1 and 2: they both contain b.

It is easy to rewrite G7.13 as an unambiguous grammar. The simplest equivalent unambiguous grammar is

G7.14   Selection Set
  1. S → bS   {b}
  2. S → b   {b}

which, unfortunately, is not LL(1). But there is another simple unambiguous grammar that is, in fact, LL(1):

G7.15   Selection Set
  1. S → bB   {b}
  2. B → bB   {b}
  3. B → λ   {#}

Converting an ambiguous grammar to an LL(1) always requires the elimination of the ambiguity. However, just eliminating the ambiguity does not guarantee that the result is LL(1), as demonstrated by G7.14 above.

Like ambiguous grammars, left-recursive grammars are never LL(1). Here is the basis for this assertion: Suppose a grammar contains a left-recursive production, A → Ax. Then it must also contain at least one more A production, A → y. Otherwise A would be a dead nonterminal, which, in itself, would make the grammar non-LL(1) [by definition, an LL(1) grammar cannot contain any dead or unreachable nonterminals]. The selection set of A → Ax contains everything in FIRST(Ax), which contains everything in FIRST(A), which—because we have the production A → y—contains everything in FIRST(y). But the selection set for A → y also includes everything in FIRST(y). Thus, the selection sets for the two productions have the elements in the FIRST(y) in common, making the grammar non-LL(1). To complete our argument, we have to consider the special case in which FIRST(y) is empty. We leave this as an exercise (see Problem 35).

Let us consider the following example of a left-recursive grammar:

G7.16   Selection Set
  1. S → Sb   {d, e}
  2. S → Sc   {d, e}

3. S → d   {d}
4. S → e   {e}

Notice the overlap in selection sets. Let us eliminate the left recursion in G7.16 and see if the resulting grammar is LL(1). Each string in the language starts with either d or e and is followed by a list of zero or more b's and/or c's. We eliminate the left recursion by creating a grammar that generates the strings in the language left to right. The result is LL(1):

G7.17   Selection Set
  1. S → dL   {d}
  2. S → eL   {e}
  3. L → bL   {b}
  4. L → cL   {c}
  5. L → λ   {#}

Another example—a very important example—of a conversion to an LL(1) grammar by the elimination of ambiguity and left recursion is illustrated by the four grammars for arithmetic expressions in Section 4.2. We repeat the four grammars here as G7.18, G7.19, G7.20, and G7.21. G7.18 has two types of ambiguities—precedence and associativity— and is, therefore, not LL(1):

G7.18
  1. expr → expr "+" expr
  2. expr → expr "*" expr
  3. expr → "b"
  4. expr → "c"
  5. expr → "d"
  6. expr → "(" expr ")"

G7.19 results by eliminating the precedence ambiguity in G7.18. Since G7.19 still has the associativity ambiguity, it is not LL(1):

G7.19
  1. expr → expr "+" expr
  2. expr → term   (one-way street)
  3. term → term "*" term
  4. term → "b"
  5. term → "c"
  6. term → "d"
  7. term → "(" expr ")"

G7.20, which results from G7.19 by eliminating the remaining ambiguity, is still not LL(1) because it uses left recursion:

G7.20
  1. expr   →   expr "+" term   (left recursive)
  2. expr   →   term
  3. term   →   term "*" factor   (left recursive)
  4. term   →   factor

```
5. factor  →  "b"
6. factor  →  "c"
7. factor  →  "d"
8. factor  →  "(" expr ")"
```

The final grammar, G7.21, obtained by eliminating the left-recursion in G7.20 is LL(1):

G7.21

```
 1. expr        →  term termList
 2. termList    →  "+" term termList
 3. termList    →  λ
 4. term        →  factor factorList
 5. factorList  →  "*" factor factorList
 6. factorList  →  λ
 7. factor      →  "b"
 8. factor      →  "c"
 9. factor      →  "d"
10. factor      →  "(" expr ")"
```

G7.21 is a grammar that anyone who has constructed a top-down parser for arithmetic expressions knows (and appreciates), since it is LL(1) and, therefore, can be used in a top-down parser. Moreover, it captures the correct the operator precedence and associativity. In Chapter 4, we commented that the operator precedence and associativity implied by G4.4 (which is repeated above as G7.21) is not obvious. For example, consider the parse tree for b + c + d in Figure 7.10.

What associativity for the addition operator is implied by this parse tree? We know from Section 6.2 that a top-down parse determines the left-most derivation of the input string. Moreover, during a top-down parse, we process nodes in depth-first order with preference given to the leftmost. In Figure 7.10, we have indicated this order with subscripts. It is this order that tells us the associativity of the addition operation implied by the parse tree. Note that we process the left addition operator, along with its operands

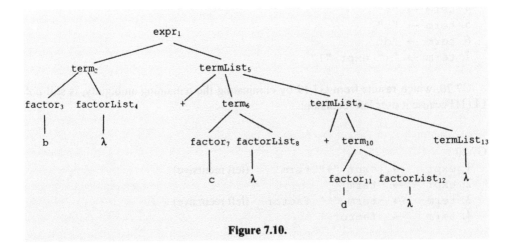

Figure 7.10.

(term$_2$ and term$_6$), before we process the right addition. The result of the left addition functions as the left operand of the right addition. Its right operand is term$_{10}$. Thus, the implied associativity is left. That is, the left addition operation is performed before the right addition operation, *even though the right addition is lower in the tree.*

The order associated with depth-first processing tells us the precedence and associativity implied by a parse tree for a top-down parse.

Exercise 7.6

Convert the following grammar to an equivalent LL(1) by eliminating left recursion:

		Selection Set
1. S → SSb		{c}
2. S → c		{c}

Answer:

Each string in the language starts with c followed by a list of zero or more occurrences of Sb. The grammar that generates this language left to right is

		Selection Set
1. S → cL		{c}
2. L → SbL		{c}
3. L → λ		{#}

■

A third conversion technique is *left factoring.* In left factoring, a common initial part of the right sides of two or more productions with the same left side is "factored" out. The best way to describe the technique is through an example. Consider the following grammar:

G7.22	Selection Set
1. S → eBd	{e}
2. S → eCd	{e}
3. B → bB	{b}
4. B → λ	{d}
5. C → c	{c}

G7.22 is not LL(1) because the two S productions have overlapping selection sets. Through left factoring, however, we can combine the two S productions into a single production. In particular, we factor out the left portion of the right sides that are common to both productions (i.e., e) and let a new nonterminal R generate the remaining portions (i.e., Bd and Cd) of the two right sides:

G7.23	Selection Set
1. S → eR	{e}
2. R → Bd	{b, d}
3. R → Cd	{c}
4. B → bB	{b}
5. B → λ	{d}
6. C → c	{c}

The first three productions in G7.23 generate what the first two productions in G7.22 generate. In G7.23, however, there is only one S production. We have eliminated the problem associated with the two S productions, making the new grammar LL(1).

Another example of left factoring is given by

G7.24	Selection Set
1. S → b,S	{b}
2. S → b	{b}

This grammar generates a list of one or more b's, with commas separating successive b's. Similar lists occur frequently in programming languages (e.g., in variable declarations). To convert the grammar to an LL(1) grammar, we factor out the leading b in both productions, leaving ",S" in the first production and the null string in the second production. Again, in the new grammar, we use a new nonterminal R to generate the two "leftovers":

G7.25	Selection Set
1. S → bR	{b}
2. R → ,S	{,}
3. R → λ	{#}

Exercise 7.7

Convert the following grammar to an equivalent LL(1) grammar by left factoring:

	Selection Set
1. S → bA	{b}
2. S → b	{b}
3. A → bb	{b}
4. A → bc	{b}

Answer:

	Selection Set
1. S → bR	{b}
2. R → A	{b}
3. R → λ	{#}
4. A → bT	{b}
5. T → b	{b}
6. T → c	{c}

An extension of left factoring is *left–right factoring*. In left–right factoring, we factor out the common left and right sides. For example, in G7.22, we can factor out both e on the left and d on the right in the two S productions. We get

G7.26	Selection set
1. S → eMd	{e}
2. M → B	{b, d}
3. M → C	{c]
4. B → bB	{b}

5. B → λ   {d}
6. C → c   {c}

One advantage of left–right factoring over left factoring is that the right factor appears only once in the resulting grammar. For example, in G7.26, the right factor, d, appears in only production 1. Thus, the processing of d in a top-down parser would appear in only one location. In contrast, with left factoring, d appears twice (see productions 2 and 3 in G7.23), and, therefore, its processing would appear in two locations in a top-down parser.

Our final conversion technique is *corner substitution*. A *corner* is the leftmost symbol of the right side of a production (unless the production is a lambda production, in which case a corner does not exist). In corner substitution, all the productions for a corner are used to replace that corner. For example, consider

G7.27   Selection Set
    1. S → bA   {b}
    2. S → Ac   {b, c}
    3. A → bA   {b}
    4. A → λ   {c, #}

In production 2, A is the corner. We substitute for this A using the two A productions. The two new productions that result—productions 2 and 3 in G7.28 below—replace production 2 in G7.27:

G7.28   Selection Set
    1. S → bA   {b}
    2. S → bAc   {b}
    3. S → c   {c}
    4. A → bA   {b}
    5. A → λ   {c, #}

Our new grammar is still not LL(1). However, we can now left factor productions 1 and 2. We factor out bA in both productions, leaving the null string in production 1 and c in production 2. The result is an LL(1) grammar:

G7.29   Selection Set
    1. S → bAR   {b}
    2. S → c   {c}
    3. R → λ   {#}
    4. R → c   {c}
    5. A → bA   {b}
    6. A → λ   {c, #}

Exercise 7.8

Convert the following grammar to an equivalent LL(1) grammar by using corner substitution:

                     Selection Set
1. S → bA   {b}
2. A → Sb   {b}
3. A → b   {b}

Answer:

Corner substitution on production 2 produces

		Selection Set
1. S → bA		{b}
2. A → bAb		{b}
3. A → b		{b}

Left factoring b in productions 2 and 3 produces

		Selection Set
1. S → bA		{b}
2. A → bR		{b}
3. R → Ab		{b}
4. R → λ		{b, #}
5. A → b		{b}

which, unfortunately is still not LL(1). Thus, we must study the grammar to "understand" the language defined and then to write a completely new grammar. Our study reveals the language is (bb)+, which is generated left to right by

		Selection Set
1. S → bbB		{b}
2. B → bbB		{b}
3. B → λ		{#}

Alas! An LL(1) grammar.

∎

7.10 PARSING WITH AN AMBIGUOUS GRAMMAR

An ambiguous grammar is a grammar for which at least one input string exists that has two or more distinct parse trees. If we perform a top-down parse on such an input string, which parse tree will the parse construct? Let us perform a top-down parse with an ambiguous grammar and see what happens. Consider the following grammar:

G7.30		Selection Set	
1. S → λ		{c, #}	
2. S → bSQ		{b}	
3. Q → cS		{c}	
4. Q → λ		{c, #}	delete c to disambiguate

G7.30 is ambiguous as demonstrated by the two parse trees for bbc in Figure 7.11.

Let us perform the top-down parse for the input string bbc to determine which of these two distinct parse trees will be constructed. Figure 7.12 shows the parse.

In each of the first three steps, the current token determines the production to use. In Figure 7.12a, the current token is b. Thus, we use production 2. Similarly, in Figure 7.12b, the current token is again b, again requiring the use of production 2. In Figure 7.12c, the current token is c, which cannot be generated by either S production. Thus, we must eliminate the S (with production 1 and let what follows the S generate the c. After these three steps, the parse produces what the two parse trees in Figure 7.11 have in com-

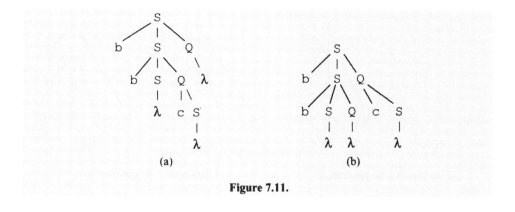

Figure 7.11.

mon (compare Figure 7.12d with Figure 7.11). What happens next determines which of the two possible variants in Figure 7.11 ultimately results. We can allow either the lower or upper Q in Figure 7.12d to generate c, with the other Q generating λ. This choice is reflected by the presence of c in the selection sets for both Q productions. If we select production 3 at this point, then the lower Q generates the c. If, on the other hand, we select production 4, then the upper Q must generate the c. Figs. 7.12e through 7.12g show what happens for each choice. The parse trees on the left corresponds to the lower-Q choice and those on the right correspond to the upper-Q choice.

Clearly, every top-down parser based on an ambiguous grammar must be faced with a choice when the input string has multiple parse trees. This choice must be reflected in the selection sets of the grammar. In particular, there must be at least two productions with the same left side that do not have disjoint selection sets. We can conclude that an ambiguous grammar is never LL(1).

What should we do if we wish to parse strings in a language defined by an ambiguous grammar? One approach, of course, is to convert the ambiguous grammar to an equivalent unambiguous LL(1) grammar, and then construct the parser based on this new grammar. Another approach is to construct a parser based on the ambiguous grammar. The parser, if it is to be deterministic, must be forced to make a particular choice whenever one exists. To do this, we simply delete elements from the offending selection sets until all productions with the same left side have disjoint selection sets. We then construct a parser according to these new selection sets. We call this process *disambiguating the grammar*. For example, for G7.30, we simply delete the c in the selection set for production 4. Thus, in the corresponding parser, there is never a choice. Whenever the current token is c and Q must be expanded, the parser uses production 3. For those strings in L(G7.30) that have only one parse tree, our parser determines that tree. For those strings that have multiple parse trees (for example, bbc), our parser determines one particular variant—namely, the variant that is produced when Q is always expanded with production 3 when the current token is c.

Our disambiguating technique does not always work (in fact, for most ambiguous grammars it does not work). The problem with disambiguating is that the corresponding parser may be constrained from constructing any parse tree for certain input strings. For example, consider the following ambiguous grammar that generates bb*:

G7.31   Selection Set
1. S → SS   {b}
2. S → b   {b}

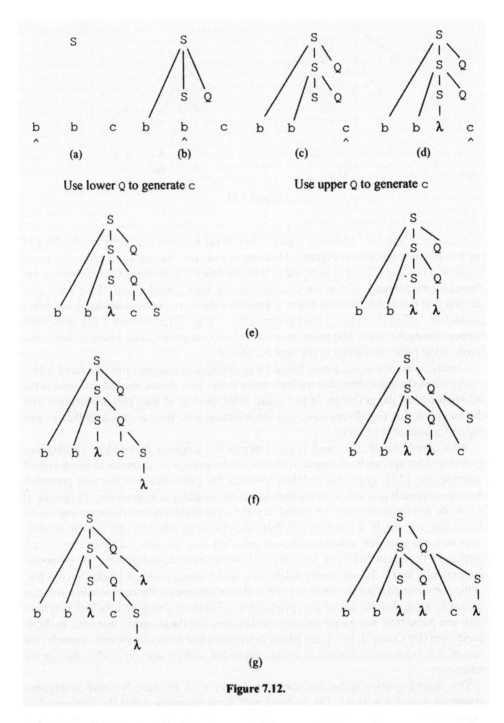

Figure 7.12.

If we delete the b in the first selection set, the corresponding parser can construct the parse tree only for the input string b. For all other input strings in L(G7.31), the parser fails. If, instead, we delete the b from the second selection set, then the corresponding parser fails for all input strings (the parser would use production 1 ad infinitum). Thus, disambiguating fails for G7.31. However, for this grammar, it is not hard to write an equivalent grammar that is LL(1):

G7.32   Selection Set
   1. S → bL   {b}
   2. L → bL   {b}
   3. L → λ   {#}

7.11   COMPUTING FIRST AND FOLLOW SETS

Up to now, we have computed FIRST and FOLLOW sets using an odd collection of techniques. Our last task in this chapter is to collect and formalize these techniques. In so doing, we achieve several benefits. First, formalization provides a check on the completeness and correctness of our techniques. Second, formalization forces us to "think through" and thoroughly understand our techniques. Finally, formalization provides a precise and organized form for our techniques that can serve as the basis of a computer program for computing FIRST and FOLLOW sets.

Here is our approach: we will construct a *FIRST/FOLLOW graph* that represents all the FIRST and FOLLOW relationships that can be determined from each production, *taken one at a time*, in the grammar. You may be confused by the term "graph." It has two very different meanings:

1. A graph is a structure that consists of a set of axes on which points are plotted.
2. A graph is a structure that consists of nodes and arrows. The arrows connect the nodes and represent a relationship on the nodes.

The graph that we will construct corresponds to the second definition. Each node represents a set. Each arrow connecting two nodes indicates that the set pointed from is a subset of the set pointed to. For example, the graph

FIRST(A) → FIRST(S)

indicates that FIRST(A) is a subset of FIRST(S).

The first step in the construction of the graph is to determine the nullable nonterminals in the grammar using the algorithm in Section 3.6. Next, we create a node for the FIRST set of each nonterminal, for the FOLLOW set of each nonterminal, for each input symbol, and for the end-of-input marker #. Then we add an arrow to the graph from {#} node to the FOLLOW(S) node [since FOLLOW(S) always contains #]. Last, we inspect the grammar, one production at a time. For each production, we determine all the set relationships that we can from that production in isolation, adding an arrow to the graph for each relationship we determine.

Let us apply this graphical approach to the following grammar:

G7.33

   1. S → BC
   2. B → bB
   3. B → λ
   4. C → c
   5. C → λ

We start by determining the nullable nonterminals. S, B, and C are nullable. Next, we create nodes for FIRST(S), FIRST(B), FIRST(C), FOLLOW(S), FOLLOW(B), FOLLOW(C), {b}, {c}, and {#} (see Figure 7.13). We then draw an arrow from {#} to FOLLOW(S) and additional arrows for each relationship that can be determined from the productions. For example, from production 1, S → BC, we know from our whatever-follows-left-follows-rightmost rule that FOLLOW(S) is a subset of both FOLLOW(B) (since C is nullable) and FOLLOW(C). Furthermore, we know that FIRST(C) is a subset of both FOLLOW(B) (since C follows B in production 1) and FIRST(S) (since C appears on the right side of production 1 with only a nullable to its left). We also know FIRST(B) is a subset of FIRST(S) (because B starts the right side of the production). We, therefore, add five arrows to our graph corresponding to these five relationships derived from production 1 alone. In Figure 7.13, we have labeled the arrows with the production number from which they are derived.

In our completed graph, a path exists from an input symbol to a set if and only if the set contains that input symbol. For example, in Figure 7.13, the path that exists from {#} to FOLLOW(B) implies FOLLOW(B) contains #. Similarly, the paths from {#} to FOL-LOW(S) and FOLLOW(C) indicate these sets also contain #. Thus, the problem of determining FIRST and FOLLOW sets is transformed to the problem of constructing a graph and determining paths in it. We can readily incorporate this process—the construction of the graph and the determination of the FIRST and FOLLOW sets implied by its paths—into in a computer program.

Let's complete our example. From Figure 7.13, we get

FIRST(S) = {b, c}   FOLLOW(S) = {#}
FIRST(B) = {b}   FOLLOW(B) = {c, #}
FIRST(C) = {c}   FOLLOW(C) = {#}

Exercise 7.9

a) Construct the FIRST/FOLLOW graph for

1. S → BCD
2. B → b
3. C → c
4. C → λ
5. D → d

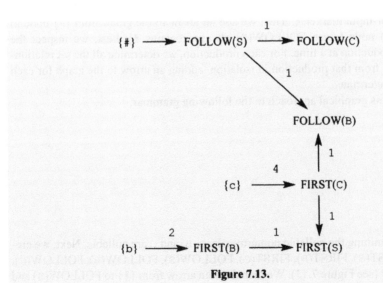

Figure 7.13.

b) Using the FIRST/FOLLOW graph, determine the FIRST and FOLLOW sets of each non-terminal.

Answers:

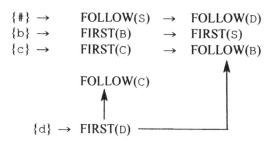

	FIRST	FOLLOW
S	{b}	{#}
B	{b}	{c, d}
C	{c}	{d}
D	{d}	{#}

PROBLEMS

1. Determine the selection sets for G7.18, G7.19, G7.20, and G7.21.

2. a) Determine the selection sets for

     1. S → Ad
     2. A → Bf
     3. B → Cb
     4. C → Dc
     5. D → e

  b) Construct the parse table for this grammar.

  c) Show the sequence of input-stack configurations that occurs when your stack parser operates on the input strings `ecbfd` and `ecbff`.

  d) Implement the stack parser.

3. Same as question 7.2 but for the input strings d and dd and the grammar

     1. S → A
     2. A → B
     3. B → C
     4. C → d

4. Same as question 7.2 but for the input strings `bccdddeeee` and `bccdddeee` and the grammar

     1. S → BCDE
     2. B → b
     3. C → cc
     4. D → ddd
     5. E → eeee

5. Same as question 7.2 but for the input strings bcdcde, bcde, bde, e, and bcd and the grammar

   1. S → ABCe
   2. A → bB
   3. A → λ
   4. B → cC
   5. B → λ
   6. C → d
   7. C → λ

6. Same as question 7.2 but for the input string bcdcd and grammar

   1. S → ABC
   2. A → bB
   3. A → λ
   4. B → cC
   5. B → λ
   6. C → d
   7. C → λ

7. Same as question 7.2 but for the input strings d and dd and the grammar

   1. S → ABCD
   2. A → λ
   3. B → λ
   4. C → λ
   5. D → d

8. Same as question 7.2 but for the input string λ and d and the grammar

   1. S → ABCD
   2. A → λ
   3. B → λ
   4. C → λ
   5. D → λ

9. Is the following grammar LL(1)?

   1. S → λ
   2. S → Ad
   3. A → bAS
   4. A → λ

10. Determine the selection sets for

   1. S → ABC
   2. A → bAS
   3. A → λ
   4. B → cASB
   5. B → λ
   6. C → AB

11. Convert the following grammar to an equivalent LL(1) grammar by eliminating left recursion:

    1. S → S+S
    2. S → S* S
    3. S → b

12. Convert the following grammar to an equivalent LL(1) grammar:

    1. S → SS+
    2. S → SS*
    3. S → b

    Note: + and * are terminal symbols in this grammar.

13. Suppose corner substitution is performed on a grammar that is already LL(1). Is the resulting grammar always LL(1)?

14. Suppose substitution (not necessarily corner substitution) is performed on a grammar that is already LL(1). Is the resulting grammar always LL(1)?

15. Convert the following grammar to an equivalent LL(1) grammar by left factoring:

    1. S → BCe
    2. S → Bd
    3. S → BCc
    4. B → b
    5. C → c

16. Convert the following grammar to an equivalent LL(1) grammar by left–right factoring:

    1. S → BCe
    2. S → Bde
    3. S → BCee
    4. B → b
    5. C → c

17. Convert the following grammar to an equivalent LL(1) grammar:

    1. S → Bd
    2. S → bcd
    3. B → bB
    4. B → λ

18. Give an example of an unambiguous grammar that is not LL(k) for any k.

19. Show that the language defined by the following grammar has no LL(1) grammar that defines it:

    1. S → aSa
    2. S → bSb
    3. S → λ

20. Give an example like G7.30 in which disambiguating works. Hint: Consider the control structures in Java.

21. Does disambiguating work for

   1. S → bS
   2. S → Sb
   3. S → c

22. Suppose the end-of-input symbol were always included in the selection set of any production whose right side is nullable. Would the top-down parser using these selection sets still work, that is, ultimately accept all and only input strings generated by the grammar?

23. Construct the FIRST/FOLLOW graph for G7.6. Using the graph, determine the FIRST and FOLLOW sets for each nonterminal.

24. Construct the FIRST/FOLLOW graph for G7.7. Using the graph, determine the FIRST and FOLLOW sets for each nonterminal.

25. Construct the FIRST/FOLLOW graph for G7.8. Using the graph, determine the FIRST and FOLLOW sets for each nonterminal.

26. Construct the FIRST/FOLLOW graph for G7.9. Using the graph, determine the FIRST and FOLLOW sets for each nonterminal.

27. Construct the FIRST/FOLLOW graph for G7.10. Using the graph, determine the FIRST and FOLLOW sets for each nonterminal.

28. Construct the FIRST/FOLLOW graph for G7.11. Using the graph, determine the FIRST and FOLLOW sets for each nonterminal.

29. Construct the FIRST/FOLLOW graph for G7.12. Using the graph, determine the FIRST and FOLLOW sets for each nonterminal.

30. Construct the FIRST/FOLLOW graph for

   1. S → ABC
   2. S → BC
   3. S → C
   4. A → aAb
   5. A → B
   6. B → dAb
   7. B → C
   8. C → cd
   9. C → c

   Using the graph, determine the FIRST and FOLLOW sets for each nonterminal.

31. If a grammar G is LL(k), does there necessarily exist an LL(1) grammar equivalent to G?

32. Show that for an arbitrary nonterminal A, if FOLLOW(A) = {}, then A is useless.

33. In an LL(1) grammar, can more than one production with the same left side have a nullable right side? Justify your answer.

34. Determine the selection sets for

   1. S → eBbCD
   2. S → λ
   3. B → bBc
   4. B → BSe
   5. B → λ
   6. C → CC

7. C → d
8. C → λ
9. D → SdD
10. D → λ

35. Suppose a grammar has two productions of the form

1. A → Ax
2. A → y

Show that these productions do not have disjoint selection sets when FIRST(y) is empty.

36. Construct the parse table for the following grammar:

1. S → CDe
2. C → cC
3. C → λ
4. D → dD
5. D → λ

Optimize the S row of the operational table as much as possible.

37. Determine the selection sets for

1. S → BCD
2. B → BcCc
3. B → λ
4. C → CSc
5. C → λ
6. D → dBf

38. Consider the following grammar:

1. S → ABSdC
2. S → ABC
3. A → BbSAfA
4. A → Ba
5. A → λ
6. B → BeB
7. B → Sc
8. B → λ
9. C → SgC
10. C → λ

Given that A, B, and C are nullable, does the second production, S → ABC, imply that FIRST(A), FIRST(B), and FIRST(C) are subsets of FIRST(S)? What other relations on the FIRST sets do the other productions imply? What can you say about all the FIRST sets? What does the production S → ABC imply about FOLLOW(S), FOL-LOW(A), FOLLOW(B), and FOLLOW(C). What other relations on the FOLLOW sets do the other produtions imply? What can you say about all the FOLLOW sets. What is the selection set for each productions of the grammar?

8

TABLE-DRIVEN STACK PARSER (OPTIONAL)

8.1 INTRODUCTION

In Chapter 6, we examined a Java program (see Figure 6.12) that implements a stack parser for a particular grammar (G6.5). Recall that the heart of this program is a `switch` statement that selects and executes the operation sequence called for by the top of the stack and the current token. If we wanted this program to perform a parse for another grammar, we would, of course, have to change the `switch` statement to reflect this new grammar.

Now consider this very important question: Is there some way to implement a stack parser so that it can handle different grammars without modification? You might think that this is a clear impossibility but that is not the case. We can implement our stack parser with two distinct parts: a data part and a code part. The data part consists of tables that describe a particular grammar. The code part contains the instructions that perform the parse for the grammar described in the data part. Nothing in the code part itself has any dependency on the particular grammar for which it is parsing. Thus, the code part works without modification for any grammar. The parser can be set up to handle any grammar simply by "plugging in" the data part that describes that grammar. We call a stack parser implemented in this way a *table-driven stack parser* because its operation is controlled by the tables in the data part.

The table-driven approach makes it easy to construct a stack parser for a given grammar. We can even write a program to do it for us. We call such a program is a *stack-parser generator* (see Figure 8.1). A stack-parser generator typically inputs a grammar and outputs the tables that make up the data part of a table-driven stack parser. These tables are then combined with the code part of the stack parser to produce a complete parser for the input grammar. We have a really remarkable capability here: A stack-parser generator automates the entire process of implementing a complex piece of software. Moreover, once we have completely debugged our stack-parser generator, we are certain to produce a bug-free parser every time. Our only obligation is to provide the parser generator with the correct LL(1) grammar.

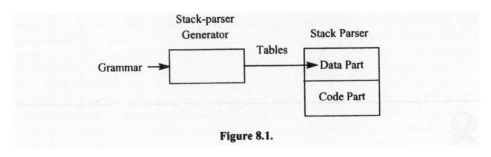

Figure 8.1.

In this chapter, we will design two table-driven stack parsers. Our first stack parser will be as simple as possible, and, therefore, will be somewhat limited in its capabilities. The second parser, will be a modification of the first that will not have the limitations of the first parser.

8.2 UNIFYING THE OPERATIONS OF A STACK PARSER

In Chapters 6 and 7, we learned a variety of rules for determining the operation sequences corresponding to the productions in a grammar. Recall that the operation sequence depends on the form of the production. For example, if the production has a leading terminal on its right side, then its operation sequence includes an advance operation. Otherwise, it does not. Let us see if we can come up with an operation sequence that works for any production and does not depend on the production's form.

Consider the stack parser based on the following grammar (notice that the productions are numbered starting from 0 instead of the usual 1; we will give the reason for this later):

G8.1   Selection Set
0. S → fBC   {f}
1. B → bb   {b}
2. B → CD   {c, d, e}
3. C → cC   {c}
4. C → λ   {d, e, #}
5. D → dD   {d}
6. D → e   {e}

The initial input-stack configuration in a parse of the string fe is

Input   Stack
fe#   S$
^

Recall that $, #, and ^ are the markers for the bottom of the stack, the end of input, and the current token, respectively.

In its first step, the stack parser selects production 0 and performs its corresponding operation sequence: namely, pop, push in reverse order the right side of production 0 (except for the leading terminal), and advance. The stack-input configuration becomes

fe#   BC$
^

There is, however, a different operation sequence that a stack parser can perform when applying production 0: It can replace S on the stack with the entire right side of production 0 and *not* advance. If we apply this operation sequence to the initial configuration, we get

```
fe#              fBC$
  ^
```

This new configuration makes perfect sense. Here is why: The initial configuration asserts that S can generate fe. Since, in a leftmost derivation of fe, S is replaced by fBC, it follows that fBC can generate fe, which is what our new configuration asserts. Furthermore, since fBC can generate fe, it follows that BC can generate e. Thus, it makes sense for the parser in its next step to get rid of both the f on the stack (by popping) and the f in the current token (by advancing). The configuration then becomes

```
fe#              BC$
  ^
```

This configuration is the same as the one that results from the original operation sequence for production 0. The difference between the two operation sequences is that the new sequence has an additional step in which the f pushed on the stack is popped and the current token marker is advanced. In the original sequence, the f is never pushed on the stack so we can avoid this extra step.

We know from Chapter 7 that the operation sequence for a production whose right side does not start with a terminal is a pop followed by a push of the entire right side. From our example above, we see that this sequence of operations also works if the production's right side starts with a terminal. Thus, it works for *any* production. We call a stack parser that uses this single type of operation sequence for every production a *uniform stack parser* because it treats every production uniformly.

A uniform stack parser is easier to construct because the parser (and the person writing the parser or the parser generator) does not have to treat productions with leading terminals as special cases. The parser does, however, take extra steps when applying productions that start with leading terminals, or whose operation sequences would have been optimized in a nonuniform parser.

Let us construct the parse table for the uniform stack parser that is based on G8.1. The table is given in Figure 8.2.

Since a uniform stack parser pushes the entire right side of every production it applies during a parse, every terminal symbol is also a stack symbol. Accordingly, in Figure 8.2, there is a row as well as a column for every terminal symbol. Whenever a terminal symbol is on top of the stack and a matching symbol is the current token, the parser discards both by popping and advancing.

We can considerably abbreviate Figure 8.2 without losing any essential information. Since every operation sequence is a pop followed by a push in reverse order of the right side of some production, we can specify an operation sequence unambiguously with just the number of the corresponding production. In addition, we can eliminate the rows in the parse table corresponding to the terminal symbols since the parser always treats a terminal on top of the stack in the same way, regardless of the grammar. For the same reason, we can omit the row corresponding to the bottom-of-stack marker $. With these changes, the parse table given in Figure 8.2 becomes the abbreviated parse table given in Figure 8.3.

Current token

		b	c	d	e	f	#
	S					pop push(C) push(B) push(f)	
	B	pop push(b) push(b)	pop push(D) push(C)	pop push(D) push(C)	pop push(D) push(C)		
	C		pop push(C) push(c)	pop	pop		pop
Symbol on top of stack	D			pop push(D) push(d)	pop push(e)		
	b	pop advance					
	c		pop advance				
	d			pop advance			
	e				pop advance		
	f					pop advance	
	$						accept

Figure 8.2.

	b	c	d	e	f	#
S					0	
B	1	2	2	2		
C		3	4	4		4
D			5	6		

Figure 8.3.

Exercise 8.1:

Construct the abbreviated parse table for the following grammar:

0. S → BC
1. B → bB
2. B → λ
3. C → ccc

Answer:

	b	c	#
S	0	0	
B	1	2	
C		3	

■

8.3 IMPLEMENTING A TABLE-DRIVEN STACK PARSER

A good starting point for any software design is to consider the data structures that are needed. Here are the data structures that we need for our table-driven stack parser:

1. `java.util.Stack stk`
2. `int [ ][ ] parseTable`

   `parseTable` is a two-dimensional integer array that corresponds to our abbreviated parse table discussed in Section 8.2. Entries that correspond to reject configurations contain -1. All other entries contain production numbers. The stack parser must translate the top of the stack symbol and the current token into the appropriate row and column index, respectively, before it can access the parse table. `parseTable` for G8.1 is essentially what appears in Figure 8.3, except that

   - All blank (i.e., reject) entries contain -1.
   - Row and column indices are integers starting from zero.

   The declaration in Java of this array is

   ```
   int[ ][ ] parseTable  =
   {
       {-1,  -1,  -1,  -1,   0,  -1},
       { 1,   2,   2,   2,  -1,  -1},
       {-1,   3,   4,   4,  -1,   4},
       {-1,  -1,   5,   6,  -1,  -1}
   };
   ```

3. `String[ ] pTab`

   `pTab` is a `String` array that contains the right side of each production *in reverse order*. For example, if production 0 is S → fBC, then `pTab[0]` is the string "CBf." Since indexing in Java starts from zero, it is convenient to number productions starting from zero. Then the production number is the index of that production in pTab. The Java declaration for the grammar in G8.1 is

```
String[ ] pTab =
{
    "CBf",
    "bb" ,
    "DC" ,
    "Cc" ,
    "" ,
    "Dd",
    "e"
} ;
```

4. String nonTerms

Since parseTable has integer indices, the parser must translate a nonterminal symbol on top of the stack to its corresponding row index in parseTable. This translation makes use of nonTerms. nonTerms holds a string consisting of the nonterminal symbols arranged in the same order as their corresponding rows in parseTable. Rows 0 through 3 in parseTable correspond to nonterminals S, B, C, and D. Thus, nonTerms contains "SBCD." Whenever a nonterminal is on top of the stack, the stack parser searches for that nonterminal in nonTerms. The index of the nonterminal in nonTerms gives the row index of that nonterminal in the parseTable. The Java declaration of nonTerms for G8.1 is

```
String nonTerms = "SBCD";
```

5. String tokens

tokens functions like nonTerms except it is used to map token symbols to parseTable column indices. The Java inputs for G8.1 is

```
String tokens = "bcdef#";
```

The complete listing for the table-driven stack parser appears in Figure 8.4. Its basic structure is similar to the stack parser that we implemented in Chapter 6 (see Figure 6.12). The principal difference is inside the loop. Our table-driven stack parser uses parseTable to determine the appropriate operation sequence whereas our parser in Chapter 6 uses a rather complicated switch statement. Both parsers use the same token manager, ArgsTokenMgr (see Figure 6.12).

Each time through the loop, the table-driven stack parser converts the current token into a column index into parseTable:

```
75          tokenIndex = tokens.indexOf(currentToken);
```

It also converts the symbol on top of the stack into a row index into parseTable:

```
83          nonTermIndex = nonTerms.indexOf(stk.peek());
```

If the top of the stack contains a terminal symbol, indexOf returns –1 (because the terminal symbol does not appear in the nonTerms string). If, on the other hand, the top of

```
1  /* Figure 8.4: Top-down table-driven stack parser for
2
3                  Selection set
4     0) S -> fBC      { f}
5     1) B -> bb       { b}
6     2) B -> CD       { c, d, e}
7     3) C -> cC       { c}
8     4) C -> lambda {d, e, #}
9     5) D -> dD       { d}
10    6) D -> e        { e}
11 */
12 import java.util.*;  // import Stack and Scanner classes
13 //=========================================================
14 class Fig0804
15 {
16   public static void main(String[] args)
17   {
18     // construct token manager (see Figure 6.12)
19     ArgsTokenMgr tm = new ArgsTokenMgr(args);
20
21     // construct parser, pass it the token manager
22     Fig0804Parser parser = new Fig0804Parser(tm);
23
24     parser.parse();                       // do parse
25   }
26 }                                // end of Fig0804
27 //=========================================================
28 interface DataPart
29 {
30   // These constants are available to any class that
31   // implements this interface.
32
33   String tokens = "bcdef#";      // list of tokens
34   String nonTerms = "SBCD";      // list of non-terminals
35
36   // right-hand sides of productions in reverse order
37   String[] pTab = { "CBf", "bb", "DC", "Cc","","Dd","e"};
38
39   int[][] parseTable =
40   {
41     { -1, -1, -1, -1,  0, -1},  // -1 means reject
42     {  1,  2,  2,  2, -1, -1},  // Non-neg numbers are
43     { -1,  3,  4,  4, -1,  4},  // production numbers
44     { -1, -1,  5,  6, -1, -1}
45   };
46 }                                // end of DataPart
47 //=========================================================
48 class Fig0804Parser implements DataPart
49 {
```

Figure 8.4.

```
50    private ArgsTokenMgr tm;
51    private Stack<Character> stk;
52    private char currentToken;
53    //---------------------
54    public Fig0804Parser(ArgsTokenMgr tm)
55    {
56      this.tm = tm;                      // save tm
57      advance();                         // prime currentToken
58      stk = new Stack<Character>();  // create stack
59      stk.push('S');          // init stack with start symbol
60    }
61    //---------------------
62    private void advance()
63    {
64      currentToken = tm.getNextToken();
65    }
66    //---------------------
67    public void parse()
68    {
69      int nonTermIndex, tokenIndex, pNumber;
70
71      while (true)
72      {
73
74        // convert current token into index
75        tokenIndex = tokens.indexOf(currentToken);
76
77        // check if bad token or stk empty
78        if (tokenIndex == -1 || stk.empty())
79          break;
80
81        // convert top-of-stack symbol to index
82        // get -1 if top of stack is terminal
83        nonTermIndex = nonTerms.indexOf(stk.peek());
84
85        if (nonTermIndex >= 0)  // nonterm on top of stk?
86        {
87          // get production number
88          pNumber = parseTable[ nonTermIndex][ tokenIndex];
89
90          if (pNumber < 0)        // -1 means reject
91            break;
92
93          // apply production whose number is // pNumber
94          stk.pop();
95          for (int i = 0; i < pTab[ pNumber] .length(); i++)
96            stk.push(pTab[ pNumber] .charAt(i));
97        }
98
```

Figure 8.4 *Continued.*

```
99          else
100         // does term on top of stack match current token?
101         if (currentToken == stk.peek())
102         {
103            stk.pop();     // discard term on top of stack
104            advance();     // discard matching current token
105         }
106         else
107            break;
108      }
109
110      // test if in accept configuration
111      if (currentToken == '#' && stk.empty())
112         System.out.println("accept");
113      else
114         System.out.println("reject");
115   }
116 }                                    // end of Fig0804Parser
```

Figure 8.4. *Continued.*

the stack contains a nonterminal symbol, then indexOf returns a nonnegative value which is then assigned to nonTermIndex. In this case, the parser retrieves a production number from parseTable using nonTermIndex and tokenIndex as indices:

```
88            pNumber = parseTable[nonTermIndex][tokenIndex];
```

It then pops the nonterminal off the stack and pushes—character by character—the string it retrieves from pTab onto the stack:

```
94            stk.pop();
95            for (int i = 0; i < pTab[pNumber].length(); i++)
96               stk.push(pTab[pNumber].charAt(i));
```

Otherwise, if the symbol on top of the stack is a terminal that matches the current token, it pops and advances:

```
101           if (currentToken == stk.peek())
102           {
103              stk.pop();     // discard term on top of stack
104              advance();     // discard matching current token
105           }
```

Whenever an accept or reject configuration occurs, the loop terminates (via the break statements on lines 79, 91, or 107). The test that follows the loop determines if the final configuration is an accept or reject configuration:

```
111           if (currentToken == '#' && stk.empty())
112              System.out.println("accept");
```

```
113      else
114        System.out.println("reject");
```

8.4 IMPROVING OUR TABLE-DRIVEN STACK PARSER

The table-driven stack parser that we described in the previous section follows the same convention for context-free grammars that we have been using in most of our examples: Uppercase letters designate nonterminals and lowercase letters designate inputs. Although convenient, this convention leads to some unnecessary limitations on our stack parser. In particular, we cannot handle any grammar with more than 26 (the number of uppercase letters) nonterminals. Although this restriction has not been a problem with any of our examples so far, any grammar for a real programming language is likely to exceed this 26 nonterminal limit.

We need to rewrite our table-driven stack parser to make it more versatile. Here are the distinguishing features of our new table-driven stack parser: The stack is now a stack of integers instead of characters. We use the nonpositive integers, 0, -1, -2, etc., to represent the nonterminal symbols, with 0 always designating the start symbol. For example, for G8.1 the nonterminals S, B, C, and D are represented on the stack by 0, -1, -2, and -3, respectively. We represent tokens (i.e., input symbols) with positive integers.

Using the zero and negative integers for the nonterminal symbols has some advantages. First, the parser can easily determine if the symbol on top of the stack is a nonterminal (by checking if its value is less than or equal to zero). Second, the parser does not have to use indexOf to convert the symbol on top of the stack into a row index into parseTable. Instead, it simply negates the integer representing a nonterminal to obtain the correct index. For example, for G8.1, -3 represents D. Its negation, 3, is the row index of D in parseTable.

Changing the stack requires changes to some of the tables in the parser. Since the parser now pushes integers onto the stack, we represent the right sides of productions as arrays of integers. We this new approach, the Java declaration for pTab for G8.1 is

```
int[ ][ ]  pTab =
{
  { -2, -1 'f' },      // 0) S → fBC
  { 'b', 'b' },        // 1) B → bb
  { -3, -2},           // 2) B → CD
  { -2, 'c' },         // 3) C → cC
  { },                 // 4) C → lambda
  { -3, 'd'},          // 5) D → dD
  { 'e'}               // 6) D → e
}
```

Note that in pTab, we are representing characters with their binary codes, all of which are positive integers. The integers 0, -1, -2, and -3 represent S, B, C, and D, respectively (0 does not appear in the pTab for G8.1 only because S does not appear on the right side of any production). For example, row 0,

```
{ -2, -1, 'f' }
```

represents "BCf", the reversed right side of S → fBC.

8.5   PARSERS THAT ARE NOT DETERMINISTIC—A DIGRESSION ON THEORY (OPTIONAL)

A *palindrome* is a string that reads the same forwards and backwards. For example, "otto" is a palindrome. A grammar that defines all even-length palindromes over the alphabet {b, c} is

G8.2   Selection Set
  1. S → bSb   {b}
  2. S → cSc   {c}
  3. S → λ   {b, c, #}

As we can see from the selection sets, G8.2 is not LL(1). To parse the language defined by this grammar, a stack parser must first push all inputs up to the middle of the string onto the stack (we call this activity the "pushing phase"). It then must switch to a "comparing phase" in which it compares the contents of the stack with the remaining input. If they are identical, then the original string is a palindrome. The transition from pushing to comparing must occur exactly at the middle of the input string. Unfortunately, the only way for the stack parser to determine the middle of the input string is to first look ahead to determine the location of the end of the input string. Because there is no upper bound on the length of input strings for this grammar, the length of the lookahead that the parser has to perform has no upper bound. Thus, this grammar is not only not LL(1), it is not LL(k) for any k.

Although G8.2 is not LL(k) for any k, we can still construct a stack parser for it in our usual way. However, the parser will lack determinism. It will necessarily allow a choice, reflecting the fact that the selection sets for S are not disjoint. Such a parser is not suitable for a compiler. It is, however, interesting from a theoretical point of view. Consider the parse table for G8.2 in Figure 8.5. Notice that when S is on top of the stack and the input is b, there are two distinct operation sequences: push(b), push(S), push(b) (the actions for production 1), or pop (the action for production 3). That is, we

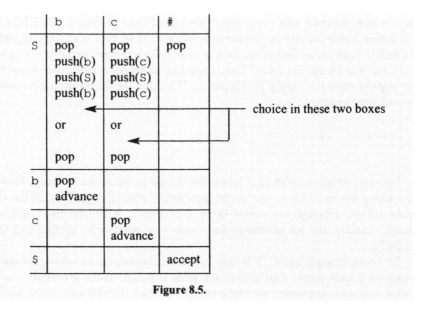

Figure 8.5.

have a choice. We have a similar situation when S is on top of the stack and c is the current token.

Let us see what happens when our stack parser parses bccb:

Input	Stack	
bccb# ^	S$	pushing phase
bccb# ^	bSb$	
bccb# ^	Sb$	
bccb# ^	cScb$	
bccb# ^	Scb$	pop S and change to comparing phase here
bccb# ^	cb$	
bccb# ^	b$	
bccb# ^	$	accept

In this particular parse, the parser applies production 1 or 2 until it reaches the middle of the input string. It then applies production 3, which eliminates the S nonterminal on the stack. By eliminating S from the stack, the parser forces a change from the pushing phase to the comparing phase. The parser then repeatedly compares the top of the stack with the current token. On each match, it gets rid of both the symbol on top of the stack and the matching input by popping and advancing, ultimately yielding an accept configuration.

The parse above ended in an accept configuration because the parser made the transition from pushing to comparing (by applying production 3) in the middle of the input string. If it makes this transition at any other point, the parse will fail. If it applies production 3 before the middle of the input, then the parse necessarily fails; even if all the compares match, the stack will empty before the end of input. Similarly, if the parser applies production 3 after the middle, the parser necessarily fails; even if all the compares match, the end of input occurs before the stack is empty. For example, initially S is on top of the stack and b is the current token. Thus, according to the parse table, one choice is to simply pop the stack (i.e., apply production 3). If it does, the following reject configuration immediately results:

bccb# ^	$	

For every string in L(G8.2), it is possible for our parser above to accept. However, for any string not in L(G8.2), our parser necessarily rejects, regardless of the choices it makes. Thus, although our parser lacks determinism, it still precisely defines a language—namely, the set of strings *for which it is possible to accept;* and this set is L(G8.2).

From our example above, it is easy to see that for any context-free grammar, we can construct a stack-parser than defines the same language as the grammar on which it is based. For some grammars, the stack-parser may lack determinism, but it, nevertheless, precisely defines the same language as the grammar on which it is based. It is also true (but not easy to show) that any language that can be defined by a stack-parser can also be defined by a context-free grammar. Thus, context-free grammars and stack parsers have exactly the same power to define languages.

If you read any textbooks on formal language theory, you will probably encounter a discussion of pushdown automata. A *pushdown automaton* is an abstraction of a stack parser. It uses a stack in exactly the same way a stack parser uses a stack. You will find in most formal language textbooks a proof of the equivalence of context-free languages and languages defined by pushdown automata, that is, a proof that every language that can be defined by a context-free grammar can be defined by a pushdown automaton, and vice versa. If you would like to experiment with the pushdown automaton model, see the files pda.txt and p.txt in the J1 Software Package.

Exercise 8.2:

Show the successive input-stack configurations that occur when the parser in Figure 8.5 parses bb. Make choices that result in an accept configuration.

Answer:

```
bb#            S$
^

bb#            bSb$
^

bb#            Sb$
 ^

bb#            b$
 ^

bb#            $        accept
  ^
```

■

PROBLEMS

1. Construct the full and abbreviated parse tables for the following grammars:

   a) S → b
      S → c
   b) S → λ
   c) S → ABCD
      A → λ
      B → λ
      C → λ
      D → λ
   d) G7.1
   e) G7.3
   b) G7.8
   g) G7.12

2. Implement the improved table driven stack parser described in Section 8.4.

3. a) Show the nondeterministic parse table for

    $S \rightarrow bSb$

    $S \rightarrow b$

    b) Show a successful parse of bbb.

    c) Give a grammar that defines the same language whose parse table is deterministic. Show its parse table.

    d) Show a parse of bbb corresponding to your parser in part c.

4. Is it possible to construct a stack parser for $\{ww : w \in \{b, c\}^*\}$?

5. Is it possible to construct a deterministic stack parser for $\{b^i c^j d^k : i = j \text{ or } i = k\}$?

6. Construct a deteministic parse table for for $\{b^i c^{2i} : i \geq 0\}$. Show a parse of bcc.

7. Construct a deterministic parse table for $\{b^i c^i : i \geq 1\} | \{c\}$. Show a parse of bc, bcc, and c.

8. Are there any regular languages for which no deterministic stack parser exist? Try to find one such regular language.

9

RECURSIVE-DESCENT PARSING

9.1 INTRODUCTION

Recursive-descent parsers—like the stack parsers we studied in the previous chapters—perform a top-down parse. They are particularly easy to implement. We simply write a method for each nonterminal in the grammar. Because the structure of each of these methods closely parallels the structure of the corresponding production, we do not have to do any creative programming. The productions for each nonterminal symbol, along with their selection sets, tell us precisely how to write the corresponding method.

Recursive-descent parsers have one important advantage over a stack parser: They are easy to extend so that they support translation. To do this, we simply embed calls to the code generator within the methods that make up the parser. These calls pass information on the source program collected by the parser to the code generator. With this information, the code generator can output the target program.

If the productions for a nonterminal are recursive, then the corresponding method in a recursive-descent parser is also recursive—hence, the use of "recursive" in the name "recursive-descent parsing." "Descent" refers to the top-to-bottom action of the parser.

In this chapter, we will learn how to implement recursive-descent parsers. Then, in the next chapter, we will learn how to extend them so that they support translation.

9.2 A SIMPLE RECURSIVE-DESCENT PARSER

Let us write a simple recursive-descent parser corresponding to

G9.1   Selection Set
  1. S → BD   {b, c}
  2. B → bB   {b}
  3. B → c   {c}
  4. D → de   {d}

This grammar defines the language b*cde. The b*c part comes from B in production 1; the de part comes from D in production 1.

Let us call any terminal string that can be generated by S an S string. Similarly, let us call any string that can be generated by B and D a B string and a D string, respectively. Thus, in bbcde, the substring bbc is a B string, de is a D string, and the entire string, bbcde, is an S string.

Suppose we have a method B() that advances in the input stream across a B string, after which the current token is the first token after the B string. For example, suppose the current token is at the beginning of the following string (the caret marks the current token):

```
bbcde#
^
```

Notice that for this string, the initial substring bbc is a B string. If we call the B() method at this point, it will advance in the input stream to just *beyond* the end of the B string:

```
bbcde#
   ^
```

If the current token is not at the beginning of a B string when we call B(), the B() method throws an error exception. For example, if we call B() when the current token is at the beginning of

```
bdbcde#
^
```

B() throws an error exception because no substring starting at the current token is a B string.

Let us also assume we have a D() method that behaves like B(), except that it advances across a D string. For example, if we call D() when we have

```
bbcde#
   ^
```

then it advances to # (the first character beyond the end of the D string de):

```
bbcde#
     ^
```

Like B(), D() throws an error exception if the current token initially is not at the start of the appropriate string. For example, if we call D() when the current token is d in

```
bbcd#
   ^
```

then D() throws an error exception because a single d is not a D string.

Once we have our B() and D() methods, we can easily write an S() method that behaves similarly—that is, it advances across any S string, or, if the string is not an S string, throws an exception. Our S() method simply calls B() and then D(), the combined effect of which is to advance across an S string.

In our implementation of the B () and D () methods, we will use a consume method that tests the current token and advances past it. For example, if we call consume with

```
consume('d');
```

consume checks if the current token is d. If it is, consume advances to the next token in the input stream. Otherwise it throws an exception that contains the message Expecting "d". The catch block that subsequently catches the exception displays this message. Here is the implementation of the consume method (the line numbers are from Figure 9.1):

```
51    private void consume(char expected)
52    {
53      if (currentToken == expected)
54        advance();
55      else
56        throw new RuntimeException(
57                  "Expecting \"" + expected + "\"");
58    }
```

advance(), which consume calls, gets the next token from the token manager and assigns it to currentToken:

```
46    private void advance()
47    {
48      currentToken = tm.getNextToken();
49    }
```

Let us now implement the B () method. Because there are two B productions, the B () method has to determine which production to apply. If currentToken is in {b} (the selection set of the first B production), B () applies the first production. If currentToken is in {c} (the selection set of the second B production), B () applies the second production. Otherwise, B () throws an exception. A switch statement nicely implements this test and multi-way branch, giving us the following structure for B ():

```
switch(currentToken)
{
  case 'b':
    apply first production here
    break;
  case 'c':
    apply second production here
    break;
  default:
    throw exception
}
```

What should B () do when it "applies" production 2 (B → bB)? Recall that B () is obliged to advance past the substring that comes from the right side of the production. To do this, B () first advances past initial b by calling consume('b'). It then advances past the part of the substring that comes from the recursive B by simply calling B() recursively. To apply production 3 (B → c), B() simply advances past the c by calling consume('c'). Thus, the code for B() is

```
74    private void B()
75    {
76      switch(currentToken)
77      {
78        case 'b':
79          consume('b');               // apply B -> bB
80          B();
81          break;
82        case 'c':
83          consume('c');               // apply B -> c
84          break;
85        default:
86          throw new RuntimeException(
87                          "Expecting \"b\" or \"c\"");
88      }
89    }
```

When we call B(), the current token should be either b or c. Thus, the default case in B() gets control only if the current token is neither b nor c. In that case, B() throws an exception that contains the message Expecting "b" or "c". Here, the error message lists the expected tokens at the point the error occurs. Alternatively, we can indicate the category of the expected token. For example, for B(), we could use the message Expecting B string. However, we should use a category in a message only if the category would be meaningful to the intended recipient.

Now let us implement the D() method. The D() method should advance past a de sequence. To do this, it can simply make two calls to consume:

```
91    private void D()
92    {
93      consume('d');                 // apply D -> de
94      consume('e');
95    }
```

Because there is only one D production, we do not need a switch statement as we did in the B() method. The first call of consume checks if the current token is 'd'. If it is not, consume throws an exception. Similarly, the second call of consume checks if the current token toke is 'e'.

Our only S production is S → BD. Thus, to implement S(), we simply call B() and D():

```
68    private void S()
69    {
70      B();                          // apply S -> BD
71      D();
72    }
```

Using S(), B(), and D(), we can now write our parse() method, which calls S() to perform the parse:

```
60    public void parse()
61    {
62      S();
63      if (currentToken != '#')     // trailing-garbage test
64        throw new RuntimeException(
65                              "Expecting end of input");
66    }
```

In addition to calling S() to parse the input string, parse() checks the final current token (i.e., the current token after the call of S()). If the current token is not the end-of-input marker #, then some garbage follows the S string, in which case parse() throws a RuntimeException.

main() creates the token manager (identical to the one we used for our stack parsers in Chapters 6 and 8) and the parser and then calls the parse() method in the parser object. If a RuntimeException does not occur during the parse (which indicates the parse completed successfully), main() displays accept. Otherwise, it displays reject.

The complete parser corresponding to G9.1 appears in Figure 9.1. Note that the parser contains the consume method, which calls advance(), which in turn calls getNext-Token() in the token manager to get the next token from to input stream.

Let us examine the calling structure that occurs when the program in Figure 9.1 parses bcde. We depict this structure in Figure 9.2. Figure 9.2 shows each terminal symbol under the method call that consumes it. For example, under the D() method call, we have d and e, because this call consumes d and e. We have labeled each node in Figure 9.2 with a subscript that indicates the order in which that node is processed.

The parse method starts by calling S(). S(), in turn, calls B(), which consumes b and then recursively calls B(). This recursive call consumes c and then returns to the previous call of B(), which, in turn, returns to S(). S() then calls D() consumes d and e. D() then returns to S(), at which point S() is done.

This structure is clearly the parse tree for the input string bcde. This result is no surprise because at every step, a recursive-descent parser processes the leftmost symbol not yet processed. The parser, in effect, traverses the parse tree of the input string in depth-first order—the order associated with a leftmost derivation.

Exercise 9.1

Convert the following set of B productions to the corresponding recursive-descent method:

B → bBdD
B → c

Answer:

```
private void B()
{
  switch(currentToken)
  {
    case 'b':
```

```
1  /* Figure 9.1: Recursive-descent parser for
2
3                 Selection set
4     1) S -> BD    {b, c}
5     2) B -> bB    {b}
6     3) B -> c     {c}
7     4) D -> de    {d}
8  */
9  import java.util.Scanner;
10 //=========================================================
11 class Fig0901
12 {
13   public static void main(String[] args)
14   {
15     // Construct token manager (see Figure 6.12)
16     ArgsTokenMgr tm = new ArgsTokenMgr(args);
17     // Construct parser
18     Fig0901Parser parser = new Fig0901Parser(tm);
19
20     try
21     {
22       parser.parse();                    // do parse
23     }
24     catch (RuntimeException e)
25     {
26       System.err.println(e.getMessage());
27       System.err.println("reject");
28       System.exit(1);
29     }
30     // reach here then accept
31     System.out.println("accept");
32   }
33 }                                      // end of Fig0901
34 //=========================================================
35 class Fig0901Parser
36 {
37   private ArgsTokenMgr tm;
38   private char currentToken;
39   //---------------------
40   public Fig0901Parser(ArgsTokenMgr tm)
41   {
42     this.tm = tm;
43     advance();           // prime currentToken
44   }
45   //---------------------
46   private void advance()
47   {
48     currentToken = tm.getNextToken();
```

Figure 9.1.

```
49    }
50    //----------------------
51    private void consume(char expected)
52    {
53      if (currentToken == expected)
54        advance();
55      else
56        throw new RuntimeException(
57                    "Expecting \"" + expected + "\"");
58    }
59    //----------------------
60    public void parse()
61    {
62      S();
63      if (currentToken != '#')     // trailing-garbage test
64        throw new RuntimeException(
65                              "Expecting end of input");
66    }
67    //----------------------
68    private void S()
69    {
70      B();                          // apply S -> BD
71      D();
72    }
73    //----------------------
74    private void B()
75    {
76      switch(currentToken)
77      {
78        case 'b':
79          consume('b');             // apply B -> bB
80          B();
81          break;
82        case 'c':
83          consume('c');             // apply B -> c
84          break;
85        default:
86          throw new RuntimeException(
87                              "Expecting \"b\" or \"c\"");
88      }
89    }
90    //----------------------
91    private void D()
92    {
93      consume('d');                // apply D -> de
94      consume('e');
95    }
96 }                               // end of Fig0901Parser
```

Figure 9.1. *Continued.*

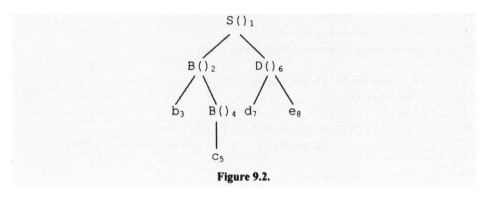

Figure 9.2.

```
      consume('b');
      B();
      consume('d');
      D();
      break;
    case 'c';
      consume('c');
      break;
    default:
      throw new RuntimeException("Expecting B string");
  }
}
```

■

9.3   HANDLING LAMBDA PRODUCTIONS

How should a recursive-descent parser handle a lambda production? Recall that each method in a recursive-descent parser corresponding to a nonterminal advances across the substring generated by that nonterminal symbol, and then returns to the caller. Because a lambda production does not generate any terminal symbols, the method in a recursive-descent parser should simply return to the caller when it applies a lambda production. For example, the S() method for the following grammar

G9.2   Selection Set
1. S → bS   {b}
2. S → λ   {#}

is

```
  private void S()
  {
    switch(currentToken)
    {
      case 'b':        // {b} is selection set for prod 1
        consume('b'); // apply production 1
        S();
        break;
```

```
    case '#':          // {#} is selection set for prod 2
      ;                // apply lambda production
    break;
  default:
    throw new RuntimeException(
                     "Expecting \"b\" or end of input");
  }
}
```

If the current token is b, S() applies production 1 (by consuming 'b' and recursively calling S()). If the current token is #, S() applies production 2 by executing the null statement (a statement that consists of the semicolon only), after which control returns to the caller. Because the null statement does nothing, the effect is simply to return to the caller. Equivalently, we could have omitted the null statement or replaced it with a return statement. We include it to emphasize that we are applying a lambda production.

Exercise 9.2

What are the productions that correspond to the following B() method:

```
 private void B()
{
  switch(currentToken)
  {
    case 'b':
      consume('b');
      B();
      C();
      D();
      consume('e');
      break;
    case 'c':
      ;
      break;
    case 'd':
      consume('d');
      break;
    default:
      throw new RuntimeException("Expecting B string");
  }
}
```

Answer:

B → bBCDe
B → λ
B → d

■

Another possible S() method for G9.2 is

```
 private void S()
{
```

```
switch(currentToken)
{
  case 'b':
    consume('b');
    S();
    break;
  default: // do not perform selection set test
    ;       // apply lambda production
    break;
}
}
```

In this version, the lambda production is the default production. That is, S() applies the second production (the lambda production) whenever it cannot apply the first production (i.e., whenever the current token is not b). When it applies the lambda production, it does *not* first check to see if the current token is in the selection set of the lambda production. Because the first production generates a leading b, it makes sense to apply it only if the current token is b. However, the second production—the lambda production—does not generate anything. Thus, it is reasonable to apply it no matter what the current token is as long as the current token is not b. Our second version of S() behaves just like the first version if the current token is b or #. However, the two versions behave differently if the current token is neither b nor #: The first version generates an error message; the second version simply returns to the caller. For example, suppose the input is

    bb?

This input consists of a string from S ("bb") followed by some garbage ("?") at the end. The first version of S() flags this trailing garbage. The second version, however, does not. When it reaches the garbage, it applies the lambda production, the effect of which is to cause S() to return to its caller. No error message is generated. Moreover, the error will not be detected later in the parse because the parse is essentially done at this point. Our first S() method detects trailing garbage because it performs a selection set test for each production. Our second S() method does not detect trailing garbage because it does not perform a selection set test for each production.

To ensure that trailing garbage is detected, our parsers should perform the following trailing-garbage test:

> **After calling the start-symbol method, the top-level caller of the start-symbol method should check if the current token is the end of input. If it is not, trailing garbage is present.**

Then if our parsing methods do not detect trailing garbage, the trailing-garbage test will. Notice that we included a trailing-garbage test in Figure 9.1 on line 63 after the call of S():

```
62    S();
63    if (currentToken != '#')    // trailing-garbage test
64      throw new RuntimeException("Expecting end of input");
```

If we perform a selection set test for every production in a grammar, can we omit the trailing-garbage test? We cannot because performing selection set tests for every production does not guarantee that trailing garbage will be detected. For example, consider the following grammar:

G9.3   Selection Set
  1. S → be   { b}

Its corresponding method is

```
private void S()
{
   consume('b');
   consume('e');
}
```

Here, the first call to consume performs the selection set test (it checks if the current token is 'b'). If the input is "be?," the S() method advances past the "be" sequence by calling consume('b') and consume('e'). It then returns to its caller *without detecting the trailing garbage.*

Why does the standard parsing method for S in G9.2 detect trailing garbage but the standard parsing method for S in G9.3 does not? Both perform a selection set test for each production (for G9.3, the selection set test is perfomed by the consume method). The reason has to do with the structure of the languages defined by these grammars. G9.2 generates a list. If a string in a language is a list, and something follows an element of the list, it, of course, should be another element of the list or the end of input. If is not, we have an error. For example, a Java program consists of a list of classes. If a class in a Java program is followed by something, that something should be another class. Thus, if something follows a class, the compiler will naturally start compiling it. If it is trailing garbage, the compiler will, of course, generate an error message. Because of the list structure of a Java program, a Java compiler will naturally detect trailing garbage.

Now consider G9.3. It does not generate a list. An S string is a single "be" sequence. A parser for G9.3 only has to consume the b and e to complete the parse. There is no reason for the parser to continue parsing beyond the e. Thus, a parser will not detect trailing garbage unless it has an explicit trailing-garbage test. A programming language with a structure like the language of G9.3 is Pascal. A standard Pascal program has the following form:

```
Program program name
declarations
begin
   .
   .
   .
end
```

The end keyword that balances the initial begin keyword marks the end of the program. Thus, there is no reason for a Pascal compiler to compile beyond the terminating end. Unless a Pascal compiler performs an explicit trailing-garbage test after the parse of the program has completed, it will not detect trailing garbage. If you have access to a Pascal compiler, try compiling a valid program that has trailing garbage. Most likely, it will not detect the trailing garbage.

We have seen that an error may go undetected if a parser applies a lambda production as the default production, that is, if it applies the production without checking if the current token is in the production's selection set. In most cases, if there is an error, it will be detected, but later in the parse as the parse proceeds. But if the parse is done, then there is no further parsing that will detect the error. We, however, can ensure that errors will not go undetected by including a trailing garbage test in the parser. As long as we do that, then there is nothing fundamentally wrong with applying a lambda production as the default production. In fact, there is a benefit: We do not have to compute the selection set for the lambda production. One further consideration, the error message may be affected (see Exercise 9.20).

Exercise 9.3

Construct the S() method and two versions of the B() method for the following grammar.

1. S → Bd   { b, d}
2. B → bB   { b}
3. B → λ   { d}

One version of B() should perform a selection set test for production 3; the other should not. Compare the error messages generated by both versions for the inputs bbbf.

Answer:

```
private void S()
{
   B();                            // apply production 1
   consume('d');
}
//-------------------
private void B()    // version 1
{
  switch(currentToken)
  {
    case 'b':
      consume('b');                // apply production 2
      B();
      break;
    case 'd':
      ;                            // apply production 3
      break;
    default:
      throw new RuntimeException(
                        "Expecting \"b\" or \"d\"");
  }
}
//-------------------
private void B()    // version 2
{
   switch(currentToken)
   {
      case 'b':
```

```
            consume('b');            // apply production 2
            B();
            break;
        default:
            ;
            break;
    }
}
```

The first version produces the error message `Expecting "b" or "d"`; the second version produces the error message `Expecting  "d"` (from the call of `consume` in the `S()` method), which is misleading because b is also a possible input.

◼

9.4   A COMMON ERROR

Suppose a grammar has the following Q productions:

```
Q → ;   {;}
Q → λ   {d}
```

What is the `Q()` method corresponding to these productions? The first production generates a single terminal symbol (`';'`). Thus, the `Q()` method should advance past this symbol for this case. The second production is a lambda production. Thus, the `Q()` method should do nothing for this case (i.e., it should execute the null statement). The corresponding `Q()` method is

```
private void Q()
{
  switch(currentToken)
  {
    case ';':
      consume(';');  // apply Q -> ;
      break;
    case 'd':
      ;                // apply Q -> lambda
      break;
    default:
      throw new RuntimeException(
                     "Expecting \";\" or \"d\"");
  }
}
```

Note that if the current token is a semicolon, we consume it, as required by the first Q production. If the current token is `'d'`, we simply return (by executing the null statement) as required by the second Q production. If you are not thinking carefully when you write this method, you might incorrectly write

```
private void Q()
{
  switch(currentToken)
```

```
  {
    case ';':
      ;              // null statement here is wrong!
      break;
    case 'd':
      consume('d'); // consume here is wrong!!!
      break;
    default:
      throw new RuntimeException(
                    "Expecting \";\" or \"d\"");
  }
}
```

Do not make this mistake!

9.5 JAVA CODE FOR PRODUCTIONS

Let us summarize the code we need in a recursive-descent parser for the various components of the right side of a production.

Component on right side of production	Java code
terminal t	consume('t');
nonterminal N	N();
λ	; (the null statement)

For example, if the right side of a production is bBCd, the corresponding Java code is

```
consume('b');
B();
C();
consume('d');
```

Because a simple correspondence exists between productions and their corresponding Java code in a recursive-descent parser, writing this code is a trivial process. In fact, because of this correspondence, it is possible to write a program that will write the Java code for a recursive-descent parser for us. We simply supply the grammar. We call such a program a *parser generator*. We will learn more about recursive-descent parser generators in Chapters 13.

Exercise 9.4

Construct the method that corresponds to the following Q productions:

```
Q → bBDe
Q → Ec         assume selection set is {c}
Q → λ          assume selection set is {d, e}
```

Answer:

```
private void Q()
{
```

```
switch(currentToken)
{
  case 'b':
    consume('b');
    B();
    D();
    consume('e');
    break;
  case 'c':
    E();
    consume('c');
    break;
  case 'd':
  case 'e':
    ;
    break;
  default:
    throw new RuntimeException(
                "Expecting \"b\", \"c\", \"d\", or \"e\"");
  }
}
```

■

9.6   LEFT FACTORING IN A RECURSIVE-DESCENT PARSER

Consider the following grammar:

G9.4   Selection set
  1. S → dB   {d}
  2. S → dC   {d}
  3. S → f   {f}
  4. B → b   {b}
  5. C → c   {c}

This grammar is not LL(1). The selection sets for the first two S productions both contain d. Thus, if the current token is d, a top-down parser with a lookahead of 1 would not be able to decide which S production to apply. We, however, can easily transform G9.4 to an equivalent LL(1) grammar using left factoring, the technique we studied in Section 7.9. By factoring out the leading d in the two S productions, we get the following LL(1) grammar:

G9.5   Selection Set
  1. S → dR   {d}   new S production
  2. S → f   {f}
  3. R → B   {b}   production added by left factoring
  4. R → C   {c}   production added by left factoring
  5. B → b   {b}
  6. C → c   {c}

The S() method corresponding to the S nonterminal in G9.5 is

```
private void S()
{
  switch(currentToken)
  {
    case 'd':
      consume('d');
      R();
      break;
    case 'f':
      consume('f');
      break;
    default"
      throw new RuntimeException(
                  "Expecting S string");
  }
}
```

The R() method corresponding to the R nonterminal is

```
private void R()
{
  switch(currentToken)
  {
    case 'b':
      B();
      break;
    case 'c':
      C();
      break;
    default:
      throw new RuntimeException(
                  "Expecting \"b\" or \"c\"");
  }
}
```

Notice that the S() method calls R() only once. Thus, a simple alternative is to place the body of R() into S() at the point of call, and eliminate the separate R() method. If we do this, we get the following S() method:

```
private void S()
{
  switch(currentToken)
  {
    case 'd':
      consume('d');

      // start of body of R() method ===================
      switch(currentToken)
```

```
    {
      case 'b':              '
        B();
        break;
      case 'c':
        C();
        break;
      default:
        throw new
          RuntimeException("Expecting \"b\" or \"c\"");
    }
    // end of body of R() method =====================

    break;
  case 'f':
    consume('f');
    break;
  default:
    throw new RuntimeException("Expecting S string");
  }
}
```

The two versions of S() work identically. The only difference is that the second version is slightly more efficient because it does not have the overhead associated with the call to R(). This difference in efficiency, however, is insignificant. Thus, either approach is perfectly acceptable. However, if the R nonterminal introduced by left factoring represents a set of strings that we would like to view as a separate syntactic category, then it probably makes sense to use a separate R() method. Otherwise, it makes sense to eliminate the R() method by placing its code into the S() method. If we do the latter, it is helpful to rewrite the S productions in G9.5 so that there is a closer correspondence between them and the S() method. Here is the new grammar:

G9.6
    1. S → d (B|C)
    2. S → f
    3. B → b
    4. C → c

In production 1, we are using the vertical bar to specify a choice within the right side of one production. Associated with each alternative is a selection set: We choose B if the current token at that point is in FIRST(B); we choose C if the current token at that point is in FIRST(C). Thus, the first S production above has three selections sets:

FIRST(d (B|C)) = {d} = the selection set for the entire production
FIRST(B)   = {b} = the selection set for the B alternative
FIRST(C)   = {c} = the selection set for the C alternative

The analysis above on left factoring also applies to left–right factoring (see Section 7.9). Specifically, when we left–right factor, we can either create a new nonterminal and its corresponding method, or we can simply include this code within the method for the nonterminal that is left–right factored.

If an alternative within a production can be null, then the selection set for that alternative includes inputs than can follow it in that production as well as inputs in its FIRST set. For example, suppose the S production in a grammar is

```
S → d (B|C) e
```

and B is nullable but C is not. Then the selection set for the B alternative would be FIRST(B) |{ e} , and the selection set for the C alternative would be FIRST(C). To determine the selection of an alternative, it is helpful to rewrite a grammar so that the choices are represented with a new nonterminal. For example, we can rewrite the production above as

	Selection Set	
S → bMe	{b}	
M → B	FIRST(B) | FOLLOW(M)	(assuming B is nullable)
M → C	FIRST(C)	(assuming C is not nullable)

In this form, we can easily determine the selection set of the B alternative: Our rules for selection sets tell us it is FIRST(B) | FOLLOW(M). The selection set for the C alternative is FIRST(C). Because FOLLOW(M) = {e}, the structure in pseudocode of the M nonterminal is

```
switch(currentToken)
{
  case FIRST(B) or 'e':
    B();
    break;
  case FIRST(C):
    C();
    break;
  default:
    error
}
```

and this is the code we would embed in the S () method if we did not want to create a separate M method—that is, if we wanted to implement S () in the form that matches

```
S → b (B | C) e
```

Notice that the selection set for the B alternative is *not* FIRST(B)|FOLLOW(B). Instead, it is FIRST(B) plus whatever can follow *this particular instance of* B.

Let's consider one more example. Suppose the S production is

```
S → b (B | C) D
```

where both B and D but not C are nullable. Then the selection set for the C alternative is FIRST(C). However, the selection set for the B alternative is FIRST(B)|FIRST(D)|FOLLOW(S). Because B has only nullables to its right, we get, from the whatever-follows-left-follows-rightmost rule, that whatever follows S also follows B. Thus, we should include FOLLOW(S) in the selection set for the B alternative.

Exercise 9.5

Write the S method corresponding to the productions below. Use left factoring. Do not introduce any new nonterminals. Then redo with left–right factoring. Again, do not introduce any new nonterminals.

S → bcd
S → bed

For each of your answers, give an S production whose form matches the form of your S() method.

For these productions, which is better: left factoring or left–right factoring?

Answers:

Left-factored version: S → b(cd | ed)

```
private void S()
{
  consume('b');

  switch(currentToken)
  {
    case 'c':
      consume('c');
      consume('d');
      break;
    case 'e':
      consume('e');
      consume('d');
      break;
    default:
      throw new RuntimeException(
                "Expecting \"c\" or \"e\"");
  }
}
```

Left–right-factored version: S → b(c | e)d

```
private void S()
{
      consume('b');

      switch(currentToken)'
      {
        case 'c':
          consume('c');
          break;
        case 'e':
          consume('e');
          break;
        default:
          throw new RuntimeException(
                    "Expecting \"c\" or \"e\"");
```

```
        }

        consume('d');
    }
```

Left–right factoring is more space efficient—only one call to `consume('d');`   ■

9.7 ELIMINATING TAIL RECURSION

If any of the productions for a nonterminal are recursive, then the corresponding method in a recursive-descent parser is also recursive. Recursive methods, unfortunately, involve some extra overhead. Each recursive call takes time to execute and requires space on a run-time stack. Thus, if the recursion proceeds to a great depth, the time or space overhead can become significant. The stack may even overflow, causing the parse to fail. Thus, we should be careful when we use recursion. In some cases, we can use a simple loop in place of a recursive structure.

Let us examine the operation of the recursive method r1 in Figure 9.3. Suppose we invoke this method with

```
    r1(2);
```

After 2 is assigned to the parameter n, we execute the `if` part of the `if-else` statement (line 5) because n is greater than zero. That is, we execute

```
5           System.out.println(n);
```

which displays 2. We then execute the recursive call on line 6:

```
6           r1(n-1);                        // tail recursion
```

Because n equals 2, the value of the argument in this call is 1. Thus, when we reenter r1, the value of parameter n is 1. We again execute the `if` part of the `if-else` statement, displaying 1. When we again execute the recursive call on line 6, we reenter r1 with n equal to 0. At this point, there are three instances of the parameter n, one for each level of the recursion. At the bottom level, n equals 0. At the next level up, n equals 1, and above that n equals 2 (see Figure 9.4).

```
 1  public void r1(int n)
 2  {
 3  if (n > 0)
 4  {
 5    System.out.println(n);
 6    r1(n-1);                          // tail recursion
 7  }
 8  else
 9    System.out.println("goodbye");
10  }
```

Figure 9.3.

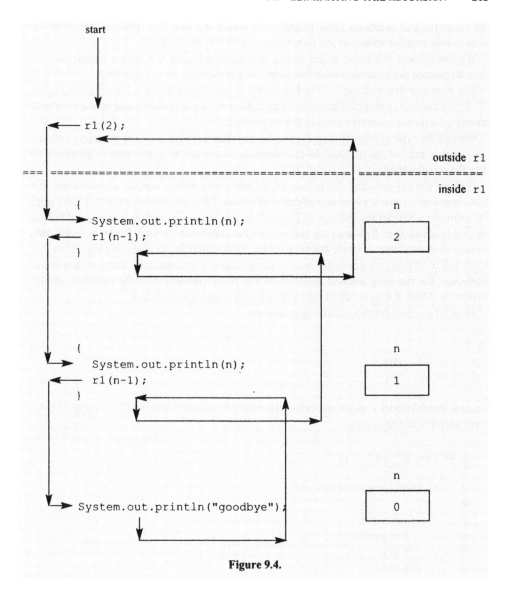

Figure 9.4.

When we enter r1 with n equal to 0, we execute the else part of the if-else statement because the true/false expression in the if statement is now false. The else part
displays goodbye and then returns to the caller one level up. But when it does, there is
nothing more to do at that level because there is nothing to be executed following the call
of r1 on line 5. Thus, that level immediately returns to the next higher level. This returning action continues until we reach the initial call of the method. Figure 9.4 shows the sequence of events (follow the arrows).

By examining Figure 9.4, we can see that we execute the println statement that displays n once for each positive value of n starting at 2 working down to 0. When n is equal to
0, we execute the println statement that displays goodbye once. The output displayed is

```
2
1
goodbye
```

The recursive call creates a loop, in effect, in which the line 5 is repeated executed for successively smaller values of the parameter n until 0 is reached.

We can achieve the same effect as the recursion in Figure 9.3 with a simple `while` loop. Replacing the recursion with this loop, we get the method in Figure 9.5.

The nonrecursive method `nr1` in Figure 9.5 is equivalent to the `r1` method in Figure 9.3. Moreover, it is more efficient because it does not have the time and space overhead associated with the recursive calls in the `r1` method.

We call the type of recursion in Figure 9.3 *tail recursion* because the recursive call appears at the "tail" of the method. In tail recursion, there are no statements to be executed after the recursive call.

We can always simulate the action of tail recursion with a simple `while` loop. We have, however, a much more complicated situation if the recursion is *not* tail recursion. For example, consider the method in Figure 9.6. The recursive call on line 6 is not tail recursive because it is followed by the `println` statement on line 7. As a result, this method does not have a simple looping action. Unfortunately, to eliminate recursion that is not tail recursion, we generally need a complicated logic structure along with a stack. Moreover, the resulting method may not be any more efficient than the recursive implementation. Thus, it is generally best to not eliminate nontail recursion.

Now let us consider the following grammar:

G9.5
1. S → bS {b}
2. S → d   {d}

Because production 1 is right recursive, the method corresponding to S in a recursive-descent parser is tail recursive:

```
 1 private void S()
 2 {
 3    switch(currentToken)
 4    {
 5      case 'b':
 6        consume('b');
 7        S();                // tail recursion
 8        break;
 9      case 'd':
10        consume('d');
11        break;
```

```
1  void nr1(int n)
2  {
3     while (n > 0)
4     {
5        System.out.println(n);
6        n = n - 1;
7     }
8     System.out.println("goodbye");
9  }
```

Figure 9.5.

```
1   public void r2(int n)
2   {
3     if (n > 0)
4     {
5       System.out.println(n);
6       r2(n-1);        // not tail recursion
7       System.out.println(n);
8     }
9     else
10      System.out.println("goodbye");
11  }
```

Figure 9.6.

```
12      default:
13          throw new RuntimeExcéption("Expecting S string");
14  }
15 }
```

Notice that the recursive call of S() (line 7), in effect, forms a loop in which initial b's are consumed by line 6, after which the final d is consumed (line 10). If we now apply the same type of transformation we used on the recursive method in Figure 9.3, we get

```
private void S()
{
  while (currentToken == 'b')
    consume('b');
  consume('d');
}
```

This new form of S() makes sense: Each input string in the language of G9.5 is a list of zero or more b's followed by a single d. The while loop is a simple structure that processes the list of b's.

We should use with care these techniques for eliminating tail recursion in a recursive-descent parser. When we eliminate recursion from a method for a nonterminal, the structure of the method no longer parallels the structure of the productions for that nonterminal. Thus, errors are more likely to creep into our implementation. Moreover, the improvement in run-time performance may be insignificant. Thus, we risk more bugs without gaining any significant reduction in run time.

Exercise 9.6

Without using recursion, write the S() method corresponding to the following productions

S → bcS
S → λ

Answer:

```
private void S()
{
```

```
  while (currentToken == 'b')
  {
    consume('b');
    consume('c');
  }
  if (currentToken == '#')
    ;
  else
    throw new RuntimeException(
                  "Expecting \"b\" or end of input");
}
```

∎

9.8 TRANSLATING THE STAR, PLUS , AND QUESTION MARK OPERATORS

One of the advantages of extended Backus—Naur form (BNF; see Section 4.4) is that it can explicitly specify lists. For example, using the variant of BNF that uses * and + to specify lists, we can define the language consisting of zero or more b's followed by d with

```
S : ("b")*"d"
```

whose corresponding code is

```
private void S()
{
  while (currentToken == 'b')
    consume('b');
  consume('d');
}
```

Similarly, we can define the language consisting of one or more b's followed by d with

```
S : ("b")+"d"
```

whose corresponding code is

```
private void S()
{
  do {
    consume('b');
  }
  while (currentToken == 'b');
  consume('d');
}
```

Notice that the star operator corresponds to a `while` loop. Because the star operator allows for zero occurrences of the starred item, we need to determine if we have any occurrences *before* we enter the loop body that processes the starred item. Thus, we need the leading exit test of a while loop. The plus operator, on the other hand, requires at least one occurrence of the plussed item. Thus, we should *always* enter the loop body that processes the plussed item. This requirement is met by the trailing exit test of the do-while loop. The question mark operator corresponds to an if statement. For example, if we have the grammar

```
S : ("b")? "d"
```

then the corresponding code uses an if statement:

```
private void S()
{
  if (currentToken == 'b')
    consume('b');
  consume('d');
}
```

In the preceding examples, the starred, plussed, and question-marked items are all single terminals. What if these items were complex sequences of nonterminals and/or terminals? In that case, the corresponding code would still have the same structure as the preceding examples. We would simply perform tests with FIRST sets rather than with a single terminal. For example, suppose Q is an arbitrary sequence of nonterminals and/or terminals. Then the code for

```
S : (Q)* "d"
```

would have the following structure:

```
private void S()
{
  while (currentToken in FIRST(Q))
    Q();
  consume('d');
}
```

For example, if the FIRST(Q) = {b, c}, then our s() method would be

```
private void S()
{
  while (currentToken == 'b' || currentToken == 'c')
    Q();
  consume('d');
}
```

If we wish to parse lists using loops rather than recursion, it makes sense to write our grammar using the star and plus operators of extended BNF. With a grammar in this form, we can determine the required loops from the grammar in an obvious way. We simply use the following rules:

> The starred structure becomes a while loop.
> The plussed structure becomes a do-while loop.
> The question-marked structure becomes an if statement.

9.9   DOING THINGS BACKWARD

The recursive method r1 in Figure 9.3 has a println statement before the recursive call that displays the value of the parameter n. Thus, as r1 recurses down, it displays the successive values of the parameter. For example, if we pass 2 to r1, it will display 2 and 1 in that order, followed by goodbye. Suppose we reposition the println statement so that it immediately follows the recursive call (i.e., switch lines 5 and 6). Then r1 will display the successive values of the parameter n as it recurses *up*. Now if we pass 2 to r1, it will display goodbye followed by 1 and 2 in that order. Notice the order is reversed (follow the arrows in Figure 9.7) from that produced by original r1 method.

From Figures 9.4 and 9.7, we can see a very important pattern that occurs when we execute recursive methods:

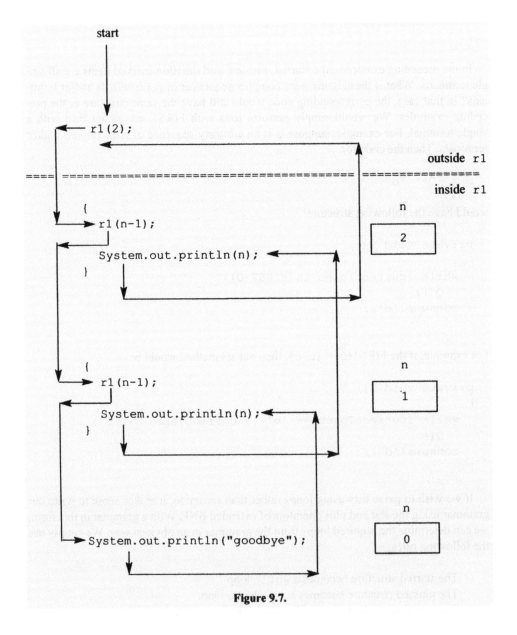

Figure 9.7.

1. As we recurse down, we execute the statement(s) *before* the recursive call.
2. We hit bottom.
3. As we recurse back up, we execute the statement(s) *after* the recursive call.

With recursion, we have a choice of the order in which actions are performed. If we place actions before the recursive call, they will be performed in the normal order. If, however, we place actions after the recursive call, they will be performed in reverse order. For another example, see the `traverse` method in Figure 9.8. It traverses a linked list in which each node consists of a `data` field and a `link` field. Each `link` field, except the last, contains the reference to the next node on the list. The last `link` field contains null.

Because the `println` statement follows the recursive call, it displays the data in the linked list in reverse order (i.e., from the last node to the first). If, on the other hand, the `println` statement preceded the recursive call, it would display the data in its normal order (i.e., from first node to last).

> With recursion, we can process the elements of a list in their given order or in their reverse order.

Using recursion to process lists in reverse order is a common technique used in parsers. For example, we will encounter a parser in Chapter 16 that has to associate successive integers (starting from 2) with the parameters in a method definition in *right-to-left* order. For example, in the method definition that starts with

```
void f(int b, int c, int d)
```

the parser has to associate 2, 3, and 4, with the parameters d, c, and b, respectively. Unfortunately, this task is not easy because the parser parses the parameter list in *left-to-right* order. When it parses the first parameter, it does not know its corresponding integer because it depends on the number of parameters. In this example, b should be associated with 4. If, however, there were 10 parameters, then b should be associated with 11. We do, however, have an elegant solution for this problem: With recursion, we can scan the list left to right but process it right to left. We will see the details of this technique in Chapter 16.

```
void traverse(Node p)
{
  if (p != null)
  {
    traverse(p.link);            // recursive call
    System.out.println(p.data);  // follows recursive call
  }
}
```

Figure 9.8.

PROBLEMS

1. Implement a recursive-descent parser for

   1. E → +EE
   2. E → -EE

3. E → *EE

4. E → /EE

5. E → b

6. E → c

7. E → d

Test your program with b, c, d, +bc, -/bc*cd, +-*/bcbcd, bc, +b, *bcd, and λ.

2. Implement a recursive-descent parser for

1. S → BCD

2. B → bB

3. B → λ

4. C → cC

5. C → λ

6. D → dD

7. D → λ

Test your program with λ, b, c, d, bc, bd, cd, ccc, bcb, db, and dc.

3. Implement a recursive-descent parser for the same language processed by the stack parser in Figure 6.12. Test your program with cbd, bcbdcbcbcd, cbdd , bcd, ddd, and λ.

4. Implement a recursive-descent parser for the same language processed the stack parser in Figure 8.4. Test your program with fbb, fbbcc, fccdec, bb, fbbed, and λ.

5. Implement a recursive-descent parser for G4.4. Test your program with b, (b), (((b)), (b+c*d), (b+c)*d, bb, b),)b(, and λ.

6. What is the B() method corresponding to

B → bBbBbB

B → cccc

B → e

7. Write both a recursive and a nonrecursive S() method for

S → bS

S → cS

S → d

8. Write the S() method corresponding to

S → bSc

S → λ

9. Implement a top-down nonrecursive parser for the grammar in problem 8. Do this in two ways:

a) Implement a stack parser.

b) Eliminate the recursion in the S() method of a recursive-descent parser.

Test your two programs with λ, bc, bbcc, bcb, bbccc, bbc, ccbb, and bcbc. Compare your two parsers. In what ways are they similar?

10. Implement a recursive-descent parser for the language $\{ wdw^r : w \in$ (b|c)*$\}$. Note: w^r is the reverse of w. Test your program with d, bcdcb, cdc, bcdcbb, bccdcb, and λ.

11. Convert the following grammar to an LL(1) grammar by left factoring.

    1. S → bcC
    2. S → bcDf
    3. C → dD
    4. D → eD
    5. D → λ

12. Write the S(), C(), D(), and R() methods for the grammar in problem 11. Note: R() corresponds to the nonterminal R that left factoring introduces.

13. Incorporate the code body of R() in problem 12 into S().

14. Rewrite G4.4 in extended BNF.

15. Implement a recursive-descent parser for G4.4. Do not use recursion in your methods for termList and factorList. Test your program as specified by problem 5.

16. Write a Java program that creates a linked list and then traverses it in its natural order and in reverse order using recursive methods.

17. Write a Java program that displays the contents of an array in bottom-to-top order and top-to-bottom order using recursive methods.

18. In a LL(1) grammar, there can never be more than one production with the same left side that is nullable. Why? In a recursive-descent parser, we do not have to test if the current token is in the selection set for this nullable production. Why? Thus, the only selection sets we have to compute are the selection sets for the nonnullable productions. What does this imply about the computation of FOLLOW sets?

19. Will a recursive-descent parser always detect trailing garbage at the end of the input if the parser performs selection set tests for every production?

20. Does a parser that performs a selection set test for every production produce better error messages than a parser the performs a selection set test only when it is absolutely necessary?

21. Show the structure of the code for

    ```
    S : (Q)* "d"
    ```

22. Show the structure of the code for

    ```
    S : (Q)*
    ```

23. Show the structure of the code for

    ```
    S: (A)* "b" | (B)* "d" | (C)* "d"
    ```

    Assume A and C but not B are nullable.

24. What is the problem with converting the following grammar to parser code:

    ```
    S: (B)* "d"
    B: "b" | "d"
    ```

25. Write the recursive method corresponding to

    S → bS
    S → λ

Write the iterative method corresponding to

```
S :  (b)*
```

In what way will the two methods behave differently?

26. Implement the parser for the following extended BNF grammar:

```
S : B* "e"? D+
B : "b" B | "c"
D : "d" L
L : "d" L | λ
```

Use recursion in your B() and L() methods. Use loops (for B* and D+) in your S() method. Test your parser with the following input strings:d, ed, cd, ced, bced, bbceddd, b, bedb, λ.

27. Under what circumstances can a call of the advance() method be used in place of a call of the consume method . Is the result more efficient code? Consider the following grammar:

1. S → b
2. S → c
3. S → dBe
4. B → bB
5. B → d

10

RECURSIVE-DESCENT TRANSLATION

10.1 INTRODUCTION

We can easily extend a recursive-descent parser so that it both parses and translates. We do this by embedding *actions* in the various methods of the parser. These actions perform the translation function. An action is usually a call to a method in the code generator.

When the parser calls a method in the code generator, the parser generally has to pass it information obtained earlier in the parse. Thus, one of the additional jobs of the parser in a parser/translator is to collect this information and provide it to the actions that require it. We can easily implement this flow of information in a recursive-descent parser/translator using Java's `return` statement and its parameter-passing mechanism. Using `return` statements, we can pass information up a chain of method calls; using parameters, we can pass information down a chain of method calls. The parser can also provide information to the code generator via shared data structures.

In the previous chapter, we learned that an LL(1) grammar and its corresponding recursive-descent parser have parallel structures. The grammar, along with its selection sets, is essentially a flowchart that tells us how to implement the parser. If we augment our grammar with symbols that represent the actions performed by a parser/translator, then the augmented grammar becomes, in effect, a flowchart of a parser/translator. We call a grammar augmented in this way is a *translation grammar*. A translation grammar uses a syntax-defining mechanism (the grammar) to define not only a language but also its translation. Accordingly, we call a translation based on a translation grammar a *syntax-directed translation*.

10.2 A SIMPLE TRANSLATION GRAMMAR

The following grammar defines the language bc^*d:

G10.1a   Selection Set
1. $S \rightarrow bCd$ {b}
2. $C \rightarrow cC$ {c}
3. $C \rightarrow \lambda$ {d}

We can also represent this grammar in extended Backus–Naur form (see Section 4.4). We get

G10.1b
```
S : "b" C "d"
C : "c" C | λ
```

In this form, we group all the productions with the same left side and separate their right sides with vertical bars. We also replace "→" with " : ", and enclose terminal symbols with double quotes.

Let us add an action to G10.1b specifying that c should be outputted whenever c in the input string is parsed. The natural location for this action is between the c and C on the right side of first C production:

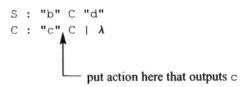

```
S : "b" C "d"
C : "c" C | λ
```

— put action here that outputs c

In the corresponding parser, this point corresponds to the point right after the advance past c in the input string. Thus, if the parser outputs c at this point, it will output c for each c in the input. Because we not do have a similar action for b and d, the output string will contain only c's. That is, it will be the input string from which the initial b and the final d have been stripped.

A convenient way to represent an action is to use the Java statement that performs that action, enclosed in braces. For example, we can specify the action that outputs c with the Java statement

```
{System.out.print('c');}
```

We will write translation grammars using extended Backus–Naur form within a structure that is similar to a Java method. For each nonterminal in the grammar, there will be a corresponding Java-method-like structure that contains the productions for that nonterminal. For example, the translation grammar that corresponds to G10.1b with the embedded action that outputs c is

G10.2
```
void S(): {}          ◄——— use S() in place of S  and : in place of →
{
    "b" C() "d"       ◄——— use C() in place of C
}

void C(): {}          ◄——— use C() in place of C
{
    "c" {System.out.print('c');} C()
|                     ◄——— the vertical bar separates alternatives
    {}                ◄——— empty action represents λ
}
```

It contains two Java-like methods, S() and C(), that represent the S and C productions, respectively. Like Java itself, a translation grammar can be formatted in a variety of ways. For clarity, we place the right side of each production and each vertical bar on a separate line. Notice that we enclose the action in the C() method in braces, and we represent nonterminals with their corresponding method names. We represent λ with a line on which only an action appears. The action can be empty. That is, we can use { } to represent λ. As in Backus–Naur form, we use ":" in place of "→", and we separate the right sides of productions with vertical bars. The empty braces that immediately follow ":" are for local variables (we will discuss local variables in Section 10.3).

10.3 CONVERTING A TRANSLATION GRAMMAR TO JAVA CODE

It is easy to convert a translation grammar to Java code. We simply use the procedure we learned in Chapter 9 to convert grammars to Java code. The only feature that is new in translation grammars are actions. These we simply carry over, as is, to the Java code.

The following table summarizes the Java code we need in a parser/translator for the various components of a translation grammar:

Translation grammar	Java code
terminal "t"	consume('t');
nonterminal N() within a method	N(); (i.e., call the N() method)
λ represented with { }	; (i.e., the null statement)
{action written in Java}	action written in Java

In a translation grammar, we list the alternatives for a nonterminal, separating each from the next with a vertical bar. This multichoice structure converts to a switch statement in the corresponding Java code. For example, the Java code that corresponds to G10.2 is

```
private void S()
{
  consume('b');
  C();
  consume('d');
}
//----------------------------
private void C()
{
  switch(currentToken)
  {
    case 'c':
            // apply first C production
      consume('c');
      System.out.print('c');     // action
      C();
      break;
    case 'd':
            // apply second C production
      ;
```

```
        break;
    default:
        throw new RuntimeException("Expecting \"c\" or \"d\"");
    }
}
```

Consider the `C()` method. The action `{System.out.print('c');}` in the translation grammar is carried over to the `C()` method. We test `currentToken` with a `switch` statement to determine which `C` production to apply. If `currentToken` is in the selection set for the first `C` production (its selection set is `{c}`), we apply the first production. Similarly, if `currentToken` is in the selection set for the second `C` production (its selection set is `{d}`), we apply the second production.

A translation grammar and its corresponding Java code are similar in structure. So be sure to not confuse the two. A common error is to use `switch` statements and calls to `consume` in a translation grammar. Remember that it is the Java code that has `switch` statements and calls to `consume`, not the translation grammar.

The translation grammar G10.2 specifies not only a language bc* d, but also the translation of each string in this language. Although the form of a translation grammar that we are using may be confusing at first, you will quickly get used it. Its form is not unlike that of Java methods. With this form we can precisely specify not only grammars but translations as well.

10.4 SPECIFICATIONS FOR A TRANSLATION GRAMMAR

Let us more precisely define the form of our translation grammars. We will observe the thirteen conventions listed below. They allow us to specify a source language and its translation. Given such a translation grammar, we can easily—indeed, mechanically—convert it to the Java code that performs the specified translation.

1. To emphasize the correspondence between nonterminals in the grammar with method calls in a recursive-descent parser, we will represent nonterminals with their corresponding method calls. For example, in place of the nonterminal S, we will use `S()`. Thus, `S()` represents both a nonterminal symbol and the method in a recursive-descent parser corresponding to it. We will also use meaningful names for methods and their corresponding nonterminals. For example, we will use `expr()` rather than `e()` for the method that parses expressions.

2. We will separate the parts of the right side of each production with spaces.

3. We will use ":" in place of "→" to separate the left and right sides of a production.

4. We will enclose terminal symbols in double quotes. For a sequence of terminal symbols, we can either enclose each symbol in quotes or enclose the entire sequence. However, the two alternatives are not equivalent. If we specify

    `"b" "c" "d"`

    then spaces are allowed between `"b"` and `"c"` and between `"c"` and `"d"`. However, if we specify

    `"bcd"`

    then the three characters must be contiguous, that is, have no intervening spaces.

5. We will start the specification of each production using a form similar to method definitions in Java. For example, suppose that the N() method corresponding to the N nonterminal in a grammar returns an int value, has an double parameter d, and uses a local String variable s. Then the specification of N in a translation grammar would start with

```
int N(double d)  :  {String s;}
```

indicates N() uses local String variable s
indicates N() is passed an double argument
indicates N() returns an int value

If N() does not return a value, does not use any parameters, and does use any local variables, then the specification of N() would start with

```
void N()  :  {}
```

Note that we must include the braces for local variables even if the method does not use any local variables.

6. We will group together productions with the same left side, separating the successive right sides with "|" (without the quotes), and enclosing the list of right sides with braces. Let us look as an example. Suppose the B productions in a grammar are

```
B → CD
B → DE
B → b
```

and have no embedded actions. If the corresponding B() method does not return a value, does not use any parameters, and does not return a value, then we would represent these productions in a translation grammar with

```
void B()  :  {}
{
   C() D()
 |
   D() E()
 |
   "b"
}
```

7. We will enclose actions within braces. For a sequence of actions, we can either surround each individual action with braces or surround the entire sequence with just one set of braces.

8. An alternative that consists solely of an action represents λ. We will use an empty action to represent λ when no action is required. For example, in the translation grammar below, the second alternative for S() and Q() both consist of an action alone. Thus, they both represent λ.

```
void S(): {}
{
    "b" Q()
 |
     {}  ←—— action alone represents λ
}
```

```
void Q(): {}
{
    "c"
 |
    { System.out.println("bye");}   ←——— action alone represents λ
}
```

9. We will omit the semicolon at the end of method calls corresponding to nonterminal symbols but not omit it within the Java code that specifies actions. For example, we will write

```
S()
```

without a terminating semicolon, but we will write

```
{ System.out.print('b');}
```

with the terminating semicolon at the end of the `print` statement.

10. If a token corresponds to a category, we will represent that token with an uppercase descriptive name surrounded by angle brackets. For example, suppose a category of tokens is unsigned integer. We will represent such tokens with `<UNSIGNED>`.

11. We can use the star operator (meaning zero or more), the plus operator (meaning one or more), or the question mark operator (meaning zero or one). For example, consider the following grammar that specifies a list consisting of one or more b's:

```
list     → "b" listTail
listTail → "b" listTail
listTail → λ
```

In a translation grammar, we represent these productions with

```
void list() : {}
{
    "b" listTail()
}
void listTail(): {}
{
    "b" listTail()
  |
    {}   ←——————— use action alone to represent λ
}
```

However, in a translation grammar, we can specify the same list with

```
void list(): {}
{
    "b" ("b")*
}
```

Here, the asterisk means zero or more. Thus, we are specifying a list that consists of an initial "b" followed by zero or more additional occurrences of "b". In a translation grammar, the item to which the asterisk, plus, or question mark is applied *must* be enclosed in parentheses. For example, we must write ("b")* rather than "b"*.

12. We can specify comments in a translation grammar in the same way we specify comments in a Java program: Start a one-line comment with "//"; bracket a multiline comment with "/*" and "*/".

13. The vertical bar (also known as the *alternation operator*) separates one alternative from the next. For example, in the following translation grammar, the alternation operator divides the S() into two alternatives: one that displays hello and parses b, and the other that parses c and displays goodbye:

```
void S(): {}
{
    { System.out.println("hello");
    "b"
  |
    "c"
    { System.out.println("goodbye");
}
```

Thus, if the input is b, the output is hello. If the input is c, the output is "goodbye". The corresponding Java code is

```
private void S()
{
    switch(currentToken)
    {
      case 'b':
        System.out.println("hello");
        consume('b');
        break;
      case 'c':
        consume('c');
        System.out.println("bye");
        break;
      default:
        throw new RuntimeException("Expecting S string");
    }
}
```

Using parentheses, we can restrict the scope of the alternation operator. For example, in the following grammar, the parentheses restrict the scope of the alternation operator so that it does not include the two println statements:

```
void S(): {}
{
    { System.out.println("hello");
    (
       "b"
     |
       "c"
    )
  { System.out.println("goodbye");
}
```

Thus, if the input is b, the output is `hello` followed by `goodbye`. If the input is c, the output is also `hello` followed by `goodbye`. Because the actions are out of the scope of the alternative operator, they are executed regardless of which alternative is taken. The corresponding Java code is

```java
private void S()
{
  System.out.println("hello");
  switch(currentToken)
  {
    case 'b':
      consume('b');
      break;
    case 'c':
      consume('c');
      break;
    default:
      throw new RuntimeException("Expecting S string");
  }
  System.out.println("bye");
}
```

For most translation grammars, we will provide the selection sets on the right. The selection sets, however, are not part of the translation grammar. The form of our translation grammars is essentially extended Backus–Naur form (see Section 4.4), further extended to allow the specification of actions, parameter passing, and value returning.

When writing a translation grammar, be sure to remember this semicolon rule: A nonterminal on the right side of a production in a translation grammar is *not* followed with a semicolon. For example, the right side of the production B → CD is represented in a translation grammar with

```
C() D()
```

rather than with the method calls

```
C(); D();
```

In the corresponding Java code, however, nonterminals on the right side of a production in a translation grammar become method calls in Java, which, of course are terminated with semicolons.

Exercise 10.1

Modify G10.2 so that it also outputs a newline character at the end of the output string.

Answer:

```
void S(): {}                                        Selection Set
{
   "b" C() "d" {System.out.println();}                 {"b"}
}
```

```
void C(): {}                                         Selection Set
{
    "c" {System.out.println('c');} C()                 {"c"}
|
    {}                                                 {"d"}
}
```

■

Let us examine the recursive-descent parser/translator in Figure 10.1 that is based on G10.2.

The action in G10.2 corresponds to line 85 in Figure 10.1. We execute this line whenever the current token is c. Thus, for every c in the input string, line 85 outputs a matching c. There is, however, no similar action if the current token is b or d. Thus, the output string produced is the input string from which the initial b and final d have been stripped. When we run this program with the input bccd, the computer display screen will show the following:

```
input = bccd
cc              ◄——— this is the output string produced by the parser/translator
```

Notice that in Figure 10.1 we consume a terminal whenever when we reach a point where the grammar *generates* a terminal. On line 74, we consume b; on line 84, we consume c; on line 76, we consume d. However, we do not consume anything on line 89. On this line, we are applying a lambda production which, of course, does not generate a terminal symbol. The code corresponding to a lambda production is simply the null statement.

Because we are now focusing on translation, we did not include in our parser/translator in Figure 10.1 the statements that display accept and reject. The program, however, still generates an error message if the input string is invalid.

The program in Figure 10.1 is actually a simple compiler. It contains the three essential components of any compiler: the token manager, the parser, and the code generator. Of course, its code generator is minimal; just a single action statement (line 85) embedded in the parser.

Figure 10.2 shows the parse tree for bccd using G10.2. We have subscripted each node of the tree with a number that indicates the order in which the node is processed during a recursive-descent parse.

If we read the leaf nodes left to right, excluding the actions, we get the input string bccd. If, instead, we read the actions left to right, we get the actions in the order in which they are executed.

Let us now consider a more complex translation grammar:

G10.3
```
void S(): {}
{                                                    Selection Set
    "b" S() {System.out.print('b');}                   {"b"}
|
    "c" S() {System.out.print('c');}                   {"c"}
|
    {}                                                 {"#"}
}
```

```
1  /* Figure 10.1: Recursive-descent parser/translator for
2
3      void S() : {}                              Selection Set
4      {
5         "b" C() "d"                                  { "b"}
6      }
7
8      void C(): {}
9      {
10        "c" { System.out.println('c');} C()     { "c"}
11     |
12        {}                                      { "d"}
13     }
14 */
15 import java.util.Scanner;
16 //=========================================================
17 class Fig1001
18 {
19   public static void main(String[ ] args)
20   {
21     // construct token manager (see Figure 6.12)
22     ArgsTokenMgr tm = new ArgsTokenMgr(args);
23     // Construct parser
24     Fig1001Parser parser = new Fig1001Parser(tm);
25
26     try
27     {
28       parser.parse();                // parse and translate
29     }
30     catch (RuntimeException e)
31     {
32       System.err.println();
33       System.err.println(e.getMessage());
34       System.exit(1);
35     }
36   }
37 }                                     // end of Fig1001
38 //=========================================================
39 class Fig1001Parser
40 {
41   private ArgsTokenMgr tm;
42   private char currentToken;
43   //-----------------------
44   public Fig1001Parser(ArgsTokenMgr tm)
45   {
46     this.tm = tm;
47     advance();                   // prime currentToken
48   }
49   //-----------------------
```

Figure 10.1.

```
50    private void advance()
51    {
52      currentToken = tm.getNextToken();
53    }
54    //---------------------
55    private void consume(char expected)
56    {
57      if (currentToken == expected)
58        advance();
59      else
60        throw new RuntimeException(
61                       "Expecting \"" + expected + "\"");
62    }
63    //---------------------
64    public void parse()
65    {
66      S();
67      if (currentToken != '#')
68        throw new RuntimeException(
69                       "Expecting end of input");
70    }
71    //---------------------
72    private void S()
73    {
74      consume('b');             // apply production S -> bCd
75      C();
76      consume('d');
77    }
78    //---------------------
79    private void C()
80    {
81      switch(currentToken)
82      {
83        case 'c':               // apply production C -> cC
84          consume('c');
85          System.out.print('c');      // this is an action
86          C();
87          break;
88        case 'd':
89          ;                     // apply lambda production
90          break;
91        default:
92          throw new RuntimeException(
93                         "Expecting \"c\" or \"d\"");
94      }
95    }
96 }                                    // end of Fig1001Parser
```

Figure 10.1. *Continued.*

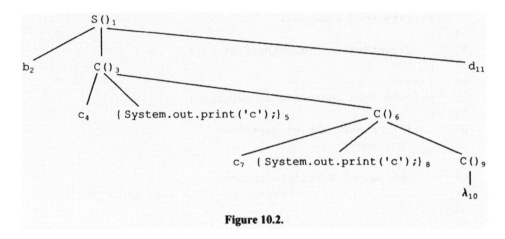

Figure 10.2.

When production 1 generates b, it also outputs b, but only after all the actions associated with the intervening S() nonterminal have completed. Thus, the b that is outputted corresponding to the initial b in the input string appears last in the output string. Look at the parse tree for bbc in Figure 10.3. The input string, read left to right, is bbc, but the actions, left to right (which is the order in which they are executed) display cbb. The output string is the reverse of the input string. In Figure 10.3, we have numbered the nodes in the order in which they are processed during a recursive-descent parse. Notice that this numbering confirms that the actions are performed in left-to-right order.

Exercise 10.2

What would be the effect of inserting System.out.println() in the empty action on the right side of the last production in G10.3?

Answer:

The println() would output a newline character at the *beginning* of the output string.

∎

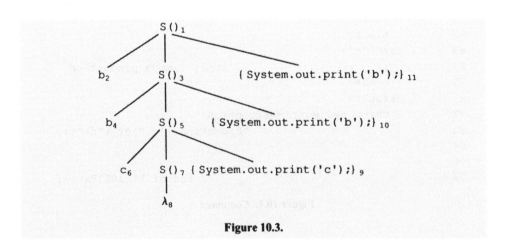

Figure 10.3.

Exercise 10.3

Modify G10.3 so that a newline character appears at the end of the output string.

Answer:

```
void newStart(): {}
{
    S() {System.out.println();}
}


void S() : {}
{
    "b" S() {System.out.print('b');}
  |
    "c" S() {System.out.print('c');}
  |
     {}
}
```

Another interesting translation grammar is

G10.4

```
  void S():  {}                                         Selection Set
  {
     expr() {System.out.println();}          {"+", "-", "*",
                                                "/", "b", "c", "d"}
  }

  void expr()  : {}
  {
    "+" expr() expr() {System.out.print('+');}   {"+"}
  |
    "-" expr() expr() {System.out.print('-');}   {"-"}
  |
    "*" expr() expr() {System.out.print('*');}   {"*"}
  |
    "/" expr() expr() {System.out.print('/');}   {"/"}
  |
    "b" {System.out.print('b');}                 {"b"}
  |
    "c" {System.out.print('c');}                 {"c"}
  |
    "d" {System.out.print('d');}                 {"d"}
  }
```

This translation grammar specifies the translation of arithmetic expressions in prefix notation to their corresponding postfix notation. In *prefix notation*, the operator precedes its operands. In *postfix notation*, the operator follows its operands. In *infix notation* (the notation we use in everyday mathematics), the operator is between its operands. For example, the prefix expression + + b c d, the postfix expression b c + d +, and the infix expression b + c + d are equivalent. They all specify the addition of b, c, and d in left-to-right order.

In the prefix expression + + b c d, the operands for the second + are b and c (the two operands that follow it). The operands for the first + are the result of the computation for the second + and d. Thus, this expression specifies the addition b and c, followed by the addition of d. That is, it specifies a left-to-right order of evaluation. Similarly, in the postfix expression b c + d +, the first + operates on the b and c that precedes it. The second + operates on the result of the first addition and d. Thus, this expression, too, specifies the addition of b, c and d in left-to-right order. The infix expression b + c + d does not specify an order of evaluation. However, by convention, additions are performed left to right, unless parentheses indicate otherwise. Thus, we view this expression as also specifying a left-to-right order of evaluation.

In prefix notation, as well as in postfix notation, we never need parentheses. We can specify any order of evaluation by simply arranging the operands and operators in the appropriate order. For example, the prefix expression for the sum of b, c, and d added in right-to-left order is +b+cd; the postfix expression for the same sum is bcd++. In the equivalent infix expression, we have to use parentheses: b+(c+d).

The last three productions in G10.4 output operands as soon as they are parsed. However, the four productions that start with an operator defer outputting the operator until after their two operands have been parsed. Thus, in the output, each operator follows its operands. That is, each output string is the postfix expression equivalent to the prefix string in the input.

The method call of expr() in S() in G10.4 parses the input string, and outputs an output string. The output string appears on one line because of the use of the System.out.print method (which does not advance the cursor to the beginning of the next line) within the expr() method. On return to S(), the System.out.println action positions the display screen cursor at the beginning of the next line.

The recursive descent parser/translator for G10.4 in given in Figure 10.4. When we run this program and enter the prefix string +/bcd, the computer screen will display the following:

```
input = +/bcd
bc/d+  ◄────────── this is the output string produced by the parser/translator
```

Exercise 10.4

Construct the parse tree for *b+cd in G10.4. What is the corresponding output string? Abbreviate the action { System.out.print} with { print}

Answer:

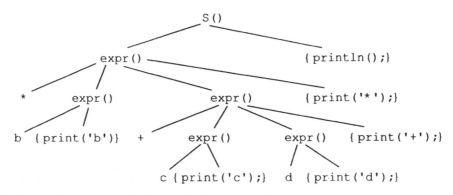

The output string is bcd+* followed by the new line.

```
 1  // Figure 10.4
 2  import java.util.Scanner;
 3  //========================================================
 4  class Fig1004
 5  {
 6    public static void main(String[] args)
 7    {
 8      // construct token manager (see Figure 6.12)
 9      ArgsTokenMgr tm = new ArgsTokenMgr(args);
10      // construct parser
11      Fig1004Parser parser = new Fig1004Parser(tm);
12
13      try
14      {
15        parser.parse();            // parse and translate
16      }
17      catch (RuntimeException e)
18      {
19        System.err.println();
20        System.err.println(e.getMessage());
21        System.exit(1);
22      }
23    }
24  }                                     // end of Fig1004
25  //========================================================
26  class Fig1004Parser
27  {
28    private ArgsTokenMgr tm;
29    private char currentToken;
30    //---------------
31    public Fig1004Parser(ArgsTokenMgr tm)
32    {
33      this.tm = tm;
34      advance();                 // prime currentToken
35    }
36    //---------------
37    private void advance()
38    {
39      currentToken = tm.getNextToken();
40    }
41    //---------------
42    private void consume(char expected)
43    {
44      if (currentToken == expected)
45        advance();
46      else
47        throw new RuntimeException(
48                    "Expecting \"" + expected + "\"");
49    }
```

Figure 10.4.

```
50    //----------------
51    public void parse()
52    {
53      S();
54      if (currentToken != '#')
55        throw new RuntimeException(
56                              "Expecting end of input");
57    }
58    //----------------
59    private void S()
60    {
61      expr();
62      System.out.println();
63    }
64    //----------------
65    private void expr()
66    {
67      switch(currentToken)
68      {
69        case '+':
70          consume('+');
71          expr();
72          expr();
73          System.out.print('+');
74          break;
75        case '-':
76          consume('-');
77          expr();
78          expr();
79          System.out.print('-');
80          break;
81        case '*':
82          consume('*');
83          expr();
84          expr();
85          System.out.print('*');
86          break;
87        case '/':
88          consume('/');
89          expr();
90          expr();
91          System.out.print('/');
92          break;
93        case 'b':
94          consume('b');
95          System.out.print('b');
96          break;
97        case 'c':
98          consume('c');
```

Figure 10.4. *Continued.*

```
 99         System.out.print('c');
100         break;
101      case 'd':
102        consume('d');
103        System.out.print('d');
104        break;
105      default:
106        throw new RuntimeException(
107                   "Expecting prefix expression");
108    }
109  }
110 }                              // end of Fig1004Parser
```

Figure 10.4. *Continued.*

10.5 PASSING INFORMATION DURING THE PARSE

In the translation grammars we have seen so far, the actions do not need information from earlier in the parse. For example, in the production

```
void S(): {}
{
    "b" S() { System.out.print('b');}
  |
        .
        .
        .
}
```

the action { System.out.println('b');} is completely defined. It does not need information from earlier in the parse.

Now consider the following incomplete translation grammar:

G10.5
```
  void S(): {}                            Selection Set
  {
     Q() { output what Q() generates}     {"b", "c"}
   |
     {}                                   {"#"}
  }


  void Q() : {}
  {
     "b"                                  {"b"}
   |
     "c"                                  {"c"}
  }
```

In production 1, the action is supposed to output whatever Q() to its left generates. If Q() generates b, the action should output b; if Q() generates c, the action should output c.

Thus, Q() must provide to S() information it uncovers during the parse, namely, the terminal symbol it generates. S() can then pass this information to the action so that the action can output it.

We can easily implement the flow of information required by G10.5 using the return statement and the parameter passing mechanism in Java. Q() simply uses a return statement to return the terminal symbol it generates. S() saves this terminal symbol in a local variable r. S() then passes r to the action. The translation grammar that describes the required information flow is

G10.6

```
void S(): {char r;}                    Selection Set
{
    r=Q(){ System.out.print(r);}       {"b", "c"}
  |
    {}                                 {#}
}

char Q():  {}
{
    "b" {return 'b';}                  {"b"}
  |
    "c" {return 'c';}                  {"c"}
}
```

Notice that within the braces that follow " : " in the S() production, we declare the local variable r. From the first S() production, we can see that Q() returns a value which is then assigned to r. r is then passed to the System.out.print action. The Q() productions indicate that Q() returns either b or c, depending on the terminal symbol it generates. Notice that we have prefixed the specification of Q() with char to explicitly indicate the type of value Q() returns. With this additional information in the translation grammar, the grammar specifies precisely how it should be converted into a computer program (see Figure 10.5)

Recall from Section 9.2 that a recursive-descent parser, in effect, traverses the parse tree of the input string in a depth-first order with preference given to the leftmost. Associated with this type of traversal are three directions of motion: down, up, and across.

Any information the parser uncovers during a parse can be passed to any point later on in the traversal. In Figure 10.5, when the direction of the traversal is up (from Q() back to S()), we use the return statement to carry the information. When the direction is across a production (from the call of Q() in the S() method to the action System.out.print(r) to its right), we use a local variable to carry the information. And when the direction is down (from S() to the action System.out.print(r)), we use the parameter passing mechanism in Java to carry the information.

Another interesting translation grammar is

G10.7

```
void S(): {int r;}                     Selection Set
{
    r=B(0) {System.out.println(r);}    {"b", "#"}
}
```

```
 1 void private S()
 2 {
 3   char r;
 4   switch(currentToken)
 5   {
 6     case 'b':
 7     case 'c':
 8       r = Q();
 9       System.out.print(r);
10       break;
11     default:
12       throw new RuntimeException(
13                       "Expecting \"b\" or \"c\"");
14   }
15 }
16 //————————————
17 char private Q()
18 {
19   switch(currentToken)
20   {
21     case 'b':
22       consume('b');
23       return 'b';
24     case 'c':
25       consume('c');
26       return 'c';
27     default:
28       throw new RuntimeException(
29                       "Expecting \"b\" or \"c\"");
30   }
31 }
```

Figure 10.5.

```
int B(int p): { int t;}                    Selection Set
{
    "b" t=B(p+1) { return t;}              {"b"}
  |
    { return p;}                           {#}
}
```

In this translation grammar, the method that corresponds to the B() nonterminal returns an integer value, uses a local integer variable t, and is passed an integer value. Accordingly, its specification in the translation grammar starts with

```
int B(int p): { int t;}
```

G10.7 translates a string of zero or more b's to the number of b's in the input string. For example, if the input string is bbb, then the output string is 3 (which is the number of b's in the input string). Notice that

```
t=B(p+1)
```

in the specification of B() is both an action (an assignment to t) and a nonterminal (B). Because it includes a nonterminal, we do not enclose it in braces.

The easiest way to understand G10.7 is to examine the implementation of the S() and B() methods corresponding to the S() and B() nonterminals in G10.7 (see Figure 10.6).

When B() applies its first production, it consumes b (line 25) and then recursively calls itself (line 26), passing a count one more than it received from its caller. Because the count starts at 0 (S() passes 0 to B() on line 9), the count at any point in the parse is equal to the number of b's in the input string processed so far. B() applies its second production when the current token is the end-of-input marker. At this point, the count that B() receives is the final count because the entire input string has been processed. This last invocation of B() echoes this count back to its caller, which, in turn, returns it to its

```
1 void private S()
2 {
3    int r;                    // final count
4
5    switch(currentToken)
6    {
7      case 'b':
8      case '#':
9        r = B(0);             // pass initial count 0
10       System.out.println(r);   // display final count
11       break;
12     default:
13       throw new RuntimeException(
14                   "Expecting \"b\" or end of input");
15   }
16 }
17 //————————————————
18 int private B(int p)
19 {
20   int t;
21
22   switch(currentToken)
23   {
24     case 'b':
25       consume('b');
26       t = B(p+1);          // increase count
27       return t;
28     case '#':
29       return p;            // return final count
30     default:
31       throw new RuntimeException(
32                   "Expecting \"b\" or end of input");
33   }
34 }
```

Figure 10.6.

caller, and so on, until it reaches S(). S() saves it in a local variable r (line 9), and then passes the value in r to the println method. For this example, the information flow is first down the parse tree (by means of Java's parameter passing mechanism), then up the tree (by means of Java's return statement), horizontally across the tree (by means of the local variable r in S()), and finally down to the println action (by means of the parameter passing mechanism). The information flow follows the parser as it performs, in effect, a depth-first traversal of the parse tree.

Exercise 10.5

Rewrite B() in Figure 10.6 without using t.

Answer:

```
int private B(int p)
{
   switch(currentToken)
   {
     case 'b':
       consume('b');
       return(B(p+1));                    // increase count
     case '#':
       return p                           // return final count
     default:
       throw new RuntimeException("b" or end of input);
   }
}
```

Exercise 10.6

In G10.7, the b's are counted as we recurse "down" (i.e., as the recursive calls are occurring). For each b in the input string, we call B() recursively. For each recursive call, we add one to the parameter. Thus, the parameter at each level equals the number of b's processed so far. When we reach "bottom" (i.e., when currentToken is #), the value of the parameter is equal to the total number of b's in the input string. We then pass this final value back "up" as each level returns to the level above it. To summarize, we count as we recurse "down". As we recurse back "up", we simply return the final count.

An alternative approach is to count as we return back "up" rather than as we recurse "down". In this approach, we start with a count of 0 when we reach "bottom". Then as we recurse back "up" (i.e., as each level returns to the level above it), we add one to the value returned as each level. Thus, when B() finally returns to S(), the value returned will be equal to the number of b's in the input string. Write a translation grammar that corresponds to this approach.

Answer:

```
void S(): { int r;}
{
   r=B() { System.out.println(r);}
}
```

```
int B(): { int t;}
{
    "b" t=B() { return t+1;}   // counting as we recurse "up"
  |
    { return 0;}
}
```

∎

Exercise 10.7

Write a translation grammar that outputs the input string if the length of the input string is even. Otherwise, it should output the input string plus one additional 'b'. The input string is any string of zero of more b's. You may use an if statement as an action within a translation grammar. Hint: one solution to this problem is a simple extension of G10.7

Answer:

```
void S():  { int r;}              Selection Set
{
    r=B(0)                        {"b", "#"}
    { if (r mod 2 == 1)
       System.out.println('b');
      else
       System.out.println():
    }
}
int B(int p) : { int t;}
{
    "b" {System.out.print('b');}    {"b"}
    t=B(p+1) { return t;}
  |
    { return p;}                     {"#"}
}
```

∎

10.6   L-ATTRIBUTED GRAMMARS

When the code in Figure 10.6 is executed, a value (equal to 0) is passed from S() to B(). B(), in turn, passes a value (equal to 1) to B() in a recursive call. B() repeatedly calls itself (line 26), once for each b in the input string. At the end of the input string, the recursion "hits bottom", at which point the final count of b's is returned (line 29) to the next level up, where it, in turn, is returned to the next level up. This process continues all the way up to the S() method. When the final count is returned to S() on line 9, S() then passes the final count to the a println statement (line 10). We can see that associated with each call of B() are two values: the value passed to it from above, and the value returned to it from below. The println action has one value associated with it (the value S() passes to it). Figure 10.7 shows the parse tree corresponding to the input string bb. We have labeled each B() node with a pair of values. The first value is the value passed to it from above; the second value is the value returned to it from below. We also show

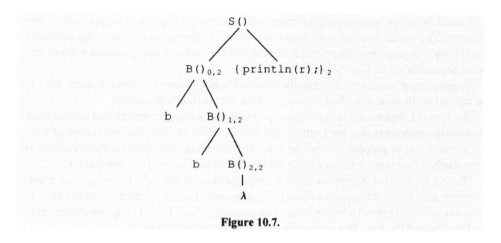

Figure 10.7.

the `println` statement labeled with the argument 2—the value it receives from `S()`. We call the values associated with symbols and actions in a parse tree—like the pair of values on each `B()` node and the argument in the `println` statement in Figure 10.7—*attributes*. A translation grammar defines these attributes: what they are and how they are computed. For example, from the definition of `B()` in G10.7, we can see that one of the attributes of `B()` comes from above in the parse tree (the parameter p that is passed to `B()`), and one comes from below (the value returned by the recursive call).

There are two types of attributes in an attributed grammar: synthesized and inherited. A *synthesized attribute* is an attribute that depends on the attributes of symbols below it in the parse tree. In Figure 10.7, the second number on each `B()` node is a synthesized attribute because it comes from below in the parse tree. An *inherited attribute* is an attribute that depends on the attributes of symbols above it or on the same level in a parse tree. In Figure 10.7, the first number on each `B()` node is an inherited attribute since it comes from above in the parse tree. The value of the argument in the `println` statement is also an inherited attribute. Its value comes from the `B()` node to its left in the parse tree.

Dependencies can exist between attributes. For example, in G10.7, the inherited attribute of the `println` statement (i.e., its argument) depends on the synthesized attribute of the `B()` nonterminal to its left.

For our compilers, we would like translation grammars with attribute dependencies that have no forward dependencies. For example, when the parser reaches the `println` statement in G10.7, its inherited attribute (i.e., the value of its argument) is available from the *preceding* call of `B()`. Now suppose the `println` action preceded rather than followed the call of `B()`. That is, suppose we define the `S()` production as follows:

```
void S(): { int r;}                     Selection Set
{
    { System.out.println(r);}  r=B(0)     { "b", "#"}
}
```

When the parser reaches the `println` action, it has not yet determined its inherited attribute (i.e., the value of its argument). The value depends on the *following* call of `B(0)`. Thus, we cannot perform this action when we reach it in a top-down parse because it has a forward dependency.

Parsers based on translation grammars with no forward dependencies are easy to implement. The parser computes attributes as it proceeds through the parse using attributes previously computed and, therefore, available. We call a translation grammar without forward dependencies an *L-attributed grammar*.

Programming languages are usually designed without forward dependencies. Java is an exception: In Java, a method call can precede the method's definition.

No forward dependencies in a language yield translation grammars that do not have forward dependencies that are L-attributed. For example, in Java, the declaration of a local variable has to precede the use of that variable. Thus, any use of a local variable is necessarily a backward reference to its declaration, which necessarily precedes it.

Having no forward dependencies in a language is good not only for translation grammars but also for us humans; it makes programs easier to read because we never have to look ahead to understand a line of code. The meaning of any line of code can depend only on that line and the lines that precede it, never the lines that follow it.

Can a compiler be constructed that is based on a grammar that is not L-attributed? The answer is yes, but the compiler will necessarily be more complex. Such a compiler would typically create some representation of the parse tree in which nodes have associated attributes (like the tree in Figure 10.7). On the first pass, it would create the parse tree and enter all the attribute values it can compute. It would then make additional passes over the tree to determine the values of attributes associated with forward references.

10.7   A NEW TOKEN MANAGER

Up to now, all the input languages for which we have written token managers have a simple token structure: Each token is a single character. Thus, all our token managers have been quite simple. They get the next token simply by returning the next character in the input string. However, our next translation grammar will require a more complex token manager. It will specify the translation of arithmetic expressions in prefix notation (i.e., expressions in which the operator precedes its two operands) to their corresponding values. For example, if the input string is "+ 17 * 2 5", then the output string is "27". Notice that in our input string, "17" is a multiple-character token. Our token manager has to

```
class Token
{
    // integer that identifies kind of token
    public int kind;

    // location of token in source program
    public int beginLine, beginColumn, endLine, endColumn;

    // String consisting of characters that make up token
    public String image;

    // link to next Token object
    public Token next;
}
```

Figure 10.8.

identify these multiple-character tokens, and return each to the parser as a single unit. It also has to filter out whitespace (i.e., spaces, tabs, newlines, and carriage returns). For example, the sequence of tokens in "+ 17 * 2 5" is "+", "17", "*", "2", and "5".

Our new token manager handles input differently from the token managers we have seen so far. It inputs from a file rather than from the command line. It reads one line at a time. Each time the token manager reads a line, it stores it in a buffer. It then processes the characters in the buffer one at a time. After processing all the characters in the buffer, the token manager then reads the next line into the buffer, and so on.

The principal method in our new token manager is the method getNextToken(), which returns the next token from the input stream in the form of an object. This object, which is instantiated from the class Token (see Figure 10.8), contains all the information that the parser requires of a token. The Token class contains the following fields:

- `public int kind`

  kind contains an integer that identifies the token kind (i.e., category). The kind values for the various tokens handled by our new token manager are defined in the following interface:

  ```
  interface Fig1010Constants
  {
      // integers that identify token kinds
      public int EOF = 0;
      public int UNSIGNED = 1;
      public int PLUS = 2;
      public int MINUS = 3;
      public int TIMES = 4;
      public int DIVIDE = 5;
      public int ERROR = 6;
          . . .
  }
  ```

  For example, the kind value for an unsigned integer token is UNSIGNED (which is equal to 1). The kind value for a "+" token is PLUS (which is equal to 2).
- `public int beginLine, beginColumn, endLine, endColumn`

  These fields specify the position in the source file of the first character of the token (beginLine and beginColumn) and the last character of the token (endLine and endColumn).

- `public String image`

  image contains the string of characters that make up the token. For example, for the token "17", image would contain the string "17". The image of the end-of-file token is set to "<EOF>".

- `public Token next`

  next contains a link to the next token.

Figure 10.9 shows the values in the Token object returned by getNextToken() for a source file with a single line containing

```
+ 17 * 2 5
```

token	+	17	*	2	5	EOF
kind	2	1	4	1	1	0
beginLine	1	1	1	1	1	1
beginColumn	1	3	6	8	10	11
endLine	1	1	1	1	1	1
endColumn	1	4	6	8	10	11
image	"+"	"17"	"*"	"2"	"5"	"<EOF>"

Figure 10.9.

With our new token manager in place, the parser identifies a token during the parsing process by examining its `kind` field. For example, to determine if `currentToken` is a "+" token, the parser checks if `currentToken.kind` is equal to PLUS (PLUS is the `kind` value for a "+" token). Let us examine an example. Suppose our translation grammar contains the following alternative:

```
"+" expr() expr()
```

With our old token manager, it would translate to

```
switch (currentToken)
{
    case '+':
      consume('+');
      expr();
      expr();
      break;
      ...
}
```

We identify the token by inspecting the character in `currentToken`. We also specify to the `consume` method the expected token by passing it the expected character. `consume` then compares this character with the character in `currentToken`. Now compare this code with the code we need with our new token manager:

```
switch(currentToken.kind)   // test kind value in currentToken
{
    case PLUS:
      consume(PLUS);   // pass kind value to consume
      expr();
      expr();
      break;
      ...
}
```

We identify the token by inspecting `currentToken.kind`. We also specify the expected token to `consume` by passing it the `kind` value of the expected token. `consume` then compares this `kind` value with the `kind` value in `currentToken`.

10.8   SOLVING THE TOKEN LOOKAHEAD PROBLEM

Let us examine what our new token manager must do when the parser calls its `getNextToken()` method. `getNextToken()` triggers the processing of the next token in the input stream. When `getNextToken()` is processing an unsigned integer constant, it must *look ahead,* that is, it must read one character beyond the end of the constant to determine where constant ends. For example, when `getNextoken()` reads the "7" in "17", it has no way of knowing that it has reached the end of the constant. It must repeatedly read characters until it reads a nondigit. Only then does it know where the end of the integer constant is. But then when `getNextToken()` is again called, it may already have read in on its previous call the first character of the next token. So `getNextToken()` should never start with a read because an initial read would overlay the last character read in from the previous call. Instead, it should always start by processing the character it already has from the previous call. But that means that `getNextToken()` should read one character past *every* token, including those (like + and *) whose ends can be determined without reading past them. In other words, if the token manager looks ahead when it processes some types of tokens, then it should look ahead for *every* type of token.

10.9   CODE FOR THE NEW TOKEN MANAGER

At this point, the structure of our new token manager may seem complex to you. You will see that it is, in fact, quite straightforward. Let us examine its code, which appears on lines 58 to 186 of Figure 10.10. Note that Figure 10.10 shows the code for the entire prefix expression compiler, which, of course, includes the token manager. In this section, we will examine only the token manager portion of Figure 10.10. In the subsequent sections, we will consider the rest of the compiler.

Notice on line 81 that `getNextToken()` accesses the value in `currentChar` without first reading a value into it:

```
81      while (Character.isWhitespace(currentChar))
82         getNextChar();
```

This sequence make sense because `getNextToken()` always reads one character beyond the end of a token. Thus, on every call, except the first, it already has a character in `currentChar` to process. If this character is whitespace, `getNextToken()` discards it by calling `getNextChar()`(`getNextChar()` places the next character in `currentChar`). If not, it falls through to line 85 where it creates an object of type `Token`:

```
85      token = new Token();
```

On line 102, `getNextToken()` tests `currentChar` to determine if it is a digit:

```
102     if (Character.isDigit(currentChar))
```

```
1  // Figure 10.10: Compiles a prefix expr to its value.
2  import java.io.*;
3  import java.util.Scanner;
4  //========================================================
5  class Fig1010
6  {
7    public static void main(String[] args) throws
8                                          IOException
9    {
10     if (args.length != 1)
11     {
12       System.err.println("Wrong number cmd line args");
13       System.exit(1);
14     }
15
16     // create the objects that make up the compiler
17     Scanner inFile = new Scanner(new File(args[0]));
18     Fig1010TokenMgr tm = new Fig1010TokenMgr(inFile);
19     Fig1010Parser parser = new Fig1010Parser(tm);
20
21     // parse and translate
22     try
23     {
24       parser.parse();
25     }
26     catch (RuntimeException e)
27     {
28       System.err.println(e.getMessage());
29       System.exit(1);
30     }
31   }
32 }                                    // end of Fig1010
33 //========================================================
34 interface Fig1010Constants
35 {
36   // integers that identify token kinds
37   public int EOF = 0;
38   public int UNSIGNED = 1;
39   public int PLUS = 2;
40   public int MINUS = 3;
41   public int TIMES = 4;
42   public int DIVIDE = 5;
43   public int ERROR = 6;
44
45   // tokenImage provides string for each kind
46   String[] tokenImage =
47   {
48     "<EOF>",
49     "<UNSIGNED>",
```

Figure 10.10.

```
50      "\ "+\ "",
51      "\ "-\ "",
52      "\ "*\ "",
53      "\ "/\ "",
54      "<ERROR>"
55      };
56 }                              // end of Fig1010Constants
57 //=========================================================
58 class Fig1010TokenMgr implements Fig1010Constants
59 {
60    private Scanner inFile;
61    private char currentChar;
62    private int currentColumnNumber;
63    private int currentLineNumber;
64    private int lineLength;
65    private String inputLine;      // holds 1 line of input
66    private Token token;           // holds 1 token
67    private StringBuffer buffer;   // token image built here
68    //----------------------
69    public Fig1010TokenMgr(Scanner inFile)
70    {
71       this.inFile = inFile;
72       currentChar = '\n';         //  \n will trigger read
73       currentColumnNumber = 0;
74       currentLineNumber = 0;
75       buffer = new StringBuffer();
76    }
77    //----------------------
78    public Token getNextToken()
79    {
80      // skip whitespace
81      while (Character.isWhitespace(currentChar))
82        getNextChar();
83
84      // create token to be returned to the parser
85      token = new Token();
86      token.next = null;
87
88      // save start-of-token position
89      token.beginLine = currentLineNumber;
90      token.beginColumn = currentColumnNumber;
91
92      // check for EOF
93      if (currentChar == EOF)
94      {
95         token.image = "<EOF>";
96         token.endLine = currentLineNumber;
97         token.endColumn = currentColumnNumber;
98         token.kind = EOF;
```

Figure 10.10. *Continued.*

```
 99      }
100
101     else  // check for unsigned int
102     if (Character.isDigit(currentChar))
103     {
104       buffer.setLength(0);     // set length to 0
105       do                       // process unsigned int
106       {
107         // append currentChar to buffer
108         buffer.append(currentChar);
109
110         // save token end location
111         // must do this before calling getNextChar()
112         token.endLine = currentLineNumber;
113         token.endColumn = currentColumnNumber;
114
115         getNextChar();
116       } while (Character.isDigit(currentChar));
117       token.image = buffer.toString();
118       token.kind = UNSIGNED;
119     }
120
121     else  // process one-character token
122     {
123       switch(currentChar)
124       {
125         case '+':
126           token.kind = PLUS;
127           break;
128         case '-':
129           token.kind = MINUS;
130           break;
131         case '*':
132           token.kind = TIMES;
133           break;
134         case '/':
135           token.kind = DIVIDE;
136           break;
137         default:
138           token.kind = ERROR;
139           break;
140       }
141
142       // save currentChar as String in token.image
143       token.image = Character.toString(currentChar);
144
145       // save end-of-token position
146       token.endLine = currentLineNumber;
147       token.endColumn = currentColumnNumber;
```

Figure 10.10. *Continued.*

```
148
149        getNextChar();   // read 1 char beyond end of token
150      }
151
152      // token trace appears as comments in output file
153      System.out.printf(
154        "kd=%3d bL=%3d bC=%3d eL=%3d eC=%3d im= %s%n",
155        token.kind, token.beginLine, token.beginColumn,
156        token.endLine, token.endColumn, token.image);
157
158      return token;
159    }
160    //---------------------
161    private void getNextChar()
162    {
163      if (currentChar == EOF)
164        return;
165
166      if (currentChar == '\n')          // need line?
167      {
168        if (inFile.hasNextLine())      // any lines left?
169        {
170          inputLine = inFile.nextLine();   // get next line
171          inputLine = inputLine + "\n";    // mark line end
172          currentColumnNumber = 0;
173          currentLineNumber++;
174        }
175        else  // at end of file
176        {
177          currentChar = EOF;
178          return;
179        }
180      }
181
182      // get next character from inputLine
183      currentChar =
184                inputLine.charAt(currentColumnNumber++);
185    }
186 }                                      // end of Fig1010TokenMgr
187 //=========================================================
188 class Fig1010Parser implements Fig1010Constants
189 {
190    private Fig1010TokenMgr tm;
191    private Token currentToken;
192    private Token previousToken;
193    //---------------------
194    public Fig1010Parser(Fig1010TokenMgr tm)
195    {
196      this.tm = tm;
```

Figure 10.10. *Continued.*

```
197      currentToken = tm.getNextToken();   // prime
198      previousToken = null;
199    }
200    //---------------------
201    public void parse()
202    {
203      S();                                 // do parse
204      if (currentToken.kind != EOF)   // check for garbage
205        throw genEx("Expecting <EOF>");
206    }
207    //---------------------
208    // Construct and return an exception that contains
209    // a message consisting of the image of the current
210    // token, its location, and the expected tokens.
211    //
212    private RuntimeException genEx(String errorMessage)
213    {
214      return new RuntimeException("Encountered \"" +
215        currentToken.image + "\" on line " +
216        currentToken.beginLine + " column " +
217        currentToken.beginColumn +
218        System.getProperty("line.separator") +
219        errorMessage);
220    }
221    //---------------------
222    // Advance currentToken to next token.
223    //
224    private void advance()
225    {
226      previousToken = currentToken;
227
228      // If next token is on token list, advance to it.
229      if (currentToken.next != null)
230        currentToken = currentToken.next;
231
232      // Otherwise, get next token from token mgr and
233      // put it on the list.
234      else
235        currentToken =
236                currentToken.next = tm.getNextToken();
237    }
238    //---------------------
239    // getToken(i) returns ith token without advancing
240    // in token stream.  getToken(0) returns
241    // previousToken.  getToken(1) returns currentToken.
242    // getToken(2) returns next token, and so on.
243    //
244    private Token getToken(int i)
245    {
```

Figure 10.10. *Continued.*

```
246      if (i <= 0)
247        return previousToken;
248
249      Token t = currentToken;
250      for (int j = 1; j < i; j++)  // loop to ith token
251      {
252        // if next token is on token list, move t to it
253        if (t.next != null)
254          t = t.next;
255
256        // Otherwise, get next token from token mgr and
257        // put it on the list.
258        else
259          t = t.next = tm.getNextToken();
260      }
261      return t;
262   }
263   //---------------------
264   // If the kind of the current token matches the
265   // expected kind, then consume advances to the next
266   // token. Otherwise, it throws an exception.
267   //
268   private void consume(int expected)
269   {
270      if (currentToken.kind == expected)
271        advance();
272      else
273        throw genEx("Expecting " + tokenImage[ expected] );
274   }
275   //---------------------
276   private void S()
277   {
278      int p;
279
280      p = expr();
281      System.out.println(p);   // display value of expr
282   }
283   //---------------------
284   private int expr()
285   {
286      int p, q;
287      Token t;
288
289      switch(currentToken.kind)
290      {
291        case PLUS:
292          consume(PLUS);
293          p = expr();          // get value of first operand
294          q = expr();          // get value of second operand
```

Figure 10.10. *Continued.*

```
295          return p + q;       // compute/return expr value
296        case MINUS:
297          consume(MINUS);
298          p = expr();         // get value of first operand
299          q = expr();         // get value of second operand
300          return p - q;       // compute/return expr value
301        case TIMES:
302          consume(TIMES);
303          p = expr();         // get value of first operand
304          q = expr();         // get value of second operand
305          return p * q;       // compute/return expr value
306        case DIVIDE:
307          consume(DIVIDE);
308          p = expr();         // get value of first operand
309          q = expr();         // get value of second operand
310          return p / q;       // compute/return expr value
311        case UNSIGNED:
312          t = currentToken;              // save in t
313          consume(UNSIGNED);             // consume token
314          p = Integer.parseInt(t.image); // now use t
315          return p;                      // return int val
316        default:
317          throw genEx("Expecting operator or " +
318                              tokenImage[ UNSIGNED] );
319      }
320    }
321 }                              // end of Fig1010 parser
```

Figure 10.10. *Continued.*

If it is, then it is the start of an unsigned integer constant, which is then proocessed with

```
105        do                       // process unsigned int
106        {
107          // append currentChar to buffer
108          buffer.append(currentChar);
109
110          // save token end location
111          // must do this before calling getNextChar()
112          token.endLine = currentLineNumber;
113          token.endColumn = currentColumnNumber;
114
115          getNextChar();
116        } while (Character.isDigit(currentChar));
```

The do-while loop reads in the digits that make up an unsigned integer constant. After it reads each digit, it appends it to buffer (line 108). Thus, when the do-while loop is done, buffer holds the complete sequence of characters corresponding to the unsigned integer constant. From line 116, we can see that the do-while loop iterates until currentChar becomes a nondigit. Thus, for unsigned integer constants, getNextToken() reads one character beyond the end of the token.

Following the do-while loop, getNextToken() converts the sequence of characters in buffer to a string and assigns it to the image field of the token object:

```
117          token.image = buffer.toString();
```

Next, getNextToken() assigns UNSIGNED to the kind field in the token object:

```
118          token.kind = UNSIGNED;
```

UNSIGNED is the constant 1 defined in the Fig1010Constants interface (see line 38). Because the class Fig1010TokenMgr implements this interface (see line 58), UNSIGNED is available to the methods in the Fig1010TokenMgr class.

If a token does not start with a digit, the do-while loop within getNextToken() is skipped. Instead, the switch statement on line 123, which sets the kind field of the token object according to currentChar is executed:

```
123          switch(currentChar)
124          {
125            case '+':
126              token.kind = PLUS;
127              break;
128            case '-':
129              token.kind = MINUS;
130              break;
131            case '*':
132              token.kind = TIMES;
133              break;
134            case '/':
135              token.kind = DIVIDE;
136              break;
137            default:
138              token.kind = ERROR;
139              break;
140          }
```

For example, if currentChar contains the plus sign, then token.kind is assigned PLUS, the constant defined in the constants interface with

```
39       public int PLUS = 2;
```

The character in currentChar is then converted to type String and assigned to token.image:

```
143          token.image = Character.toString(currentChar);
```

token.endLine and token.endColumn fields are then set:

```
146          token.endLine = currentLineNumber;
147          token.endColumn = currentColumnNumber;
```

After processing a single-character token, `getNextToken()` reads the next character by calling `getNextChar()`:

```
149         getNextChar();   // read 1 char beyond end of token
```

This call is necessary because the code at the beginning of `getNextToken()` (line 81) assumes that `getNextToken()` always reads one character past the end of every token. Thus, `getNextToken()` must work in that way for every token.

Before any calls of `getNextToken()`, currentChar is initialized to the newline character:

```
72          currentChar = '\n';           // \n will trigger read
```

This initialization ensures that `currentChar` has a value when it is tested on line 81 during the first call of `getNextToken()`. In response to the newline character, `getNextToken()` calls `getNextChar()` to get the next (i.e., first) character from the source file. Because `currentChar` is initialized to `'\n'` (which indicates the end of a line), this first call of `getNextChar()` reads a line from the source file:

```
166     if (currentChar == '\n')         // need line?
167     {
168       if (inFile.hasNextLine())       // any lines left?
169       {
170         inputLine = inFile.nextLine();  // get next line
```

Because the `nextLine()` method in the `Scanner` class returns the input line without a line separator, `getNextChar()` attaches a newline with

```
171         inputLine = inputLine + "\n";   // mark line end
```

Then after incrementing the line number and resetting the column number, it assigns the first character in `inputLine` to `currentChar`:

```
183     currentChar =
184                  inputLine.charAt(currentColumnNumber++);
```

On subsequent calls of `getNextChar()`, `getNextChar()` simply retrieves the next character in `inputLine` until it reaches the newline character.

Each time `getNextToken()` is entered after its initial call, `currentChar` contains the character in the input that follows the last character of the token processed on the previous call.

Lines 37 to 43 of the `Fig1010Constants` interface define the constants that identify the various tokens:

```
37      public int EOF = 0;
38      public int UNSIGNED = 1;
39      public int PLUS = 2;
40      public int MINUS = 3;
41      public int TIMES = 4;
42      public int DIVIDE = 5;
43      public int ERROR = 6;
```

The array `tokenImage` provides a descriptive string for each token kind:

```
46    String[ ] tokenImage =
47    {
48      "<EOF>",
49      "<UNSIGNED>",
50      "\ "+\ "",
51      "\ "-\ "",
52      "\ "*\ "",
53      "\ "/\ "",
54      "<ERROR>"
55    };
```

For example, `tokeImage[UNSIGNED]` provides the descriptive string `"<UN-SIGNED>"`. The `consume` method in the parser uses `tokenImage` when it creates an error message:

```
268    private void consume(int expected)
269    {
270      if (currentToken.kind == expected)
271        advance();
272      else
273        throw genEx("Expecting " + tokenImage[expected]);
274    }
```

`consume` first checks if `currentToken.kind` matches the kind of the expected token (given by the parameter `kind`). If there is a match, `consume` advances to the next token. Otherwise, `consume` throws an exception. The error message in this exception includes the descriptive string of the expected token obtained from the `tokenImage` array (see line 273).

To advance to the next token, the parser calls its `advance()` method. `advance()` first saves the `currentToken` in `previousToken`:

```
226      previousToken = currentToken;
```

If the next token is already available via the `next` field of the current token, `advance()` moves `currentToken` to it:

```
229      if (currentToken.next!=null)
230        currentToken = currentToken.next;
```

Otherwise, `advance()` calls `getNextToken()` in the token manager:

```
234      else
235        currentToken =
236                  currentToken.next = tm.getNextToken();
```

`advance()` assigns the token that `getNextToken()` returns to the `next` field of `currentToken`. It then assigns this token to `currentToken` itself (note that the two assignments on lines 235 and 236 are performed right to left). Figure 10.11 shows the pictures before and after lines 235 and 236 are executed.

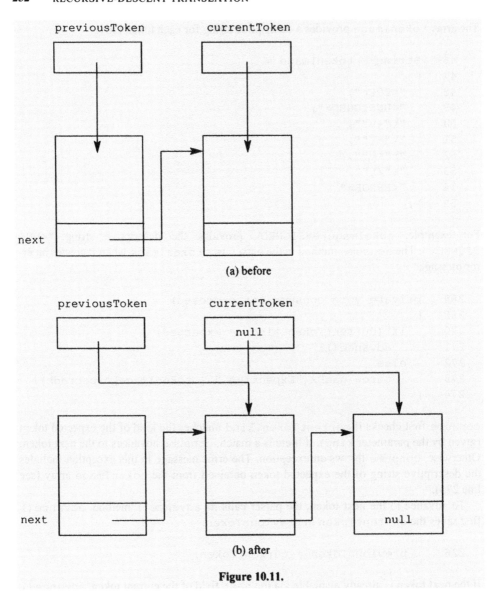

Figure 10.11.

The parser in Figure 10.10 chains all the tokens together using the `next` field in each token. However, it does not make use of this chain. We will see in later chapters that the chaining of tokens can be very useful. In particular, it allows the parser to look ahead in the token stream to make parsing decisions [which is necessary if the grammar in not LL(1)]. The parser in Figure 10.10 does not need to look ahead. Thus, it does not make use of the token chain it creates.

`currentToken` and `previousToken` are fields within the parser object. Thus, the parser has access to the current and previous tokens via these fields.

If the parser needs to advance to the next token but needs to save information on the current token, it can simply save `currentToken` in a local variable. For example on line 312, the parser saves `currentToken` in a local variable `t`:

```
312             t = currentToken;              // save in t
```

where t is defined with

```
287      Token t;
```

If the parser needs to know anything about the saved token in t, it can simply examine the fields of the object referenced by t. For example, to obtain the image of the saved token, the parser accesses t.image on line 314:

```
314           p = Integer.parseInt(t.image); // now use t
```

Just before getNextToken() returns a token to the parser, it displays on the display screen the fields of the token it is returning:

```
153      System.out.printf(
154        "kd=%3d bL=%3d bC=%3d eL=%3d eC=%3d im= %s%n",
155        token.kind, token.beginLine, token.beginColumn,
156        token.endLine, token.endColumn, token.image);
```

For example, if the source file contains

```
+ 17 * 2 5
```

then the trace displayed is

```
kd=  2 bL=  1 bC=  1 eL=  1 eC=  1 im= +
kd=  1 bL=  1 bC=  3 eL=  1 eC=  4 im= 17
kd=  4 bL=  1 bC=  6 eL=  1 eC=  6 im= *
kd=  1 bL=  1 bC=  8 eL=  1 eC=  8 im= 2
kd=  1 bL=  1 bC= 10 eL=  1 eC= 10 im= 5
kd=  0 bL=  2 bC=  1 eL=  2 eC=  1 im= <EOF>
```

This trace is useful when debugging the token manager.

10.10 TRANSLATION GRAMMAR FOR PREFIX EXPRESSION COMPILER

From a parser's point of view, each token provided by the token manager is a single terminal symbol. Thus, although an unsigned integer constant can consist of multiple characters, the parser treats every unsigned integer constant as a single terminal symbol. "Unsigned integer constant" represents a category of tokens. We represent such token categories in a grammar with an uppercase name enclosed in angle brackets. In G10.8 below, the right side of production 6 is <UNSIGNED>. This name identifies a token corresponding to the category "unsigned integer constant". Be sure to understand that <UNSIGNED> represents a terminal symbol. It is *not* a nonterminal.

G10.8

```
1. S    → expr
2. expr → "+" expr expr
3. expr → "-" expr expr
4. expr → "*" expr expr
```

```
5. expr → "/" <expr> expr
6. expr → <UNSIGNED>
```

Recall that in a translation grammar, we represent nonterminals with method names that are not enclosed with angle brackets. Suppose we specified token categories like <UNSIGNED> without angle brackets. Then, we might confuse them with nonterminals symbols. For this reason, we always enclose token categories in a grammar with angle brackets.

Let us now create a translation grammar based on G10.8 that specifies the translation of a prefix expression to its value. The prefix expression will be read in from an input file; its value will be outputted to the display screen. This particular translation is somewhat unusual. Typically, compilers translate one language to another. In contrast, our proposed translation grammar is going to specify the translation of a prefix expression to its value. For example, this translation would convert the prefix expression

```
+ 20 30
```

to 50. To do this, the parser/translator has to perform the computation specified by the prefix expression. Thus, we should expect in the translation grammar actions that perform computations.

The two key considerations are

1. Where to perform the addition, subtraction, multiplication, and division actions
2. How to pass the required values to these actions

During the parse, we can perform a computation using the value of an expression only after that expression has been parsed (because only then is its value available). Clearly, we have to perform the addition operation at the end of production 2 in G10.8. The action should add the values of the two expressions to its left. Similarly, the other operations should be performed at the end of their corresponding productions. We should also have an action (a println) on the far right of production 1 that displays the value of the expression to its left.

The expr() method should return the value of the expression it parses. Then in productions 2 to 5, the two calls of expr() would provide the required values for the actions at the right of those productions. Similarly, the call of expr() in production 1 would provide the required value for the println action to its right. G10.9 shows the complete translation grammar.

G10.9

```
void S(): { int p;}                              Selection Set
{
    p=expr() { System.out.println(p);}          {"+", "-", "*",
                                                  "/", <UNSIGNED>}
}
//------------------
int expr() : { int p, q; Token t}
{
    "+" p=expr() q=expr() { return p+q;}         {"+"}
  |
    "-" p=expr() q=expr() { return p-q;}         {"-"}
  |
```

```
                                                        Selection Set
   "*" p=expr() q=expr() { return p*q;}               {"*"}
 |
   "/" p=expr() q=expr() { return p/q;}               {"/"}
 |
   t=<UNSIGNED>                                        {<UNSIGNED>}
   { p=Integer.parseInt(t.image);}
   { return p;}
}
```

Note the the assignments in G10.9 to p, q, and t are actions, but they involve nonterminal or terminal symbols. For example, in

```
p=expr()
```

expr() is a nonterminal, and in

```
t=<UNSIGNED>
```

<UNSIGNED> is a terminal. Because these actions involve nonterminals or terminals, they are not enclosed in braces. If we did enclose them in braces, they would effectively be removed from the grammar. For example, if we wrote the first alternative for expr() this way,

```
"+" {p=expr()} {q=expr()} { return p+q;}
```

with braces surrounding the two assignment actions, then this line would represent the production

```
expr →  "+"
```

rather than

```
expr →  "+" expr expr
```

Notice that in the last production in G10.9, we have the following assignment statement:

```
t=<UNSIGNED>
```

The left side of this statement is a local variable of type Token, and its right side is the token in the input corresponding to <UNSIGNED>. This statement represents the assignment to t of the token object that getNextToken() creates for an unsigned integer constant. The corresponding code in the parser is

```
312             t = currentToken;                    // save in t
```

When the parser parses a token (i.e., a terminal symbol), it calls consume to advance past that token. For example, consider the code that corresponds to

```
t=<UNSIGNED>
```

in G10.9. When the parser reaches the unsigned integer token, it calls `consume`:

```
313              consume(UNSIGNED);
```

However, the line

```
t=<UNSIGNED>
```

in the translation grammar implies that the assignment to `t` occurs before the call to the `consume`. Accordingly, on line 312, the parser saves `currentToken` by assigning it to `t` before calling `consume` on line 313:

```
311          case UNSIGNED:
312              t = currentToken;            // save in t
313              consume(UNSIGNED);           // consume token
```

Because our actions in this translation grammar perform numerical computations, we need to convert the image of the unsigned integer constant (which has type `String`) to type `int`, which we do with the action

```
314              p = Integer.parseInt(t.image);  // now use t
```

Here, the `parseInt` method in the `Integer` class converts the string of digits in `t.image` to its corresponding `int` value. For example, if `t.image` contains the string `"17"`, `parseInt` converts this string to the `int` value 17, which is then assigned to the `int` variable `p`. The value in `p` is then returned with

```
315              return p;                        // return int val
```

It not hard to come up with the translation grammar G10.9. It requires just a little common sense. And once we have our translation grammar, it is simple to write the corresponding Java code in Figure 10.10.

If the parser in Figure 10.10 detects an error, it throws a `RuntimeException` created with a call to `genEx`:

```
212    private RuntimeException genEx(String errorMessage)
213    {
214      return new RuntimeException("Encountered \"" +
215        currentToken.image + "\" on line " +
216        currentToken.beginLine + " column " +
217        currentToken.beginColumn +
218        System.getProperty("line.separator") +
219        errorMessage);
220    }
```

This method creates a `RuntimeException` object whose error message contains the current token's image and location, and the expected token. The caller of `genEx` passes to it a string describing the error via parameter `errorMessage`. `genEx` appends this string to the error message with an intervening line separator. Thus, it appears as a second line. The line separator is system dependent. On Microsoft systems, it is a carriage return/newline sequence. On most non-Microsoft systems is simply a newline character. The call of

`System.getProperty("line.separator")` on line 218 returns this system-dependent line separator.

Let us look at an example of an error and its corresponding error message. The following input string

```
+ 2
```

is missing a second operand. This operand can be either another prefix expression or an unsigned integer. In the former case, the missing operand would start with an operator. Thus, either an operator or an unsigned integer is missing immediately following the 2 in the preceding input. The error message that `genEx` creates for this case is

```
Encountered "<EOF>" on line 1 column 4
Expecting operator or <UNSIGNED>
```

The second line of this error message originates in the call of `genEx` and is passed to `genEx` as a parameter:

```
317            throw genEx("Expecting operator or " +
318                            tokenImage[UNSIGNED] );
```

To run the program in Figure 10.10, we must first compile it with

```
javac Fig1010.java
```

We then run the program by entering the `java` command. When entering this command, we have to specify both the `Fig1010` compiler and the file that contains the prefix expression to be translated. For example, suppose the file `prefix.txt` contains the following expression:

```
+ 17 * 2 5
```

If we enter the `java` command to run the compiler and specify the file `prefix.txt` on the command line, the compiler will display a token trace and the value of the expression provided by the file `prefix.txt`:

```
java Fig1010 prefix.txt
kd=  2 bL=  1 bC=  1 eL=  1 eC=  1 im= +
kd=  1 bL=  1 bC=  3 eL=  1 eC=  4 im= 17
kd=  4 bL=  1 bC=  6 eL=  1 eC=  6 im= *
kd=  1 bL=  1 bC=  8 eL=  1 eC=  8 im= 2
kd=  1 bL=  1 bC= 10 eL=  1 eC= 10 im= 5
kd=  0 bL=  2 bC=  1 eL=  2 eC=  1 im= <EOF>
27
```

10.11   AN INTERESTING USE OF RECURSION (OPTIONAL)

In C, C++, and Java, we use a list to declare variables. Preceding the list we specify the type of the variables on the list. A semicolon terminates the list. For example, in

```
int x, y;
```

we are declaring x and y to be of type int. When a compiler processes such a list, it typically makes an entry into a symbol table recording the name of each variable and its type. If it needs to know the type of any variable later on, it can simply look up that variable in the symbol table. Compilers typically use an arbitrary code to represent the various types stored in the symbol table. For example, it might use 0 to represent the type int, 1 to represents the type long, and so on. Figure 10.12 shows the entries in the symbol table corresponding to the preceding declaration of x and y.

To make a complete entry into the symbol table, the compiler has to know both the variable name and its type. Because the type precedes the identifier list in C, C++, and Java, the compiler can make complete entries into the symbol for each variable as soon as it parses that variable's name. For example, as soon as it parses "x", it can enter "x" and the type int (represented by the integer 0) into the symbol table.

In some languages (Pascal is one example), the type in a declaration comes at the end of the list of variable names, rather than at the beginning. For example, to declare x and y of type int, we use

```
x, y: int;
```

Unfortunately, with the type at the end, the compiler cannot make complete entries into the symbol table as it parses the variable names in the list. It does not know the type until after it parses the type at the very end of the statement. Because of this awkwardness, the designers of C, C++, and Java wisely decided to place the type at the beginning of a declaration list.

With the type at the end of a declaration list, how can the compiler make the proper entries into the symbol table? Let us consider two approaches that work. In the first approach, when the compiler is about to start parsing the list of variable names, it saves currentIndex (the index of the next available slot in the symbol table) in a variable named savedIndex. As the compiler then parses the names of the variables on the list, it enters only the name of each variable into the symbol table, incrementing currentIndex after each entry. When it ultimately parses and determines the type, the compiler can then enter that type into those symbol table slots whose indices run from savedIndex up to but not including currentIndex (see Figure 10.13).

The translation grammar that describes this method is (we have numbered each line for easy reference)

G10.10

```
1 void declaration(): { int savedIndex, r;}
2 {
3    (savedIndex=symTab.getCurrentIndex();}
4    identifierList() ":" r=type() ";"
5    { symTab.updateSymbolTable(savedIndex, r);}
```

Symbol	Type
"x"	0
"y"	0

Figure 10.12.

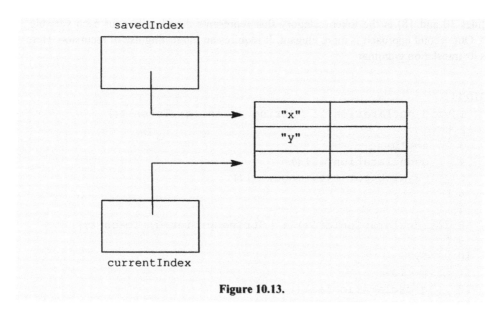

Figure 10.13.

```
 6 }
 7
 8 void identifierList() : { Token t;}
 9 {
10    t=<ID>
11    { symtab.enter(t.image} ;}
12    identifierTail()
13 }
14
15 void identifierTail() :  { Token t;}
16 {
17    ","
18    t=<ID>
19    { symtab.enter(t.image);}
20    identifierTail()
21  |
22    {}
23 }
```

symTab is the symbol table object. In the declaration() method, the getCurrentIndex() method in the symTab object returns the current index of the symbol table, which is then saved in savedIndex (line 3). On line 4, declaration() then parses the list of identifiers (by calling identifierList(), the colon, the type (by calling type()), and the semicolon. The call of type() on line 4 returns the type parsed, which is then assigned to r. Finally, updateSymbolTable is called to which savedIndex and r is passed. updateSymbolTable updates the entries just created. updateSymbolTable is in the symbol table object. Thus, it has access to currentIndex. Using r, savedIndex and currentIndex, it updates those entries in the symbol table with indices from savedIndex up to but not including currentIndex. In the identifierList and identifierTail modules, the enter method enters the identifiers only into the symbol table (lines 11 and 19). <ID>

(lines 10 and 18) is the token category that represents the identifier for each variable.

Our second approach is more elegant. It requires an interesting use of recursion. Here is its translation grammar:

G10.11

```
 1 void declaration(): {String p; int q; Token t;}
 2 {
 3     t=<ID>
 4     q=declarationTail()
 5     {symTab.enter(t.image, q);}
 6 }
 7
 8 int declarationTail() : {String p; int q; Token t;}
 9 {
10     ","
11     t=<ID>
12     q=declarationTail()
13     {symTab.enter(t.image,q); return q;}
14   |
15     ":" q=type() ";"
16     {return q;}
17 }
```

Let us see what happens when the parser applies the declaration() production. It first parses <ID>, saving it in t (line 3). It then calls declarationTail() (line 4) which recurses until it parses the colon, the type, and the semicolon (line 15). declarationTail() then returns the type (line 16) to all its callers, all the way up to declaration(), where it is saved in q (line 4). t.image and q are then passed to the enter method (line 5), which makes a complete entry into the symbol table. Similarly, when the parser applies the first declarationTail() production, it gets the type from the recursive call of declarationTail() (line 12). This type can then be passed to the call of the enter method (line 13).

Figure 10.14 shows an abbreviated parse tree for the input string

```
x, y: int;
```

It shows how recursive calls of declarationTail() proceed down the tree until declarationTail() calls type(). type() returns the type to its caller declarationTail(), which returns it to its caller—also declarationTail()— which passes the type and "y", to the enter method. Finally, this call of declarationTail() returns the type to declaration(), which passes the type and "x" to the enter method.

Notice that the call of enter in production 1 is the last action performed. That is, the first variable listed in the input string is entered into the symbol table last. This technique enters the variable names in reverse order from the order in which they appear in the input string. We expect this reversal because the call of enter in declarationTail() follows the recursive call. As we learned in Section 9.9, this calling structure processes a list in reverse order.

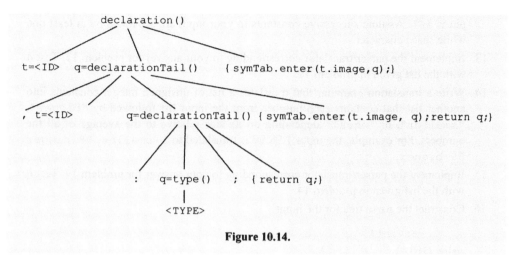

Figure 10.14.

PROBLEMS

1. Show the parse tree for bccd in G10.2.

2. Show the parse tree for +* /bcbc in G10.4

3. Write a translation grammar whose input language is bb*. Each output string should be the same as the input string, but with a comma separating successive b's. For example, if the input string is "bbb", the output string should be "b,b,b".

4. Implement the parser/translator corresponding to your answer for problem 3. Test it with b, bb, bbb, dd, and λ.

5. Write a translation grammar whose input language is (b|c)*. Each output string should be the input string with its characters rearranged so that all the b's precede all the c's.

6. Implement the parser/translator corresponding to your answer for problem 5. Test it with λ, b, c, cbcb, and cccbbbb.

7. Write·a translation grammar whose input language is (b|c)*. Each output should be the number of b's minus the number of c's. For example, if the input string is bbbc, the output should be 2; if the input string is cbccccb, the output should be -3.

8. Write a translation grammar whose input language is (b|c) (, (b|c))*. This language consists of nonnull lists of b's and c's with successive letters separated by a comma. The output string should be the same as the input string, but with its first element removed and appended on the end. For example, if the input string is "b,b,c", the output string should be "b,c,b".

9. Implement a parser/translator corresponding to your answer in Problem 10.8. Test it with "b", "c", "b,c", "c,b", and "b,c,c,c".

10. Write a translation grammar that translates an arithmetic expression in infix notation to its corresponding decimal value. Limit your grammar to the addition and multiplication operations.

11. Implement the parser/translator corresponding to your answer for problem 10. Test it with 21, ((22)), 3*(4+5), and 3*4+5.

12. Write a translation grammar that translates a list of unsigned integer constants to the maximum constant on the list. For example, if the input is 54 341 6 17 then the out-

put is 341. Assume successive constants in your input are separated by at least one white space character.

13. Implement the parser/translator corresponding to your answer for problem 12. Test it with the list given in problem 12.

14. Write a translation grammar that translates a list of unsigned integer constants into another list that contains each number from the input list followed by "bigger", "smaller", or "equal" depending on its size relative to the average of all the numbers. For example, the input 1 98 99 is translated to 1 smaller 98 bigger 99 bigger.

15. Implement the parser/translator corresponding to your answer for problem 14. Test it with the list given in problem 14.

16. Construct the parse tree for the input

```
x, y, z: int;
```
using G10.11.

17. On line 314 in the prefix expression compiler in Figure 10.10, the parser converts the image of an unsigned integer constant to type int. Would it be better if the token manager performed this conversion and supplied the resulting int value to the parser via the token object the token manager returns?

18. Would the program in Figure 10.10 work correctly if it used the following version of the getNextChar() method:

```
private void getNextChar()
{
   if (currentColumn = inputLine.length())
     if (inFile.hasNextLine())
     {
        inputLine = inFile.nextLine();
        currentLine++;
        currentColumn = 0;
        currentChar = inputLine.charAt(currentColumn++);
     }
     else
        currentChar = EOF;
   else
     currentChar = inputLine.charAt(currentColumn++);
}
```

19. Convert the following grammar to a translation grammar that translates each input string to its maximum nesting level:

1. S → (S)
2. S → λ

For example, the null string should be translated to 0; the string "(())" should be translated to 2.

Provide three translations grammars: (1) Count the left parentheses as you recurse "down" to the center of the input string. As you recurse "up", return the final count. (2) Count the right parentheses as you recurse "up". (3) Like approach 1, except do not return the final count as you recurse "up". Instead, display the final count when you reach the center of the string.

20. Implement the parser/translators for your answers in problem 19. Test with the input strings λ, ( ), (( )), ((, and ( )).

21. Implement the parser/translator corresponding to G10.4. Test your program with the input strings b, +bc, +b* cd, +* /−bbcde, +b, +bcd, and λ.

22. Convert G10.8 to a translation grammar that translates prefix expressions to infix expressions.

23. Implement the parser/translatior for your answer in problem 22. Test with the input strings b, c, d, +bc, /cd, +b+cd, * b−cd.

24. Write a translation grammar that defines b* dd* and translates each input string by outputting each b in the input but only the first d. For example, bbdd should be translated to bbd, and ddd should be translated to d.

25. Why is the getToken() method in Figure 10.10 in the parser rather than in the token manager? What does it do?

26. Why are tokens chained by the parser in Figure 10.10 rather than by the token manager?

11

ASSEMBLY LANGUAGE

11.1 INTRODUCTION

The only instructions the *central processing unit* (CPU) of a computer can directly execute are *machine language instructions. Assembly language instructions* are essentially machine language instructions written in symbolic form. Before the CPU can execute a program written in assembly language, the program must be assembled, that is, translated to a machine language program. We call the program that translates assembly language to machine language an *assembler.*

Compilers typically translate the source programs they input to an assembly language, and then translate the assembly language to machine language using an internal assembler. The compilers that we will write, however, will simply translate to assembly language. We will then use an external assembler to translate to machine language.

Each computer type has its own unique machine language and corresponding assembly language. Our compilers will translate to the assembly language for the *J1 computer.* The J1 computer is well suited to our purposes for several reasons. First, its assembly language is easy to learn. Second, the J1 Software Package that accompanies this textbook will make your computer act like a J1 computer. Thus, you will be able to execute J1 programs on your own computer. Third, the J1 Software Package has several features that we will put to good use. For example, it can determine if the compilers you write are working correctly.

11.2 STRUCTURE OF THE J1 COMPUTER

The J1 computer consists of a central processing unit (CPU), main memory, a keyboard input device, and a display output device. The two principal registers in the CPU are the *pc* (program counter) register and the *sp* (stack pointer) register (see Figure 11.1). A *register* in the J1 computer is a memory area within the CPU that can hold 16 bits of information.

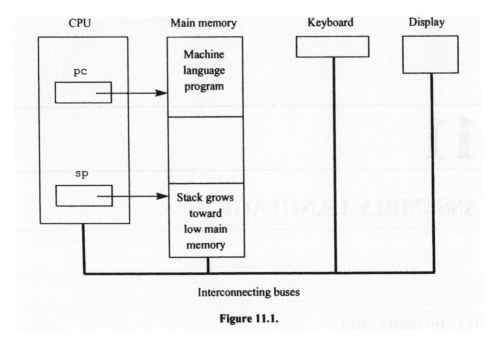

Interconnecting buses

Figure 11.1.

The pc register points to (i.e., contains the address of) the machine instruction in main memory that the CPU will execute next. The sp register points to the top of the stack in main memory. The stack grows downward in main memory. That is, as items are pushed onto the stack, the top of the stack moves toward location 0 in main memory. Figure 11.2 shows the stack before and after the value 5 is pushed onto the stack. Notice that the top of the stack is at location 711 before the push and 710 after the push.

Main memory consists of 4096 cells, each 16 bits wide. Thus, main memory addresses run from 0 to 4095 in decimal. 4095 in decimal equals 111111111111 in binary—a 12-bit number.

Because an address in the J1 computer is only 12 bits wide, only the rightmost 12 bits of the pc and sp registers are needed to hold an address. J1 ignores the leftmost four bits of these registers.

The *word size* of the J1 computer is 16 bits. That is, the circuits in the CPU of the J1 computer operate on data items that are 16 bits wide. A *word* is any 16-bit item stored in the J1 computer. Because each register and each memory location is 16 bits wide, each can hold exactly one word.

11.3 MACHINE LANGUAGE INSTRUCTIONS

Most machine instructions on the J1 computer consist of an opcode followed by either the address of an operand or by the operand itself. The *opcode* specifies the operation (add, subtract, multiply, etc.) that the CPU is to perform. The *operand* is the item on which the instruction operates. For example, in the following machine language instruction,

12-bit address of the operand

4-bit opcode for push

Before

Main memory

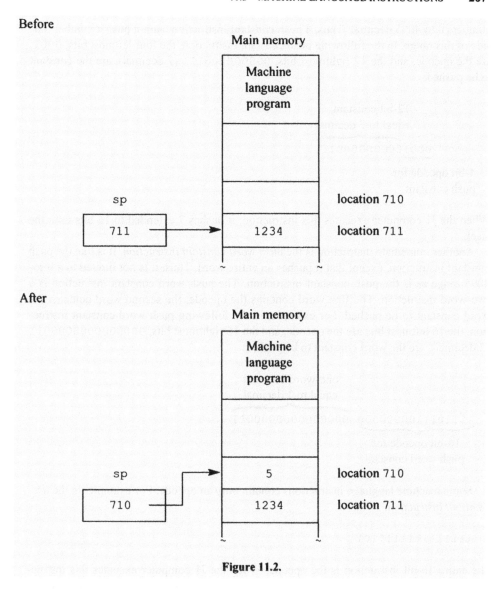

Figure 11.2.

the first four bits, 0000, is the opcode. This particular opcode specifies the *push* operation. The 12 bits to the right of the opcode in the machine instruction (000000000100
in this example, which equals 4 decimal), is the main memory address of the operand.
When the J1 computer executes this instruction, it goes to location 4 in main memory,
makes a copy of the 16-bit word at that location, and then pushes the copy onto the
stack.

Some machine language instructions contain the operand itself rather than the address
of the operand. For example, in the *push constant instruction,* the operand to be pushed is
in the instruction itself. Thus, the operand is "immediately" available to the CPU once the
machine instruction is in the CPU. Accordingly, we call the push constant instruction an
immediate instruction, that is, an instruction that contains the operand rather than the address of the operand. In the push constant instruction, the four leftmost bits are the opcode, leaving the 12 rightmost bits for the operand. With 12 bits, we can represent the

numbers 0 to 4095 decimal. Thus, a push constant instruction cannot push a number outside of this range. In the following push constant instruction, the four leftmost bits, 0001, are the opcode, and the 12 rightmost bits, 000000000111 (7 decimal), are the constant to be pushed:

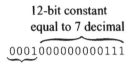

When the J1 computer executes this instruction, it pushes 7 extended to 16 bits onto the stack.

Another immediate instruction is the *push word constant instruction*. It is like the push constant instruction, except that it pushes an entire word. Thus, it is not limited to a 0-to-4095 range as is the push constant instruction. The push word constant instruction is a two-word instruction. The first word contains the opcode; the second word contains the word constant to be pushed. For example, in the following push word constant instruction, the 16 leftmost bits are the opcode, and the 16 rightmost bits, 0000000000000011 (3 decimal), are the word constant to be pushed:

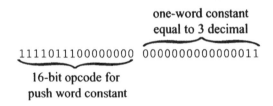

Some machine language instructions contain only an opcode. For example, in the *decimal out instruction,*

1111111111111101

the entire 16-bit instruction is the opcode. When the J1 computer executes this instruction, it pops the binary number on top of the stack, converts it to decimal, and displays it on the display monitor. Another instruction with a 16-bit opcode is the *halt instruction:*

1111111111111111

This instruction causes a program to terminate execution.

11.4   ASSEMBLY LANGUAGE INSTRUCTIONS

A useful reference at this point is Appendix A. This appendix also appears in the file stack.txt in the J1 Software Package. It describes the instruction set for the J1 computer. We call this instruction set the *stack instruction set* because its instructions make use of a stack. Its basic structure is similar to that of the Java Virtual Machine (the virtual machine on which Java programs execute).

Assembly language instructions are symbolic forms of machine language instructions. For example, the following assembly language instructions correspond to the machine instructions we discussed in the preceding section:

```
p        4        ; push the word at address 4
pc       7        ; push 7
pwc      3        ; push 3
dout              ; pop and display
halt              ; terminate program
```

In assembly language, we use a *mnemonic* (an easy-to-remember name) in place of the opcode, and a decimal number in place of a binary constant or address. The mnemonics for the push, push constant, push word constant, decimal out, and halt instructions are p, pc, pwc, dout, and halt, respectively. We start single-line comments in the assembly language for the J1 computer with the semicolon. We, however, can also start a single-line comment with either a single slash or, as in Java, with double slashes.

In assembly language, we can specify data as well as instructions. For example, the following assembly language statement defines a data word (dw stands for "define word") that contains the binary number equivalent to 15 decimal:

```
dw       15
```

The assembler translates this statement to 0000000000001111, the 16-bit binary number equal to 15 decimal.

The J1 computer cannot execute a program in assembly language form. It can execute only machine language instructions. Thus, to execute an assembly language program, we first have to translate it to a machine language program. We, however, do not have to do this translation ourselves. A computer program, called an assembler, will do it for us.

11.5 PUSHING CHARACTERS

The J1 computer uses ASCII to represent characters. In ASCII, each character is represented by a unique number. For example, 'A' is represented by 65, 'B' by 66, 'C' by 67, and '\n' (the newline character) by 10. Thus, to push a character onto the stack, we simply push the number that represents it using a pc instruction. For example, to push '\n', we can use

```
pc       10
```

A better approach, however, is to specify the character itself in the pc instruction. That way, we do not have to remember the ASCII codes for the characters we want to push. For example, to push '\n', we can use

```
pc       '\n'
```

When the assembler translates this instruction to machine code, it replaces the character '\n' with 10, its ASCII code.

The ASCII codes ranges from 0 to 127. Thus, they are all within the 0-to-4095 range of the pc instruction.

11.6 aout INSTRUCTION

When the aout (ASCII out) instruction is executed, an ASCII code should already be on top of the stack. The aout instruction pops this ASCII code and displays its corresponding character if it is displayable. If, however, the code is for a control character (such as newline), then the indicated control operation is performed. For example, the following sequence displays A:

```
        pc       'A'          ; push 'A' onto the stack
        aout                  ; pop and display ASCII
```

Note that we get a different result if we use dout in place of aout:

```
        pc       'A'          ; push 'A' onto the stack
        dout                  ; pop and display decimal code
```

dout displays in decimal the value of the item popped from the stack. Thus, this sequence displays 65, the ASCII code for 'A'.

The sequence

```
        pc       '\n'         ; push newline character
        aout                  ; pop and move cursor
```

causes the cursor on the display screen to move to the beginning of the next line on the screen.

11.7 USING LABELS

In assembly language, we can use a label to represent the location (i.e., the address) of a line of code. For example, consider the program in Figure 11.3. The label x at the beginning of the third line (the dw statement) represents the address of that line. Addresses start at 0 and increase by one for each line of code. Thus, the address corresponding to the label x in Figure 11.3 is 2.

A label is a *symbolic address*. In Figure 11.3, x is a symbolic address that corresponds to the *absolute address* 2. When the assembler translates an assembly statement to machine language, it translates labels to their corresponding absolute addresses. It also translates mnemonics to their corresponding opcodes. For example, in Figure 11.3, the assembler would translate p and x in the first instruction to 0000 (the opcode for p) and 000000000010 (the absolute address of x) to get the machine instruction 0000000000000010. When this instruction is executed, it pushes the value at address 2 (which is 12) onto the stack.

```
        p       x        ; this instruction is at address 0
        halt             ; this instruction is at address 1
x:      dw      12       ; this data item is at address 2
```

Figure 11.3.

We can also write the p instruction in Figure 11.3 as

```
        p         2
```

in which case we would not need the label x on the dw statement. However, the version that uses the label x is better because we then do not have to determine the address of the operand. The assembler will do that for us. Because the program in Figure 11.3 is so short, it is easy to determine that the operand 12 is at the address 2. However, if the program were long and the operand 12 appeared at its end, it would be far more difficult to determine the address of the operand (we would have to count all the lines of code up to the operand). Fortunately, we do not have to determine the addresses of operands. We simply use labels. Then the assembler determines their addresses for us.

The label x does not convey any information about the constant it labels. A better approach is to use labels on constants that do provide useful information. Accordingly, for a nonnegative integer constant, we will use a label that starts with "@" followed by the number written in decimal; for a negative integer constant, we will use a label that starts with "@_" followed by the absolute value of the number written in decimal. For example, to define the constants 3 and −3 in an assembly language program, we will use

```
@3:         dw          3
@_3:        dw          -3
```

If we then see the labels @3 or @_3 in a program, we will immediately know their corresponding values. We will not have to search for their dw statements to determine their values.

A label at the beginning of a statement must be separated from the rest of the statement with a colon. The label/colon pair can either appear on the statement to which it applies or it can precede it. For example, in the following code, the label start precedes the p instruction, but nevertheless, applies to it:

```
start:
        p         x
```

This code is equivalent to

```
start:    p         x
```

We can also use multiple labels for one statement, as long as each one is on a different line. For example, in the following code, the labels dog, cat, and bird all apply to the p instruction:

```
dog:
cat:
bird:     p         x
```

The following format, however, is illegal:

```
dog: cat: bird:    p         x          ; illegal format
```

The mnemonic and the operand of an instruction must be on the same line. Thus, the following format is illegal:

```
        p
                    x               ; illegal format
```

The columns in which the parts of an assembly language instruction start are not critical. However, to make our programs easy to read, we will always start a label/colon sequence in column 1, a mnemonic in column 11, and the operand or operand address in column 21.

Labels may consists any sequence of letters, digits, "@", "$", and "_" that does not start with a digit.

11.8   USING THE ASSEMBLER

Let us write, assemble, and run a simple assembly language program that adds 1, 2, and 4 and displays the result. To add 1, 2, and 4, we have to push them on the stack. To do this, we can use the p instruction, the pc instruction, or the pwc instruction. To illustrate all three approaches, we will use the p, pc, and pwc instruction to push 1, 2, and 4, respectively (see Figure 11.4).

In this program, we first push 1 (with a p instruction) and 2 (with a pc instruction). Next we add these two numbers with the add instruction. This instruction pops the top two items, adds them, and pushes the sum back onto the stack. Next we push 4 with the pwc instruction. Thus, the stack now has two items: 4 and 3 (the 3 is the sum of 1 and 2 from the add instruction). When we execute the second add instruction, the 4 and 3 are popped and added. The sum, 7, is pushed back onto the stack. dout then pops and displays this result. The second pc instruction pushes the newline character onto the stack. The aout instruction then pops the newline character and moves the cursor to the beginning of the next line. Finally, the halt instruction terminates execution.

Suppose the current directory on your computer system is the directory that contains the J1 Software Package. The file fig1104.a in this directory contains the program in Figure 11.4. We can assemble fig1104.a by entering

```
    a fig1104.a
```

a is the name of the assembler in the J1 Software Package. If you are using a non-Microsoft system and it cannot find the a program, try entering

```
    ./a fig1104.a
```

The leading period (which represents the current directory) in this command forces your operating system to search for the a program in your current directory (see the file readme.txt in the J1 Software Package for more details).

When you invoke the a assembler program with one of the commands above, it reads in fig1104.a and outputs the corresponding machine language program to the file fig1104.e. We use the extension ".a" for files containing assembly language code, and ".e" for files containing executable machine code. You must specify the ".a" extension on the input file name when you invoke a. Thus, you may not enter

```
    a fig1104   <-- wrong because missing the ".a" extension
```

In addition to an ".e" file (which contains the executable machine code), the a program outputs a list file whose base name matches the base name of the input file and whose ex-

```
              p          @1     ; push 1
              pc         2       ; push 2
              add                ; pop twice,add,push
              pwc        4       ; push 4
              add                ; pop twice,add,push
              dout               ; pop and display
              pc         '\n' ; push newline
              aout               ; pop and output
              halt               ; terminate
      @1:     dw         1       ; data
```

Figure 11.4.

tension is ".lst". For example, if the input file is fig1104.a, then the assembler produces the list file fig1104.lst. List files produced by the a program show the assembly language source code and its corresponding addresses and machine code (see Figure
11.5).

To execute the program in fig1104.e (the executable file produced by the assembler
when it assembles fig1104.a), we enter either

    e fig1104

or

    e fig1104.e

```
a Assembler Version 1.7     Mon Mar 07 14:50:21 2011


     LOC     MACHINE       ASSEMBLY
   hex*dec   CODE          CODE


   0  *0     000A          p          @1    ; push 1
   1  *1     1002          pc         2      ; push 2
   2  *2     F100          add               ; pop twice, add, push
   3  *3     F700          pwc        4      ; push 4
   4  *4     0004
   5  *5     F100          add               ; pop twice, add, push
   6  *6     FFFD          dout              ; pop and display
   7  *7     100A          pc         '\n' ; push newline
   8  *8     FFFB          aout              ; pop and output
   9  *9     FFFF          halt              ; terminate
   A  *10    0001   @1:    dw         1      ; data
   B  *11    ========= end of fig1104.a =========================

asm in  = fig1104.a
asm out = fig1104.e
asm lst = fig1104.lst
```

Figure 11.5.

On a non-Microsoft system, if your operating system cannot find the e program, try entering . /e in place of e in the commands above. e is the program in the J1 Software Package that makes your computer act like the J1 computer.

The first time you run e, it will start by prompting you for your family name, first name, and middle initial. After you enter this information (you may omit the middle initial), e runs the program in fig1104.e, the effect of which is to display 7 on the screen. e also creates a log file named fig1104.*<family name>*.log, that contains a record of the run (see Figure 11.6). The *<family name>* component of the log file name is the family name that you enter when you run e for the first time.

The log file shows your name, the results of your run, and some statistics on your program. Machine code size is the number of words in the executable program. Machine inst count is the total number of machine instructions executed. Execution time is a precise relative measure of the execution time of the program. Because the actual execution time depends on the computer on which you are running e, this statistic provides only a relative measure of execution time. For example, suppose you have a program whose execution time statistic is 100. You then modify this program so that its execution time statistic becomes 50. This new statistic indicates that your modified program runs in exactly half the time as the original.

You can also run fig1104.e with the following command:

```
e fig1104 /c
```

The /c command line argument causes e to check your program in addition to running it. However, you can specify /c only if a check file is available for the program you are running. A check file name has the extension ".chk". Its base name should match the base name of its corresponding program. For example, the check file for fig1104.e is fig1104.chk. Because fig1104.chk is in the J1 Software Package, we can use /c when we run fig1104.e. Figure 11.7 shows the log file that e creates when we invoke it with /c. It includes the output generated by fig1104.e, enclosed within two lines of

```
e Version 1.7
Log file fig1104.dosreis.log

Your name:          DosReis Anthony J
Machinecode file:   fig1104.e

=================== Thu Jul 28 12:30:34 2011 ==============r
7


================================================================r

Report for:         DosReis Anthony J
Program output:     not tested
Machine code size:  11
Machine inst count: 9
Execution time:     101

================ r(d24b) terminated Thu Jul 28 12:30:34 2011
```

Figure 11.6.

```
e Version 1.7
Log file fig1104.dosreis.log

Your name:          DosReis Anthony J
Machinecode file:   fig1104.e
Check file:         fig1104.chk
Check data:         fa89 11 9 101 d227


=================== Thu Jul 28 12:33:01 2011 ===============r
7


============================================================r


Report for:         DosReis Anthony J
Program output:     correct
Machine code size:  11      (at limit)
Machine inst count: 9       (at limit)
Execution time:     101     (at limit)


================ r(03f5) terminated Thu Jul 28 12:33:01 2011
```

Figure 11.7.

equal signs. It also shows an evaluation of fig1104.e (which is also written to the log file), indicating whether its output is correct, and how its machine code size, machine instruction count, and execution time compare with predetermined limits. For this program, the limit on the machine code size is 11. The line

```
Machine code size:   11      (at limit)
```

indicates that the machine code size of the program is 11 and this size is at the limit, that is, it is equal to the predetermined limit. e would flag any machine code size above 11 with a warning message OVER LIMIT. For example, Figure ·11.8 shows the results e would display if fig1104.e were completely substandard, that is, if it produced incorrect output, and had a machine code size, machine instruction count, and execution time that exceeded their limits.

11.9 stav INSTRUCTION

We use the stav instruction to store a value into a memory location. For example, consider the program in Figure 11.9. Before we use the stav instruction, we have to push the address at which we want to store and the value to be stored, *in that order.* To push the address of x (which is 4), we use

```
pc        x
```

Recall from Section 11.7 that the assembler translates labels to their corresponding absolute addresses. Thus, the assembler translates this instruction to a machine instruction in which the rightmost 12 is the *address of* x. When the pc machine instruction is execut-

```
e Version 1.7
Log file fig1104.dosreis.log

Your name:           DosReis Anthony J
Machinecode file:    fig1104.e
Check file:          fig1104.chk
Check data:          fa89 11 9 101 d227

=================== Thu Jul 28 12:33:01 2011 ==============r
10


===========================================================r

Report for:          DosReis Anthony J
Program output:      NOT CORRECT                  <----- ERROR
Machine code size:   13      (2    OVER LIMIT ) <----- WARNING
Machine inst count:  11      (2    OVER LIMIT ) <----- WARNING
Execution time:      106     (5    OVER LIMIT ) <----- WARNING

================ r(03f5) terminated Thu Jul 28 12:33:01 2011
```

Figure 11.8.

ed, it pushes this address. Addresses can range from 0 to 4095. Thus, they are always within the 0-to-4095 range of the pc instruction.

> The pc instruction is, in effect, a push address instruction when its operand is a label.

After we push the address at which we want to store, we push the value we want to store. To push the value of y (which is 77), we use

```
        p           y
```

We now are ready to use the stav instruction to perform the store operation. When executed, it pops the value and address from the stack. It then stores the popped value into the location corresponding to the popped address. In Figure 11.9, the stav instruction pops 77 (the value of y) and 4 (the address of x), and then stores the 77 at location 4 in main memory.

It is easy to remember that the stav instruction requires the address and value to be pushed in that order. The "av" in the mnemonic stav indicates the required order: first "a" (the address), then "v" (the value).

```
        pc      x       ; push address of x
        p       y       ; push value of y
        stav            ; pop and store
        halt
x:      dw      0
y:      dw      77
```

Figure 11.9.

11.10   COMPILING AN ASSIGNMENT STATEMENT

Let us look at the code that corresponds to the following assignment statements:

```
b = 5000;
c = -3;
d = b + c + 7000;
```

First, we have to push the address of b onto the stack. We need the address of b on the stack so we can assign it a value with the stav instruction. Suppose b corresponds to the address 8. Then to push the address of b, we can use the following pc instruction,

```
pc          8           ; push the address of b
```

which pushes 8 (the address of b) onto the stack. However, it is better to use

```
pc          b           ; push the address of b
```

With this form, we do not have to determine the actual address that corresponds to b; the assembler does it for us. When the assembler translates this instruction, it replaces b (a symbolic address) with 8 (the absolute address of b). Thus, both instructions above yield the same machine instruction.

After pushing the address of b, we push the value of the right side of the assignment statement with

```
pwc         5000        ; push 5000 onto the stack
```

We cannot use a pc instruction here because 5000 is out of its range. To complete the assignment statement, we execute

```
stav                    ; pop twice and store 5000 in b
```

The stav instruction pops the value and the address from the stack, and then stores the value in the location specified by the address. Thus for this example, it stores 5000 in b.

We handle the next assignment statement

```
c = -3;
```

in the same way with

```
pc          c           ; push the address of c
pwc         -3          ; push -3
stav                    ; pop twice and store -3 in c
```

For the third assignment statement,

```
d = b + c + 7000;
```

we first push the address of d:

```
pc          d
```

Next, we have to perform the computation specified by the right side of the assignment statement. This computation will occur at the top of the stack, just above the address of d that we just pushed. To perform the indicated computation, we use the following sequence of push and add operations:

```
p        b          ; push the value of b
p        c          ; push the value of c
add                 ; pop twice, add, push
pwc      7000       ; push 7000
add                 ; pop twice, add, push
```

The two p instructions push the values of b and c. The first add instruction then pops and adds these values and places the result back on the stack. We then push 7000 with the pwc instruction. Thus, when we execute the second add instruction, the top two items on the stack are 7000 and the sum of b and c. This add instruction pops these two items, adds them, and pushes the result back onto the stack. At this point, the top of the stack has the sum of b, c, and 7000. Just below the top is the address of d (pushed there by the initial pc instruction). To complete the assignment, we execute the stav instruction:

```
stav                ; pop twice and store result
```

This instruction pops the value on top of the stack and the address below it and then places the popped value into the main memory location specified by the popped address.

A program containing the assembly language code above would also have a dw statement for b, c, and d. These dw statements would appear at the end of the program after the halt instruction:

```
         halt               ; terminate
b:       dw        0        ; create b variable
c:       dw        0        ; create c variable
d:       dw        0        ; create d variable
```

Figure 11.10 shows the complete sequence of assembly code needed for our three assignment statements, along with some informative comments.

To perform subtraction, multiplication, and division on the J1 computer, we have the sub, mult, and div instructions, respectively. These instructions are similar to the add instruction. Each pops the two top items from the stack, performs a computation on them, and pushes the result back onto the stack. For example, the assignment statement

```
f = b*c - d/e;
```

corresponds to the following assembly instructions:

```
pc       f          ; push the address of f
p        b          ; push the value of b
p        c          ; push the value of c
mult                ; pop twice, mult, push
p        d          ; push the value of d
p        e          ; push the value of e
div                 ; pop twice, div, push
```

```
                ;  b = 5000;
        pc          b           ; push the address of b
        pwc         5000        ; push 5000
        stav                    ; pop twice and store 5000 in b


                ;  c =      -3;
        pc          c           ; push the address of c
        pwc         -3          ; push -3
        stav                    ; pop twice and store -3 in c


                ;  d = b + c + 7000;
        pc          d           ; push the address of d
        p           b           ; push the value of b
        p           c           ; push the value of c
        add                     ; pop twice, add, push
        pwc         7000        ; push 7000
        add                     ; pop twice, add, push
        stav                    ; store result in d


        halt                    ; terminate execution
b:      dw          0           ; create b variable
c:      dw          0           ; create c variable
d:      dw          0           ; create d variable
```

Figure 11.10.

```
        sub                     ; pop twice, sub, push
        stav                    ; store result in f
        halt
b:      dw          0
c:      dw          0
d:      dw          0
e:      dw          0
f:      dw          0
```

Exercise 11.1

Write the assembly language statements that correspond to the following statements:

```
        x = b + -20 + c;
```

Answer:

```
        pc          x
        p           b
        pwc         -20
        add
        p           c
        add
        stav
        halt
```

```
x:          dw          x
b:          dw          0
c:          dw          0
```

■

11.11 COMPILING print AND println

The print and println statements output values to the display screen. For example,

```
print(q);
```

displays the value of q in decimal on the current line of the display, and

```
println(q);
```

similarly displays the value of q but also outputs a newline character, causing the cursor to move to the beginning of the next line on the display. These statements have the following assembly code counterparts. For

```
print(q);
```

we have

```
        p           q
        dout
```

For

```
println(q);
```

we have

```
        p           q
        dout
        pc          '\n'
        aout
```

Exercise 11.2

Write an assembly language statements that correspond to the following statements:

```
x = (b+c)* (d+e)  -  f/g;
println(x);
```

Answer:

```
        pc          x
        p           b
        p           c
        add
        p           d
```

```
        p           e
        add
        mult
        p           f
        p           g
        div
        sub
        stav

        p           x
        dout
        pc          '\n'
        aout

        halt
x:      dw          0
b:      dw          0
c:      dw          0
d:      dw          0
e:      dw          0
f:      dw          0
g:      dw          0
```

■

11.12 OUTPUTTING STRINGS

Strings in an assembly language program are defined with dw statements. For example, to define the string "Dog" and label it with @L0, use

```
@L0:       dw              "Dog"
```

This single statement is translated to four consecutive words: one word for the ASCII code of each character in the string plus a fourth word at the end that holds the null character. The null character (a word with all zero bits) marks the end of the string. The label is optional.

When the assembler translates assembly code to machine code, it replaces labels with absolute addresses. Thus, for the pc instruction in the following program,

```
        pc          @L0     ; pushes the address of @L0
        sout                ; outputs the string "Dog"
        halt
@L0:    dw          "Dog"   ; address of this dw is 3
```

the assembler will output a machine instruction consisting of the opcode for the pc instruction and the address corresponding to the label @L0 (which is 3 in this example). Thus, the immediate operand that the pc instruction pushes is the address of @L0 (which is the address of the string "Dog"). The sout (string out) instruction then pops this address and outputs the string that starts at this address to the display monitor. Thus, in this example, it outputs Dog.

In the example above, we placed the `dw` statement for the string constant, `"Dog"`, at the bottom of the program, out of the flow of control. It would be wrong to place the `dw` statement between the `sout` and `halt` instructions, like so:

```
            pc          @L0
            sout
@L0:        dw          "Dog"       ; WRONG!   CPU will execute.
            halt
```

If we did this, the program would assemble without error. However, during its execution, the CPU would attempt to fetch and execute the string constant `"Dog"` because it is in the "flow of control." To avoid this problem, we must position the `dw` statement in the program so that it cannot be executed by the CPU. Placing it after the `halt` instruction, as we did in the correct version, satisfies this requirement. Another alternative, however, is to precede the label on the `dw` statement with the caret symbol `"^"`. When the assembler scans a line with a caret, it automatically places that line at the end of the program, out of the flow of control. For example, in the following program, the string `"Dog"` appears in line with instructions:

```
            pc          @L0
            sout
^@L0:       dw          "Dog"
            halt
```

However, because of the caret on the label `@L0`, the assembler places the string at the end of the machine language program, after the `halt` instruction. The list file that the assembler produces (the file with the `".lst"` extension) shows the string in the position it occupies in the machine language program (see Figure 11.11). Note that the string constant `"Dog"` appears after the `halt` instruction.

```
    a Assembler Version 1.7      Thu Jul 28 12:39:18 2011


    LOC     MACHINE         ASSEMBLY
   hex* dec  CODE            CODE


    0  *0    1003            pc          @L0
    1  *1    FFF7            sout
    2  *2    FFFF            halt
                        ;===================== ^-lines follow ======
    3  *3    0044   @L0:     dw          "Dog"
    4  *4    006F
    5  *5    0067
    6  *6    0000
    7  *7    ========= end of fig1111.a ========================

    asm in  = fig1111.a
    asm out = fig1111.e
    asm lst = fig1111.lst
```

Figure 11.11.

Let us examine some statements that output a string, along with the corresponding assembly code. The following statements

```
y = -2;
x = y;
print("x = ");
println(x);
```

output

```
x = -2
```

The `print` statement outputs the string `"x = "` but does not advance to the next line. Thus, the `println` statement outputs the value of x on the same line and then advances to the next line. The corresponding assembly code is in Figure 11.12. The string `"x = "` is defined with a `dw` statement. The `pc-sout` sequence outputs this string.

We will follow the convention of labeling strings with labels that start with `"@L"` followed by sequence numbers starting from 0. That is, we will use the labels `@L0`, `@L1`, `@L2`, and so on.

11.13 INPUTTING DECIMAL NUMBERS

The `din` (decimal in) inputs decimal numbers from the keyboard. `din` converts the number entered on the keyboard from decimal to binary and pushes the binary value onto the

```
         pc      y              ; y = -2
         pwc     -2
         stav

         pc      x              ; x = y;
         p       y
         stav

         pc      @L0            ; print("x = ");
         sout
^@L0:    dw      "x = "

         p       x              ; println(x);
         dout
         pc      '\n'
         aout                   ; advance cursor to next line

         halt
y:       dw      0
x:       dw      0
```

Figure 11.12.

stack. Let us look at an example that reads in a decimal number and stores it in the location whose label is x. We first push the address of x with

```
        pc          x
```

We do this because we ultimately want to store a value into x using the stav instruction. So we need to push the address of x onto the stack. Next, we read in a decimal number and push its binary equivalent onto the stack with

```
        din
```

After the din executes, the inputted value in binary is on top of the stack with the address of x right below it. Thus, if we then execute

```
        stav
```

the inputted value is stored in x.

Whenever we use din, we should precede it with the instructions that display an appropriate prompt message to inform the user that keyboard input is expected. For example, the following sequence of instructions displays a prompt message ("Enter integer\n") and reads in a decimal value into x:

```
        pc          @L0         ; push address of prompt message
        sout                    ; display prompt message
^@L0:   dw          "Enter integer\n"
        pc          x           ; push address of x
        din                     ; input decimal number
        stav                    ; store inputted value in x
```

We included the newline character ('\n') at the end of the prompt message to force the user input to start on the next line. Thus, when this sequence is executed, the display would look like this (assuming we enter 23):

```
Enter integer
23
```

If, however, we define the prompt message with

```
^@L0:      dw          "Enter integer: "
```

then the display would look like this:

```
Enter integer: 23
```

Either approach works well.

11.14 ENTRY DIRECTIVE

In all the assembly language programs we have examined so far, execution starts at the physical beginning of the corresponding machine code. For example, the execution of the machine code corresponding to the following assembly program starts with the initial p instruction.

```
            p        x        // execution starts here
            p        y
            add
            dout
            halt
   x:       dw       3
   y:       dw       4
```

We call the location within a program at which execution starts its *entry point.*

Using the *entry directive,* we can specify any entry point we want. For example, the entry directive in the following program indicates that execution should start at the label cat (which is at the first p instruction following the x and y data):

```
            entry    cat         ; specifies entry point
   x:       dw       3
   y:       dw       4
   cat:     p        x
            p        y
            add
            dout
            halt
```

If we omit the entry directive in this program, the CPU would start execution at the the physical beginning of the program. That is, it would attempt to execute the data at x as if it were an instruction.

An entry directive can appear on any line in a program. In the example above, we placed it at the very beginning. Alternatively, we could have placed it at the end or anywhere in between.

11.15   MORE ASSEMBLY LANGUAGE

In the next chapter, we will write our first serious compiler. It translates simple assignment and println statements to the assembly code. We will call this first compiler S1. Because we already know enough assembly for S1, we will dispense for now with our investigation of assembly language. As we develop more powerful compilers in later chapters, we will concurrently learn the additional assembly language required by those compilers.

PROBLEMS

1. Translate to an assembly language program:

```
b = 1;
c = 2;
e = 3;
d = b - c;
e = e*e/d;
```

```
println(b);
println(c);
println(d);
println(e);
```

Do not optimize. For example, do not initialize b, c, and e to 1, 2, and 3, respectively, in their dw statements. Instead, initialize them to 0 in their dw statements. Place your program in a file named p1101.a. Assemble and run with

```
a p1101.a
e p1101 /c
```

2. Assemble and run the following program. What happens?

```
start:          pc          5
                dout
                ja          start
```

The ja instruction is the "jump always" instruction.

3. Translate the following statements to assembly language. Do not optimize. For example, for the first statement, you should provide assembly code that performs all the specified additions. Specifically, after pushing the address of x, push the operands, 1, 2, ..., 10. Then perform the specified additions, followed by a stav instruction. Use the pc instruction to push each constant.

```
x = (1 + (2 + (3 + (4 + (5 + (6 + (7 + (8 + (9 + 10)))))))));
print("x = ");
println(x);
```

Place your program in a file name p1103.a. Assemble and run with

```
a p1103.a
e p1103 /c
```

Change your program so that it pushes the constants with the pwc instruction instead of the pc instruction. Assemble and run. Compare the two log file reports. Which version is better? Why?

4. Translate the following statements to assembly language. Do not optimize. For example, for the first statement, you should provide assembly code that performs all the specified additions. Specifically, after pushing the address of x, push 1 and 2, then add. Then push 3 and add. Continue in this fashion until all ten numbers have been added. Use the pwc instruction to push the constants.

```
x = 1 + 2 + 3 + 4 + 5 + 6 + 7 + 8 + 9 + 10;
print("x = ");
println(x);
```

Place your program in a file name p1104.a. Assemble and run with

```
a p1104.a
e p1104 /c
```

5. Compare the efficiencies of the assembly language programs for problems 3 and 4. Are they different?

6. Assemble and run the following program. What happens? Why?

```
dout
halt
```

7. Which bits of the `sp` register are used to determine where in memory an item is pushed? All 16 bits?

8. The stack pointer initially contains 0. What is the address of the memory location that receives the first value pushed? Hint: the stack pointer is decremented by 1 before each push operation.

9. Without using the `mult` instructions, write the most efficient assembly language sequence you can that multiplies 23 by 48 and displays the result. Display the result with no newline after the result and with no labels. Assemble and run with

```
a p1109.a
e p1109 /c
```

Hint: You may want to use the `dupe` instruction. It duplicates the top of the stack. For example, if 5 is on top of the stack and you execute `dupe`, then an additional 5 is pushed onto the stack.

10. Which instruction below is better? Why?

```
pc          5
```

or

```
p           @5
```

where @5 is defined with

```
@5:         dw          5
```

Which instruction below is better? Why?

```
pwc         5
```

or

```
p           @5
```

where @5 is defined shown above.

11. Write an assembly language program that prompts the user for two integers, adds the two integers, and displays the sum. Your program should produce output that looks exactly like that in the sample session below:

```
Enter integer
1
Enter integer
2
Sum = 3
```

After outputting the sum, your program should position the cursor at the beginning of the line that follows the sum. Place your program in a file name `p1111.a`. Assemble and run with

```
a    p1111.a
e    p1111 /c
```

12. Suppose you delete the `entry` directive in the program in Section 11.14. What happens when the program is executed?

12

S1—A SIMPLE COMPILER

12.1 INTRODUCTION

In this chapter, we design and implement a simple compiler that translates assignment and `println` statements to the assembly language of the J1 computer. Our compiler is modest on two counts. First, the source language it processes is very restricted. Second, it makes no attempt to produce the optimal assembly code. We want our compiler to be as simple as possible because it is our first compiler for a programming language. We call this compiler S1. "S" in "S1" stands for the stack instruction set—the instruction set of the J1 computer.

Although S1 is quite simple, it, nevertheless, provides us with a base on which we can build. Once we understand its structure and operation, we can add to it, ultimately producing a compiler for a full-fledged programming language.

12.2 THE SOURCE LANGUAGE

Before we define a grammar for the source language, let us look at the following sample program:

```
x = 5000;
y = x*2 + -10;
println(y + 3);
```

This program uses two variables, x and y. Note that the program does not contain any declarations for x and y. We do not need variable declarations because all variables in our source language have the same type, namely, `int`. That is, they hold signed integers. The initial value of all variables is 0.

The expressions that appear on the right side of assignment statements and within the `println` statements are limited to the operations of addition and multiplication. Unary plus and minus are *not* supported. Thus, the following statements are illegal:

```
x = +y;          ◄——————— unary plus not legal
x = x + -y;      ◄——————— unary minus not legal
```

However, constants can be signed. For example, the following statements are legal:

```
x = +5;
x = x + -20;
```

The `println` statement must have exactly one argument. Thus, the following statements are all legal:

```
println(5);
println(5 + 20);
println(y);
println(x + y + -3);
```

but these statements are illegal:

```
println();          ◄──────── null argument list not legal
println(x, y);      ◄──────── more than one argument not legal
```

An identifier for a variable must be a sequence of letters and/or digits, it must start with a letter, and it must not be a keyword word (the only keyword in our source language is `println`).

Programs can have zero or more statements. A program with zero statements is translated to an assembly language program that contains only the `halt` instruction.

12.3   GRAMMAR FOR SOURCE LANGUAGE

Now let us write a grammar that defines our source language. We will use `program` for the start symbol. Because a program consists of a list of statements, we define `program` with

		Selection Set
`program` →	`statementList <EOF>`	`{<ID>, "println", <EOF>}`

Notice that we have placed `<EOF>` at the end of this production. Its inclusion here explicitly indicates that `<EOF>` should follow `statementList`. A `statementList` is a list of zero or more statements:

```
statementList → statement statementList    {<ID>, "println"}
statementList → λ                           {<EOF>}
```

We have two types of statements: the assignment statement and the `println` statement. So we have

```
statement → assignmentStatement             {<ID>}
statement → printlnStatement                {"println"}
```

where

```
assignmentStatement → <ID> "=" expr ";"          {<ID>}
printlnStatement    → "println" "(" expr ")" ";" {"println"}
```

The productions for an expression are

```
expr         → term termList            { "(", "+" "-", <UNSIGNED>, <ID>}
termList     → "+" term termList        { "+"}
termList     → λ                        { ")", ";"}
term         → factor factorList        { "(", "+" "-", <UNSIGNED>, <ID>}
factorList   → "*" factor factorList    { "*"}
factorList   → λ                        { ")", ";", "+"}
factor       → <UNSIGNED>               { <UNSIGNED>}
factor       → "+" <UNSIGNED>           { "+"}
factor       → "-" <UNSIGNED>           { "-"}
factor       → <ID>                     { <ID>}
factor       → "(" expr ")"             { "("}
```

Although there are a variety of grammars that define infix arithmetic expressions (see Section 4.2 and Section 7.9), most are not LL(1). As you can see from the selection sets above, this group of productions is LL(1), and, therefore, is appropriate for top-down parsing. These productions also capture the correct associativity and precedence rules for addition and multiplication.

12.4 THE TARGET LANGUAGE

We now need to convert our grammar from Section 12.3 to a translation grammar. However, to do this, we first need a thorough understanding of our target language—the stack instruction set of the J1 computer—and how it corresponds to the source language. Let us look at the target code corresponding to

```
x = 5000;
y = x*2 + -10;
println(y + 3);
```

For the statement

```
x = 5000;
```

we first need the assembler instruction that pushes the address of x:

```
        pc          x
```

Next, we need a pwc instruction that pushes 5000:

```
        pwc         5000
```

We complete the assignment of 5000 to x with

```
        stav
```

which pops the value and address from the stack and then stores the value at the address. In the instruction,

```
        y = x*2 + -10;
```

we have two constants, 2 and -10. We can push 2 but not -10 with a pc instruction (recall that a pc instruction can push constants only in the range of 0 to 4095). Rather than complicate the compiler by having it use the pc instruction to push constants within the range of a pc instruction, and the pwc instruction for other constants, our compiler will use the pwc instruction exclusively to push constants. However, our compiler will continue to use the pc instruction to push addresses. Addresses are always within the 0 to 4095 range, and, therefore, can always be pushed by the pc instruction. Here is the code for our assignment statement:

```
; code for y = x*2 + -10;
pc        y        ; push address of y
p         x        ; push value of x
pwc       2        ; push 2
mult               ; compute x*2
pwc       -10      ; push -10
add                ; compute x*2 + -10
stav               ; assign result to y
```

The println statement displays the value of y + 3 and then outputs the newline character:

```
; code for println(y + 3);
p         y        ; push value of y
pwc       3        ; push 3
add                ; compute y + 3
dout               ; pop and display in decimal
pc        '\n'     ; push newline character
aout               ; pop and output
```

Finally, we have some "endcode" (i.e., code the compiler outputs after it has completed the parsing of the source program) consisting of the halt instruction followed by the dw statements that the program requires:

```
          halt
x:        dw       0
y:        dw       0
```

12.5   SYMBOL TABLE

Because the compiler outputs at the end of the assembly language program a dw statement for each variable, it obviously has to create a data structure during the compilation process in which it records the names of each variable. We call this data structure a *symbol table*. The symbol table in S1 is a separate object constructed from the class S1SymTab. We use the variable st to reference this object. The symbol table uses an ArrayList<String> named symbol to record the names of the variables used in the program. In addition to symbol, the symbol table object contains an enter method (which makes an entry into the symbol table), a getSymbol method (which retrieves a symbol table entry at a specific index), and a getSize method (which returns the size of the symbol ArrayList).

12.6   CODE GENERATOR

The code generator in S1 is a separate object constructed from the class `S1CodeGen`. We use the variable `cg` to reference this object. Its two principal methods are `emitInstruction` and `endCode`. The `emitInstruction` method *emits* (i.e., outputs to the assembly language file the compiler creates) an assembly language instruction. For example,

```
cg.emitInstruction("mult");
```

emits the instruction

```
        mult
```

`emitInstruction` can take one or two `String` arguments. For example, if `t.image` is `"x"`, then

```
cg.emitInstruction("pc", t.image);
```

emits the instruction

```
        pc        x
```

The `endcode` method emits a `halt` instruction and the `dw` statements—one for each entry in the symbol table—that appear at the end of the assembly language program. For example, if the symbol table has two entries `"x"` and `"y"`, then `endCode` emits

```
        halt
x:      dw        0
y:      dw        0
```

12.7   token CLASS

The token manager in S1 is essentially the token manager for the prefix expression compiler we studied in Section 10. 9. Recall that this token manager provides tokens to the parser in the form of objects of the following type:

```
class Token
{
   // integer that identifies kind (i.e., category) of token
   public int kind;

   // location of token in source program
   public int beginLine, beginColumn, endLine, endColumn;

   // String consisting of characters that make up token
   public String image;

   // link to next Token object
   public Token next;
}
```

The `kind` field contains an integer that represents the token's kind (i.e., category). For example, the `kind` field value for unsigned integer constants is UNSIGNED. In S1, UNSIGNED is a named constant defined with

```
int UNSIGNED = 2;
```

The `kind` field value for all identifiers is ID (equal to 3 in S1). The `kind` field value for a "println" token is PRINTLN (equal to 1 in S1).

The `beginLine`, `endLine`, `beginColumn`, and `endColumn` fields specify the location of the token in the source code.

The `image` field contains the string consisting of the characters from the source code that make up the token. For example, the `image` field in the `Token` object for 123 would contain the string "123".

The `next` field links each token object to the next one in the order in which tokens appear in the source program.

12.8 WRITING THE TRANSLATION GRAMMAR

Once we understand the output that our compiler has to generate, it is easy to figure out where to put actions in our grammar to accomplish the required translation. Let us start by considering the assignment statement

```
x = y + 1;
```

The corresponding assembly code is

```
pc       x     ; push address of x onto stack

p        y     ; push value of y onto stack
pwc      1     ; push 1 onto stack
add            ; double pop, add, and push sum

stav           ; pop and store value at address
```

When the `stav` instruction is executed, the address of x and the value of y + 1 are on the stack, with the latter on top. The `stav` instruction pops both the value and the address, and then stores the value at the address. In addition to generating the assembly code above, the compiler has to enter "x" and "y" into the symbol table. Note that the order of operations in the assembly code above is

1. The initial `pc` instruction that pushes the address of the variable on the left side of the assignment statement
2. The code corresponding to the expression on the right side of the assignment statement
3. The `stav` instruction

The placement of actions in the `assignmentStatement` production will reflect this order.

Actions in a translation grammar, in general, require information. For example, the action

```
{ cg.emit("pc", t.image);}
```

requires the information in `t.image`. The longer we postpone an action, the longer we have to maintain the information the action needs. Thus, a good rule to follow regarding the placement of actions is

Place actions in a translation grammar as early as possible.

We call this rule the *early-as-possible* rule. Keeping this rule in mind, let us determine at what points to put actions in the production for the assignment statement. We have identified the five possible points within the production:

```
void assignmentStatement(): { Token t;}
{
                    ←————————— point 1
    t=<ID>
                    ←————————— point 2
    "="
                    ←————————— point 3
    expr()

                    ←————————— point 4
    ";"
                    ←————————— point 5
}
```

Let us first consider the point at which we should enter the identifier into the symbol table with the following action:

```
{ st.enter(t.image);}
```

where `st` is the reference to the symbol table object, and `t` is a local variable of type `To-ken` to which the `<ID>` token is assigned. Thus, `t.image` is the image of the identifier. This action can appear at points 2, 3, 4, or 5. It must appear *after* point 1 because at point 1 we have not yet parsed the identifier so we do not yet have access to it. Applying our early-as-possible rule, we will place it at point 2.

There are two constraints on where we emit the `pc` instruction: It must be after point 1 because we need the identifier for the operand in the `pc` instruction). It must also precede the assembly code associated with `expr()`. Thus, we have a choice: point 2 or point 3. Applying our early-as-possible rule, we will place it at point 2. We emit the `pc` instruction with

```
{ cg.emit("pc", t.image);}
```

where `cg` is the reference to the code generator object, and `t` is the local variable to which the identifier token is assigned.

The point at which we emit the `stav` instruction must follow the code for `expr()`. Thus, it can appear at point 4 or 5. Using our early-as-possible rule, we will place it at point 4. We emit the `stav` instruction with

```
{ cg.emit("stav");}
```

Incorporating these actions into the assignment statement production, we get

```
void assignmentStatement(): { Token t;}
{
    t=<ID>
    { st.enter(t.image);}
    { cg.emitInstruction("pc", t.image);}
    "="
    expr()
    { cg.emitInstruction("stav");}
    ";"
}
```

We need a local variable `t`. Thus, we declare it within the first set of braces (that is where local variables are declared in a translation grammar). Note that we do not need to include any actions corresponding to `expr()`. The `expr()` production itself will provide those actions.

Our actions include the following two methods:

1. `public void enter(String s)`

This is a method in the `st` object (the symbol table) that makes an entry into the symbol table. `enter` is passed `t.image` (the image of the identifier). If the identifier is already in the symbol table, then `enter` simply returns to its caller.

2. `public void emitInstruction(String op)`
   `public void emitInstruction(String op, String opnd)`

This is a method in the `cg` object (the code generator) that outputs an assembly language instruction. It is passed either a mnemonic alone (for instructions like `stav` that consist of a mnemonic only) or a mnemonic and an operand (for instructions like `pc` that consist of a mnemonic and an operand). For example, if `t.image` is `"x"`, then the action

```
{ cg.emitInstruction("pc", t.image);}
```

outputs to the output file the instruction

```
            pc          x
```

The translation grammar entry for the `println` statement is even simpler than the entry for the assignment statement:

```
void printlnStatement(): {}
{
```

```
     "println"
     "("
     expr()
     { cg.emitInstruction("dout");}
     { cg.emitInstruction("pc",  "'\\n'");}
     { cg.emitInstruction("aout");}
     ")"
     ";"
}
```

We call `emitInstruction` three times. The first call outputs the `dout` instruction. The second call outputs

```
        pc              '\n'
```

In second argument of the second call, we use a double backslash to represent a single backslash. If the second call were

```
    { cg.emitInstruction("pc",  "'\n'");}     // wrong!
```

we would get three characters in the operand: two single quotes surrounding the newline character. What we want is four characters: single quotes surrounding a backslash and the letter n. The third call of `emitInstruction` in the translation grammar entry for `println` outputs the `aout` instruction.

The actions for the productions associated with `termList` are also simple to determine. Consider the `termList` production:

```
    termList   →  "+" term termList
```

Right after we parse the input corresponding to `term` on the right side of this production, we should emit an `add` instruction, which adds the value of this `term` with the value of the `term` that is to the left of the "+". The term to the left of "+" comes from higher up in the parse tree and earlier in the parse (see Figure 12.1).

The entry in the translation grammar for `termList` is

```
  void termList(): {}
  {
     "+"
     term()
     { cg.emitInstruction("add");}
     termList()
   |
     {}          // the empty set represents lambda
  }
```

We similarly output the `mult` instruction after `factor` in

```
    factorList →  "*" factor factorList
```

The entry for `factorList` *in the translation grammar is*

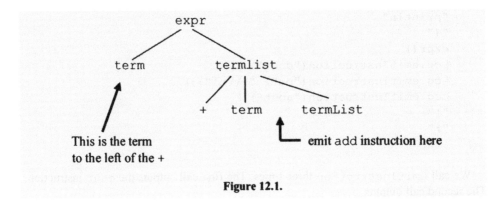

Figure 12.1.

```
void factorList(): {}
{
    "*"
    factor()
    {cg.emitInstruction("mult");}
    factorList()
  |
    {}                  // the empty set represents lambda
}
```

The only additional actions we need are for the productions

```
factor → <UNSIGNED>
factor → "+" <UNSIGNED>
factor → "-" <UNSIGNED>
factor → <ID>
```

For the first three of these productions, we emit a `pwc` instruction that pushes the constant. For the fourth factor production, we enter the identifier into the symbol table, and we emit a `p` instruction that pushes the value of the identifier. For example, if the identifier is x, we enter "x" into the symbol table and emit

```
        p        x
```

We do not need any actions for the `factor` production that generates another expression within parentheses:

```
        factor → "(" expr ")"
```

For this production, the actions required will be provided by the `expr` production.
The entry in the translation grammar for `factor` is

```
void factor(): { Token t;}
{
    t=<UNSIGNED>
    {cg.emitInstruction("pwc", t.image);}
  |
```

```
    "+"
    t = <UNSIGNED>
    { cg.emitInstruction("pwc", t.image);}
  |
    "-"
    t = <UNSIGNED>
    { cg.emitInstruction("pwc", "-" + t.image);}
  |
    t=<ID>
    { st.enter(t.image);}
    { cg.emitInstruction("p", t.image);}
  |
    "("
    expr()
    ")"
}
```

The entry in the translation grammar for program is

```
void program(): {}
{
    statementList()
    { cg.endCode();}
    <EOF>                          // make sure no garbage at end
}
```

It contains the action, { cg.endcode()} , which outputs the halt instruction and the dw statements that appear at the end of the assembly language object program. Notice that the <EOF> token follows statementList(). The inclusion of <EOF> at this point indicates that the <EOF> token must immediately follow the tokens that correspond to statementList(). That is, we test for end of file after parsing statementList. Thus, if garbage were to follow the last statement in a program, and it was not detected by statementList() or any of the methods below it, the end-of-file test in program() would trigger a parsing error, as it should.

The complete translation grammar for S1 appears in Figure 12.2. It is also in the file S1.tg in the J1 Software Package.

12.9 IMPLEMENTING THE S1 COMPILER

Our last step in creating the S1 compiler is to write the Java code corresponding to the translation grammar in Figure 12.3. This step is the least creative. We simply follow the structure specified by the translation grammar, using selection sets to determine which production to apply. The token manager in S1 is essentially the token manager in the prefix expression compiler we studied in Chapter 10 (see Figure 10.10). The Java code for the S1 compiler is in the file S1.java in the J1 Software Package. A listing of this file appears in Figure 12.3.

Most of the code in Figure 12.3 should be self-explanatory. For a discussion of the token manager in S1, see the discussion of the token manager for the prefix expression compiler in Section 10.9. These two token managers are nearly identical. One minor dif-

```
 1  // Translation grammar for S1 =============================
 2
 3  void program(): {}
 4  {
 5      statementList()
 6      { cg.endCode();}
 7      <EOF>
 8  }
 9  //----------------
10  void statementList(): {}
11  {
12      statement()
13      statementList()
14  |
15      {}
16  }
17  //----------------
18  void statement(): {}
19  {
20      assignmentStatement()
21  |
22      printlnStatement()
23  }
24  //----------------
25  void assignmentStatement(): { Token t;}
26  {
27      t=<ID>
28      { st.enter(t.image);}
29      { cg.emitInstruction("pc", t.image);}
30      "="
31      expr()
32      { cg.emitInstruction("stav");}
33      ";"
34  }
35  //----------------
36  void printlnStatement(): {}
37  {
38      "println"
39      "("
40      expr()
41      { cg.emitInstruction("dout");}
42      { cg.emitInstruction("pc", "'\\n'");}
43      { cg.emitInstruction("aout");}
44      ")"
45      ";"
46  }
47  //----------------
48  void expr(): {}
49  {
50      term()
```

Figure 12.2.

```
 51    termList()
 52 }
 53 //----------------
 54 void termList(): {}
 55 {
 56    "+"
 57    term()
 58    { cg.emitInstruction("add");}
 59    termList()
 60  |
 61    {}
 62 }
 63 //----------------
 64 void term(): {}
 65 {
 66    factor()
 67    factorList()
 68 }
 69 //----------------
 70 void factorList(): {}
 71 {
 72    "*"
 73    factor()
 74    { cg.emitInstruction("mult");}
 75    factorList()
 76  |
 77    {}
 78 }
 79 //----------------
 80 void factor(): { Token t;}
 81 {
 82    t=<UNSIGNED>
 83    { cg.emitInstruction("pwc", t.image);}
 84  |
 85    "+"
 86    t = <UNSIGNED>
 87    { cg.emitInstruction("pwc", t.image);}
 88  |
 89    "-"
 90    t = <UNSIGNED>
 91    { cg.emitInstruction("pwc", "-" + t.image);}
 92  |
 93    t=<ID>
 94    { st.enter(t.image);}
 95    { cg.emitInstruction("p", t.image);}
 96  |
 97    "("
 98    expr()
 99    ")"
100 }
```

Figure 12.2. *Continued.*

```
1  // Hand-written S1 compiler
2  import java.io.*;
3  import java.util.*;
4  //=========================================================
5  class S1
6  {
7    public static void main(String[ ] args) throws
8                                          IOException
9    {
10      System.out.println("S1 compiler written by ...");
11
12      if (args.length != 1)
13      {
14        System.err.println("Wrong number cmd line args");
15        System.exit(1);
16      }
17
18      // set to true to debug token manager
19      boolean debug = false;
20
21      // build the input and output file names
22      String inFileName = args[ 0] + ".s";
23      String outFileName = args[ 0] + ".a";
24
25      // construct file objects
26      Scanner inFile = new Scanner(new File(inFileName));
27      PrintWriter outFile = new PrintWriter(outFileName);
28
29      // identify compiler/author in the output file
30      outFile.println("; from S1 compiler written by ...");
31
32      // construct objects that make up compiler
33      S1SymTab st = new S1SymTab();
34      S1TokenMgr tm =  new S1TokenMgr(inFile, outFile, debug);
35      S1CodeGen cg = new S1CodeGen(outFile, st);
36      S1Parser parser = new S1Parser(st, tm, cg);
37
38      // parse and translate
39      try
40      {
41        parser.parse();
42      }
43      catch (RuntimeException e)
44      {
45        System.err.println(e.getMessage());
46        outFile.println(e.getMessage());
47        outFile.close();
48        System.exit(1);
49      }
50
51       outFile.close();
```

Figure 12.3.

```
 52    }
 53  }                                              // end of S1
 54  //=========================================================
 55  interface S1Constants
 56  {
 57     // integers that identify token kinds
 58     int EOF = 0;
 59     int PRINTLN = 1;
 60     int UNSIGNED = 2;
 61     int ID = 3;
 62     int ASSIGN = 4;
 63     int SEMICOLON = 5;
 64     int LEFTPAREN = 6;
 65     int RIGHTPAREN = 7;
 66     int PLUS = 8;
 67     int MINUS = 9;
 68     int TIMES = 10;
 69     int ERROR = 11;
 70
 71     // tokenImage provides string for each token kind
 72     String[] tokenImage =
 73     {
 74        "<EOF>",
 75        "\"println\"",
 76        "<UNSIGNED>",
 77        "<ID>",
 78        "\"=\"",
 79        "\";\"",
 80        "\"(\"",
 81        "\")\"",
 82        "\"+\"",
 83        "\"-\"",
 84        "\"*\"",
 85        "<ERROR>"
 86     };
 87  }                                     // end of S1Constants
 88  //=========================================================
 89  class S1SymTab
 90  {
 91     private ArrayList<String> symbol;
 92     //---------------------
 93     public S1SymTab()
 94     {
 95        symbol = new ArrayList<String>();
 96     }
 97     //---------------------
 98     public void enter(String s)
 99     {
100        int index = symbol.indexOf(s);
101
102        // if s is not in symbol, then add it
```

Figure 12.3. *Continued.*

```
103      if (index < 0)
104         symbol.add(s);
105    }
106    //---------------------
107    public String getSymbol(int index)
108    {
109      return symbol.get(index);
110    }
111    //---------------------
112    public int getSize()
113    {
114      return symbol.size();
115    }
116 }                                   // end of S1SymTab
117 //==========================================================
118 class S1TokenMgr implements S1Constants
119 {
120    private Scanner inFile;
121    private PrintWriter outFile;
122    private boolean debug;
123    private char currentChar;
124    private int currentColumnNumber;
125    private int currentLineNumber;
126    private String inputLine;     // holds 1 line of input
127    private Token token;          // holds 1 token
128    private StringBuffer buffer; // token image built here
129    //---------------------
130    public S1TokenMgr(Scanner inFile,
131                      PrintWriter outFile, boolean debug)
132    {
133      this.inFile = inFile;
134      this.outFile = outFile;
135      this.debug = debug;
136      currentChar = '\n';          //  '\n' triggers read
137      currentLineNumber = 0;
138      buffer = new StringBuffer();
139    }
140    //---------------------
141    public Token getNextToken()
142    {
143      // skip whitespace
144      while (Character.isWhitespace(currentChar))
145        getNextChar();
146
147      // construct token to be returned to parser
148      token = new Token();
149      token.next = null;
150
151      // save start-of-token position
152      token.beginLine = currentLineNumber;
153      token.beginColumn = currentColumnNumber;
```

Figure 12.3. *Continued.*

```
154
155      // check for EOF
156      if (currentChar == EOF)
157      {
158        token.image = "<EOF>";
159        token.endLine = currentLineNumber;
160        token.endColumn = currentColumnNumber;
161        token.kind = EOF;
162      }
163
164      else  // check for unsigned int
165      if (Character.isDigit(currentChar))
166      {
167        buffer.setLength(0);  // clear buffer
168        do  // build token image in buffer
169        {
170          buffer.append(currentChar);
171          token.endLine = currentLineNumber;
172          token.endColumn = currentColumnNumber;
173          getNextChar();
174        } while (Character.isDigit(currentChar));
175        // save buffer as String in token.image
176        token.image = buffer.toString();
177        token.kind = UNSIGNED;
178      }
179
180      else  // check for identifier
181      if (Character.isLetter(currentChar))
182      {
183        buffer.setLength(0);  // clear buffer
184        do  // build token image in buffer
185        {
186          buffer.append(currentChar);
187          token.endLine = currentLineNumber;
188          token.endColumn = currentColumnNumber;
189          getNextChar();
190        } while (Character.isLetterOrDigit(currentChar));
191        // save buffer as String in token.image
192        token.image = buffer.toString();
193
194        // check if keyword
195        if (token.image.equals("println"))
196          token.kind = PRINTLN;
197        else  // not a keyword so kind is ID
198          token.kind = ID;
199      }
200
201      else  // process single-character token
202      {
203        switch(currentChar)
204        {
```

Figure 12.3. *Continued.*

```
205        case '=':
206          token.kind = ASSIGN;
207          break;
208        case ';':
209          token.kind = SEMICOLON;
210          break;
211        case '(':
212          token.kind = LEFTPAREN;
213          break;
214        case ')':
215          token.kind = RIGHTPAREN;
216          break;
217        case '+':
218          token.kind = PLUS;
219          break;
220        case '-':
221          token.kind = MINUS;
222          break;
223        case '*':
224          token.kind = TIMES;
225          break;
226        default:
227          token.kind = ERROR;
228          break;
229      }
230
231      // save currentChar as String in token.image
232      token.image = Character.toString(currentChar);
233
234      // save end-of-token position
235      token.endLine = currentLineNumber;
236      token.endColumn = currentColumnNumber;
237
238      getNextChar();  // read beyond end of token
239    }
240
241    // token trace appears as comments in output file
242    if (debug)
243      outFile.printf(
244        "; kd=%3d bL=%3d bC=%3d eL=%3d eC=%3d im=%s%n",
245        token.kind, token.beginLine, token.beginColumn,
246        token.endLine, token.endColumn, token.image);
247
248    return token;      // return token to parser
249  }
250  //----------------------
251  private void getNextChar()
252  {
253    if (currentChar == EOF)
254      return;
255
```

Figure 12.3. *Continued.*

```
256      if (currentChar == '\n')           // need next line?
257      {
258        if (inFile.hasNextLine())         // any lines left?
259        {
260          inputLine = inFile.nextLine();  // get next line
261          // output source line as comment
262          outFile.println("; " + inputLine);
263          inputLine = inputLine + "\n";   // mark line end
264          currentColumnNumber = 0;
265          currentLineNumber++;
266        }
267        else  // at end of file
268        {
269          currentChar = EOF;
270          return;
271        }
272      }
273
274      // get next char from inputLine
275      currentChar =
276                  inputLine.charAt(currentColumnNumber++);
277
278      // in S2, test for single-line comment goes here
279   }
280 }                                        // end of S1TokenMgr
281 //=========================================================
282 class S1Parser implements S1Constants
283 {
284   private S1SymTab st;
285   private S1TokenMgr tm;
286   private S1CodeGen cg;
287   private Token currentToken;
288   private Token previousToken;
289   //---------------------
290   public S1Parser(S1SymTab st, S1TokenMgr tm,
291                                      S1CodeGen cg)
292   {
293     this.st = st;
294     this.tm = tm;
295     this.cg = cg;
296     // prime currentToken with first token
297     currentToken = tm.getNextToken();
298     previousToken = null;
299   }
300   //---------------------
301   // Construct and return an exception that contains
302   // a message consisting of the image of the current
303   // token, its location, and the expected tokens.
304   //
305   private RuntimeException genEx(String errorMessage)
306   {
```

Figure 12.3. *Continued.*

```
307    return new RuntimeException("Encountered \"" +
308      currentToken.image + "\" on line " +
309      currentToken.beginLine + ", column " +
310      currentToken.beginColumn + "." +
311      System.getProperty("line.separator") +
312      errorMessage);
313    }
314    //---------------------
315    // Advance currentToken to next token.
316    //
317    private void advance()
318    {
319      previousToken = currentToken;
320
321      // If next token is on token list, advance to it.
322      if (currentToken.next != null)
323        currentToken = currentToken.next;
324
325      // Otherwise, get next token from token mgr and
326      // put it on the list.
327      else
328        currentToken =
329                  currentToken.next = tm.getNextToken();
330    }
331    //---------------------
332    // getToken(i) returns ith token without advancing
333    // in token stream.  getToken(0) returns
334    // previousToken.  getToken(1) returns currentToken.
335    // getToken(2) returns next token, and so on.
336    //
337    private Token getToken(int i)
338    {
339      if (i <= 0)
340        return previousToken;
341
342      Token t = currentToken;
343      for (int j = 1; j < i; j++)  // loop to ith token
344      {
345        // if next token is on token list, move t to it
346        if (t.next != null)
347          t = t.next;
348
349        // Otherwise, get next token from token mgr and
350        // put it on the list.
351        else
352          t = t.next = tm.getNextToken();
353      }
354      return t;
355    }
356    //---------------------
357    // If the kind of the current token matches the
```

Figure 12.3. *Continued.*

```
358    // expected kind, then consume advances to the next
359    // token. Otherwise, it throws an exception.
360    //
361    private void consume(int expected)
362    {
363      if (currentToken.kind == expected)
364        advance();
365      else
366        throw genEx("Expecting " + tokenImage[ expected] );
367    }
368    //---------------------
369    public void parse()
370    {
371      program();    // program is start symbol for grammar
372    }
373    //---------------------
374    private void program()
375    {
376      statementList();
377      cg.endCode();
378      if (currentToken.kind != EOF)   //garbage at end?
379        throw genEx("Expecting <EOF>");
380    }
381    //---------------------
382    private void statementList()
383    {
384      switch(currentToken.kind)
385      {
386        case ID:
387        case PRINTLN:
388          statement();
389          statementList();
390          break;
391        case EOF:
392          ;
393          break;
394        default:
395          throw genEx("Expecting statement or <EOF>");
396      }
397    }
398    //---------------------
399    private void statement()
400    {
401      switch(currentToken.kind)
402      {
403        case ID:
404          assignmentStatement();
405          break;
406        case PRINTLN:
407          printlnStatement();
408          break;
```

Figure 12.3. *Continued.*

```
409        default:
410           throw genEx("Expecting statement");
411    }
412  }
413  //----------------------
414  private void assignmentStatement()
415  {
416    Token t;
417
418    t = currentToken;
419    consume(ID);
420    st.enter(t.image);
421    cg.emitInstruction("pc", t.image);
422    consume(ASSIGN);
423    expr();
424    cg.emitInstruction("stav");
425    consume(SEMICOLON);
426  }
427  //----------------------
428  private void printlnStatement()
429  {
430    consume(PRINTLN);
431    consume(LEFTPAREN);
432    expr();
433    cg.emitInstruction("dout");
434    cg.emitInstruction("pc", "'\\n'");
435    cg.emitInstruction("aout");
436    consume(RIGHTPAREN);
437    consume(SEMICOLON);
438  }
439  //----------------------
440  private void expr()
441  {
442    term();
443    termList();
444  }
445  //----------------------
446  private void termList()
447  {
448    switch(currentToken.kind)
449    {
450      case PLUS:
451        consume(PLUS);
452        term();
453        cg.emitInstruction("add");
454        termList();
455        break;
456      case RIGHTPAREN:
457      case SEMICOLON:
458        ;
459        break;
```

Figure 12.3. *Continued.*

```
460        default:
461          throw genEx("Expecting \"+\", \")\", or \";\"");
462      }
463  }
464  //---------------------
465  private void term()
466  {
467    factor();
468    factorList();
469  }
470  //---------------------
471  private void factorList()
472  {
473    switch(currentToken.kind)
474      {
475        case TIMES:
476          consume(TIMES);
477          factor();
478          cg.emitInstruction("mult");
479          factorList();
480          break;
481        case PLUS:
482        case RIGHTPAREN:
483        case SEMICOLON:
484          ;
485          break;
486        default:
487          throw genEx("Expecting op, \")\", or \";\"");
488      }
489  }
490  //---------------------
491  private void factor()
492  {
493    Token t;
494
495    switch(currentToken.kind)
496      {
497        case UNSIGNED:
498          t = currentToken;
499          consume(UNSIGNED);
500          cg.emitInstruction("pwc", t.image);
501          break;
502        case PLUS:
503          consume(PLUS);
504          t = currentToken;
505          consume(UNSIGNED);
506          cg.emitInstruction("pwc", t.image);
507          break;
508        case MINUS:
509          consume(MINUS);
510          t = currentToken;
```

Figure 12.3. *Continued.*

```
511              consume(UNSIGNED);
512              cg.emitInstruction("pwc", "-" + t.image);
513              break;
514          case ID:
515              t = currentToken;
516              consume(ID);
517              st.enter(t.image);
518              cg.emitInstruction("p", t.image);
519              break;
520          case LEFTPAREN:
521              consume(LEFTPAREN);
522              expr();
523              consume(RIGHTPAREN);
524              break;
525          default:
526              throw genEx("Expecting factor");
527          }
528      }
529 }                                        // end of S1Parser
530 //=========================================================
531 class S1CodeGen
532 {
533    private PrintWriter outFile;
534    private S1SymTab st;
535    //----------------------
536    public S1CodeGen(PrintWriter outFile, S1SymTab st)
537    {
538      this.outFile = outFile;
539      this.st = st;
540    }
541    //----------------------
542    public void emitInstruction(String op)
543    {
544      outFile.printf("          %-4s%n", op);
545    }
546    //----------------------
547    public void emitInstruction(String op, String opnd)
548    {
549      outFile.printf("          %-4s     %s%n", op,opnd);
550    }
551    //----------------------
552    private void emitdw(String label, String value)
553    {
554      outFile.printf(
555            "%-9s dw       %s%n", label + ":", value);
556    }
557    //----------------------
558    public void endCode()
559    {
560      outFile.println();
561      emitInstruction("halt");
```

Figure 12.3. *Continued.*

```
562
563      int size = st.getSize();
564      // emit dw for each symbol in the symbol table
565      for (int i=0; i < size; i++)
566        emitdw(st.getSymbol(i), "0");
567   }
568 }                                          // end of S1CodeGen
```

Figure 12.3. *Continued.*

ference concerns the token trace. The token manager in Section 10.9 always generates a
token trace. The token manager in S1 generates a token trace only if debug is set to true
(see lines 19 and 242 in S1).

The service methods in the parser—genEx, advance, getToken, and consume—
are identical to the corresponding methods with the same names that we studied in
Section 10.10. genEx (see lines 305 to 313 in S1) constructs and returns an exception
object that contains a detailed error message. When calling genEx, you should pass it
a string that lists or describes the tokens that are expected at the point of the error.
genEx then incorporates this string in the error message it creates. advance (see lines
317 to 330 in S1) advances in the token stream to the next token. consume (see lines
361 to 367 in S1) determines if the current token is the expected token. If it is, consume advances in the token stream by calling advance. Otherwise, it throws an exception. getToken provides a lookahead capability. Let us examine getToken more
closely:

```
337      private Token getToken(int i)
338      {
339        if (i <= 0)
340          return previousToken;
341
342        Token t = currentToken;
343        for (int j = 1; j < i; j++)   // loop to ith token
344        {
345          // if next token is on token list, move t to it
346          if (t.next != null)
347            t = t.next;
348
349          // Otherwise, get next token from token mgr and
350          // put it on the list.
351          else
352            t = t.next = tm.getNextToken();
353        }
354        return t;
355      }
```

S1 does not use getToken. But you may want to use it in a more advanced compiler you
build from S1. Do not confuse this method with the getNextToken method in the token
manager. getToken in the parser returns any token from previousToken (the token
just before the current token) onward, depending on the argument it is passed. For example, getToken(0) returns previousToken; getToken(1) returns currentToken;

`getToken(2)` returns the token following the current token, and so on. The argument passed to `getToken` should be nonnegative.

`getToken` places any tokens it obtains from the token manager on the linked list of tokens (see line 352). Thus, when the parser subsequently advances to these tokens, it obtains them from the linked list rather than from the token manager (see lines 321 to 323 in S1).

A lookahead beyond the current token is necessary if the parser is based on a grammar which is not LL(1). For example, suppose a translation grammar contains the following two alternatives:

```
{
    "b"
    "c"
    "d"
    { System.out.println("hello");}
  |
    "b"
    "c"
    "e"
    { System.out.println("bye");}
}
```

Each alternative starts with a "b", "c" sequence. Thus, the grammar is not LL(1). However, we can decide between these two alternatives by looking at `getToken(2)` and `getToken(3)` (the two tokens following the current token). Assume that the `kind` values for the tokens "b", "c", "d", and "e" are the named constants B, C, D, and E, respectively. Then the corresponding Java code is

```
switch (currentToken.kind)
{
  case B:
    if (getToken(2).kind == C && getToken(3).kind == D)
    {
      consume(B);
      consume(C);
      consume(D);
      System.out.println("hello");
    }
    else
    if (getToken(2).kind == C && getToken(3).kind == E)
    {
      consume(B);
      consume(C);
      consume(E);
      System.out.println("bye");
    }
    break;
  default:
    throw genEx("Expecting \"bcd\" or \"bce\"");
}
```

In the example above, the grammar is LL(3). It, however, can be easily converted to an equivalent LL(1) grammar by left factoring. Thus, an alternative approach is to create the parser from the equivalent LL(1) grammar, in which case `getToken` would not be needed. If, however an LL(1) grammar were not easily obtainable, then the lookahead capability provided by `getToken` could be put to good use.

12.10   TRYING OUT S1

To use S1, we first have to compile it. We do this by entering

```
javac S1.java
```

which compiles our `S1.java` compiler to the file `S1.class`. We can then use `S1.class` to translate the sample source program in `S1.s` (included in the J1 software package). `S1.s` is the test program for the S1 compiler. It performs a computation (the result of which should be 4107). It then displays the result of the computation and 4107. Thus, it should display 4107 twice. To compile `S1.s`, enter

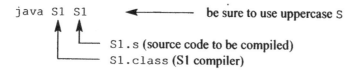

```
java S1 S1        ◄——————— be sure to use uppercase S
```
S1.s (source code to be compiled)
S1.class (S1 compiler)

The `java` interpreter assumes the extension `".class"` for the first command line argument (the first `S1` in the preceding command line). The S1 compiler assumes the extension `".s"` for the source code file (the second `S1` in the command line above). Thus, the first argument in the command line above specifies `S1.class` (the compiler), and the second argument specifies `S1.s` (the source code file the S1 compiler is to translate). When the S1 compiler compiles `S1.s`, it outputs the corresponding assembly code to the file `S1.a`.

Next, we have to assemble `S1.a`. We do this with

```
a S1.a        ◄——————— you must specify the ".a" extension
```

The a assembler will then produce the file `S1.e` containing the executable program. You must specify the `".a"` extension in the input file name when you invoke the a program. It you do not, it will assume the extension `".o"`, which is the extension for an object file (we discuss object files in Chapter 16).

After assembling `S1.a` to get `S1.e`, we can run `S1.e` with

```
e S1 /c
```

e is the program that simulates the J1 computer. The optional `/c` command line argument causes e to check the correctness of the `S1.e` program. It also causes e to provide input to the program if it requires any. With or without `/c`, e produces a log file named `S1.<`*family name*`>.log` that contains the results of the run (the first time you run e, it will prompt you for your name). Figure 12.4 shows the `S1.s`, `S1.a`, and `S1.<`*family name*`>.log` files. Note that the `S1.a` file contains *as comments* the source code and, optionally, the token trace (if `debug` on line 19 is true). If your token manager is not work-

a) S1.s (the source program)

```
x = +3 + -2 + 1;
y = x;
z = x* (2 + y) + (((4099)));
println(z + x + -2);
println(4107);
```

b) S1.a (the assembler program produced by the S1 compiler)

```
; S1 compiler written by ...
;     x = +3 + -2 + 1;
            pc        x
            pwc       3
            pwc       -2
            add
            pwc       1
            add
            stav
;     y = x;
            pc        y
            p         x
            stav
;     z = x* (2 + y) + (((4099)));
            pc        z
            p         x
            pwc       2
            p         y
            add
            mult
            pwc       4099
            add
            stav
;     println(z + x + -2);
            p         z
            p         x
            add
            pwc       -2
            add
            dout
            pc        '\n'
            aout
;     println(4107);
            pwc       4107
            dout
            pc        '\n'
            aout

            halt
x:          dw        0
y:          dw        0
z:          dw        0
```

Figure 12.4.

c) `S1.dosreis.log` **(the log file produced by the** `e` **program)**

```
e Version 1.7
Log file S1.dosreis.log


Your name:            DosReis Anthony J
Machinecode file:     S1.e
Check file:           S1.chk
Check data:           bafd 42 32 440 4dfb



================== Mon Mar 07 08:59:27 2011 ==============r
4107
4107




===========================================================r


Report for:           DosReis Anthony J
Program output:       correct
Machine code size:    42       (at limit)
Machine inst count:   32       (at limit)
Execution time:       440      (at limit)

=============== r(bf2e) terminated Mon Mar 07 08:59:27 2011
```

d) `S1.dosreis.log` **(the log file produced by the** `e` **program)**

```
e Version 1.7
Log file s1.dosreis.log


Your name:            DosReis Anthony J
Machinecode file:     s1.e
Check file:           s1.chk
Check data:           bafd 42 32 440 4dfb



================== Mon Mar 07 09:01:21 2011 ==============r
4117
4107



===========================================================r


Report for:           DosReis Anthony J
Program output:       NOT CORRECT             <--- ERROR
Machine code size:    48     (6    OVER LIMIT ) <--- WARNING
Machine inst count:   37     (5    OVER LIMIT ) <--- WARNING
Execution time:       518    (78   OVER LIMIT ) <--- WARNING

=============== r(f1fd) terminated Mon Mar 07 09:01:21 2011
```

Figure 12.4. *Continued.*

ing correctly, you should be able to isolate the problem by examining the token trace in the output file.

S1.s, like all our test cases, displays not only the result of a computation but also what the result should be. Thus, when we run the translated program with e, we should see two identical numbers displayed. For the test case S1.s, we see 4107 displayed twice (see Figure 12.4c). The first 4107 is the computed result; the second 4107 is what the computed result should be. Because the two values displayed in Figure 12.4c are equal, we know immediately that our compiler has translated S1.s correctly. If you invoke e with the /c argument, then the report in the log file explicitly indicates whether the output is correct. With or without /c, the log file also provides the size, instruction count (i.e., the number of machine language instructions executed), and execution time of the translated program. But if you use the /c argument when you invoke e, the log file also indicates how the size, instruction count, and execution time compare with predefined limits. If the translated program is over any of these limits, then your compiler is generating inefficient code. Figure 12.4d shows a log file for a S1 compiler that is not working correctly.

12.11   ADVICE ON EXTENDING THE S1 COMPILER

Now that you understand the structure and operation of S1, you should extend S1 as specified in Section 12.12. Call the extended compiler S2. You should copy S1.java in the J1 Software Package to S2.java, and then change all occurrences of "S1" in S2.java to "S2". Then extend the code in S2.java as specified in Section 12.12. Be sure to insert your name into the statements that output the name of the author of the compiler (see lines 10 and 30 in S1).

Although our list of extensions to S1 to get S2 is extensive, implementing S2 should, in fact, be quite straightforward. The translation grammar, which we give in Figure 12.5, completely defines the parser. Thus, implementing the parser should be a "no-brainer." The symbol table, the code generator, and the main() method in S1 and in S2 are essentially identical. The only difference is that in S2, the class names start with "S2" rather than "S1". The token manager in S2 has to support a few new token types and single-line comments. The code that adds this support is not complex and is similar to the code already in the token manager for S1. Thus, if you understand the token manager for S1, you should be able to extend it easily so that it works for S2. The new tokens for S2 also require a few simple additions to the constants interface (lines 55 to 87 in S1).

12.11.1   Updating the Token Manager

The token manager for S2 has to recognize two new tokens: the keyword readint and "/" (the division operator). Thus, the constants interface should be updated with constants for these new tokens. Use constants named READINT and DIVIDE. The token-Image array in the constants interface should also be extended in accordance with these new tokens.

Because keyword tokens start with letters, they are processed by the do-while loop in the token manager that handles identifiers (lines 184–190 in S1). Following this loop, check the token image. If it is "println" or "readint", set the token's kind field to PRINTLN or READINT, respectively. If the token image is not either of these keywords, then set the kind field to ID.

Do not forget to set the kind field of the keyword tokens.

Recall from Section 10.8, we solved the token lookahead problem by having the token manager read one character beyond the end of every token even if doing so is not necessary to determine the end of the token. This requirement is the reason for the call of `get-NextChar` on line 238 in S1.

> **Do not forget that for every token, the token manager should read one character beyond the token's end before returning that token to the parser.**

12.11.2 Debug Your Token Manager First

The parser depends on the token manager. So what looks like a parser error may, in fact, be a token manager error.

> **Make sure your token manager is working correctly by inspecting the token trace before you debug your parser.**

To generate a token trace, set the `debug` variable to true (see line 19 in S1). Reset it back to false once you have your token manager working correctly.

12.11.3 Selection Sets

The source language for S2 is an extension of the source language for S1. Thus, its grammar is different from the grammar for S1. Whenever a grammar changes, selection sets also change, necessitating changes to the cases in the `switch` statements in the parser. One of the errors you will make most likely make when you implement S2 is to forget to update the parser code according to the new selection sets that result from changes to the grammar.

> **Be sure your implementation of the parser is based on the correct selection sets.**

12.11.4 Using the Required Break Statements

Each method in the parser corresponding to a multiple-production nonterminal uses a `switch` statement to determine which production to apply.

> **Do not forget to include a `break` statement at the end of each alternative in the `switch` statements, except for the cases in which a `throw` statement appears.**

If you include a `break` statement following a `throw` statement, the Java compiler will flag it because the `break` statement in that case would be unreachable.

12.11.5 Using the Required Calls to the Consume Method

A translation grammar does not explicitly indicate where the calls of the `consume` method should appear. But it is not hard to determine where they belong: they are wherever a terminal symbol is parsed.

> **Do not forget to include in the S2 parser a call of consume wherever a to-
> ken is parsed. To consume the current token, pass the consume method
> the kind field value of the expected token.**

For example, to consume an unsigned integer token, call consume with

```
consume(UNSIGNED);
```

To consume a "+" token, call consume with

```
consume(PLUS);
```

Note that UNSIGNED is the kind field value for unsigned integer tokens, and PLUS is the
kind field value for "+" tokens. Do not pass consume the token object itself or its image.
For example, do *not* do this:

```
consume(currentToken);    // wrong!
consume('+');             // wrong!
```

12.11.6   Interpreting the Translation Grammar Correctly

In several places in the translation grammars for S1 and S2, a Token variable t and a token category appear in an assignment statement. For example, in the factor() productions in the translation grammar for S2 (see line 120 in Figure 12.5), we have the assignment

```
t = <UNSIGNED>
```

The Java code in the parser that corresponds to this statement is an assignment of the current token (which is in the variable currentToken) to t. Thus, the Java code for this
statement is

```
t = currentToken;      // correct
```

Do not do this:

```
t = UNSIGNED;          // wrong!
```

We want to assign the current token to t. UNSIGNED is *not* the current token. Rather, it is
a constant declared in the constants interface that is the value in the kind field for an unsigned integer token.

12.12   SPECIFICATIONS FOR S2

The S2 compiler is the S1 compiler with the following extensions:

1. The subtraction and division operations are supported. Subtraction and division
   have the same precedence as addition and multiplication, respectively. Thus, the
   parser should handle subtraction like addition, and division like multiplication. You
   need to add the following productions to your grammar:

```
termList   → "-" term termList
factorList → "/" factor factorList
```

2. The null statement—the statement that consists of the semicolon only—is supported. You need to add the following productions to your grammar:

```
statement      → nullStatement
nullStatement  → ";"
```

The code generator should generate no code for the null statement. But if that is the case, what good is a null statement? Situations can occur in programming where a statement that does nothing is useful. For example, suppose in Java we want the else to associate with the first if in the following structure:

```
if (...)
   if (...)
      statement 1
else                 // associates with second if
   statement 2
```

In this structure, however, the else associates with the nearer (i.e., the second) if. If, however, we use another else and a null statement, we can force the else on statement 2 to associate with the first if:

```
if (...)
   if (...)
      statement 1
   else          // this else associates with the 2nd if
      ;          // use null statement here
else             // this else now associates with the 1st if
   statement 2
```

The first else associates with the second if. Thus, the second else is now forced to associate with the first if.

3. The compound statement is supported. You will need it when you add support for the if and while statements in the next chapter. You need to add the following productions to your grammar:

```
statement          → compoundStatement
compoundStatement  → "{" statementList "}"
```

4. The print statement is supported. The print statement works like the println statement except that it does not output the newline character after it outputs the value of its argument. You need to add the following production to your grammar:

```
printStatement     → "print" "(" expr ")" ";"
```

5. Single-line comments in the source program are supported. These comments start with a double slash, "//". The best place to check for comments is in the get-NextChar() method in the token manager (line 278 in S1). Just before returning from the getNextChar() method, check if the character in currentChar and inputLine[currentColumn] are both '/'. If they are, then reassign '\n' to currentChar. This action effectively terminates the line right at the beginning of the comment. On the next invocation of getNextChar(), the '\n' in currentChar forces getNextChar() to read the next line from the input file.

The complete translation grammar for S2 appears in Figure 12.5. It is also in the file S2.tg in the J1 Software Package.

```
 1 // Translation grammar for S2
 2
 3 void program(): {}
 4 {
 5     statementList()
 6     { cg.endCode();}
 7     <EOF>
 8 }
 9 //----------------
10 void statementList(): {}
11 {
12     statement()
13     statementList()
14  |
15     {}
16 }
17 //----------------
18 void statement(): {}
19 {
20     assignmentStatement()
21  |
22     printlnStatement()
23  |
24     printStatement()
25  |
26     nullStatement()
27  |
28     compoundStatement()
29 }
30 //----------------
31 void assignmentStatement(): { Token t;}
32 {
33     t=<ID>
34     { st.enter(t.image);}
35     { cg.emitInstruction("pc", t.image);}
36     "="
37     expr()
38     { cg.emitInstruction("stav");}
39     ";"
40 }
41 //----------------
42 void printlnStatement(): {}
43 {
44     "println"
45     "("
46     expr()
47     { cg.emitInstruction("dout");}
48     { cg.emitInstruction("pc", "'\\n'");}
49     { cg.emitInstruction("aout");}
50     ")"
51     ";"
52 }
53 //----------------
```

Figure 12.5.

```
54 void printStatement(): {}
55 {
56     "print"
57     "("
58     expr()
59     { cg.emitInstruction("dout");}
60     ")"
61     ";"
62 }
63 //---------------
64 void nullStatement(): {}
65 {
66     ";"
67 }
68 //---------------
69 void compoundStatement(): {}
70 {
71     "{ "
72     statementList()
73     "} "
74 }
75 //---------------
76 void expr(): {}
77 {
78     term()
79     termList()
80 }
81 //---------------
82 void termList(): {}
83 {
84     "+"
85     term()
86     { cg.emitInstruction("add");}
87     termList()
88 |
89     "-"
90     term()
91     { cg.emitInstruction("sub");}
92     termList()
93 |
94     {}
95 }
96 //---------------
97 void term(): {}
98 {
99     factor()
100    factorList()
101 }
102 //---------------
103 void factorList(): {}
104 {
105    "* "
106    factor()
```

Figure 12.5. *Continued.*

```
107     {cg.emitInstruction("mult");}
108     factorList()
109   |
110     "/"
111     factor()
112     {cg.emitInstruction("div");}
113     factorList()
114   |
115     {}
116 }
117 //---------------
118 void factor(): {Token t;}
119 {
120     t=<UNSIGNED>
121     {cg.emitInstruction("pwc", t.image);}
122   |
123     "+"
124     t = <UNSIGNED>
125     {cg.emitInstruction("pwc", t.image);}
126   |
127     "-"
128     t = <UNSIGNED>
129     {cg.emitInstruction("pwc", "-" + t.image);}
130   |
131     t=<ID>
132     {st.enter(t.image);}
133     {cg.emitInstruction("p", t.image);}
134   |
135     "("
136     expr()
137     ")"
138 }
```

Figure 12.5. *Continued.*

PROBLEMS

1. Copy S1.java to S2.java. Then replace every occurrence of "S1" in S2.java
   with "S2". Enter your name in S2.java on lines 10 and 30. Modify S2.java so
   that it meets the specifications for S2 described in Section 12.12. Compile your S2
   compiler with

   ```
   javac S2.java
   ```

   Compile S2.s (which is in the J1 Software Package) with your S2 compiler with

   ```
   java S2 S2
   ```

   Assemble the output file S2.a created by your S2 compiler with

   ```
   a S2.a
   ```

   Finally run the executable program in S2.e created by the assembler with

   ```
   e S2 /c
   ```

Submit to your instructor S2.java, S2.a and S2.*<family name>*.log (the log file that the e program creates when it runs S2.e).

2. Is it possible to output the dw for a variable as soon as that variable is encountered in the source program. If that is the case, can we eliminate the symbol table from S1? Hint: see the discussion of caret lines in Section 11.12.

3. Give two examples for which a null statement in Java is useful.

4. S1 does not close the input file. It this a bug? What problem results if S1 does not close the output file?

5. In the translation grammar for the assignment statement, we emit the stav instruction before we parse the semicolon at the end of the statement (see line 32 in Figure 12.2). Is the reverse order possible? Is the reverse order better?

6. If we were to change our target assembly language, we would have to change the parser in S1. That is, our parser implementation is dependent on the target language. Is it possible to implement the parser in S1 so that it is largely independent of the target language? What would be the advantage of such an implementation?

7. Copy S1.java to S1207.java. Change all occurrences of "S1" in S1207.java to "S1207". Then rewrite S1207.java so that the expr() method corresponds to the production

```
expr → term ("+" term)*
```

and the term() method corresponds to the production

```
term → factor ("*" factor)*
```

That is, use loops instead of recursion for these productions. Test your new compiler by entering

```
javac S1207.java
java S1207 S1
a S1.a
e S1 /c
```

8. What error message does S1 generate if the source program is

```
x = 3; &
```

What error message does S1 generate if the source program is

```
x = 3; y
```

9. To support comments, you have to check in getNextChar() if the current character and the character that follows it are both '/'. Before you check for the second '/', do you have to make sure that you are not already at the end of inputLine? Could an index-out-of-bounds exception occur?

10. What does your S2 compiler do when it compiles

```
x = 32768;
y = 5555555555;
```

Assemble the resulting assembly language program. What happens? Why?

11. Why are the assignments to endLine and endColumn inside the loop rather than after the loop on lines 171, 172, 187, and 188 in S1? Would not executing the assignments to endLine and endColumn once suffice?

12. The token managers in S1 and S2 perform a serial search to determine if an identifier token is actually a keyword (see lines 195 to 198 in S1). An alternative approach is a binary search of a table preloaded with all the keywords in ascending order. In S1, there is only one keyword ("println"). Thus, is does not make sense to use the more complicated binary search in place of a serial search. How many keywords would justify using a binary search?

13. Copy S2.java to S1213.java. Change all occurrences of "S2" in S1213.java to "S1213". Modify S1213.java so that it using a binary search to detect keywords (see Problem 12.12). Test your compiler as specified in Problem 12.1.

14. Examine the assembly code that your S2 compiler produces for the source code in S2.s. Try to write by hand more efficient code. Assemble with a and run with e using the /c command argument. Examine the performance statistics in the log file. How much better is your hand-written assembly code?

15. Copy S1.java to S1215.java. Change all occurrences of "S1" in S1215.java to "S1212". Then rewrite S1215.java so that it uses the following optimization technique: Evaluate constant expressions at compile time rather than at run time. This technique is called *constant folding*. For example, translate the following statement

```
x = 1 + 2;
```

by evaluating the expression at compile time to get 3. Then generate the assembly code

```
pc        x
pwc       3
stav
```

Without this optimization technique, S2 would generate assembly code that performs the addition at run time:

```
pc        x
pwc       1
pwc       2
add
stav
```

Run your optimized S1215 compiler against S1.s. Examine the performance statistics in the log file. Is the code generated more efficient that the code generated by S1?

16. The main method in S1 outputs the compiler/author information to the output file (see line 30 in Figure 12.3). Would it be better for the code generator's constructor to output this information?

17. Copy S1.java to S1217.java. Change every occurrence of "S1" in S1217.java to "S1217". Then rewrite S1217.java so that it compiles directly to machine code. That is, it should output a machine code file (with extension ".e") rather and an assembly code file. Test your compiler by entering

```
javac S1217.java
java S1217 S1
e S1 /c
```

The machine code file that your S1217 compiler produces should start with the ASCII code for the capital letter "T" followed by the machine code in binary.

The best way to implement S1217 is to have its code generator enter machine code into an int array whose contents are then outputted at the end of the compile.

Let us call this array code. Note that the index of an instruction in the code array is also the address of that instruction.

When the code generator enters an instruction that references a variable into the code array, it should enter its instruction's index into the symbol table entry for that variable. For example, suppose the instruction at index 0 references x. Then 0 should be recorded in the symbol table entry for x. If the instruction at index 4 also references x, then 4 should also be recorded in the symbol table entry for x. Thus, the symbol table entry for x will contain a list of indices—an index for every instruction that references x.

For each symbol in the symbol table, the endcode() method should

1. Insert the index of the next available slot in the code array into every instruction that references that symbol. endcode() can determine where these instructions are in the code array by examining the list of indices for that symbol table entry.

2. Insert 0 into the code array (this action allocates the variable and gives it an initial value).

After processing the symbol table, endcode() should then output in binary the ASCII code for the capital letter "T" (54 in hex) followed by the contents of the code array.

For example, consider the source program

```
x = 1;
println(x);
```

The corresponding machine and assembly code is

```
1009         pc      x        ; x = 1
F700 0001    pwc     1
F300         stav

0009         p       x        ; println(x);
FFFD         dout
100A         pc      '\n'
FFFB         aout
FFFF         halt
0000         dw      0
```

When the code generator in S1217 enters the machine code for the intial pc instruction into the code array, it does not know the address of x. Thus, it enters the machine code for a pc instruction with zero in its address field. For the same reason, the p instruction will have 0 in its address field. Then, when endcode() starts processing the symbol table, the code array will contain

```
1000              0  in address of pc  instruction
F700
0001
F300
0000              0  in address of p  instruction
FFFD
100A
FFFB
FFFF
```

        x will go here. This slot has index 9.

At this point, the zero value for x has not yet been entered into the code array. Thus, the next available slot in the code array corresponds to x. This slot has index 9. Thus, the address of x is 9. When endcode() processes the symbol table entry for x, it has to insert 9 (the address of x) into all the instructions in the code array that reference x. Using the symbol table entry for x, endcode() can determine that the instructions at indices 0 and 4 reference x. Thus, encode() then inserts (by adding) 9 into the code array at indices 0 and 4. It then enters 0 into the next slot of the code array (this is the slot for x). Finally, endcode() outputs in binary the ASCII code for the capital letter "T" (54 in hex) followed by the contents of the code array.

18. Could the code that produces the token trace in the S1 compiler be placed in the parser rather than in the token manager? Could the code that outputs the source code as comments be placed in the parser rather than in the token manager?

19. Copy S1.java to S1219.java. Change every occurrence of "S1" in S1219.java to "S1219". Then rewrite S1219.java so that so that it uses the pc instruction in place of the pwc instruction wherever possible. Using your modified compiler, compile the source code in S1.s. How does the modified compiler compare with the original S1 compiler with respect the size and execution time of the generated target code? Next, further modify your compiler so that it uses the p instruction in place of the pwc instruction. A p instruction that replaces a pwc instruction requires a dw for the constant. For example, the following pwc instruction,

```
pwc     -1
```

can be replaced by

```
p       @_1
```

where @_1 is defined with

```
@_1:        dw      -1
```

How does this modification affect the size or execution time of the S1.s program?

20. The genEx method in S1 returns a RuntimeException to its caller (which the caller throws). Would it be better if genEx threw the exception rather than return it?

21. The error messages on line 461 and 487 in S1 include the right parenthesis even when a right parenthesis is not an expected token for the given input. For example, when S1 compiles the following program

```
x = 2
```

it displays the error message

```
Expecting op, ")", or ";"
```

even though the right parenthesis is not expected after 2 (because there is no preceding left parenthesis). Modify S1 so that it does not include the right parenthesis in an error message if it is not among the expected tokens.

22. Could the kind value of single-character tokens be the character itself? What changes would be required to S1? How does this approach compare with the approach used by S1.

23 Is it possible for line 379 in S1 to be executed? If so, give a source program that will cause it to be executed.

24. Would the following replacement for the statementList() method in S1 work correctly? In what way, if any, would S1 behave differently?

```
private void statementList()
{
  switch(currentToken.kind)
  {
    case ID:
    case PRINTLN:
      statement();
      statementList();
      break;
    default:
      break;
  }
}
```

25. Modify S1 so that on a parsing error, a `ParsingException` rather than a `RuntimeException` is thrown, where `ParsingException` is a class of your own creation. What is the advantage of doing this?

26. Modify S1 so that it appends the ".s" extension to the input file name only if it does not have an extension.

13

JAVACC (OPTIONAL)

13.1 INTRODUCTION

We can use a program—a *token manager generator* (often called a *lexical analyzer generator*)—to write a token manager for us. We simply input regular expressions that define the tokens we want to identify. The token manager generator will then output the corresponding token manager in Java code or in some other programming language (see Figure 13.1).

We can also use a program—a *parser generator*—to write a parser for us. We input a grammar and the parser generator outputs the corresponding parser in Java code or in some other programming language (see Figure 13.2).

There are two distinct types of parser generators: those that generate top-down parsers and those that generate bottom-up parsers. In this chapter, we will examine an example of the former (JavaCC); in Chapter 23, we will examine an example of the latter (yacc).

There is more than one way a parser generator can accomplish its task. In one approach, the parser generates tables based on the grammar it is provided. These tables are then combined with a code part to form a complete parser (see Figure 13.3). The code part

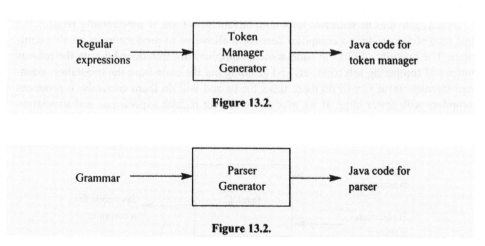

Regular expressions → Token Manager Generator → Java code for token manager

Figure 13.2.

Grammar → Parser Generator → Java code for parser

Figure 13.2.

Compiler Construction Using Java, JavaCC, and Yacc, First Edition. Anthony J. Dos Reis
© 2012 the IEEE Computer Society, Inc. Published 2012 by John Wiley & Sons, Inc.

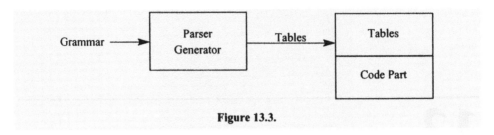

Figure 13.3.

is fixed. That is, every parser generated uses exactly the same code part. yacc, a parser generator that generates bottom-up parsers, uses this approach.

Another approach a parser generator can take—one that works well for parser generators that generate top-down parsers—is to do precisely what we do when we write a top-down recursive-descent parser by hand: namely, write a method for each nonterminal based on the productions in the grammar and their selection sets. JavaCC uses this approach.

If we give a parser generator a grammar, the parser generator creates a parser. If, however, we give it a translation grammar, a parser generator creates a parser/translator—code that not only parses but also translates. Thus, given the appropriate input, a parser generator can output not only the parser but also the code generator components of a compiler. A parser generator, together with a token manager generator, can produce all three essential components of a compiler: the token manager, the parser, and the code generator.

JavaCC is a program that combines a token manager generator with a parser generator. It inputs a file that contains regular expressions (that specify how the token manager should work) and a translation grammar (that specifies how the parser/translator should work). It outputs a file that contains Java code for the corresponding compiler (see Figure 13.4). That is, JavaCC writes the entire compiler for us!

JavaCC performs a translation. It translates its input—regular expressions and a translation grammar—to a compiler. Thus, we can view JavaCC, itself, as a compiler, whose "source program" consists of regular expressions and a translation grammar, and whose "target program" is Java code for the corresponding compiler. For this reason, we call JavaCC a *compiler-compiler*—that is, a compiler of a compiler. The two C's in "JavaCC" stand for "compiler-compiler."

JavaCC provides us with two important advantages. First, it substantially reduces the time required to produce a compiler. Second, it allows us to produce more reliable compilers. The majority of bugs in hand-written compilers are introduced during the tedious process of computing selection sets and grinding out the code from the translation grammar. Because JavaCC will do these tasks for us and will do them correctly, it produces compilers with fewer bugs. If we give it the correct regular expressions and translation grammar, it will give us a bug-free compiler.

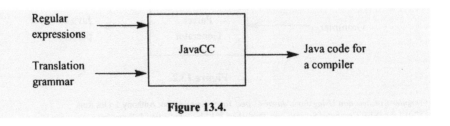

Figure 13.4.

In this chapter, we will learn how to use JavaCC. There is really not much to learn. The form of translation grammar that JavaCC requires is precisely the form we have been using.

Once we learn how to use JavaCC, we will then use it to produce S1j, the JavaCC equivalent to our handwritten compiler S1 from Chapter 12 ("S1j" stands for "S1 JavaCC version"). By doing so, we will get a good sense of how writing a compiler by hand compares with writing one with JavaCC

13.2 JavaCC EXTENDED REGULAR EXPRESSIONS

In the extended regular expressions used by JavaCC, symbols of the underlying alphabet or strings of these symbols are enclosed in double quotes. For example, the expression representing "b" or "c" is

```
"b"|"c"
```

The quotes enclosing alphabetical symbols allow us to distinguish them from symbols not in the underlying alphabet, such as the operators and parentheses. For example, in the preceding expression, the vertical bar is an operator. We know this because it is not enclosed in quotes. Thus, this expression represents "b" or "c". In contrast, the expression

```
"b|c"
```

represents the single string "b|c". Here, the vertical bar is not the union operator because it is enclosed in quotes.

In JavaCC extended regular expressions, we can use the * (zero or more), the + (one or more), and the ? (zero or one) operators (see Section 1.14 for a discussion of these operators). JavaCC requires that the item to which these operators apply be enclosed in parentheses. For example, to indicate zero or more b's, we write

```
("b")*
```

not

```
"b"*
```

Using square brackets, we can specify a set of individual characters. For example, to specify the set containing, "b", "c", and "d", we can use

```
[ "b","c","d"]
```

Note that we must separate successive items within square brackets with commas. We, of course, can also specify the same set with

```
"b"|"c"|"d"
```

The advantage of the square-bracket approach, however, is that it allows us to specify ranges of symbols with hyphens. For example, to specify all the upper- and lower-case letters in the English alphabet, we can specify the ranges "A" through "Z" and "a" through "z" within square brackets:

```
[ "A"-"Z","a"-"z"]
```

This expression is very convenient shorthand for the longer expression

```
[ "A", "B", ..., "Z", "a", "b", ..., "z"]
```

that lists all 52 letters. We use square brackets to specify sets of *individual characters only*. We cannot specify any elements that are character sequences. For example, in

```
[ "b", "cd", "\n"]    ◄——— "cd"  is illegal within square brackets
```

"b" and "\n" are both legal because they are both single characters ("\n" represents the newline character, which is a single character). However, "cd" is not legal because it is a character sequence.

The complement operator, ~, can be applied only to a set defined by square brackets. For example,

```
~[ "b"]
```

represents every single character except for "b". Thus, the following expression is not legal:

```
~"b"    ◄——— not legal
```

Unlike the *, +, and ? operators, parentheses should not be used with the ~ operator. For example, the following expressions are not legal:

```
~ ([ "b"] )    ◄——— not legal
~ ("b")    ◄——— not legal
```

As you would expect, [ ] represents the empty set. Thus, ~[ ] is the complement of the empty set, and represents the complete alphabet—that is, the entire set of characters available.

Exercise 13.1

Write a JavaCC extended regular expression that represents the universe of strings.

Answer:

(~[ ])*

By starring the alphabet ~[ ] , we get the universe. Notice we have to use a pair of parentheses for the "*" operator but not for the "~" operator.   ■

Any spaces not inside quotes in a JavaCC extended regular expression are ignored. Thus,

```
"b" | "c"
```

and

```
"b"   |   "c"
```

are equivalent. However,

```
"b" | "c"
```

and

```
"b " | "c"
```

are not because the space following the b in the latter expression is within quotes.

Let us define the unsigned integer token category with an extended regular expression. An unsigned integer consists of one or more digits. We can define this token category with

```
([ "0"-"9"] ) +
```

Suppose, however, we wanted to specify numbers that include both unsigned integers and numbers with a decimal point. For example, we want to include all these numbers:

```
32
3.20
45.
.11
```

An expression that appears to define these numbers is

```
([ "0"-"9"] )*   "."   ([ "0"-"9"] )*
```

Preceding and following the decimal point in the middle, we can have zero or more digits. This expression specifies all the numbers we listed above, except 32 (every number defined by the regular expression above necessarily has a decimal point—thus, it cannot define 32 without a decimal point). Moreover, it also specifies a nonnumber: a decimal point without any preceding or following digits. To get just the decimal point, we take zero occurrences (as allowed by the star operators) of the parenthesized expressions before and after the decimal point. To get a correct expression for our numbers—one that does not include nonnumbers—we need to consider four possibilities for our numbers:

1. Digits but no decimal point (like 32)
2. Digits both before and after the decimal point (like 3.20)
3. Digits only before the decimal point (like 45.)
4. Digits only after the decimal point like (.11).

We can construct a correct expression by simply defining each of these four possibilities separately and combining them with the vertical bar. We get

```
([ "0"-"9"] ) +                              |
([ "0"-"9"] ) +   "."   ([ "0"-"9"] ) +      |
([ "0"-"9"] ) +   "."                        |
                  "."   ([ "0"-"9"] ) +
```

If we make the left side of the second alternative optional, we do not need the fourth alternative. We can make it optional either by using "* " (which allows zero occurrences) in place of "+" or by applying the question mark operator to it. Using the former approach, we get

```
([ "0"-"9"] )+                              |
([ "0"-"9"] )*    "."    ([ "0"-"9"] )+     |
([ "0"-"9"] )+    "."
```

Exercise 13.2

Suppose an identifier consists of an initial letter followed by zero or more letters and/or digits. Give the corresponding JavaCC extended regular expression.

Answer:

```
[ "A"-"Z","a"-"z"] ([ "A"-"Z","a"-"z","0"-"9"] )*
```

■

The double quote and backslash characters are special characters in a string. Thus, if we want to specify an ordinary double quote or backslash, we must backslash them. For example, to specify the string consisting of "A", backslash, double quote, and "B", we have to write

```
"A\\\"B"
```

The first two backslashes represent a single ordinary backslash; the third backslash and the following double quote represent an ordinary double quote (which, therefore, does not terminate the string). A few ordinary characters, if backslashed, have special meanings. For example, "\n", "\r", and "\t" represent the newline, return, and tab characters, respectively.

Exercise 13.3

1. What will "A\nB" match?
2. What will "A\\nB" match?

Answers:

1. the sequence "A", newline, "B"
2. the sequence "A", backslash, "n", "B"

■

JavaCC allows us to associate names with regular expressions. To do this, we enclose the name and regular expression in angle brackets, separating the two with a colon. For example, to associate the name UNSIGNED with the regular expression for unsigned integers, we write

```
<UNSIGNED:  ([ "0"-"9"] )+>
```

By convention, we use all capital letters for the names of regular expressions. Once we give a regular expression a name, we can refer to the token category it specifies by that name. For example, consider the definition of factor() in the translation grammar for S1 given in Chapter 12:

```
  void factor(): { Token t;}
  {
     t=<UNSIGNED>
     { cg.emitInstruction("pwc", t.image);}
   |
     "+"
     t = <UNSIGNED>
     { cg.emitInstruction("pwc", t.image);}
   |
     "-"
     t = <UNSIGNED>
     { cg.emitInstruction("pwc", "-" + t.image);}
   |
     t=<ID>
     { symTab.enter(t.image);}
     { cg.emitInstruction("p", t.image);}
   |
     "("
     expr()
     ")"
  }
```

If we provide this definition of factor() to JavaCC along with the following named
regular expressions

```
  <UNSIGNED: ([ "0"-"9"] )+>
```

and

```
  <ID: [ "A"-"Z","a"-"z"] ([ "A"-"Z","a"-"z","0"-"9"] )*>
```

then JavaCC will interpret <UNSIGNED> and <ID> in the definition of factor() accordingly. That is, it will view them as tokens defined by their corresponding regular expressions.

If we give a name to a regular expression, we can use that name (with angle brackets) in
the definitions of other regular expressions. For example, suppose we have the definition

```
  <DIGIT: [ "0"-"9"] >
```

Then we can use <DIGIT> in other definitions. For example, we can define an expression
for unsigned integers with

```
        <UNSIGNED: (<DIGIT>)+>
```

13.3 JavaCC INPUT FILE

By convention, we use the extension ".jj" for a JavaCC input file. For example,
S1j.jj in the J1 Software Package contains the JavaCC input file that defines the S1j
compiler. Figure 13.5 shows the structure of a typical ".jj" file. Java-style comments

```
options
{
    // JavaCC options go here.
}

PARSER_BEGIN (name of parser class)

    // The parser class and other classes go here.

PARSER_END (name of parser class)

TOKEN_MGR_DECLS:
{
    // Declarations of variables and methods for use
    // by the token manager go here.
}

SKIP:
{
    // Regular expressions that describe tokens that
    // the token manager should not pass to the parser
    // go here.
}

TOKEN:
{
    // Regular expressions that describe tokens that
    // the token manager should pass to the parser go here.
}

    // Translation grammar goes here.
```

Figure 13.5. JavaCC input file format.

are allowed in a JavaCC input file, either single-line comments that start with "//" or multiple-line comments that are bracketed with "/* " and "*/".

The options block is used to set options for JavaCC. For example, the following statement in the options block

```
STATIC = false;
```

sets the STATIC option to false. This setting causes JavaCC to generate nonstatic rather than static methods from the translation grammar it is provided. All the JavaCC options have default values. The default value of the STATIC option is true. Thus, if we want STATIC to be false, we have to set it to false. To see a list of all the JavaCC options and their default values, enter javacc on the command line without any arguments.

The PARSER_BEGIN/PARSER_END block contains the Java code we want to provide to JavaCC. This block must contain at the least the parser class. The parser class is required because it is this class into which JavaCC places the Java code it produces when it translates the translation grammar in the ".jj" file. Because the PARSER_BE-GIN/PARSER_END block may optionally contain additional classes (such as the symbol table or code generator classes), you must tell JavaCC which class in this block is the

parser class. You do this by specifying the parser class name within parentheses in the
PARSER_BEGIN and PARSER_END statements. For example, if the parser class is
named Sample, then you should use

```
PARSER_BEGIN(Sample)
   ...
PARSER_END(Sample)
```

The parser class within the PARSER_BEGIN/PARSER_END block does not have to contain any Java code. It can be an empty shell. For example, we can have

```
PARSER_BEGIN(Sample)
public class Sample
{
}
PARSER_END(Sample)
```

In this case, the Sample class that JavaCC outputs will contain only the Java code produced by JavaCC from the translation grammar it is provided. Alternatively, we can include some methods (such as main()) in the parser class. For example, we can have

```
PARSER_BEGIN(Sample)
class Sample
{
    public static void main(String[] args)
    {
        ...
    }
}
PARSER_END(Sample)
```

In this case, the Sample class that JavaCC outputs will contain main() as well as the
methods corresponding to the translation grammar. If we also include the symbol table
and code generator classes in the PARSER_BEGIN/PARSER_END block, then JavaCC
will output a complete compiler. This is what we do in S1j.jj. Figure 13.6 shows the
structure of the PARSER_BEGIN/PARSER_END block for S1j.jj.

The TOKEN_MGR_DECLS block in a ".jj" file contains declarations of variables and
methods for use by the token manager. In Section 13.3, we will see an example that
makes use of the TOKEN_MGR_DECL block.

A SKIP block in a ".jj" file contains regular expressions for those tokens the token
manager should *not* pass to the parser. For our S1j compiler, we want the token manager
to skip whitespace (space, newline, carriage return, and tab). So the SKIP block should
contain a regular expression for each whitespace character (see Figure 13.7).

The TOKEN block contains regular expressions for the tokens the token manager
should pass to the parser. It should also provide names for the tokens that we use in the
translation grammar. For the S1j compiler, we can use the TOKEN block in Figure 13.8.

Because we have associated the names PRINTLN, ID, and UNSIGNED with the regular
expressions in this TOKEN block, we can use these names (enclosed in angle brackets) in
the translation grammar to represent the corresponding tokens.

The order we list regular expressions in a TOKEN block can be significant. If two regular expressions match the same image from the input stream, then the JavaCC-generated

```
PARSER_BEGIN(S1j)
import java.io.*;
import java.util.ArrayList;
class S1j
{
    public static void main(String[] arg)
    {
        ...
    }
}
//=========================================
class S1jSymTab
{
    ...
}
//=========================================
class S1jCodeGen
{
    ...
}
PARSER_END(S1j)
```

Figure 13.6.

token manager will use the first one listed. For example, suppose "println" appears in the input stream that the token manager is processing. Both the <PRINTLN> and <ID> regular expressions in the TOKEN block in Figure 13.8 match this image. Because, the PRINTLN expression is listed before the ID expression, the token manager treats a "println" in the input stream as a <PRINTLN> token. If, however, the <ID> expression preceded the <PRINTLN> expression in the TOKEN block, then "println" would be treated as an <ID> token. Then the parse of a println statement would fail because it would get from the token manager an <ID> token instead of the expected <PRINTLN> token. Because of this leading bogus <ID> token, the parser would think it had an assignment statement and would proceed to parse it accordingly. The parser would then detect an error on the next token, which should be "=" for an assignment statement but would be "(" for the actual println statement it is parsing.

Because the <PRINTLN> token corresponds to the single string "println", we may use the string itself instead of <PRINTLN> in a translation grammar (see Figure 13.9).

```
SKIP:
{
    " "
    |
    "\n"
    |
    "\r"
    |
    "\t"
}
```

Figure 13.7.

```
TOKEN:
{
    <PRINTLN: "println">
  |
    <UNSIGNED: ([ "0"-"9"] )+>
  |
    <ID: [ "A"-"Z","a"-"z"] ([ "A"-"Z","a"-"z","0"-"9"] )*>
}
```

Figure 13.8.

```
void printlnStatement(): {}
{
    "println"    ◄──────  using the token itself rather than <PRINTLN>
    "("
    expr()
    { cg.emitInstruction("dout");}
    { cg.emitInstruction("pc",  "'\\n'");}
    { cg.emitInstruction("aout");}
    ")"
    ";"
}
```

Figure 13.9.

If we do this, then we do not have to give "println" a name in the TOKEN block. We still must list it, however, in the TOKEN block. Moreover, we must list it before the <ID> token for the reason given above. We call unnamed tokens, like "println" in Figure 13.10, *anonymous tokens*.

What if we we list neither "println" nor <PRINTLN: "println"> in the TOKEN block but we use "println" in the translation grammar? Then JavaCC will, in effect, place the "println" token *at the end* of the TOKEN block. In other words, JavaCC builds a token manager as if the TOKEN block included "println" after the listed tokens, as in Figure 13.11.

But then the <ID> regular expression, not "println", would match a "println" in the input stream, resulting in a parsing error on a valid println statement. Note that we do not have to list anonymous single character tokens such as "=", "(", and ")". All these tokens do not match any of the expressions in the TOKEN block in Figure 13.11. So when JavaCC places them at the end of the TOKEN block, incorrect matches cannot occur.

```
TOKEN:
{
    "println"   ◄──────  not giving the token expression a name
  |
    <UNSIGNED: ([ "0"-"9"] )+>
  |
    <ID: [ "A"-"Z","a"-"z"] ([ "A"-"Z","a"-"z","0"-"9"] )*>
}
```

Figure 13.10.

```
TOKEN:
{
    <UNSIGNED: ([ "0"-"9"] )+>
  |
    <ID: [ "A"-"Z","a"-"z"]  ([ "A"-"Z","a"-"z","0"-"9"] )*>
  |
    "println"
}
```

Figure 13.11.

We *must* delimit each alternative listed in a TOKEN and SKIP block with angle brackets if it is *not* a quoted string. For example, the first alternative in the following SKIP block is illegal because it is neither a quoted string nor a string enclosed in angle brackets:

```
SKIP:
{
    ("b")+  ◀———— Illegal (must surround with angle brackets)
  |
    "hello" ◀———— okay with or without angle brackets
}
```

The correct SKIP block is

```
SKIP:
{
    <("b")+> ◀———— angle brackets required
  |
    "hello"  ◀———— okay with or without angle brackets
}
```

Because the second alternative, "hello", is a quoted string, we do not need angle brackets. However, we can still use them if we want. That is, we could have used

```
        <"hello">
```

for the second alternative above.

The token manager that JavaCC generates follows two rules when it matches regular expressions in the SKIP and TOKEN blocks with the characters in the input stream:

1. Always use the longest match possible. For example, suppose a TOKEN block is

```
TOKEN:
{
<T1:  ("b")+>
}
```

and the input to the token manager is "bbbccc". Then <T1> matches three substrings of the input: the first "b", the first two b's. and all three b's. The token manager in this case returns the longest matched token, which is "bbb".

2. If more than one expression provides the longest match, then use the one listed the first. We have already seen this rule in action with "println" and the expression for ID. Both match "println". So the order in which we list them in the TOKEN block determines which one is used when "println" appears in the input stream.

Exercise 13.4

If the input to the token manager is "ABCDEF" and the TOKEN block is

```
TOKEN:
{
    <T1: "ABC">
  |
    <T2: "ABCDEF">
}
```

Which token is returned?

Answer:

T2 because it matches the longer substring.

■

With the TOKEN block in Figure 13.10, the JavaCC-generated token manager will match those tokens listed ("println", <UNSIGNED>, and <ID>) plus all those tokens JavaCC automatically includes in TOKEN block. The latter are all the quoted strings in the translation grammar that are not already listed in the TOKEN block. For S1j, these tokens are "=", ";", "(", ")", "+", and "*". Now suppose the JavaCC-generated token manager scans the following input:

```
x = ^ 3;
```

The token manager will have no problem with the first two tokens, "x" and "=". However, when it reaches "^", it will throw an exception because no expression in the TOKEN block can match it. Unlike the parser, the token manager does not know what is expected in the input stream at the point the invalid character appears. As a result, the error message associated with the exception thrown by the token manager will lack some important information. A better approach is for the token manager to return the bad token to the parser. The parser would then detect the error and throw an exception with a more informative error message. We would not have to modify the parser in any way: It already includes a catch block that catches parse exceptions and displays their associated error messages.

To force the JavaCC-created token manager to return bad tokens to the parser rather than throwing exceptions, we simply include the following expression *at the bottom* of the TOKEN block:

```
<ERROR: ~[ ] >
```

The regular expression ~[ ] is the complement of the empty set. Thus, it represents *any* single character. It will match any single character that is not matched by the expressions above it in the TOKEN block. Unfortunately, if we use single-character tokens such as "=" in the translation grammar, then JavaCC includes them in the TOKEN block *after* the ER-

ROR expression. Then when a single character token, such as "=", appears in the input stream, the ERROR expression will be first expression in the TOKEN block to match it. Thus, the token manager will return the ERROR token to the parser, incorrectly causing an error. If we want to use the ERROR token, we must explicitly list *all* the possible tokens in the TOKEN block *before* the ERROR token. Then the token manager will return the ERROR token only on an invalid character.

Although the TOKEN block in Figs. 13.8 will work for S1j, the best TOKEN block to use is the TOKEN block in Figure 13.12, in which we list all possible tokens, with the ERROR token at the end.

Although the only token names we use in the translation grammar for S1j are <UN-SIGNED> and <ID>, we have given names to all the token expressions in Figure 13.11. That way, if we ever need the name of a token expression, one is available.

Here are some good rules to follow when creating a TOKEN block:

> **Always list a regular expression for every possible token in the TOKEN block. Give every expression a name. List the ERROR expression last.**

13.4 SPECIFYING ACTIONS FOR REGULAR EXPRESSIONS

Actions can be associated with the regular expressions we use in a ".jj" file to define the operation of the token manager. If a regular expression has an action associated with it, that action is executed whenever that regular expression is used in a match. We specify actions in the same way we specify them in a translation grammar: with Java code en-

```
TOKEN:
{
    <PRINTLN: "println">
  |
    <UNSIGNED: ([ "0"-"9"] )+>
  |
    <ID: [ "A"-"Z","a"-"z"] ([ "A"-"Z","a"-"z","0"-"9"] )*>
  |
    <ASSIGN: "=">
  |
    <SEMICOLON: ";">
  |
    <LEFTPAREN: "(">
  |
    <RIGHTPAREN: ")">
  |
    <PLUS: "+">
  |
    <MINUS: "-">
  |
    <TIMES: "*">
  |
    <ERROR: ~[ ]>
}
```

Figure 13.12.

closed in braces. An action should follow the regular expression to which it applies. Let us look at an example. Suppose we define an unsigned integer with

```
TOKEN:
{
        ...
  |
    <UNSIGNED: ([ "0"-"9"] )+>
    { System.out.println("UNSIGNED");}
  |

        ...
}
```

Then every time the token manager scans an unsigned integer in the input stream, it would display UNSIGNED just before it returns the unsigned integer token to the parser.

When the token manager has found a match with a regular expression and is about to return a token to the parser, the reference to that token is available in the variable matchedToken. The actions in TOKEN and SKIP blocks can make use of this variable. For example, if we define an unsigned integer with

```
TOKEN:
{
        ...
  |
    <UNSIGNED: ([ "0"-"9"] )+>
    { System.out.println("image is " + matchedToken.image);}
  |
        ...
}
```

then every time the token manager scans an unsigned integer, it would display the image field of its token. Thus, if the input were

```
123 456
```

then the token manager would display

```
image is 123
image is 456
```

Suppose we wanted the token manager to display the image for *every* token returned to the parser, not just unsigned integer tokens. We, of course, could add the action to do this to every regular expression in the TOKEN block. But there is an easier way: We simply place the action in a method named CommonTokenAction, and place this method in the TOKEN_MGR_DECLS block. We also set the COMMON_TOKEN_ACTION option to true in the options block. Then the token manager will call the CommonTokenAction method, passing it the current token, each time it is about to return the token to the parser. Figure 13.13 shows the structure of a ".jj" file in which we use this technique with the TOKEN block from S1j.

```
options
{
    STATIC = false;
    COMMON_TOKEN_ACTION = true;
    // other options can go here
}
//============================================================
PARSER_BEGIN(name of parser class)


    // The parser class and other classes go here


PARSER_END(name of parser class)
//============================================================
TOKEN_MGR_DECLS:
{
    void CommonTokenAction(Token t)
    {
        System.out.println("image is " + t.image);
    }
}
//============================================================
SKIP:
{
    " "
  |
    "\n"
  |
    "\r"
  |
    "\t"
}
//============================================================
TOKEN:
{
    <PRINTLN: "println">
  |
    <UNSIGNED: (["0"-"9"])+>
  |
    <ID: ["A"-"Z","a"-"z"] (["A"-"Z","a"-"z","0"-"9"])*>
  |
    <ASSIGN: "=">
  |
    <SEMICOLON: ";">
  |
    <LEFTPAREN: "(">
  |
    <RIGHTPAREN: ")">
  |
    <PLUS: "+">
  |
```

Figure 13.13.

```
   <MINUS: "-">
 |
   <TIMES: "*">
 |
   <ERROR: ~[ ] >
 }

 // Translation grammar goes here ===============================
```

Figure 13.13. *Continued.*

Given the input

```
   x = 17;
```

the token manager corresponding to Figure 13.13 would display

```
image is x
image is =
image is 17
image is ;
```

We can set JavaCC options, like STATIC and COMMON_TOKEN_ACTION, with either an assignment statement in the options block (see the options block in Figure 13.13) or with a command line argument. For example, suppose we invoke JavaCC with

```
javacc -NOSTATIC -COMMON_TOKEN_ACTION Fig1313.jj
```

Then the -NOSTATIC and -COMMON_TOKEN_ACTION arguments would set the corresponding options to false and true, respectively, when JavaCC processes Fig1313.jj.

Each true/false option has two possible corresponding arguments: one with a "NO" prefix, and one without a "NO" prefix. The NO variation sets the option to false; the variation without NO sets the option to true. For example, the argument -STATIC sets the STATIC option to true, but -NOSTATIC sets it to false. The default value for the STATIC option is true. Thus, if we want it to be false, we must set it to false in the options block or on the command line with the -NOSTATIC option. Similarly, the default value for the COMMON_TOKEN_ACTION option is false. Thus, if we want it to be true, we must set it to true in either the options block or on the command line with the -COMMON_TOKEN_ ACTION argument. If we use both the options block and a command line argument for an option, the command line argument dominates.

The CommonTokenAction method in Figure 13.13 provides a useful debugging capability. It displays a token trace. Specifically, it displays the image of every token returned to the parser. With a token trace, we can easily check if our token manager is working correctly. Once we confirm that the token manager is working correctly, we can create a new token manager that does not produce the token trace: We simply run JavaCC again, supplying it with a ".jj" file in which the -COMMON_TOKEN_ACTION option in the options block is set to false or omitted (in which case it defaults to false). Alternatively, we can supply JavaCC the original ".jj" file but specify -NOCOMMON_TO-KEN_ACTION on the command line.

Rather than use the `CommonTokenAction` method to display token information, we can have JavaCC provide token information automatically. We simply set the `DEBUG_TOKEN_MANAGER` option to true. Then the token manager that JavaCC generates will display voluminous information on the tokenizing process and on each token it provides the parser. Similarly, you can get information useful for debugging the parser by setting the `DEBUG_PARSER` option to true.

13.5 JavaCC INPUT FILE FOR S1j

The listing of the JavaCC input file `S1j.jj` for the S1j compiler appears in Figure 13.14. The file `S1j.jj` is in the J1 Software Package. The symbol table and code generator classes in `S1j.jj` are identical to those classes in the hand-written S1 compiler.

The translation grammar in `S1j.jj` (lines 200 to 299) is identical to the translation grammar for S1 that we provided in Chapter 12. It assumes that tokens are provided to the parser in the form of `Token` objects, where `Token` is a class generated by JavaCC. The JavaCC-generated `Token` class is similar to the `Token` class we used in our handwritten S1 compiler. It has `kind`, `beginLine`, `endLine`, `beginColumn`, `endColumn`, `image`, and `next` fields, just like our `Token` class in S1. It also has a few additional fields that we will discuss later. The compiler JavaCC produces for `S1j.jj` behaves exactly like our handwritten S1 compiler with one exception: The source code does not appear as comments in the output file. In S1, these comments are generated by our handwritten token manager (see line 262 in Figure 12.4). However, in our S1j compiler, our token manager is generated for us by JavaCC, and this generated token manager does not output source lines as comments. If we want our JavaCC-generated token manager to output the source code as comments, we have to provide JavaCC with the code that performs that function (see problem 34). Alternatively, we can have the parser do it (see Section 13.12).

The code generator and the symbol table classes in the `PARSER_BEGIN`/`PARSER_END` block are essentially identical to those we used in S1. The only difference is that `S1j` appears in the class names in place of `S1`. However, the `main()` method in the `PARSER_BEGIN`/`PARSER_END` block is slightly different from the `main()` method in S1. This difference is because the two versions use different token managers and parsers. In S1, we use our handwritten versions; in `S1j.jj`, we use the JavaCC-produced versions. In addition, `main()` is in its own class in S1 but within the parser class in `S1j.jj`. Another difference is the type of exception thrown. Notice that line 59 of the `S1j.jj` file catches a `ParseException` rather than a `RuntimeException`. In S1, a `RuntimeException` is thrown on a parse error. However, in S1j, a `ParseException` is thrown on a parse error.

Because the `TOKEN_MANAGER_USES_PARSER` option is set to true on line 10 in `S1j.jj`, the reference to the parser is passed to the token manager, which stores it in a variable named `parser`. Via this variable, the token manager can access the public methods and variables in the parser. For example, on line 160, the `CommonTokenAction` method in the token manager invokes the `makeComment` method in the parser via the `parser` reference, passing it the reference to the current token. `makeComment` then writes the fields of the token it is passed in the form of a comment to the output file, the effect of which is to create a token trace in the output file. This mechanism is in effect, however, only if `COMMON_TOKEN_ACTION` is set to true (see line 7). In S1, the token manager creates the token trace. But in S1j, the parser creates the token trace. Why doesn't the token manager in S1j create the token trace? It does not have direct access to the output file. Specifically, it does not have access to `outFile`, the reference to the output file.

```
 1 // S1j.jj JavaCC input file for S1j compiler
 2 options
 3 {
 4   STATIC = false;           // generate non-static methods
 5
 6   // set to true to debug token manager
 7   COMMON_TOKEN_ACTION = false;
 8
 9   // pass parser reference to the token manager
10   TOKEN_MANAGER_USES_PARSER = true;
11 }                                   // end of options block
12 //=========================================================
13 PARSER_BEGIN(S1j)
14 import java.io.*;
15 import java.util.ArrayList;
16 class S1j
17 {
18   private PrintWriter outFile;
19   private S1jSymTab st;
20   private S1jCodeGen cg;
21   //----------------------
22   public static void main(String[] args) throws
23                                         IOException
24   {
25     System.out.println("S1j compiler written by ...");
26
27     if (args.length != 1)
28     {
29       System.err.println("Wrong number cmd line args");
30       System.exit(1);
31     }
32
33     // build input and output file names
34     String inFileName = args[0] + ".s";
35     String outFileName = args[0] + ".a";
36
37     // construct file objects
38     FileInputStream inFile =
39                       new FileInputStream(inFileName);
40     PrintWriter outFile = new PrintWriter(outFileName);
41
42     // identify compiler/author in output file
43     outFile.println("; from S1j compiler written by ...");
44
45     // construct objects that make up compiler
46     S1jSymTab st = new S1jSymTab();
47     S1jCodeGen cg = new S1jCodeGen(outFile, st);
48     S1j parser = new S1j(inFile);
49
50     // initialize parser's instance variables
51     parser.outFile = outFile;
52     parser.st = st;
53     parser.cg = cg;
```

Figure 13.14.

```
54
55     try
56     {
57       parser.program();
58     }
59     catch(ParseException e)
60     {
61       System.err.println(e.getMessage());
62       outFile.println(e.getMessage());
63       outFile.close();
64       System.exit(1);
65     }
66
67     outFile.close();
68   }
69   //---------------------
70   // If COMMON_TOKEN_ACTION is true, the token manager
71   // calls makeComment for each token to create the
72   // token trace.
73   //
74   public void makeComment(Token t)
75   {
76     outFile.printf(
77       "; kd=%3d bL=%3d bC=%3d eL=%3d eC=%3d im= %s%n",
78         t.kind, t.beginLine, t.beginColumn, t.endLine,
79         t.endColumn, t.image);
80   }
81 }                                        // end of S1j
82 //========================================================
83 class S1jSymTab
84 {
85   private ArrayList<String> symbol;
86   //---------------------
87   public S1jSymTab()
88   {
89     symbol = new ArrayList<String>();
90   }
91   //---------------------
92   public void enter(String s)
93   {
94     int index = symbol.indexOf(s);
95
96     // if s is not in symbol, then add it
97     if (index < 0)
98       symbol.add(s);
99   }
100  //---------------------
101  public String getSymbol(int i)
102  {
103    return symbol.get(i);
104  }
105  //---------------------
106  public int getSize()
```

Figure 13.14. *Continued.*

```
107   {
108       return symbol.size();
109   }
110 }                                      // end of S1jSymTab
111 //============================================================
112 class S1jCodeGen
113 {
114   private PrintWriter outFile;
115   private S1jSymTab st;
116   //---------------------
117   public S1jCodeGen(PrintWriter outFile, S1jSymTab st)
118   {
119     this.outFile = outFile;
120     this.st = st;
121   }
122   //---------------------
123   public void emitInstruction(String op)
124   {
125     outFile.printf("          %-4s%n", op);
126   }
127   //---------------------
128   public void emitInstruction(String op, String opnd)
129   {
130     outFile.printf(
131                   "          %-4s        %s%n", op, opnd);
132   }
133   //---------------------
134   public void emitdw(String label, String value)
135   {
136     outFile.printf(
137             "%-9s dw        %s%n", label + ":", value);
138   }
139   //---------------------
140   public void endCode()
141   {
142     outFile.println();
143     emitInstruction("halt");
144
145     int size = st.getSize();
146     // emit dw for each symbol in the symbol table
147     for (int i=0; i < size; i++)
148       emitdw(st.getSymbol(i), "0");
149   }
150 }                                      // end of S1jCodeGen class
151 PARSER_END(S1j)
152
153 // Specification of the S1j token manager ==============
154
155 TOKEN_MGR_DECLS:
156 {
157   // called for each token returned to parser
158   void CommonTokenAction(Token t)
159   {
```

Figure 13.14. *Continued.*

```
160        parser.makeComment(t);
161    }
162 }
163 //----------------
164 SKIP:  // these tokens are not returned to parser
165 {
166    " "
167  |
168    "\n"
169  |
170    "\r"
171  |
172    "\t"
173 }
174 //----------------
175 TOKEN:   // these tokens are returned to parser
176 {
177    <PRINTLN: "println">  // must precede <ID>
178  |
179    <UNSIGNED: ([ "0"-"9"] )+>
180  |
181    <ID: [ "A"-"Z","a"-"z"]  ([ "A"-"Z","a"-"z","0"-"9"] )*>
182  |
183    <ASSIGN: "=">
184  |
185    <SEMICOLON: ";">
186  |
187    <LEFTPAREN: ")">
188  |
189    <RIGHTPAREN: ")">
190  |
191    <PLUS: "+">
192  |
193    <MINUS: "-">
194  |
195    <TIMES: "*">
196  |
197    <ERROR: ~[]>   // matches any single character
198 }
199
200 // Translation grammar for S1j and S1 ====================
201
202 void program(): {}
203 {
204    statementList()
205    { cg.endCode();}
206    <EOF>
207 }
208 //----------------
209 void statementList(): {}
210 {
211    statement()
212    statementList()
```

Figure 13.14. *Continued.*

```
213  |
214     {}
215 }
216 //---------------
217 void statement(): {}
218 {
219     assignmentStatement()
220  |
221     printlnStatement()
222 }
223 //---------------
224 void assignmentStatement(): { Token t;}
225 {
226     t=<ID>
227     { st.enter(t.image);}
228     { cg.emitInstruction("pc", t.image);}
229     "="
230     expr()
231     { cg.emitInstruction("stav");}
232     ";"
233 }
234 //---------------
235 void printlnStatement(): {}
236 {
237     "println"
238     "("
239     expr()
240     { cg.emitInstruction("dout");}
241     { cg.emitInstruction("pc", "'\\n'");}
242     { cg.emitInstruction("aout");}
243     ")"
244     ";"
245 }
246 //---------------
247 void expr(): {}
248 {
249     term()
250     termList()
251 }
252 //---------------
253 void termList(): {}
254 {
255     "+"
256     term()
257     { cg.emitInstruction("add");}
258     termList()
259  |
260     {}
261 }
262 //---------------
263 void term(): {}
264 {
265     factor()
```

Figure 13.14. *Continued.*

```
266     factorList()
267 }
268 //---------------
269 void factorList(): {}
270 {
271     "*"
272     factor()
273     {cg.emitInstruction("mult");}
274     factorList()
275   |
276     {}
277 }
278 //---------------
279 void factor(): { Token t;}
280 {
281     t=<UNSIGNED>
282     {cg.emitInstruction("pwc", t.image);}
283   |
284     "+"
285     t = <UNSIGNED>
286     {cg.emitInstruction("pwc", t.image);}
287   |
288     "-"
289     t = <UNSIGNED>
290     {cg.emitInstruction("pwc", "-" + t.image);}
291   |
292     t=<ID>
293     {st.enter(t.image);}
294     {cg.emitInstruction("p", t.image);}
295   |
296     "("
297     expr()
298     ")"
299 }
```

Figure 13.14. *Continued.*

To convert `S1j.jj` to a Java program, enter

```
javacc S1j.jj
```

JavaCC will then create a Java program from `S1j.jj` and output it to the file `S1j.java`.

To compile the Java program produced by JavaCC, enter

```
javac S1j.java
```

To then use our new compiler to compile `S1.s`, enter

```
java S1j S1
```

This command invokes the S1j compiler, which then creates an assembly language program from the source program in `S1.s` and places it in a file named `S1.a`.

To assemble the assembly language program `S1j.a`, enter

```
a S1.a
```

which creates the file `S1.e` containing the executable program. To then execute the executable program in `S1.e` and verify its correctness, enter

```
e S1 /c
```

13.6 FILES PRODUCED BY JavaCC

When JavaCC processes the input file `S1j.jj`, it outputs the following files:

```
S1j.java
ParseException.java
Token.java
S1jConstants.java
S1jTokenManager.java
TokenMgrError.java
SimpleCharStream.java
```

`S1j.java` contains all the Java code that we provide in the PARSER_BEGIN/PARSER_END block. In addition, it contains the Java code produced by JavaCC corresponding to the translation grammar. This code is inserted into the `S1j` parser class within the PARSER_BEGIN/PARSER_END block.

The `S1j.java` also contains the `getToken()` method. This method returns a token without advancing the current input. `getToken(i)` returns the *i*th token relative to the current token. For example, `getToken(1)` returns the current token, `getToken(2)` returns the next token, and so on. The argument we pass to `getToken()` should not be a negative integer. However, we can pass it 0. `getToken(0)` returns the token preceding the current token.

The token returned by `getToken()` depends on the context in which the call of `getToken()` appears. For example, in the sequence

```
void printlnStatement(): { Token t;}
{
    "println"
    ...
    ")"
    { t=getToken(1);}
    ";"
  }
```

`getToken(1)` returns the `")"` token. However, in the sequence

```
(statement())*
{ t=getToken(1);}
  ";"
```

`getToken(1)` returns the `";"` token. In the latter case, the parser has to reach the `";"` before it can determine that the statement list has ended. Thus, when `getToken(1)` is executed the current token is already " ; ". However, in the former case, getToken(1) is called just before the parser advances past the ") ". So it returns the ") " token.

To obtain the token at the very beginning of a sequence, you should call getToken(1) before the initial token. For example, in the sequence

```
void printlnStatement(); { Token t;}
{
    { t=getToken(1);}
    "println"
    "("
    ...
}
```

getToken(1) returns the "println" token. This behavior makes sense: For the parser to select this sequence, the parser has to have already reached the "println" token. Thus, the initial call of getToken(1) returns the "println" token.

The S1j class implements the S1jConstants interface (see Figure 13.15). Thus, all the constants in S1jConstants.java are available to the parser.

When the parser generated by JavaCC detects an error, it generates a ParseException. This type of exception is defined in the file ParseException.java.

Token.java is similar to the Token class that we used in S1. It contains the same fields as the Token class in S1 (kind, beginLine, beginColumn, endLine, endColumn, image, and next) as well as additional fields that support some advanced functions.

S1jConstants.java (see Figure 13.15) corresponds to the S1Constants interface we used in S1. As in S1, the tokenImage array provides a displayable string for every token kind. Note that all the strings in the tokenImage array include the quotes, except for the token categories <EOF>, <UNSIGNED>, and <ID>. For example,

```
System.out.println(tokenImage[ID] );
```

would display

```
<ID>
```

without quotes. However,

```
System.out.println(tokenImage[ASSIGN] );
```

would display

```
"="
```

with the quotes. JavaCC includes the quotes in the latter to make it easier to construct error messages. For example, to construct and display the message

```
Expecting "="
```

we would not have to insert the quotes enclosing the equal sign. We simply use the entry in the tokenImage array. This entry already has the quotes.

```
 1  /* Generated By:JavaCC: Do not edit this line.
       S1jConstants.java */
 2
 3  /**
 4   * Token literal values and constants.
 5   * Generated by org.javacc.parser.OtherFilesGen#start()
 6   */
 7  public interface S1jConstants {
 8
 9    /** End of File. */
10    int EOF = 0;
11    /** RegularExpression Id. */
12    int PRINTLN = 5;
13    /** RegularExpression Id. */
14    int UNSIGNED = 6;
15    /** RegularExpression Id. */
16    int ID = 7;
17    /** RegularExpression Id. */
18    int ASSIGN = 8;
19    /** RegularExpression Id. */
20    int SEMICOLON = 9;
21    /** RegularExpression Id. */
22    int LEFTPAREN = 10;
23    /** RegularExpression Id. */
24    int RIGHTPAREN = 11;
25    /** RegularExpression Id. */
26    int PLUS = 12;
27    /** RegularExpression Id. */
28    int MINUS = 13;
29    /** RegularExpression Id. */
30    int TIMES = 14;
31    /** RegularExpression Id. */
32    int ERROR = 15;
33
34    /** Lexical state. */
35    int DEFAULT = 0;
36
37    /** Literal token values. */
38    String[] tokenImage = {
39      "<EOF>",
40      "\" \"",
41      "\"\\n\"",
42      "\"\\r\"",
43      "\"\\t\"",
44      "\"println\"",
45      "<UNSIGNED>",
46      "<ID>",
47      "\"=\"",
48      "\";\"",
49      "\"(\"",
50      "\")\"",
51      "\"+\"",
```

Figure 13.15.

```
52      "\ "-\ "",
53      "\ "*\ "",
54      "<ERROR>",
55    } ;
56
57  }
```

Figure 13.15. *Continued.*

As we mentioned earlier, if we associate a name with a regular expression in a TOKEN block, then that name, enclosed in angle brackets, represents that type of token in a translation grammar. Thus, a statement such as

```
t=<PLUS>
```

in a translation grammar represent the assignment of a <PLUS> token to the Token variable t. If, however, we specify PLUS *without* the angle brackets in a translation grammar, then we get the value defined for the PLUS constant in the constants interface. We see from line 26 of Figure 13.15 that we would get the value 12. This value is the index into the tokenImage[ ] array corresponding to a <PLUS> token. It is also the value in the kind field for a <PLUS> token. Of course, it would be incorrect to assign PLUS (without the angle brackets) to t:

```
t=PLUS      // ERROR: need angle brackets around PLUS
```

This statement attempts to assign the integer constant PLUS (which is 12) to the Token variable t. However, we might want to use PLUS (without the angle brackets) in the following way in the translation grammar for some future compiler:

```
if (t.kind == PLUS)
{
    ...
}
```

Here we are testing the kind field of token t to determine if t is a PLUS token. We never have to perform this test in S1j.jj. However, we will see (in the next section) that there are circumstances in which we do need to perform such a test.

> **In a translation grammar, a token's name enclosed in angle brackets represents the token's object. A token's name *without* angle brackets represents the value in the kind field of the token. It is also the index into the tokenImage array for that token kind.**

JavaCC also generates the file S1jTokenManager.java that contains the S1jTokenManager class (the token manager). This class contains the method getNextToken() which the parser calls each time it needs a token. Like getNextToken() in S1, it returns the next token in the form of an object. On an error, the JavaCC-generated getNextToken() method throws a TokenErrorException, which is defined in TokenMgrError.java.

JavaCC also generates an input stream defined in SimpleCharStream.java. The token manager uses this stream for character input.

13.7   USING THE STAR AND PLUS OPERATORS

Up to now, we have avoided using the star and plus operators in grammars (see Section 9.8 for a discussion on the use of these operators in grammars). For example, we have avoided using

```
expr → term ("+" term)*
```

preferring instead the recursive equivalent

```
expr        → term termList
termlist    → "+" term termList
termList    → λ
```

Both approaches are perfectly acceptable. If we use the star approach, it makes sense to use loops in the corresponding parser. If, in the other hand, we use the recursive approach, it makes sense to use recursion in the corresponding parser. By using the structure in the parser that more closely parallels the productions in the grammar, we minimize the possibility of introducing bugs in our code.

In translation grammars we provide JavaCC, we can use the star and plus operators to represent lists, or we can avoid them by using recursive productions. JavaCC will generate correct code with either approach. However, the star and plus operators yield slightly more efficient code (loops, in general, are more efficient than recursive code).

Let us look at some of the changes we can make to our translation grammar for S1 if we use the star and plus operators. Currently, we define expr() andd term() with

```
void expr(): {}
{
    term()
    termList()
}
//-------------------
void termList(): {}
{
    "+"
    term()
    { cg.emitInstruction("add");}
    termList()
  |
    {}
}
```

We can replace all this with

```
void expr(): {}
{
    term()
    (
        "+"
        term()
```

```
        { cg.emitInstruction("add");}
    )*
}
```

Wherever we have specified a list in the translation grammar in Figure 13.14, we can, alternatively, specify it using the star or plus operator. If we do so, we may produce a more efficient compiler (see Problem 13.6). Incidentally, we can also use the question mark operator in the translation grammars for which we provide JavaCC.

Recall that S2 is the extension of S1 that we implemented in Chapter 12. S2 supports both the addition and subtraction operators. If we try to use the star and plus operators to replace some of the recursive productions in the translation grammar for S2, we run into a problem. Consider the productions for expr() and termList() in the translation grammar for S2:

```
void expr(): {}
{
    term()
    termList()
}
//------------------
void termList(): {}
{
    "+"
    term()
    { codeGen.emitInstruction("add");}
    termList()
  |
    "-"
    term()
    { codeGen.emitInstruction("sub");}
    termList()
  |
    {}
}
```

If we attempt to simplify expr() by using the star operator, we get

```
expr(): {}
{
    term()
    (
        ("+"|"-")
        term()
        { codeGen.emitInstruction(???); }
    )*
}
```
— "add" or "sub" here?

Which assembly instruction—add or sub—should the emitInstruction method output? It, of course, depends on the operator in between the two terms just parsed. If the operator is "+", then we should output add; if it is "-", then we should output sub.

To solve this problem, we have to save the operator when we parse it. Then we can test it later to determine which instruction—add or sub—to emit. Using this approach, we get

```
void expression(): { Token t;}
{
    term()
    (
        (t="+"|t="-")              // save operator in t
        term()
        {
            if (t.kind == ?????)  ◄────── what is the kind of a "+" token?
                codeGen.emitInstruction("add" );
            else
                codeGen.emitInstruction("sub"
        }
    )*
}
```

But now we run into another problem: We have to test t to determine if it is a "+" token. But to do that, we need to know the value in the kind field of a "+" token. But this value is given by PLUS—the name we gave the regular expression for the plus operator in the Token block (see line 26 Figure 13.15). We can then specify the kind of the "+" token with PLUS (without the angle brackets). With this approach, our expr() production becomes

```
void expr(): { Token t;}
{
    term()
    (
        (t="+"|t="-")              // save operator in t
        term()
        {
            if (t.kind == PLUS)
                codeGen.emitInstruction("add" );
            else
                codeGen.emitInstruction("sub");
        }
    )*
}
```

For the sake of consistency, you can then replace "+" and "-" in the translation grammar with <PLUS> and <MINUS>, respectively. In that case, the line

```
        (t="+"|t="-")                      // save operator in t
```

becomes

```
        (t=<PLUS>|t=<MINUS>)         // save operator in t
```

This example illustrates the reason why it is important to give names to the token regular expressions in the TOKEN block. These given names provide the values in the kind fields of the corresponding tokens.

13.8 CHOICE POINTS AND LOOKAHEAD

Let us put the following grammar into the form JavaCC requires:

G13.1
1. S → bcd
2. S → def

We get

G13.2
```
PARSER_BEGIN(G1302)
class G1302
{
}
PARSER_END(G1302)
void S(): {}
{
```
```
    "b" "c" "d"  ◄──────  selection set is {"b"}
  |
    "d" "e" "f"  ◄──────  selection set is {"d"}
}
```
with the annotations: `◄──────────────────────` choice point is here

The S() method specifies two alternatives, each corresponding to an S production. If we provide this translation grammar to JavaCC, it will produce the corresponding parser. This parser chooses between the two alternatives that we list in the grammar on the basis of the selection set for each production. Because the selection set for the first alternative is {"b"}, the parser uses this alternative if the current token is a "b". If, however, the current token is "d", the parser uses the second alternative because its selection set is {"d"}.

We call the point in a translation grammar corresponding to the location in the corresponding parser at which a choice is made between alternatives a *choice point*. The choice point in the grammar above is just before the two alternatives. A choice has to be made there to determine which alternative to take.

If a grammar is LL(1), then at every choice point, the choice is completely determined by the current token. Thus, the parser never has to guess which alternative is the correct one to take. If, however, a grammar is not LL(1), then there will be choices not completely determined by the current token. For example in the grammar

G13.3
```
PARSER_BEGIN(G1303)
class G1303
{
}
PARSER_END(G1303)
void S(): {}
{
    "b" "c" "d"  ◄──────  selection set is {"b"}
  |
    "b" "e" "f"  ◄──────  selection set is {"b"}
}
```

the selection set for both alternatives is {"b"} , so the parser cannot determine the correct alternative from the current token alone. If, however, it were to look ahead at the token following the current token, it could determine the correct alternative. If it is "c", then the current token/next token sequence is "b" "c", so the parser should use the first alternative. If the next token is "e", the parser should use the second alternative.

The parser that JavaCC generates looks at, by default, only the current token at each choice point. If there are multiple alternatives possible for the current token, the one listed first in the grammar is the one the parser takes. For the grammar above, if the input stream is "bcd", the parser takes the first alternative, which matches the "b", "c", and "d" in the input stream. So the parse completes successfully. If, on the other hand, the input stream is "bef", the parser also takes the first alternative (it does not know at the choice point that the second token is "e"—it is looking at only the current token "b" at the choice point). The first alternative matches the current token "b", but not the "e" that follows it. The parser, accordingly, throws a parse exception when it reaches the "e". Although this grammar is defective, JavaCC nevertheless, converts it to a parser. However, it does generate a warning message of this form:

```
"Warning: choice conflict ...".
```

We can fix the problem with G13.3 by forcing the parser to look ahead when it is at the choice point. Specifically, we can force it to look at two tokens: the current token and the next. We do this with the LOOKAHEAD(2) directive placed at the choice point as G13.4 illustrates:

G13.4
```
PARSER_BEGIN(G1304)
class G1304
{
}
PARSER_END(G1304)
void S(): {}
{
    LOOKAHEAD(2)          // Put LOOKAHEAD(2) at choice point
    "b" "c" "d"
|
    "b" "e" "f"
}
```

Because of the LOOKAHEAD(2) directive, the parser that JavaCC generates will look at two tokens—the current and the next—at the choice point, allowing it to choose the correct alternative. The argument in the LOOKAHEAD directive determines the number of tokens used in the lookahead. For G13.4, we need only a lookahead of 2. JavaCC, however, permits larger lookaheads if you need them.

Exercise 13.5

Fix the following grammar using the LOOKAHEAD directive:

```
void S(): ()
{
    "b" "c" "d"
```

```
    |
        "b" "c" "e"
}
```

Answer:

Insert LOOKAHEAD(3) before the first alternative. By looking at three tokens (the current token and the next two), the parser can choose the correct alternative.

∎

Now let's consider a variation of G13.3:

G13.5
```
    PARSER_BEGIN(G1305)
    class G1303
    {
    }
    PARSER_END(G1305)
    void S(): {}
    {
        "bcd"  ◄———————  selection set is {"bcd"}
      |
        "bef"  ◄———————  selection set is {"bef"}
    }
```

In this grammar, "bcd" and "bef" are both *single* tokens. Thus, if "bcd" is in the input stream, the token manager produced by JavaCC returns the single token "bcd". It does not return three tokens, "b" then "c" then "d", as was the case for G13.3. Similarly, if "bef" is in the input stream, the token manager returns the single token "bef". This grammar is, in fact, LL(1). The two alternatives have disjoint selection sets. Thus, we do not need a LOOKAHEAD directive as we did in G13.3.

LOOKAHEAD directives can appear only at choice points. For example, in Figure 13.16, we cannot place a LOOKAHEAD directive before or immediately after the B() alternative because these points are not choice points. However, we can put one just before the C() alternative.

Choice points occur when we use "|". They also occur when we use "*", "+", and "?" because these operators involve choices as well. Figure 13.16 shows the location of the choice points for these operators.

```
    void S(): {}
    {
            ◄———————  cannot put LOOKAHEAD directive here
      B()
            ◄———————  cannot put LOOKAHEAD directive here
      (
            ◄———————  this is a choice point so can put LOOKAHEAD directive here
          C()
        |
          D()
      )
    }
```

Figure 13.16.

```
                    void S(): {}
                    {
                        (
                                  ◄──────── choice point for first " | "
                            B()
                        |
                                  ◄──────── choice point for second " | "
                            C()
                        |
                            D()
                        )

                        (
                                  ◄──────── choice point for "? "
                            E()
                        )?

                        (
                                  ◄──────── choice point for "* "
                            F()
                        )*

                        (
                                  ◄──────── choice point for "+"
                            G()
                        )+
                    }
```

Figure 13.17.

At the choice point for the star operator, the parser decides if it should proceed with the parse using the starred expression or what follows it. For example, the structure of the code in a JavaCC-created parser for

```
(   "b" "c")* "d"
 ▲
 └─ choice point (LOOKAHEAD(2) not needed here)
```

is

```
while (current token is "b")
{
    consume "b"
    consume "c"
}
consume "d"
```

The choice point corresponds to the exit test for the `while` loop. The exit test ensures that whenever the first *consume* in the loop body is executed, the current token is "b". Note that the exit test here checks only the current token. If, however, we place LOOKA-HEAD(2) at the choice point (right after the left parentheses), then the structure of the JavaCC-generated code becomes

```
while (current token is "b" and the next token is "c")
{
      consume "b"
      consume "c"
}
consume "d"
```

In this example, the LOOKAHEAD(2) directive is not needed because the current token alone is enough to determine if the body of the `while` loop should be executed. However, in the following structure, we do need the LOOKAHEAD(2) directive:

```
(LOOKAHEAD(2) "b" "c")* "b" "d"
```
        ⬆
        └─ choice point (LOOKAHEAD(2) needed here)

Here, the body of the `while` loop corresponding to the starred expression should be executed only if "b" is the current token, and it is followed by a "c". This test requires a lookahead of 2. The corresponding code is

```
while (current token is "b" and the next token is "c")
{
      consume "b"
      consume "c"
}
consume "b"
consume "d"
```

The code structure for a plus expression is like that for a star expression except that it corresponds to a do-while loop instead of `while` loop. For example, the structure for

```
(LOOKAHEAD(2) "b" "c")+ "b"
```

is

```
do
{
   consume "b"
   consume "c"
} while (current token is "b" and the next token is "c")
```

Note that the choice occurs after the first "b" is consumed. However, the choice point in the grammar (i.e., the location at which a LOOKAHEAD statement can be inserted) is before the first "b".

The code structure for a question mark expression is an `if` statement. For example, the code structure of

```
("b")?
```

is

```
if  (current token is "b")
{
    consume "b"
}
```

Exercise 13.6

Fix the problem with the following production:

```
void S(): {}
{
    ( "b" "c")*
    "b"
}
```

Answer:

```
void S(): {}
{
    (
        LOOKAHEAD(2)
        "b" "c"
    )*
    "b"
}
```

■

13.9   JavaCC'S CHOICE ALGORITHM

Consider the following two productions:

```
A → B
A → C
```

If B and C are both nullable, then we know from Section 7.6 that the selection set of each production contains FOLLOW(A). Because the selection sets of the two productions include FOLLOW(A), we do not have an LL(1) grammar. It follows that in an LL(1) grammar, for each group of productions with the same left side, there can be *at most one production with a nullable right side.*

Suppose P is nonterminal in an LL(1) grammar with the following productions:

```
P → Q
P → R
P → T
```

then there is at most one production that has a nullable right side. Let us assume it is the last one we listed, P → T. Because it has a nullable right side, its selection set is FIRST(T) | FOLLOW(P). Because the other productions do not have nullable right sides, their selections sets are simply the FIRST sets of their right sides. Figure 13.18a shows the structure of the corresponding method in a recursive descent parser. However, the parser does not have to perform a selection set test for the last production. It can simply call T() as the default option when the current token is neither in FIRST(Q) nor FIRST(R). With this approach, we get the structure in Figure 13.18b. Selection set tests precede the calls of Q() and R(), but not the call of T(). With this approach, the nullable alternative has to be last. By not performing a selection set test on the nullable alternative, we benefit in the following way: We *do not need to compute any FOLLOW sets* because the selection sets for the nonnullable alternatives are simply their FIRST sets.

When JavaCC generates parser code, it uses the approach illustrated by 13.18b. The code it generates for a production whose right side is nullable does not perform a selection set test. It simply applies the production unconditionally if the preceding alternatives do not apply. Thus, we must always list the nullable alternative last. If we do not, we will not get a correct parser. For example, consider the JavaCC input file in Figure 13.19. Notice that the first alternative for the S() productions consists of an action only. It does not generate any terminals or nonterminals. Thus, it corresponds to a lambda production. Because this alternative is nullable, we should have listed it last. Although the grammar in Figure 13.19 is LL(1), JavaCC complains that the first alternative "can expand to the empty token sequence." This message is an indication that we have not listed the nullable alternative last. JavaCC, nevertheless, generates the parser. The code created by JavaCC for S() is

```
final public void S() throws ParseException {
   System.out.println("hello");
}
```

Because the first alternative is nullable, the code for it has no selection set test. It is executed unconditionally. But then the code for the second alternative is unreachable. Unreachable code is useless, so JavaCC does not even generate it. The fix for the grammar in Figure 13.11 is simple: reverse the order of the two alternatives.

```
void P()
{
    switch (current token)
    {
        case current token in FIRST(Q):
            Q();
            break;
        case current token in FIRST(R):
            R();
            break;
        case current token in FIRST(T)/FOLLOW(P)):
            T();
            break;
        default:
            throw exception
    }
}

              (a)
```

```
void P()
{
    switch (current token)
    {
        case current token in FIRST(Q):
            Q();
            break;
        case current token in FIRST(R):
            R();
            break;
        default:
            T();
            break;
    }
}

              (b)
```

Figure 13.18.

```
 1 // Figure 13.19
 2 options
 3 {
 4    STATIC = false;
 5 }
 6 //================================================
 7 PARSER_BEGIN(Fig1319)
 8 import java.io.*;
 9 class Fig1319
10 {
11   public static void main(String[] args) throws
12                              IOException, ParseException
13   {
14     Fig1319 parser =
15             new Fig1319(new FileInputStream(args[ 0] ));
16     parser.S();
17   }
18 }
19 PARSER_END(Fig1319)
20 //================================================
21 SKIP:
22 {
23    " "|"\n"|"\r"|"\t"
24 }
25 //================================================
26 void S(): {}
27 {
28    {System.out.println("hello");}   // Sel set is {<EOF>}
29  |
30    "b" S()                          // Sel set is {"b"}
31 }
```

Figure 13.19.

Notice in the JavaCC input file for S1j (see Figure 13.14) that we test for < EOF> at the end of the `program()` method:

```
202 void program(): {}
203 {
204     statementList()
205     { cg.endCode();}
206     <EOF>
207 }
```

Suppose we omitted this test. Let us see what would then happen if the source program is

```
x = 5; 7
```

The parser should, of course, detect the error in this program (the extraneous "7" at the end of the program). We start by calling `program()` which, in turn, calls `statementList()`:

```
209 void statementList(): {}
210 {
211     statement()
212     statementList()
213   |
214     {}
215 }
```

statementList() calls statement() (line 211) which parses the assignment statement. It then calls itself recursively (line 212). At this point "7" is the current token. In this call of statementList(), we take the second alternative because "7" is not in the selection set of the first alternative. But the second alternative is λ, represented by the empty action. Because no selection set test is performed for the nullable alternative, the error (the "7") is not detected. Instead, statementList() simply returns to its caller (also statementList), which, in turn, returns to program(), which (assuming we omit line 206) returns to main(). We have a problem here: The parser terminates without detecting the error. This problem occurs because the JavaCC parser does not perform a selection set test for second alternative in statementList(). To fix this problem, we must force a test for the end of input on return to program(). We do this by specifying the <EOF> token on line 206 in program().

If JavaCC processes a translation grammar without complaint, the grammar may still be defective. For example, consider the grammar in Figure 13.20. The parser that JavaCC generates for this grammar can successfully parse "bb" but not "b", although the grammar can generate both strings. When attempting to parse "b", the JavaCC parser uses the first alternative for the Q() productions to match the "b" in the input. But then there are no more occurrences of "b" left in the input to match the "b" in the S() production. To parse a single "b", we have to use the second alternative in the Q() method. This alternative specifies lambda so it does not consume the "b" in the input, making it available to match the "b" in the S() production. This grammar is, in fact, not LL(1). The selection sets for the two Q() alternatives are both { "b"}. Unfortunately, JavaCC does not detect this because it does not compute the selection set for the second alternative in Q(). Thus, JavaCC does not know that the Q() alternatives violate the requirements of an LL(1) grammar. In this case, JavaCC generates a defective parser without giving us any warning.

```
void S(): {}
{
    Q() "b"
}
//----------------
void Q(): {}
{
    "b"        // selection set is { "b"}
  |
    {}         // selection set is { "b"}
}
```

Figure 13.20.

13.10 SYNTACTIC AND SEMANTIC LOOKAHEAD (OPTIONAL)

In the examples of the LOOKAHEAD directive we have seen so far, we have specified the lookahead with a number. For example, in

```
void S(): {}
{
    LOOKAHEAD(2)
    B()
  |
    C()
}
```

the LOOKAHEAD directive specifies the number 2. This number indicates that the parser should examine two tokens (the current token and the next token) to determine which alternative (B() or C()) to take. There are, however, two other forms in which we can specify a lookahead: syntactic and semantic.

In *syntactic lookahead*, we specify the syntactic expectation for the first alternative. If the input meets this expectation, the parser takes the first alternative. Otherwise, it takes the next alternative. For example, consider the LOOKAHEAD directive in Figure 13.21. The LOOKA-HEAD directive specifies two syntactic components, D() and "b". Accordingly, the parser

```
 1 void S(): {}
 2 {
 3     LOOKAHEAD(D() "b")
 4     B()
 5 |
 6     C()
 7 }
 8 //-----------------
 9 void B(): {}
10 {
11     D()
12     "b"
13     "b"
14 }
15 //-----------------
16 void C(): {}
17 {
18     D()
19     "c"
20     "c"
21 }
22 //-----------------
23 void D(): {}
24 {
25     "d"
26     "d"
27 }
```

Figure 13.21.

will look ahead in the input stream (starting at the current token) for a substring that corresponds to D(), followed by "b". If it is successful, it takes the first alternative B(). Otherwise it takes the next alternative. Thus, if the input stream is "ddbb", then the parser takes the B() alternative. We could have also used a LOOKAHEAD(3) directive. But this lookahead works in this example only because the string corresponding to D() has a fixed length of 2. Thus, a lookahead of 3 provides the parser with the token that follows the D() substring in the input from which it can determine the correct alternative. If, on the other hand, D() were defined as

```
void D() : {}
{
    ("d")+
}
```

then no fixed-size lookahead would work since the D() substring can be arbitrarily long. However, the syntactic lookahead that we used in Figure 13.14 would still work.

In *semantic lookahead,* the lookahead is a true/false condition enclosed within braces. If the condition is true, the parser takes the first alternative. Otherwise, it takes the next alternative. For example, consider the example of semantic lookahead in Figure 13.22. The semantic lookahead checks if the current and the next tokens are <UNSIGNED> and <ID>, respectively. If they are, the parser takes the first alternative E(). Otherwise, it takes the second alternative F(). Recall that getToken returns the specified token without advancing in the input stream. getToken(1) returns the current token; getToken(2) returns the token that follows the current token.

13.11 USING JavaCC TO CREATE A TOKEN MANAGER ONLY

We can use JavaCC to generate a token manager only. We simply omit the translation grammar. Then JavaCC does not generate any parser code. Moreover, we can use the

```
 1 void S() : {}
 2 {
 3   LOOKAHEAD({ getToken(1).kind==UNSIGNED &&
 4                              getToken(2).kind==ID} )
 5      E()
 6   |
 7      F()
 8 }
 9 //-----------------
 0 void E() : {}
11 {
12      <UNSIGNED>
13      <ID>
14 }
15 //------------------
16 void F() : {}
17 {
18      <UNSIGNED>
19      <UNSIGNED>
20 }
```

Figure 13.22.

PARSER_BEGIN/PARSER_END block for Java code that uses the token manager. For example, the JavaCC input file in Figure 13.23 creates only a token manager. Its class name is Fig1323TokenManager. The main() method creates the token manager (line 20). It then calls getNextToken() repeatedly to get each token (lines 24 and 29). For each token, it displays the token name and image (line 27).

Because main() in Figure 13.23 displays the image of each token, it is handy for checking the correctness of the token manager as specified by the SKIP and TOKEN blocks. We simply run it against a test file to see the tokens that getNextToken() returns. For example, if we have a test file test.txt that contains

```
123println xy z+
```

and we enter

```
javacc Fig1323.jj
javac  Fig1323.java
java   Fig1323 test.txt
```

We should see on the screen

```
<UNSIGNED> 123
"println" println
<ID> xy
<ID> z
<ERROR> +
```

13.12   USING THE TOKEN CHAIN

The token objects that the token manager returns to the parser are chained together by their next fields. For example, suppose the token manager returns token objects for "b", "c", and "d" in that order to the parser. Then the token for "b" points to (i.e., has the reference of) the token for "c", which, in turn, points to the token for "d" (see Figure 13.24). In other words, the next field of each token contains the reference of the next token.

Given a reference to a token, we can easily get the reference to the next token. We simply access the given token's next field. However, we cannot get the reference to the *previous* token. For example, given a reference to the "c" token in Figure 3.24, we can get the reference to the "d" token but not the "b" token. The token chain is a "one-way street": we can go forward but not backward.

Suppose the parser saves the reference to the "b" token when it receives the "b" token from the parser. Then at any time later on in the parse, the parser can use the saved reference to access not only the "b" token but also all the tokens that follow the "b" token. It can do this simply by traversing the token chain starting with the token for "b".

The S1j.jj compiler does not comment the assembly code for each statement with the corresponding source statement. However, we can, in fact, implement this feature using the token chain. We simply save the reference to the current token when we are about to parse a statement. We then parse the statement (which causes assembly code for the statement to be outputted). We then output all the tokens from the saved token up to but not including the current token by traversing the token chain. These tokens are the tokens

```
 1 // Figure 13.23
 2 // JavaCC input file for token manager only
 3 options
 4 {
 5   STATIC = false;
 6 }
 7
 8 PARSER_BEGIN(Fig1323)
 9 import java.io.*;
10 class Fig1323
11 {
12   public static void main(String[] args) throws
13                                         IOException
14   {
15     Token t;
16     FileInputStream inFile =
17                       new FileInputStream(args[ 0] );
18
19     // create token manager
20     Fig1323TokenManager tm = new Fig1323TokenManager(
21                       new SimpleCharStream(inFile));
22
23     // display each token's image
24     t = tm.getNextToken();
25     while (t.kind != EOF)
26     {
27       System.out.println(tokenImage[ t.kind] + " " +
28                                         t.image);
29       t = tm.getNextToken();
30     }
31   }
32 }
33
34 PARSER_END(Fig1323)
35
36 // Specification of the token manager ====================
37
38 SKIP:
39 {
40     " "
41   |
42     "\n"
43   |
44     "\r"
45   |
46     "\t"
47 }
48
49 TOKEN:
50 {
51     "println"
52   |
```

Figure 13.23.

```
53    <UNSIGNED: ([ "0"-"9"] )+>
54    |
55    <ID: [ "A"-"Z","a"-"z"]  ([ "A"-"Z","a"-"z", "0"-"9"] )*>
56    |
57    <ERROR: ~[ ] >
58 }
```

Figure 13.23. *Continued.*

that make up the statement just parsed. Incorporating this technique into S1j.jj and then compiling S1.s we get the assembly output in Figure 13.25. The source code for each statement appears as a comment *following* its corresponding assembly code. Figure 13.26 shows the two changes to S1j.jj that are required: we overload the makeComment() method by adding two new versions to the parser, and we modify the statement() method in the translation grammar..

Before parsing a statement, we save the reference to the current token in t (line 22). After the statement is parsed, we call makeComment (line 30), which traverses the token list from the saved token t up to the current token (given by getToken(1)), writing the image of each token to the output file. Finally, makeComment terminates the comment line with a call to println() (line 10). The outComment variable allows us to inhibit the call of makeComment() on line 30. We will want to do this for the statements that contain statements, such as the compound statement. For example, to inhibit the call to makeComment() for a compound statement, we set outComment to false for the compoundStatement() alternative within the statement() method:

```
    ...
|
    printlnStatement()
|
    compoundstatement()
    { outComment=false;}
|
    ...
```

After a compound statement has been parsed, all the statements within its braces have already been parsed and outputted as comments. Thus, if we call makeComment() for a compound statement, the source code for the statements within the compound statement

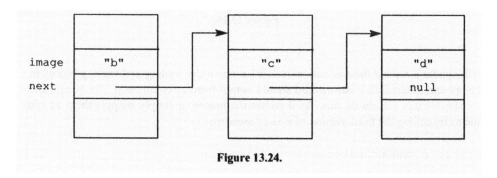

Figure 13.24.

```
                    ; from S1j compiler written by ...
                         pc          x
                         pwc         3
                         pwc         -2
                         add
                         pwc         1
                         add
                         stav
                    ; x = + 3 + - 2 + 1 ;
                         pc          y
                         p           x
                         stav
                    ; y = x ;
                         pc          z
                         p           x
                         pwc         2
                         p           y
                         add
                         mult
                         pwc         4099
                         add
                         stav
                    ; z = x * ( 2 + y ) + ( ( ( 4099 ) ) ) ;
                         p           z
                         p           x
                         add
                         pwc         -2
                         add
                         dout
                         pc          '\n'
                         aout
                    ; println ( z + x + - 2 ) ;
                         pwc         4107
                         dout
                         pc          '\n'
                         aout
                    ; println ( 4107 ) ;

                         halt
                  x:     dw          0
                  y:     dw          0
                  z:     dw          0
```

Figure 13.25.

will appear a *second time* as comments. What about the leading and trailing braces in a compound statement? What method should output them as comments? The `compound-Statement()` should do this. As it parses the braces, it simply outputs them as comments by calling the third version of `makeComment()`:

```
void compoundStatement(): { Token t;}
{
    "{ "
```

```
 1 // second makeComment method
 2 public void makeComment(Token t1, Token t2)
 3 {
 4   outFile.print("; "); // start comment
 5   while (t1 != t2)
 6   {
 7     outFile.print(t1.image + " ");
 8     t1 = t1.next;
 9   }
10   outFile.println();   // terminate comment
11 }
12 //=================================================
13 // third makeComment method
14 public void makeComment(String s)
15 {
16   outFile.println("; " + s);
17 }
18 //=================================================
19 // modified statement() in the translation grammar
20 void statement(): { Token t; boolean outComment;}
21 {
22   { t = getToken(1);}        // save current token
23   { outComment = true;}
24   (
25       assignmentStatement()
26   |
27       printlnStatement()
28   )
29   // output tokens from t to current token
30   { if (outComment) makeComment(t, getToken(1));}
31 }
```

Figure 13.26.

```
{ makeComment("{ ");}
statementList()
"} "
{ makeComment("} ");}
}
```

13.13 SUPPRESSING WARNING MESSAGES

Whenever a choice occurs during the execution of a JavaCC-generated parser, the parser will apply the first alternative listed. For example, consider the following definition of the Q productions in a JavaCC translation grammar:

```
void Q(): {}
{
   "b" T()    // selection set is { "b"}
 |
   U()        // selection set is { "b", "e", "f"}
}
```

Suppose the selection sets for the first and second alternatives are {"b"} and {"b", "e", "f"}, respectively. Because "b" is in the selection sets of both alternatives, a choice occurs whenever the corresponding Q() method in the generated parser is called and the current token is "b". Q(), in this case, will resolve the choice in favor of the first alternative listed. That is, it will consume "b" and call T() rather than call U(). If resolving a choice in favor of the first alternative in Q() is precisely the behavior you want the parser to have, then this translation grammar needs no modification. However, in that case you would probably want to suppress the warning message that JavaCC generates. To do this, simply insert a LOOKAHEAD(1) statement before the first alternative:

```
void Q(): {}
{
    LOOKAHEAD(1)
    "b" T()    // selection set is { "b"}
  |
    U()    // selection set is { "b", "e", "f"}
}
```

The only effect of the LOOKAHEAD(1) statement here is to suppress the "choice conflict" warning message that JavaCC would otherwise generate.

PROBLEMS

1. Implement S2 as described in Chapter 12 using JavaCC. Call your JavaCC-generated compiler S2j. You should
   a. Copy S1j.jj to S2j.jj.
   b. Insert your name into S2j.jj on lines 25 and 43.
   c. Replace the translation grammar in S2j.jj with S2.tg.
   d. Add an entery to the SKIP block that defines a single-line comment. Hint: a single-line comment consists of two slashes, followed by zero or more occurrences of any character except \n and \r.
   e. Add entries to the TOKEN block for the new tokens: "print", "/", "{ ", "} ".
   f. Add actions so that source code is output as comments (see Section 13.12).
   g. Test your compiler by entering

   ```
   javacc S2j.jj
   javac S2j.java
   java S2j S2
   a S2.a
   e S2 /c
   ```

   Submit to your instructor S2j.jj, S2.a, and S2.<*family name*>.log (the log file that the e program creates).

2. Compile

   ```
   x = ? 5;
   ```

   with the S1j compiler. Then delete the ERROR entry in the TOKEN block in S1j.jj. With this modified S1j compiler, compile the above statement. How do the error messages of the two versions of S1j compare?

3. Move the ERROR entry in the TOKEN block in S1j to the beginning of the TOKEN block. Compile S1.s with the modified S1j compiler. What happens? Why?

4. Is this translation grammar acceptable to JavaCC?

```
void S(); {}
{
    {int x;}      // declare local variable as action
    x = B()
    {System.out.println(x);}
}
int B(): {}
{
    {return 5;}
}
```

5. A JavaCC input file consists of several components: the PARSER_BEGIN/PARS-ER_END block, the SKIP block, the TOKEN block, and the translation grammar. Can these components be placed in any order? Experiment with JavaCC to determine your answer.

6. Represent all the lists in the translation grammar in S1j.jj using the star or plus operators. Compare the resulting code with that produced by that in the original S1j.jj. Is it smaller? Is it faster?

7. Write a JavaCC extended regular expression that defines all strings with one or more occurrences of the substring "bc". Test your expression using JavaCC against the following input:

   b, c, bc, cb, bbbbbbcccccccc, cccbbb

8. Write a JavaCC extended regular expression that defines all strings with exactly one occurrence of the substring "bc". Test your expression using JavaCC against the following input:

   b, c, bc, cb, bccbc, bcbbbbbbbbbbbbbbc

9. Write a JavaCC extended regular expression that defines a Java multiple-line comment (i.e., a comment bracketed with "/* and */" that can span lines). Assume nested comments are not allowed. Test your expression using JavaCC.

10. Determine if command line arguments for JavaCC are case sensitive.

11. Write a JavaCC extended regular expression that defines a quoted string that can span multiple lines as long each newline is backslashed. Test your expression using JavaCC.

12. Suppose an expression in the SKIP block and an expression in the TOKEN block both match the same string. Which expression has precedence? Does the order in which the SKIP and TOKEN blocks appear matter?

13. Implement the compiler in Figure 10.10 using JavaCC. Call your JavaCC version Fig1010j.jj. Test by entering the expression

   + * - / 10 9 8 7 6

14. In what ways does S1j function differently from S1 from Chapter 12?

15. What are the disadvantages of using JavaCC compared to writing the compiler yourself?

16. Fix the following grammar with a LOOKAHEAD directive:

```
void S(): {}
{
    B() "b" "c"
}
void B(): {}
{
    ("b" "c")*
}
```

17. Fix the following grammar with a LOOKAHEAD directive:

```
void S(): {}
{
    ("b" "c")+ "b" "d"
}
```

18. Can the last alternative for a nonterminal be applied without first performing a selection set test if the alternative is not nullable?

19. Show the structure of the code corresponding to

```
void S(): {}
{
("b"|"c")?
}
```

20. Show the structure of the code corresponding to

```
void S(): {}
{
("b" "c")+ "b" "b"
}
```

Repeat but with LOOKAHEAD(2) inserted at the choice point.

21. Suppose we delete line 206 in Figure 13.14. What would the S1j compiler do if the source program is

```
x = 5;
7 = 8;
y = 9;
```

22. What will the following regular expression match:

```
<WHAT: ~[] ~[] >
```

23. Create a Java program with JavaCC that inputs a text file and outputs the same text file with a line number inserted at the beginning of each line. For example, if the input file contains

```
aaa
bbb
 .
 .
 .
jjj
```

then the output file would be

```
1 aaa
2 bbb
.

.

.
10 jjj
```

The line numbers in the output file should be right justified and have a field width of 3.

24. Create a program with JavaCC that inputs a text file and outputs the number of words in the file. Test your program with a file that contains

> Let us, you and I , have a really good time studying compilers.

Your program should produce a count of 12 for this file.

25. Compile the following program using the S1j compiler:

```
x = - 32768;
println(x);
```

Then assemble. Try the do the same with

```
x = 5 - 32768;
println(x);
```

What happens? Why?

26. How are the symbol table and token manager objects passed to the parser in S1? In S1j?

27. Can an identifier for a regular expression be used before its definition in a Token block in a JavaCC input file? For example, is the following sequence legal:

```
<UNSIGNED: (<DIGIT>)+>
<DIGIT: [ "0"-"9"] >
```

28. Would it be correct to test only getToken(2).kind on line 3 in Figure 13.22? Try a test case with JavaCC to confirm your answer.

29. Can syntactic and semantic lookahead in JavaCC be placed at the multiple choice points in a list of alternatives? Confirm your answer with a test case.

30. Can you test the image field of a token instead of the kind field to determine the token type? For example, can you do this:

```
if (t.image.equals("+"))
{
...
}
```

What are the disadvantages of this approach?

31. Does the JavaCC-generated parser perform a selection set test for a nonterminal if there is only one production in the grammar with that nonterminal on the left side? Determine your answer by inspecting the code JavaCC generates for this case.

32. What happens if you move the SKIP block in S1j.jj to after the TOKEN block?

33. Why does the parser rather than the token manager produce the token trace?

34. Replace the SimpleCharStream class that JavaCC generates with a class you write. It should implement the interface CharStream, which Java CC generates if the USER_CHAR_STREAM option is set to true.

14

BUILDING ON S2

14.1 INTRODUCTION

In this chapter, we build on the S2 compiler described in Chapter 12 to get a more powerful compiler we call S3. If you have mastered the principles of compiler construction we have presented so far, you should have little trouble implementing S3. If you like, you may use JavaCC to generate the S3 compiler. But if you do, call it S3j to distinguish it from the handwritten S3 compiler.

S3 supports a cascaded assignment statement, that is, a single statement that performs multiple assignments. For example, the following cascaded assignment statement

```
x = y = z = 7;
```

assigns 7 to z, y, and x, in that order. The grammar will we use for the cascaded assignment is not LL(1). Thus, the S3 parser has to look ahead in the token stream to make parsing decisions when it processes a cascaded assignment statement. The parser can easily look ahead *without advancing in the token stream*. It simply calls the getToken method in the parser, specifying the index of the desired token.

Be sure you do not confuse the getToken method in the parser with the getNextToken method in the token manager (the former permits lookahead and the latter returns the next token). You do not have to create getToken yourself; it appears fully implemented in the S1 compiler (see lines 337–355 in Figure 12.3)

S3 also supports strings in the print and println statements, unary plus and minus, and the readint statement. The readint statement reads an integer constant from the keyboard.

14.2 EXTENDING println AND print

The S3 compiler allows the argument in the println and print statements to be either an expression or a string. It also allows the println statement to have no arguments. For example, the following statements are legal for the S3 compiler:

Compiler Construction Using Java, JavaCC, and Yacc, First Edition. Anthony J. Dos Reis
© 2012 the IEEE Computer Society, Inc. Published 2012 by John Wiley & Sons, Inc.

```
print("hello");      // display hello
println();           // go to next line
println("bye");      // display bye, go to next line
```

The `print` statement displays `hello`. The first `println`, with no arguments, moves the cursor to the beginning of the next line. The second `println` statement displays `bye` and then moves the cursor to the beginning of the next line. The output produced looks like this:

```
hello
bye
```

Let us examine the assembly code corresponding to the following `println` statement:

```
println("up\ndown");
```

It first outputs the string with an `sout` instruction, and then outputs the newline character with an `aout` instruction:

```
          pc        @L0
          sout
^@L0:     dw        "up\ndown"
          pc        '\n'
          aout
```

where `@L0` is a *compiler-generated* (i.e., compiler-created) label. The caret symbol (^) causes the assembler to place the `dw` for `"up\ndown"` at the end of the program, out of the flow of control (see Section 11.12). The `aout` instruction outputs the newline character, causing the display cursor to move to the beginning of the next line. The backslash-n sequence in the `dw` also causes the cursor to move to the next line. Thus, when executed, this code outputs up and down on successive lines and positions the cursor at the beginning of the line following down. Note that the string constant in the source code is carried over as is—including the backslash-n sequence—to the `dw` statement in the assembly code. Thus, the token manager does not have to modify a string constant it reads before passing it to the parser. It simply passes it, *as is,* to the parser which outputs it, *as is,* in a `dw` statement in the assembly code. Thus, a backslash-n sequence (two characters) in a string constant in the source code appears as a backslash-n (two characters) in the corresponding string constant in the assembly code. The loop in the token manager that processes strings should simply place all the characters in the string, including the initial and final quotes, into the `image` field of the `Token` object it creates for the string constant.

If you are using JavaCC to create the S3j compiler, it is easy to extend the token manager so that it supports strings. A string consists of a double quote, followed by zero or more characters other than the newline, return, or double quote, followed by a terminating double quote. Simply define a regular expression that captures this definition and place it in the TOKEN block.

A `println` statement with no arguments simply causes the cursor to move to the beginning of the next line. Thus, the assembly code for

```
println();
```

is

```
pc          '\n'
aout
```

To support string constants, we have to add another loop to the `getNextToken` method in the token manager. This loop is executed if the current character at the beginning of a token is the double quote. The loop executes until the matching quote is found. The token image that the loop constructs should *include* the quotes. For example, if the string in the source code is `"yes"` (with the quotes), then the image provided by `getNextToken` should be `"yes"` (also with the quotes). We keep the quotes for the following reason: If we were to strip them from a string constant, the code generator would have to reinsert them when it outputs the string constant to the assembly language program. By keeping the quotes as part of the image, they do not have to be reinserted later on. `getNextToken` should set the `kind` field to `STRING` (defined as an appropriate integer constant in the constants interface). Be sure you set the `endLine` and `endColumn` fields of a `String` constant correctly—they should reflect the position of the quote at the end of the string.

The source language that S3 handles does not allow a string to span a line. For example, the following statement is illegal:

```
        println("up
down");
```

If a string spans a line, the token manager should return a token whose `kind` field is ER-ROR, where `ERROR` is a constant defined in the constants interface. This `ERROR` token will cause the parser to generate an error message. It is easy to detect if a string spans a line: simply check if it contains any line separator character (i.e., `'\n'` or `'\r'`). The string in the preceding `println` statement contains a line separator between `up` and `down` (that is why `down` appears on a separate line). The string in

```
println("up\ndown");
```

does *not* contain a line separator, and, therefore, should be regarded as a legal string by the S3 compiler. But what about the backslash-n sequence in this statement? This sequence is not a newline character. It is, in fact, a two-character sequence in the source program: the backslash and the letter n.

Whenever the parser parses a string constant within a `print` or `println` statement, it should execute the following code:

```
t = currentToken;              // save string token
consume(STRING);
label = cg.getLabel();         // get label for string
cg.emitInstruction("pc", label);
cg.emitInstruction("sout");
cg.emitdw("^" + label, t.image);
```

where `t` is a local `Token` variable, `label` is a local `String` variable, and `cg` is the code generator. On each call of `cg.getLabel()`, it returns the next string in the sequence `"@L0"`, `"@L1"`, `"@L2"`, and so on. This string is assigned to `label`. For example, suppose the string in

```
println("hello");
```

is the first string in a program. Then during the parse of this statement, getLabel() would return "@L0", which would be assigned to label. The call of emitdw would then output

```
^@L0:      dw          "hello"
```

We implement getLabel() in the code generator class with a simple method that concatenates "@L" to a sequencing number, which is incremented on each call of getLabel():

```
public String getLabel()
{
    return "@L" + labelNumber++;
}
```

where labelNumber is an instance variable within the code generator that is initialized to 0.

When S3 parses a string in the source program, it outputs a dw statement for it, even if the string is identical to a string previously encountered. For example, the two instruction sequence,

```
print("hello");
print("hello");
```

would produce the following assembly code:

```
           pc         @L0
           sout
^@L0:      dw         "hello"

           pc         @L1
           sout
^@L1:      dw         "hello"
```

A more space-efficient approach is to output

```
           pc         @L0
           sout
           pc         @L0
           sout
```

and then have a single dw at the end of the program for "hello":

```
@L0:       dw          "hello"
```

However, this optimization should be used only for source languages, like Java, in which strings are immutable. In a language, like C, in which strings can be modified, this optimization might cause problems. For example, consider the following C code:

```
char *p, *q;
p = "hello";
*p = 'm';              // overlays 'h' with 'm'
q = "hello";
printf("%s", q);       // displays mello
```

The statement

```
*p = 'm';              // overlays 'h' with 'm'
```

stores `'m'` in the location to which p points. p points to the first character in `"hello"`. Thus, this assignment statement overlays the `'h'` in `"hello"` with `'m'`. Suppose at the assembly level there were only one dw for `"hello"`. Then both p and q would point to this single instance of `"hello"`. In that case, any modification of the string to which p points would affect the string assigned to q. The `printf` of q would display `mello` rather than `hello`, even though q appears to be assigned `"hello"`. This problem does *not* occur in C because C compilers generate a separate dw for each occurrence of a string. Thus, in the preceding C code, the modification of the `"hello"` to which p points would not affect the `"hello"` to which q points. Let us assume that the compilers we are developing will ultimately support a source language that can modify strings. Thus, our compilers, like C compilers, should generate a dw for every occurrence of a string.

Let us see what productions we need to define our new `println` and `print` statements. For S2, the `println` and `print` productions are

```
printlnStatement → "println" "(" expr ")" ";"
printStatement   → "print" "(" expr ")" ";"
```

When extending a grammar, it is most natural to simply add productions to those we already have. Thus, the most natural set of productions for our extended `println` and `print` statements are the preceding two to which we add

```
printlnStatement → "println" "(" <STRING> ")" ";"
printlnStatement → "println" "(" ")" ";"
printStatement   → "print" "(" <STRING> ")" ";"
```

However, with the addition of these productions, our grammar is no longer LL(1). The three `printlnStatement` productions start with `"println"`. Thus `"println"` is in each of their selection sets. Similarly, the two `printStatement` productions start with `"print"`. Thus `"print"` is in each of their selection sets.

We, however, can easily convert this new set of productions to an equivalent LL(1) set by left–right factoring (see Sections 7.9 and 9.6). We get

```
printlnStatement → "println" "(" (printArg|λ) ")" ";"
printStatement   → "print" "(" printArg ")" ";"
```

where `printArg` is defined with

```
printArg → expr
printArg → <STRING>
```

On the right side of the preceding `printlnStatement` production, we have two alternatives: `printArg` and λ, separated by the "|". We can use exactly the same structure in the corresponding translation grammar (see Figure 14.1). Note that we must surround the list of alternatives with parentheses. We need them to specify the scope of the alternatives. The first parenthesis (without the quotes) marks the beginning of the first alternative; the balancing right parenthesis marks the end of the last alternative. Without the parentheses, the first alternative would include the initial `"println"` and `"("` tokens; the last alternative would include the two calls of the `emitInstruction` method at the end.

14.3 CASCADED ASSIGNMENT STATEMENT

In a cascaded assignment, the assignment operations are performed right to left. For example, when the following statement is executed,

```
x = y = z = 7;
```

7 is assigned to z, y, and x, in that order. We say that the assignment operator is *right associative* because of its right-to-left order of evaluation.

Recall from Section 4.3 that right recursive productions imply right-associativity. So let us define a cascaded assignment using right-recursive productions:

```
assignmentStatement  →  <ID> "=" assignmentTail
assignmentTail        →  <ID> "=" assignmentTail
assignmentTail        →  expr ";"
```

The first `assignmentTail` production is right recursive. Thus, these productions will capture the right associativity of the cascaded assignment operator. Unfortunately, the two `assignmentTail` productions make the grammar not LL(1). Both productions have `<ID>` in their selection sets. Left factoring is awkward here because the two produc-

```
 1 void printlnStatement(): {}
 2 {
 3    "println"
 4    "("
 5
 6    // this paren starts a list of alternatives
 7    (
 8      printArg()          // first alternative
 9    |
10      {}                  // second alternative
11    ) // this paren ends the list of alternatives
12
13    { cg.emitInstruction("pc", "'\\n'");}
14    { cg.emitInstruction("aout");}
15    ")"
16    ";"
17 }
```

Figure 14.1.

tions do not start with the same prefix: one starts with <ID>, the other starts with expr. So we will use the productions as is. How then does the parser decide which assignmentTail production to apply? It simply looks one token beyond the current token. If it is "=", then the production to apply is necessarily the first assignmentTail production above. Otherwise, it is the second assignmentTail production.

The translation grammar for the assignment statement is given in Figure 14.2. In this translation grammar, we specify the required lookahead with the LOOKAHEAD(2) directive on line 13. The argument 2 here indicates that the choice should be based two consecutive tokens, starting with the current token. That is, it should be based on the current token and the token that follows it. Similarly, LOOKAHEAD(3) would indicate that the choice should be based on the three consecutive tokens starting from the current token. In general, LOOKAHEAD(*n*), where *n* is a positive integer, indicates that the choice should be based on the *n* consecutive tokens starting from the current token.

The parser can easily look ahead in the token stream using the getToken method. This method can provide any token from the one preceding the current token forward. getToken(*n*), where *n* is a positive integer, returns the *n*th token relative to the current token. For example, getToken(0) returns the token preceding the current token, getToken(1) returns the current token, getToken(2) returns the token following the currentToken(), and so on.

The structure of the parser code that implements the LOOKAHEAD(2) function for the cascaded assignment statement is

```
if (getToken(1).kind == ID &&
    getToken(2).kind == ASSIGN)
  apply first assignmentTail production
else
  apply second assignmentTail production
```

When getToken looks ahead in the token stream, all the tokens it reads from the input file are placed on the token chain linked by the next field in each token (see Section 10.9). Thus, these tokens will be available to the parser when it continues to access the token stream.

If you are using JavaCC, then to implement the lookahead mechanism you simply place LOOKAHEAD(2) at the choice point in the translation grammar as shown on line 13 in Figure 14.2.

When the stav instruction performs a store operation, it pops the value to be stored. Thus, this value is no longer available on the stack. If we want to perform multiple stores with the same value, we need to duplicate the value on the stack before each time we execute stav. If we do that, the duplicated value is available for the next stav operation.

To perform the cascaded assignment, we use the dupe and rot instructions as well as the stav instruction. dup duplicates the top item on the stack. rot pops the top item and then reinserts it into the stack so it is the third item from the top. Figure 14.3 shows the stack activity during the execution of the statement

```
x = y = z = 7;
```

The address of each variable is pushed onto the stack in left-to-right order. The value 7 is then pushed onto the stack (see Figure 14.3a). Next, a dupe/rot/stav sequence (see lines 19, 20, and 21 in Figure 14.2) is executed. The dupe instruction duplicates the 7 on the stack (see Figure 14.3b). The rot instruction then moves the top 7 on the stack down

```
 1 void assignmentStatement(): {Token t;}
 2 {
 3      t=<ID>
 4      { st.enter(t.image, "0");}
 5      { cg.emitInstruction("pc", t.image);}
 6      "="
 7      assignmentTail()
 8      { cg.emitInstruction("stav");}
 9 }
10 //---------------
11 void assignmentTail(): {Token t;}
12 {
13      LOOKAHEAD(2) · // <----lookahead specified here
14      t=<ID>
15      { st.enter(t.image, "0");}
16      { cg.emitInstruction("pc", t.image);}
17      "="
18      assignmentTail()
19      { cg.emitInstruction("dupe");}
20      { cg.emitInstruction("rot");}
21      { cg.emitInstruction("stav");}
22  |
23      expr()
24      ";"
25 }
```

Figure 14.2.

two positions (see Figure 14.3c). The stav instruction then pops the top 7 and the address of z, and performs the assignment to z, leaving the stack in a configuration (see Figure 14.3d) that allows this sequence to be repeated (so that 7 can be subsequently assigned to y and then x).

Now let's consider the code that our S3 compiler has to generate for a cascaded assignment statement. When assignmentStatement() parses the leftmost variable (x in our example), it emits code that pushes the variable's address onto the stack (line 5 in Figure 14.2). It then calls the recursive assignmentTail(). Recall from Section 9.9 that the statements preceding a recursive call are executed as the recursion recurses "down". Thus, on each recursive call of assignmentTail(), it emits code that pushes the address of the next variable (line 16). When it hits "bottom" (line 23), assignmentTail() parses the expression at the right of the cascaded assignment, the effect of which is to emit code that pushes the expression's value onto the stack. Recall from Section 9.9 that the statements that follow a recursive call are executed as the recursion proceeds back "up". Thus, the dupe/rot/stav sequence (lines 19, 20, 21) is repeatedly emitted as assignmentTail() recurses "up." For example, the code emitted corresponding to

    x = y = z = 7;

is

pc	x	◄―――	pushes address of x
pc	y	◄―――	pushes address of y
pc	z	◄―――	pushes address of z
pwc	7	◄―――	pushes value of expr

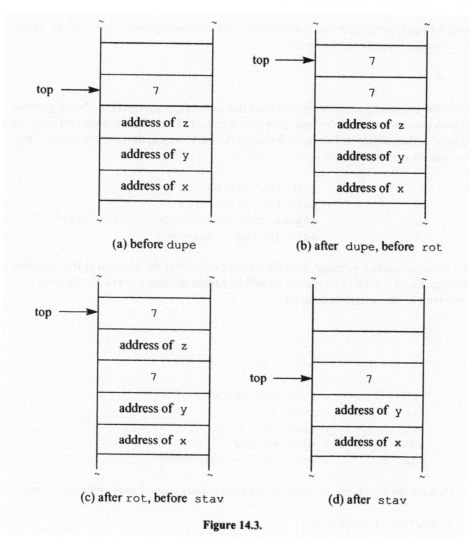

(a) before dupe   (b) after dupe, before rot

(c) after rot, before stav   (d) after stav

Figure 14.3.

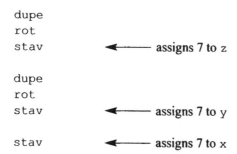

dupe
rot
stav   ◄——— assigns 7 to z

dupe
rot
stav   ◄——— assigns 7 to y

stav   ◄——— assigns 7 to x

14.4   UNARY PLUS AND MINUS

S3 supports the unary plus and minus operators. The unary plus operator is easy to handle. On a factor that starts with a unary plus, the compiler simply consumes the plus and then calls `factor()` to parse the rest of the factor. However, for the unary minus, the compiler has to generate a `neg` assembler instruction after it parsers the rest of the factor. For example, consider the statement

```
y = -x;
```

When the compiler parses the right side of this assignment statement, it should generate code to push the value of the right side onto the stack. To do that, it must first push the value of x, then negate it. To negate the top of the stack, we use the `neg` instruction. Thus, the code for this statement is

```
pc        y    ; push the address of y
p         x    ; push the value of x
neg            ; negate the value on top of the stack
stav           ; perform the assignment
```

If a minus precedes a constant, then S3 simply carries over the constant to the assembler code, prefixing it with a minus sign. S1 and S2 handle constants in exactly the same way. For example, the assembler code for

```
z = +3 + -4;
```

is

```
pc        z    ; push the address of z
pwc       3    ; push 3
pwc       -4   ; push -4
add            ; compute sum
stav           ; perform the assignment
```

Here are the new factor productions we need to fully support unary plus and minus:

```
1. factor → <UNSIGNED>
2. factor → <ID>
3. factor → "(" expr ")"
4. factor → "+" factor
5. factor → "-" <UNSIGNED>
6. factor → "-" <ID>
7. factor → "-" "(" expr ")"
8. factor → "-" "+" factor
9. factor → "-" "-" factor"
```

If a factor starts with a plus, then what follows the plus is also a factor. We generate such factors with the preceding production 4. Similarly, if a factor starts with a minus, then what follows the minus is also a factor. However, we do *not* generates such factors with

```
factor → "-" factor
```

Although this production would correctly generate the factors that start with minus, it does not distinguish among the different types of factors that can follow the minus. Thus, in the translation grammar, we would not be able to specify different actions for the different types of factors that can follow the minus. For example, if 5 (a constant) follows the minus, the corresponding action should output

```
pwc        -5
```

If, however, x (an identifier) follows the minus, the action should output

```
p          x
neg
```

Following a unary minus, we have five possibilities: a constant, an identifier, an expression within parentheses, unary plus, or another unary minus. By having a separate production for each of the possibilities (see the preceding productions 5, 6, 7, 8, and 9), we can specify a distinct action for each in the translation grammar. Unfortunately, our grammar is not LL(1) because productions 5 to 9 all start with the same terminal symbol. However, we can easily convert it to the following equivalent LL(1) grammar by left factoring:

```
factor → <UNSIGNED>
factor → <ID>
factor → "(" expr ")"
factor → "+" factor
factor → "-" (

               <UNSIGNED>

            |

               <ID>

            |

               "(" expr ")"

            |

               "+" factor

            |

               "-" factor"

         )
```

Figure 14.4 shows the `factor` portion of the translation grammar. Note that if a minus sign follows the minus sign, then the two minus signs cancel each other out. Thus, in this case, the parser simply parses the factor that follows the second minus sign (see line 35). It does not output a `neg` instruction. For example, S3 would translate

```
y = - -x;
```

to the following assembler code:

```
pc         y
p          x
stav
```

14.5 `readint` STATEMENT

When the following `readint` statment is executed,

```
readint(x);
```

```
 1 void factor(): { Token t;}
 2 {
 3     t=<UNSIGNED>
 4     { cg.emitInstruction("pwc", t.image);}
 5   |
 6     t=<ID>
 7     { st.enter(t.image);}
 8     { cg.emitInstruction("p", t.image);}
 9   |
10     "(" expr() ")"
11   |
12     "+"
13     factor()
14   |
15     "-"
16     (
17         t=<UNSIGNED>
18         { cg.emitInstruction("pwc", "-" + t.image);}
19       |
20         t=<ID>
21         { st.enter(t.image);}
22         { cg.emitInstruction("p", t.image);}
23         { cg.emitInstruction("neg");}
24       |
25         "("
26         expr()
27         ")"
28         { cg.emitInstruction("neg");}
29       |
30         "+"
31         factor()
32         { cg.emitInstruction("neg");}
33       |
34         "-"
35         factor()
36     )
37 }
```

Figure 14.4.

execution stops until the user enters a decimal integer. When the user enters an integer and hits the Enter key, execution of the `readint` proceeds: It converts the decimal integer entered to the equivalent binary number and stores it in x. The assembly code that corresponds to this statement is

```
pc        x
din
stav
```

The `pc` instruction pushes the address of x in preparation for the `stav` instruction that will perform the store. Next, the `din` (decimal in) instruction reads in the number, converts it to binary, and pushes it on the stack. Finally, the `stav` performs the store.

You need to add the following productions to your grammar for `readint`:

```
statement          →  readintStatement
readintStatement  →  "readint" "(" <ID> ")" ";"
```

14.6   CONTROLLING THE TOKEN TRACE FROM THE COMMAND LINE

In S3, the token trace is controlled from the command line when the compiler is invoked. Specifically, if `-debug_token_manager` is specified on the command line when S3 is invoked, then S3 creates a token trace. Otherwise, it does not. Implementing this feature is simple. The `debug` variable in `main` should be initialized to false. If `debug_token_manager` is specified on the command line, S3 should set `debug` to true.

When the `debug_token_manager` argument is specified, it should precede the input file name on the command line. For example, to compile `S3.s` with the S3 compiler and generate a token trace, enter

```
java S3 -debug_token_manager S3
```

To compile S3 with no token trace, enter

```
java S3 S3
```

For the token trace to be optional in the handwritten S3 compiler, S3 has to be able to access the command line to determine if the `-debug_token_manager` argument is specified. S3 accesses this argument with `args[ 0]`, where `args` is the `String` array parameter for `main`.

Like `-debug_token_manager`, any command line arguments we support in the future will be specified on the command line *before* the input file name. Because the input file name is last, it can always be accessed with `args[ args.length - 1]`.

The comparison tests performed on the command line arguments should be case insensitive. Test if `args[0]` is the `-debug_token_manager` argument using the `equalsIgnoreCase()` method in the following `if` statement:

```
if (args[0].equalsIgnoreCase("-debug_token_manager"))
    . . .
```

`equalsIgnoreCase()` performs a case insensitive comparison of strings.

The token trace is already controllable from the command line in S1j and S2j (the JavaCC versions of S1 and S2). Thus, if you are creating S3j by extending S1j or S2j, you do not have to do anything to make the token trace controllable from the command line. To get a token trace with your S3j compiler, specify the `-COMMON_TOKEN_ACTION` argument (in upper or lower case) on the command line *when you invoke JavaCC*. For example, to create a S3j compiler that generates a token trace, enter

```
javacc -COMMON_TOKEN_ACTION S3j.jj
```

14.7 SPECIFICATIONS FOR S3

S3 is the S2 compiler with the following extensions:

1. The `println` allows zero arguments.
2. Both `println` and `print` can take a string (as defined in Section 14.2) as an argument.
3. Unary plus and minus are supported.
4. Cascaded assignments are supported. For example, in S3, the following statement is legal:

   ```
   x = y = z = 7;
   ```

   Support this statement using recursive productions that require a lookahead, as described in Section 14.3.
5. The `readint` statement is supported. It reads in a single integer from the keyboard, converts it to binary, and places the binary value in the variable specified in the `readint` statement. For example,

   ```
   readint(x);
   ```

   reads an integer into `x`.
6. The token trace is optional. S3 (the handwritten version) should generate a token trace only if the `debug_token_manager` argument (case insensitive) is specified before the input file name on the command line when the S3 compiler is invoked. The S3j compiler(the JavaCC version of S3) should generate a token trace only if the S3j compiler is created with a `javacc` command in which you specify the `-COMMON_TOKEN_ACTION` argument before the input file name.
7. The assembly language file generated by the compiler should contain the source code as comments.

PROBLEMS

1. Implement the handwritten S3 compiler or the equivalent JavaCC-generated S3j compiler by extending your S2 or S2j compiler. Test your compiler by entering

   ```
   javac S3.java    or    javacc S3j.jj
   java S3 S3              javac S3j.java
   a S3.a                 java S3j S3
   e S3 /c                a S3.a
                          e S3 /c
   ```

   Submit to your instructor your source file (`S3.java` or `S3j.jj`), the assembly file created by your compiler, and the log file. Do not generate a token trace on the final version you submit. Note: you will probably get OVER LIMIT warnings when you execute the compiled program because your compiler does not produce optimal code for the unary minus operator (see problem 2).
2. Modify Figure 14.4 so that two unary minus operators separated by one or more unary plus operators are optimized out. For example, the statement

   ```
   y = - + + -x;
   ```

should be translated to

```
pc        y
p         x    // no neg instructions needed
stav
```

Hint: Change line 30 in Figure 14.4 so that it matches one or more unary plus signs. Also change line 31 so that if the current token at that point is a unary minus, `factor()` is called but not `emitInstruction("neg")`. This action optimizes out the current token unary minus along with the unary minus on line 15. If, on the other hand, the current token at line 31 is not a unary minus, then both `factor()` and `emitInstruction("neg")` should be called (for this case, we need the `neg` instruction for the unary minus on line 15). The selection sets for both of these alternatives will include the unary minus sign. Thus, the modified grammar will not be LL(1). However, you can still use it for deterministic parsing: Simply perform the first alternative whenever it is consistent with the current token. This approach is precisely what JavaCC-generated parsers do when they encounter a choice—they perform the first choice given in the grammar. Thus, if you are using JavaCC to implement S3j, you can use Figure 14.4 modified as we have described. However, you may want to add `LOOKAHEAD(1)` directives to suppress the "choice conflict" messages that JavaCC will generate (see Section 13.13). You will need two `LOOKAHEAD(1)` statements—one for the choice conflict on the modified line 30 and one for the choice conflict on the modified line 31.

3. What does your S3 compiler do if a string is specified in the source program that is missing the terminating quote?

4. Execute the following Java code. Do p and q point to the same object?

```java
String p, q;
p = "hello";
q = "hello"
if (p == q)
    System.out.println("p, q sharing one string object");
else
    System.out.println("p, q not sharing");
```

5. Execute the following C++ code. Do p and q point to the same string?

```cpp
char *p, *q;
p = "hello";
q = "hello"'
if (p == q)
    cout << "p, q sharing one string";
else
    cout << "p, q not sharing";
```

6. A unary minus preceding a constant is detected and handled by the `factor()` method. Why not have the `getNextToken()` detect and handle a unary minus preceding a constant. For example, for -5000, it would return the token <INTEGER>, whose image is "-5000".

7. Do these productions indicate a good way to add support for unary plus and minus?

```
factor → <UNSIGNED>
factor → <ID>
```

```
factor → "(" expr ")"
factor → "+" factor
factor → "-" factor
```

Is the language defined any different from the source language for S3?

8. What error message does S3 generate if the source program is

```
x = 3; &
```

What if the source program is

```
x = 3; y
```

9. What happens if during the execution of the `readint` statement, the user enters a noninteger or an integer too big?

10. If you define <STRING> is S3j.jj with

```
<STRING: "\" (~[ "\n", "\r"] )* "\"">
```

what happens when you compile

```
println("ABC"DEF");
```

11. Using EBNF and no recursion, define the cascaded assignment statement.

12. Compile the following statements with a C or C++ compiler:

```
y = - +  - + - - -x;
```

When you invoke the compiler, specify the command line argument that causes the compiler to output an assembly listing of the translated program. From this listing, determine if the generated code performs any negation operations. Repeat with a Java compiler. To get the JVM assembly code for a Java class file X.class, enter

```
javap -c X
```

13. Can you think of any reason why consecutive unary minus signs should *not* be optimized out—that is, not be translated to any code. For example, is there any reason why a compiler should generate six negation operations for the statement in Problem 12? What changes to Figure 14. 4 are required if consecutive unary minus signs are not to be optimized out?

14. Copy your version of S3 or S3j to S1414.java or S1414j.jj, respectively. Then extend S1414.java or S1414j.jj so that it supports the increment operator (++) and the decrement operator (–). Test your compiler by entering

```
java S1414 S1414     or    java S1414j S1414
a S1414.a                  a S1414.a
e S1414 /c                 e S1414 /c
```

15

COMPILING CONTROL STRUCTURES

15.1. INTRODUCTION

In this chapter, we enhance our S3 compiler from Chapter 14. We add support for

- The `while` statement
- The `if` statement
- The `do-while` statement
- Strings with embedded double quotes
- Strings that span lines
- Error recovery

We call the resulting compiler S4. If you prefer, you may use JavaCC to generate the S4 compiler. But if you do, call it S4j to distinguish it from the handwritten S4 compiler.

We will see that control structures—like the `while`, `if`, and `do-while` statements—require the parser to pass labels. These labels function as the targets of jump instructions in the target program.

We will add support for the `while`, `if`, and `do-while` statement to our compiler by performing the following five steps:

1. Determine the productions for the new statement.
2. Analyze the assembly code required by the new statement.
3. Determine the actions required to produce the required translation.
4. Write the translation grammar.
5. Convert the translation grammar to Java code by hand or by using JavaCC.

15.2. `while` STATEMENT

The `while` statement requires instructions that transfer control from one point in a program to another. We call these instructions *jump instructions*. The J1 computer has nine

Compiler Construction Using Java, JavaCC, and Yacc, First Edition. Anthony J. Dos Reis.
© 2012 the IEEE Computer Society, Inc. Published 2012 by John Wiley & Sons, Inc.

types of jump instructions. However, we will need only three: `ja` (jump always), `jz` (jump on zero), and `jnz` (jump on nonzero). The `ja` instruction is an unconditional jump instruction. When it is executed, it always causes a transfer of control to the target label. For example,

```
ja    @L0
```

causes an unconditional jump to the label `@L0`.

The `jz` and `jnz` instructions are conditional jump instructions. When they are executed, they cause a transfer of control only if a certain condition is true. The `jz` and `jnz` instructions pop and test the value from the top of the stack. The `jz` instruction transfers control if this value is zero; the `jnz` instruction transfers control if this value is nonzero.

The production for the `while` statement is

```
whileStatement -> "while" "(" expr ")" statement
```

where `expr` represents the arithmetic expressions that we handled in the S3 compiler. As in C and C++, an arithmetic expression in S4 is interpreted as true or false if its value is nonzero or zero, respectively. Note that a single statement constitutes the body of a `while` loop. But recall that one of the productions for `statement` in S3 is

```
statement → compoundStatement
```

Thus, the body of a `while` loop can be a compound statement consisting of multiple statements surrounded by braces.

Let us examine the assembly code that corresponds to the following `while` statement:

```
while (x)
{
    print(x);
    x = x - 1;
}
```

The `while` statement has a leading exit test. That is, the exit test is performed before the body of the loop is executed. For this `while` loop, the exit test determines if `x` is false (i.e., zero). If it is false, the exit occurs; otherwise, the body of the loop is executed. Figure 15.1 shows the corresponding assembly code.

The assembly code uses two labels. In the example in Figure 15.1, the labels are `@L0` and `@L1`. Both appear in the exit test code at the beginning of the loop (`@L0` as a label and `@L1` as an operand in a jump instruction). Both also appear at the end of the loop. The parser has to call the code generator at the corresponding points during the parse to output these labels. At the beginning of the `while` loop, the parser obtains the two labels and provides them to the code generator (which uses them in the code for the exit test). The parser then reuses the same labels when it is at the end of the `while` loop it is processing.

Each label, of course, must be unique. Once we use `@L0` and `@L1`, we cannot reuse them for another loop. The parser obtains a unique label each time it requires one by calling `cg.getLabel()`, a method in the code generator. This method generates labels by generating strings that start with `"@L"` concatenated to sequencing numbers that start from 0:

```
@L0:                              ; first label
            p       x             ; code generated by expr()
            jz      @L1           ; jump on false to exit loop

            p       x             ; body of loop
            dout
            pc      x
            p       x
            pwc     1
            sub
            stav

            ja      @L0           ; jump back to exit test
    @L1:                          ; second label
```

Figure 15.1.

```
public String getLabel()
{
    return "@L" + labelNumber++;
}
```

where labelNumber is an integer variable in the code generator whose initial value is 0. We have already used this method in S3 to generate labels for string constants.

Now let us look at the production for the while statement and compare it with the assembly code in Figure 15.1 to determine where in the production we need actions. From Figure 15.1, we can see we need a label at the beginning of the loop. Immediately after expr is parsed, we need our exit test (a jz that jumps to the second label). After the body of the loop, we need an unconditional jump to the first label. On the next line, we need the second label:

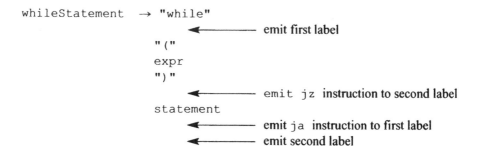

Once we have identified the actions we need, it is simple to write the translation grammar. Let us use cg.emitLabel(*label*) to emit a target label, cg.emitInstruction ("jz", *label*) to emit a jz instruction, and cg.emitInstruction("ja", *label*) to emit a ja instruction, where *label* is the appropriate String label. We get the translation grammar in Figure 15.2.

Let us go through the translation grammar in Figure 15.2 step by step to see what happens during the parse of

```
while (x)
{
```

```
    void whileStatement(): { String label1, label2;}
    {
        "while"
        { label1=cg.getLabel();}
        { cg.emitLabel(label1);}
        "("
        expr()
        ")"
        { label2=cg.getLabel();}
        { cg.emitInstruction("jz", label2);}
        statement()
        { cg.emitInstruction("ja", label1);}
        { cg.emitLabel(label2);}
    }
```

Figure 15.2.

```
    print(x);
    x = x - 1;
}
```

Let us assume labels @L0 through @L10 have been used earlier in the parse. Thus, the first label the parser gets from cg.getLabel() when it parses the preceding while statement is @L11. After parsing the while keyword, the parser gets a label that it saves in the local variable label1:

```
label1 = cg.getLabel();
```

It then executes

```
cg.emitLabel(label1);
```

which emits the label in label1:

```
@L11:
```

expr() then parses the expression within parentheses. When it does this, it emits code that, when executed, will place the value of the expression on top of the stack. For the expression x, it emits

```
        p           x
```

The parser then executes

```
label2 = cg.getLabel();
cg.emitInstruction("jz", label2);
```

which emits

```
        jz          @L12
```

statement() then emits the code for the loop body:

```
p        x
dout
pc       x
p        x
pwc      1
sub
stav
```

Finally, the parser executes

```
cg.emitInstruction("ja", label1);
```

which emits the jump back to the exit test

```
        ja          @L11
```

and

```
cg.emitLabel(label2);
```

which emits the label used in the exit test:

```
@L12:
```

15.3. if STATEMENT

To determine the translation grammar for the if statement, we use the same approach we used for the while statement: We determine the grammar, analyze the assembly code, determine the actions, and, finally, write the translation grammar. As in the while statement, the parser gets the required labels from cg.getLabel() and passes them to the code generator at various points during the parse of the if statement. There are, however, two aspects of the if statement that make it more difficult to handle. First, there are two variations of the if statement: one without an else part and one with an else part. Here are the productions that define both variations:

```
ifStatement  →  "if" "(" expr ")" statement elsePart
elsePart     →  "else" statement
elsePart     →  λ
```

Second, this grammar, which is the standard grammar for the if statement, is ambiguous. We can demonstrate this by showing two parse trees for the nested if statement

```
if (a)
  if (b)
    c = 1;
  else
    d = 2;
```

One parse tree associates the else with the first if (see Fig 15.3a); the other associates the else with the second if (see Figure 15.3b).

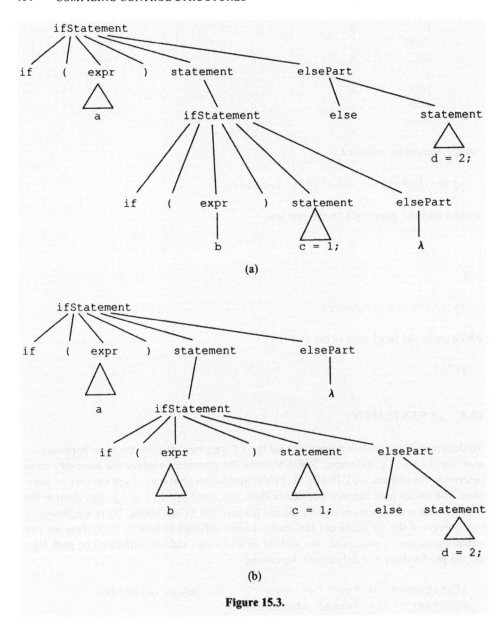

Figure 15.3.

As we learned in Section 3.5, an ambiguous grammar cannot be LL(1). Thus, it is no surprise that the selection sets for the two `elsePart` productions have a common member, the token `"else"`:

	Selection Set
elsePart → "else" statement	{ "else"}
elsePart → λ	{ "else", <ID>, "println",
	"print", ";", "{ ", "} ",
	"while", "if", "do" }

_____ delete this `else`

Suppose we delete else from the selection set of the elsePart lambda production, and then write the elsePart() method accordingly. How will our parser handle our nested if statement in Figure 15.3? Figure 15.4 shows its top-down parse at the point in the parse at which else is the current token. At this point, the input remaining is

```
else d = 2;
```

and the lower elsePart nonterminal in Figure 15.4 is to be expanded next.

With "else" in the selection set for the production elsePart → λ the parser has a choice at this point in the parse. This choice determines which parse tree in Figure 15.3 results. However, with "else" deleted from the selection set for the elsePart → λ production, there is no choice: Our parser must expand elsePart with

```
elsePart →  "else" statement
```

The right side of this production will then generate the remaining input. The upper elsePart on the parse tree will generate the null string. The result is the tree in Figure 15.3b. Our selection set modification forces the else to associate with the nearest unassociated if. The if statement in C, C++, and Java works this way, and it is precisely how the if statement in the S4 source language should work. If we are using JavaCC to construct S4, we should simply list the nonnull elsePart alternative first. Then the parser will always select it whenever the current input is else.

The ambiguity in our grammar for the if statement does not present a serious problem. We simply delete a member from a selection set to disambiguate the parsing process. However, we cannot always use this trick. Sometimes if we delete a member from a se-

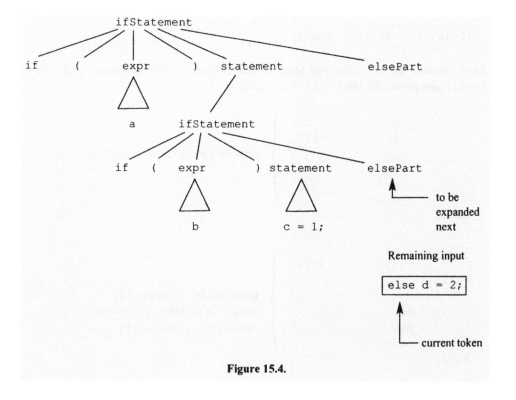

Figure 15.4.

lection set, the parser will not be able to successfully parse the input string in any way (see Section 7.10 for an example).

Let us now look at the assembly code for

```
if (b) c = 2;
```

Let us assume the parser has used the labels @L0 through @L20 earlier in the parse. Thus, the first label it gets from cg.getLabel() when it process the preceding if statement will be @L21. Then the corresponding assembly code for this if statement is

```
        p       b
        jz      @L21          ⎫
                              ⎬  emitted by ifStatement()
        pc      c             ⎪
        pwc     2             ⎪
        stav                  ⎭


@L21:                         ⎬  emited by elsePart()
```

ifstatement(), the method corresponding to ifstatement, first parses "if", " (", b, and ")". It then gets "@L21" by calling cg.getLabel(). It then emits the jz instruction that jumps to this label. elsepart(), the method corresponding to elsePart, then emits this label at the end of the statement. Thus, ifstatement() must pass "@L21" to elsepart().

Now consider the assembly code for

```
if (b) c = 2; else c = 3;
```

Again, assume the next available label is @L21. Then for this statement, ifstatement() also passes the label "@L21" to elsePart():

```
        p       b
        jz      @L21          ⎫
                              ⎬  generated by ifStatement()
        pc      c             ⎪
        pwc     2             ⎪
        stav                  ⎭



        ja      @L22          ⎫
@L21:                         ⎪
                              ⎬  generated by elsePart()
        pc      c             ⎪  (@L21 is the label ifStatement()
        pwc     3             ⎪  passes to elsePart())
        stav                  ⎭
@L22:
```

But for this case, `elsePart` does not immediately emit the label it is passed (`"@L21"` in this example). Instead, it emits it after emitting an unconditional jump to the end of the entire statement. This `ja` instruction is executed if the expression tested by the `if` statement is true. It causes a transfer of control over the `elsepart` code.

Once we understand the assembly code for the `if` statement, we can easily write its translation grammar (see Figure 15.5).

15.4. do-while STATEMENT

The `do-while` loop in C, C++, and Java creates a loop with a trailing exit test. That is, the exit test occurs after the body of the loop has been executed. The `do-while` loop in the S4 source language works the same way. Let us consider the following example:

```
do
{
  print(x);
  x = x - 1;
} while (x);
```

This loop executes until x goes false (i.e., equals zero). Like the body of the `while` loop, the body of a `do-while` loop must consist of a single statement. But this single statement can be a compound statement. Thus, the body of a `do-while` loop can, in fact, contain multiple statements as long as they are surrounded by braces (which makes them into a single compound statement).

```
void ifStatement(): { String label1;}
{
    "if"
    "("
    expr()
    ")"
    { label1=cg.getLabel();}
    { cg.emitInstruction("jz", label1);}
    statement()
    elsePart(label1)
}

void elsePart(String label1): { String label2;}
{
    "else"
    { label2=cg.getLabel();}
    { cg.emitInstruction("ja", label2);}
    { cg.emitLabel(label1);}
    statement()
    { cg.emitLabel(label2);}
|
    { cg.emitLabel(label1);}          // if no else part
}
```

Figure 15.5.

You should analyze the assembly code required by the `do-while` statement, determine the actions you need, and write the translation grammar for it. Then incorporate the required Java code into the S4 compiler. This procedure is not difficult—simply parallel the steps we used to handle the `while` loop.

15.5. RANGE CHECKING OF NUMERICAL CONSTANTS

Suppose we use our S3 compiler to compile

```
x = 5555555;
```

This statement is illegal because the integer constant is too large. However, S3 does not detect this error because it does not perform range checking on numerical constants. It generates the following assembly code:

```
; from S3 compiler written by ...
;    x = 555555;
        pc      x
        pwc     555555
        stav

        halt
x:      dw      0
```

However, when we assemble this code, the assembler will detect the error in the constant. It produces the following error message:

```
ERROR on line 4 (decimal)
        pwc      555555
Address or operand out of range
```

Although the assembler ultimately detects this error, it would be better if the compiler detected it. Then we would not waste time attempting to assemble an invalid program. But more important, the compiler would be able to produce a more useful error message. For example, it could specify the line number of the error *in the source code* file. The assembler, in contrast, provides the line number of the error in the *assembly code* file. We have to fix the source code, not the assembly code. Obviously, the line number of the error in the source code would be more useful.

Within the compiler, should the token manager or the parser detect out-of-range numerical constants? Before we answer that question, let us consider the following two statements.

```
x = -32768;        // legal
y = 5 - 32768;     // not legal
```

In the first statement, the minus sign is part of the integer constant. That is, -32768 here is a *negative integer constant*. Because this value is within range (the range of an integer constant on the J1 computer is from –32768 to 32767), this statement is legal. But in the second statement, the minus sign is the subtraction operator. It is followed by the *positive integer constant* 32768. This constant it out of range. We have two instances of 32768, one of which is legal and one of which is illegal. Clearly, to determine if an integer constant is out of range, we sometimes need to know the context in which it appears (as the two statements above illustrate). Whenever the parser processes an integer constant, it knows the context in which it appears. Thus, it is better able to perform out-of-range checking than the token manager.

Let us see how we can modify our translation grammar so that it specifies an out-of-range check on integer constants. Consider the `factor` productions of the translation grammar for S1 in Figure 15.6. `<UNSIGNED>` on line 11 has a minus sign on line 10 that precedes it. Together, they represent a negative integer constant. Thus, at line 11, the maximum legal value for `<UNSIGNED>` is 32768. `<UNSIGNED>` on line 7 has a preceding plus sign. Together, they represent a positive integer constant. Thus, at line 7, the maximum legal value for `<UNSIGNED>` is 32767, not 32768. The `<UNSIGNED>` on line 3 might be preceded by a minus sign. But if it is, the minus sign is the subtraction operator and not the unary minus of a negative constant. Thus, here the maximum value is also 32767.

To specify range checking in our translation grammar, we simply insert actions to perform the required checks. We insert

```
{
    if (t.image.length() > 5 ||
            Integer.parseInt(t.image) > 32767)
        throw genEx("Expecting integer (-32768 to 32767)");
}
```

```
 1 void factor(): { Token t;}
 2 {
 3       t=<UNSIGNED>
 4       { cg.emitInstruction("pwc", t.image);}
 5   |
 6       "+"
 7       t = <UNSIGNED>
 8       { cg.emitInstruction("pwc", t.image);}
 9   |
10       "-"
11       t = <UNSIGNED>
12       { cg.emitInstruction("pwc", "-" + t.image);}
13   |
14       t=<ID>
15       { symTab.enter(t.image);}
16       { cg.emitInstruction("p", t.image);}
17   |
18       "("
19       expr()
20       ")"
21 }
```

Figure 15.6.

after lines 3 and 7 in Figure 15.8, and we insert

```
{
    if (t.image.length() > 5 ||
            Integer.parseInt(t.image) > 32768)
        throw genEx("Expecting integer (-32768 to 32767)");
}
```

after line 11.

15.6. HANDLING BACKSLASH-QUOTE IN A STRING

In addition to supporting the control structures that we described above, S4 should also support escape sequences within strings. For example, we should be able to compile the statement

```
print("hello\ngoodbye");
```

in which an escape sequence appears within a string. For this statement, the S4 compiler should generate the following code (assuming @L0 is the next available label):

```
        pc          @L0
        sout
^@L0:   dw          "hello\ngoodbye"
```

Notice that the string in the dw statement is identical to the string in the print statement. Thus, the token manager simply has to pass the string, as is, to the parser. When the assembler processes this dw statement, it will substitute a newline character for the escape sequence '\n'. The translation of the escape sequence '\n' to the newline character *occurs at assembly time,* not at compile time. Thus, we do not need to have any special code in our token manager to support this particular escape sequence.

Now consider the statement

```
print("hello\"goodbye");
```

Again the dw statement in the assembly code should contain a string identical to the string in the print statement:

```
^@L1:   dw          "hello\"goodbye"
```

However, for this case, our token manager must have special code to handle it. The problem here is the quote embedded within the string. If we do not program our token manager to handle it properly, it will incorrectly think that the embedded quote is the *terminating quote* (i.e., the quote that marks the end of the string). In that case, it would incorrectly return the token "hello\" rather than "hello\"bye". To avoid this problem, the token manager must check if a quote is preceded by a backslash. If it is, it should treat the quote as an embedded quote—not as the quote that marks the end of the string.

To add support for quotes embedded within strings does not appear at first to be a difficult task. Unfortunately, there are complications. Consider the following statement:

```
print("hello\\");
```

Here the second quote should be treated as the terminating quote even though it is preceded by the backslash. The double backslash sequence represents a single ordinary backslash. So in reality, the second quote is not escaped with a backslash. Consider also

```
print("hello\\\"goodbye");
```

Here the embedded quote is escaped with a backslash. The first two backslashes represent the ordinary backslash. So the third backslash starts a backslash-quote escape sequence. From these two examples, we can formulate the following rule:

> **If a quote in a string constant is preceded by an even number (including zero) of backslashes, the quote is the terminating quote. If, however, it is preceded by an odd number of backslashes, then it is not the terminating quote.**

To support embedded quotes, the token manager must use this rule to distinguish embedded quotes from the terminating quote. When it encounters a string, it should move all its characters, including the initial and the terminating quote into the image field of the token it creates.

15.7.   HANDLING BACKSLASH-QUOTE WITH JAVACC (OPTIONAL)

How do we add support for the backslash-quote escape sequence in a string if we are using JavaCC to generate our token manager? One obvious approach is to determine a regular expression that correctly describes strings that can have this escape sequence. We can then use that regular expression in the TOKEN block to define a STRING token. For example, in S3j.jj (the JavaCC file for the S3 compiler), we can define a string with

```
<STRING: "\"" (~[ "\n", "\r", "\""] )* "\"">
```

It defines a string that starts with a quote and ends with a quote with no newline, carriage return, or quote in between. Unfortunately, this expression does not work correctly when the string contains the backslash-quote sequence. It works for the S3j compiler only because the S3j compiler does not support the backslash-quote escape sequence. But the S4 and S4j compilers are supposed to support the backslash-quote sequence.

To see the problem with the STRING expression above, consider the following statement:

```
println("hello\");
```

This string has no terminating quote (the second quote is backslashed, so it should be treated as an embedded quote). Thus, the compiler should generate an error message for it. However, the STRING expression above will match it. Thus, the token manager that JavaCC generates will return "hello\" as a valid string to the parser. The parser will then output assembly code that contains this invalid string.

We need to replace the STRING expression above with one that correctly captures strings that allow backslash-quote. Although such a regular expression exists, it would be difficult to determine. An alternative approach is to use two features of JavaCC we have yet to discuss: MORE blocks and lexical states.

A MORE block, like a TOKEN block, contains regular expressions that the token manager uses to identify tokens in the input stream. However, if an expression in a MORE block matches the next token in the input, the token manager does not return it to the parser. Instead, it saves it. It continues to save the strings matched by expressions from the MORE block, concatenating all of them together, until a match occurs with an expression in a block that is not a MORE block. Then the entire saved string plus the last string matched is returned to the parser as a single token.

Let us look at an example. Suppose we have the following MORE and TOKEN blocks:

```
MORE:
{
    "x"
}
TOKEN:
{
   <T1: "y">
}
```

If the input stream is "xxxy", the MORE block expression matches and saves the three x's. The Token block expression then matches the "y" and returns a <T1> token whose image is "xxxy".

The token manager that JavaCC generates is initially in the DEFAULT state. However, we can force it to change state whenever a match occurs. Let us look at the following example:

```
TOKEN:                       // Active when in DEFAULT state
{
    <T1: "A">   : DOG        // On match, change to DOG state
}

<DOG>
TOKEN:                       // Active when in DOG state
{
    <T2: "A">  : DEFAULT  // on match, change to DEFAULT state
}
```

The second TOKEN block is prefixed with the state name DOG inside angle brackets. This state prefix means that the TOKEN block that follows it is active only when the token manager is in the DOG state. The first TOKEN block, on the other hand, has no state prefix so it is active only when the token manager is in the DEFAULT state.

Now suppose the input stream is "AAA". Both the T1 and T2 expressions match the initial "A" in the input stream. But only the first TOKEN block is active since the token manager is initially in the DEFAULT state. Thus, the token manager returns the T1 token with the image "A". However the T1 match also triggers a state change to the DOG state because of the ": DOG" construct that follows the T1 definition:

```
<T1: "A">   : DOG
```

Thus, the first TOKEN block becomes inactive and the second becomes active. With the second TOKEN block active, T2 matches the next "A" in the input stream, triggering a state change back to DEFAULT:

```
<T2: "A">   : DEFAULT
```

For successive A's, the token manager provides tokens alternating between <T1> and <T2>. For the input "AAA", it provides the token sequence <T1>, <T2>, <T1>.

Notice that in the example above, the same input token ("A") can be matched by different expressions, depending on the state of the token manager. This capability is precisely what we need to handle strings with embedded quotes. We need to treat a quote within a string differently from the quotes that start and end a string. With lexical states, we can do this easily. We can put the token manager in the IN_STRING state whenever it is within a string, and in the DEFAULT state whenever it is outside a string. The default block can then handle the initial quote, and the IN_STRING TOKEN block can handle "inside" and terminating quotes. Figure 15.7 shows specification of the token manager for S3j extended to support embedded quotes. At the beginning of a string (i.e., at the initial quote), the default MORE block saves the initial quote and switches to the IN_STRING state:

```
15 MORE:
16 {
17    "\"": IN_STRING        // matches initial quote in string
18 }
```

When the token manager subsequently reaches the terminating quote, the IN_STRING TOKEN block returns the entire string as a <STRING> token, switching back to the DEFAULT state:

```
65 <IN_STRING>
66 TOKEN:
67 {
68    <STRING: "\"">            // matches terminating quote
69 }
```

Between the initial and terminating quotes, the IN_STRING MORE block accumulates and saves the characters that make up the string:

```
55 <IN_STRING>
56 MORE:
57 {
58    "\\\""            // matches backslash, quote (embedded)
59  |
60    "\\\\"            // matches backslash, backslash
61  |
62    <~[ "\"","\n","\r"] >   // matches all except ", \n, \r
63 }
```

Line 68 should match only a terminating quote. If it were able to match an embedded quote, then it would incorrectly treat an embedded quote as the terminating quote. For example, it would match the second quote in the string in the following statement

```
1 // S3j token manager extended to support embedded quotes
2 SKIP:
3 {
4     " "
5 |
6     "\n"
7 |
8     "\r"
9 |
10    "\t"
11 |
12    <"//" (~[ "\n", "\r"])*>   // matches one-line comment
13 }
14 //---------------
15 MORE:
16 {
17    "\"": IN_STRING        // matches initial quote in string
18 }
19 //---------------
20 TOKEN:
21 {
22    <PRINTLN: "println">
23 |
24    <PRINT: "print">
25 |
26    <READINT: "readint">
27 |
28    <UNSIGNED: ([ "0"-"9"])+>
29 |
30    <ID: [ "A"-"Z","a"-"z"] ([ "A"-"Z","a"-"z","0"-"9"])*>
31 |
32    <ASSIGN: "=">
33 |
34    <SEMICOLON: ";">
35 |
36    <LEFTPAREN: "(">
37 |
38    <RIGHTPAREN: ")">
39 |
40    <PLUS: "+">
41 |
42    <MINUS: "-">
43 |
44    <TIMES: "*">
45 |
46    <DIVIDE: "/">
47 |
48    <LEFTBRACE: "{ ">
49 |
50    <RIGHTBRACE: "} ">
51 |
52    <ERROR: ~[ ] >
53 }
```

Figure 15.7.

```
54 //----------------
55 <IN_STRING>
56 MORE:
57 {
58    "\\\""            // matches backslash, quote
59  |
60    "\\\\"            // matches backslash, backslash
61  |
62    <~[ "\"","\n","\r"]>  // everything else except ", \n, \r
63 }
64 //----------------
65 <IN_STRING>
66 TOKEN:
67 {
68    <STRING: "\"">      // matches terminating quote
69    <ERROR: ~[ ] )
70 }
```

Figure 15.7. *Continued.*

```
println("hello\");
```

in which case an invalid string, `"hello\"`, would be returned to the parser as a valid string. This error, however, cannot occur because of line 58:

```
58    "\\\""            // matches backslash, quote (embedded)
```

An embedded quote—that is, a quote preceded by an escaping backslash—is always matched by line 58. Thus, an embedded quote cannot be matched by line 68 (which treats a quote as the terminating quote). In other words, an embedded quote always gets treated an as embedded quote (by line 58); a terminating quote always gets treated as a terminating quote (by line 68).

In a sequence of consecutive backslashes within a string, each pair of backslashes is matched by

```
60    "\\\\"            // matches backslash, backslash
```

in the IN_STRING MORE block. Thus, only the rightmost backslash in a backslash sequence of odd length can escape a quote. For example, suppose the string ends with exactly four backslashes:

```
...\\\\"
```

Then the two pairs of backslashes are matched by line 60. The terminating quote, therefore, cannot be matched by line 58 because the backslashes have already been matched by line 60. Thus, the terminating quote will be matched by line 68, as it should. If, on the other hand, we have exactly three backslashes preceding an embedded quote

```
...\\\"...
```

then the first pair would be matched by line 60. Then the remaining backslash-quote would be matched by line 58. Thus, line 68 would not be able to match the embedded quote.

15.8. UNIVERAL BLOCKS IN JAVACC (OPTIONAL)

Recall from Section 13.3 that it is advisable to include at the bottom of your TOKEN block the "catch-all" expression

```
<ERROR: ~[ ] >
```

Then, if an invalid character appears in the input stream, this expression matches it. In that case, the token manager returns an ERROR token to the parser. The parser then detects the invalid token and throws an exception. If we did not include the ERROR expression in our token block, then the token manager, not the parser, would throw an exception on an invalid character. It is better for the parser to throw the exception because it, in general, produces more meaningful error messages. For example, the parser knows what is expected in the input stream at the point of the error. Thus, it can include this information in the error message. Suppose we use several TOKEN blocks that have the following structure:

```
TOKEN:  // active when token manager in the DEFAULT state
{
   ...
 |
   <ERROR:~[ ]>    // catch-all expression
}
//=========================================================
<DOG>         // active when token manager is in DOG state
TOKEN:
{
   //  no catch-all expression in this block
}
//=========================================================
<CAT>         // active when token manager is in CAT state
TOKEN:
{
   //  no catch-all expression in this block
}
```

Each TOKEN block is associated with a different state. Suppose only the first TOKEN block has the ERROR catch-all expression. Thus, the ERROR expression can be used only when the token manager is in the DEFAULT state. If an invalid character occurs when the token manager is in the DOG or CAT states, the token manager will not match the invalid character, and, therefore, throw an exception. To insure that the token manager matches all possible inputs, we can include the ERROR expression for every possible state (note that we did this in Figure 15.7). Then, regardless of the current state of the token manager, any invalid input would be matched by one of these ERROR expressions.

An alternative approach to placing the same expression in all the TOKEN blocks is to include it only once in a universal TOKEN block. A universal TOKEN block is active for all states. We designate a universal block by preceding the block with "<*>". Applying this approach to the example above, we get

```
TOKEN:  // active when token manager in the DEFAULT state
{
```

```
      // no catch-all expression in this block
}
//==========================================================
<DOG>           // active when token manager is in DOG state
TOKEN:
{
    //  no catch-all expression in this block
}
//==========================================================
<CAT>           // active when token manager is in CAT state
TOKEN:
{
    //  no catch-all expression in this block
}
//==========================================================
<*>             // <*> marks a universal block
TOKEN:
{
    <ERROR: ~[ ] >
}
```

Now the DEFAULT, DOG, and CAT blocks do not have the catch-all expressions. But the universal block at the bottom does. Thus, regardless of the state, the token manager will use the catch-all expression in the universal block if none of the expressions in the active TOKEN block match the current input.

Another use of a universal TOKEN block is to associate an action with the end of the source file. End of file obviously can occur at any point, regardless of the state of the token manager. Thus, we should specify the expression to match the end-of-file condition in a universal block. For example, suppose we wanted the token manager to display the total number of tokens in the source file when it encountered end of file. To do this, we

1. Set the COMMON_TOKEN_ACTION option to true (see Section 13.4).
2. Include the following TOKEN_MGR_DECLS block (see Section 13.4):

   ```
   TOKEN_MGR_DECLS:
   {
       int tokenCount = 0;
       void CommonTokenAction(Token t)
       {
           tokenCount++;
       }
   }
   ```
3. Include the following universal TOKEN block after the other TOKEN blocks:

   ```
   <*>
   TOKEN:
   {
       <EOF>
       { System.out.println("Token count = " + tokenCount);}
   }
   ```

With this setup, for each token matched, the `CommonTokenAction()` method is executed, the effect of which is to increment `tokenCount`. The `<EOF>` expression in the universal block matches the end-of-file condition, resulting in the display of the final count in `tokenCount` on end of file.

15.9. HANDLING STRINGS THAT SPAN LINES

The string constant in the following statement does not span a line:

```
println("hello\nbye");
```

All the characters from the initial quote to the terminating quote are on the same line. Of course, when the machine code for this statement is ultimately executed, the display will show two lines. Nevertheless, the string *in the source code* is all on one line. Note that the sequence \n in this string is *not* the newline character. It is a two-character sequence—the backslash followed by the letter n—that ultimately is translated by the assembler to the newline character.

Now let us consider a string that does span a line. Here is an example:

```
    println("hello\
bye");
```

The string here appears on two lines because it contains a *line separator* (i.e., the newline character, the return character, or the return–newline sequence, depending on the system) right after the slash.

We require line separators within strings to be backslashed to minimize the impact of forgetting to include the terminating quote. For example, consider

```
    println("hello\
bye);    ←————— missing quote detected when newline here is scanned
```

The missing terminating quote in the string would be detected by the token manager when it reaches the line separator that follows the semicolon on the second line (because this line separator occurs within a string, and it does not have the required backslash). But suppose we did not require line separators to be backslashed, and we made the same error in the following sequence of instructions:

```
    println("pro
blem 1);    ←————— missing terminating quote
    x = 1;
    y = 2;
    println(x + y);
```

In this example, the token manager would consume all the characters from the quote in the `println` to the end of the program, looking for the terminating quote. Thus, it would flag the last line rather than the line that is missing the quote (the second line). This example clearly demonstrates that requiring backslashes before line separators in strings is a good policy: it allows the detection of a missing quote on the line on which the error occurs.

The a assembler does not support strings that span lines. If the token manager passes, as is, a string that spans lines to the parser, we will get that same string in the assembly code. For example, the string in

```
    println("good\
bye");
```

would appear in the assembly code as

```
^@L0:     dw      "good\
bye"
```

which is illegal assembly code. But what if the token manager passed the string to the parser with the backslash–line separator sequence removed, that is, it passed the string `"goodbye"`? Then the assembly code would contain the legal statement

```
^L0:      dw      "goodbye"
```

Thus, to handle strings that span lines, the token manager simply passes them to the parser with their backslash–line separator sequences removed. Here is the rule on how the token manager should handle all the escape sequences:

> **Pass all escape sequences, as is, to the parser, except for the backslash–line separator sequence. Backslash–line separator sequences should be removed before the string is passed to the parser. The backslash–n sequence, on the other hand, should be passed *as is* to the parser.**

15.10. HANDLING STRINGS THAT SPAN LINES USING JAVACC (OPTIONAL)

Supporting strings that span lines is easy if you are using JavaCC. Simply remove any backslash–line separator sequence in a string token before it is returned to the parser. We can do this by modifying the `matchedToken` variable. Recall that on a match, the token manager returns `matchedToken` to the parser (see Section 13.4). Thus, we can change the token returned by the parser simply by changing the `matchedToken` token. Figure 15.8, the specification of the S3j token manager, illustrates this technique.

Line 72 matches the terminating quote in a string constant. When a match occurs with this expression, the token manager returns `matchedToken` to the parser. However, before it does, it performs the associated actions on lines 74 to 79. These actions remove any backslash–line separator sequences in the image field of the `Token` object to be returned (by replacing them with the null string `""`). The `replace` method is a method in `String` objects (`matchedToken` has the type `String`).

The `": DEFAULT"` construct on line 80 causes a switch to the `DEFAULT` state. To cause a state switch, we can alternatively call the `SwitchTo` method. For example, if we insert

```
SwitchTo(DEFAULT);
```

between lines 79 and 80, we then can omit the `": DEFAULT"` construct on line 80. The `SwitchTo` method is useful when we want to specify conditional state switches within actions. For example, the following action

```
 1 // removes escaped line breaks from matchedToken
 2 SKIP:
 3 {
 4    " "
 5  |
 6    "\n"
 7  |
 8    "\r"
 9  |
10    "\t"
11  |
12    <"//" (~[ "\n", "\r"])*>   // matches one-line comment
13 }
14 //----------------
15 MORE:
16 {
17    "\"": IN_STRING        // matches initial quote in string
18 }
19 //----------------
20 TOKEN:
21 {
22    <PRINTLN: "println">
23  |
24    <PRINT: "print">
25  |
26    <READINT: "readint">
27  |
28    <UNSIGNED: ([ "0"-"9"])+>
29  |
30    <ID: [ "A"-"Z","a"-"z"] ([ "A"-"Z","a"-"z","0"-"9"])*>
31  |
32    <ASSIGN: "=">
33  |
34    <SEMICOLON: ";">
35  |
36    <LEFTPAREN: "(">
37  |
38    <RIGHTPAREN: ")">
39  |
40    <PLUS: "+">
41  |
42    <MINUS: "-">
43  |
44    <TIMES: "*">
45  |
46    <DIVIDE: "/">
47  |
48    <LEFTBRACE: "{">
49  |
50    <RIGHTBRACE: "}">
51 }
52 //——————————
53 <IN_STRING>
```

Figure 15.8.

```
54 MORE:
55 {
56     "\\\""                          // matches backslash quote
57   |
58     "\\\\"                          // matches backslash backslash
59   |
60     "\\\r\n"                        // matches backslash \r \n
61   |
62     "\\\n"                          // matches backslash \n
63   |
64     "\\\r"                          // matches backslash \r
65   |
66     <~[ "\"","\n","\r"] >           // all except ", \n, and \r
67 }
68 //---------------
69 <IN_STRING>
70 TOKEN:
71 {
72     <STRING: "\"">                  // matches terminating quote
73     {
74         matchedToken.image  =
75            matchedToken.image.replace("\\\r\n","");
76         matchedToken.image  =
77            matchedToken.image.replace("\\\r","");
78         matchedToken.image  =
79            matchedToken.image.replace("\\\n","");
80     }  : DEFAULT
81 }
82 //---------------
83 <*>
84 TOKEN:
85 {
86     <ERROR: ~[ ] >                  // catch-all expression
87 }
88
```

Figure 15.8. *Continued.*

```
{
    if (flag)
        SwitchTo(DOG);
    else
        SwitchTo(DEFAULT);
}
```

switches to either the DOG or DEFAULT state depending of the true/false value of flag.

The approach we used in Figure 15.8 removes the backslash–line separator sequence in the image field of a string token *after* the creation of the token object. An alternative approach is to create a modified version of the image field *during* the creation of the to-ken. We do this by modifying a special variable in the token manager whose type is StringBuffer. As the token manager scans the characters that make up a token, it places them in this special variable. We can monitor this variable during this process. Whenever a backslash–line separator sequence is placed in this special variable, we can immediately remove it. Thus, when the token manager completes the scan of the token, this special variable has the image we desire. We can then assign it to the image field of matchedToken. When the token manager then returns matchedToken to the parser, the token object has the desired image (i.e., the string with all backslash–line separator sequences removed). Now for the confusing part: the name of this special variable is image. image, unfortunately is also the name of a field in a Token object. Do not confuse these two quite distinct uses of the name image. Figure 15.9 illustrates this technique.

The expressions on lines 56, 59, and 62 match the possible backslash–line separator sequences. When any of these three expressions match the input, we remove it from the image variable by resetting its length back by 2 or 3 using the setLength() method, depending on the length of the line separator sequence. Then when the expression on line 75 matches the terminating quote, the string in the image variable (which has all the backslash–line separator sequences removed) is converted to type String (line 77) and assigned to the image field of the matchedToken object.

15.11. SPECIAL_TOKEN BLOCK IN JAVACC (OPTIONAL)

We have seen three types of blocks that determine how the token manager works: the TOKEN block, the SKIP block, and the MORE block. A fourth type of block, the SPECIAL_TOKEN block, causes the token manager to save the strings it matches in the form of a chain. Let us look at a simple example that illustrates the effect of a SPECIAL_TOKEN block. Suppose we have the following blocks and the input stream is "dbce":

```
SPECIAL_TOKEN:
{
    <B: "b">
  |
    <C: "c">
}
TOKEN:
{
    <D: "d">
  |
    <E: "e">
}
```

The "d" in the input stream is matched by the TOKEN block. In response, the token manager creates a token object for "d", and returns this token to the parser (see Figure 15.10.a). Next, the "b" in the input stream is matched by the SPECIAL_TOKEN block. In response, the token manager creates a token object for "b", but it does *not* return this object to the parser (see Figure 15.10b). Next, "c" is matched by the SPECIAL_TOKEN block. The token manager creates a token for it, and chains it to the previous special token using the specialToken field of the token object (see Figure 15.10c). This token, like the previous special token, is not returned to the parser. Finally, "e" is matched by the TOKEN block. The token manager creates a token for "e". It chains the previous regular token (the token with "d") to this new token using the next field. It also chains this new token to the previous special token using the specialToken field (see Figure 15.10d). It then returns this token to the parser. Thus, the parser does, in fact, receive special tokens from the token manager, but not directly. Special tokens are, in effect, skipped. But,

```
 1 // removes escaped line breaks on the fly
 2 SKIP:
 3 {
 4     " "
 5   |
 6     "\n"
 7   |
 8     "\r"
 9   |
10     "\t"
11   |
12     <"//" (~[ "\n", "\r"])*>   // matches one-line comment
13 }
14 //---------------
15 MORE:
16 {
17     "\"": IN_STRING        // matches initial quote in string
18 }
19 //---------------
20 TOKEN:
21 {
22     <PRINTLN: "println">
23   |
24     <PRINT: "print">
25   |
26     <READINT: "readint">
27   |
28     <UNSIGNED: ([ "0"-"9"])+>
29   |
30     <ID: [ "A"-"Z","a"-"z"] ([ "A"-"Z","a"-"z","0"-"9"])*>
31   |
32     <ASSIGN: "=">
33   |
34     <SEMICOLON: ";">
35   |
36     <LEFTPAREN: "(">
37   |
38     <RIGHTPAREN: ")">
39   |
40     <PLUS: "+">
41   |
42     <MINUS: "-">
43   |
44     <TIMES: "*">
45   |
46     <DIVIDE: "/">
47   |
48     <LEFTBRACE: "{ ">
49   |
50     <RIGHTBRACE: "} ">
51 }
52 //---------------
53 <IN_STRING>
```

Figure 15.9.

```
54 MORE:
55 {
56     "\\\n"      // remove backslashed newline from image
57     { image.setLength(image.length() - 2);}
58   |
59     "\\\r"      // remove backslashed ret from image
60     { image.setLength(image.length() - 2);}
61   |
62     "\\\r\n"  // remove backslashed ret/newline from image
63     { image.setLength(image.length() - 3);}
64   |
65     "\\\""                     // matches backslash, quote
66   |
67     "\\\\"                     // matches backslash, backslash
68   |
69     <~[ "\"","\n","\r"]>       // all except ", \n, \r
70 }
71 //---------------
72 <IN_STRING>
73 TOKEN:
74 {
75     <STRING: "\"">             // matches terminating quote
76     // set image field in token to StringBuffer image
77     { matchedToken.image = image.toString();}  : DEFAULT
78 }
79 //--------------
80 <*>
81 TOKEN:
82 {
83     <ERROR: ~[ ]>             // catch-all expression
84 }
85
```

Figure 15.9. *Continued.*

at the same time, they are available to the parser if it wants them via the `specialToken` chain.

One use of a `SPECIAL_TOKEN` block is to process comments. Comments then are not directly returned to the parser so they do not interfere with the parsing process. However, the parser can still access them if it, for example, wants to output them to the target file it is creating.

15.12.   ERROR RECOVERY

Our S1, S2, and S3 compilers have no *error recovery* capability. That is, they do not continue to compile once they detect an error. On an error, they simply generate a message and terminate. If we want S1, S2, or S3 to detect the next error in the source program, we have to fix the first error and recompile. A better approach is for the compiler to recover from an error, that is, to continue compiling in spite of the error. That way, the compiler can flag multiple errors in a single run. A compiler designer must implement error recovery very carefully. Improperly implemented, error recovery can result in a cascade of bogus error messages.

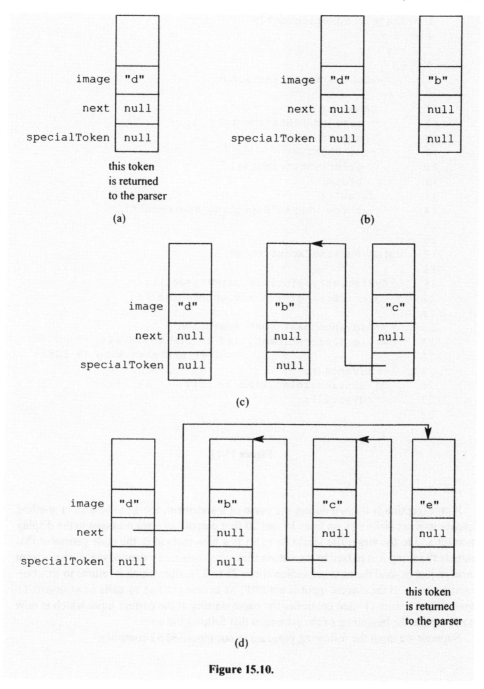

Figure 15.10.

The implementation of error recovery we describe here works well. In most cases, it will not result in bogus error messages. Here is how it works: On an error, the parser advances in the input stream to just beyond the next semicolon. Because the semicolon is a statement terminator, advancing past the next semicolon positions the parser at the beginning of the statement that follows the error. The parser can then recommence parsing at that statement. The code to implement this approach to error recovery is quite simple. Figure 15.11 shows the changes required to the statement() method in the S1 compiler.

```
 1 private void statement()
 2 {
 3   try
 4   {
 5     switch(currentToken.kind)
 6     {
 7       case ID:
 8         assignmentStatement();
 9         break;
10       case PRINTLN:
11         printlnStatement();
12         break;
13       default:
14         throw genEx("Expecting statement");
15     }
16   }
17   catch(RuntimeException e)
18   {
19     System.err.println(e.getMessage());
20     cg.emitString("; " + e.getMessage());
21
22     // advance past next semicolon
23     while (currentToken.kind != SEMICOLON &&
24                        currentToken.kind != EOF)
25       advance();
26     if (currentToken.kind != EOF)
27       advance();
28   }
29 }
```

Figure 15.11.

If an exception is thrown during the parse of a statement, the statement() method catches it. statement() on lines 19 and 20 first outputs an error message to the display monitor and to the target file (emitString is a new method in the code generator that outputs the string it is passed to the output file). statement() then advances the current input to just beyond the next semicolon (lines 23 to 27), after which it returns to statementList(). If the current input is not EOF, statementList() calls statement() again. statement() then continues the parse starting at the current input which is now positioned at the beginning of the statement that follows the error.

Suppose we input the following program to our modified S1 compiler:

```
x = 3 3;
y = 4;
z == 5;
```

Figure 15.12 shows the corresponding output file. We can see that the modified S1 compiler flags the error on the first line, correctly translates the second line, and flags the error on the third line. A single compile yields an error message for every error in the source program.

Our implementation of error recovery in S1 is not quite complete. Consider the following source program:

```
                      ; from S4 compiler written by ...
                      ; x = 3 3;
                              pc           x
                              pwc          3
                      Encountered "3" on line 1 column 7
                      Expecting op, ")", or ";"
                      ; y = 4;
                              pc           y
                              pwc          4
                              stav
                      ; z == 5;
                              pc           z
                      Encountered "=" on line 3 column 4
                      Expecting factor
                      ;

                              halt
                      x:      dw           0
                      y:      dw           0
                      z:      dw           0
```

Figure 15.12.

```
      x = 1;
  7   y = 2;
      z == 3;
```

statementList() in our modified S1 calls statement() for the first statement, which advances the current input to the 7 at the beginning of the second line. It then calls itself recursively (line 8 in Figure 15.13a). However, on this call, statementList() does not call statement() because at this point "7", the current input, cannot be the start of any statement. statementList() calls statement() only if the current input is an identifier or "println" (see lines 5 and 6). Thus, at this point in the parse, statementList() throws an exception (line 14). This exception propagates back to main() where it is caught, resulting in the termination of the compile. For this case, our modified S1 compiler terminates at the first error.

Error recovery does not work for this case because the error is detected at the statementList() level, but our error recovery mechanism is at the statement() level, which is below the statementList() level. Our error recovery mechanism works only for errors detected at or below the statement() level. We can fix this problem with a simple modification to the statementList() method: We modify it so it always calls statement() unless the current token is EOF (see line 3 in Figure 15.13b). Thus, statement() in this example will now detect and recover from the "7" input.

Note that the implementation of statementList() in Figure 15.13b is consistent with selection set criteria. statementList() represents two productions:

```
      statementList → statement statementList
      statementList → λ
```

The selection set for the lambda production is {EOF}. statementList() performs a selection test for the lambda production (by testing if the current token is EOF). The other production is the default to be applied whenever the lambda production cannot be applied.

```
 1 private void statementList()
 2 {
 3   switch(currentToken.kind)
 4   {
 5     case ID:
 6     case PRINTLN:
 7       statement();
 8       statementList();
 9       break;
10     case EOF:
11       ;
12       break;
13     default:
14       throw genEx("Expecting statement or <EOF>");
15   }
16 }
```

(a) Original code in S1 for `statementList()`

```
 1 private void statementList()
 2 {
 3   if (currentToken.kind == EOF)
 4     return;
 5   statement();
 6   statementList();
 7 }
```

(b) New `statementList()` method for error recovery

Figure 15.13.

With the modifications in Figure 15.11 and Figure 15.13b, error recovery will work well in S1. Unfortunately, when we carry these changes over to S2 and later versions of our compiler, they create a bug: the parse of a compound statement fails. The reason for the failure is a selection set error. Recall that a compound statement is defined with

```
compoundstatement → "{ " statementList "} "
```

Thus, with a compound statement in our language, the selection set for

```
statementList → λ
```

includes the right brace as well as EOF. Thus, we should change line 3 in Figure 15.13b to

```
if (currentToken.kind == EOF ||
    currentToken.kind == RIGHTBRACE)
```

This change fixes the compound statement problem. But it also disables error recovery slightly. Consider what happens when the following program is compiled:

```
} x = 2;
  y = 3;
  z = 4;
```

Here, statementList() does not call statement() at all (because the initial token is the right brace). Instead, it returns to program(), which throws an exception. No error recovery occurs for this case.

The correct way to fix the.compound statement problem is to

1. Leave statementList() as it is in Figure 15.13b to keep error recovery fully in effect.

2. Create a new nonterminal compoundList() similar to statementList() in Figure 15.13b:

```
private void compoundList()
{
   if (currentToken.kind == RIGHTBRACE)
     return;
   statement();
   compoundList();
}
```

3. Replace the call of statementList() in compoundStatement() with a call of compoundList().

With these changes, the selection set for

statementList → λ

becomes {EOF}. Thus, the version of statementList() in Figure 15.13b is now correct. We have eliminated the compound statement problem, and, at the same time, we have a fully enabled error recovery mechanism.

15.13.   ERROR RECOVERY IN JAVACC (OPTIONAL)

We can implement error recovery for the JavaCC-generated S1j compiler using exactly the same approach that we described above for S1. Figure 15.14 shows the new version of statement() that implements error recovery.

In our modified S1j compiler, program() always calls statementList(), and statementList() always calls statement() unless the current input is EOF. statement() catches any exceptions and advances the current input to just beyond the next semicolon in the source program. Our modified S1j compiler works exactly like our modified S1 compiler. Note that we write try and catch blocks in a JavaCC translation grammar *without* enclosing braces. We do not distinguish try and catch blocks from the grammatical symbols in the grammar with any special delimiters, as we do with actions. getNextToken() is a method in the S1j compiler that corresponds to the advance() method in S1. Like S1, it calls getNextToken() (a method with the same name) in the token manager to get the next token.

For versions that include the compound statement, you should define a compoundStatement() without using statementList() to avoid the selection set problem with compoundStatement() that we discussed in preceding section. For example, you can use

```
 1 void program(): {}
 2 {
 3    statementList()
 4    { codeGen.endCode();}
 5    <EOF>
 6 }
 7 //---------------
 8 void statementList(): {}
 9 {
10    { if (getToken(1).kind==EOF) return;}
11    statement()
12    statementList()
13 }
14 //---------------
15 void statement(): {}
16 {
17   try
18   {
19      assignmentStatement()
20    |
21      printlnStatement()
22   }
23   catch(ParseException e)
24   {
26     System.err.println(e.getMessage());
27     cg.emitString(e.getMessage());
28
29     while (getToken(1).kind != SEMICOLON &&
30            getToken.kind != EOF)
31       getNextToken();                // like advance() in S1
32     if (getToken(1).kind != EOF)
33       getNextToken();                // like advance() in S1
34   }
35 }
```

Figure 15.14.

```
void compoundStatement(): { Token t;}
{
   "{ "
   (statement())*
   "} "
}
```

15.14. SPECIFICATIONS FOR S4

S4 is the S3 compiler with the following extensions:

1. The while, if, if-else, and do-while control statements are supported. Do *not* support relational or boolean operators and expressions. The true/false expressions in the while, if, if-else, and do-while statements are all arithmetic. A zero value represents false; a nonzero value represents true.

2. Perform range checking on integer constants.

3. String constants with embedded quotes are supported. An embedded quote must be preceded by an odd number of backslashes. For example, the following statement is now legal:

```
println("He said \"Hello\" to me.");
```

The string in this statement should be passed as is by the token manager to the parser.

4. String constants that span multiple lines are supported. Every line separator in a string constant must be preceded immediately by a backslash. For example, the following statement has two line separators, each preceded by a backslash:

```
    println("one\
two\
three");
```

Because the assembler does not support strings that span lines, a multiple-line string constant should be returned by the token manager to the parser as a single-line string (i.e., with its backslash–line separator sequences removed). For example, the string in the preceding statement should be returned as "onetwothree".

5. Error recovery as described in Sections 15.12 and 15.13 is supported.

PROBLEMS

1. Implement the S4 or S4j compiler. Test your compiler by entering

```
javac S4.java    or    javacc S4j.jj
java S4 S4              javac S4j.java
a S4.a                  java S4j S4
e S4 /c                 a S4.a
                        e S4 /c
```

Also enter

```
java S4 p1501 or java S4j p1501
```

Your compiler should recover from all the errors in p1501.s (this file is in the J1 Software Package). Submit S4.java or S4j.jj, the assembly files produced by your compiler, and the log files to your instructor.

2. Modify S1j.jj so that the S1j compiler can handle both single-line comments that start with "//" and multiline comments that are bracketed with "/*" and "*/". Your modified S1j compiler should not comment the assembly code file with the source code it is translating. Test your modified compiler by compiling the file p1502.s (in the J1 Software Package) by entering

```
javacc S1j.jj
javac S1j.java
java S1j p1502
a p1502.a
e p1502 /c
```

Submit to your instructor your modified S1j.jj, p1502.a, and p1502.<*family name*>.log (the log file that the e program creates).

3. Further modify S1j.jj from Problem 2 so that the S1j compiler's output includes as comments the source code in the input file (see Section 13.11). Test your modified S1j compiler as specified in Problem 2. Use a SPECIAL_TOKEN block to capture the comments in p1502.s so you can output them to the assembly file.

4. Write the translation grammar for the do-while statement.

5. Using your S4/S4j compiler, compile the following program:

```
x = -32768;
y = 32767;
z = 5 - 32768;
```

What error messages, if any, does your compiler produce?

6. If the do-while loop below were legal, what ambiguity would we encounter?

```
do
  x = x + 1;
  y = y + 1;
while (x);
```

7. Why does C, C++, and Java have a do-while but not a do-until statement.

8. Write a translation grammar for a loop statement defined by

```
loopStatement → "loop" expr statement
```

When executed, a loop statement will execute its body (a statement) the number of times equal to the value of the expression following the keyword loop. If the value of the expression is less than or equal to 0, then the statement is not executed.

9. Write out the assembly code corresponding to the code below that your S4/S4j compiler should generate. Then check your answer by compiling the code with your compiler and examining the output file.

```
if (b)
if (c)
if (d)
d = 1;
else
d = 2;
else
c = 1
else
b = 1;
```

10. Write out the assembly code corresponding to the code below that your S4/S4j compiler should generate. Then check your answer by compiling the code with your compiler and examining the output file.

```
while (a)
while (b)
while (c)
{
    a = 0;
    b = 0;
    c = 0;
}
```

11. Suppose a compiler labels a point in the assembly code it generates with multiple labels. For example,

```
L3:
L2:
L1:
        pc        x
        .
        .
        .
```

Do these multiple labels cause a space or time inefficiency in the executable code to which the assembly code is translated?

12. Write a nonambiguous grammar for the `if` statement. Is your grammar suitable for top-down parsing?

13. Compute the selection set for the production

$$elsepart \rightarrow \lambda$$

in the grammar for the S4 compiler. Explain why it includes "`;`", "`{`", and "`}`".

14. Describe what happens when the token manager defined by Figure 15.7 processes the input string "`A\nB`". What matches the backslash? What matches the "`n`"?

15. The productions for the `if` statement are not LL(1). Why does JavaCC accept the `if` statement productions without complaint?

16. What happens when S4/S4j, modified with error recovery as described in Sections 15.12 and 15.13, translates

```
if (x)
{
x = 5;
else
x = 6;
```

17. Give a source program for which the error recovery mechanism as described in Sections 15.12 and 15.13 does a poor job.

18. Where does your S4j compiler detect the error in

```
println("hello
goodbye");
println("yes");
```

19. Would it be all right to move the MORE block on lines 15 to 18 to after the TOKEN block on lines 20 to 53 in Figure 15.7? Justify your answer.

20. Would error recovery work correctly if `program()` were changed to

```
void program(): {}
{
    (statement())*
    { codeGen.endCode();}
    <EOF>
}
```

Justify your answer.

21. Modify your S4/S4j compiler so that error recovery is at the `statementList` level rather than at the `statement` level. Run your modified compiler against `p1521.s` and `p1501.s`. Compare with the error recovery for your original S4/S4j compiler. Are there any differences?

22. Will this definition of a string constant

    ```
    <STRING:  "\""  (~[ "\n",  "\r"] )*  "\"">
    ```

    match the entire string in

    ```
    println("abc\"cde");
    ```

    Use JavaCC to check your answer. Does this definition of a string correctly handle embedded quotes?

16

COMPILING PROGRAMS IN FUNCTIONAL FORM

16.1 INTRODUCTION

In this chapter, our source programs finally start looking like programs written in a real programming language. With the exception of the input/output statements, our source language is a subset of C. In C, we organize code segments into functional units called functions. Functions in C are like static methods in Java. We will call the hand-written compiler that handles this source language S5, and the JavaCC version S5j.

If we examine a program in the source language for S5, we will see that it consists mostly of lists. A program is a list of global declarations and function definitions. A global declaration is a list of variables with optional initial values. Within a function definition, we have a parameter list and local variable declarations. Each local variable declaration is a list of variables with optional initial values. In short, lists are everywhere.

We, of course, know how to handle lists. We can write grammars that define them (Section 2.10). We know how to process them recursively or iteratively (Section 9.7). We know how to process them left to right or right to left (Section 9.9). We can do just about anything we want with lists. So our job in this chapter should not be too difficult.

Our first step is to learn more about the assembly language for the J1 computer. Specifically, we need to learn how to handle separately assembled modules, function calls, returns, and relative instructions (we use relative instructions to access parameters and local variables). Next, we extend our grammar for S4 so that it encompasses all the new features to be handled by S5. Finally, we incorporate actions into our grammar that generate the required target language.

16.2 SEPARATE ASSEMBLY AND LINKING

It is possible to create a large program in a single file. However, a better approach is to break up a large program into small modules, each in its own file. We can then indepen-

Compiler Construction Using Java, JavaCC, and Yacc, First Edition. Anthony J. Dos Reis
© 2012 the IEEE Computer Society, Inc. Published 2012 by John Wiley & Sons, Inc.

dently compile, assemble, and test each module. To create a complete executable program, we have to combine the separate modules into a single executable file using a program called a *linker*.

The a program in the J1 Software Package is both an assembler and a linker. If the input file to a is a complete program, it translates it directly to an executable file (a file with the extension ".e"). Otherwise, it translates the input file to an *object module* (a file with the extension ".o"). An object module contains machine code. However, it is not a complete program. So we have to link it with other object modules to get an executable file.

Every C program consists of one or more modules. When these modules are compiled and assembled, we get the corresponding object modules. To create an executable program, these object modules, along with a special module called *start-up code,* have to be linked together. When the resulting executable program is run, start-up code always gets control first. After performing some necessary initializations, start-up code calls the main function. Thus, every C program must have at least the main function.

When the main function in a C program completes, it returns control back to the start-up code. The start-up code then performs a final "clean-up" and returns to the operating system.

Just like C, the modules that our S5 compiler generates have to be linked with start-up code. Let us consider an example in which we create an executable program. Suppose we have two source modules m1.s and m2.s that together constitute a single program (see Figure 16.1a). The use of x in the print statement in m1.s is an *external reference.* That is, it is a reference to an item defined outside of m1.s. The extern statement in m1.s informs the compiler that x is defined externally. Without it, the compiler would flag the print statement with the message

```
Undeclared Symbol
```

To create an executable program, we first have to compile m1.s and m2.s with our S5 compiler by entering

```
java S5 m1
java S5 m2
```

These two compiles produce two assembly modules m1.a and m2.a (see Figure 16.1b) Next, we assemble these modules and link their resulting object modules with the object module for the start-up code. This start-up code is in the file sup.o. We can do all this with just one command:

```
a m1.a m2.a sup.o          you may omit the ".o" extension on sup.o
```

The a program will then assemble m1.a and m2.a and link the resulting object modules with sup.o, producing the executable file m1.e. The base name of the executable file is obtained from the base name of the first file specified on the command line when the a program is invoked. Because the first file specified by the preceding command is m1.a, the name of the executable file is m1.e. We can now execute our executable program in m1.e with

```
e m1
```

or

```
e m1 /c
```

```
        m1.s                                  m2.s

  extern int x;                       int x = 5;
  void main()
  {
     print(x);
  }
```

(a)

```
m1.a                                        m2.a

        extern    x                          public    x
        public    main          x:           dw        5
  main:   .
          .
          .
        p         x
        dout
          .
          .
          .
```

(b)

Figure 16.1.

The reference to x in the p instruction in m1.a is an external reference. Thus, when the assembler assembles m1.a, it has no way of knowing the location of x. It is completely unaware of the m2.a module and the definition of x within it. Thus, when it assembles the p instruction, it places 0 in the address field of the instruction. However, when we link the two modules, the linker will find the actual address of x and insert it into the p instruction. Thus, when the program is ultimately executed, the p instruction will correctly access x.

Notice in Figure 16.1, m1.a contains the statement

```
     extern    x
```

This statement informs the assembler that x is an external symbol. Without this statement, the assembler would view the x in the p instruction as an undefined label, in which case, it would flag the p instruction with the following error message:

```
Undefined label in operand field
```

A call of a function in one module from a different module is also an external reference, and, therefore, requires an extern statement. For example, if an assembly module contains the call

```
     call      f
```

and f is in another, separately assembled module, then the call of f here is an external reference. Thus, the module that contains this call must also contain

```
     extern    f
```

In `m2.a`, we have the statement (see Figure 16.1b)

```
public    x
```

This statement makes the scope of x global. Without it, x would be unknown outside the `m2.a` module, in which case the linker would not be able to find the address of x (which it needs for the p instruction in `m1.a`). Without the `public` statement, `m2.a` would assemble without error. However, at link time, the linker would complain with the message

```
LINK ERROR: Unresolved external symbol x
```

and terminate without creating an executable program. Similarly, `main` in `m1.a` must also be declared `public` so start-up code can call it.

Every assembly module that contains the definition of a function should contain a `public` statement for the name of that function. Every global variable should also have a `public` statement. The effect of these `public` statements is to make the scope of function and global variable names global. For example, corresponding to the source code

```
int x;
void f()
{
    .
    .
    .
}
```

is the assembly code

```
          public    x
x:        dw        0

          public    f
f:          .
            .
            .
```

`public` and `extern` statements may appear on any line in an assembly language program. They can appear at the beginning, in the middle, or at the end.

The assembler does not translate `public` and `extern` statements to machine code. The purpose of these statements is to direct the assembler to treat identifiers in a certain way. For this reason, we call them *assembler directives*.

Only one identifier may appear on each `public` or `extern` statement in an assembly language program. Thus, we cannot use

```
        public x, y, z      ; illegal
```

Instead, we should use

```
        public x            ; legal
        public y
        public z
```

16.3 CALLING AND RETURNING FROM FUNCTIONS

To call a function in assembly lanaguage, we use the `call` instruction, specifying the name of the function. For example, the assembler code corresponding to

```
f();  // calls the f function
```

is

```
        call        f
```

The `call` instruction not only transfers control to the specified function, it also pushes the return address (the address of the instruction that physically follows the `call` instruction) onto the stack. To return to its caller, the called function executes the `ret` instruction. This instruction pops the return address off the stack into the `pc` register, causing the desired return (see Figure 16.2).

Consider the following function call:

```
f(2, y, y + 3);
```

Just before the `call` instruction, we must push the values of the arguments onto the stack. Immediately after the call, we must remove them from the stack. Thus, the code for the above function call is

```
        ; push values of args onto stack to create
        ; the corresponding parameters
        pwc         2
        p           y
        p           y
        pwc         3
        add

        ; call the function f
        call        f

        ; add 3 to sp which effectively pops three values previously pushed
        asp         3
```

The `asp` instruction after the call adds three to the `sp` register, effectively popping the three values previously pushed onto the stack. Unlike C, which pushes the values of argu-

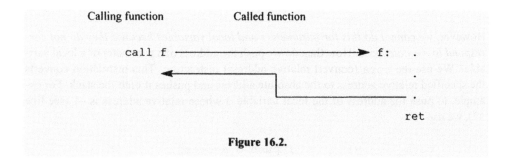

Figure 16.2.

ments in a function call in right-to-left order, our language pushes arguments values in left-to-right order (translation is easier for the left-to-right approach).

By pushing the values of the arguments in a function call, we create and initialize the corresponding parameters. For example, suppose the definition of f starts with

```
void f(int a, int b, int c)
```

Pushing the values of 2, y, and y + 3 in the call

```
f(2, y, y + 3);
```

creates the parameters a, b, and c.

Let us look at the complete example of a function call and return in Figure 16.3.

Figure 16.4a shows what the stack looks like immediately after we execute the call instruction on line 21. The sp register points to the return address pushed by the call instruction. Above the return address (i.e., at higher memory addresses), we have the three parameters c, b, a initialized, respectively, to 4, 1, and 2.

The first instruction we execute when we enter the f function is the esba instruction. Its effect is to save the current value in the bp register by pushing it onto the stack. It then copies the sp register to the bp register.

We then create the local variables d and e, respectively, by subtracting 1 from the sp register to create d (line 34) and by pushing 5 to create and initialize e. Thus, d has no guaranteed initial value but e has the initial value of 5. Figure 16.4b shows the stack at this point.

bp is the base register. It provides the base address from which we access items on the stack. For example, to access c (which is two slots above the slot to which bp is pointing), we use the pr (push relative) instruction

```
pr        2
```

The address in this instruction is a *relative address*. That is, it is the address relative to the location to which bp points. To access the parameters c, b, and a, we use the relative addresses 2, 3, and 4, respectively. Note that the relative address of the rightmost parameter is always 2. To access the local variables d and e, we use the relative addresses −1 and −2 (we use negative numbers because the local variables are below the base address in bp). The relative address of the first local variable is always −1.

The global variables are created with dw statements (lines 2 and 4). Thus, we can refer to them using their corresponding labels. For example, to push the address of x, we use

```
pc        x
```

However, *we cannot do this for parameters and local variables because they do not correspond to dw statements.* How then do we push the address of a parameter or a local variable? We use the cora (convert relative address) instruction. This instruction converts the specified relative address to the absolute address and pushes it onto the stack. For example, to push the address of the local variable d whose relative address is −1 (see line 47), we use

```
cora      -1        ; push d address
```

```
 1 int x, y = 1;                    public   x      ; x global
 2                             x:   dw    0
 3                                  public   y      ; y global
 4                             y:   dw    1
 5
 6 void main()                      public   main   ; main global
 7                             main:
 8
 9
10                                  esba            ; set up bp
11 {
12
13    f(2, y, y + 3);               ; create parms a, b, and c
14                                  pwc   2         ; create a
15                                  p     y         ; create b
16                                  p     y         ; push y value
17                                  pwc   3         ; push 3
18                                  add             ; create c
19
20                                  ; transfer control to f
21                                  call  f
22
23                                  ; remove parms a, b, and c
24                                  asp   3
25
26 }                                reba            ; prepare for ret
27                                  ret             ; to sup code
28
29
30 void f(int a, int b, int c)      public f
31                             f:
32 {                                esba            ; set up base reg
33
34    int d, e = 5;                 asp   -1        ; allocate d
35                                  pwc   5         ; allocate/init e
36
37    x = y;                        pc    x         ; push x address
38                                  p     y         ; push y value
39                                  stav            ; do assignment
40
41    a = b + c;                    cora  4         ; push a address
42                                  pr    3         ; push b value
43                                  pr    2         ; push c value
44                                  add             ; compute b + c
45                                  stav            ; do assignment
46
47    d = e;                        cora  -1        ; push d address
48                                  pr    -2        ; push e value
49                                  stav            ; do assignment
50
51 }                                reba            ; prepare for ret
52                                  ret             ; return to main
```

Figure 16.3.

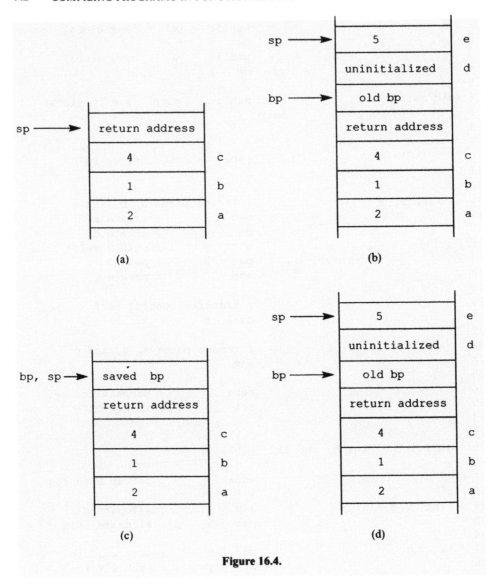

Figure 16.4.

Thus, the assembler code for

```
d = e;
```

is

```
cora      -1      ; push address of d
pr        -2      ; push e value
stav              ; do assignment
```

Just before the called function returns, it executes the reba instruction (line 51). This instruction copies the bp register contents into the sp register, the effect of which is to pop all the local variables. It then pops the top of the stack into the bp register which restores bp with its previous value. The stack at this point is back to the configuration in Figure 16.4a. The ret instruction (line 52) then pops the return address into the pc register, returning control to the asp instruction on line 24 in main. The asp instruction then removes the three parameters from the stack by adding 3 to the sp register, completing the call.

16.4   SOURCE LANGUAGE FOR S5

The source language for S5 is essentially the source language for S4 extended to support the program structures illustrated by Figure 16.3. Here are the distinguishing features of S5 and its source language:

1. All variables must be declared before they can be used.
2. The scope of a global variable starts from the point of declaration and extends to the end of the file. It also extends to other files that contain an extern declaration for that variable, starting at the point of the extern declaration and extending to the end of the file.
3. The scope of a local variable starts from the point of declaration and extends to the end of the function in which it is declared. A local variable with the same name as a global variable has precedence over that global variable. For example, suppose we have both a global variable x and a local variable x. If the following statement is in he scope of both the local and global x variables,

    ```
    x = 1;
    ```

    then S5 treats the x in this statement as the local x.
4. Local variable declarations, if any, in a function must appear before any executable statements in that function.
5. The return type of all functions must be void. That is, a function cannot return a value.
6. S5 does *not* check if the argument list in a function call is compatible with the parameter list of the corresponding function.
7. S5 allows references to external variables (i.e., variables defined in a separately compiled file). However, such references must be preceded by extern declarations. For example, in the following main function, we are making external references to x and y:

    ```
    extern int x;
    extern int y;

    void main()
    {
        x = y;   // external reference to x and y
    }
    ```

Thus, we must precede main with the extern declarations to explicitly indicate that x and y are external symbols. An extern declaration in the source language can list one or more identifiers. For example, in the example above we could have used

```
extern int x, y;
```

in place of the two `extern` declarations. However, in the corresponding assembler program, we must have a separate `extern` statement for each external symbol. For the preceding `extern` statement, S5 outputs the following assembler code:

```
extern x
extern y
```

8. S5 treats a function call without an accompanying function definition as an external reference. For example, the following module,

```
void main()
{
  h();
}
```

does not contain a definition of the function `h()`. Thus, S5 assumes that the definition of `h()` is in a separately compiled module. Accordingly, S5 includes an `extern` declaration for `h` in the assembler code it outputs:

```
        public   main
main:
        esba
        call     h
        reba
        ret

        extern   h   ; h assumed to be an external symbol
```

S5 has to wait until it reaches the end of the input file before it can output this `extern` statement because it is only then that S5 can confirm that the definition of `h()` is not in the input file.

16.5 SYMBOL TABLE FOR S5

The symbol table class for S5 uses three parallel ArrayLists: `symbol`, `relAdd`, and `category` (see Figure 16.5b). `relAdd` holds the relative address of local items (i.e., parameters and local variables). It is not used for nonlocal items. So for those items, `relAdd` entries are set to zero. Each entry in `category` holds one of five possible category constants. These constants indicate the type of the entry:

LOCAL—a parameter or local variable

GLOBALVARIABLE—global variable

EXTERNVARIABLE—external variable declared with the `extern` statement

FUNCTIONDEFINITION—function definition

FUNCTIONCALL—a function call for which there is no matching function definition in the input file

For example, when the parser process lines 1 through 5 in Figure 16.5a, it enters "q", "r", "main", and "x" into the symbol table with categories GLOBALVARIABLE, EXTERNVARIABLE, FUNCTIONDEFINITION, and LOCAL, respectively. When the parser

```
 1   int q;            // entered as GLOBALVARIABLE
 2   extern r;         // entered as EXTERNVARIABLE
 3   void main()       // entered as FUNCTIONDEFINITION
 4   {
 5       int x = 70;
 6       g(x);         // entered as a FUNCTIONCALL1
 7   }
 8   void g(int a)     // change g entry to FUNCTIONDEFINITION
 9   {
10       println("hello");
11       h();          // entered as a FUNCTIONCALL
12   }
```

(a)

	symbol (String)		relAdd (Integer)	category (Integer)
0	"q"		0	GLOBALVARIABLE
1	"r"		0	EXTERNVARIABLE
2	"main"	|	0	FUNCTIONDEFINITION
3	"x"	|	-1	LOCAL
	"g"		0	FUNCTIONDEFINITION
5	"a"		2	LOCAL
6	"h"		0	FUNCTIONCALL

(b)

Figure 16.5.

reaches line 6, it first enters "g" as a FUNCTIONCALL. But when it then reaches the definition of g on line 8, it converts this entry to a FUNCTIONDEFINITION entry. On line 11, the parser enters "h" as a FUNCTIONCALL. Because the definition of the h() function does not appear in this file, this entry remains a FUNCTIONCALL entry. At the end of the parse, the endCode() method outputs an extern statement for each FUNCTIONCALL entry. Figure 16.5b shows the final symbol table.

The symbol table class has the following methods:

```
public void enter(String sym, int ra, int cat)
```

If sym does not match any entry in the table, sym, ra, and cat are added to the symbol, relAdd, and category ArrayLists, respectively.

If sym matches an entry in the table, what happens depends on the parameter cat and the category of the matched symbol in the table as indicated in the following table:

cat	Category of matched symbol in table	Action
FUNCTIONCALL	FUNCTIONCALL	none
FUNCTIONCALL	FUNCTIONDEFINITION	none
FUNCTIONDEFINITION	FUNCTIONCALL	change category of matched symbol in table to FUNCTIONDEFINITION
LOCAL	GLOBALVARIABLE or EXTERNVARIABLE	add new LOCAL entry

For other matches, enter throws an exception.

```
public int find(String sym)
```

This searches symbol for sym. If it finds it, it returns its index. Otherwise, it throws an exception. find searches in reverse order, that is, from the most recent entry to the least recent entry.

```
public String getSymbol(int i)
```

This returns symbol entry at index i.

```
public Integer getRelAdd(int i)
```

This returns relAdd entry at index i.

```
public Integer getCategory(int i)
```

This returns category entry at index i.

```
public int getSize()
```

This returns the size of the symbol table.

```
public void localRemove()
```

This removes all LOCAL entries in the symbol table.

16.6 CODE GENERATOR FOR S5

The code generator for S5 has the following methods:

```
public void emitString(String s)
```

which calls outFile.println(s).

```
public void emitInstruction(String op)
```

which outputs instruction that consists of the mnemonic op only.

```
public void emitInstruction(String op, String opnd)
```

which outputs instruction that consists of a mnemonic op and an operand opnd.

```
public void emitdw(String label, String value)
```

which outputs label, ":", "dw", and value by calling printf().

```
public void endCode()
```

which outputs an extern statement for every FUNCTIONCALL entry in the symbol table.

```
public String getLabel()
```

which returns the strings in the sequence "@L0", "@L1", ... to serve as labels for string constants and for the jump instructions.

```
public void emitLabel(String label)
```

which outputs label followed by ":"

```
public void push(int p)
```

If the index p corresponds to a non-LOCAL entry, push outputs the p mnemonic followed by the variable name obtained with st.getSymbol(p) (st is the reference to the symbol table). For example,

```
    p      x          ; global
```

For a LOCAL entry, push outputs the pr mnemonic followed by the variable's relative address (obtained by st.getRelAdd(p)). For example,

```
    pr     -1         ; local
```

```
public void pushAddress(int p)
```

Similar to push, except it outputs the mnemonics pc or cora if the variable is non-LOCAL or LOCAL, respectively. For example, for the global variable x, it outputs

```
    pc     x
```

For the local variable with relative address –1, it outputs

```
    cora   -1          ; local
```

16.7 TRANSLATION GRAMMAR FOR S5

Figure 16.6 shows a partial translation grammar for S5 (it is available in the file S5.tg in the J1 Software Package). Components of this grammar that are identical to components

```
1  // Translation grammar for S5
2  // No range checking or error recovery
3
4  void program(): {}
5  {
6      programUnitList()
7      { cg.endCode();}
8      <EOF>
9  }
10 //---------------
11 void programUnitList(): {}
12 {
13     { if (getToken(1).kind == EOF) return;}
14     programUnit()
15     programUnitList()
16 }
17 //---------------
18 void programUnit(): {}
19 {
20     externDeclaration()
21  |
22     globalDeclaration()
23  |
24     functionDefinition()
25 }
26 //---------------
27 void externDeclaration(): { Token t;}
28 {
29     "extern"
30     "int"
31     t=<ID>
32     { st.enter(t.image, 0, EXTERNVARIABLE);}
33     { cg.emitInstruction("extern", t.image);}
34     (
35         ","
36         t=<ID>
37         { st.enter(t.image, 0, EXTERNVARIABLE);}
38         { cg.emitInstruction("extern", t.image);}
39     )*
40     ";"
41 }
42 //---------------
43 void globalDeclaration(): {}
44 {
45     "int"
46     global()                // process one global variable
47     (
48         ","
49         global()            // process one global variable
50     )*
51     ";"
52 }
53 //---------------
```

Figure 16.6.

```
54 void global(): {Token t1, t2; String initVal;}
55 {
56    t1=<ID>
57    {cg.emitInstruction("public", t1.image);}
58    {initVal="0";}
59    (                    // do if global variable initialized
60       "="
61       {initVal = "";}
62       (<PLUS> | <MINUS> {initVal = "-";})?
63       t2=<UNSIGNED>
64       {initVal = initVal + t2.image;}
65    )?
66    {st.enter(t1.image, 0, GLOBALVARIABLE);}
67    {cg.emitdw(t1.image, initVal);}
68 }
69 //---------------
70 void functionDefinition(): {Token t;}
71 {
72    "void"
73    t=<ID>
74    {cg.emitString(
75       "; =============== start of function " + t.image);}
76    {st.enter(t.image, 0, FUNCTIONDEFINITION);}
77    {cg.emitInstruction("public", t.image);}
78    {cg.emitLabel(t.image);}
79    "("
80    (parameterList())?
81    ")"
82    "{ "
83    {cg.emitInstruction("esba");}
84    localDeclarations()
85    statementList()
86    "} "
87    {cg.emitInstruction("reba");}
88    {cg.emitInstruction("ret");}
89    {cg.emitString(
90       "; =============== end of function " + t.image);}
91    // remove locals from symbol table
92    {st.localRemove();}
93 }
94 //---------------
95 void parameterList(): {Token t; int p;}
96 {
97    t=parameter()
98    p=parameterR()
99    {st.enter(t.image, p, LOCAL);}
100 }
101 //--------------
102 Token parameter(): {Token t;}
103 {
104    "int"
105    t=<ID>
106    {return t;}
```

Figure 16.6. *Continued.*

```
107 }
108 //----------------
109 int parameterR(): { Token t; int p;}
110 {
111     ","
112     t = parameter()
113     p = parameterR()         // p is the rel address
114     { st.enter(t.image, p, LOCAL);}
115     { return p + 1;}         // return next relative address
116   |
117     { return 2;}             // at end of parameter list
118 }
119 //----------------
120 void localDeclarations(): { int relativeAddress = -1;}
121 {
122     (
123         "int"
124         local(relativeAddress-)      // process 1 local var
125         (
126             ","
127             local(relativeAddress-) // process 1 local var
128         )*
129         ";"
130     )*
131 }
132 //----------------
133 void local(int relativeAddress): { Token t; String sign;}
134 {
135     t=<ID>
136     { st.enter(t.image, relativeAddress, LOCAL);}
137     (
138         (                    // do if local variable initialized
139             "="
140             { sign = "";}
141             (<PLUS> | <MINUS> { sign = "-"; })?
142             t=<UNSIGNED>
143             { cg.emitInstruction("pwc", sign + t.image);}
144         )
145     |
146         { cg.emitInstruction("asp", "-1");}
147     )
148 }
149 //----------------
150 void statementList(): {}
151 {
152     { if (getToken(1).kind == RIGHTBRACE) return;}
153     statement()
154     statementList()
155 }
156 //----------------
157 void statement(): {}
158 {
159     LOOKAHEAD(2)
```

Figure 16.6. *Continued.*

```
160      assignmentStatement()        // starts with <ID>
161   |
162      functionCall()               // also starts with <ID>
163   |
164      printlnStatement()
165   |
166      printStatement()
167   |
168      nullStatement()
169   |
170      compoundStatement()
171   |
172      readintStatement()
173   |
174      whileStatement()
175   |
176      ifStatement()
177   |
178      doWhileStatement()
179 }
180 //---------------
181 void assignmentStatement(): { Token t; int index;}
182 {
183      t=<ID>
184      { index=st.find(t.image);}
185      { cg.pushAddress(index);}
186      "="
187      assignmentTail()
188      { cg.emitInstruction("stav");}
189 }
190 //---------------
191 void assignmentTail(): {Token t; int index;}
192 {
193      LOOKAHEAD(2)
194      t=<ID>
195      { index=st.find(t.image);}
196      { cg.pushAddress(index);}
197      "="
198      assignmentTail()
199      { cg.emitInstruction("dupe");}
200      { cg.emitInstruction("rot");}
201      { cg.emitInstruction("stav");}
202   |
203      expr()
204      ";"
205 }
206 //---------------
207 void printlnStatement(): {}
208 {
209      // as in S4
210 }
211 //---------------
212 void printlnArg(): {Token t; String p;}
```

Figure 16.6. *Continued.*

```
213 {
214     // as in S4
215 }
216 //---------------
217 void printStatement(): {}
218 {
219     // as in S4
220 }
221 //---------------
222 void printArg(): {Token t; String p;}
223 {
224     // as in S4
225 }
226 //---------------
227 void nullStatement(): {}
228 {
229     // as in S4
230 }
231 //---------------
232 void compoundStatement(): { int p;}
233 {
234     // as in S4
235 }
236 //---------------
237 void readintStatement(): {Token t; int index;}
238 {
239     "readint"
240     "("
241     t=<ID>
242     {index=st.find(t.image);}
243     {cg.pushAddress(index);}
244     {cg.emitInstruction("din");}
245     {cg.emitInstruction("stav");}
246     ")"
247     ";"
248 }
249 //---------------
250 void whileStatement(): {String label1, label2; Token t;}
251 {
252     // as in S4
253 }
254 //---------------
255 void ifStatement(): {String label1; Token t;}
256 {
257     // as in S4
258 }
259 //---------------
260 void elsePart(String label1): {String label2;}
261 {
262     // as in S4
263 }
264 //---------------
265 void doWhileStatement(): {String label; Token t;}
```

Figure 16.6. *Continued.*

```
266 {
267     // as in S4
268 }
269 //---------------
270 void functionCall(): { Token t; int count;}
271 {
272     t=<ID>
273     { st.enter(t.image, 0, FUNCTIONCALL);}
274     "("
275     { count = 0;}
276     (count = argumentList())?
277     { cg.emitInstruction("call", t.image);}
278     {
279         if (count > 0)
280             cg.emitInstruction("asp",
281                                 Integer.toString(count));
282     }
283     ")"
284     ";"
285 }
286 //---------------
287 int argumentList(): { int count;}
288 {
289     expr()
290     { count = 1;}
291     (
292         ","
293         expr()
294         { count++;}
295     )*
296     { return count;}
297 }
298 //---------------
299 void expr(): { Token t;}
300 {
301     // as in S4
302 }
303 //---------------
304 void term(): { Token t;}
305 {
306     // as in S4
307 }
308 //---------------
309 void factor(): { Token t; int index;}
310 {
311     t=<UNSIGNED>
312     { cg.emitInstruction("pwc", t.image);}
313 |
314     t=<ID>
315     { index=st.find(t.image);}
316     { cg.push(index);}
317 |
318     "(" expr() ")"
```

Figure 16.6. *Continued.*

```
319   |
320     "+"
321     factor()
322   |
323     "-"
324     (
325       t=<UNSIGNED>
326       { cg.emitInstruction("pwc", "-" + t.image);}
327     |
328       t=<ID>
329       { index=st.find(t.image);}
330       { cg.push(index);}
331       { cg.emitInstruction("neg");}
332     |
333       "("
334       expr()
335       ")"
336       { cg.emitInstruction("neg");}
337     |
338       (
339         LOOKAHEAD(1)   // suppress warning message
340         "+"
341       )+
342       (
343         LOOKAHEAD(1)   // suppress warning message
344         "-"
345         factor()
346       |
347         factor()
348         { cg.emitInstruction("neg");}
349       )
350     |
351       "-"
352       factor()
353     )
354 }
```

Figure 16.6. *Continued.*

in the translation grammar for S4 have been omitted. The specification of range checking and error recovery has also been omitted. The translation grammar for S5j (the JavaCC version of S5) is the same except that it has additional actions that output the source code as comments (see Section 13.12). These actions are not needed by S5 because in S5 the token manager outputs the source code as comments.

Wherever possible, we have used the "*" operator rather than recursion to represent lists in our translation grammar for S5. For example, the production for `globalDeclaration()` is

```
43 void globalDeclaration(): {}
44 {
45     "int"
46     global()                    // process one global variable
```

```
47      (
48          ","
49          global()              // process one global variable
50      )*
51      ";"
52  }
```

We use the " * " operator on line 50 to specify a list of zero of more occurrences of the sequence

```
","
global()
```

We, however, have used recursion to specify the list associated with the `parameterList()` production:

```
 95  void parameterList(): { Token t; int p;}
 96  {
 97      t=parameter()
 98      p=parameterR()
 99      { st.enter(t.image, p, LOCAL);}
100  }
```

`parameter()` on line 97 parses the first parameter in a parameter list. Then `parameterR()`, a recursive method, parses the remaining parameters. We use recursion here because we have to enter the parameters into the local symbol table in right-to-left order. Right-to-left order is necessary to determine the relative address for each parameter. For example, in the parameter list in

```
        void f(int a, int b, int c)
```

the relative addresses of a, b, and c are 4, 3, and 2, respectively. The relative address of the first parameter depends on the number of parameters. Thus, the parser cannot determine this relative address until it has parsed all the parameters. If, however, the parser processes the parameter list *right to left*, it can simply assign the relative address 2 to the rightmost parameter and successively higher addresses to the other parameters as it moves to the left through the list. Here is where recursion is very handy. Recall from Section 9.9 that we can use recursion to process a list in reverse order. We simply perform the required processing after the recursive call. This is precisely what we do in `parameterR()`:

```
109  int parameterR(): { Token t; int p;}
110  {
111      ","
112      t = parameter()
113      p = parameterR()         // p is the rel address
114      { st.enter(t.image, p, LOCAL);}
115      { return p + 1;}          // return next relative address
116  |
117      { return 2;}              // at end of parameter list
118  }
```

parameterR() recurses to the right end of the parameter list. When it reaches the end, it returns 2 (line 117), the relative address of the rightmost parameter. At the next level up, parameterR() assigns this address to p (line 113). The enter method then enters t.image (the name of the parameter), p (the parameter's relative address), and the LO-CAL category into the symbol table (line 114). Next, parameterR() returns p + 1 (line 115), the relative address of the next parameter to the left (which is one more than the relative address in p of the current parameter). As parameterR() continues to recurse back to the leftmost parameter, it returns successively higher relative addresses. Thus, at each level on the way back to the leftmost parameter, it can make the required entry into the local symbol table.

localDeclarations() processes local declarations, if any, within a function definition. These declarations must appear right after the opening brace of the function's body. Each time we call the local method (which processes one local variable) from within localDeclarations(), we pass it the current value of relativeAddress and then decrement this value:

```
120 void localDeclarations(): { int relativeAddress = -1;}
121 {
122     (
123         "int"
124         local(relativeAddress-)      // process 1 local var
125         (
126             ","
127             local(relativeAddress-) // process 1 local var
128         )*
129         ";"
130     )*
131 }
```

Thus, each local variable is given a relative address of one less than its predecessor. Because we initialize relativeAddress to –1 (line 120), these relative addresses form the sequence –1, –2, –3, ... These are the correct relative addresses for local variables (recall from Figure 16.4d that local variables appear on the stack just below the location to which the bp register points, and, therefore, have relative addresses –1, –2, –3, ...).

local() processes one local variable declaration:

```
133 void local(int relativeAddress): { Token t; String sign;}
134 {
135     t=<ID>
136     { st.enter(t.image, relativeAddress, LOCAL);}
137     (
138         (                    // do if local variable initialized
139             "="
140             { sign = "";}
141             (<PLUS> | <MINUS> { sign = "-"; } )?
142             t=<UNSIGNED>
143             { cg.emitInstruction("pwc", sign + t.image);}
144         )
145     |
```

```
146          { cg.emitInstruction("asp", "-1");}
147      )
148 }
```

On line 136, `local` enters the local variable's name into the symbol table with the correct relative address and the LOCAL category. If an initial value is specified for the local variable, `local` then outputs a `pwc` instruction (line 143) that both creates and initializes the variable. Otherwise, it outputs an `asp` instruction (line 146), which creates but does not initialize the variable.

On line 276 in `functionCall()`, `argumentList()` returns the count of the number of arguments in the argument list it has just parsed:

```
276      (count = argumentList())?
```

The parser needs this count because it has to generate an `asp` instruction that removes the parameters from the stack (see line 24 in Figure 16.3). The number of parameters is equal to the number of arguments in the function call. Thus, this count is the number of parameters to remove. The operand in the `asp` instruction should be this count. For example, if the count is 3, then the `asp` instruction should be

```
asp         3
```

The productions for `statement()` (lines 157 to 179) are not LL(1) because both an assignment statement and a function call start with an < ID>. We resolve this problem by placing a LOOKAHEAD(2) directive on line 159.

16.8 LINKING WITH A LIBRARY

The a program not only assembles modules but links them as well. If external references still exist after the a program links all the modules specified on the command line, it will then search a library for modules that will satisfy the remaining external references. If it finds such modules, it will link them with the modules it has already linked to create a complete executable program.

A *library* is a collection of object modules combined into a single file. Each module in a library typically performs some general-purpose function. If you write an assembly language program that needs one or more of these modules, you can simply call those modules from your program. The a program will then automatically link those modules with your program. For example, suppose the library has a module named m that you would like to use in your program. To call m from your program, you simply include the following code in your assembly language program:

```
extern m
call   m
```

If you have additional calls of m in the same program, just specify the `call` instruction. Do not repeat the `extern` statement.

The a program uses the library in the file a.1, if one exists. You can easily create your own a.1 library with the 1 (this is a lowercase "L") program in the J1 Software Package. For example, suppose you want to create a library containing the m1, m2, and m3 modules obtained from the `m1.a`, `m2.a`, and `m3.a` files, respectively. To do this, we first assemble (but not link) the three assembly modules with

```
a /a m1.a m2.a m3.a
```

The `/a` command line argument suppresses the link step that the a program normally performs. Thus, this command only assembles the three modules, yielding the three object modules `m1.o`, `m2.o`, and `m3.o`. To create the `a.l` library containing these modules, we invoke the `l` program specifying the three object modules (we do not have to include the `".o"` extensions):

```
l m1 m2 m3
```

16.9   SPECIFICATIONS FOR S5

S5 is S4 extended to support

1. Function definitions and function calls
2. Parameter passing but not checking for argument–parameter compatibility
3. Global and local `int` variables, both initialized and uninitialized
4. Separate compilation and linking

To test your S5 compiler, enter

```
javac S5.java          (compile S5 compiler)
java S5 S5a            (compile S5a.s)
java S5 S5b            (compile S5b.s)
a S5a.a S5b.a sup     (assemble S5a.a, S5b.b and link with start-up code sup.o)
e S5 /c               (execute and verify S5.e)
```

16.10   EXTENDING S5 (OPTIONAL)

S6 is the extension of S5 that includes the following added features:

1. Functions can return values. The assembler code for

    ```
    y = f(x);
    ```

    is

    ```
              pc        y     ; push address of y
              asp       -1    ; reserve slot for return value
              p         x     ; push value of x, creating parm
              call      f
              asp       1     ; remove parameter
              stav            ; store returned value in y
    ```

    The assembler code for

    ```
    int f(int z)
    {
    ```

```
    return z + 1;
}
```

is

```
        public    f
f:
        esba
        cora      3      ; push address of reserved slot
        pr        2      ; push z
        pwc       1      ; push 1
        add              ; compute and push value of z+1
        stav             ; store value in address
        reba
        ret
```

Figure 16.7 shows the stack just before the `stav` instruction in the `f` method is executed.

2. S6 supports the relational operators ($<$, $<=$, $>$, $>=$, ==, !=) and the remainder operator (%). Operator precedence from highest to lowest is

```
*, /, %
+, -
<, <=, >, >=
==, !=
```

Use the `cmps` (signed compare) instruction to perform comparisons. The `cmps` instruction pops and compares the top two numbers on the stack. If any of the relational conditions tested for are true, the `cmps` instruction pushes true (i.e., 1) onto the stack; otherwise it pushes false (i.e., 0). The conditions to be tested are specified by a mask in the `cmps` instruction. For example, in the following instruction

```
cmps        6
```

the mask is 6 (110 in binary). The three bits in the mask, left to right, correspond to the conditions $<$, ==, and $>$, respectively. A 1 bit indicates that the corresponding

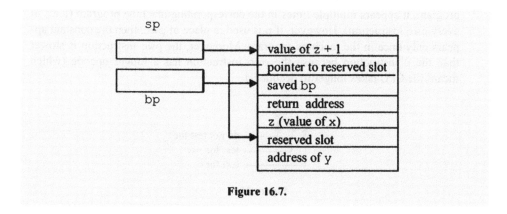

Figure 16.7.

test should be performed. Thus, the mask 110 specifies that the tests for the < and == conditions should be performed (see Figure 16.8).

When an cmps instruction with a mask of 6 is executed, it pops the top two numbers from the stack. It then compares the second number popped with the first number popped. If the second number is less than or equal to the first number, it pushes true (i.e., 1); otherwise, it pushes false (i.e., 0). For example, the code for

```
if (x <= y)
    x = 0;
```

is

```
        p       x
        p       y
        cmps    6       ; 6 = 110, tests for < and ==
        jz      @L0     ; jump on false to @L0
        pc      x       ; x = 0;
        pwc     0
        stav
@L0:
```

3. S6 supports the break statement, which causes an immediate exit from a loop.

4. S6 supports /* */ comments. A /* */ comment may span lines. It starts with any occurrence of /* outside a string constant or a comment. It ends with the *next* occurrence of */, regardless of the context in which the */ appears. Thus, */ will terminate a comment even if it appears within a string constant or a single-line comment.

5. S6 pushes integer constants with a p instruction instead of a pwc instruction. For example, the code for

```
x = 2;
```

where x is a global variable is

```
        pc      x
        p       @2
        stav
```

where @2 is defined with

```
@2:     dw      2
```

Using p in place of pwc results in more efficient code. The pwc instruction contains the constant it pushes. Thus, if a constant appears multiple times in the source program, it appears multiple times in the corresponding machine program (once in every pwc instruction). However, if p is used in place of pwc, then the constant appears only once in the machine program. Moreover, the pwc instruction is slower than the p instruction because the pwc instruction has a longer opcode (which means the CPU takes longer to decode it).

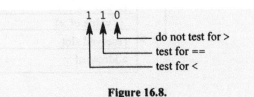

Figure 16.8.

PROBLEMS

1. Implement the handwritten S5 compiler or the S5j JavaCC version. A partial translation grammar for S5 (Figure 16.6) is available in the J1 Software Package in S5.tg.
   Test your S5 or S5j compiler by entering

   ```
   javac S5.java       or        javacc S5j.jj
   java S5 S5a                    javac S5j.java
   java S5 S5b                    java S5j S5a
   a S5a.a S5b.a sup             java S5j S5b
   e S5a /c                      a S5a.a S5b.a sup
                                 e S5a /c
   ```

   Submit S5.java or S5j.jj, the assembly files created by your compiler and the
   log file, to your instructor. Also test error recovery by entering

   ```
   java S5 p1601   or    java S5j p1601
   ```

2. What happens if you link S5a.o and S5b.o without sup.o? Does the link complete? If so, what happens when you execute the resulting program?

3. Create an a.l library that contains the S5b.o module created in problem 1. Then
   link the S5a.o with S5b.o in the library by entering

   ```
   a S5a sup
   ```

   Test the resulting S5a.e executable module.

4. Implement the handwritten S6 compiler or the S6j JavaCC version. Test your S6 or
   S6j compiler by performing the following steps:

   a. Compile S6b.s with your S6 or S6j compiler.
   b. Using the l program, create a library containing the object module S6b.o ob-
      tained from S6b.s.
   c. Enter

   ```
   a S6a.a sup
   e S6a /c
   ```

   Submit S6.java or S6j.jj, S6a.a, S6b.a and the log file to your instructor.

5. Would it be difficult for the parser to generate code to push the values of the arguments in a function call in right-to-left order? How would this approach affect the
   implementation of parameterList()? See Problem 17.

6. Describe how you would implement parameterList() nonrecursively.

7. Describe how you would implement the for statement.

8. Why does the compiler prefix the labels it generates with "@"?

9. An alternate structure for the while loop is

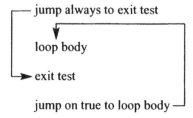

In what way is this structure superior to the structure we have been using for the `while` loop? Incorporate this structure into your S5 compiler. Test your modified S5 compiler with `S5a.s` and `S5b.s`, as specified in Problem 16.1.

10. Create an `a.l` library that contains three modules. One displays `"left"`, one displays `"middle"`, and one displays `"right"`. Write an assembly language program that displays

    ```
    left middle right
    ```

    by calling these three modules. Place your program in a file named `p1610.a`. Assemble and run with

    ```
    a p1610.a sup
    e p1610
    ```

11. Modify `S5.java` or `S5j.jj` so that a local variable can be declared anywhere within a function definition body. The scope of a local variable should start at the point of declaration and extend to the end of the function body. Test your new compiler as specified in problem 1. Also use your compiler to compile `p1611.s`, which is in the J1 Software Package. Assemble, link with `sup.o` and run with

    ```
    a p1611.a sup
    e p1611
    ```

12. Modify your compiler from Problem 11 so that the scope of a local variables ends at the end of the block in which it is declared. Thus, if it declared within a compound statement, it ends at the end of the compound statement. Test your new compiler as specified in Problem 1. Also use your compiler to compile `p1612.s`, which is in the J1 Software Package. Assemble, link with `sup.o`, and run with

    ```
    a p1612.a sup
    e p1612
    ```

13. Add support to your S5 or S5j compiler for the scope resolution operator `"::"`. When this operator precedes an identifier, it indicates that the identifier should be interpreted as the globally defined one even if it is within the scope of an identically named local identifier. Test your new compiler as specified in Problem 1. Also use your compiler to compile `p1613.s`, which is in the J1 Software Package. Assemble, link with `sup.o`, and run with

    ```
    a p1613.a sup
    e p1613
    ```

14. Suppose the `find` method for a LOCAL symbol returned its negated index, but for a non-LOCAL symbol returned its nonnegated index. Could `push` and `pushAddress` then be implemented more efficiently. If so, how?

15. Are the local entries in the symbol table always grouped together at the bottom of the symbol table? If so, can you make the method `localRemove` more efficient?

16. Would it be better to have all local entries in the symbol table in a separate table? In that case, how would the `find` method work?

17. Modify your S5 or S5j compiler so that it pushes arguments in right-to-left order (the same order C and C++ uses). Then the relative address of the parameters are num-

bered starting from 2 from left to right. Test your compiler as specified in Problem 16.1.

18. Is there any reason *not* to use the star operator to define the list of statements in `statementList()` (lines 150 to 155 in Figure 16.6)?

19. Evaluate the effectiveness of the error recovery mechanism you implemented in S5/S5j. Extend your recovery mechanism so that it recovers from most errors.

17

FINITE AUTOMATA

17.1 INTRODUCTION

Regular expressions, regular grammars, context-free grammars, and context-sensitive grammars all define languages. Regular expressions and regular grammars are equally powerful in defining languages (we have yet to show this equivalence). That is, if we can define a language with a regular expression, we can also define it with regular grammar, and vice versa. Context-free grammars are more powerful than regular expressions and regular grammars. Context-sensitive grammars, in turn, are more powerful than context-free grammars. In this chapter, we will study another mechanism for defining languages: the finite automaton. Finite automata ("automata" is the plural form of "automaton") have the same power to define languages as regular expressions and regular grammars. Finite automata are important for three reasons:

1. A simple algorithm exists that will optimize any finite automaton—that is, convert it to the least complex finite automaton that defines the same language.
2. We can use a finite automaton directly to determine if an arbitrary string is in the language defined by that finite automaton. That is, a finite automaton not only defines a language, it is essentially an algorithm that determines if an arbitrary string is in that language.
3. It is often easier to work with finite automata than with regular expressions or regular grammars.

In this chapter, we will learn how to convert between regular expressions, regular grammars, and finite automata. The conversions are important for two reasons. First, they establish that regular expressions, regular grammars, and finite automata are equally powerful in defining languages. Second, they allow us to obtain the form of language definition that is best suited for the task at hand. For example, suppose we are given a regular expression, and our job is to create an algorithm that will determine if an arbitrary string

Compiler Construction Using Java, JavaCC, and Yacc, First Edition. Anthony J. Dos Reis

© 2012 the IEEE Computer Society, Inc. Published 2012 by John Wiley & Sons, Inc.

465

is in the language defined by the given regular expression. If we simply convert the regular expression to the equivalent finite automaton, we are done. The equivalent finite automaton, itself, is the algorithm we need. JavaCC, which generates token managers for us, does precisely this. We give it regular expressions that describe the various tokens in the source language. It converts these regular expressions to finite automata. The token manager it generates then uses these finite automata to identify the various tokens that appear in the source programs it processes.

17.2   DETERMINISTIC FINITE AUTOMATA

There are two variations of finite automata: *deterministic finite automata* (DFA) and *nondeterministic finite automata* (NFA). An DFA does not allow choice in its operation, but a NFA does. Both variations contain a finite number of states; hence, the name "finite automata."

Let us examine the DFA in Figure 17. 1. The circles in Figure 17.1 represent the *states* of the DFA. We typically give each state a name. In Figure 17.1, the states are named q0, q1, q2, q3, and q4. Exiting each state are labeled arrows. We call these labeled arrows *transitions*. The labels on these arrows are characters from the alphabet of the DFA. The alphabet for this DFA is { b,   c} . Each state has exactly one arrow exiting it for each character in the alphabet of the DFA, labeled with that character. Because the alphabet for this DFA has two characters, b and c, each state has two arrows exiting it, one labeled with b and one labeled with c. A single arrow with multiple labels is a shorthand representation of multiple arrows, one for each label. For example, the arrow from q0 to q1 labeled with b and c represents two arrows, one labeled with b and one labeled with c. Exactly one state in a DFA, designated by the arrowhead, is the *start state*. In Figure 17.1, q0 is the start state. Zero or more states, designated by concentric circles, are *accept states*. All states that are not accepting (i.e., those that are not designated by concentric circles) are *reject states*. In Figure 17.1, q2 and q3 are the accept states; q0, q1, and q4 are reject states.

Let us list the components that make up the DFA in Figure 17.1:

1. The set of states Q = { q0,   q1,   q2,   q3,   q4}
2. The input alphabet Σ   = { b,   c}
3. The initial state q0 ∈ Q
4. The set of accept states A = { q2,   q3} ⊆ Q

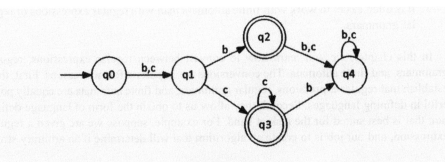

Figure 17.1.

5. The set of arrows. These arrows constitute a function that maps each state/character pair to a state (the state to which the arrow points). For example, the arrow from q0 labeled with b that points to q1 maps the q0/b pair to q1.

When we input a string to a DFA, the DFA starts in the start state. As we input each character of the string, the DFA follows the arrow with the same character. For example, when we input bcc to the DFA in Figure 17.1, the following sequence occurs:

1. The initial b takes the DFA from q0 to q1.
2. The first c then takes the DFA from q1 to q3.
3. The second c takes the DFA from q3 back to q3.

Because q3, the state in which the DFA ends when we input bcc, is an accept state, we say that the DFA *accepts* the input string bcc.

Now let us input bcbb to our DFA. The string takes the DFA from q0 to q1 to q3 to q4 and, finally, back to q4. Here, the last state, q4, is a reject state. We say the DFA *rejects* the input string bcbb. Note that the DFA rejects this string even though its input causes the DFA at one point to be in state q3, an accept state. Acceptance and rejection of a string depend only on the state in which the DFA ends.

As we input a string to a DFA, there is never any choice on which arrow to take. There is always exactly one arrow whose label matches the next character in the input string. Its operation at any step is completely determined. Hence, we call this type of automaton *deterministic*.

The language defined by a DFA is the set of strings it accepts. That is, it is the set of strings that take the DFA from the start state to some accept state. For the DFA in Figure 17.1, the regular expression for the set of strings that take the DFA to q2 or q3 (the two accept states) are (b|c)b and (b|c)cc*, respectively. Thus, the regular expression for the language defined by this DFA is the two preceding expressions joined by the union operator:

(b|c)b|(b|c)cc*

which equals (by factoring out (b|c)),

(b|c)(b|cc*)

Note that the loop at q3 in the DFA corresponds to the star operator in the corresponding regular expression.

Inputting λ (i.e., the null string) to a DFA does not cause a state transition. Thus, when the input string is λ, the DFA stays and, therefore, ends in the start state. Thus, a DFA accepts λ if an only if its start state is an accept state.

q4 in Figure 17.1 is a rejecting state from which the DFA can never leave (because both b and c loop on q4). We call such states *trap states*. Suppose the first portion of a string causes a DFA to enter a trap state. Then regardless of what remains in the string, the DFA will necessarily reject the string. Not all DFAs have trap states. For example the DFA whose alphabet is { b, c} that defines (b|c)* obviously cannot because it must accept every string over the alphabet { b, c} .

Exercise 17.1

Give a DFA that defines (b|c)*.

Answer:

Exercise 17.2

Convert the following DFA to a regular expression:

Answer:

    bcc* | cbc*

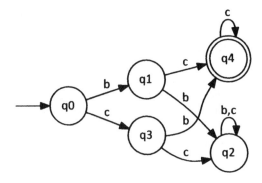

17.3   CONVERTING A DFA TO A REGULAR EXPRESSION

An algorithm exists that converts an arbitrary DFA to a regular expression that defines the same language. Because this algorithm is difficult to describe precisely, we will not cover it here. Instead, we will describe a simple technique that will allow us to determine for many DFAs the corresponding regular expression by inspection. This technique is based on the following observation: If a string is accepted by a DFA, it must take the DFA from the start state to an accept state and optionally loop on that accept state. A regular expression defining these strings has

1. An initial part that takes the DFA from the start state to the accept state for the first time

2. A second part that corresponds to strings that cause the DFA to loop on the accept state

To determine the regular expression for a DFA, we simply determine the regular expressions for these two parts and concatenate them together. Let us consider the DFA in Figure 17.2. To go from q0 (the start state) to q1 (the accept state) the first time, we optionally loop with c's at q0 and then go to q1 on a b. The corresponding regular expression is c*b. At q1, there are two loops. One corresponds to a single c. The other corresponds to a b, followed by a c, followed by zero or more c's, followed by one more b. We can describe the strings corresponding to one circuit of the first loop with c; we can describe the strings corresponding to one circuit of the second loop with bcc*b. When the DFA reaches q1, it can follow either loop any number of times (including zero times). Thus, the regular expression corresponding to the two loops at q1 is (c|bcc*b)*. By concatenating the regular expression corresponding to strings that get us from the start state to the accept state the first time (c*b) with the regular expression corresponding to loops at q1 (c|bcc*b)*, we get the regular expression for the entire DFA:

```
c*b(c|bcc*b)*
```

In general, the regular expression for the strings accepted by accept state q is given by

```
alpha (beta₁ | beta₂ | ... | betaₙ)*
```

where `alpha` is the regular expression for the strings that takes the DFA from the start state to q for the first time, and $beta_1$, $beta_2$, ..., $beta_n$ are the regular expressions corresponding to one circuit of the loops at q.

Exercise 17.3

Convert the following DFA to a regular expression that defines the same language:

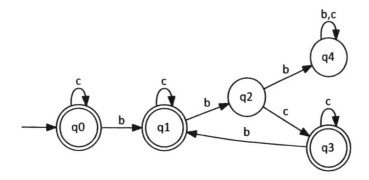

Answers:

For q0: c*
For q1: c*b(c|bcc*b)*
For q3: c*bc*bc(c|bc*bc)*

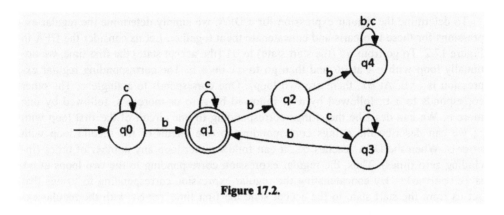

Figure 17.2.

For the entire DFA (the three expressions joined by the union operator):

c* | c* b (c | bcc* b) * | c* bc* bc (c | bc* bc) *   ■

Suppose we want to determine a regular expression for the type of comment allowed in Java programs that starts with " /* " and end with "* / ". Between the " /* " and "* / " delimiters, any characters can appear except for a "* / " sequence. Because it is easier to construct the DFA than the regular expression for this type of comment, we will first construct the DFA and then convert it to a regular expression.

One of the problems we immediately encounter when we try to construct the DFA for comments is the size of its alphabet. It contains *every* character that can appear within a comment: all the letters, digits, and special symbols. Every state in our DFA has to have an arrow exiting it for each character in its alphabet. Thus, every state will have about 100 arrows exiting it—one for each symbol in the alphabet. However, there is a simple technique we can use to minimize the number of arrows we have to draw: We represent all the arrows that exit some state p that point to some state q with a single arrow from p to q. We then label this single arrow with the set of characters that correspond to this transition. For example, suppose a " /" causes a transition from state q0 to q1, and all other characters cause a transition from state q0 to q5 (see Figure 17.3b). We can then draw a single arrow from q0 to q1 labeled with " /", and a single arrow from q0 to q5 labeled with ~["/"] . The operator ~ is the complement operator. But note that here it specifies the complement *with respect to the alphabet of the DFA,* not with respect to the set of all strings over that alphabet. Thus ~["/"] is the set of all single characters in the alphabet except for " /". To ensure that there is no ambiguity in this notation, we will double quote the characters from the alphabet that make up the strings in the language we are defining. The special symbols, like ~, [, and] , will be unquoted. That way, we can always distinguish characters of the alphabet from the special symbols (the former will be quoted; the latter will not be quoted).

A good starting point in the construction of the required DFA is to create the states and arrows that will accept the shortest possible comment, namely /* * /. This input requires five states with arrows from one to the next labeled with " /", "* ", "* ", and " /" (see Figure 17.3a).

Next, we add all the missing arrows (see Figure 17.3b). We use ~["* "] to represent all characters except "* " Similarly, we use ~["* ", "/"] to represent all characters except "* " and " /".

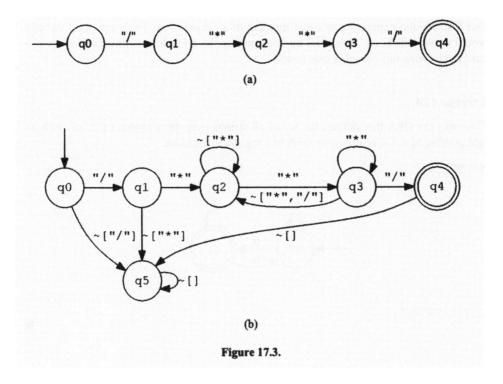

Figure 17.3.

q2 is the state that corresponds to the inside of the comment (i.e., inside the delimiting "/∗ " and "∗ /"). When in q2, if we get anything other than "∗ ", we remain inside the string. Thus, we should stay in q2. If, however, we get "∗ ", we have to go to a different state, q3, because the asterisk might be the beginning of the terminating "∗ /" sequence. When we are in q3, if we get a "/", we are done—we have a complete comment. If, instead, we get another "∗ ", we stay in q3 (this new asterisk might also be the beginning of the terminating "∗ /" sequence). And if we get any character other than "/" or "∗ ", we are back inside the comment, so we should go back to q2. q5 is the trap state we go to if some input makes it impossible for the input string to be a comment.

Now that we have our DFA, we can easily convert it to a regular expression. We will do this in four steps:

1. Determine the regular expression describing the strings that take the DFA from q0 to q3 for the first time. We get

    "/∗ " (~["∗ "])∗ "∗ "

2. Determine the regular expression associated with looping on q3. Note that there are two distinct loops. We get

    ("∗ " | ~["∗ ","/"] (~["∗ "])∗ "∗ ")∗

3. Concatenate the expression from step 1 with the expression from step 2. We get

    "/∗ " (~["∗ "])∗ "∗ " ("∗ " | ~["∗ ","/"] (~["∗ "])∗ "∗ ")∗

    This expression corresponds to the set of strings that start at q0 and end at q3.

4. Concatenate the expression from step 3 with "/":

    "/∗ " (~["∗ "])∗ "∗ " ("∗ " | ~["∗ ","/"] (~["∗ "])∗ "∗ ")∗ "/"

Our final regular expression is a real monster of an expression. To determine it directly would be very difficult. However, by constructing the DFA for comments first, we can easily determine this complex expression.

Exercise 17.4

Construct the DFA that defines the set of all strings over the alphabet { b, c} with an odd number of b's. Convert your DFA to a regular expression.

Answer:

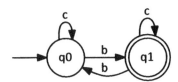

```
c*b(c|bc*b)*
```

17.4   JAVA CODE FOR A DFA

A DFA provides us with a step-by-step procedure to determine if an arbitrary string is in the language defined by the DFA. We simply input the string to the DFA and examine the state in which the DFA ends. If it is an accept state, then the string is in the language. Otherwise, it is not. Because a string, by definition, is of finite length, this procedure necessarily halts in a finite number of steps. Thus, a DFA meets the standard definition of an algorithm: a precise, step-by-step procedure that always halts.

Given an algorithm in the form of a DFA, we can, of course, convert it to other forms. For example, Figure 17.4 shows the Java code for the DFA in Figure 17.1. It uses our standard `advance()` method. Each time `advance()` is called, it updates `currentToken` with the next character in the input string. `currentState` holds the number of the current state of the DFA. The input string is provided on the command line. For example, to process the string `bcc`, enter

```
java Fig1704 bcc
```

The program will respond by displaying

```
input = bcc
accept
```

The Java code in Figure 17.4 consists of a `while` loop that executes once for each character in the input string. Each state is represented by one case in the `switch` statement. For each case, the `if-else` statement determines the next state and assigns its number to the `currentState` variable. After the loop completes, `accept` or `reject` is displayed depending on the final current state.

```
 1 class Fig1704
 2 {
 3   public static void main(String[] args)
 4   {
 5     // create token manager (see Fig. 6.12)
 6     ArgsTokenMgr tm = new ArgsTokenMgr(args);
 7
 8     // create DFA, pass it the token manager
 9     Fig1704DFA m = new Fig1704DFA(tm);
10
11     m.runDFA();
12   }
13 }                                   // end of Fig1704
14 //=========================================================
15 class Fig1704DFA
16 {
17   ArgsTokenMgr tm;
18   private char currentToken;
19   //---------------------
20   public Fig1704DFA(ArgsTokenMgr tm)
21   {
22       this.tm = tm;
23   }
24   //---------------------
25   public void advance()
26   {
27     // get next token and save in currentToken
28     currentToken = tm.getNextToken();
29   }
30   //---------------------
31   public void runDFA()
32   {
33     int currentState = 0;        // 0 is the start state
34     advance();                   // get first char
35
36     while (currentToken != '#')
37     {
38       switch(currentState)
39       {
40         case 0:
41           if (currentToken == 'b') currentState = 1;
42           else
43           if (currentToken == 'c') currentState = 1;
44           break;
45         case 1:
46           if (currentToken == 'b') currentState = 2;
47           else
48           if (currentToken == 'c') currentState = 3;
49           break;
50         case 2:
51           if (currentToken == 'b') currentState = 4;
52           else
53           if (currentToken == 'c') currentState = 4;
```

Figure 17.4.

```
54          break;
55        case 3:
56          if (currentToken == 'b') currentState = 4;
57          else
58          if (currentToken == 'c') currentState = 3;
59          break;
60        case 4:
61          if (currentToken == 'b') currentState = 4;
62          else
63          if (currentToken == 'c') currentState = 4;
64          break;
65     }
66       advance();
67     }
68
69     if (currentState == 2 || currentState == 3)
70       System.out.println("accept");
71     else
72       System.out.println("reject");
73 }
74 }                                              // end of DFA
```

Figure 17.4. *Continued.*

17.5 NONDETERMINISTIC FINITE AUTOMATA

A nondeterministc finite automaton (NFA) has the same general structure as a DFA. However, it is allowed to have some features not allowed in a DFA:

1. There can be more than one arrow leaving a state with the same label. For example, it can have

2. There can be no arrow leaving a state for one or more of the characters of the alphabet. For example, suppose the alphabet of an NFA is { b, c, d} . It can have

3. An arrow can be labeled with λ. For example, it can have

The NFA can follow an arrow labeled with λ regardless of the current input. Moreover, when the NFA follows an arrow labeled with λ, the NFA does not advance in the input. In contrast, when the NFA follows an arrow labeled with a character from the alphabet, the current input must be that character, and the NFA must advance to the next character in the input. In other words, when an NFA follows an arrow labeled with a character, it necessarily "consumes" that character in the input stream.

Let us examine the NFA in Figure 17.5. Its start state has a choice for a b input: the NFA can go to either state q1 or state q2. There is no arrow at all for c. In states q1 and q4, there are no arrows for b; in states q0, q2, q3, and q4, there are no arrows for c.

Let us see what the NFA in Figure 17.5 does for various input strings.

- For   c, the NFA runs into a "dead end" in state q0 because there is no outgoing arrow labeled with c. Whenever, a dead-end situation occurs, the NFA immediately rejects the input string. Thus, any string that starts with c is immediately rejected.

- For b in state q0, we have a choice: we can go to either state q1 or state q3. Both states are accept states. Thus, regardless of the choice we make, the NFA accepts the input string.

- For bc, the NFA accepts this string if we make the right choices. In state q0, if we go to state q1 on the initial b, then the c takes us back to state q1. The NFA accepts. However, in state q0, if we go to state q2 on the initial b, then we run into a dead end on the c. In this case, the NFA rejects.

From the three cases above, we see that the NFA in Figure 17.5 necessarily rejects some strings (like c), necessarily accepts some strings (like b), and for some strings (like bc), it accepts or rejects depending on the choices we make. What then is the language defined by this NFA? Does this language include bc (because this NFA can accept it) or exclude it (because this NFA can reject it)? The language defined by an NFA is the set of strings for which *it is possible to accept*. Thus, bc is in the language defined by the NFA in Figure 17.5 because, with the correct choices, the NFA can accept it.

The language defined by the NFA in Figure 17.5 is the set of strings that take can take the NFA from state q0 to one of its accept states: states q1, q2, and q4. The sets of strings that can take the NFA to these states are bc*, b, and bbb. Thus, the language defined by this NFA is bc* | b | bbb. Note that b is in the language defined by bc*. Thus, a simpler but equivalent expression is bc* | bbb.

Exercise 17.5

What language is defined by

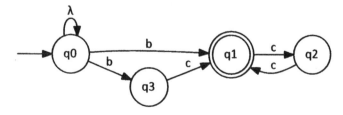

Answer:

```
b(cc)*|bc(cc)* = (b|bc)(cc)*
```

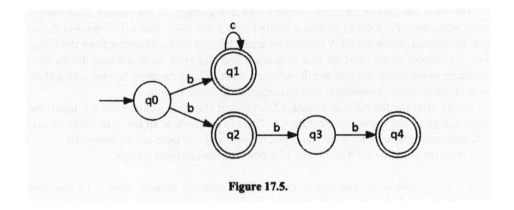

Figure 17.5.

The NFA in Figure 17.6 contains a λ-transition. A λ-transition is a "one-way street": it allows the NFA to move from one state to the next in the direction of the arrow, but not in the reverse direction.

Remember, when a NFA follows a λ-transition, it does not consume the current input character. The start state in the NFA in Figure 17.6 is q0. Without consuming any input, the NFA can immediately take the λ-transition to q1, an accept state. Thus, the NFA accepts λ (i.e., the null string). If we input one or more b's, the NFA loops on q0. After we input the b's, the NFA ends up in state q0. However, it can then take the λ-transition to the accept state q1. Thus, the NFA can accept any string of b's. It also can accept any string of c's. To accept a string of c's, the NFA starts by taking the λ-transition to q1. It then loops on q1 as we input the string of c's. It ends in q1. Any string of b's followed by c's can also be accepted. The NFA loops on q0 as we input the b's. It then takes the λ-transition to q1 where it loops as we input the c's. Clearly, this NFA accepts any string consisting of zero or more b's followed by zero or more c's. Thus, it defines the language b* c* . Because of the "one-way" property of the λ-transition, the c's must follow the b's.

17.6   USING AN NFA AS AN ALGORITHM

A DFA is clearly an algorithm. It provides a precise step-by-step procedure for recognizing strings in the language defined by the DFA. Is an NFA also an algorithm? An NFA allows choice during its operation. So can it be considered an algorithm? The answer is that an NFA is, indeed, an algorithm. However, the algorithm it specifies is more complex than the algorithm a DFA specifies. For a DFA, we have to keep track of only the current state at each step of the input process. For an NFA, we have to keep track of all the states

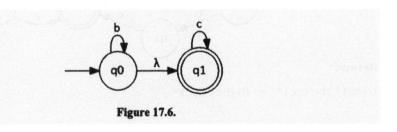

Figure 17.6.

the NFA might be in at every step of the input process. Because an NFA allows choice, it can be in more than one state at each step of the input process. Thus, we have to keep track of the set of these possible current states. After applying the entire input string, we check the last set of states. If this set contains at least one accept state, then the input string is in the language defined by the NFA.

Let us use the NFA in Figure 17.7 to determine if bbb is in language it defines. The start state is q0. Because we can reach q3 and q4 from q0 via one or more λ-transitions, the state set (i.e., set of possible states) initially is

{ q0, q3, q4}

When we input the first b in bbb, we hit dead ends at q3 and q4. However, we can go from q0 to q1. Thus, our state set becomes { q1} . When we input the second b in bbb, we go from q1 to q2. Moreover, from q2 we optionally can go back to q1 via a λ-transition. Thus, our set of possible current states becomes { q1, q2} . When we input the third b in bbb, we hit a dead end at q2. However, we go from q1 to q2, and optionally from q2 we can go back to q1 via the λ-transition. Thus, our final state set is { q1, q2} . These are all the possible states the NFA can be in after we input bbb. Because this set contains an accept state (q1 is an accept state), we know it is possible for the NFA to accept the input string (by making the right choices during the input of bbb). Thus, bbb is in the language defined by the NFA.

Suppose X is a set of states. We call the set obtained from X by *adding to it* any state reachable from some state in X via λ-transitions exclusively the λ-closure of X. For example, for the NFA in Figure 17.7, the λ-closure of { q0} is { q0, q3, q4} because q3 and q4 are reachable from q0 via λ-transitions exclusively. Let us describe the process of inputting a string to an NFA using the concept of λ-closure. We start by taking the λ-closure of the set containing just the start state. For example, for the NFA in Figure 17.7, we take the λ-closure of { q0} . The set we obtain—{ q0, q3, q4} for the NFA in Figure 17.7—is the set of possible starting states. Then for each input character,

1. We obtain the set of states reachable from the current state set via that character.
2. We take the λ-closure of the set we get in step 1.

The set that results from step 2 is the set of all possible states at that point in the input process. For example, when the current state set is { q1} in Figure 17.7, and we input b,

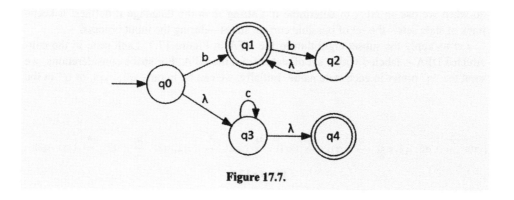

Figure 17.7.

the set of reachable states via b is { q2} . We then take the λ- closure of { q2} to get { q1, q2} . Thus, the current state set becomes { q1, q2} .

Figure 17.8 shows the complete sequence of sets we get when we input bbb to the NFA in Figure 17.7. The arrows with λ correspond to the λ-closures.

Exercise 17.6

Show the sequence of state sets when bbcc is input to the NFA in Figure 17.6. Is bbcc in the language defined by the NFA?

Answer:

$$\{ q0\} \xrightarrow{\lambda} \{ q0,q1\} \xrightarrow{b} \{ q0\} \xrightarrow{\lambda} \{ q0,q1\} \xrightarrow{b} \{ q0\} \xrightarrow{\lambda} \{ q0,q1\} \xrightarrow{c} \{ q1\}$$

$$\xrightarrow{\lambda} \{ q1\} \xrightarrow{c} \{ q1\} \xrightarrow{\lambda} \{ q1\}$$

bbcc is in the language.

■

Exercise 17.7

What is the state set when λ is applied to the NFA in Figure 17.7? Is λ in the language defined by the NFA?

Answer:

$$\{ q0\} \rightarrow \{ q0, q3, q4\}$$

Because the final state set includes an accept state (q4), λ is in the language defined by the NFA.

■

17.7 CONVERTING AN NFA TO A DFA WITH THE SUBSET ALGORITHM

An NFA allows choice and λ-transitions but it does not require them. Thus, every DFA is a special case of an NFA, but not vice versa. However, we can convert every NFA to an equivalent DFA. Thus, DFAs and NFAs have equal power to define languages.

The algorithm to convert an NFA to an equivalent DFA is called the *subset algorithm.* It constructs a DFA that keeps track of the set of current states the NFA can be in at each step of the input process. The set of current states is, of course, a subset of the states in the NFA; hence, the name "subset algorithm." The constructed DFA does precisely what we do when we use an NFA to determine if a string is in the language it defines: it keeps track of state sets—the set of possible current states—during the input process.

Let us apply the subset algorithm to the NFA in Figure 17.7. Each state in the constructed DFA is labeled with a set of states from the NFA. For space considerations, we omit the "q" prefix in each state name. Initially, we can be in only q0, q3, or q4 in the

$$\{ q0\} \xrightarrow{\lambda} \{ q0,q3,q4\} \xrightarrow{b} \{ q1\} \xrightarrow{\lambda} \{ q1\} \xrightarrow{b} \{ q2\} \xrightarrow{\lambda} \{ q1,q2\} \xrightarrow{b} \{ q2\} \xrightarrow{\lambda} \{ q1,q2\}$$

Figure 17.8.

NFA in Figure 17.7. Thus, we label the initial state of the DFA with {0, 3, 4} (see Figure 17.9a). On a b, we can end up in q1 only. Thus, in our DFA, we go from the initial state to a state labeled {1} on a b (see Figure 17.9b). On a c in q1, we hit a dead end. Accordingly, in the DFA we go on a c to a state labeled with the empty set (see Figure 17.9c). Reaching this state in the DFA for some input means that in the NFA there are no states reachable for the same input. Thus, the DFA should reject regardless of what input follows. If the DFA reaches this state, it stays in it, that is, it is a trap state (see Figure 17.9d). We continue constructing the DFA in this fashion, adding new states in the DFA as we need them until we have completed the DFA (see Figure 17.9e). This process has to terminate because there are only a finite number of subsets of the states in the NFA. The final step in the subset algorithm is to double circle (i.e., make an accept state) any state in the constructed DFA labeled with a state set that includes at least one accept state from the NFA (see Figure 17.9f).

Exercise 17.8

Convert the NFA in Figure 17.6 to an equivalent DFA using the subset algorithm.

Answer:

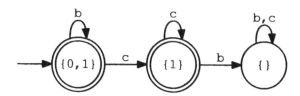

17.8   CONVERTING A DFA TO A REGULAR GRAMMAR

It is simple to convert a DFA to a regular grammar. The procedure consists of three steps:

1. Give a capital letter name to each state in the DFA. Give the start state the name S. These names will be the nonterminals in the equivalent regular grammar. For example, in Figure 17.10, we give the names S, B, and T to the three states q0, q1, and q2, respectively.

2. For each arrow, create a production of the form P → bQ, where P is the name of the state from which the arrow leaves, b is the label on the arrow, and Q is the name of the state to which the arrow points. For example, in Figure 17.10, there is an arrow from the S state to the B state labeled with the letter c. This arrow yields the production S → cB. We also have an arrow from the S state back to the S state labeled with b. This arrow yields S → bS. We have four arrows associated with state T. These arrows yield the productions

   B → bT
   B → cT
   T → bT
   T → cT

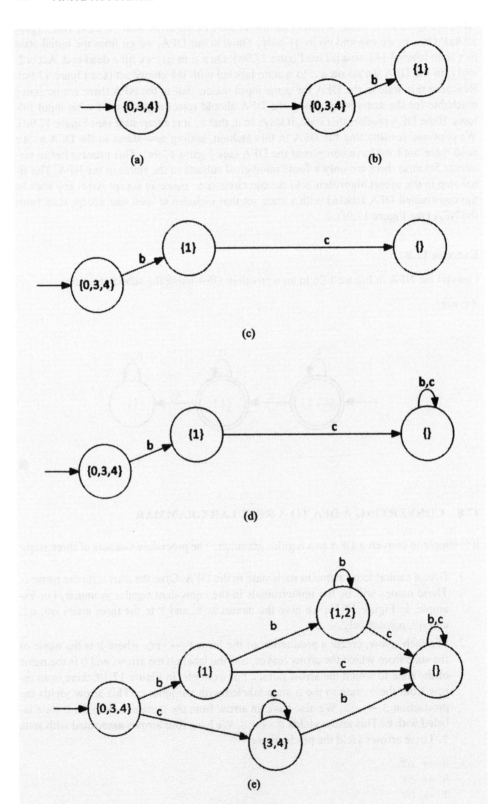

Figure 17.9.

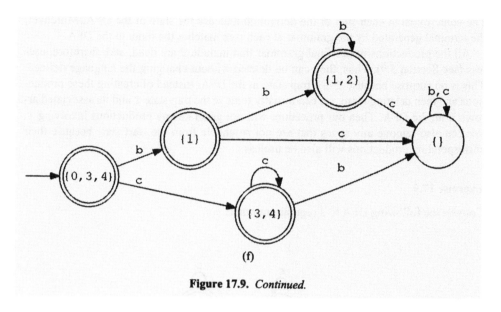

(f)

Figure 17.9. *Continued.*

3. For every accept state, we include a λ production whose left side is the name of the accept state. For example, in Figure 17.10, B is an accept state. Thus, we include the production B → λ.

Our final grammar is

S → bS
S → cB
B → bT
B → cT
T → bT
T → cT
B → λ

In a derivation of a terminal string in this grammar, the nonterminal takes the place of the current state in the DFA. For example, consider the following derivation of bbc, below which we have displayed the state transitions in the DFA:

S ⇒ bS ⇒ bbS ⇒ bbcB ⇒ bbc

$$S \xrightarrow{b} S \xrightarrow{b} S \xrightarrow{c} B$$

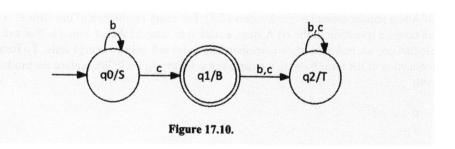

Figure 17.10.

The nonterminal at each step of the derivation matches the state of the DFA. Moreover, the terminal generated by the grammar at each step matches the input to the DFA.

All the productions in our final grammar that include T are dead, and, therefore, useless (see Section 3.9). Thus, they can be deleted without changing the language defined. This is no surprise because T is a trap state in the DFA. Instead of creating these productions and then deleting them, we can initially remove the trap state T and its associated arrows from the DFA. Then our procedure will not generate any productions involving T. We can also remove any states that are not reachable from the start state because their corresponding productions will also be useless.

Exercise 17.9

Convert the following DFA to a regular grammar:

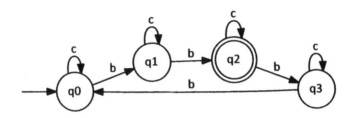

Name q0, q1, q2, and q3 S, A, B, and C, respectively.

Answers:

$$S \rightarrow cS$$
$$S \rightarrow bA$$
$$A \rightarrow cA$$
$$A \rightarrow bB$$
$$B \rightarrow cB$$
$$B \rightarrow \lambda$$
$$B \rightarrow bC$$
$$C \rightarrow cC$$
$$C \rightarrow bS$$

17.9   CONVERTING A REGULAR GRAMMAR TO AN NFA

To convert a regular grammar to an NFA, we do the reverse of the procedure to convert a DFA to a regular grammar (see Section 17.8). For every production of the form P → bQ, we create a transition in the NFA from a state P to state Q labeled with a b. For every λ-production, we make the state corresponding to its left side an accept state. To handle a production of the form P → b, we can use the following trick: We replace the production with

$$P \rightarrow bX$$
$$X \rightarrow \lambda$$

where X is a new nonterminal. This modification does not change the language defined by the grammar. We can then create the transition corresponding to P → bX: namely, a transition from state P to state X labeled with a b, where X is an accept state. The start state in our DFA is the state labeled with the start symbol of the grammar. For example, let us convert

    S → bS
    S → b

to an NFA. First, let us replace the second production to get a new grammar:

    S → bS
    S → bX
    X → λ

Next, create states for each nonterminal:

Finally, add transitions, make S the start state, and make states accepting as required by the modified grammar. We get the following NFA:

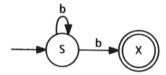

If we want a DFA that corresponds to the grammar, we can convert the preceding NFA to a DFA using the subset algorithm (see Section 17.7)

Exercise 17.10

Convert the following grammar to a NFA. Then convert the NFA to a DFA.

    S → λ
    S → bS
    S → cC
    C → cC
    C → cS

Answers:

NFA:

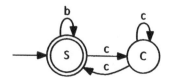

DFA:

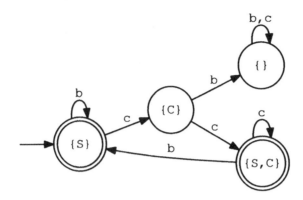

17.10 CONVERTING A REGULAR EXPRESSION TO AN NFA

Recall from Section 1.14 that a regular expression over the alphabet {b, c} is defined inductively:

- Base regular expressions
    ϕ (the empty set)
    λ (the null string)
    b
    c
- Construction rules:
    If r and s are regular expressions, then (r), r|s, rs and r* are also regular expressions.

We can provide NFAs for the base regular expressions. Moreover, whenever we construct a new regular expression with a construction rule, we can construct in parallel the equivalent NFA (i.e., the NFA that defines the same language). Thus, for every regular expression, we can construct an equivalent NFA. The NFAs we construct will all have the following properties:

1. They have exactly one accept state.
2. No state will have more than two arrows leaving it.
3. For every state with two arrows leaving it, at least one of the arrows will be labeled with λ.
4. The accept state has no arrows leaving it.

Let us see how we can construct an NFA for any regular expression over the alphabet { b, c} . First, we provide NFAs for the base regular expressions:

ϕ

λ

b

c

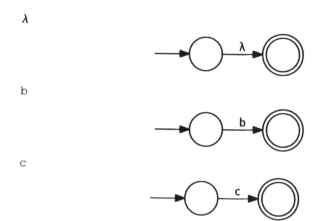

Note that all four of these NFAs have properties 1 to 4.

Now suppose we have regular expressions r and s and their corresponding NFAs that satisfy properties 1 to 4 above. We show only the start states (r0 and s0) and the accept states (ra and sa):

NFA for r

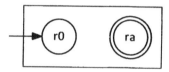

NFA for s

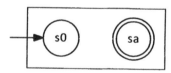

Then for each regular expression we construct with a construction rule, we can construct an NFA as follows.

NFA for (r)
Same as the NFA for r

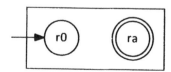

r|s
Add two new states, t0 and ta. t0 becomes the start state. ta becomes the accept state. ra and sa are no longer accept states. Add λ-transitions as shown.

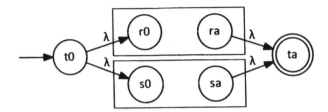

`rs`

`r0` stays the start state. `sa` stays the accept state. `ra` is no longer an accept state. Add the λ-transition as shown.

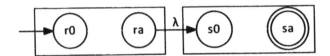

`r*`

Add two new states, `t0` and `ta`. `t0` becomes the start state. `ta` becomes the accept state. `ra` is no longer an accept state. Add λ-transitions as shown.

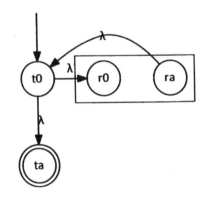

Note that if the NFAs for `r` and `s` have properties 1 to 4 listed above, then all the constructed NFAs also have these properties.

Let us construct the NFA for `bc | d*`. First, we construct the NFA for `b` and `c`:

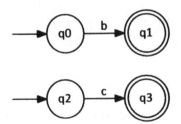

Next we construct the NFA for bc using our NFAs for b and c:

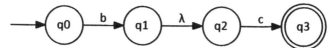

Next we construct the NFA for d:

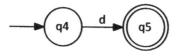

Next we construct the NFA for d* using our NFA for d:

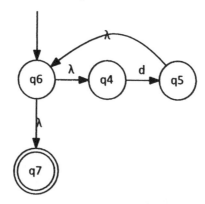

Finally, we construct the NFA for bc | d* using our NFAs for bc and d* :

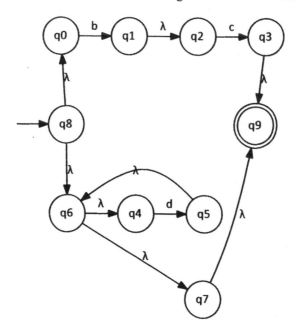

Exercise 17.11

Construct the NFA for b* c* .

Answer:

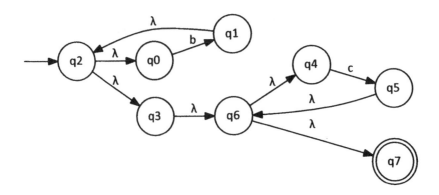

17.11   FINDING THE MINIMAL DFA

Suppose e1 and e2 are two states in a DFA. If we start in state e1 and apply some input string x, we end up in some state. Similarly, if we start is state e2 and apply the same string x we end up in some state. Suppose for *all* strings x (including λ), the two ending states are either both accept states or both reject states. We then say that e1 and e2 are *equivalent* or *indistinguishable*. If this is not the case (that is, if there is at least one string for which the two ending states are not both accept states or both reject states), then we say that e1 are e2 are *distinguishable*.

For example, let us apply λ to states q0 and q2 in Figure 17.11. If we apply λ to q0, we of course, end up in q0 (λ does not cause a transition in a DFA). Similarly, if we apply λ to q2, we end up in q2. Both ending states (q0 and q2) are reject states. Now let us apply b to q0 and q2. If we start in q0, we end up in q1; if we start in q2, we end up in state q3. Both ending states (q1 and q3) are accept states. In fact, for all strings x, if we apply x to q0 and q2, the two ending states will be either both accept or both reject. Thus, q0 and q2 are equivalent.

Now let us apply b to q0 and q1 in Figure 17.11. The ending states are q1 and q2. q1 is accepting; q2 is rejecting. Thus, q0 and q1 are not equivalent. The string b distinguishes between these two states. That is, it results in one ending state accepting and one rejecting. λ also distinguishes between q0 and q1 (for λ, the two ending states are the rejecting q0 and the accepting q1). c, however, does not distinguish between q0 and q1. For c, the ending states are both q4. Nevertheless, q0 and q1 are not equivalent because there is at least one string (such as λ or b) that distinguishes them.

Suppose the following conditions hold in a DFA (see Figure 17.12a):

1. e1 and e2 are equivalent states.
2. The input z takes the DFA from e1 to s1.
3. The input z takes the DFA from e2 to s2.

What can we conclude about s1 and s2? They must be both accepting or both nonac-

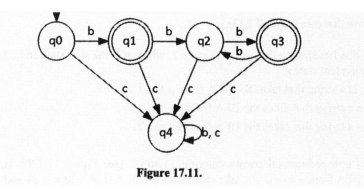

Figure 17.11.

cepting, otherwise, e1 and e2 would not be equivalent because the string z would distin-guish between them. In fact, we can make an even stronger assertion about s1 and s2: they would have to be equivalent. Suppose, to the contrary, that s1 and s2 were not equivalent. Then, by definition, there would be some string u that distinguishes between s1 and s2. But then zu would distinguish between e1 and e2, and e1 and e2 would not be equivalent (see Figure 17.12b). In other words, the nonequivalence of s1 and s2 im-plies the nonequivalence of e1 and e2, or, equivalently, the equivalence of e1 and e2 im-plies the equivalence of s1 and s2. To summarize:

> **Equivalent states on the same input go to equivalent states. States that go to nonequivalent states on the same input are necessarily non-equivalent.**

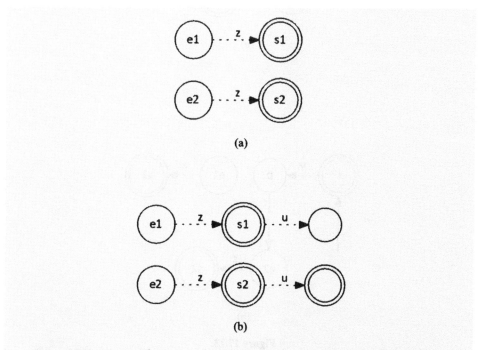

Figure 17.12. If s1 and s2 are not equivalent then e1 and e2 are not equivalent.

Suppose that (see Figure 17.13a)

1. a DFA has states s, e1, e2, s1, and s2, where s is the start state and e1 and e2 are equivalent states.
2. *y*b is a string that takes the DFA from s to e1.
3. *z* is a string that takes the DFA from e1 to s1.
4. *z* is a string that takes the DFA from e2 to s2.

Let us now redirect all arrows entering e1 to e2 (see Figure 17.13b). *y*bz takes the original DFA from s to s1. *y*bz takes the modified DFA from s to s2. s1 and s2 must be both accepting or both rejecting because e1 and e2 are equivalent. Thus, redirecting arrows entering e1 to e2 does not affect the accept/reject result for the string *y*bz (or, for the same reason, any other string that causes the DFA to visit e1). Nor does it affect the accept/reject result of any string that does not cause the DFA to visit state e1 at some

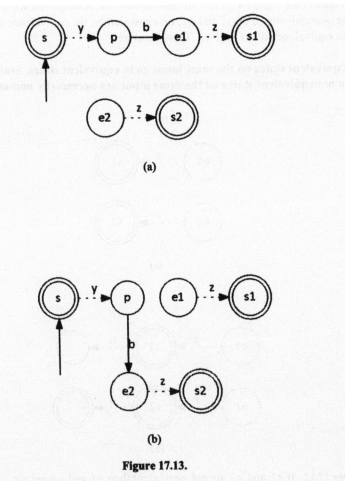

(a)

(b)

Figure 17.13.

point (how could it if e1 is never visited?). Thus, our redirection of arrows does not affect the accept/reject result of any string. It follows that

> **Redirecting all arrows entering a state to an equivalent state does not affect the language defined by a DFA.**

Moreover, the state away from which arrows are directed becomes unreachable from the start state. Thus, we can remove it and all its outgoing arrows without affecting the language defined by the machine.

If a DFA has a group of states which are all equivalent to each other, we can use our redirection technique to eliminate all the states in the group except one: we keep one to which the incoming arrows to the other states are redirected. If we do this state reduction for every group of equivalent states, and we remove any states that are inaccessible from the start states (inaccessible states can be removed without affecting the language defined), we get the *minimal DFA*. Let M represent the original DFA, and let L represent the language it defines. Then the minimal DFA we obtain from M is the best (i.e., having the fewest states) DFA that defines L.

In Figure 17.12b, we saw that two states are necessarily nonequivalent if on the same input they go to nonequivalent states. For example, suppose on a b input, states p and q go to distinguishable states r and s, respectively. Because r and s are distinguishable, there must be some string x that distinguishes then. But then the string bx would distinguish p from q. Using this property, we can easily determine the equivalent and nonequivalent states in any DFA.

Let us illustrate the technique by applying it to the DFA in Figure 17.11. We first partition the set of states into two blocks: rejecting and accepting states. We identify these blocks with Roman numerals I and II, respectively. If we start in a block I state and input λ, we simply stay in the same block I state (inputting λ does not cause a transition in a DFA). Thus, we end in a rejecting state. On the other hand, if we start in a block II state, and input λ, we end in the same block II state. That is, we end in an accepting state. λ distinguishes every state in block I from every state in block II. Thus, every state in block I is nonequivalent to every state in block II.

Next, we construct a table that shows the next block for each state and input character (see Figure 17.14a). For example state q0 on a b goes to state q1, which is in block II. Thus, in the q0 row and b column of our table, we show II. We also group states in the table by block. Thus, we list states q0, q2, and q4 first (block I states), and then q1 and q3 (block II states). Examining our table, we can see that state q4 on b goes to a block I state; q0 and q2 on b go to a block II state. Because every block I state is nonequivalent to every block II state, q4 must be nonequivalent to q0 and q2. Thus, block I breaks up into two subblocks: block Ia (q0 and q2) and block Ib (q4). Each of our three blocks—Ia, Ib, and II—contain states that are nonequivalent to the states in the other two blocks. Next, we again construct our table. But this time, the table entries are Ia, Ib, or II (see Figure 17.14b), reflecting the three blocks of the latest partition. Now, however, we get no further break-up of any of our blocks. This condition means that all the states in each block are equivalent. Specifically, q0 and q2 are equivalent, and q1 and q3 are equivalent. We then eliminate q0 and q1 using the arrow-redirection technique to get Figure 17.11d. We label each state in the minimal DFA with all the states from the original DFA that correspond to that state. For example, we label the start state with q0q2, indicating that it is the representative of states q0 and q2 in the original DFA.

	b	c
q0	II	I
q2	II	I
q4	I	I
q1	I	I
q3	I	I

Block I states: q0, q2, q4
Block II states: q1, q3

(a)

	b	c
q0	II	Ib
q2	II	Ib
q4	Ib	Ib
q1	I	Ib
q3	I	Ib

Block 1a states: q0, q2
Block 1b states: q4
Block II states: q1, q3

(b)

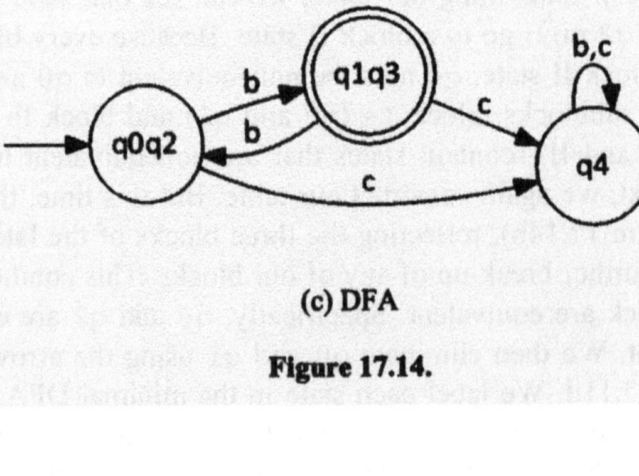

(c) DFA

Figure 17.14.

Exercise 17.12

Construct the minimal DFA equivalent to

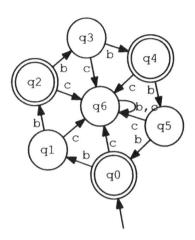

Answer:

States $q0$, $q2$, and $q4$ are equivalent; states $q1$, $q3$, and $q5$ are equivalent. The minimal DFA is

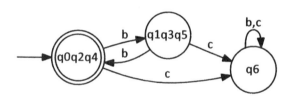

■

17.12   PUMPING PROPERTY OF REGULAR LANGUAGES

Suppose we input a string of length one to a DFA. The DFA will either loop on the state it is in (see Figure 17.15a) or move to another state (see Figure 17.15b). In both cases, the DFA visits two states, not necessarily distinct. Similarly, if we input a string of length two, the DFA will visit three states, not necessarily distinct. Generalizing, if we input a string of length n, the DFA will visit $n + 1$ states.

Suppose we have an infinite regular language L. Then, by definition, we can define L with some DFA. Let n denote the number of states in this DFA. We know that if we input a string whose length is n or greater, the DFA will visit at least $n + 1$ states. Because the DFA has only n states, it follows that the DFA has to visit at least one state more that once during the input of the first n characters. In other words, there *has to be a state repetition at some point during the input of the first n characters.*

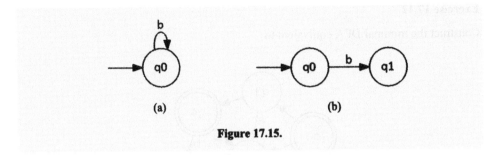

Figure 17.15.

Let us input a string whose length is greater than or equal to n, the number of states in the DFA. Suppose this input string is accepted by the DFA. Let us denote the first state to repeat during the input process with s, and state in which the DFA ends when the input is complete with t (see Figure 17.16). Because the DFA accepts our input string, t is necessarily an accept state. Let x be the initial portion of the input string that brings the DFA from the initial state to s for the first time. Let y be that portion of the input string between the initial visitation of s and its first repetition. Let z be the input string from the first repetition of s to the end of the string.

Now let us consider what occurs when we input the string xz to the DFA (xz is the original input string with its y portion extracted). The initial x portion will take the DFA to state s. The z portion will then take the DFA from s to t (we can see that z will do this from Figure 17.16). Because t is an accepting state, xz will also be accepted by the DFA. Using similar reasoning, it is easy to see that $xyyz$ will also be accepted by the DFA (x takes the DFA to s; yy causes the DFA to loop twice on s; z then takes the DFA from state s to state t). Similarly, $xyyyz$ is also accepted. In fact, we can "*pump*" (i.e., replicate) y within xyz any number of times. All the resulting strings are accepted by the DFA. Each occurrence of y simply causes the DFA to loop on s. When we then input z, the DFA goes from s to the accept state t, and, therefore, accepts the input string. That all these strings are accepted by the DFA is called the *pumping property* of regular languages. Let's formally state this property:

> Let L be an infinite regular language. There exists an n such that if u is in L and $|u| \geq n$, then $u = xyz$ where
>
> (i) $|y| > 0$
> (ii) $|xy| \leq n$
> (iii) $xy^i z \in L$ for all $i \geq 0$

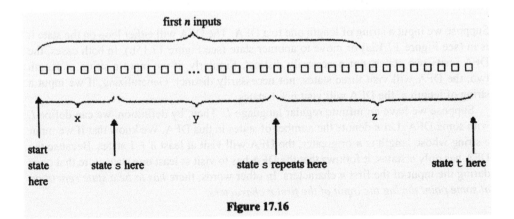

Figure 17.16

n is the number of states in the defining DFA. y takes the DFA from s back to s. This loop requires the input of at least one character. Thus, (i) is true. The first state repetition has to occur by the nth character. Thus, (ii) is true. Because y corresponds to the state s-to-state-s-loop, it can be replicated any number of times (including zero times) without affecting the acceptance of the resulting string. Thus, (iii) is true.

Note that to apply the pumping property to a string in a regular language, the string must be "long enough." That is, its length must be equal to at least the number of states in the defining DFA.

The pumping property is a property of every infinite regular language. Thus, if an infinite language does not have this property, it cannot be regular. What about finite languages? All finite languages are regular.

To prove an infinite language is not regular, we perform the following two steps:

1. Assume that the language is regular.
2. Show that the language does not have the pumping property, from which we conclude that our initial assumption (that the language is regular) is false.

For example, consider the language

$$PAIRED = \{b^i c^i : i \geq 0\} = \{\lambda, \text{ bc, bbcc, bbbccc, bbbbcccc, } \ldots \}$$

Let us assume that $PAIRED$ is a regular language. The string $b^k c^k$ is in $PAIRED$ for all value of $k \geq 0$. There is no upper limit on k. So let us use a value of k that is greater than or equal to the n in the pumping property. Then $b^k c^k$ is more than long enough for the pumping property to apply. By the pumping property, there must exist an x, y, and z such that

$$b^k c^k = xyz$$

such that (i), (ii), and (iii) of the pumping property are satisfied. By (ii), we know that y is exclusively in the b portion of $b^k c^k$. Moreover, from (i), we know y is nonnull. Thus, xz necessarily has fewer b's than c's and, therefore, cannot be in $PAIRED$. But, by (iii) xz has to be in $PAIRED$. We resolve this contradiction by concluding that our initial assumption (that $PAIRED$ is regular) is false.

PROBLEMS

1. What is the difference between a nondeterministic FA and an FA that is not deterministic?

2. Construct a DFA that defines b* c* d* . Write a computer program that simulates its operation. Test it with λ, b, c, d, bc, bd, cd, bcd, bbdd, bcb, bcdc, and dc.

3. Construct a DFA that defines b* cb* . Write a computer program that simulates its operation. Test it with c, bc, cb, bcb, bbcb, bb, bcbc, and bccb.

4. Construct a four-state NFA that defines all strings over $\{b, c\}$ that end in bcc. Using the subset algorithm, convert your NFA to an equivalent DFA.

5. Construct a four-state NFA that defines the set of strings over $\{b, c\}$ that contains at least one occurrence of bcc. Using the subset algorithm, convert your NFA to an equivalent DFA.

6. Construct a DFA that defines the set of strings that contain at least one occurrence of bcc and at least one occurrence of ccb.

7. Construct a DFA that defines C-type strings. In C-type strings, embedded quotes and line separators are permitted as long as they are immediately preceded by a back-slash. Thus, the string

"A\ "B\ \ C\
D"

is legal. Convert your DFA to a regular expression.

8. Convert the following grammar to an NFA. Then convert your NFA to a DFA using the subset algorithm.

S → bS
S → bB
B → bB
B → cC
C → c

9. Convert the following grammar to a NFA. Then convert your NFA to a DFA using the subset algorithm.

S → bB
B → bS
B → b
B → cC
C → cC
C → λ

10. Convert the DFA in Figure 17.11 to a regular grammar.

11. Convert the DFA in Figure 17.14 to a regular grammar.

12. Using the construction technique in Section 17.10, construct the NFA for b | c | d.

13. Using the construction technique in Section 17.10, construct the NFA for b★★★.

14. Using the construction technique in Section 17.10, construct the NFA for bcd.

15. Using the construction technique in Section 17.10, construct the NFA for b★ | (c★) | d★.

16. Construct the minimal DFA for

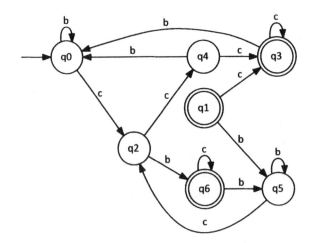

17. Construct the minimal DFA for

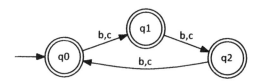

18. Construct the minimal DFA for

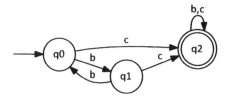

19. Prove that the set of all strings over $\{b, c\}$ in which the number of b's equals the number of c's is not regular.

20. Show that the regular languages are closed under union, intersection, and complementation.

21. Prove that $\{b^i c^j : i \neq j\}$ is not regular. Hint: take the complement of this language and intersect it with $b\star c\star$. What language do you get? Also see Problem 20.

22. Prove that $\{b^i c^j : i > j\}$ is not regular.

23. Prove that $\{b^i : i$ is a perfect square$\}$ is not regular.

24. Prove that $\{b^i : i$ is a prime$\}$ is not regular.

25. Prove that the union of a nonregular language and a finite language is always nonregular. That is, you can never change a nonregular language into a regular one by adding only a finite number of strings.

18

CAPSTONE PROJECT: IMPLEMENTING GREP USING COMPILER TECHNOLOGY

18.1 INTRODUCTION

In this chapter, we will design and implement grep. grep is a standard utility program available on Linux and other operating systems. When you invoke grep, you provide it with a regular expression and one or more files. It then searches the files for any substrings that match the regular expression. For example, if you enter

```
grep bo*t f.txt
```

grep will search the `f.txt` file for substrings that "match" the regular expression `bo*t`. That is, it searches for substrings that are in the language defined by the regular expression. Thus, in this example, it would search for substrings that start with b, are followed by zero or more o's, and end with t. grep displays each line of the file in which it finds such a substring.

Implementing grep is an ideal capstone project in your study of compilers for the following reasons:

1. It illustrates the broad applicability of compiler design techniques. grep is not a compiler in the traditional sense, but its design and implementation uses compiler design techniques.

2. It requires you to put into practice virtually all the compiler design theory you have learned.

3. It illustrates the usefulness of finite state automata theory. Many compiler textbooks present this theory without showing how it can be put to good use.

4. A translation grammar and its corresponding Java code are so similar that it is hardly a mystery how the parser generator component of JavaCC works. But how does

Compiler Construction Using Java, JavaCC, and Yacc, First Edition. Anthony J. Dos Reis.

499

its token manager generator component work? Right now, you could probably write your own parser generator but not your own token manager generator. However, by implementing grep, you will learn the techniques essential for implementing a token manager generator.

Using Java, we will implement grep in three stages. In the first stage, we implement G1. G1 is the "front end" of our grep program. It parses the regular expression provided on the command line. If the expression is a regular expression, G1 simply terminates. If, however, the expression is not a regular expression, G1 displays an error message and then terminates. For example, if we enter

```
java G1 bc
```

G1 simply terminates because bc is a regular expression. If, however, we enter

```
java G1 )b
```

then G1 responds by displaying

```
Encountered ")" at position 1 in regular expression
Expecting factor
```

because ")b" is not a regular expression. G1 includes a token manager and a parser, but no code generator.

In stage two, we add a code generator to G1. We call the resulting program G2. The code generator constructs a nondeterministic finite automaton (NFA) from the regular expression provided on the command line. For example, if we enter

```
java G2 bc
```

G2 constructs the NFA that defines the same language as the regular expression bc. G2 is a compiler in every sense. It has a token manager (to tokenize the regular expression), a parser (to parse the regular expression), and a code generator (to output the NFA corresponding to the regular expression). The source language is the set of regular expressions. The target language is the set of corresponding NFAs. Thus, it is entirely accurate to call G2 a *regular expression compiler.*

In stage three, we add a pattern-matching capability to G2. We call the resulting program G3. G3 is our finished grep program. When we invoke G3, we specify both a regular expression and a file. For example, in the following command,

```
java G3 be f.txt
```

we are specifying the regular expression be and the file f.txt. In response, G3 constructs an NFA corresponding to the regular expression be. It then determines which lines in f.txt have a substring accepted by the NFA, and, therefore, match the regular expression. G3 displays all such lines.

That portion of JavaCC that creates the token manager is similar to G3. Like G3, JavaCC converts the regular expressions it is provided to finite automata. It then outputs a program (the token manager) that uses these automata to identify the corresponding tokens.

18.2 REGULAR EXPRESSIONS FOR OUR GREP PROGRAM

When you invoke G1, G2, or G3, you specify a regular expression on the command line. This expression can be any regular expression in the form described in Section 1.14, except λ and ϕ. The regular expression can also use the period, which acts as a wild-card character, that is, it matches any *single* character. For example, the regular expression b.t matches bat, but, b7t, and b!t, but not bt or boot.

You should surround the regular expression on the command line with quotes if it contains any characters that are treated in a special way by the shell program of the operating system you are using. The use of quotes on the regular expression on the command line ensures that the shell program of the operating system passes it as is to your grep program. Suppose, for example, you omit the quotes around the regular expression, as in the following command:

```
java G1 bc*
```

On some systems, the shell program would expand bc* to a list of file names that start with bc. In that case, G1 would not be passed the regular expression.

An asterisk in a regular expression represents the star operator. But what if we want to represent an "ordinary" asterisk (i.e., an asterisk that is not the star operator)? To specify an "ordinary" asterisk, we simply prefix the asterisk with a backslash. For example "b*c" matches a b followed by an asterisk and a c (here the asterisk is an "ordinary" character). But "b*c" matches zero or more b's followed by a c (here the asterisk is the star operator). Similarly, to represent the ordinary versions of any of the other special characters (the period , vertical bar, left parenthesis, right parenthesis, backslash, and quote), simply backslash the character. For example, to represent a sequence consisting of an ordinary period, an ordinary vertical bar, and an ordinary backslash, use "\.\|\\".

18.3 TOKEN MANAGER FOR REGULAR EXPRESSIONS

In a nutshell, here is how the our grep program works: It compiles the regular expression obtained from the command line to an NFA. It then scans the specified input file using this NFA to detect matches. Thus, the first part of our grep program is a regular expression compiler that translates a regular expression to its corresponding NFA. Just like the compilers we have already written, this compiler consists of a token manager, a parser, and a code generator.

Let us start by considering the design of the token manager for our regular expression compiler. We will represent each token with an object of type Token—the same class we used for our compilers in previous chapters (see Figure 10.8).

However, we will use only the kind, beginColumn, and image fields.

For ordinary characters, the kind field contains the constant CHAR defined in the G1Constants interface (see Figure 18.1), and the image field contains the character in string form. For the special characters period, left parenthesis, right parenthesis, vertical bar, and asterisk, the kind field contains the constants PERIOD, LEFTPAREN, RIGHT-PAREN, OR, or STAR, respectively, all of which are defined in the G1Constants interface. To mark the end of the regular expression, a token whose kind field contains the constant EORE is used. For example, consider the regular expression b**. It consists of a b, a star operator, and an escape sequence that represents an "ordinary" asterisk. It yields the sequence of tokens in Figure 18.2.

```
 1 interface G1Constants
 2 {
 3    int EORE = 0;            // end of regular expression
 4    int CHAR = 1;
 5    int PERIOD = 2;          // PERIOD matches any character
 6    int LEFTPAREN = 3;
 7    int RIGHTPAREN = 4;
 8    int OR = 5;
 9    int STAR = 6;
10    int ERROR = 7;
11
12    int CONCAT = 8;          // no corresponding token
13
14    String[] tokenImage =
15    {
16      "<EORE>",
17      "<CHAR>",
18      "\".\"",
19      "\"(\"",
20      "\")\"",
21      "\"|\"",
22      "\"*\"",
23      "<ERROR>"
24    };
25 }
```

Figure 18.1.

In most cases, each token corresponds to a single character in the regular expression. Thus, the logic for the `getNextToken()` method in the token manager is simple:

1. If at the end of the regular expression, return an EORE token.
2. If the current character is a special character, return a special character token (i.e., a token with PERIOD, LEFTPAREN, RIGHTPAREN, OR, or STAR in its kind field and the character in string form in its image field).
3. If the current character is the backslash, advance to and return the next character as CHAR token (i.e, a token with CHAR in its kind field and the character in its image

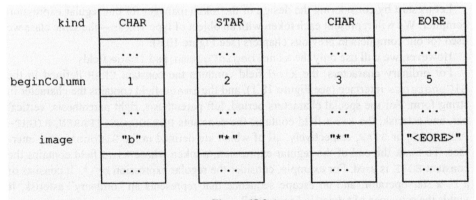

Figure 18.2.

field). For example, for the escape sequence \ *, getNextToken() returns the asterisk as a CHAR token rather than as a STAR token. Thus, an escaped asterisk specifies an "ordinary" asterisk. getNextToken() handles all escape sequences this way. Thus, for \n, \r, and \t, it returns "n", "r", and "t", respectively, not the newline, carriage return, and tab characters.

4. Otherwise, return the current character as a CHAR token (i.e., a token with CHAR in its kind field and the character in String form in its image field).

In addition, for all tokens the beginColumn field should be set to the starting position of the token in the regular expression.

The regular expression to be compiled is obtained from args[0], where args is the parameter in the main method. To provide the token manager with the regular expression, we simply pass args[0] to the token manager constructor:

```
G1TokenMgr tm = new G1TokenMgr(args[0]);
```

18.4   GRAMMAR FOR REGULAR EXPRESSIONS

G18.1 is the grammar for our regular expressions. It is similar to the grammar we have been using for arithmetic expressions.

G18.1

```
  1. expr        → term termList
  2. termList    → "|" term termList
  3. termList    → λ
  4. term        → factor factorList
  5. factorList  → factor factorList
  6. factorList  → λ
  7. factor      → <CHAR> factorTail
  8. factor      → <PERIOD> factorTail
  9. factor      → "(" expr ")" factorTail
 10. factorTail  → "*" factorTail
 11. factorTail  → λ
```

In regular expressions, successive factors have no intervening operator; we simply concatenate factors together. Thus, the first factorList production does not start with an operator symbol. The factorTail productions add zero or more star operators to the end of a factor.

At this point, you should implement G1—the first version of our grep program that only parses the regular expression it is provided. It should display an error message if the expression provided is not a valid regular expression.

The structure of G1 is given in Figure 18.3.

18.5   TARGET LANGUAGE FOR OUR REGULAR EXPRESSION COMPILER

Our next step is to extend our G1 regular expression parser to a regular expression compiler, which we will call G2. Accordingly, its various classes will have names prefixed with "G2" rather than "G1." G2 translates the regular expression it is provided when it is

```
 1 class G1
 2 {
 3   public static void main(String[] args)
 4   {
 5     // Check here if number of arguments is correct
 6
 7     G1TokenMgr tm = new G1TokenMgr(args[ 0] );
 8     G1Parser parser = new G1Parser(tm);
 9
10     try
11     {
12       // parse regular expression
13       parser.parse();
14     }
15     catch (RuntimeException e)
16     {
17         System.err.println(e.getMessage());
18         System.exit(1);
19     }
20 }
21 //=========================================================
22 interface G1Constants
23 {
24   // see Fig. 18.1
25 }
26 //=========================================================
27 class G1TokenMgr implements G1Constants
28 {
29   // Contains constructor and getNextToken method
30 }
31 //=========================================================
32 class G1Parser implements G1Constants
33 {
34   // Contains constructor, parse, advance, and consume
35   // methods.  Also contains the methods for the recursive
36   // descent parser based on the grammar in Fig. 18.3
37 }
```

Figure 18.3.

invoked to an NFA that corresponds to that regular expression. Thus, the target language for our G2 compiler is the set of nondeterministic finite automata (NFAs) corresponding to the regular expressions we can provide G2. The source language is the set of regular expressions we can provide to G2. A new class G2CodeGen (the code generator) provides the methods that construct the required NFAs.

G2 represents each state of the NFA it builds with an object of type NFAState (see Figure 18.4). The NFAState class includes a static method displayNFA that displays an NFA, given its start state. The implementation of this method is not shown in Figure 18.4. However, the complete NFAState class is in the file NFAState.java in the J1 Software Package.

Each state has at most two exiting arrows. NFAState has two fields—arrow1 and arrow2—to represent these arrows. Note that there is a label1 field for arrow1 in NFAState (see line 4 in Figure 18.4). The second arrow, if there is one, necessarily has λ

```
 1 class NFAState
 2 {
 3    public NFAState arrow1;
 4    public char label1;
 5    public NFAState arrow2;        // arrow2 always lambda
 6    public NFAState acceptState;
 7    //---------------------
 8    public NFAState()
 9    {
10      arrow1 = arrow2 = acceptState = null;
11      label1 = 0;                  // zero represents lambda
12    }
13    //---------------------
14    public static void displayNFA(NFAState startState)
15    {
16      // display NFA
17    }
18 }
```

Figure 18.4.

as its label. Thus, a `label2` field for `arrow2` is unnecessary. The `acceptState` field points to the accept state of the NFA (there is only one). However, this field is valid only for the start state of the NFA.

G2 constructs NFAs as described in Section 17.10. Using the construction technique described there, G2 produces NFAs that have the following properties:

1. One and only one state is an accept state.
2. Each state has at most two arrows leaving it.
3. If a state has two arrows leaving it, one necessarily is labeled with λ.
4. The accept state has no arrows leaving it.

Thus, the representation of a state need include only

1. `arrow1` and `arrow2`, which represent the two arrows (at most) that leave a state. A lack of an arrow leaving a state is indicated with a null value. For example, if `arrow2` is null, then the state has no second arrow leaving it.
2. `label1`, the label on `arrow1`. The label λ is represented with 0. We do not need `label2`, the label for `arrow2`, because `arrow2`, if used, always has the label λ.
3. `acceptState`, the pointer to the accept state of the NFA. All states have this field. However, it is valid only for the start state of the NFA. That is, only the `acceptState` field of the start state necessarily points to the accept state of the NFA.

The methods that make up the parser pass states via the parameter and return mechanisms of Java. For example, let us consider the productions for `expr` and `termList`:

```
expr      → term termList
termList  → "|" term termList
termList  → λ
```

The corresponding translation grammar is in Figure 18.5. The `expr` production tells us that the `expr` method calls the `term` method and then the `termList` method (lines 5 and 6 in Figure 18.5). `term` returns to `expr` the pointer (i.e., reference) to the start state of the NFA corresponding to the term it just parsed. `expr` then calls `termList`, passing it this pointer. `termList` parses the rest of the expression and returns the pointer to the start state of the NFA for the entire expression. The `expr` method then returns this pointer to its caller.

   `termList` calls `term` (line 18 in Figure 18.5). `term` parses the input corresponding to the next term in the regular expression and constructs its corresponding NFA. It then returns the pointer to the start state of this NFA to `termList`. Now `termList` has access to pointers to two start states:

1. p, the pointer it is passed (see line 10).
2. q, the pointer returned by the call of `term` (see line 18).

`termList` then passes the constant OR (which represents the vertical bar operator), p, and q to the `make` method in the code generator (line 19). This method constructs a new NFA from the NFAs associated with p and q, and returns the pointer to its start state. This new NFA is the combination of the p and q NFAs as required by the OR (i.e., vertical

```
1    private NFAState expr()
2    {
3      NFAState p;
4
5      p = term();
6      p = termList(p);
7      return p;
8    }
9    //--------------------
10   private NFAState termList(NFAState p)
11   {
12     NFAState q;
13
14     switch (currentToken.kind)
15     {
16       case OR:
17         consume(OR);
18         q = term();
19         p = cg.make(OR, p, q);
20         p = termList(p);      // pass new NFA to termList
21         break;
22       case RIGHTPAREN:
23       case EORE:
24         ;
25         break;
26       default:
27         throw genEx("\"|\", \")\", or <EORE>");
28     }
29     return p;
30   }
```

Figure 18.5.

bar) operator. `termList` then calls itself (line 20), passing it the start state of the new NFA. Through recursive calls, `termList` repeats this process—once for each additional term in the expression, each time building an increasingly more complex NFA that includes the latest term just parsed. When the end of the expression is reached (which is signaled by the appearance of a right parenthesis or `EORE` in the input), the recursion of `termList` stops. Lines 25 and 29 are executed. At this point, the parameter p points to the final NFA (the NFA for the entire expression). Line 29 returns this pointer to the caller of `termList`, which, in turn, returns it to its caller, and so on, all the way back to `expr`. `expr` then returns it to its caller (see line 7). For example, suppose an expression consists of four terms:

$$term_1 \mid term_2 \mid term_3 \mid term_4$$

On its first call, `termList` constructs (by calling `make`) the NFA for $term_1 \mid term_2$ using the NFAs for $term_1$ and $term_2$. On its first recursive call, `termList` constructs the NFA for $term_1 \mid term_2 \mid term_3$ using the NFA just constructed for $term_1 \mid term_2$ and the NFA for $term_3$. On its second recursive call, `termList` constructs the NFA for $term_1 \mid term_2 \mid term_3 \mid term_4$ using the NFA just constructed for $term_1 \mid term_2 \mid term_3$ and the NFA for $term_4$. Each recursive call uses the NFA constructed on the previous recursive call by `make`. Finally, on its third (and last) recursive call, `termList` stops recursing. Instead, it returns the pointer to the NFA it was just passed (which is the pointer to the NFA for $term_1 \mid term_2 \mid term_3 \mid term_4$). This pointer is then returned back up the call chain, all the way to `expr`, which, in turn, returns it to its caller.

The structure of the `term` and `factorList` methods parallels that of `expr` and `termList`. `factorList` calls `make` with

```
p = cg.make(CONCAT, p, q);
```

Because the first argument in this call of `make` is `CONCAT`, `make` constructs the NFA that results from the concatenation of the p and q NFAs.

`factor` calls `make` to construct the NFAs corresponding to `CHAR` and `PERIOD` tokens. For example, when `factor` is parsing b, it calls `make` to construct the corresponding NFA. This NFA has a start state, an accept state, and one arrow from the start state to the accept state labeled with b (see lines 32–38 in Figure 18.7).

`factorTail` calls `make` to construct NFAs corresponding to a starred expression. Whenever it is called, it is passed the pointer to the start state of an NFA for a factor in the regular expression. If it then consumes a `STAR` operator, it calls `make` to construct the NFA corresponding to that factor starred (see Figure 18.6). There are two `factorTail` productions, one of which is a lambda production (see G18.1). In `factorTail`, the lambda production is the default production, that is, it is applied by default if the other production cannot be used.

Figure 18.7 shows the structure of the `make` method in the code generator. It is an overloaded method that can take a variety of arguments. Note that some of the code has been omitted (see lines 19, 40, and 54). Figure 18.7 is available in the J1 Software package in the file `make.java`.

Let us examine the operation of `make` when it is passed the `OR` operator and the pointers p and q to the start states of two NFAs (see Figure 18.8a). Note that in Figure 18.8, each state is labeled with the pointer variable that points to it. For example, the state to which p points is labeled with p. Thus, when we say "the p state," we mean the state labeled with p, that is, the state to which p points.

```
1    private NFAState factorTail(NFAState p)
2    {
3       switch(currentToken.kind)
4       {
5          case STAR:
6             consume(STAR);
7             p = cg.make(STAR, p);
8             p = factorTail(p);
9             break;
10         default:
11            ;              // apply lambda production
12            break;
13      }
14      return p;
15   }
```

Figure 18.6.

On lines 9 and 10 in Figure 18.7, make creates the s and a states (see Figure 18.8b). On lines 11 and 12, it creates arrows from the s state to the p and q states (see Figure 18.8c). The labels on these arrows default to λ. Next, on lines 14 and 15, it creates arrows from the accept states of the p and q NFAs to the a state (see Figure 18.8d). Finally, on line 16, it sets the acceptState field in the s state to a (see Figure 18.8e). It then returns s, the pointer to the start state of the new NFA.

At this point, you should extend your G1 program so that it compiles the regular expression it is provided to an NFA. Call this version of your grep program G2. The expr method should return to the parse method the start state of the final NFA. parse should then return this start state to main. main should then call displayNFA, passing it the start state returned to parse.

18.6   USING AN NFA FOR PATTERN MATCHING

Our last step in the creation of our grep program is to extend G2 so that it can perform pattern matching using the NFA it constructs. We call the resulting program G3. It includes a G3Matcher class that provides the pattern matching function. This class contains three methods:

```
private boolean lambdaClosure()
private void applyChar(char c)
public void match()
```

lambdaclosure performs the λ-closure operation described in Section 17.6. apply-Char determines the set of states reachable from the current set of states via the character it is passed. match calls lambdaClosure and applyChar to determine if a match occurs on any line on the input file. match displays any line on which a match occurs.

The G3Matcher class contains the following instance variables:

- ArrayList<NFAState> currentStates, which contains all the possible current states at each step of the input process. Remember that there can be more than one current state in an NFA as it processes its input.

```
 1    public NFAState make(int op, NFAState p, NFAState q)
 2    {
 3      // s is new start state; a is new accept state
 4      NFAState s, a;
 5
 6      switch(op)
 7      {
 8        case OR:
 9          s = new NFAState();
10          a = new NFAState();
11          s.arrow1 = p;          // make s point to p and q
12          s.arrow2 = q;
13          // make accept states of p and q NFAs point to a
14          p.acceptState.arrow1 = a;
15          q.acceptState.arrow1 = a;
16          s.acceptState = a;     // make a the accept state
17          return s;
18        case CONCAT:
19          ...
20        default:
21          throw new RuntimeException("Bad call of make");
22      }
23    }
24    //--------------------
25    public NFAState make(int op, Token t)
26    {
27      // s is new start state; a is new acccept state
28      NFAState s, a;
29
30      switch(op)
31      {
32        case CHAR:
33          s = new NFAState();
34          a = new NFAState();
35          s.arrow1 = a;          // make s point to a
36          s.label1 = t.image.charAt(0);
37          s.acceptState = a;     // make a the accept state
38          return s;
39        case PERIOD:
40          ...
41        default:
42          throw new RuntimeException("Bad call of make");
43      }
44    }
45    //--------------------
46    public NFAState make(int op, NFAState p)
47    {
48      // s is new start state; a is new accept state
49      NFAState s, a;
50
51      switch(op)
52      {
53        case STAR:
54          ...
55        default:
56          throw new RuntimeException("Bad call of make");
57      }
58    }
```

Figure 18.7.

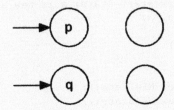

(a) Component NFAs p and q

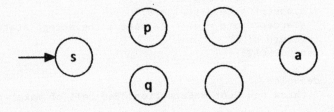

(b) Create s and a states

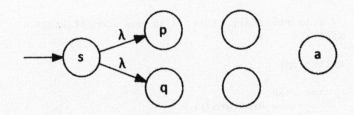

(c) Create λ-transitions leaving s

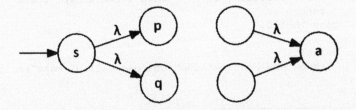

(d) Create λ-transitions to a

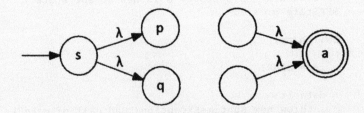

(e) Mark a accepting (by setting the acceptState field in s to a)

Figure 18.8.

- `ArrayList<NFAState> nextStates`, which is used to hold the set of states reachable from the current state set when a character is applied to the NFA.
- State `startState`, which contains the pointer to the start state of the NFA
- `Scanner inFile`, which provides access to the input file.

Let's now examine the methods in `G3Matcher` more closely. `lambdaClosure` performs the λ-closure operation (see Section 17.6) on the set of states in `currentStates`. Its pseudocode is in Figure 18.9.

In addition to performing the λ-closure operation, `lambdaClosure` returns a true/false value in the variable `gotAccept` that indicates if the set of current states includes the accepting state of the NFA. This return value is used by the `match` method to determine if a match has occurred. The initial `if` statement checks if `startState.acceptState` (the accept state of the NFA) is `s`, where `s` is one of the current states.

The `applyChar` method determines which states are reachable from the current states via the character it is passed. It uses a local variable `nextStates` whose type is `ArrayList<NFAState>`. Its pseudocode is in Figure 18.10.

Now let us consider what `match` must do to process one line of the input file. The NFA might match a substring that starts at column 1 of the current line. If it does, `match` should display the line, and move on to the next line. If, however, it does not match the substring starting in column 1, it has to move on to column 2 in the same line and repeat the test. That is, it has to check to see if the substring starting in column 2 provides a match. Again, if a match is detected, `match` displays the line and moves on to the next line. If a match does not occur, it moves on to the next column of the current line. It continues this process until either a match is detected or the line has been completely tested. Figure 18.11 shows the Java code in `match` that processes one line of the input file (this code is in the file `match.java` in the J1 Software Package). `match` has to execute this code for every line in the input file. `buf` holds the current input line.

set gotAccept *to false*

for each state s *in* currentStates
{
      if startState.acceptState *is* s
      then set gotAccept *to true*

      if s.arrow1 *is non-null (i.e., there is an outgoing arrow) and*
            s.label1 *is 0 (i.e.,* λ*) and*

            s.arrow1 *is not already in* currentStates
      then add s.arrow1 *to* currentStates.

      if s.arrow2 *is non-null (i.e., there is an outgoing arrow) and*
            s.arrow2 *is not already in* currentStates
      then add s.arrow2 *to* currentStates.
}

return gotAccept

Figure 18.9. Pseudocode for `lambdaClosure()`.

clear nextStates

for each state s in currentStates
{

    if s.arrow1 *is non-null (i.e.,there is an outgoing arrow and*
    s.arrow1 *is not already in* nextStates *and*
    (s.label1 *is* PERIOD *or* s.label1 *matches* c))
    then add s.arrow1 *to* nextStates

}

swap currentStates *and* nextStates

Figure 18.10. Pseudo code for applyChar(char c).

With the G3Matcher class, you can easily extend your G2 regular expression compiler to get G3. Figure 18.12 shows the structure of the main method in G3. On line 20, main passes the constructor for G3Matcher both the input file and the NFA (whose start state is given by startState).

G3 displays the lines in the input file on which a match occurs. If the expression provided to G3 is not a valid regular expression, G3 displays an appropriate error message.

```
1    // process input line in buf
2    for (startIndex = 0; startIndex < buf.length();
3                                        startIndex++)
4    {
5      currentStates.clear();
6      currentStates.add(startState);
7      bufIndex = startIndex;
8
9      // apply substring starting at bufIndex to
10     // NFA.  Exit on an accept, end of substring,
11     // or trap state
12     while (true)
13     {
14       gotAccept = lambdaClosure();
15       if (gotAccept            // accept state entered
16         || bufIndex >= buf.length() // end substring
17         || currentStates.size() == 0)  // trap state
18         break;
19       applyChar(buf.charAt(bufIndex++));
20     }
21
22     // display line if match occurred somewhere
23     if (gotAccept)
24     {
25       System.out.println(buf);
26       break;                         // go to next line
27     }
28   }   // end of for loop
```

Figure 18.11.

```
 1  class G3
 2  {
 3    public static void main(String[] args) throws
 4                                          IOException
 5    {
 6
 7      // test here if the numbers of args is correct
 8
 9      G3TokenMgr tm = new G3TokenMgr(args[0]);
10      G3CodeGen cg = new G3CodeGen();
11      G3Parser parser = new G3Parser(tm, cg);
12      Scanner inFile = new Scanner(new File(args[1]));
13
14      try
15      {
16        // parse reg expression, return start state
17        NFAState startState = parser.parse();
18
19        // Search for matches in input file using NFA
20        G3Matcher m = new G3Matcher(inFile, startState);
21        m.match();
22      }
23      catch (RuntimeException e)
24      {
25          System.out.println(e.getMessage());
26          System.exit(1);
27      }
28  }
29  }
```

Figure 18.12.

PROBLEMS

1. Implement G1. Test your program with b, bc, b | c, b*, ((b)), bc | b*, b |, * b, b),
   (b, b | * c, λ. Be sure to surround the regular expressions that contain the star opera-
   tor with quotes when you enter them on the command line. Also try b\ (b followed
   by a backslash), both with and without surrounding quotes.

2. Implement G2. Test your program with the regular expressions from Problem 18.1.

3. Implement G3. Test your program by entering

   ```
   java G3 xyz grep.txt > p1803a.txt
   java G3 "n.t|bo*t" grep.txt > p1803b.txt
   java G3 "b\*t" grep.txt > p1803c.txt
   ```

   grep.txt is in the J1 Software Package. Hand in your G3 program, p1803a.txt,
   p1803b.txt, and p1803c.txt.

4. In the implementation of grep described in this chapter, every state has an accept-
   State field. An alternate approach is to represent an NFA with an object that has
   both the start state and the accept state. Then each state would not have to have an
   acceptState field. Rewrite your implementation of G3 using this approach. How
   does it compare with the original approach?

5. Add support to your implementation of G3 for the + (one or more) and ? (zero or one) operators. Call this version G4. Test your program by entering

```
java G4 xyz grep.txt > p1805a.txt
java G4 "n.t|bo*t" grep.txt > p1805b.txt
java G4 "b\*t" grep.txt > p1805c.txt
java G4 "n.?t grep.txt > p1805d.txt
java G4 "bo+t" grep.txt > p1805e.txt
```

grep.txt is in the J1 Software Package. Hand in your G4 program, p1805a.txt, p1805b.txt, p1805c.txt, p1805d.txt, and p1805e.txt.

6. Add support of the command line arguments −v (invert match) and −n (line numbers) to your G3 program. Call this version G5. If −v is specified, G5 displays every line *not* matched by the given regular expression. If −n is specified, G5 displays the line number within the input file of every line displayed. Test your program by entering

```
java G5 -v -n xyz grep.txt > p1806a.txt
java G5 -n -v xyz grep.txt > p1806b.txt
```

grep.txt is in the J1 Software Package. Hand in your G5 program, p1806a.txt, and p1806b.txt.

7. Would it make sense to convert the NFA that your grep program creates to a DFA and then use the DFA for pattern matching? How would you represent the DFA?

8. Would it be better to use an array representation of the NFA rather than a linked structure? Describe the structure of the array that you would use.

9. Implement a grep program that supports JavaCC-type regular expressions.

10. Using the standard grep program (for example, the grep on a Linux system), determine what strings are matched by the following regular expressions:

```
b\ |c         (do not enter with enclosing quotes)
"b\ "|c"      (enter with enclosing quotes)
"b|c"         (enter with enclosing quotes)
```

Now repeat using the standard egrep program.

19

COMPILING TO A REGISTER-ORIENTED ARCHITECTURE

19.1 INTRODUCTION

The J1 computer that we have been using has a stack-oriented architecture. Most the instructions in its instruction set operate on operands obtained from the stack. For example, the assembly code for

```
z = x + y;
```

is

```
pc      z     ; push address onto the stack
p       x     ; push value in x onto stack
p       y     ; push value in y onto stack
add           ; pop top two, add, and push result
stav          ; pop value and address, store value
```

All five of these assembly instructions involve pushing and/or popping items from the stack. The J1 computer, however, has a second, alternate architecture—one that is register oriented. In a register-oriented architecture, the CPU uses registers (one-word storage areas within the CPU) rather than a stack to hold operand values and to accumulate results. For example, to add x and y and place the result in z when the J1 computer is configured with its register-oriented architecture, we would use the following assembly instructions:

```
ld      x     ; load value of x into ac register
add     y     ; add value of y to ac register
st      z     ; store value in ac register in z
```

Compiler Construction Using Java, JavaCC, and Yacc, First Edition. Anthony J. Dos Reis
© 2012 the IEEE Computer Society, Inc. Published 2012 by John Wiley & Sons, Inc.

The ld instruction loads the contents of the main memory location specified by x into the ac register. The add instruction adds the contents of the main memory location specified by y to the ac register. Finally, the st instruction stores the value in the ac register into the main memory location specified by z. The ld, add, and st instructions work only with the ac register. Thus, the specific register to be loaded, added to, or stored does not have to be (and should not be) specified in these instructions. The ac register is typically used to accumulate the result of a computation, hence the name ac (which stands for "accumulator"). Comparing the two assembly sequences above, we see that the sequence for the register-oriented architecture is shorter. A more dramatic difference appears if we compare the total number of main memory accesses. For the stack-oriented architecture, we get 14 (one for pc, one for each p, three for add, three for stav, and one for each instruction to fetch it from main memory). For the register-oriented architecture, we get only six (one for ld, one for add, one for st, and one to fetch each instruction from main memory). The number of memory accesses is important because memory accesses are time-consuming. The total number of memory accesses is a rough measure of the execution time of an instruction sequence. The stack-oriented architecture is clearly inferior in this respect. Unless it has special circuits to speed up accesses to its stack, it will generally be significantly slower than a comparably priced register-oriented architecture. A register-oriented architecture does have some disadvantages, however. In this chapter, we will see that compiling to a register-oriented architecture is more difficult than compiling to a stack-oriented architecture. Moreover, compilers for register-oriented architectures, unlike compilers for stack architectures, generally produce significantly less-than-optimal code unless they use special techniques to optimize the generated code. Thus, a good compiler for a register-oriented architecture is typically more complicated and more difficult to write than one for a stack-oriented architecture.

When the J1 computer is configured with its stack-oriented architecture (this is its default configuration), its instruction set is the *stack instruction set*. When configured with its register-oriented architecture, its instruction set is the *register instruction set*. We will call the S1 compiler from Chapter 12 modified to generate code in the register instruction set the R1 compiler.

19.2 USING THE REGISTER INSTRUCTION SET

To use the register instruction set on the J1 computer, we simply place a !register directive at the beginning of our assembly language program. With this directive, both the a and e programs in the J1 software package reconfigure to the register instruction set. For example, Figure 19.1 shows a complete assembly language program that uses the register instruction set. It adds x and y and displays the sum. Note the !register directive on the first line.

The sout, dout, and aout instructions in the register instruction set work the same way they do in the stack instruction set except that they use the ac register instead of the top of the stack. For example, sout displays the string pointed to by the ac register (not the string pointed to by the top of the stack); dout displays the value in the ac register (not the value on top of the stack). The ldc instruction is like the pc instruction in the stack instruction set, except that it moves the immediate value into the ac register instead of pushing it onto the stack. For example, in the instruction

```
ldc       @L0
```

```
               !register        ; configure to register inst set
               ld        x       ; load x into ac
               add       y       ; add y to ac
               st        sum     ; store result in sum
               ldc       @L0     ; load ac with address of @L0
               sout              ; display string pointed to by ac
               ld        sum     ; load sum into ac
               dout              ; display decimal value
               ldc       '\n'    ; load newline into ac
               aout              ; move to next line on display
               halt
     x:        dw        2
     y:        dw        3
     sum:      dw        0
     @L0:      dw        "Sum = "
```

Figure 19.1.

the immediate value in the machine instruction is the memory address corresponding to @L0. Thus, when executed, this instruction loads the address of @L0 into the ac register.

With the register instruction set, the J1 computer has two modes: absolute and relative. In the absolute mode, the addresses in the ld, st, add, sub, div, and mult instructions are treated as absolute addresses. In the relative mode, the addresses in these instructions are treated as relative addresses—relative to the location to which the bp register points. For example, suppose bp points to location 100 and the J1 computer is in the relative mode. Then

```
          ld        3
```

would load the ac register from location 103. The same instruction, however, would load from location 3 if the J1 computer were in the absolute mode.

The start-up code for the register instruction set is in the file rup.o in the J1 Software Package (see Section 16.2). For a description of all the instructions in the register instruction set, see Appendix B or the register.txt file in the J1 Software Package.

19.3 MODIFICATIONS TO THE SYMBOL TABLE FOR R1

The endcode method in our S1 compiler for the stack instruction set outputs dw statements all of whose values are zero. Because the value of every symbol is zero, it is not necessary to record the value of each symbol in the symbol table. However, in the R1 compiler, the dw statements that endCode generates can have nonzero as well as zero values. For example, the assembly code R1 generates for

```
     x = y + 5000;
```

is

```
          ld        y
          add       @5000
          st        x
```

For this statement, endCode in R1 has to output three dw statements, one of which has a nonzero value:

```
x:          dw          0
y:          dw          0
@5000:      dw          5000
```

To record the value of each symbol, the symbol table in R1 uses an ArrayList named symbol (to record the symbol) and an ArrayList named dwValue (to record the symbol's value). These two ArrayLists (as well as a third ArrayList named needsDW, which we will discuss shortly) are parallel structures. Whenever the enter method adds a symbol to symbol, it also adds its corresponding value to dwValue (see Figure 19.2a).

Our S1 compiler for the stack instruction set did very little passing of information from one point in the parse to another. However, our R1 compiler will have to do considerably more passing of information. The best way to pass information on a variable encountered during a parse is to pass its symbol table index. A symbol table index provides easy access to not only a variable's name but any other information on that variable that is in the symbol table. Moreover, a symbol table index uniquely identifies a variable, whereas the variable's name does not. For example, a source program could have two variables named x: one global and one local. The two variables have the same name, but they would have distinct symbol table indices.

In all our compilers for the stack instruction set, the endCode method in the code generator emits a dw statement for every entry in the symbol table. What if we want to pass something via its symbol table index but do not want a dw statement generated for it? We will not need to do this in R1 but we will for more advanced compilers that use the register instruction set. In anticipation of this future requirement, we will use in R1's symbol table a third ArrayList of type boolean named needsDW. For each symbol in the symbol table, the corresponding element in needsDW indicates if a dw statement should be generated by endCode. enCode outputs a dw statement only for those symbols whose needsDW value is true (see Figure 19.2b). The symbol table also includes some new accessor and mutator methods (see Figure 19.2c).

19.4   PARSER AND CODE GENERATOR FOR R1

Let us consider the stack instruction set code that is generated by our S1 compiler when it parses the expression x + y:

```
p           x
p           y
add
```

Where in S1 is the add instructions produced? Recall that when the current token is "+", the termList method parses "+" and term, and then recursively calls itself (see Figure 19.3).

Between the call of term and the recursive call, termList generates an add instruction (line 5 in Figure 19.3. The call of term() produces the code that pushes the right operand of the add operator onto the stack. Under this operand on the stack is the left operand, pushed there by code emitted earlier in the parse. Thus, the code we need to add

```
 1 public int enter(String s, String v, boolean b)
 2 {
 3   int index = symbol.indexOf(s);
 4   if (index >= 0)     // s already in symbol?
 5     return index;     // yes, then return its index
 6
 7   index = symbol.size();
 8   symbol.add(s);      // add symbol
 9   dwValue.add(v);     // add value
10   needsdw.add(b);     // add needsdw value
11   return index;
12 }
```

(a)

```
 1 public void endCode()
 2 {
 3   outFile.println();
 4   outFile.println("          halt");
 5
 6   int size = st.getSize();
 7   // emit a dw if corresponding needsdw value is true
 8   for (int i=0; i < size; i++)
 9     if (st.getNeedsdw(i))
10       emitdw(st.getSymbol(i), st.getdwValue(i));
11 }
```

(b)

```
 1 public boolean getdwValue(int index)
 2 {
 3   return dwValue.get(index);
 4 }
 5 //----------------------
 6 public boolean getNeedsdw(int index)
 7 {
 8   return needsdw.get(index);
 9 }
10 //----------------------
11 public void setNeedsdw(int index)
12 {
13   needsdw.set(index, true);
14 }
```

(c)

Figure 19.2.

these two operands is simply an add instruction. At execution time, the two operands will be the top two items on the stack. The add instruction pops them, adds them and places the result back on the stack. Now let us see what kind of add instruction we need when we are compiling to the register instruction set. Unfortunately, determining the appropriate add instruction is considerably more complex when we use the register instruction set. Consider, for example, the expression x + y. For this expression, termList should

```
1 void termList(): {}
2 {
3     "+"
4     term()
5     { codeGen.emitInstruction("add");}
6     termList()
7 |
8     {}
9 }
```

Figure 19.3.

emit not only an add instruction (which adds the right operand), but also a ld instruction which loads the left operand:

```
ld        x
add       y
```

Thus, both left and right operands must be passed to termList. Could the code to load the left operand be generated when term or factor parses the left operand? But if term or factor did that, it would also do it for the right operand. Thus, we would get the code

```
ld        x
ld        y
```

The second load (of y) would overlay the value loaded by the first load (of x). Thus, if termList then generated

```
add       y
```

the resulting code would incorrectly add y and y instead of x and y. We conclude that both left and right operands must be passed to termList so it can generate the necessary ld as well as the add instruction. Similarly, both left and right operands in a multiplication must be passed to factorList (the method that generates the multiplication code).

Now consider the expression x + y + z. For this expression, termList is called twice, once to parse "+ y" and once to parse "+ z". On its first call, termList should emit a ld and an add:

```
ld        x
add       y
```

However, on its second call, it should emit only an add of the right operand:

```
add       z
```

because the left operand is already in the ac register by virtue of the first add instruction.

We have seen that under some circumstances, termList should generate both a ld and add instruction. But under other circumstances, it should generate only an add of the right operand. Now consider x + y* z. For this expression, termList calls term, which, by calling factorList, generates

```
ld          y
mult        z
```

Thus, `termList` in this case should generate an `add` of the left (not the right) operand:

```
add         x
```

Clearly, to generate the correct instruction, `termList` has to consider the special cases: sometimes it should emit a `ld` and an `add`, sometimes only an `add` of the right operand, sometimes only an `add` of the left operand. But there is yet another complication. Consider w* x + y* z. When w* x is parsed, we get the code

```
ld          w
mult        x
```

When executed, this code leaves the result in the `ac` register. But we cannot simply leave the result in the `ac` register because the `ac` register is needed to evaluate the second term, y* z. The code we need for this expression must save the value of w* x in a temporary location, thereby making the `ac` register available for the evaluation of y* z. Here is the code we need:

```
ld          w
mult        x
st          @t0       ; save value of w* x in @t0

ld          y
mult        z         ; value of y* z now in ac reg
add         @t0       ; add value of w* x to value of y* z
```

where `@t0` is a *temp* variable (a compiler-generated variable whose name is selected from the sequence `@t0`, `@t1`, `@t2`, . . .) defined by

```
@t0:    dw          0
```

To make our R1 compiler as simple as possible, we will design `termList` to handle all cases we discussed above in a uniform way. Specifically, we will pass both the left and right operands to `termList`. `termList` will then emit code to

1. Load the left operand
2. Add the right operand
3. Store the result in a temp

With this approach, we will not get efficient code (we will fix this shortcoming in the next chapter). On the positive side, our compiler will be as simple as possible. We will design `factorList`, which generates the `mult` instruction, with the same approach. That is, it will emit code to

1. Load the left operand
2. Multiply by the right operand
3. Store the result in a temp

Let us examine the translation grammar in Figure 19.4 for our simplified `termList` method, which we will use for R1. When we call `termList`, we pass it `left`, the symbol table index of the left operand (see line 1). On line 4, we call `term`, which returns the symbol table index of the right operand. Then on line 5, we call the `add` method in the code generator, passing it the left and right operands. `add` emits the required `ld-add-st` sequence. It also returns the symbol table index of the temp it uses in the `st` instruction. This temp becomes the left parameter in the recursive call of `termList` on line 6. Thus, as `termList` recurses, the left parameter represents that portion of the expression parsed so far. When `termList` finally reaches the end of the expression, the second alternative is taken (line 9). At this point, the `left` parameter is the symbol table index of the item that holds the value of the entire expression. `termList` returns this index to its caller, which, in turn, returns it to its caller, and so on, all the way back to `expr`. Figure 19.5 shows the code for the `add` and `getTemp` methods in the code generator. `add` first emits the `ld` and `st` instructions. It then calls `getTemp` to get the next available temp in the sequence `@t0`, `@t1`, `@t2`, ... It then emits a `st` to this temp and returns its symbol table index. `getTemp` creates the temp, enters it into the symbol table, and returns its symbol table index. We have to enter the temp into the symbol table so we have an index to return. We also have to enter it so that a `dw` statement will ultimately be generated for it by `endCode`.

```
 1 int termList(int left): {int right, int temp, expVal;}
 2 {
 3     "+"
 4     right=term()
 5     { temp = cg.add(left, right);}   // emits ld/add/st
 6     expVal=termList(temp)
 7     { return expVal;}
 8 |
 9     { return left;}        // do this at end of expression
10 }
```

Figure 19.4.

```
public int add(int left, int right)
{
    emitInstruction("ld", left);
    emitInstruction("add", right);
    int temp = getTemp();       // returns index
    emitInstruction("st", temp);
    return temp;
}
```

(a)

```
private int getTemp()
{
    String temp = "@t" + tempIndex++;     // create temp
    return st.enter(temp, "0", true); // return index
}
```

(b)

Figure 19.5.

Let us see what assembly code we get using our new `termList` method for several expressions. For x + y, we get

```
ld    x
add   y
st    @t0
```

For x* y + z, we get

```
ld    x
mult  y
st    @t1


ld    @t1
add   z
st    @t2
```

For w* x + y* z, we get

```
ld    w
mult  x
st    @t3


ld    y
mult  z
st    @t4


ld    @t3
add   @t4
st    @t5
```

Figure 19.6 gives the entire translation grammar for the parser in R1. The translation grammar for R1 differs from the translation grammar for S1 in two significant ways. First, it does not directly call the `emitInstruction` method in the code generator. `emitInstruction` is now a private method in the code generator. For example, to emit code for the assignment statement, the R1 parser calls the `assign` method in the code generator (see line 31 in Figure 19.6) which, in turn, calls `emitInstruction`. Second, the `factor` method does not emit any code. It simply returns a symbol table index. The code to load a factor into the `ac` register is emitted by either the `add` method in `termList` or the `mult` method in `factorList`.

The methods in the R1 code generator that are not in the S1 code generator are

```
public void assign(int left, int expVal)
```

This outputs the `ld-st` sequence for an assignment statement by making calls to `emitInstruction` (see line 31 in Figure 19.6). `left` and `expVal` are symbol table indices.

```
public void println(int expVal)
```

```
 1 // Translation grammar for R1
 2
 3 void program(): {}
 4 {
 5     statementList()
 6     { cg.endCode();}
 7     <EOF>
 8 }
 9 //---------------
10 void statementList(): {}
11 {
12     statement()
13     statementList()
14 |
15     {}
16 }
17 //---------------
18 void statement(): {}
19 {
20     assignmentStatement()
21 |
22     printlnStatement()
23 }
24 //---------------
25 void assignmentStatement(): { Token t; int left, expVal;}
26 {
27     t=<ID>
28     { left = symTab.enter(t.image, "0", true);}
29     "="
30     expVal=expr()
31     { cg.assign(left, expVal);}
32     ";"
33 }
34 //---------------
35 void printlnStatement(): { int expVal;}
36 {
37     "println"
38     "("
39     expVal = expr()
40     { cg.println(expVal);}
41     ")"
42     ";"
43 }
44 //---------------
45 int expr(): { int left, expVal;}
46 {
47     left=term()
48     expVal=termList(left)
49     { return expVal;}
50 }
51 //---------------
52 int termList(int left): { int right, temp, expVal;}
53 {
```

Figure 19.6.

```
54     "+"
55     right=term()
56     { temp = cg.add(left, right);}
57     expVal=termList(temp)
58     { return expVal;}
59   |
60     { return left;}
61  }
62  //---------------
63  int term(): { int left, termVal;}
64  {
65     left=factor()
66     termVal=factorList(left)
67     { return termVal;}
68  }
69  //---------------
70  int factorList(int left): { int right, temp, termVal;}
71  {
72     "*"
73     right=factor()
74     { temp = cg.mult(left, right);}
75     termVal=factorList(temp)
76     { return termVal;}
77   |
78     { return left;}
79  }
80  //---------------
81  int factor(): {Token t; int index;}
82  {
83     t=<UNSIGNED>
84     { index = st.enter("@" + t.image, t.image, true);}
85     { return index;}
86   |
87     "+"
88     t = <UNSIGNED>
89     { index = st.enter("@" + t.image, t.image, true);}
90     { return index;}
91   |
92     "-"
93     t = <UNSIGNED>
94     { index = st.enter("@_" + t.image, "-" + t.image, true);}
95     { return index;}
96   |
97     t=<ID>
98     { index = st.enter(t.image, "0", true);}
99     { return index;}
100  |
101    "("
102    index=expr()
103    ")"
104    { return index;}
105 }
```

Figure 19.6. *Continued.*

This outputs the `ld-dout-ldc-aout` sequence for a `println` statement by making calls to `emitInstruction` (see line 40 in Figure 19.6). `expVal` is a symbol table index.

```
public void add(int left, int right)
```

This outputs the `ld-add-st` sequence for an add operation by making calls to `emitIn-struction` (see Figure 19.5a and line 56 in Figure 19.6). `left` and `right` are symbol table indices.

```
public void mult(int left, int right)
```

This outputs the `ld-mult-st` sequence for a multiplication operation by making calls to `emitInstruction` (see line 74 in Figure 19.6). `mult` is similar to `add`.

```
private int getTemp()
```

This generates the next temporary variable from the sequence `"@t0"`, `"@t1"`, `"@t2"`, ... , enters it into the symbol table, and returns its symbol table index (see Figure 19.5b). `getTemp` is called by `add` and `mult` (see Figure 19.5a).

```
private void emitInstruction(String op, int opndIndex)
```

The code in this method consists of the following call to the `emitInstruction` method that has two string parameters :

```
emitInstruction(op, st.getSymbol(opndIndex));
```

PROBLEMS

1. Implement the hand-written R1 compiler or the equivalent JavaCC-generated R1j compiler. R1 is S1 modified to generate code in the register instruction set. Test your compiler by entering

```
javac R1.java       or       javacc R1j.jj
java R1 S1                    javac  R1j.java
a S1.a                       java R1j S1
e S1 /c                      a S1.a
                             e S1 /c
```

   Start by copying `S1.java` to `R1.java` or `S1j.jj` to `R1j.jj`. Then modify `R1.java` or `R1j.jj`. Because you are compiling `S1.s`, the performance statistics that the program generates will be relative to the S1 compiler. You will probably find that R1 is over the limit in size but under the limit in execution time.

2. Compare your S1 (or S1j) compiler with your R1 (or R1j) compiler with respect to size and execution time of the generated code. Does R1 generates inefficient code relative to the code generated by S1?

3. Do temps have to be unique? Or can they be reused?

4. What is the minimum number of temps required for each of the following statements:

```
x = b + c + d + e + f;
x = b + (c + (d + (e + f)));
```

5. Implement R2 or R2j, the register instruction version of S2 or S2j. Test your program with S2.s.

6. Implement R3 or R3j, the register instruction version of S3 or S3j. Test your program with S3.s.

7. Implement R4 or R4j, the register instruction version of S4 or S4j. Test your program with S4.s.

8. Implement R5 or R5j, the register instruction version of S5 or S5j. Test your program with S5a.s and S5b.s. Be sure to link with rup.o, not sup.o. rup.o is the start-up code for the register instruction set.

9. Implement R6 or R6j, the register instruction version of S6 or S6j. Test your program with S6a.s and S6b.s. Be sure to link with rup.o, not sup.o. rup.o is the start-up code for the register instruction set.

20

OPTIMIZATION

20.1 INTRODUCTION

We observed in the Chapter 19 that the code generated by our R1 compiler (the register instruction set version of S1) is inefficient. In this chapter, we will fix this shortcoming by incorporating the following code optimization techniques in our R1 compiler:

1. Use the `ldc` instruction in place of the `ld` instruction to load constants in the range 0–4095. The `ldc` instruction does not require a `dw` for the constant (the constant is in the `ldc` instruction itself). Moreover, an `ldc` instruction executes faster than an `ld` instruction. Thus, using `ldc` in place of `ld` saves both time and space.

2. Reuse temps (i.e., temporary variables) to minimize their number. For example, suppose a program consisted of three assignment statements, each requiring a single temporary variable. Without the reuse of temps, the compiler would create `@t0`, `@t1`, and `@t2`. With reuse, the compiler would create only `@t0` and use it for all three assignment statements. Reuse of temps reduces the size but not the execution time of the target program.

3. Constant folding. With constant folding, constant expressions (i.e., expressions or subexpressions containing constants exclusively) are evaluated at compile time rather than at run time. For example, without constant folding, the code for the expression 5000 + 6000 is

```
ld      @5000
add     @6000
```

where `@5000` and `@6000` are defined with

```
@5000:    dw      5000
@6000:    dw      6000
```

The computation—adding 5000 and 6000—is performed at run time, when the target program is executed. With constant folding, however, the code is

```
ld      @11000
```

where @11000 is defined by

```
@11000:   dw        11000
```

The computation—adding 5000 and 6000—is performed by the compiler at compile time. Constant folding reduces both the size and execution time of the target program.

4. Register allocation. With register allocation, the compiler keeps track of what will be in registers during execution time. It can then generate code that accesses these values via the registers that contain them. For example, without register allocation, the code for

```
x = y;
z = x;
```

is

```
ld        y
st        x

ld        x
st        z
```

The first st instruction stores the value in the ac register into the x variable in main memory. Thus, after its execution, the value of x is also in the ac register. With register allocation in effect, the compiler records this fact. Then, when it translates the second assignment statement, it knows it does not have to emit a ld instruction to load the value of x into the ac register. It can simply emit a st instruction to store the value in the ac register (which already is the value of x by virtue of the preceding st instruction) into z. The code produced is

```
ld        y
st        x

st        z
```

The register allocation technique is easy to implement. Moreover, it can yield an impressive improvement in both the size and execution time of the target program.

5. Peephole optimization. In peephole optimization, the compiler passes a "peephole" over the generated code. In any given position, the peephole allows the viewing of only a few lines. For each position of the peephole, the viewable code is optimized, if possible. For example, suppose the peephole is currently viewing the two-instruction sequence

```
st        x
ld        x
```

In this sequence, the compiler can eliminate the ld instruction because the ac register already contains the value of x by virtue of the preceding st instruction. Peephole optimization is a localized optimization technique. That is, for each position of the peephole, the optimization that occurs is based on only the viewable code, not on the code that precedes it or follows it.

In this chapter, we will implement several extensions of R1 using various optimization techniques. These compilers are

R1a   R1 with ldc in place of ld wherever possible

R1b   R1a with temporary variable reuse

R1c   R1b with constant folding

R1d   R1c with register allocation

R1e   R1c with peephole optimization

By comparing the performance of these compilers, we will get a good sense of the effectiveness of these optimization techniques. We will also see how compiler-generated code for the register instruction set compares to compiler-generated code for the stack instruction set (see Problems 6 and 7 at the end of the chapter).

20.2   USING THE ldc INSTRUCTION

R1 emits an ld instruction in the assign, println, add and mult methods in the code generator. To emit an ldc instruction in place of the ld instruction wherever possible, we simply replace the code that emits a ld instruction with a call of a new method emit-Load. For example, in assign, we replace

```
emitInstruction("ld", expVal);
```

with

```
emitLoad(expVal);
```

emitLoad checks if the value corresponding to the symbol table index it is passed is in the range is 0–4095 (see Figure 20.1). If it is, it emits a ldc instruction; otherwise it emits a ld instruction.

isldcConstant is a new method in the symbol table. It accesses the item in the symbol table corresponding to the index it is passed, and checks if it is a constant (by calling another new method isConstant). If it is, it converts the constant to type int using Integer.parseInt, checks if its int value is in the range 0–4095, and returns true or false accordingly.

You should now do Problem 1 at the end of the chapter (implement R1a by extending R1 so that it uses ldc wherever possible). R1a has the following new methods:

- In the symbol table:

    ```
    public boolean isConstant(int index)
    ```

```
private void emitLoad(int opndIndex)
{
  if (st.isldcConstant(opndIndex)
    emitInstruction("ldc", st.getdwValue(opndIndex));
  else
    emitInstruction("ld", opndIndex);
}
```

Figure 20.1.

Returns true if the symbol at the given index is a constant (i.e., if the symbol starts with "@" or "@_" followed by at least one digit). Otherwise, it returns false.

```
public boolean isldcConstant(int index)
```

Determines if the symbol at given index is a constant (by calling isConstant). If it is, and if its value is in the range 0–4095, returns true. Otherwise, it returns false.

- In the code generator:

```
private void emitLoad(int opndIndex)
```

Emits an ldc in place of an ld if opndIndex corresponds to a constant in the range 0–4095 (see Figure 20.1).

20.3   REUSING TEMPORARY VARIABLES

Temps (i.e., temporary variables) are never accessed more that once for the value they are holding. Thus, whenever they are accessed, they immediately become available for reuse. Consider the code R1 generates for

```
a = b + c + d;
```

It contains two temps, @t0 and @t1:

```
ld      b
add     c
st      @t0
ld      @t0     ; @t0 reusable at this point
add     d
st      @t1     ; can use @t0 here
ld      @t1     ; can use @t0 here
st      a
```

When the compiler emits

```
ld      @t0
```

@t0 becomes available for reuse. Thus, at this point the compiler should free (i.e., mark as available for reuse) @t0. Then, when the compiler subsequently needs another temp (it needs one to hold the result when d is added), it will reuse @t0 instead of using @t1. With temp reuse in effect, the code for the assignment statement above is

```
ld      b
add     c
st      @t0
ld      @t0     ; @t0 reusable at this point
add     d
st      @t0     ; reuse @t0
ld      @t0
st      a
```

```
1 public int getTemp()
2 {
3     String temp = "@t" + tempIndex++;
4     return st.enter(temp, "0", true);
5 }
```

Figure 20.2.

In R1, temps are provided by the `getTemp` method (see Figure 20.2). The specific temp that `getTemp` provides depends on the value of `tempIndex`. For example, if `tempIndex` is equal to 0, then a call to `getTemp` returns `@t0` (or, more precisely, it returns the symbol table index of `@t0`). It also increments `tempIndex` so the next call of `getTemp` will provide the next temp in the sequence. Thus, after providing `@t0`, get-Temp increments `tempIndex` to 1. How does the compiler subsequently free `@t0` so that it can be reused? The compiler simply decrements `tempIndex` back down to 0. get-Temp will then provide `@t0` again on its next call. Each time the compiler decrements `tempIndex`, it frees the most recently created temp.

When multiple temps are in use at the same time, they are accessed in reverse order to which they were created. Thus, they should be freed in reverse order as well. That is, it will never be the case that when temps `@t0`, `@t1`, and `@t2` are in use, `@t0` is accessed (and therefore should be freed) but not `@t1` or `@t2`. For example, consider the assembly code in Figure 20.3 that corresponds to

```
a = (b + c) +((d + e) + (f + g));
```

After the sum of `f` and `g` is stored in `@t2` (line 9 in Figure 20.3), three temps—`@t0`, `@t1`, and `@t2`—are is use. `@t1` and `@t2` are then accessed. Thus, the compiler should immedi-

```
1     ld      b
2     add     c
3     st      @t0
4     ld      d
5     add     e
6     st      @t1
7     ld      f
8     add     g
9     st      @t2     ; @t0, @t1, @t2 in use at this point
10
11    ld      @t1     ; accessing @t1 and @t2 so free them
12    add     @t2
13
14    st      @t1     ; @t0 and @t1 in use at this point
15
16    ld      @t0     ; accessing @t0 and @t1 so free them
17    add     @t1
18
19    st      @t0     ; using @t0 at this point
20    ld      @t0     ; accessing @t0 so free it
21    st      a
```

Figure 20.3.

ately free them for reuse. Since these two temps were the most recently created temps, the compiler can free them simply by decrementing `tempIndex` twice.

The decrementation of `tempIndex` is performed by the `freeTemp` method in Figure 20.4a. `freeTemp` decrements `tempIndex` only if the index it is passed corresponds to a temp in the symbol table. This check is necessary because `freeTemp` is sometimes passed an index that does not correspond to a temp. For example, consider the code for the `assign` method (see Figure 20.4b).

On line 3 of Figure 20.4b, `assign` emits a load instruction that loads the value of the expression on the right side of an assignment statement. If this expression is represented by a temp, the call of `freeTemp` on line 4 frees it immediately. However, the expression may not be represented by a temp. For example, in the call of `assign` for

```
x = y;
```

the indices of x and y would be passed to the parameters `left` and `expVal`, respectively, in `assign`. `assign` would then call `freeTemp` passing it `expVal` (the index of y). `freeTemp` in this case should not decrement `tempIndex` because y is not a temp. For the `add` method (see Figure 20.4c), both the left and right operands may or may not be temps. Accordingly, `add` calls `freeTemp` twice, once for each operand (see lines 5 and 6). `freeTemp` decrements `tempIndex` only if they are temps.

```
1 public void freeTemp(int opndIndex)
2 {
3     if (st.isTemp(opndIndex))
4         tempIndex--;
5 }
```

(a)

```
1 public void assign(int left, int expVal)
2 {
3     emitLoad(expVal);
4     freeTemp(expVal);
5     emitInstruction("st", left);
6 }
```

(b)

```
1 public int add(int left, int right)
2 {
3     emitLoad(left);
4     emitInstruction("add", right);
5     freeTemp(left);
6     freeTemp(right);
7     int temp = getTemp();
8     emitInstruction("st", temp);
9     return temp;
10 }
```

(c)

Figure 20.4.

The isTemp method that freeTemp calls (line 3 in Figure 20.4a) is a new method in the symbol table. It determines if an index corresponds to a temp by checking if the corresponding symbol is longer than two characters and starts with "@t".

You should now do Problem 2 at the end of the chapter (implement R1b by extending R1a so that it reuses temps). R1b has the following new methods:

- In the symbol table:

```
public boolean isTemp(int index)
```

Returns true if the symbol corresponding to index is a temp.
- In the code generator:

```
public void freeTemp(int opndIndex)
```

Decrements tempIndex if the symbol corresponding to opndIndex is a temp.

20.4 CONSTANT FOLDING

Constant folding requires a simple modification to the termList and factorList methods in the parser. Before we consider these modifications, lets review the structure of the termList method as it is in the R1 compiler (see Figure 20.5). On line 9, termList calls term to parse the right operand of the plus operator. The left operand is provided by the parameter left. termList then calls add, passing it the left and right operands (line 10). add emits the required ld-add-st sequence and returns the temp (or more precisely, the index of the temp) it uses in the st instruction. This temp then becomes the left parameter in the recursive call of termList on line 11. Thus, as termList recurses, the left parameter represents that portion of the expression parsed so far. When termList finally reaches the end of the expression, it executes line 15. At this point, left is the symbol table index of the entry that will hold the value of the entire expression at execu-

```
1 private int termList(int left)
2 {
3   int right, temp, expVal;
4
5   switch(currentToken.kind)
6   {
7     case PLUS:
8       consume(PLUS);
9       right = term();
10      temp = cg.add(left, right);    // emits ld/add/st
11      expVal = termList(temp);
12      return expVal;
13    case RIGHTPAREN:
14    case SEMICOLON:
15      return left;      // do this at end of expression
16    default:
17      throw genEx("Expecting \"+\", \")\", or \";\"");
18  }
19 }
```

Figure 20.5.

tion time. `termList` returns this index to its caller, which, in turn, returns it to its caller, and so on, all the way back to `expr`.

To support constant folding is easy: If the left and right operands are both constants, the compiler does not emit assembly code to compute the result. Instead, it adds the two constants, creates a new constant corresponding to their sum, and then continues the parse using this new constant. In other words, the compiler computes the sum at compile time rather than generating assembly code to compute the sum. Figure 20.6 gives the specifics of the code we need in place of line 10 in Figure 20.5.

If the left and right operands are not both constants, then we do what we normally do (line 13): call `add`, which emits the assembly code to perform the addition. However, if both operands are constants, then we convert their values to type `int`, add them, create a new constant for their sum, and then continue the parse using this new constant.

To convert the values of constants to type `int`, we first get their values from the symbol table using the `getdwValue` method (see Figure 19.2c). Because the values returned by `getdwValue` are type `String`, we have to convert them to type `int` (using `Integer.parseInt`) before we can add them.

Note that the second argument in the call of `enter` on lines 8 and 10 in Figure 20.6 is

```
"" + result
```

`enter` requires its second parameter to be type `String`. But `result` is type `int`. Thus, to pass a string, we concatenate the null string to `result`, which yields a string. For example, if result is the `int` -7, the concatenation of `""` to result yields the string `"-7"`.

Note that the third argument on lines 8 and 10 is false. This value is assigned to the `needsdw` flag for the new constant in the symbol table (see Figure 19.2a). We do this because we will not necessarily need a `dw` for the new constant. For example, consider the following assignment statement:

```
x = -1 + 3 + -7;
```

The corresponding assembly code with constant folding is

```
ld      @_5
st      x
```

```
1  if the left and right operands are both constants
2  {
3      set leftValue  to int value of left operand
4      set rightValue  to int value of right operand
5
6      result = leftValue + rightValue;
7      if (result >= 0)
8          temp=st.enter("@" + result, "" + result, false);
9      else
10         temp=st.enter("@_" + -result, "" + result, false);
11 }
12 else
13     temp = cg.add(left, right);
```

Figure 20.6.

On its first call, `termList` creates the constant @2 whose value is "2" by adding −1 and 3. Thus, on the recursive call, the left and right operands are 2 and −7. On this call, `termList` creates the constant @_5 whose value is "−5" by adding 2 and −7. The constant 2 is folded with the constant −7. Thus, constant 2 never appears in the assembly code. So we do not need a dw for it. However, we do need a dw for some constants, for example, for @_5 in the current example. To get the dw statements we need, we simply monitor the assembly code that is emitted. If an instruction is emitted that uses a constant, then the `needsdw` flag for that constant is set to true at that time. Then, when `endCode` is subsequently executed, it will emit a dw for that constant. Figure 20.7 shows the required modification. Of the three `emitInstruction` methods, we have to modify only one—the one with a `String` parameter and an `int` parameter.

To complete the implementation of constant folding, we have to modify `factorList` in the same way we modified `termList`. Then a sequence of factors that are constants will fold into a single constant. For example, the assembly code for

```
x = 2*3 + 4*5;
```

will be

```
    ldc         26
    st
```

In this statement, 2 and 3 are folded into 6; 4 and 5 are folded into 20. Then 6 and 20 are folded into 26. Because 26 is in the range 0–4095, an `ldc` is used to load it. We do not need any dw statements!

You should now do Problem 3 at the end of the chapter (implement R1c by extending R1b so that it performs constant folding). R1c does not require any new methods. However, it requires modifications to the `termList`, `factorList`, `factor`, and `emitInstruction` methods.

20.5 REGISTER ALLOCATION

Register allocation is a technique that can produce substantial reductions in the size and runtime of the target programs produced by a compiler. The impact of register allocation is particularly significant on computers with multiple registers available to hold operands. But even with only one register available, as is the case with the J1 computer configured for the register instruction set, register allocation can yield substantial improvements.

To support register allocation, the code generator *at compile time* keeps track of what variable or temp will be in the `ac` register *at execution time*. It uses a variable named `ac` for this purpose. This variable holds the symbol table index of the item whose value will

```
1 private void emitInstruction(String op, int opndIndex)
2 {
3    if (st.isConstant(opndIndex))
4       st.setNeedsdw(opndIndex);
5    emitInstruction(op, st.getSymbol(opndIndex));
6 }
```

Figure 20.7.

be in the `ac` register during execution time. For example, consider the code for the assign method in Figure 20.8.

Suppose that during the execution of `assign`, `left` contains the index of the variable x. Then `emitInstruction` on line 6 would emit the instruction

```
st          x
```

Thus, at this point at execution time, the `ac` register would contain the value of x. On line 7, `assign` records this fact by assigning `left` (which contains the index of x) to the `ac` variable in the code generator. Now suppose the next statement in the source code is the assignment statement

```
y = x;
```

When `assign` is called for this statement, the parameter `expVal` will have the index of x. Because at this point the index of x is in the `ac` variable, the `if` statement on line 3 will not execute the call of `emitLoad`. Thus, the unnecessary `ld` from x will not be emitted. For this assignment statement, the code generator emits

```
st          y
```

instead of

```
ld          x          ; unnecessary load
st          y
```

With register allocation, temps are initially held in the `ac` register. Store instructions that store a temp in main memory are emitted only if they are necessary. For example, consider the statement

```
x = (a + b) + (c + d);
```

a + b is evaluated first, the result of which is represented by `@t0`. Immediately after this evaluation, the `ac` register holds the result of a + b. But the `ac` register then has to be used to evaluate c + d. Thus, `@t0`, the temp that represents a + b, has to be stored before the evaluation of c + d can proceed. The corresponding assembly code is

```
ld          a
add         b
st          @t0  ; must store @t0 because ac reg needed

ld          c
add         d    ; c + d now in ac reg
add         @t0  ; a + b in @t0

st          x
```

Figure 20.9 gives the code for the `add` method modified to support register allocation. If the left operand is in the `ac` register, then an `add` from the right operand is emitted (line 4). We obviously do not need a `ld` because the left operand will already be in the `ac` reg-

```
1 public void assign(int left, int expVal)
2 {
3   if (ac != expVal)
4     emitLoad(expVal);
5   freeTemp(expVal);
6   emitInstruction("st", left);
7   ac = left;
8 }
```

Figure 20.8.

ister at execution time If, on the other hand, the right operand is in the ac register, then an add from the left operand is emitted (line 7). Again, we do not need a ld. If neither is the case, then a ld has to be emitted (line 15). However, before the ld is emitted, a st into a temp is emitted (line 12) if ac has the index of a temp. A st into a temp necessitates a dw for that temp. Thus, if a st is emitted, its needsdw value is set to true (line 13). A temp is created to represent the result of the add operation (line 20). However, a st into this temp is not emitted. Instead, the ac variable is assigned the index of the temp, which effectively allocates the temp to the ac register (see line 21).

When temps are created by getTemp, their needsdw value should initially be false. If a store instruction is emitted that stores a temp in main memory, then the needsdw for that temp is changed to true (for example, by line 13 in Figure 20.9).

You should now do Problem 4 at the end of the chapter (implement R1d by extending R1c so that it performs register allocation). R1d does not require any new methods. However, it requires modifications to the getTemp, assign, add and mult methods.

```
1 public int add(int left, int right)
2 {
3   if (ac == left)
4     emitInstruction("add", right);
5   else
6   if (ac == right)
7     emitInstruction("add", left);
8   else
9   {
10     if (st.isTemp(ac))
11     {
12       emitInstruction("st", ac);
13       st.setNeedsdw(ac);
14     }
15     emitLoad(left);
16     emitInstruction("add", right);
17   }
18   freeTemp(left);
19   freeTemp(right);
20   int temp = getTemp();
21   ac = temp;
22   return temp;
23 }
```

Figure 20.9.

20.6   PEEPHOLE OPTIMIZATION

The peephole optimizer in the code generator monitors the instructions to be emitted. If the code generator is to emit a st-ld sequence with matching operands, then the peephole optimizer emits only the st instruction. For example, when the code generator is to emit

```
st        x
ld        x
```

the peephole optimizer emits only the st instruction. We don't need the ld instruction because the ac register and x would already have identical values by virtue of the preceding st instruction. If, however, we had the following sequence,

```
st        y
ld        x
```

then the ld instruction is necessary. From these two examples, we can make the following observation: the decision to emit a ld instruction depends on the instruction that *precedes* it.

If the code generator is to emit a st-ld sequence with matching operands that are temps, the peephole optimizer emits neither instruction. For example, in the sequence

```
st        @t0
ld        @t0
```

we do not need the ld instruction because the value we need in the ac register is already there. Moreover, we also do not need the st instruction because we will never need this temp value again. Thus, we do not have to store the temp in memory for later access. If, however, we had the following sequence

```
st        @t0
ld        x
```

then we would need both the st and the ld. From these two examples, we can make the following observation: the decision to emit a st into a temp in main memory depends on the instruction that *follows* it.

To modify the code generator in R1c to support peephole optimization, we add a peephole method that performs the peephole optimization. We change every call of emitInstruction or emitLoad to a call of the peephole method. Thus, all instructions go through peephole. For example, on lines 5, 6, 10, and 11 in the add method in Figure 20.10a, we can see the calls to peephole that were calls to emitInstruction in R1c. Similarly, on lines 3, 5, 6, and 7 in the println method in Figure 20.10b, we have calls to peephole that were calls to emitInstruction in R1c.

When add emits the ld instruction (line 5 or 10 in Figure 20.10a), it selects the operand that is a temp, if there is one. For example, suppose the left and right parameters are the indices of x and @t0, respectively. Then add emits

```
ld        @t0
add       x
```

```
1 public int add(int left, int right)
2 {
3     if (!st.isTemp(left) && st.isTemp(right))
4     {
5         peephole("ld", right);
6         peephole("add", left);
7     }
8     else
9     {
10        peephole("ld", left);
11        peephole("add", right);
12    }
13    freeTemp(left);
14    freeTemp(right);
15    int temp = getTemp();
16    peephole("st", temp);
17    return temp;
18 }
```

(a)

```
1 public void println(int expVal)
2 {
3     peephole("ld", expVal);
4     freeTemp(expVal);
5     peephole("dout");
6     peephole("ldc", "'\\n'");
7     peephole("aout");
8 }
```

(b)

Figure 20.10.

It emits a ld is from right (the temp). If, on the other hand, the left and right parameters are the indices of @t0 and x, respectively, then add would emit a ld from left (which now is the temp). Thus, we would get the same sequence:

```
ld        @t0
add       x
```

add gives precedence to the temp if there is one when it is emitting the ld instruction to make possible the following peephole optimization: A ld from a temp is often preceded by a st into the same temp, in which case the peephole optimizer would emit neither the ld nor the preceding st. For example, if the preceding ld-st sequences were preceded by

```
st        @t0
```

then the peephole optimizer would emit neither the st nor the ld. If, however, add emitted the ld from x rather than @t0, then this optimization would not be possible. That is, if it emitted

```
ld        x
add       @t0
```

```
1   public void peepHole(String op, int opndIndex)
2   {
3       String opnd = st.getSymbol(opndIndex);
4
5       // replace ld with ldc if possible
6       if (opnd is a constant)
7       {
8           if (
9                   current instruction is a ld
10                          and
11                  the constant is in the range 0–4095
12              )
13          {
14              set op to ldc
15              set opnd to st.getdwValue(opndIndex);
16          }
17          else
18              set needsdw to true for the constant
19      }
20
21      // check if okay not to emit current instruction
22      if (
23              previous op is st and current op is ld and operands match
24                                  or
25              current instruction is a st into a temp
26          )
27          don't emit current instruction
28      else
29      {
30          // must emit previous inst if st into temp
31          if previous instruction is st into a temp
32          {
33              emit previous instruction
34              set needsdw to true for temp in previous instruction
35          }
36          emit current instruction
37      }
38
39      // save current instruction
40      previousOp = op;
41      previousOpnd = opnd;
42      previousOpndIndex = opndIndex;
43  }
```

(a)

```
1   public void peephole(String op, String opnd)
2   {
3       if previous instruction st into a temp
4       {
5               emit previous instruction
6               set needsdw to true for temp in previous instruction
7       }
8
```

Figure 20.11.

```
9          emit current instruction
10
11         previousOp = op;
12         previousOpnd = opnd;
13         previousOpndIndex = -1;
14      }
```

(b)

```
1      public void peephole(String op)
2      {
3          peephole(op, "");
4      }
```

(c)

Figure 20.11. *Continued.*

and the `ld` were preceded by

```
       st        @t0
```

all three instructions would be necessary.

When we call `peephole`, we normally pass it a string and an `int` (as on lines 5, 6, 10, and 11 in Figure 20.10a). However, we can also pass `peephole` a string only (as on lines 5 and 7 in Figure 20.10b), or two strings (as on line 6 in Figure 20.10b). Thus, `peephole` must be an overloaded method to accommodate these three variations in arguments.

Figure 20.11a shows the structure of the principal version of `peephole` (the one that has a `String` parameter and an `int` parameter). Before returning to the caller, `peephole` stores the operation, operand, and the operand index of the current instruction in `previousOp`, `previousOpnd`, and `previousOpndIndex`, respectively. Thus, on the next call, `peephole` has access to the instruction passed to it on that call (in `op`, `opnd`, and `opndIndex`) as well as the instruction passed to it on the preceding call (in `previousOp`, `previousOpnd`, and `previousOpndIndex`). In addition to peephole optimization, the `peephole` methods performs the `ldc` optimization. That is, it uses an `ldc` in place of a `ld`, if possible (see lines 6 to 19 in Figure 20.11a).

The structure of the two-string version of `peephole` is given in Figure 20.11b. It is simpler than the version in Figure 20.11a because it is never passed a `st` or `ld` instruction. The one-string version of `peephole` is given in Figure 20.11c. It simply calls the two-string version, passing the null string as the second argument.

You should now do Problem 5 at the end of the chapter [implement R1e by extending R1c (not R1d) so that it performs peephole optimization]. R1e requires three new methods: the three variations of `peephole` that we described above. `emitLoad` from R1c is not needed in R1e because its function is assumed by `peephole` in R1e.

PROBLEMS

1. Implement R1a by extending R1 so that it replaces `ld` with `ldc` wherever possible. Test your compiler with `S1.s`.

2. Implement R1b by extending R1a so that it supports the reuse of temps. Test your compiler with `S1.s`.

3. Implement R1c by extending R1b so that it supports constant folding. Test your compiler with S1.s.

4. Implement R1d by extending R1c so that it supports register allocation. Test your compiler with S1.s.

5. Implement R1e by extending R1c (not R1d) so that it supports peephole optimization. Test your compiler with S1.s

6. Incorporate the following optimizations into the S1 compiler:

   a) Use the pc instruction in place of pwc instruction wherever possible.

   b) Use the p instruction in place of those instances of the pwc instruction not replaced by the pc instruction. For example,

   ```
   pwc        -5
   ```

   should be replaced with

   ```
   p          @_5
   ```

   where @_5 is defined with

   ```
   @_5:       dw          -5
   ```

   c) Constant folding

   Call this compiler S1c.

7. Create a chart that shows the size and execution time of the S1.s program as created by the S1, S1c (see Problem 6), R1, R1a, R1b, R1c, R1d, and R1e compilers. How do the S1 and S1c compilers compare with the register instruction set compilers?

8. Suppose the following code is compiled with a compiler that uses the register allocation technique described in Section 20.5:

   ```
   x = 7;
   while(x - 5)
   {
       x = x - 1;    // ac variable has index of x
   }
   y = x;            // no ld x emitted
   ```

   After the assignment statement in the while loop is compiled , the ac variable used in register allocation will contain the index of x. Thus, the compiler will not emit a ld instruction that loads from x for the assignment statement after the loop (because the ac variable indicates that the value of x is already in the ac register). But will the ac register have the value of x at this point during execution time? Describe how you would modify the register allocation scheme so that ld instructions are emitted whenever they are necessary.

9. In the register instruction set, why is it better to use a ld instruction with a dw than a ldw instruction without a dw? Similarly, in the stack instruction set, why is it better to use a p instruction with a dw than a pwc instruction without a dw?

10. What code is generated by R1c for

    ```
    x = 2 + 3 + y;
    x = 2 + y + 3;
    x = y + 2 + 3;
    ```

11. Extend the constant folding mechanism in R1c so it can fold variables whose values can be determined at compiler time. For example, the assembly code for

```
x = 5;
y = x + 7;
```

should be

```
ldc      5
st       x
ldc      12    ; x and 7 folded to get 12
st       y
```

In this example, the compiler can determine the value of x in the second assignment statement. Thus, it folds this value with 7 to get 12. Call your compiler R1cc. Test your compiler with S1.s. How does it compare with R1c?

12. The code R1d produces for the following program

```
x = 3;
x = x + 5;
```

is

```
ldc      3           ; version 1
st       x
add      @5
st       x
halt
x:       dw           0
@5:      dw           5
```

Because x is assigned the constant 3 before it is used, would it make sense to initialize x to 3 in its dw and then dispense with the instruction that stores into x? If the compiler did this, it would generate

```
ld       x           ; version 2
add      @5
st       x
halt
x:       dw           3
@5:      dw           5
```

Serially reusable code is code that can be used by multiple users as long as one user finishes before the next one starts. A fresh copy of the program does not have to be loaded into memory for each user. Which version above is serially reusable?

In the following problems, the letter in a compiler's name indicates the optimizations supported:

a   use of ldc in place of ld wherever possible
b   a optimizations plus reuse of temps
c   b optimizations plus constant folding
d   c optimizations plus register allocation
e   c optimizations plus peephole optimization

The number in a compiler's name indicates the level of language support. 1, 2, 3, 4, 5, and 6 corresponds to the levels supported by the S1, S2, S3, S4, S5, and S6 compilers, respectively.

13. What assembly code should be generated by R4c for

```
x = 5;
while (x)
{
    x = x - 1;
    y = y + 1;
}
x = y;
do
{
    y = y - 1;
    x = x - 1;
} while (x);
```

14. What assembly code should be generated by R4c for

```
if (x)
    y = 3;
z = y;
if (x)
    y = 4;
else
    x = y;
```

15. What assembly code should be generated by R5c for

```
extern int x, y;
void f()
{
    x = 5;
    g();
    y = x;
}
```

16. Implement R2a, R2b, R2c, R2d, and R2e compilers. Test your compilers with S2.s.

17. Implement R3a, R3b, R3c, R3d, and R3e compilers. Test your compilers with S3.s.

18. Implement R4a, R4b, R4c, R4d, and R4e compilers. Test your compilers with S4.s.

19. Implement R5a, R5b, R5c, R5d, and R5e compilers. Test your compilers with S5a.s and S5b.s.

20. Implement R6a, R6b, R6c, R6d, and R6e compilers. Test your compilers with S6a.s and S6b.s.

21. Why is line 12 in Figure 20.9 executed only for temps?

21

INTERPRETERS

21.1 INTRODUCTION

In Chapter 10, we saw two programs that processed prefix expressions. The first (Figure 10.4) translated the prefix expression in the input to the equivalent postfix expression. The second (Figure 10.10) did something quite different: As it parsed the infix expression in the input, it performed the operations specified by it. We call the former program a compiler—it translates the source program to the target program. We call the latter program an *interpreter*—it performs the operations specified by the source program.

We can easily convert the compilers we have written to interpreters. For example, to convert S1 to an interpreter (which we will call I1), we simply replace actions that generate assembly code with actions that perform the operations specified by the source program. We keep the token manager as is, throw away the code generator, and make a few changes to the parser. We also have to make a slight change to the symbol table. In an interpreter, we use the symbol table to record the current value of each variable. For example, when the I1 interpreter processes the statement

```
x = 5;
```

it first parses it (to determine the type and structure of the statement), and then it performs its operation—it assigns 5 to x. Obviously, the interpreter has to have a slot for x in which it can store 5. A natural place for this slot is the symbol table entry for x. In I1, the symbol table consists of two parallel ArrayLists: `symbol` (to hold the name of a variable) and `value` (to hold its current value).

Whenever we "mentally execute" a program to determine how it works, we are, in effect, interpreting the program. Let us do this for the program in Figure 21.1. We read the first statement and see that it is an assignment statement. We then identify its left and right sides. What have we just done? We have, in effect, parsed the first statement. We then assign 5 to x. That is, we record in our memory or on a piece of paper that x now has the value 5. What have we just done? We have executed the statement. Next, we process the second statement in the same way: We see that it is an assignment statement. We identify its left and right sides. We determine the structure of the expression on the right side. We see that it adds x and 2. We then retrieve the previously recorded value of x, add it and 2 to get 7, which we record in our memory or on a piece of paper as the value of y. Finally, we process the last statement: We see that it is a `println` statement. We identify its argument as y. We then retrieve the previously recorded value of y and announce it as the output produced by the program.

The parsing process we engage in when we mentally execute the program in Figure 21.1 requires a tokenizing subprocess. For example, when we read the `println` statement, we see the sequence of individual letters "p", "r", "i" "n", "t", "l", and "n". We put these letters together to get "println". What have we just done? We have created a token which we then use in the parsing process. Thus, our mental execution of the program in Figure 21.1 involves the tokenizing as well as the parsing and execution of each statement. The I1 interpreter we will write will similarly perform these processes.

Interpreters are inherently inefficient because statements that are executed repeatedly are parsed repeatedly. For example, consider the following program:

```
x = 100;
do
{
  println(x);
  x = x - 1;
} while (x);
```

Because the parser in an interpreter performs the execution of statements, parsing is a necessary step in the execution of a statement. In other words, a statement has to be parsed each time it is executed. Because the statements in the preceding `do-while` loop are executed 100 times, they have to be parsed 100 times as well. In contrast, a compiler would parse them only once. Moreover, with a compiler, the parsing occurs at compile time—not at run time.

To minimize the parsing overhead in an interpreter, the source code can first be translated to an internal code that is particularly well-suited for interpretation. This internal code, rather than the original source code, can be then be interpreted. Statements within loops in this internal code still have to be repeatedly parsed. However, the internal code is so simple that interpreting it can be done quickly. We will call a program of this type a *compiler–interpreter* because it is a combination of a compiler and an interpreter. Its compiler component translates the source code to the internal code; its interpreter component interprets the internal code. We will call the other type of interpreter—the interpreter than interprets the original source code—a *pure interpreter*. Most commercial interpreters are compiler–interpreters, although they are simply called interpreters.

In this chapter, we will implement both pure interpreters and compiler–interpreters. The former will be designated by names that start with "I"; the latter, by names that start with "CI". For example, I1 is the pure interpreter version of the S1 compiler from Chapter 12; CI1 is the compiler–interpreter version of the S1 compiler. Our compiler–interpreters use an internal code that we call *s-code*.

```
x = 5;
y = x + 2;
println(y);
```

Figure 21.1.

The token managers for our interpreters are almost the same as the token managers for their corresponding compilers. For example, we can use `S1TokenMgr`—the token manager for S1—almost as is in the I1 and CI1 interpreters.

Only two changes are required to the compiler token managers to adapt them for use in our interpreters:

1. The token managers for our interpreters should not output the token trace or the the source code to the assembly language output file (the interpreters do not translate the source code to assembly language so there is no assembly language output file).

2. The token managers for our interpreters should return strings without the enclosing quotes and with escape sequences processed. For example, if the source code contains the string `"up\ndown"`, the token manager should return this string without the quotes and with the escape sequence `"\n"` replaced with the newline character.

21.2   CONVERTING S1 TO I1

It is very easy to convert the S1 compiler from Chapter 12 to the pure interpreter I1. We start by copying `S1.java` to `I1.java`, and replacing every occurrence of `"S1"` in `I1.java` with `"I1"`. We then modify `I1.java` as follows.

To execute statements, I1 has to have a slot for each variable into which it can store the variable's value. The simplest way to provide this storage is to extend the symbol table. In I1, the symbol table contains of two parallel ArrayLists, `symbol` and `value`:

```
private ArrayList<String> symbol;
private ArrayList<Integer> value;
```

I1 uses `value` to hold the values of variables whose names are stored in `symbol`. The symbol table also includes an accessor method and a mutator method for `value` (see Figure 21.2) and an `enter` method. When called, `enter` is passed a symbol in `String` form. It enters the symbol into the `symbol` ArrayList if it is not already there. It then returns the index of the symbol in the `symbol` ArrayList.

The parser for I1 performs actions where S1 outputs assembly code. For example, wherever S1 emits a push instruction, I1 has to perform a push operation. Thus, the parser in I1 needs a stack. Rather than write the code that implements a stack, we can simply create a stack in the parser with

```
s = new Stack<Integer>();
```

```
public Integer getValue(int index)
{
   return value.get(index);
}
public void setValue(int index, Integer v)
{
   value.set(index, v);
}
```

Figure 21.2.

where s is an instance variable in the parser defined with

```
private Stack<Integer> s;
```

Stack is a predefined class in the java.util package.

Now let us look at some of the code in S1 and its corresponding code in I1. The code in S1 for an unsigned integer constant in the factor method is

```
case UNSIGNED:
        t = currentToken;
        consume(UNSIGNED);
        cg.emitInstruction("pwc", t.image);
        break;
```

After parsing the unsigned integer, it emits an pwc instruction, which, when executed, pushes the constant on the stack of the J1 computer. The corresponding code in I1 does exactly the same thing except that it pushes the constant on its own stack at compile time rather than generate an assembler instruction to do it at execution time:

```
case UNSIGNED:
        t = currentToken;
        consume(UNSIGNED);
        s.push(Integer.parseInt(t.image));
        break;
```

The code for termList in S1 emits an add assembler instruction:

```
1 private void termList()
2 {
3   switch(currentToken.kind)
4   {
5     case PLUS:
6       consume(PLUS);
7       term();
8       cg.emitInstruction("add");
9       termList();
10      break;
11    case RIGHTPAREN:
12    case SEMICOLON:
13      ;
14      break;
15    default:
16      throw genEx("Expecting \"+\", \")\", or \";\"");
17  }
18 }
```

The corresponding code in I1 performs the add by popping the parser's stack twice, adding, and pushing the result back on the stack:

```
1 private void termList()
2 {
```

```
 3    int right;
 4
 5    switch(currentToken.kind)
 6    {
 7      case PLUS:
 8        consume(PLUS);
 9        term();
10        right = s.pop();
11        s.push(s.pop() + right);
12        termList();
13        break;
14      case RIGHTPAREN:
15      case SEMICOLON:
16        ;
17        break;
18      default:
19        throw genEx("Expecting \"+\", \")\", or \";\"");
20    }
21 }
```

Thus, when I1 completes the parsing of an expression, the expression's value will be on top of the parser's stack.

The code in S1 for the assignment statement emits a `pc-stav` assembly sequence:

```
 1 private void assignmentStatement()
 2 {
 3    Token t;
 4
 5    t = currentToken;
 6    consume(ID);
 7    st.enter(t.image);
 8    cg.emitInstruction("pc", t.image);
 9    consume(ASSIGN);
10    expr();
11    cg.emitInstruction("stav");
12    consume(SEMICOLON);
13 }
```

The corresponding code in I1 performs the assignment by popping stack and storing the value so obtained in the variable specified by the left side of the statement:

```
 1 private void assignmentStatement()
 2 {
 3    Token t;
 4    int left, expVal;
 5
 6    t = currentToken;
 7    consume(ID);
 8    left = st.enter(t.image);
 9    consume(ASSIGN);
10    expr();
```

```
11    st.setValue(left, s.pop());
12    consume(SEMICOLON);
13 }
```

To perform the store, I1 uses the mutator method `setValue` in the symbol table (see Figure 21.2). The `expr` method in I1 does not generate assembly code to evaluate the corresponding expression. Instead, it evaluates the expression using the parser's stack. Thus, the value of the expression will be on top of the parser's stack when the `setValue` method is called in the preceding code.

As the preceding examples illustrate, a few simple transformations will convert the S1 parser to the I1 parser. I1 does not generate any code. Thus, it does not need a code generator.

To use our I1 interpreter, we first have to compile it:

```
javac I1.java
```

We can then execute it, at which time it displays the output of the program it is interpreting. For example, to interpret the S1.s source program, enter

```
java I1 S1
```

The interpreter responds with

```
I1 interpreter written by ...
4107
4107
```

The two lines containing `4107` are the output produced by the S1.s program as I1 interprets it.

21.3 INTERPRETING STATEMENTS THAT TRANSFER CONTROL

The I4 interpreter (the interpreter that corresponds to the S4 compiler) has to handle statements that transfer control, such as the `while`, `do-while`, and `if` statements. These statements require special treatment. To see why, consider what the I4 interpreter must do when it interprets the following statement:

```
while (x + 3)
    x = x - 1;
```

Because a `while` loop has a leading exit test, the parser has to jump over the body of the loop when the exit test expression evaluates to false (i.e., zero). The only way for the parser to accurately jump over the loop body is to parse it (how else could it determine where the loop body ends?). But when it parses the loop body, it also executes it. Thus, it executes the loop body *after* the loop exit has occurred.

There are three solutions for this problem:

1. We can design our source language so that the subparts of its control structures are bracketed with special symbols so that the ends of these subparts can be accurately

identified *without* parsing. For example, suppose we require that the body of a while loop be a compound statement. Then, it would necessarily start with a left brace and end with a matching right brace. With this structure, an interpreter can identify the end of the loop body simply by advancing in the token stream until it detects the matching right brace.

2. We can design our interpreter to have two modes of operation: execute mode or no-execute mode. When the interpreter has to advance in the token stream but not execute the code it is parsing, it places itself in the no-execute mode, and parses up to the desired point in the token stream. It then places itself back in the execute mode. Although this approach is simple in concept, its implemention is somewhat messy. For example, consider the whileStatement method in Figure 21.3. The do-while that starts on line 11 repeatedly parses and executes a while loop. When the value of the exit test expression is zero, the parser should advance over the while loop body without executing it. It does this by setting the exMode flag to false on line 16. Then when the loop body is parsed on line 17, it is not executed (because exMode is false).

3. Use a compiler–interpreter rather than a pure interpreter (see Section 21.4).

21.4 IMPLEMENTING THE COMPILER-INTERPRETER CI1

Pure interpreters have the drawback of excessive parser overhead because statements that are executed repeatedly are necessarily parsed repeatedly. Moreover, as we pointed out in Section 21.3, control structures are difficult to handle unless the source language is designed in a special way. A better approach is to first translate the source program to an internal code that can be interpreted quickly, and then to interpret this internal code. The CI1 compiler–interpreter takes this approach. We call the internal code that

```
1    private void whileStatement()
2    {
3        Token t;
4
5        consume(WHILE);
6        consume(LEFTPAREN);
7
8        // save this position in token chain
9        t = currentToken;
10       boolean exModeSave = exMode;
11       do
12       {
13           currentToken = t;    // reset position in chain
14           expr();
15           consume(RIGHTPAREN);
16           if (exMode && s.pop() == 0) exMode = false;
17           statement();
18       } while (exMode);
19       exMode = exModeSave;  // reset exMode
20   }
```

Figure 21.3.

the Cl1 compiler uses *s-code*. It is the machine language for a simple stack machine we call the *s-machine*.

Cl1 does not first translate the source program to assembly language, and then translate the assembly language to s-code. Instead, it translates the source program directly to s-code. s-code consists of a sequence of integers. s-code instructions that consist of just an opcode are single integers. s-code instructions that consist of an opcode and an operand are two consecutive integers.

The code generator for Cl1 emits s-code to an internal ArrayList named `scode`—not to an external file. After the parser finishes parsing the source program, it calls the `interpret` method in the code generator. This method interprets the s-code in the `scode` ArrayList. `interpret` uses a stack `s` to hold values during the execution of the s-code. It also uses an `int` array `vtab`. `vtab` provides storage for each variable in the source program. Each slot in `vtab` corresponds to one variable. Operand addresses in s-code are indices into `vtab`. For example, the s-code instruction 12 5 is a push instruction. 12 is the opcode for `push`. 5 is the address of the variable to be pushed, that is, it is the `vtab` index of the variable to be pushed.

The size of `vtab` should equal the number of variables in the source program. Because this size is not known until the parse is done, the creation of `vtab` has to be deferred until then. The `parse()` method in the parser first calls `program()`, which parses the source program and creates the s-code (see Figure 21.4). It then calls `makevtab` in the code generator, passing it the size of the symbol table (which equals the number of variables in the source program). Finally, it calls `interpret` in the code generator in the code generator to interpret the s-code created by the parser.

Let us now examine the `interpret` method in the code generator for Cl1 (see Figure 21.5). The `interpret` method contains a `do-while` loop, each iteration of which executes one instruction of s-code. It starts by accessing the opcode of the next instruction:

```
·34        opcode = scode.get(pc++);
```

pc acts as a program counter. That is, it points to the instruction to be executed next. Each time an instruction is executed, `pc` is incremented by the size of that instruction. The `switch` statement that starts on line 37 identifies the opcode and performs the corresponding operations. For example, if the opcode is PLUS, then the `switch` statement executes the following case:

```
45        case PLUS:
46          right = s.pop();
47          s.push(s.pop() + right);
48          break;
```

```
1 public void parse()
2 {
3    program();
4    cg.makevtab(st.getSize());
5    cg.interpret();
6 }
```

Figure 21.4.

```
 1 class CI1CodeGen implements CI1Constants
 2 {
 3   private ArrayList<Integer> scode;        // holds s-code
 4   private Stack<Integer> s;    // stack used by s-machine
 5   int[] vtab;                          // table for variables
 6   private int pc;     // program ctr (index of next inst)
 7   private int opcode;    // opcode of current instruction
 8
 9   public CI1CodeGen()
10   {
11     scode = new ArrayList<Integer>();
12     s = new Stack<Integer>();
13     pc = 0; // start executing scode at index 0 in scode
14   }
15   //----------------------
16   public void emit(int inst)
17   {
18     scode.add(inst);            // emit instruction to scode
19   }
20   //----------------------
21   public void makevtab(int size)
22   {
23     vtab = new int[ size] ;   // create table for variables
24   }
25   //----------------------
26   public void interpret() // interprets s-code in scode
27   {
28     boolean doAgain = true;
29     int right;
30
31     do
32     {
33       // fetch the opcode of the next instruction
34       opcode = scode.get(pc++);
35
36       // decode opcode and execute instruction
37       switch(opcode)
38       {
39         case PRINTLN:
40           System.out.println(s.pop());
41           break;
42         case ASSIGN:
43           vtab[ scode.get(pc++)] = s.pop();
44           break;
45         case PLUS:
46           right = s.pop();
47           s.push(s.pop() + right);
48           break;
49         case TIMES:
50           right = s.pop();
51           s.push(s.pop() * right);
52           break;
53         case PUSHCONSTANT:
```

Figure 21.5.

```
54              s.push(scode.get(pc++));
55              break;
56           case PUSH:
57              s.push(vtab[ scode.get(pc++)] );
58              break;
59           case HALT:
60              doAgain = false;
61              break;
62           default:
63              doAgain = false;
64              break;
65        }
66     } while (doAgain);
67   }
68 }                                // end of CI1CodeGen class
```

Figure 21.5. *Continued.*

This case functions just like the add instruction in the stack instruction set: It pops the top two values from the stack, adds them, and pushes their sum. If the opcode is PUSH, then the switch executes the following case:

```
56           case PUSH:
57              s.push(vtab[ scode.get(pc++)] );
58              break;
```

Line 57 accesses the second integer of the instruction. This integer is the index of the variable to be pushed. It is used to index into vtab to the access the value of the corresponding variable. This value is then pushed onto the stack. Notice line 57 increments pc, making pc point to the beginning of the next instruction. Thus, the next time the switch statement is executed, pc will have the scode index of the next instruction. The constants in the switch statement (PRINTLN, ASSIGN, PLUS, etc.) are defined in the CI1constants interface.

The parser emits code by calling the emit method in the code generator:

```
16   public void emit(int inst)
17   {
18     scode.add(inst);           // emit instruction to scode
19   }
```

For example, if the current token is an unsigned integer, the factor method executes

```
case UNSIGNED:
   t = currentToken;
   consume(UNSIGNED);
   cg.emit(PUSHCONSTANT);
   cg.emit(Integer.parseInt(t.image));
   break;
```

It calls emit twice, once passing it PUSHCONSTANT (the opcode for the push constant s-code instruction) and once passing it the integer itself (the push constant instruction is a two-integer instruction). interpret executes it with

```
53          case PUSHCONSTANT:
54              s.push(scode.get(pc++));
55              break;
```

This code accesses the integer that follows the opcode and pushes it onto the stack.

The translation of source code to s-code in CI1 is easy. However, it is more complicated in CI4, the version that supports the `if` statement and loops. The added complexity comes from the transfer of control these statements trigger. For example, consider the method for the `do-while` loop in CI4 (see Figure 21.6).

Line 5 consumes the keyword `do`. Line 6 then saves the current `scode` address by storing it in the variable `address`. This address is provided by the `getCurrentAddress` method, and is equal to the current size of the `scode` ArrayList. At the bottom of the loop, a `JNZ` instruction is emitted that transfers control when executed to the address saved by line 6.

As we add support for new statements in the source language, we have to add new instructions to our s-machine to handle these new source instructions. CI4 requires the following s-code instruction in addition to those in CI1:

PRINT	pop and display the top of the stack
MINUS	double pop, subtract, and push result
DIVIDE	double pop, divide, and push result
READ	read an integer from the keyboard
DUPE	duplicate the value on top of the stack
PRINTSTRING	display string specified by the given index
NEWLINE	moves cursor to the beginning of the next line
NEG	negate the value on top of the stack
JA	jump always
JZ	pop stack and jump if zero
JNZ	pop stack and jump if non-zero

The READ operation should recover from an invalid input. Specifically, if the user enters a noninteger in response to a read, the READ operation should prompt the user to reenter

```
1     private void doWhileStatement()
2     {
3       int address;
4
5       consume(DO);
6       address = cg.getCurrentAddress();
7       statement();
8       consume(WHILE);
9       consume(LEFTPAREN);
10      expr();
11      cg.emit(JNZ);
12      cg.emit(address);
13      consume(RIGHTPAREN);
14      consume(SEMICOLON);
15    }
```

Figure 21.6.

and then read again from the keyboard. It should continue this process until the user enters a valid integer.

When CI4 parses a string, it enters it into stab, a String ArrayList in the code generator. The address of a string that appears in s-code is its index in stab. For example, consider the printArg() method in CI4 (see Figure 21.7). When it parses a string, it enters it into stab by calling the enterString method (line 11). enterString returns the index of the string just entered into stab. printArg then emits a PRINTSTRING instruction, consisting of its opcode (line 12) and the index of the string to be displayed (line 13).

21.5 ADVANTAGES OF INTERPRETERS

Interpreters have three advantages over compilers:

1. They are easier to write because you do not have to know the details of the machine on which they run. In contrast, to write a compiler, you have to know the details of the assembly and/or machine language of the target machine.

2. Interpreters are portable. For example, our I1 interpreter will run as is on any computer that supports Java, which is just about every computer there is. A compiler, however, typically will produce target code for only the target machine for which the compiler is designed. For example, if you have a C compiler that runs on a

```
1 private void printArg()
2 {
3    Token t;
4    int sindex;
5
6    switch(currentToken.kind)
7    {
8      case STRING:
9        t = currentToken;
10       consume(STRING);
11       sindex = cg.enterString(t.image);
12       cg.emit(PRINTSTRING);
13       cg.emit(sindex);
14       break;
15     case LEFTPAREN:
16     case UNSIGNED:
17     case PLUS:
18     case MINUS:
19     case ID:
20       expr();
21       cg.emit(PRINT);
22       break;
23     default:
24       throw genEx("Expecting expression or string");
25   }
26 }
```

Figure 21.7.

Macintosh that generates machine code for a Macintosh, you cannot run the machine code it generates on other types of computers.

3. It is easy to write an interpreter that produces meaningful error messages. Pure interpreters directly execute the source code. Thus, if an error occurs, an interpreter can easily identify and display the line in source code in which the error occurred.

The big disadvantage of interpreters is inefficiency. An interpreted program will typically run ten times slower than a comparable compiled program. This inefficiency is the result of the parsing that occurs during execution of an interpreted program. Compiler–interpreters minimize this inefficiency, but it is still significant for two reasons:

1. Compiler–interpreters require time to perform the initial compile. In contrast, compiled code can be executed immediately.

2. The execution of each s-code instruction requires the execution of multiple machine instructions in the computer on which the interpreter is running. For example, the execution of the `push` s-code instruction requires the execution of

```
case PUSH:
    s.push(vtab[ scode.get(pc++)] );
    break;
```

But each one of these Java statements requires the execution of multiple machine instructions in the computer which is running the CI1 program. In contrast, a push instruction in compiled code requires the execution of just itself—of just one instruction.

PROBLEMS

1. Why do interpreters but not compilers have to process escape sequences?

2. Why is it not good if a compiler–interpreter uses a very low-level internal code?

3. Evaluate the merits of this approach to interpreter design: Use an internal code that is only a slightly modified version of the source code. Only those components of the source code that have substantial structural complexity and, therefore, would require a substantial amount of time to parse should be translated to a form easier to interpret. For example, we might use an internal code that has the same form as the source code except that arithmetic expressions are replaced with their postfix equivalents.

4. Implement I1 (the interpreter version of S1). Test your program with `S1.s`

5. Implement I2 (the interpreter version of S2). Test your program with `S2.s`

6. Implement I3 (the interpreter version of S3). Test your program with `S3.s`.

7. Implement I4 (the interpreter version of S4). Test your program with `S4.s`.

8. Implement CI1 (the compiler–interpreter version of S1). Test your program with `S1.s`.

9. Implement CI2 (the compiler–interpreter version of S2). Test your program with `S2.s`.

10. Implement CI3 (the compiler–interpreter version of S3). Test your program with `S3.s`.

11. Implement CI4 (the compiler–interpreter version of S4). Test your program with `S4.s`.

12. Run both I4 and CI4 on a program that contains a loop that iterates many times. Is there a difference in execution time?

13. If we limited the integer variables in our source programs to a single lower-case letter followed by an optional single digit, how could we improve the run time of our interpreters? Note: the BASIC programming language limited its variables in this way

14. Run I4 on a program that contains a loop that iterates many times. Compile the program with S4. Run the compiled program. How does the run time for I4 compare with the run time for the compiled program? Why are the results of this test not a reliable measure of the relative run times of interpreted versus compiled code?

15. Why is `exMode` saved and then restored in the `whileStatement` method in Figure 21.3?

22

BOTTOM-UP PARSING

22.1 INTRODUCTION

In top-down parsing, we start at the top of the parse tree (with the start symbol), and we end up at the bottom of the parse tree (with the terminal string). In bottom-up parsing, we do the reverse: we start at the bottom of the parse tree and end up at the top.

Bottom-up parsing is more powerful than top-down parsing. That is, bottom-up parsing works with a larger variety of grammars than top-down parsing. For example, bottom-up parsers can use left-recursive as well as right-recursive grammars. In contrast, top-down parsers can use right-recursive but not left-recursive grammars. Bottom-up parsers, however, do have a major disadvantage: they are more complex than top-down parsers. In fact, bottom-up parsers are so complex that it is, in general, not practical to build them by hand. We can, however, use a parser generator to build them for us.

Although bottom-up parsing is more powerful than top-down parsing, it is not the case that we should always use bottom-up parsing. In most cases, top-down parsing is powerful enough to get the job done. Thus, the additional power of bottom-up parsing does not always provide any advantage.

In this chapter, we will learn how bottom-up parsers work, and how to build them by hand. Then in the next chapter we will learn how use build them with a parser generator.

22.2 PRINCIPLES OF BOTTOM-UP PARSING

Let us perform a bottom-up parse using the following grammar:

G22.1
1. S → BC
2. B → b
3. C → c

Figure 22.1 shows the bottom-up parse of bc, the only string that G22.1 generates. The symbols in this terminal string (i.e., b and c) will become the leaf nodes of the parse tree will we construct. Because we scan bc left to right, the current token (marked with a "^") is initially b (Figure 22.1a). This b results from the application of production B → b in G22.1. Accordingly, we add a B node that generates this b to the tree we are constructing (Figure 22.1b). Next, we advance in the input string so that c becomes the current token (Figure 22.1c). This c results from the application of the production C → c. So we add a C node that generates this c (Figure 22.1.d). At this point, we have two nonterminals, B and C. They obviously come the application of the production S → BC. So we add an S node that generates the B and C (Figure 22.1e). At this point, the parse is done: The tree generates the entire input string, and its top node is the start symbol of the grammar.

In the bottom-up parse in Figure 22.1, we use the productions of the grammar in this order:

B → b
C → c
S → BC

If we use these productions in reverse order, starting from S, we get the get the rightmost derivation of bc:

S ⇒ BC ⇒ Bc ⇒ bc

This is no accident. Bottom-up parsing always uncovers a rightmost derivation of the terminal string, but in reverse order. If the grammar is unambiguous, then there is only one parse tree for any terminal string defined by the grammar, and therefore, only one rightmost derivation. Thus, for unambiguous grammars, we can say that bottom-up parsing uncovers *the* rightmost derivation rather that *a* rightmost derivation.

If we use a stack, we can perform a bottom-up parse without building a parse tree. In this approach, we shift the characters in the input string one by one onto the stack. Whenever both of the following two conditions hold during this shifting process, we replace the symbols on top of the stack corresponding to the right side of the production with the left side of that production.

Condition 1: The top symbol or symbols match the right side of a production.

Condition 2: The production is the one used to generate the symbol (or symbols) on top of the stack in a rightmost derivation of the input string.

Using this approach, let us perform the bottom-up parse of bc using G22.1 (see Figure 22.2). We start with an empty stack (line 1). Recall that $ and # are the bottom-of-stack and end-of-input markers, respectively. We shift b onto the stack to get line 3. Note that

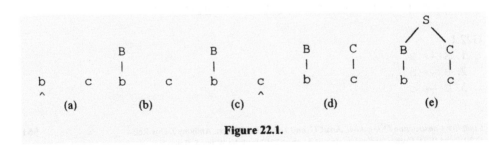

Figure 22.1.

1. b (the symbol on the top of the stack) is the right side of production 2 (i.e., condition 1 holds).

2. Production 2 is the production used that generates this b in the rightmost derivation of the input string (i.e., condition 2 holds).

We replace b (the right side of production 2) with B (the left side of production 2) to get line 5. We say that we are "reducing by production 2," and designate this operation with reduce(2). We call the symbol or symbols we replace on top of the stack when we reduce a *handle,* and the production used in the reduce operation the *handle production.* Using this terminology, we can concisely describe the steps in a bottom-up parse:

> Shift the input string onto the stack. Whenever during this shifting process a handle appears on top of the stack, reduce it using the handle production.

Continuing with our parse in Figure 22.2, we shift c onto the stack to get line 7. c is a handle so we reduce by production 3, resulting in BC on top of the stack (line 9). BC is also a handle, so we reduce by production 1, at which point S is on top of the stack (line 11), and the parse ends.

Recall that a sentential form is any string (not necessarily terminal) that can be derived from the start symbol of a grammar that can ultimately yield a terminal string. A right sentential form is any sentential form in a rightmost derivation. For example, in the rightmost derivation of bc using G22.1,

$$S \Rightarrow BC \Rightarrow Bc \Rightarrow bc$$

S, BC, Bc, and bc are all right sentential forms.

If for every line in a bottom-up parse we concatenate the stack symbols with the remaining input, we will get all the right sentential forms in the derivation of the input string. For example, if we concatenate the stack-input components of each line in the parse in Figure 22.2, we get

bc (line 1)
bc (line 3)
Bc (line 5)

	Stack	Operation	Input	
1	$		bc#	
2		shift		
3	$b		c#	(b is a handle at this point)
4		reduce(2)		
5	$B		c#	
6		shift		
7	$Bc		#	(c is a handle at this point)
8		reduce(3)		
9	$BC		#	(BC is a handle at this point)
10		reduce(1)		
11	$S		#	
12		accept		

Figure 22.2.

Bc (line 7)
BC (line 9)
S (line 11)

We get repeats whenever we shift in the parse. Eliminating the repeats, we get the following sequence of strings:

bc
Bc
BC
S

These strings are precisely all the right sentential forms in the rightmost derivation of bc.

Remember before you can reduce in a bottom-up parse, both condition 1 and 2 given above must hold. Consider, for example, the grammar

G22.2
   1. S → cS
   2. S → c

Using this grammar, let us parse cc (see Figure 22.3). We first shift the initial c. c is the right side of production 2, but the c on the stack is not a handle. The initial c in our input strings comes from production 1 and not production 2, as the rightmost derivation of cc demonstrates:

S ⇒ cS ⇒ cc

————— this c comes from production 1

The initial c by itself is not a handle because it does not satisfy condition 2. So we continue shifting. We get cc on the stack (line 5). The second c, in contrast to the first c, is a handle corresponding to production 2:

S ⇒ cS ⇒ cc

————— this c comes from production 2

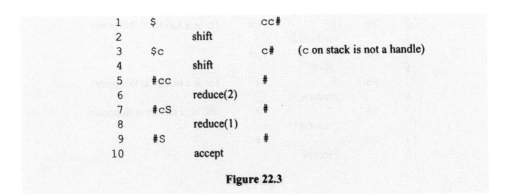

1	$		cc#	
2		shift		
3	$c		c#	(c on stack is not a handle)
4		shift		
5	#cc		#	
6		reduce(2)		
7	#cS		#	
8		reduce(1)		
9	#S		#	
10		accept		

Figure 22.3

So we reduce by production 2 to get cS on the stack (line 7). cS is a handle corresponding to production 1. So we reduce by production 1 to get S on the stack (line 9).

22.3   PARSING WITH RIGHT- VERSUS LEFT-RECURSIVE GRAMMARS

We learned in Chapter 7 that top-down parsing can use right-recursive grammars but not left-recursive grammars. Bottom-up parsing, however, can use either right-recursive or left-recursive grammars. For example, the parse in Figure 22.3 uses the right-recursive grammar G22.2. A left-recursive grammar that is equivalent to G22.2 is

G22.3
  1. S → Sc
  2. S → c

Here is the derivation of cc using this grammar:

S ⇒ Sc ⇒ cc

———— this c comes from production 2

Notice that the initial c comes from production 2. Thus, this c is a handle corresponding to production 2. Accordingly, the parse of cc using G22.3 immediately reduces after shifting the initial c onto the stack (see Figure 22.4).

For both grammars, the parser shifts twice and reduces twice. However, the order is different. With the right-recursive grammar, the two shifts occur first, then the two reduces. With the left recursive grammar, the parser alternates shifting and reducing. Which grammar is better for bottom-up parsing? The parsers for both grammars do the same about of work: one shift and one reduce for each c in the input string. However, they differ with respect to the maximum stack size. In the right-recursive case, the parser pushes the entire input string onto the stack before is reduces. The maximum stack size is equal to the size of the input string. Because there is no upper limit on the size of the input string, there is no upper limit on stack size required to parse strings. In the left-recursive case, the parser alternates shifting with reducing. Thus, the stack size never exceeds 2 regardless of the length of the input string. Although the work both parsers do is the same, the left-recursive parser is better because we do not have to worry about a possible stack overflow.

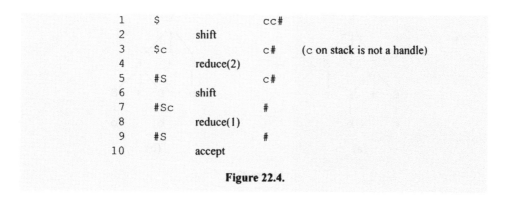

1	$		cc#	
2		shift		
3	$c		c#	(c on stack is not a handle)
4		reduce(2)		
5	#S		c#	
6		shift		
7	#Sc		#	
8		reduce(1)		
9	#S		#	
10		accept		

Figure 22.4.

> **For bottom-up parsing, left-recursive grammars are better than right-re-cursive grammars.**

Of course, we also have to consider other factors when designing the grammar. For example, a left-recursive grammar that generates a list of operands usually implies left associativity; a right-recursive grammar implies right associativity. Thus, the associativity we want would determine the type of grammar to use.

22.4   BOTTOM-UP PARSING WITH AMBIGUOUS GRAMMARS

If a grammar is ambiguous, then there necessarily is at least one string with more than one parse tree. For example, in the following grammar, two parse trees exists for the string b+b+b (see Figure 22.5):

G22.4
    1. E → E + E
    2. E → b

The parse tree in Figure 22.5a implies left associativity (i.e., the operations are performed left to right). The parse tree in Figure 22.5b implies right associativity (i.e., the operations are performed right to left).

Because there are two parse trees for b+b+b, there must be a choice at some point in the bottom-up parse of b+b+b. One alternative will lead to the tree in Figure 22.5a. The other alternative will lead to the tree in Figure 22.5b. Let us look at the parse of b+b+b in Figure 22.6. Up to line 11, there is no choice in the operations that the bottom-up parser performs. However, on line 11, there is a choice between shift and reduce. We call this situation a *shift/reduce conflict.* If the parser reduces at this point, it, in effect, creates a new E node whose children are the symbols on the stack on line 11. These stack symbols come from the initial b+b in the input string. This structure is in the parse tree in Figure 22.5a. It implies that the left addition is performed before the right addition. If, however, the parser chooses shift on line 11, then the reduce on 17b in Figure 22.6 creates a new node whose children make up the b+b substring at the end of the input string. This structure is in the parse tree in Figure 22.5b. It implies that the right addition is performed before the left addition.

In the first case (when the parser reduces on line 11), the parser reduces the left operator first (on line 12a), then the right operator (on line 20a). In the second case (when the parser shifts on line 11), it reduces the right operator first (on line 18b), then the left oper-

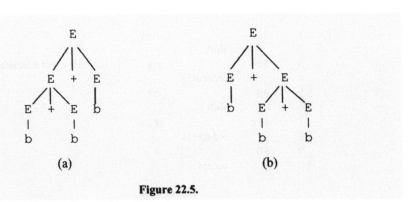

Figure 22.5.

1	$		b+b+b#
2		shift	
3	$b		+b+b#
4		reduce(2)	
5	$E		+b+b#
6		shift	
7	$E+		b+b#
8		shift	
9	$E+b		+b#
10		reduce(2)	
11	$E+E		+b#

———————————— Shift/reduce conflict at this point ————————————

choose reduce				choose shift			
12a		reduce(1)		12b		shift	
13a	$E		+b#	13b	$E+E+		b#
14a		shift		14b		shift	
15a	$E+		b#	15b	$E+E+b		#
16a		shift		16b		reduce(2)	
17a	$E+b		#	17b	$E+E+E		#
18a		reduce(2)		18b		reduce(1)	
19a	$E+E		#	19b	$E+E		#
20a		reduce(1)		20b		reduce(1)	
21a	$E		#	21b	$E		#
22a		accept		22b		accept	

Figure 22.6

ator (on line 20b). In the first case, we get a parse tree (Figure 22.5a) that implies the additions are performed left to right. In the second case, we get a parse tree (Figure 22.5b) that implies that the additions are performed right to left. From this example, we can formulate the following principle, which we call the *reduce-order principle:*

The order in which operators are reduced determines the order in which their corresponding operations are performed.

Suppose we add the production E → E * E to G22.3. With this new grammar, we can get four types of shift/reduce conflicts illustrated by the following configuations:

1. Parsing b+b+b, and the parser is in the configuration

   $E+E   +b#

2. Parsing b* b* b, and the parser is in the configuration

   $E* E   * b#

3. Parsing b* b+b, and the parser is in the configuration

   $E* E   +b#

4. Parsing b+b* b, and the parser is in the configuration

   $E+E   * b$

Assume that we want the normal associativity and precedence for addition and multiplication and higher precedence for multiplication than addition. What should the parser do in the preceding configurations? The reduce-order principle tells us we should reduce the operators in the order in which their operations should be performed. Thus, for cases 1, 2, and 3, the parser should resolve the shift/reduce conflict in favor of the reduce so the left operator is reduced first. In case 4, it should shift so that the right operator will be reduced first.

If we use the right grammar, we can avoid shift/reduce conflicts altogether. For example, if in place of G22.4 we use

G22.5

   1. E → E + b
   2. E → b

then the parse of b+b+b produces no shift/reduce conflicts. This grammar, itself, implies left associativity. Recall from Section 4.3 that a left-recursive production like production 1 in G22.5 implies left associativity. Thus, this grammar does not have the ambiguity that G22.4 has with respect to operator associativity.

Exercise 22.2

Draw the parse tree for b+b+b using G22.5. Show its bottom-up parse.

Answer:

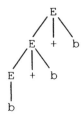

1	$		b+b+b#
2		shift	
3	$b		+b+b#
4		reduce(2)	
5	$E		+b+b#
6		shift	
7	$E+		b+b#
8		shift	
9	$E+b		+b#
10		reduce(1)	
11	$E		+b#
12		shift	
13	$E+		b#
14		shift	
15	$E+b		#
16		reduce(1)	
17	$E		#
18		accept	

Unfortunately, a simple grammar that does not produce any shift/reduce conflicts is not always available. The classic example of this is the if statement. Here is the standard grammar for an if statement:

```
ifStatement  →  "if" "(" expr ")" statement elsePart
elsePart     →  "else" statement
elsePart     →  λ
```

With this grammar, two parse trees exist for

```
if (a) if (b) c = 1; else d = 1;
```

In one parse tree, the else associates with the inner if. In the other, the else associates with the initial if. When else is the current input in a bottom-up parse of this input string, a shift/reduce conflict occurs. If the parser reduces at this point, it replaces

```
if (b) c = 1;
```

with the ifStatement production, making the inner if is a simple if statement rather than an if-else statement. Thus, a reduce at this point has the effect of associating the else with the initial if. If, instead, the parser shifts, the else associates with the inner if. Typically, we want the else to associate with the inner if. Thus, the parser should resolve this shift/reduce conflict in favor of a shift.

22.5 DO-NOT-REDUCE RULE

As we observed in Section 22.2, every configuration in a bottom-up parse corresponds to a right sentential form in the derivation of the input string. For example, consider the parse of bc using G22.1 in Figure 22.7. If for each line we concatenate the stack symbols with the remaining input, we get the following sequence of strings (with repeats omitted):

```
bc, Bc, BC, S
```

Here is the rightmost derivation of the input string bc:

$$S \Rightarrow BC \Rightarrow Bc \Rightarrow bc$$

1	$		bc#
2		shift	
3	$b		c#
4		reduce(2)	
5	$B		c#
6		shift	
7	$Bc		#
8		reduce(3)	
9	$BC		#
10		reduce(1)	
11	$S		#
		accept	

Figure 22.7.

Notice that its sentential forms are precisely the sequence of strings above, but in reverse order.

Suppose the current configuration in a bottom-up parse is

$\$\alpha\cdot$ $w\#$

where α and $\cdot$ strings over the total alphabet of the grammar and w, the remaining input, is a terminal string. If the parser reduces with the production

$B \rightarrow \alpha\cdot$

we get the configuration

$\$\alpha B$ $w\#$

The corresponding right sentential form we get by concatenating the stack part with the input part is

αBw

Because the first symbol in w follows B in this sentential form, this symbol must be in the FOLLOW set of B (see Section 7.4). For example, on line 3 in Figure 22.7, we reduce by the production $B \rightarrow b$. The right sentential form for the new configuration that results is Bc. Because Bc is necessarily a sentential form, c—the first symbol in the remaining input—is necessarily in the FOLLOW set of B.

Now suppose the current input is not in the FOLLOW set of the left side of some production. If the parser were to reduce using that production, it would result in a configuration that is not a right sentential form. Thus, to reduce by that production could not possibly be a correct step in a bottom-up parse. This observation gives us the following *do-not-reduce rule:*

> **Do not reduce by a production if the current input is not in the FOL-LOW set of the production's left side.**

22.6 SLR(1) PARSING

We now describe a specific algorithm for bottom-up parsing that is called SLR(1) parsing. The letters "S", "L", and "R", and the number 1, respectively, stand for

Simple because this parsing algorithm is simple relative to a more general technique we will study in the next section.

Left because the input is scanned left to right.

Rightmost because this parsing algorithm uncovers the rightmost derivation of the input string.

One token lookahead because the parsing actions depend on one input symbol, namely, the current token symbol, as well as the top of the stack.

How does a bottom-up parser know when it should reduce? One approach would be for the parser to examine the top of the stack and the symbols below it to determine if it contains a handle. But to examine multiple symbols on the stack would be complex and time-consuming. Here is a better approach: whenever the parser has to push a grammatical symbol onto the stack, it pushes instead a state that represents not only the grammatical symbol but what is currently on the stack. With this approach, the parser uses a stack that initially contains the state 0:

$0

The state 0 represents the empty stack. Suppose the parser has to shift b onto the stack. It would, instead, push a state that not only represents the b but also indicates what is below the b on the stack. Let us say our parser uses state 1 to indicate a b on top of stack that otherwise is empty. Then at this point, it would push 1 to get

$01

Suppose the parser now has to shift c onto the stack. It would push a state (assume it is state 2) onto the stack that represents the c on top of a b:

$012

Suppose the parser now has to shift d onto the stack. It would push a state (assume it is state 3) that represents a d on top of a c on top of a b:

$0123

Suppose the parser now has to reduce by the production

B → cd

The parser would first pop the top two symbols (these symbols—23—represent cd, the right side of the reducing production) and then push B, the left side of the production. But instead of pushing B, it would push a state (assume it is state 4) that represents a B on top of state 1, that is, a B on top of a b:

$014

With this approach, the state of top of the stack provides the parser with the information it needs about the contents of the stack. Thus, the parser never has to look below the top of the stack.

The state on the top of the stack does not have to represent the entire stack. It need represent only those aspects of the stack that the parsers needs to know to make its parsing decisions.

When a state is on top of the stack, we say the parser is "in that state." For example, when the state contains

$014

we say the parser is in state 4.

To determine the stack states needed for a given grammar, we construct a finite automaton (FA) based on the grammar. The states of this finite automaton are the states the parser pushes onto the stack during a bottom-up parse. Let us construct the required finite automaton for the following grammar:

G22.6
- 1. S → BC
- 2. B → bB
- 3. B → b
- 4. C → c

First, we create a new start symbol, Q, and add the production Q → S. Let us number this new production with the number 0. Our grammar becomes

G22.7
- 0. Q → S
- 1. S → BC
- 2. B → bB
- 3. B → b
- 4. C → c

This modification does not change the language defined by the grammar.

We will label the states of the finite automaton we construct with productions from our grammar. Each production will have an embedded period that indicates the current location of the parse in the input string. We call a production with an embedded period an *item*. For example, the item

    S → B.C

indicates that the parse is between the B and C. That is, the state for B is on top of the stack and the parser is about to process the terminals that correspond to C. In other words, the period marks the line between the stack contents and the remaining input.

We label the start state (state 0) of the finite automaton with the item

    Q → .S

The period before the S indicates that the parser is about to process the terminals in the input string that correspond to S (which should be the entire input string). If the parser is about to start to process the terminals for S, and by production 1, S goes to BC, then the parser is also about to start to process the terminals corresponding to BC in production 1. Thus, the item above implies a second item by virtue of production 1:

    S → .BC

This item indicates that the parser is about to process terminals for B. But because B goes to bB (production 2) or b (production 3), the parser is also about to process the terminals corresponding to either bB in production 2 or b in production 3. Thus, the item S → .BC implies two more items:

    B → .bB
    B → .b

The items above together represent the possible starting configurations of the parser. So we label the starting state of our finite automaton with them. We get

state 0

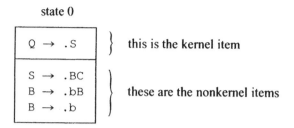

Our initial item, Q → .S, that gives rise to the other three items is called the *kernel item.*

In state 0, the period abuts S in the first item, B in the second item, and b in the third and fourth items. For each of three cases, we create a new state. The kernel items of the new state are obtained from the items in state 0 by moving the period over one position. For example, to get state 1, we move the period over one position in Q → .S to get Q → S. We also draw an arrow from state 0 to state 1 labeled with S to indicate that S causes this state change. We get

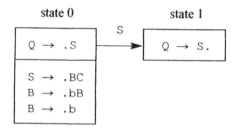

To get state 2, we move the period one position in S → .BC to get S → B.C. This item implies the item C → .c. We get

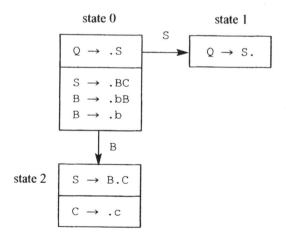

To get state 3, we move the period one position in B → .bB and B → .b in state 0 to get B → b.B and B → b. B → b.B implies B → .bB and B → .b. We get

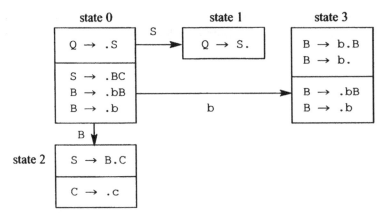

At this point, we are finished with state 0. We then continue the same process for each new state. On a C in state 2, we go to a state 4, whose kernel item is

B → BC.

On a c in state 2, we go to state 5, whose kernel item is

C → c.

On a B in state 3, we go to state 6, whose kernel item is

B → bB.

On a b in state 3, we go to a state, whose kernel items are

B → b.B
B → b.

But we already have this state (state 3). So we simply draw an arrow from state 3 to itself labeled with b. At this point, every state has all the required outgoing arrows (there should be one outgoing arrow for every distinct symbol in the item that has a period to its immediate left). Our final automaton is

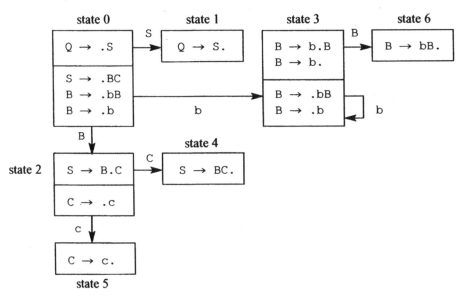

From this automaton, let us determine what the parser should do in various states. An item with the period to the extreme right indicates that a handle (the right side of the item) is on the stack. Thus, when in these states, the parser should reduce. For example in state 5, the parser should reduce using the production $C \rightarrow$ c. But remember our do-not-reduce rule. The parser should reduce using $C \rightarrow$ c only if the current input is in the FOLLOW set of C. Similarly, the parser should reduce using $S \rightarrow$ BC when in state 4 only if the current input is in FOLLOW(S). When the parser is in state 1, the parse is done. If there is no more input, the parser should accept. Otherwise it should reject. For those states that have an outgoing arrow labeled with a terminal, the parser should change state indicated by the arrow if the current input matches the label on the arrow. For example, if the parser is in state 0 (i.e., 0 is on top of the stack) and the current input is b, the parser should go to state 3 (i.e., it should push 3 onto the stack). This operation is indicated by the arrow from state 0 to state 3 labeled with b.

The operations of a parser can be specified in compact form with a parse table. In a parse table, we use the letter "s" to represent a shift operation and the letter "r" to represent a reduce operation. For example, s3 means to shift into *state 3* (i.e., push 3 onto the stack). r3 means to reduce by *production 3*. The left half of a parse table specifies the shift and reduce actions. The right half specifies the state that is pushed when a reduce is performed. The table has an entry for each arrow and for each item in which the period is on the extreme right. The blank entries in a parse table represent reject configurations. Figure 22.8 gives the parse table for the finite automaton we constructed for G22.6.

When in state 3, the parser can perform a shift or a reduce operation. We do not have a shift/reduce conflict here, however, because our do-not-reduce rule tells use the parser should not reduce by production 3 unless the current input is in the FOLLOW set of B. The FOLLOW set of B contains only c. Thus, the parser performs the r3 operation in state 3 only when the current input is c. Because the parser shifts when in state 3 only when the current input is b, the shift and reduce operations do not conflict.

		input			State to push when left side of reducing production is		
		b	c	#	S	B	C
	0	s3			1	2	
	1			accept			
	2		s5				4
state	3	s3	r3			6	
	4			r1			
	5			r4			
	6		r2				

Figure 22.8.

Let us now parse bbc using the parse table in Figure 22.8. We start in state 0:

$0   bbc#

The table tells us that in state 0 with a current input of b, the parser should s3 (i.e, push state 3). We get

$03   bc#

The next operation is another s3:

$033   c#

In state 3, when the current input is c, the parse should r3 (i.e., reduce by production 3). Production 3 is B → b. To reduce by this production, the parser pops the b (or, more precisely, the state that represents b) and then pushes B (or more precisely, the state that represents B). Thus, it pops the 3 on top, making the stack

$03

It then pushes 6, the state that represents B on top of state 3. We get this state from row 3/column B in the parse table. Thus, after the r3 operation, the configuration is

$036   c#

Next, the parser reduces by production 2, B → bB. Because the right side of this production has two symbols, the parser pops two symbols (these symbols represent bB). It then pushes 2 (from row 0/column B), the state that represents a B on top of state 0, to get

$02   c#

The next operation is s5 after which the configuration is

$025   #

The next operation is r4 (i.e., reduce by C → c). The parser pops the 5 (corresonding to the c) and pushes 4 (representing C) onto the stack:

$024   #

The next operation is r1 (i.e., reduce by production 1, S → BC). Because the right side of this production has two symbols, the parser pops the top two symbols from the stack (these symbols represent B and C). It then pushes 1, the state that represents an S on top of state 0 (see row 0/column S). The configuration becomes

$01   #

at which point the parser accepts.

22.7   SHIFT/REDUCE CONFLICTS

The SLR(1) parse table for some grammars have shift/reduce conflicts. That is, for some configurations, both a shift and a reduce are called for. For example, let us construct the SLR(1) finite automaton for the following grammar:

G22.8
  1. E → E + E
  2. E → b

First, we add a new start state Q and the production Q → E. We then construct the finite automaton (Figure 22.9a) and its corresponding parse table (Figure 22.9b). Notice that state 4 calls for a shift if the current input is +. But it also calls for a reduce by production 1 if the current input is in the follow set of E (the FOLLOW set of E is { +, #}). Thus, the parser has a shift/reduce conflict when it is in state 4 and the current input is +.

When a shift/reduce conflict occurs in a SLR(1) parser, we can often, but not always, fix the problem by

  1. Using the more complex parsing algorithm we discuss in the next section with the same grammar, or
  2. Changing the grammar so the corresponding SLR(1) parser does not have any conflicts
  3. Forcing the SLR(1) to always shift or always reduce when the shift/reduce conflict occurs

For G22.8, fixes 2 and 3 work but not fix 1. G22.8 is ambiguous. Ambiguity means that for at least one input string, there are multiple parse trees. A parsing algorithm uncovers the parse tree for the input string. Thus, for an ambiguous grammar, there must be some choice reflecting the multiple parse trees than can be constructed for some inputs. Thus, our more complex parsing technique is doomed to fail (i.e., have conflicts) for G22.8. We, however, can convert G22.8 to the following equivalent grammar:

G22.9:
  1. E → E+b
  2. E → b

The SLR(1) parser for this grammar has no conflicts. We also can force the SLR(1) grammar for G22.8 to always shift or always reduce when the shift/reduce conflict occurs. The action the parser takes at a conflict determines which of the possible parse tree it uncovers. If the SLR(1) parser for G22.8 always shifts at a conflict, then for the input string b+b+b, the parser uncovers parse tree in Figure 22.5b. If, however, the parser always reduces at a conflict, then the parser uncovers the parse tree in Figure 22.5a. We have to be careful using this technique. If the grammar is not ambiguous, a shift/reduce conflict in the SLR(1) parse means that to successfully parse some strings, the parser must sometimes shift at the conflict. But for other strings, it must reduce at the conflict. Thus, if the parser is forced to always shift or always reduce at a conflict, there neccessarily would be some input strings in the language of the grammar for which the parse would fail. For example, consider the following grammar:

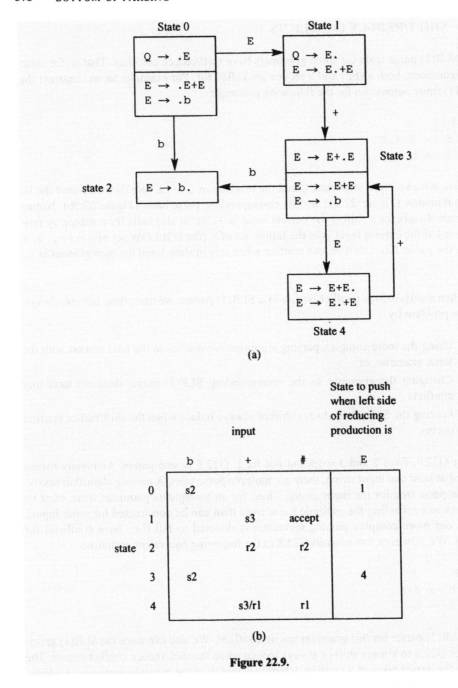

(a)

	input			State to push when left side of reducing production is
	b	+	#	E
0	s2			1
1		s3	accept	
state 2		r2	r2	
3	s2			4
4		s3/r1	r1	

(b)

Figure 22.9.

G22.10

1. S → bSb
2. S → cSc
3. S → λ

Its SLR(1) parser has shift/reduce conflicts. If you force the parse to always shift or always reduce at a conflict, then the parse will fail for all the strings in the language of the grammar except for the null string.

22.8   REDUCE/REDUCE CONFLICTS

If a parser has a choice between two reduce operations for some configuration, we say the parser has a *reduce/reduce conflict*. Let us construct the parse table for the following grammar to see if there are any reduce/reduce conflicts.

G22.11
  1. S → b
  2. S → BcB
  3. B → b

First, we add a new start state Q and the production Q → S. Next, we construct the finite automaton (Figure 22.10a) and its corresponding parse table (Figure 22.10b). We can see from the parse table that a reduce/reduce conflict occurs when the parser is in state 3 and the input is #. In this configuration, the parser has a choice between r1 and r3 when the input is #.

We can avoid the reduce/reduce conflict in the parse table in Figure 22.7b by using a grammar that does not produce any conflicts. Alternately, we can use the original grammar with the more complex bottom-up parsing algorithm that we discuss in the next section.

If the parse table for a grammar contains no shift/reduce or reduce/reduce conflicts, we say that the grammar is SLR(1). If at least one grammar exists for a language that is SLR(1), we say the language is SLR(1). G22.11 is not an SLR(1) grammar (because of the reduce/reduce conflict in its parse table). However, the language it defines is SLR(1) because the following grammar is equivalent to G22.11 and its parse table has no conflicts:

G22.12
  1. S → bX
  2. X → cb
  3. X → λ

22.9 LR(1) PARSING

The LR(1) parsing algorithm is the same as the SLR(1) parsing algorithm. The difference between an LR(1) and an SLR(1) parser is in the construction of finite automaton and its corresponding parse table. The items used in the finite automaton for an LR(1) parser contains two components:

  1. A production with an embedded period
  2. One or more lookahead inputs

For example, in the following LR(1) item,

    S → B.CbD, c/d

S → BCbD is the production and c and d are the lookahead inputs. The lookahead input in an LR(1) item indicate the possible current inputs at that point later in the parse when the states representing the right side of the production are on the stack, ready for reduc-

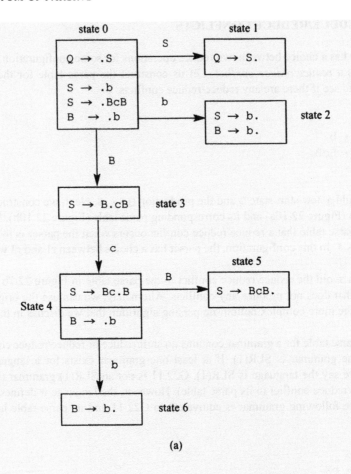

(a)

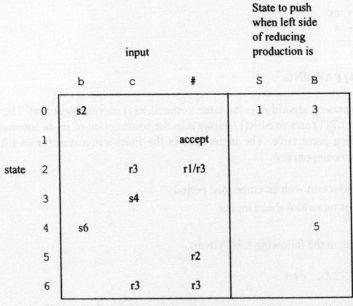

(b)

Figure 22.10

tion. For example, the lookahead tokens in the preceding LR(1) item indicate that when the states corresponding to B, C, b, and D have been pushed onto the stack, the current input should be either c or d. Thus, at that point the parse should reduce if the current input is c or d.

Let us construct the LR(1) finite automaton and parse table for

G22.13
   1. S → Sb
   2. S → c

First we add a new start state Q and the production Q → S to the grammar to get

G22.14
   0. Q → S
   1. S → Sb
   2. S → c

Next, we construct the finite automaton. The kernel item in the start state is

     Q → .S, #

The derivation of every string in the language defined by G22.14 starts with the production Q → S. Obviously, if the input string is in the language of the grammar, the S in this production must generate it. Thus, after the parser processes the input corresponding to the S in this production, the current input should be #. Accordingly, the lookahead input in the preceding above is #. The kernel item above gives rise to

     S → .Sb, #
     S → .c, #

The S of the left side of these items is the S in the kernel item. Thus, after the right sides of these productions are processed, the current input must be the same as when the input corresponding to the right side of the kernel item has been processed. Thus, these items also have the lookahead #. The first of these items,

     S → .Sb, #

gives rise to another item because the period is abutting the S on the right side. However, b follows this S. Thus, the items we get from it have a b lookahead:

     S → .Sb, b
     S → .c, b

Thus, the start state consists of these items:

     Q → .S, #
     S → .Sb, #
     S → .c, #
     S → .Sb, b
     S → .c, b

Continuing in this fashion, it is easy to construct the entire finite automaton (see Figure 22.11a). We can then construct the parse table (see Figure 22.11b). The lookahead inputs indicates the inputs for which the production should be reduced. For example, the items in state 2 indicate the parse should reduce by the production 2 if the current input is b or #.

An LR(1) grammar is a grammar whose LR(1) parse table contains no conflicts. LR(1) parsing is more powerful than SLR(1) parsing. That is, all SLR(1) grammars are also LR(1), but not all LR(1) grammars are SLR(1). In other words, if SLR(1) parsing works (i.e., no conflicts) then so will LR(1) parsing. But for some grammars, LR(1) parsing works but not SLR(1) parsing. As an example of the latter, consider G22.11, whose SLR(1) parse table is in Figure 22.10. We can see that a reduce/reduce conflict occurs in state 2. Now let us use LR(1) on the same grammar. We get the finite automata in Figure 22.12a and the corresponding parse table in Figure 22.12b.

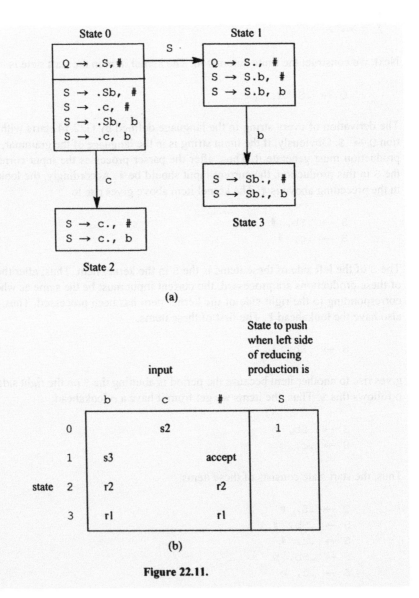

Figure 22.11.

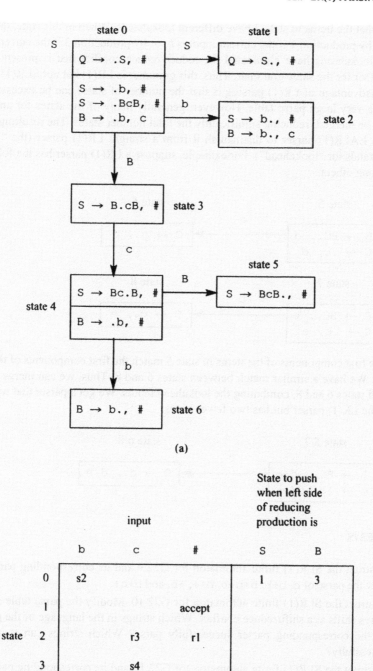

(a)

	input			State to push when left side of reducing production is	
	b	c	#	S	B
0	s2			1	3
1			accept		
state 2		r3	r1		
3		s4			
4	s6				5
5			r2		
6			r3		

(b)

Figure 22.12

Notice that the items in state 2 have different lookaheads. When in this state, the parser reduces by production 1 if the current input is #, or by production 3 if the current input is c. The lookaheads have eliminated the reduce/reduce conflict that is present in the SLR(1) parser for the same grammar. Thus, this grammar is LR(1) but not SLR(1).

One disadvantage of LR(1) parsing is that the number of states can be excessive, resulting in a very large parse table. However, generally many of the states for an LR(1) parser can be merged, reducing significantly the total number states. The resulting parser is called a LALR(1) parser to distinguish it from a straight LR(1) parser (the "LA" in "LALR" stands for "lookahead"). For example, suppose a LR(1) parser has the following states, among others:

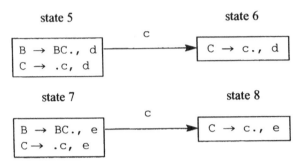

Notice the first components of the items in state 5 match the first components of the items in state 7. We have a similar match between states 6 and 8. Thus, we can merge states 5 and 7, and states 6 and 8, combining the lookahead inputs. We get a parser that works the same as the LR(1) parser but has two fewer states:

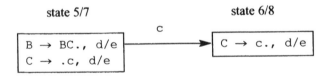

PROBLEMS

1. Construct the SLR(1) finite automaton for G22.9 and its corresponding parse table. Show the parse of b, b+b, b+b+b, b++, +b, and b+b+.

2. Construct the SLR(1) finite automaton for G22.10. Modify the parse table so that it always shifts at a shift/reduce conflict. Which strings in the language of the grammar can the corresponding parser successfully parse? Which strings can it not parse successfully?

3. Construct the SLR(1) finite automaton for G22.12 and its corresponding parse table. Are there any conflicts?

4. Construct the SLR(1) parsing table for

```
E → E + T
E → T
T → T * F
T → F
F → b
F → ( E )
```

Show the parse of b* (b+b). Implement your parser using Java. Test your parser with b+b, b* b, b+b* b, b* (b+b), bb, b*, b** b, b* b+.

5. Using Java implement the SLR(1) parser for

```
E → E + <UNSIGNED>
E → <UNSIGNED>
```

Add actions along with any necessary data structures that allow your parser to compute the value of the input expression. Test your program with 2, 2+3, and 2+3+4.

6. Construct the SLR(1) parser for

```
S → b
S → Sd
S → Bde
B → b
```

Are there any conflicts? Construct the LR(1) parser for the grammar. Are there any conflicts? Is this grammar SLR(1)? Is it LR(1)?

7. Show that the merging of states in the process of constructing a LALR(1) parser never creates a shift/reduce conflict.

8. Construct the SLR(1) parse table for G18.1 in Chapter 18.

9. Are LR(1) grammars ever ambiguous? Justify your answer.

10. Construct the LR(1) finite automata and the LALR(1) finite automaton for

```
S → BB
B → Bb
B → c
D → Dd
D → e
```

23

yacc

23.1 INTRODUCTION

yacc is a LALR(1) parser generator available on Unix systems. The letters in yacc stand for "yet another compiler compiler." This is a curious name, given that there were hardly a plethora of compiler compilers (i.e., parser generators) when yacc was released. Perhaps the yacc's name reflects the many preliminary versions that were created during its development. Because of the popularity of yacc, a number of yacc look-alike programs have been developed, most notably the GNU bison program and the Berkeley yacc.

Most versions of yacc generate C/C++ parsers only. However, one version— BYACC/J—can generate either C/C++ or Java parsers. In keeping with the Java theme of this book, we will use this version of yacc. It is available for the Microsoft, Linux, Macintosh, and SUN Solaris platforms.

yacc is different from JavaCC in two significant ways:

1. It generates a bottom-up parser rather than a top-down parser.
2. It does not include a lexical analyzer (i.e., a token manager) generator.

To use a parser created by yacc, you must provide it with a lexical analyzer method named `yylex` that provides tokens in the form required by the yacc-generated parser. You can either write the lexical analyzer by hand or use a lexical analyzer generator program to generate it for you. The lexical analyzer generator typically used with yacc is lex or its look-alike versions flex, jflex, and jlex. The latter two programs generate lexical analyzers written in Java. In this chapter, we will use both handwritten and jflex-generated lexical analyzers.

23.2 yacc INPUT AND OUTPUT FILES

A yacc input file consists of three parts (see the left side of Figure 23.1). Part 1 is divided from part 2 with a line containing %%. Similarly, part 2 is divided from part 3 with a line containing %%. Part 1 is subdivided into subparts 1a and 1b. Subpart 1a contains Java code

Compiler Construction Using Java, JavaCC, and Yacc, First Edition. Anthony J. Dos Reis
© 2012 the IEEE Computer Society, Inc. Published 2012 by John Wiley & Sons, Inc.

bracketed with %{ and %} . This code is carried over as is to the beginning of the output file (see the right side of Figure 23.1). Subpart 1b contains yacc declarations. For example, in part 1b you list the token (i.e., terminal) symbols in the translation grammar to distinguish them from the nonterminal symbols (JavaCC uses a different approach: token symbols are enclosed in angle brackets to distinguish them from the nonterminal symbols).

Part 2 contains the translation grammar in BNF (see Section 4.4). Actions are embedded in the grammar using Java code enclosed in braces. Part 3 contains Java code for additional methods. This code is carried over as is to the output file.

By convention, we use the extension ".y" in the names of yacc input files. The default output file name is Parser.java. Parser.java contains the Java code from subpart 1a in the input file followed by a class named Parser. The Parser class contains the methods generated by yacc: yyparse, which is the parser, as well as several support methods. It also contains the Java methods from part 3 of the input file.

yyparse expects two methods to be available that yacc does not generate: yylex (the lexical anaylzer) and yyerror (the method yyparse calls on a error). If we place yylex and yyerror in part 3 of the yacc input file, along with a main method, then the output file created by yacc will be a complete program.

yacc also outputs a second file named ParserVal.java. We will discuss this file in Section 23.3.

23.2 A SIMPLE yacc-GENERATED PARSER

Let us examine the simple yacc input file in Figure 23.2. The line numbers are not part of the input file—we have added them so that we can easily refer to specific lines. The trans-

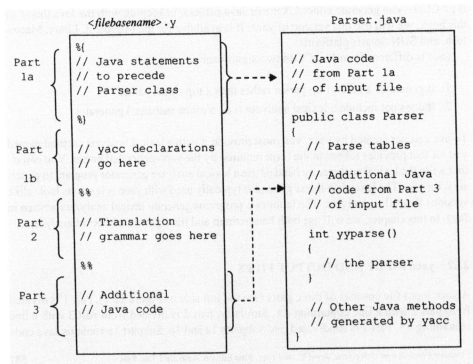

Figure 23.1.

lation grammar is in part 2 (lines 6–12). The productions for each nonterminal are terminated with a semicolon. For example, the semicolon on line 10 in Figure 23.2 terminates the B productions. The productions and actions do not have to be formatted in a particular way. For example, we could have placed each component of the B productions on a separate line, each starting in column 1 to get

```
B
:
'b'
B
{ System.out.println("Prod 2");}
|
'b'
{ System.out.println("Prod 3");}
;
```

Actions appear within braces. In the example in Figure 23.2, each production has an action to its right. These actions are performed when the corresponding production is used in a reduce operation by the parser. Character constants (such as 'b' and 'c') and any symbol declared to be a token in subpart 1b are treated as tokens (i.e., terminal symbols). Because this example does not declare any symbols to be tokens (there is no subpart 1b), the only tokens in the grammar are the character constants 'b' and 'c'. S, B, and C are the nonterminals. The left side of the first production listed is the start symbol.

A lambda production is represented in a yacc translation grammar by writing nothing on the right side of a production. For example, the following S productions

$$S \rightarrow cS$$
$$S \rightarrow \lambda$$

would appear in the following form in a yacc translation grammar as

```
S :   'c' S
  | ◄──────── nothing after vertical bar means λ
  ;
```

or, if we listed the lambda production first, as

```
S :   ◄──────── nothing before vertical bar means λ
  | c' S
  ;
```

Part 3 contains the `yylex` and `yyerror` methods that the yacc-generated parser requires. Because it also includes a `main` method, the output file produced by yacc for this example is a complete program. `yylex` returns the ASCII code for character constants, and zero on end of input. On an error, it calls `yyerror`, passing it an error message. There is no specific function `yyerror` has to perform. In this example, it simply displays the error message and terminates the program.

`yytext` is a `String` variable created by yacc. It is typically used by `yylex()` to provide the parser with the image of the current token. On line 34 in Figure 23.2, `yylex` sets `yytext` to the token image. However, the parser itself makes no use of `yytext`. To

```
1 // Fig2302.y
2
3 // no part 1
4
5 %%
6 S : B C    {System.out.println("Prod 1");}
7   ;
8 B : 'b' B {System.out.println("Prod 2");}
9   | 'b'   {System.out.println("Prod 3");}
10  ;
11 C : 'c'    {System.out.println("Prod 4 " + yytext);}
12  ;
13 %%
14 // parser expects 0 on end of file
15 private static final int EOF = 0;
16 private String input;
17 private int inputIndex = 0;
18 private char currentChar;
19 //----------------------
20 public static void main(String[] args)
21 {
22    Parser parser = new Parser();
23    parser.input = args[0];
24    parser.yyparse();    // call yacc-generated parser
25 }
26 //----------------------
27 private int yylex()   // lexical analyzer
28 {
29    if (inputIndex >= input.length())
30      return EOF;
31    else
32    {
33      currentChar = input.charAt(inputIndex++);
34      yytext = Character.toString(currentChar);
35      return currentChar;
36    }
37 }
38 //----------------------
39 private void yyerror(String s) // error handler
40 {
41    System.err.println(s);
42    System.exit(1);
43 }
```

Figure 23.2.

make parsing decisions, *the parser uses the value returned by* yylex() *via the* return
statement; it does not use what is in yytext. However, actions can access yytext, as illustrated by the C production in the translation grammar in Figure 23.2:

```
11 C : 'c'    {System.out.println("Prod 4 " + yytext);}
```

To process the input file Fig2302.y in Figure 23.2, enter

```
yacc -J Fig2302.y
```

The -J command line argument (use a capital J) causes yacc to generate Java code. Without it, yacc would generate C code. To compile the Parser.java file produced by yacc, enter

```
javac Parser.java
```

To run the parser and test it with the input string bbc, enter

```
java Parser bbc
```

The parser responds with

```
Prod 3
Prod 2
Prod 4 c
Prod 1
```

Each time the parser performs a reduce operation, an action displays the number of the production used. Now let us look at the rightmost derivation of bbc (the production in each step used is shown below the nonterminal replaced).

$$S \Rightarrow BC \Rightarrow Bc \Rightarrow bBc \Rightarrow bbc$$
$$1 \quad\quad 4 \quad\quad 2 \quad\quad\quad 3$$

We can see that the order in which the productions are used—1, 4, 2, 3—is the reverse order of the productions used in the bottom-up parse of bbc. The bottom-up parse determines the rightmost derivation, in reverse order.

If you specify the -v command line argument when you invoke yacc, yacc will output a file y.output containing the parse table used by the parser. For example, if you enter

```
yacc -v -J Fig2302.y
```

yacc outputs the file in Figure 22.3.

At the beginning of this file, we can see the grammar, augmented with a new start symbol, $accept, and a new production $accept → S:

```
0   $accept : S $end
```

$end represents the end of input that should follow the input string generated by the S in this production. Next, for each state, we have the kernel item (the nonkernel items are omitted) and a description of each arrow out of that state. Let us look at state 3:

```
state 3
  S : B . C  (1)

  'c'  shift 5
  .  error

  C  goto 6
```

The kernel item is production 1:

```
S → B.C
```

```
        0   $accept : S $end

        1   S : B C

        2   B : 'b' B
        3     | 'b'

        4   C : 'c'

    state 0
        $accept : . S $end   (0)

        'b'  shift 1
        .    error

        S   goto 2
        B   goto 3

    state 1
        B : 'b' . B   (2)
        B : 'b' .     (3)

        'b'  shift 1
        'c'  reduce 3

        B   goto 4

    state 2
        $accept : S . $end   (0)

        $end   accept

    state 3
        S : B . C   (1)

        'c'  shift 5
        .    error

        C   goto 6

    state 4
        B : 'b' B .   (2)

        .   reduce 2

    state 5
        C : 'c' .   (4)

        .   reduce 4

    state 6
        S : B C .   (1)

        .   reduce 1

    4 terminals, 4 nonterminals
    5 grammar rules, 7 states
```

Figure 23.3.

We can see that state 3 has two outgoing arrows: to state 5 on a `'c'`, and to state 6 on a C. The period in the line

```
.   error
```

represents any input other than the ones listed. Here it means any input other than `'c'`. Thus, this line indicates that any input other than `'c'` is an error. The information given for state 3 tells us that state 3 in the underlying finite automata looks like this:

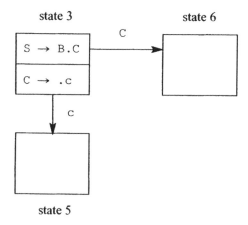

The parser performs an action for a production only when it reduces with that production. Actions are generally specified to the right of the productions to which they apply. However, they can also be specified in the interior of a production. For example, suppose we modify the translation grammar in Figure 23.2 so that it is

```
S : B
    { System.out.println("hello");}
    C
    { System.out.println("goodbye");}
    ;
B : 'b' B    { System.out.println("Prod 2");}
  | 'b'      { System.out.println("Prod 3");}
  ;
C : 'c'      { System.out.println("Prod 4");}
  ;
```

The S production contains two actions, one between the B and the C and one at the end. The one at the end is performed when the parser reduces with the S production. The one between the B and the C is performed right after the parser reduces by a B production that creates the B nonterminal in the S production. Thus, for an input of bbc, Figure 23.2 with the modified grammar would output

```
Prod 3
Prod 2
hello
Prod 4
goodbye
```

The reduction by production 3 pushes a B on the stack, but this is not the B in the S production. It is the reduction by production 2 that pushes the B in the S production. Thus, after the reduction by production 2, the first action—which displays "hello"—is performed.

yacc handles actions that are not at the end of a production by replacing the action with a nonterminal. It then adds to the grammar a lambda production for the new nonterminal with the action on its right. In the example above, yacc replaces

```
S : B
    {System.out.println("hello");}
    C
    {System.out.println("goodbye");}
    ;
```

with

```
S : B
    $$1
    C
    {System.out.println("goodbye");}
    ;
```

where $$1 is a new nonterminal. It also adds to the grammar a lambda production with $$1 on its left side with the replaced action on its right:

```
$$1 :          {System.out.println("hello");}
```

The parser, as usual, performs the action in this production when it reduces by this production. From the S production, we can see that this reduction occurs right after the reduction that pushes the B (the one in the S production) onto the stack.

The variables that are declared in part 3 of the yacc input file are included in the Parser class. Thus, all the methods in the Parser class as well as the actions have access to them. We can use these variables to pass information from yylex to the parser, or from one point in the parse to another. For example, in Figure 23.4, yylex counts the number of b's. This count is then displayed at the end of the parse when the reduction with the S production occurs. bCount (line 16) is the variable yylex uses to pass the count information to the parser. Alternatively, the parser can do the counting. The corresponding translation grammar is

```
S : B C   {System.out.println("b count = " + bCount);}
    ;
B : 'b' {bCount++;} B
    | 'b' {bCount++;}
    ;
C : 'c'
    ;
```

Here we are using bCount, a variable declared in part 3 of the input file, to accumulate information during the parse. This count is then used later in the parse in the action for the S production.

```
 1 // Fig2304.y
 2
 3 // no part 1
 4
 5 %%
 6 S : B C    {System.out.println("b count = " + bCount);}
 7  ;
 8 B : 'b' B
 9  | 'b'
10  ;
11 C : 'c'
12  ;
13 %%
14 private static final int EOF = 0;
15 private char currentChar;
16 private int bCount = 0;
17 private String input;
18 private int inputIndex = 0;
19 //----------------------
20 public static void main(String[] args)
21 {
22   Parser parser = new Parser();
23   parser.input = args[0];
24   parser.yyparse();
25 }
26 //----------------------
27 private int yylex()
28 {
29   if (inputIndex >= input.length()) // at end-of-input?
30     return EOF;
31   else
32   {
33     currentChar = input.charAt(inputIndex++);
34     if (currentChar == 'b')
35       bCount++;
36     return currentChar;
37   }
38 }
39 //----------------------
40 private void yyerror(String s)
41 {
42   System.err.println(s);
43   System.exit(1);
44 }
```

Figure 23.4.

To create the executable program from Figure 23.4, enter

```
yacc -J Fig2304.y
javac Parser.java
```

To process the input bbbc, enter

```
java Parser bbbc
```

The Parser program will then respond with

```
b count = 3
```

23.4   PASSING VALUES USING THE VALUE STACK

We learned in Chapter 22 how a bottom-up parser pushes states representing symbols onto a stack until a handle appears on top of the stack. It then reduces by the corresponding handle production. This stack is called the parsing stack. The parsers generated by yacc, however, have a second state, called a value stack. The value stack is used in parallel with the parsing stack. That is, each entry in the value stack provides the value of the corresponding item in the parsing stack.

Where do the values in the value stack come from? For the terminal symbols, the values come from the terminal symbols themselves. For example, the value of the unsigned integer token could be the string "123" or the integer 123, depending on what we want the parser to do. In the example in this section, the parser performs an arithmetic computation during the parse using the values from the tokens. Thus, in this example, the values we want for our terminals are their integer values, not their string representations.

Let us work through the example in Figure 23.5. The left side of the first production listed (line 6) is S. Thus, S is the start symbol for this grammar. On line 3, we declare UNSIGNED to be a token:

```
3 %token  UNSIGNED
```

Thus, in the grammar, UNSIGNED is a token (i.e., terminal symbol) but expr is not. '-' is also a token because it is enclosed in quotes. In response to line 3, yacc creates the following constant for UNSIGNED:

```
public final static short UNSIGNED = 257;
```

This constant, 257, represents the unsigned integer token. When yylex returns an unsigned integer token to the parse, it returns this constant (to indicate the category of the token). The integer constants yacc uses for tokens are all greater than 256. Thus, they will never conflict with any ASCII codes (all of which are less than 128).

Now look at the action on line 8:

```
8  expr :  expr '-' UNSIGNED  { $$.ival = $1.ival-$3.ival;}
```

$$ represents the left side of the production. $1 and $3 represent, respectively, the first and third symbols on the right side of the production. Thus, $$.ival represents the integer value of the left side of the production. $1.ival and $3.ival represent the integer values of the first and third symbols on the right side of the production. The action in this production subtracts the values associated with the production's right side and assigns the result to the left side.

The second production for expr (line 9) has no action. However, when no action is specified for a production, the action defaults to

```
{ $$.ival = $1.ival;}
```

```
 1 // Fig2305.y
 2
 3 %token   UNSIGNED
 4
 5 %%
 6 S    : expr { System.out.println($1.ival);}
 7      ;
 8 expr :  expr '-' UNSIGNED  {$$.ival = $1.ival-$3.ival;}
 9      |  UNSIGNED
10      ;
11 %%
12 private static final int EOF = 0;
13 private char currentChar = '\n';
14 private String input;
15 private int inputIndex = 0;
16 private StringBuffer buffer;
17 //---------------------
18 public static void main(String[] args)
19 {
20   Parser parser = new Parser();
21   parser.input = args[0];
22   parser.buffer = new StringBuffer();
23   parser.yyparse();
24 }
25 //---------------------
26 private int yylex()
27 {
28   int kind;
29
30   while (Character.isWhitespace(currentChar))
31     getNextChar();
32
33   // check if unsigned int
34   if (Character.isDigit(currentChar))
35   {
36     buffer.setLength(0);
37     do
38     {
39       buffer.append(currentChar);
40       getNextChar();
41     } while (Character.isDigit(currentChar));
42     yytext = buffer.toString();
43     kind = UNSIGNED;
44     // assign yylval object that contains value
45     yylval = new ParserVal(Integer.parseInt(yytext));
46   }
47
48   else  // return currentChar as next token
49   {
50     kind = currentChar;
51     yytext = Character.toString(currentChar);
52     yylval = null;
53     getNextChar();
```

Figure 23.5.

```
54   }
55   return kind;
56 }
57 //----------------------
58 private void getNextChar()
59 {
60   if (inputIndex >= input.length())
61     currentChar = EOF;
62   else
63     currentChar = input.charAt(inputIndex++);
64 }
65 //----------------------
66 private void yyerror(String s)
67 {
68   System.err.println(s);
69   System.exit(1);
70 }
```

Figure 23.5. *Continued.*

Thus, the action for this production is to assign the value of the right side (the UNSIGNED terminal) to the left side (the expr nonterminal). As the parse proceeds, each nonterminal in the parse tree receives its value based on the values of the node or nodes below it. When the expr nonterminal in the S production is reduced, it will have a value equal to the entire expression. This value (in $1.val) is then displayed by the action in the S production:

```
6 S     : expr { System.out.println($1.ival);}
```

The actions in the translation grammar in Figure 22.5 specify the computation that is to take place during the parse. But where do the values used in the computation originally come from? They come from yylex. For each token, yylex assigns yylval an object whose type is ParserVal (see Figure 23.6). The ParserVal object contains the token's value. The parser can then access this value via its yylval variable.

Let us examine the structure of yylex in Figure 23.5 to see how this works. This version of yylex should be familiar—it is like the token manager in the S1 compiler. Lines 30 and 31 throw out white space:

```
30   while (Character.isWhitespace(currentChar))
31     getNextChar();
```

If after white space is discarded, the current character is a digit, then that digit must be the start of an unsigned integer token. In that case, the following code is executed:

```
36     buffer.setLength(0);
37     do
38     {
39       buffer.append(currentChar);
40       getNextChar();
41     } while (Character.isDigit(currentChar));
42     yytext = buffer.toString();
```

```
43        kind = UNSIGNED;
44        // assign yylval object that contains value
45        yylval = new ParserVal(Integer.parseInt(yytext));
```

The `do-while` loop reads the digits that make up the unsigned integer token and appends them to `buffer`. At the conclusion of the loop, the sequence of characters in `buffer` is converted to a string and assigned to `yytext` (line 42). `kind` is set to UN-SIGNED (the constant yacc creates to represent an unsigned integer because of line 3). The next line (line 45) then creates a `ParserVal` object and assigns it to `yylval`. `yylval` is a variable defined by and available to the parser. Thus, whatever `yylex` assigns to `yylval` is accessible by the parser. The `Integer.parseInt` method on Line 45 converts the unsigned integer in string form in `yytext` to type `int`. This value is then passed to the `ParserVal` constructor, which stores it in the `ival` field of the `Parser-Val` object (see line 12 in Figure 23.6). The parser has access to `yylval` through which is has access the the value of the token. When on line 55 `yylex` returns to the parser, it returns `kind` (which contains UNSIGNED). The parser gets the category of the token via the return value; it gets the value of the token via the `yylval` variable.

If on entry into `yylex`, the token to be processed is not an unsigned integer, then `yylex` returns the next nonwhite-space character as the token. For this case, it sets `yyl-val` to null (line 52 in Figure 23.5) because there is no `int` value associated with this type of token.

The dollar sign notation ($1, $2, ...) we use in actions designates various slots in the value stack. Because these slots contain references to `ParserVal` objects that contain

```
 1 public class ParserVal
 2 {
 3    public int ival;
 4    public double dval;
 5    public String sval;
 6    public Object obj;
 7    public ParserVal()
 8    {
 9    }
10    public ParserVal(int val)
11    {
12       ival=val;
13    }
14    public ParserVal(double val)
15    {
16       dval=val;
17    }
18    public ParserVal(String val)
19    {
20       sval=val;
21    }
22    public ParserVal(Object val)
23    {
24       obj=val;
25    }
26 }
```

Figure 23.6.

`int` values in the `ival` field, we access these `int` values by specifying the `ival` field. For example, $3.ival in the action on line 8 in Fig 23.5,

```
8 expr : expr '-' UNSIGNED { $$.ival = $1.ival - $3.ival;}
```

specifies the value in the `ival` field in the `ParserVal` object pointed to by the $3 slot in the value stack. Because $3 corresponds to the `UNSIGNED` token on the right side of the production, $3.ival is the integer value of this token.

Let us simulate a parse of the expression 9 - 2 using the parse table that yacc constructs for Figure 23.5 (see Figure 12.7). In this simulation (see Figure 23.8), we show both the parsing stack (P$) and the value stack (V$). Whenever the parser performs a shift operation, it shifts a state onto the parsing stack. It also shifts the value of the token (i.e., the contents of `yylval`) onto the value stack. To simplify the picture of the value stack in Figure 22.7, we show the value stack as containing `int` values or "*", the latter indicating no value. But please be aware that each slot really contains a `ParserVal` reference.

Figure 23.8a shows the initial configuration. 0 is on top of the parsing stack; 9, an unsigned integer, is the current input. Our parse table in Figure 23.7 specifies s1 for this configuration. Thus, the parser shifts 1 onto the parsing stack, and 9 (more precisely, the reference to the `ParserVal` object that contains 9) onto the value stack to get the configuration in Figure 23.8b. The next step is r3, a reduction by the production on line 9 in Figure 23.5. Because the right side of this production has only one symbol, only one symbol is popped from the parsing stack, exposing the state 0, on top of which the parser has to push the state representing `expr`. Our parse table tells it to push state 3. We get the configuration in Figure 23.8c. Because this production does not have an associated action that assigns a value to the value stack, the value stack is unaffected by the reduce operation. Thus, the value on top of the value stack before the reduce is still there (compare Figure 22.8b and Figure 22.8c). Thus, the effect is as if we specified the action

```
{ $$ = $1.val;}
```

on the production on line 9 in Figure 23.5. Let us now skip ahead to the configuration in Figure 22.8e. In this configuration, the parser reduces with the production

```
8 expr :  expr '-' UNSIGNED  { $$.ival = $1.ival-$3.ival;}
```

	UNSIGNED	-	EOF	S	E
0	s1			2	3
1		r3	r3		
2			accept		
3		s4	r1		
4	s5				
5		r2	r2		

Figure 23.7.

	stacks	operation	input
a)	P$0		9 - 2 EOF
	V$*		
		s1	
b)	P$01		- 2 EOF
	V$* 9		
		r3	
c)	P$03		- 2 EOF
	V$* 9		
		s4	
d)	P$034		2 EOF
	V$* 9*		
		s5	
e)	P$0345		EOF
	V$* 9* 2		
		r2, compute 9 – 2	
		and store in	
		value stack	
f)	P$03		EOF
	V$* 7		
		r1, display 7	
g)	P$02		EOF
	V$* 7		
		accept and output 7	

Figure 23.8.

To do this, it

1. Pops three items from the parsing stack to expose the state 0
2. Pushes 3, the state that represents `expr` on top of state 0
3. Pops three items—$3, $2, and $1—from the value stack
4. Computes $1.ival - $3.ival, and pushes the result onto the value stack

We get the configuration in Figure 22.8f. In its final step, the parser reduces by production 1 and performs its action (to display $1.ival). $1.ival is the value at the top of the stack.

```
6 S     : expr { System.out.println($1.ival);}
```

When you execute the program derived from Figure 23.5, be sure to enclose the input string on the command line in quotes if it contains any embedded spaces (otherwise, it will be treated as multiple arguments). For example, to create the executable program and then use it to process 7 – 2 – 1, enter

```
yacc -J Fig2305.y
javac Parser.java
java Parser "7 - 2 - 1"
```

The `Parser` program will then respond with

4

23.5 USING yacc WITH AN AMBIGUOUS GRAMMAR

The grammar in Figure 23.9 is ambiguous with respect to both operator associativity and operator precedence. For example, there are two parse trees for 2+3+4, one implying left associativiy, the other implying right associativity. There are two parse trees for 2+3* 4, one implying addition has higher precedence than multiplication; the other implying that multiplication has higher precedence than addition. The ambiguities in this grammar manifest themselves as shift/reduce conflicts in the parser.

Suppose during a parse, the stack contains the states corresponding to

```
expr '+' expr
```

and the current input is `'+'`. The parser faces a shift/reduce conflict here. Should the parser shift or reduce? Recall from Chapter 22 the reduce-order principle:

> **The order in which operators are reduced is the order in which they are performed.**

Thus, if the parser reduces at this point, it will reduce the left `'+'` (the one on the stack) before the right `'+'` (the current input). Then by the reduce-order principle, we can conclude that a reduce here imparts left associativity to the addition operator. A shift here, on the other hand, means the right `'+'` (the current input) will be reduced before the left `'+'`(the one on the stack), thereby imparting right associativity to the addition operator. Addition should be left associative. Thus, the parser should reduce here. Unfortunately, the parser shifts by default at shift/reduce conflicts. We have a similar problem if

```
expr '*' expr
```

is on the stack and the current input is `'+'`. Here, the parser faces a shift/reduce conflict. If the parser reduces here, it imparts higher precedence to `'*'` relative to `'+'`, which is what we want. Unfortunately, the parser shifts here.

```
 1 // Fig2309.y
 2
 3 %token  UNSIGNED
 4
 5
 6 %%
 7 S    : expr { System.out.println($1.ival);}
 8      ;
 9 expr : expr '+' expr  { $$.ival = $1.ival + $3.ival;}
10      | expr '-' expr  { $$.ival = $1.ival - $3.ival;}
11      | expr '*' expr  { $$.ival = $1.ival * $3.ival;}
12      | expr '/' expr  { $$.ival = $1.ival / $3.ival;}
13      | UNSIGNED
14      ;
15 %%
16      // same part 3 as in Fig. 23.5
```

Figure 23.9.

The parse table for Figure 23.9 has 16 shift/reduce conflicts. Let us examine the parse table to locate these conflicts. To do this first, get yacc to output the parse table by entering

```
yacc -v -J Fig2309.y
```

where `Fig2309.y` is the file in the J1 Software Package that contains the input file in Figure 23.9. In response, yacc will output the file `y.output` that contains the parse table. This is what state 8 looks like:

```
8: shift/reduce conflict (shift 4, reduce 2) on '+'
8: shift/reduce conflict (shift 5, reduce 2) on '-'
8: shift/reduce conflict (shift 6, reduce 2) on '*'
8: shift/reduce conflict (shift 7, reduce 2) on '/'
state 8
     expr : expr . '+' expr   (2)
     expr : expr '+' expr .   (2)
     expr : expr . '-' expr   (3)
     expr : expr . '*' expr   (4)
     expr : expr . '/' expr   (5)


     '+'   shift 4  ⎫
     '-'   shift 5  ⎬  Shift/reduce conflicts are
     '*'   shift 6  ⎪  resolved in favor of the shift
     '/'   shift 7  ⎭

     $end   reduce 2
```

One of the items,

```
     expr : expr '+' expr .
```

calls for a reduce (because the period is rightmost) on a `'+'`, `'-'`, `'*'`, and `'/'`. But the other items in state 8 call for a shift on these inputs. In all four of these conflicts, the parser shifts (you tell this from the actions specified in state 8 for the inputs `'+'`, `'-'`, `'*'`, and `'/'`).

Let us make a small modification to Figure 23.9: change lines 4 and 5 to

```
%left '+' '-'
%left '*' '/'
```

These two lines specify the associativity (left in this example) and precedence of the four operators. Precedence is specified by the position in which the operators are listed. By listing `'*'` and `'/'` below `'+'` and `'-'`, we are indicating that the `'*'` and `'/'` should have a higher precedence than `'+'` and `'-'`. With these lines included, the parser that results will resolve shift/reduce conflicts so that `'+'`, `'-'`, `'*'`, and `'/'` have the specified associativity and precedence.

By specifying the associativity and precedence of the operators on line 8 and 9, we have, in effect, disambiguated our ambiguous grammar. Here is what state 8 now looks like:

```
state 8
    expr : expr . '+' expr   (2)
    expr : expr '+' expr .   (2)
    expr : expr . '-' expr   (3)
    expr : expr . '*' expr   (4)
    expr : expr . '/' expr   (5)

    '*'   shift 6
    '/'   shift 7
    $end  reduce 2
    '+'   reduce 2
    '-'   reduce 2
```

All the conflicts are gone. The parser now resolves shift/reduce conflicts based on the associativity and precedence specified by our new lines 4 and 5. For example, when the right side of

```
    expr : expr '+' expr
```

is on the stack and '+' is the current input, the parser now resolves the shift/reduce conflict in favor of the reduce, thereby imparting left associativity to '+'. Similarly, when the right side of

```
    expr : expr '+' expr
```

is on the stack and '*' is the current input, the parser resolves the shift/reduce conflict in favor of the shift, theereby imparting higher precedence to '*' relative to '+'.

If we add the unary minus operator to our grammar in Figure 23.5, we run into another problem: unary minus has higher precedence than subtraction (as well as addition, multiplication, and division). But both subtraction and unary minus are represented by '–'. So how can we indicate the correct precedences to yacc? We simply make up a name that represents the unary minus (let us use "UNARYMINUS") and list it below the other operators:

```
%left '+' '-'
%left '*' '/'
%right UNARYMINUS
```

We then tag the production that has the unary minus with %prec UNARYMINUS:

```
expr : expr '+' expr  { $$.ival = $1.ival + $3.ival;}
     | expr '-' expr  { $$.ival = $1.ival - $3.ival;}
     | expr '*' expr  { $$.ival = $1.ival * $3.ival;}
     | expr '/' expr  { $$.ival = $1.ival / $3.ival;}
     | '-' expr %prec UNARYMINUS { $$.ival = $2.ival;}
     | UNSIGNED
     ;
```

23.6   PASSING VALUES DOWN THE PARSE TREE

During a bottom-up parse, information is usually passed up the parse tree. For example, when the following production is used in a reduce operation, a value derived from the two expr nonterminals on the right is passed to the expr nonterminal on the left:

```
expr : expr '+' expr   { $$.ival = $1.ival + $3.ival;}
```

In the parse tree, the `expr` nonterminal on the left sits above the two `expr` nonterminals on the right. Thus, here the information flow is up the tree. We also, however, can pass information down a tree. Consider the grammar in Figure 23.10. Suppose we would like the action in the E production to display the sum of the unsigned integers that B, C, and E generate. To do this, we have to pass the unsigned integers that B and C generate down to the action in the E production. The action in the E production is performed when the parser reduces with the E production. At that point in the parse, states for B, C, and the two unsigned integers from E are on the parsing stack with their corresponding values on the value stack. For example, the parsing and value stacks would look like the following when the B, C, and E integers are 6, 7, 8, and 9, respectively and 1, 2, 4, and 5 are the states that represent, respectively, B, C, and the two integers from E:

```
P$01245
```

```
V$* 6789
```

Note that the four values we want to sum are the four top values on the stack. We can access the top two in the action for the E production with `$1.ival` and `$2.ival`. `$2.ival` is the value of the second unsigned integer in the E production. Thus, this value is on top of the stack. `$1.ival` is right below it. The two other values we need—of B and C—are right below `$1.ival` on the stack. We can access them with `$0.ival` and `$-1.ival`. Decreasing numbers in the dollar notation refer to successively lower locations on the stack. Thus, the top four values on the stack from top down can be accessed with `$2.ival`, `$1.ival`, `$0.ival`, and `$-1.ival`. We can display the sum of these values when the E production is used in a reduce by defining the E production with

```
E   : UNSIGNED UNSIGNED { System.out.println($2.ival +
                          $1.ival + $0.ival + $-1.ival);}
```

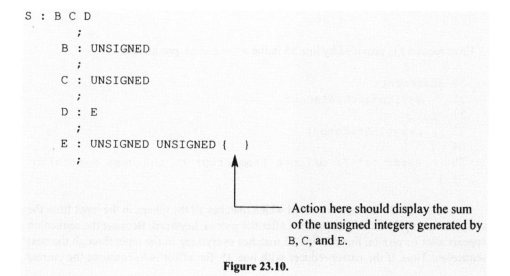

```
S : B C D
    ;
    B : UNSIGNED
    ;
    C : UNSIGNED
    ;
    D : E
    ;
    E : UNSIGNED UNSIGNED {   }
    ;
```

Action here should display the sum of the unsigned integers generated by B, C, and E.

Figure 23.10.

When we use the dollar notation with 0 and negative numbers, we are, in effect, passing information down the parse tree.

23.7 IMPLEMENTING S1y

Now that we know how to use yacc, it is easy to create a yacc-generated S1 compiler. We call this compiler compiler S1y. S1y.y, the yacc input file for the S1y compiler is in the J1 Software Package. It is also shown in Figure 23.11. Let us examine its notable features.

The S1y compiler uses the same symbol and code generator classes we used in the S1 compiler. To create the symbol table and code generator, it simply executes

```
137    S1SymTab st = new S1SymTab();
138    S1CodeGen cg = new S1CodeGen(outFile, st);
```

The lexical analyzer (i.e., token manager) in S1y (lines 154–250) works in the same way as the token manager in S1. In particular, getNextChar (lines 225–250) buffers each line and provides yylex with one character at a time. yylex records the starting and ending location of each token in the following variables:

```
111 int yybeginLine, yyendLine, yybeginColumn, yyendColumn;
```

On an error, the parser calls yyerror, passing it an error message. yyerror creates an new error message consisting of the message it is passed from the parser, the current token's image (in yytext), and the starting location (in yybeginLine and yybegin-Column). It then outputs this new message, after which it returns to the parser:

```
252 private void yyerror(String s)
253 {
254    String message =
255       s + " while scanning \"" + yytext + "\" on line " +
256       yybeginLine + " column " + yybeginColumn;
257    System.err.println(message);
258    outFile.println(message);
259 }
```

Error recovery is provided by line 35 in the statement production:

```
30 statement:
31    assignmentStatement
32 |
33    printlnStatement
34 |
35    error ';' // matches from error to the next semicolon
36 ;
```

error on line 35 is a yacc keyword which matches all the tokens in the input from the current token up to the token specified after the error keyword. Because the semicolon appears after error on line 35, line 35 matches everything in the input through the next semicolon. Thus, if the parser reduces with line 35, the effect is to consume the current

```
 1 // S1y.y yacc input file
 2 // To use, enter
 3 //    yacc -J S1y.y      (outputs compiler to Parser.java)
 4 //    javac Parser.java (compiles Parser.java)
 5 //    java Parser S1     (compiles S1.s source program)
 6 //    a S1.a             (assembles S1.a)
 7 //    e S1 /c            (executes S1.e with checking)
 8
 9 %{
10 import java.io.*;
11 import java.util.Scanner;
12 %}
13
14 %token ID
15 %token UNSIGNED
16 %token PRINTLN
17 //========================================================
18 %%
19 program:
20     statementList
21     { cg.endCode();}
22 ;
23 //---------------
24 statementList:
25     statementList statement
26 |
27     /* empty */
28 ;
29 //---------------
30 statement:
31     assignmentStatement
32 |
33     printlnStatement
34 |
35     error ';' // matches from error to the next semicolon
36 ;
37 //---------------
38 assignmentStatement:
39     ID
40     {
41       st.enter($1.sval);
42       cg.emitInstruction("pc", $1.sval);
43     }
44     '='
45     expr
46     ';'
47     { cg.emitInstruction("stav", "");}
48 ;
49 //---------------
50 printlnStatement:
51     PRINTLN
52     '('
53     expr
```

Figure 23.11.

```
54    {
55      cg.emitInstruction("dout", "");
56      cg.emitInstruction("pc","'\\n'");
57      cg.emitInstruction("aout", "");
58    }
59    ')'
60    ';'
61 ;
62 //---------------
63 expression:
64    expression
65    '+'
66    term
67    {cg.emitInstruction("add", "");}
68    |
69    term
70 ;
71 //---------------
72 term:
73    term
74    '*'
75    factor
76    {cg.emitInstruction("mult", "");}
77    |
78    factor
79 ;
80 //---------------
81 factor:
82    UNSIGNED
83    {cg.emitInstruction("pwc", $1.sval); }
84    |
85    '+'
86    UNSIGNED
87    {cg.emitInstruction("pwc", $2.sval); }
88    |
89    '-'
90    UNSIGNED
91    {cg.emitInstruction("pwc", "-" + $2.sval); }
92    |
93    ID
94    {
95      st.enter($1.sval);
96      cg.emitInstruction("p", $1.sval);
97    }
98    |
99    '('
100   expression
101   ')'
102 ;
103 //=====================================================
104 %%
105 Scanner inFile;
106 PrintWriter outFile;
```

Figure 23.11. *Continued.*

```
107 static final int EOF = 0;
108 String inputLine;
109 char currentChar = '\n';
110 int currentLine = 0, currentColumn = 0;
111 int yybeginLine, yyendLine, yybeginColumn, yyendColumn;
112 S1SymTab st;
113 S1CodeGen cg;
114 StringBuffer buffer;
115 //---------------
116 public static void main(String[] args) throws IOException
117 {
118   System.out.println("S1y compiler written by ...");
119
120   if (args.length != 1)
121   {
122     System.err.println("Wrong number cmd line args");
123     System.exit(1);
124   }
125
126   // build input and output file names
127   String inFileName  = args[0] + ".s";
128   String outFileName = args[0] + ".a";
129
130   // construct file objects
131   Scanner inFile = new Scanner(new File(inFileName));
132   PrintWriter outFile = new PrintWriter(outFileName);
133
134   outFile.println("; from S1y compiler written by ...");
135
136   // construct objects that make up the compiler
137   S1SymTab st = new S1SymTab();
138   S1CodeGen cg = new S1CodeGen(outFile, st);
139   Parser parser = new Parser();
140
141   // initialize instance variables in parser
142   parser.inFile = inFile;
143   parser.outFile = outFile;
144   parser.st = st;
145   parser.cg = cg;
146   parser.buffer = new StringBuffer();
147
148   // parse and translate
149   parser.yyparse();
150
151   outFile.close();
152 }
153 //---------------
154 private int yylex()
155 {
156   int kind;
157
158   // skip whitespace
```

Figure 23.11. *Continued.*

```
159   while (Character.isWhitespace(currentChar))
160     getNextChar();
161
162   yybeginLine = currentLine;
163   yybeginColumn = currentColumn;
164
165   // check for EOF
166   if (currentChar == EOF)
167   {
168     yytext = "<EOF>";
169     yyendLine = currentLine;
170     yyendColumn = currentColumn;
171     kind = currentChar;
172   }
173
174   else  // check for unsigned int
175   if (Character.isDigit(currentChar))
176   {
177     buffer.setLength(0);  // clear buffer
178     do
179     {
180       buffer.append(currentChar);
181       yyendLine = currentLine;
182       yyendColumn = currentColumn;
183       getNextChar();
184     } while (Character.isDigit(currentChar));
185     yytext = buffer.toString();
186     kind = UNSIGNED;
187   }
188
189   else  // check for identifier
190   if (Character.isLetter(currentChar))
191   {
192     buffer.setLength(0);  // clear buffer
193     do
194     {
195       buffer.append(currentChar);
196       yyendLine = currentLine;
197       yyendColumn = currentColumn;
198       getNextChar();
199     } while (Character.isLetterOrDigit(currentChar));
200     yytext = buffer.toString();
201
202     // check if keyword
203     if (yytext.equals("println"))
204       kind = PRINTLN;
205     else  // not a keyword so kind is ID
206       kind = ID;
207   }
208
209   else  // do this if preceding cases do not apply
210   {
```

Figure 23.11. *Continued.*

```
211      // use character itself as its kind value
212      kind = currentChar;
213      yyendLine = currentLine;
214      yyendColumn = currentColumn;
215      yytext = Character.toString(currentChar);
216      getNextChar();   // read one char beyond end of token
217    }
218
219    // return ParserVal obj containing yytext via yylval
220    yylval = new ParserVal(yytext);
221    // use return statement to return token kind
222    return kind;
223  }
224  //----------------
225  private void getNextChar()
226  {
227    if (currentChar == EOF)
228      return;
229    if (currentChar == '\n')              // need line?
230    {
231      if (inFile.hasNextLine())           // any lines left?
232      {
233        inputLine = inFile.nextLine();  // get next line
234
235        // output source line as comment
236        outFile.println("; " + inputLine);
237
238        inputLine = inputLine + "\n";   // mark line end
239        currentColumn = 0;
240        currentLine++;
241
242      }
243      else  // at EOF
244      {
245        currentChar = EOF;
246        return;
247      }
248    }
249    currentChar = inputLine.charAt(currentColumn++);
250  }
251  //--------------------
252  private void yyerror(String s)
253  {
254    String message =
255      s + " while scanning \"" + yytext + "\" on line " +
256      yybeginLine + " column " + yybeginColumn;
257    System.err.println(message);
258    outFile.println(message);
259  }
```

Figure 23.11. *Continued.*

statement—that is, the statement on which the error occurred through its terminating semicolon. The parser then continues the parse with the next statement.

The lexical analyzer places the image of each token in the `sval` field of the `Parser-Val` object. Thus, to access these images from within actions, we specify the `sval` field. For example, to access the operand for the `pwc` instruction in the following action, we use `$1.sval`:

```
83    { cg.emitInstruction("pwc", $1.sval); }
```

23.8   jflex

jflex is a lexical analyzer generator that produces lexical analyzers written in Java. We can use jflex to create the lexical analyzer for the S1y compiler instead of writing one by hand. But we can also use jflex to create a variety of useful stand-alone programs. A jflex input file consists of three parts (See Figure 23.12). By convention, we use the extension ".1" on jflex input files.

jflex outputs a file named `Yylex.java` that contains the `Yylex` class. Within this class is the lexical analyzer method `yylex`. The Java code in part 1 of the jflex input file is inserted at the beginning of `Yylex.java`, before the `Yylex` class. The Java code bracketed `%{` and `%}` in part 2 is inserted into the `Yylex` class. Part 3 contains regular expressions with actions. The Java code in `yylex` that jflex generates is based on these regular expressions and actions.

In jflex regular expressions, quotes are needed to mark a character as ordinary when it otherwise would be interpreted as special. For example, to represent a b followed by an asterisk, we use `b"*"`. We need the quotes around the asterisk because otherwise it

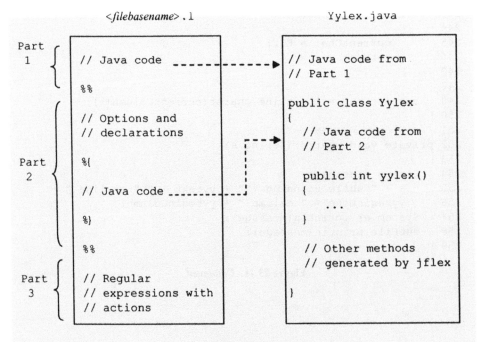

Figure 23.12.

would be interpreted as the zero-or-more operator. The backslash can also be used to mark the character that follows it as ordinary. For example, b* represents a b following by an ordinary asterisk. Within a character class (i.e., the square bracket construct), most of the characters that can be interpreted as special are not allowed. Thus, these characters within a character class are interpreted as ordinary even if they are not within quotes. For example [b* c] is the character class that consists of b, *, and c. Because it is within a character class, the asterisk here is interpreted as ordinary even though it is not enclosed in quotes. Figure 23.13 lists a variety of JavaCC regular expressions with their jflex equivalents.

Let us create a program using jflex that counts the words in a text file. Figure 23.14 is the jflex input file we need (note that the line numbers are not part of the jflex input file). The regular expression [^ \n\ r\ t] on line 26 specifies a set of characters. ^ is the complement operator. Thus, this expressions specifies the set of all characters except space, return, newline, and tab. That is, it is the set of all nonwhite-space characters. By following this expression with a + (the one-or-more operator), we get an expression that will match any word—that is, it will match any sequence of nonwhite-space characters. The lexical analyzer that jflex produces will always use the longest match possible. For example, if a file contains the word "yes", the lexical analyzer will match the entire word "yes", rather than just "y" or "ye". If more than one regular expression provides the longest match, the lexical analyzer will use the one listed first in part 3 of the jflex input file.

The period on line 27 is a wild card. It matches any single character except \ n. Thus, the regular expression . |\ n on line 27 matches any single character. However, the lexical analyzer will use it only if the expression on line 26 does not match the input. Suppose a file contains

```
yes no goodbye
```

JavaCC	jflex	Meaning
"b"	b	one b
("b")*`	b*	zero or more b's
"b""*"	b"*" or b*	b followed by ordinary asterisk
("b")+`	b+	one or more b's
("b")?`	b?	optional b
"b" "c"	bc	b followed by c
["b", "c"]	[bc]	b or c
"b"|"c"	b|c	b or c
~["b", "c"]	[^bc]	any character except b or c
["A"-"Z"]	[A-Z]	A through Z
"b" "|" "c"	b "|" c or b \ | c	b followed by | and c
["b", "|", "c"]	[b|c]	b or | or c
["-","b"]	[-b]	- or b
~[ ]	. |\ n	any character
("b"){ 2, 5}	b{ 2, 5}	two to five b's
	^	beginning of a line
	$	end of a line
	.	any character except newline
	b/c	b if followed by c

Figure 23.13.

```
 1 // Fig2314.l
 2 import java.io.*;
 3
 4 %%
 5
 6 %byaccj    // byacc/j compatibility mode
 7
 8 %{
 9 private int wordCnt = 0;
10 public static void main(String[ ] args) throws IOException
11 {
12    FileReader r = new FileReader(args[ 0] );
13
14    // create lexical analyzer
15    Yylex counter = new Yylex(r);
16
17    // call lexical analyzer
18    counter.yylex();
19
20    System.out.println("Word count = " + counter.wordCnt);
21 }
22 %}
23
24 %%
25
26 [^ \n\r\t] +   {wordCnt++;}          // match entire line
27 .|\n           {/* do nothing */} // match any single char
```

Figure 23.14.

Then the expression on line 26 will match yes, no, and goodbye, and the expression on line 27 will match all the white space. Each time the lexical analyzer matches a word with the expression on line 26, it increments wordCount. At the end of the scan, wordCount contains the number of words in the input file. This number is then displayed by line 20 in the main method.

yylex (the lexical analyzer) returns to its caller only if the action includes a return statement, or if the end of the file is reached. The actions on lines 26 and 27 do not include a return. Thus, once yylex() is called, it executes until the end of file is reached.

The declaration %byaccj on line 6 sets jflex to byacc/j compatibility mode. We have to set this mode if we are using jflex to produce a lexical analyzer for a parser generated by byacc/j. For our word count program, we are setting it only because the byacc/j compatibility mode is the easiest to use (in byacc/j compatibility mode, jflex creates a lexical analyzer that returns an int value, rather than a reference to a token object).

Suppose the jflex input file in Figure 23.14 is in the file Fig2314.l. To create the program from this file, enter

```
jflex Fig2314.l
```

jflex creates the corresponding Java program in a file named Yylex.java. To compile this program, enter

```
javac Yylex.java
```

To run the `Yylex` program with an input file `f.txt`, enter

```
java Yylex f.txt
```

The `Yylex` program will then count and display the number of words in `f.txt`.

Let us use jflex to create a program that inputs a text file and outputs the same file but with line numbers added. The required jflex input file is given in Figure 23.15. The expression on line 29 matches any single line of the input file. Its action outputs this line prefixed with its line number. `yytext()` is a method that jflex creates that returns the substring matched.

Now let us look at the jflex input file that creates the lexical analyzer we need for our Sly compiler (see Figure 23.16). The `Yylex` class that jflex creates has a `Yylex` constructor. However, this constructor is passed only the input file. We need a constructor that is passed both the input file and the parser object (the lexical analyzer needs the parser so it can access `yylval` and the token constants in the parser object). For this reason, we include a `Yylex` constructor in the jflex input file that receives both the input file and the parser (see lines 8–12 in Figure 23.16). This constructor calls the jflex-generated constructor, passing it the input file:

```
1  // Fig2315.1
2  import java.io.*;
3
4  %%
5
6  %byaccj      // byacc/j compatibility mode
7
8  %{
9  private int lineno = 1;
10 PrintWriter w;
11 public static void main(String[] args) throws IOException
12 {
13    FileReader r = new FileReader(args[0]);
14    PrintWriter w = new PrintWriter(args[1]);
15    Yylex numberFile = new Yylex(r);
16
17    // initialize instance variable in numberFile
18    numberFile.w = w;
19
20    // call lexical analyzer
21    numberFile.yylex();
22
23    w.close();
24 }
25 %}
26
27 %%
28
29 [^\n\r]+     {w.printf("%4d %s%n", lineno++, yytext());}
30 .|\n         {/* do nothing */}
```

Figure 23.15.

```
 1 // S11.1
 2 %%
 3
 4 %byaccj
 5
 6 %{
 7 private Parser parser;
 8 public Yylex(java.io.Reader inFile, Parser parser)
 9 {
10   this(inFile);
11   this.parser = parser;
12 }
13 %}
14
15 IDENT = [A-Za-z][A-Za-z0-9]*
16
17 %%
18
19 [ \n\r\t] { /* do nothing */ }   // discard whitespace
20 println   {
21                parser.yylval = new ParserVal(yytext());
22                return parser.PRINTLN;
23           }
24 [0-9]+    {
25                parser.yylval = new ParserVal(yytext());
26                return parser.UNSIGNED;
27          }
28 {IDENT}   {
29                parser.yylval = new ParserVal(yytext());
30                return parser.ID;
31          }
32         { // <- period at the start of this line
33                parser.yylval = new ParserVal(yytext());
34                return yytext().charAt(0);
35         }
```

Figure 23.16.

```
10    this(inFile);
```

It then saves the parser reference it is passed in `parser`, an instance variable in the lexical analyzer:

```
11    this.parser = parser;
```

The lexical analyzer can then access `yylval` using its `parser` variable. For example, on line 21, the lexical analyzer assigns to `yylval` the `ParserVal` object that contains in its `sval` field the image of the current token:

```
21                parser.yylval = new ParserVal(yytext());
```

It can also access the token constants defined in the parser. For example, on line 22, it accesses the `PRINTLN` token constant using `parser`:

```
22              return parser.PRINTLN;
```

On line 15, we set IDENT equal to a regular expression:

```
15 IDENT = [A-Za-z][A-Za-z0-9]*
```

We can then use IDENT in place of the regular expresson in part 3. For example, on line 28, we specify {IDENT} instead of the complicated regular expression it represents. We have to enclose IDENT in braces here to indicate that it represents a regular expression defined in part 2. Without the braces, the IDENT would match the string "IDENT", and not the string defined by the regular expression on line 15.

Line 19 discards whitespace. Line 32 starts with a period. Recall that the period matches every character except the newline character. Thus, line 32 will match anything the lines preceding it do not. For this case, the lexical analyzer returns the ASCII code of the matching character. yytext() provides the string containing the matching character. Thus, yytext().charAt(0) provides the matching character:

```
34              return yytext().charAt(0);
```

S1y.y uses our handwritten lexical analyzer. Let us copy S1y.y to S11y.y and then modify S11y.y so that it uses the jflex-generated lexical analyzer (S1y.y and S11y.y are both in the J1 Software Package). Figure 23.17 shows the new part 3 we need in

```
 1 // Part 3 of S11y.y
 2 FileReader inFile;
 3 PrintWriter outFile;
 4 S1SymTab st;
 5 S1CodeGen cg;
 6 private Yylex lexer;
 7
 8 public static void main(String[] args) throws IOException
 9 {
10   System.out.println("S11y compiler written by ...");
11
12   if (args.length != 1)
13   {
14     System.err.println("Wrong number cmd line args");
15     System.exit(1);
16   }
17
18   // build input and output file names
19   String inFileName  = args[0] + ".s";
20   String outFileName = args[0] + ".a";
21
22   // construct file objects
23   FileReader inFile = new FileReader(inFileName);
24   PrintWriter outFile = new PrintWriter(outFileName);
25
26   outFile.println("; from S11y compiler written by ...");
27
28   // construct objects that make up the compiler
```

Figure 23.17.

```
29   S1SymTab st = new S1SymTab();
30   S1CodeGen cg = new S1CodeGen(outFile, st);
31   Parser parser = new Parser();
32
33   // initialize instance variables in parser
34   parser.lexer = new Yylex(inFile, parser);
35   parser.inFile = inFile;
36   parser.outFile = outFile;
37   parser.st = st;
38   parser.cg = cg;
39
40   // parse and translate
41   parser.yyparse();
42
43   outFile.close();
44 }
45 //------------------
46 private int yylex()
47 {
48    int yyl_return = -1;
49    try
50    {
51       yyl_return = lexer.yylex();
52    }
53    catch (IOException e)
54    {
55       System.err.println(e);
56    }
57    return yyl_return;
58 }
59 //------------------
60 void yyerror(String s)
61 {
62    System.err.println(s);
63    outFile.println(s);
64 }
```

Figure 23.17: *Continued.*

S1ly.y. Line 34 creates the lexical analyzer object from the Yylex class that jflex creates:

```
34   parser.lexer = new Yylex(inFile, parser);
```

This object contains the yylex method that the parser has to call. yacc assumes yylex is a method within the parser. Thus, for the parser to call the yylex in Yylex, the yylex method in the parser (see lines 46–58) has to call the yylex method in Yylex (see line 51).

PROBLEMS

1. In a yacc-generated parser, a value can be passed up the parse tree and down the parse tree (see Section 23.6). Can a value be passed across the parse tree? That is, can a val-

ue associated with a symbol in a production be passed to a symbol or an action to the right in the same production?

2. Implement the yacc version of the S2 compiler.

3. Implement the yacc version of the S3 compiler.

4. Implement the yacc version of the S4 compiler.

5. Implement the yacc version of the S5 compiler.

6. Implement the yacc version of the G3 grep program in Chapter 18.

7. Implement the yacc version of the R1 compiler.

8. Implement the yacc version of the R1a compiler.

9. Implement the yacc version of the R1b compiler.

10. Implement the yacc version of the R1c compiler.

11. Implement the yacc version of the R1d compiler.

12. Implement the yacc version of the I1 compiler.

13. Implement the yacc version of the I2 compiler.

14. Implement the yacc version of the I3 compiler.

15. Implement the yacc version of the I4 compiler.

16. Implement the yacc version of the CI1 interpreter.

17. Implement the yacc version of the CI2 interpreter.

18. Implement the yacc version of the CI3 interpreter.

19. Implement the yacc version of the CI4 interpreter.

20. Create the parse table for the following grammar:

    S → bSc
    S → λ

    Determine the parse table yacc creates for this grammar by invoking yacc with the −v command line argument. Compare your parse table with yacc's table.

21. On line 52 in Figure 23.5, yylval is set to null if the current token is not an unsigned integer. Would it be better if yylval were assigned a reference to a parserVal object?

22. Are the values assigned to endLine and endColumn ever used in S1y.y (Figure 23.11)?

23. On line 96 in Figure 23.11, can yytext be used in place of $1.sval?

24. Create a program with jflex that outputs a file identical to the input file except that each run of spaces is replaced by a single space. Test your program with the input file p2324.txt in the J1 Software Package.

25. Create a program with jflex that capitalizes the first letter of every sentence. Test your program with the input file p2325.txt in the J1 Software Package.

26. Create a program with jflex that displays the character count, word count, and line count for the input file. Test your program with the input file p2326.txt in the J1 Software Package.

27. Create a program with jflex that displays the percent of words in the input file that contain at least one letter "e". Test your program with the input file p2327.txt in the J1 Software Package.

STACK INSTRUCTION SET

Opcode (hex)	Assembly Form	Name	Description
0	p x	Push	`mem[--sp] = mem[x];`
1	pc x	Push constant	`mem[--sp] = x;`
2	pr s	Push relative	`mem[--sp] = mem[bp + s];`
3	cora s	convert rel addr	`mem[--sp] = (bp + s)12;`
4	asp s	Add to sp	`sp = (sp + s)12;`
5	call x	Call	`mem[--sp] = pc; pc = x;`
6	ja x	Jump always	`pc = x;`
7	jct x	Jump count	`if (--ct) pc = x;`
8	jp x	Jump positive	`if (mem[sp++] > 0) pc = x;`
9	jn x	Jump negative	`if (mem[sp++] < 0) pc = x;`
A	jz x	Jump zero	`if (mem[sp++] == 0) pc = x;`
B	jnz x	Jump nonzero	`if (mem[sp++] != 0) pc = x;`
C	jodd x	Jump odd	`if (mem[sp++] % 2 == 1) pc = x;`
D	jzon x	Jump zero or neg	`if (mem[sp++] <= 0) pc = x;`
E	jzop x	Jump zero or pos	`if (mem[sp++) >= 0) pc = x;`
F0	ret	Return	`pc = mem[sp++];`

F1	add	Add	`temp = mem[sp++];`
			`mem[sp] = mem[sp] + temp;`
			`cy = carry;`

F2	sub		Subtract	`temp = mem[sp++];` `mem[sp] = mem[sp] - temp;`
F3	stav		Store addr/value	`temp = mem[sp++];` `mem[mem[sp++]] = temp;`
F4	stva		Store value/addr	`temp = mem[sp++];` `mem[temp] = mem[sp++];`
F5	load		Load	`mem[sp] = mem[mem[sp]];`
F6	awc w		Add word constant	`mem[sp] = mem[sp] + w;` `cy = carry;`
F7	pwc w		Push word constant	`mem[--sp] = w;`
F8	dupe		Dupe top of stack	`temp = mem[sp];` `mem[--sp] = temp;`
F9	esba		Estab base addr	`mem[--sp] = bp; bp = sp12;`
FA	reba		Restore base addr	`sp = bp; bp = mem[sp++];`
FB	zsp		Zero sp	`sp = 0;`

FC	cmps	y	Compare signed	`temp1 = mem[sp++];`
				`temp2 = mem[sp];`
				`mem[sp] =`
				`(y >> 2) & 1   if temp2 < temp1`
				`(y >> 1) & 1   if temp2 == temp1`
				`(y & 1)        if temp2 >  temp1`

FD	cmpu	y	Compare unsigned	`Same as scmp except` `unsigned comparison`

FE	rev		Reverse	`temp1 = mem[sp++];`
				`temp2 = mem[sp];`
				`mem[sp--] = temp1;`
				`mem[sp] = temp2;`

FF0	shll	z	Shift left logical	`mem[sp] << z; (inject 0's)`
FF1	shrl	z	Shift right logical	`mem[sp] >> z; (inject 0's)`
FF2	shra	z	Shift right arith	`mem[sp] >> z; (inject sign)`
FF3	neg		Negate	`mem[sp] = -mem[sp];`
FF4	mult		Multiply	`temp = mem[sp++];` `mem[sp] = mem[sp] * temp;`
FF5	div		Divide	`temp1 = mem[sp++];`

```
                                      temp2 = sp;
                                      if (temp1 == 0) ct = -1;
                                      else mem[sp] = mem[sp] / temp;
```

FF6	rem	Remainder	`temp = mem[sp++];`
			`if (temp == 0) ct = -1;`
			`else mem[sp] = mem[sp] % temp;`

FF7	addy	Add with carry	`temp = mem[sp++];`
			`mem[sp] = mem[sp] + temp`
			`  + carry;`
			`cy = carry;`

FF8	or	Bitwise incl or	`mem[sp] = mem[sp++]	mem[sp];`
FF9	xor	Bitwise excl or	`mem[sp] = mem[sp++] ^ mem[sp];`
FFA	and	Bitwise and	`mem[sp] = mem[sp++] & mem[sp];`
FFB	flip	Bitwise complement	`mem[sp] = ~mem[sp];`
FFC	cali	Indirect call	`temp = mem[sp]; mem[sp] = pc;` `pc = temp12;`
FFD	sct	Set ct	`ct = mem[sp++];`
FFE	rot	Rotate	rotate top 3 stack items up
FFF0	psp	Push sp	`temp = sp;` `mem[--sp] = temp;`
FFF1	bpbp	Bp to bp	`bp = mem[bp];`
FFF2	pobp	Pop bp	`bp = mem[sp++];`
FFF3	pbp	Push bp	`mem[--sp] = bp;`

FFF4	bcpy	Block copy	`temp1 = mem[sp++];`
			`temp2 = mem[sp++];`
			`while (ct--)`
			`  mem[temp2++] = mem[temp1++];`

FFF5	uout	Unsigned out	Output mem[sp++] as unsigned decimal number
FFF6	sin	String input	Input str to mem[sp++]
FFF7	sout	String output	Output str pointed to by mem[sp++
FFF8	hin	Hex input	Input hex number to mem[--sp]
FFF9	hout	Hex output	Output number in mem[sp++]
FFFA	ain	ASCII input	Input ASCII char to mem[--sp]
FFFB	aout	ASCII output	Output ASCII char in mem[sp++]

FFFC	din	Decimal input	Input decimal number (signed or unsigned) to mem[--sp]
FFFD	dout	Decimal output	Output number in mem[sp++] as a signed decimal number
FFFE	noop	No operation	None
FFFF	halt	Halt	Trigger halt

Instruction Fields

s:	12 rightmost bits of instruction,	$-4095 <= s <= 4095$
x:	12 rightmost bits of instruction,	$0 <= x <= 4095$
y:	8 rightmost bits of instruction,	$0 <= y <= 255$
z:	4 rightmost bits of instruction,	$0 <= z <= 15$
w:	Second word in instruction	$-32768 <= w <= 65535$

Registers

pc:	program counter register
sp:	stack pointer register
ct:	count register
cy:	carry register
bp:	base pointer register
temp:	designates a work register within the CPU
temp1:	designates a work register within the CPU
temp2:	designates a work register within the CPU

Note: An item followed by "12" in the instruction set descriptions denotes the 12 rightmost bits of that item. Main memory references (i.e., wherever "mem[...]" appears) use only the 12 rightmost of the address specified.

REGISTER INSTRUCTION SET

Opcode (hex)	Assembly Form		Name	Description
0	ld	x	Load	if (ar == 0) ac = mem[x]; else ac = mem[bp + x];
1	st	x	Store	if (ar == 0) mem[x] = ac; else mem[bp + x] = ac;

2	add	x	Add	if (ar == 0) ac = ac + mem[x];
				 else ac = ac + mem[bp+x];
				 cy = carry;

3	sub	x	Subtract	if (ar == 0) ac = ac - mem[x]; else ac = ac - mem[bp+x];
4	mult	x	Multiply	if (ar == 0) ac = ac * mem[x]; else ac = ac * mem[bp+x];

5	div	x	Divide	if (ar == 0) temp = mem[x];
				 else temp = mem[bp+x];
				 if (temp == 0) ct = -1;
				 else ac = ac / temp;

6	ldc	x	load constant	ac = x;
7	ja	x	Jump always	pc = x;
8	jp	x	Jump positive	if (ac > 0) pc = x;
9	jn	x	Jump negative	if (ac < 0) pc = x;
A	jz	x	Jump zero	if (ac == 0) pc = x;

B	jnz x	Jump nonzero	if (ac != 0) pc = x;
C	jzon x	Jump zero or neg	if (ac <= 0) pc = x;
D	jzop x	Jump zero or pos	if (ac >= 0) pc = x;
E	call x	Call procedure	mem[--sp] = pc; pc = x;
F0	ret	Return	pc = mem[sp++];
F1	ldi	Push indirect	ac = mem[ac];
F2	sti	Store indirect	mem[ac] = mem[sp++];
F3	push	Push onto stack	mem[--sp] = ac;
F4	pop	Pop from stack	ac = mem[sp++];
F5	asp w	Add to sp	sp = (sp + w)12;
F6	gsp	Get sp	ac = sp;
F7	ssp	Set sp	sp = ac;
F8	addw w	Add word	ac = ac + w; cy = carry;
F9	ldw w	load word	ac = w;
FA	esba	Estab base addr	mem[--sp] = bp; bp = sp12;
FB	reba	Restore base addr	sp = bp; bp = mem[sp++];
FC	cora	Convert rel addr	ac = (ac + bp)12;
FD	cmps y	Compare signed	temp = mem[sp++];
			ac =
			(y >> 2) & 1 if temp < ac
			(y >> 1) & 1 if temp == ac
			(y & 1) if temp > ac
FE	cmpu	Compare unsigned	Same as scmp but for unsigned numbers
FF0	shll z	Shift left logical	ac = ac << z; (inject 0's)
FF1	shrl z	Shift right logical	ac = ac >> z; (inject 0's)
FF2	shra z	Shift right arith	ac = ac >> z; (inject sign)
FF3	abs	Set absolute mode	ar = 0;
FF4	rel	Set relative mode	ar = 1;
FF5	neg	Negate	ac = -ac;
FF6	rem	Remainder	if (ac == 0) ct = -1;
			else ac = mem[sp++] % ac;
FF7	addy	Add with carry	ac = mem[sp++] + ac + cy; cy = carry;
FF8	or	Bitwise or	ac = ac | mem[sp++];
FF9	xor	Bitwise excl or	ac = ac ^ mem[sp++];

FFA	and	Bitwise and	ac = ac & mem[sp++];
FFB	flip	Bitwise complement	ac = ~ac;
FFC	cali	Call indirect	mem[--sp] = pc; pc = ac12;
FFD	sct	Set ct	ct = ac;
FFE	dct	Decrement ct reg	if (--ct == 0) pc++;
FFF0	sodd	Skip on odd	if (ac % 2 == 1) pc++;
FFF1	bpbp	Bp to bp	bp = mem[bp];
FFF2	pobp	Pop bp	bp = mem[sp++];
FFF3	pbp	Push bp	mem[--sp] = bp;

```
FFF4   bcpy   Block copy          temp = mem[sp++];
                                  while (ct--)
                                    mem[ac++] = mem[temp++];
```

FFF5	uout	Unsigned out	Output number in ac reg as unsigned decimal number
FFF6	sin	String input	Input str to address in ac
FFF7	sout	String output	Output str pointed to by ac
FFF8	hin	Hex input	Input hex number to ac reg
FFF9	hout	Hex output	Output number in ac in hex
FFFA	ain	ASCII input	Input ASCII char to ac reg
FFFB	aout	ASCII output	Output ASCII char in ac reg
FFFC	din	Decimal input	Input decimal number (signed or unsigned) to ac register
FFFD	dout	Decimal output	Output number in ac reg as a signed decimal number
FFFE	noop	No operation	None
FFFF	halt	Halt	Trigger halt

Instruction Fields

```
x:   12 rightmost bits of instruction,   0 <= x <= 4095  (FFF hex)
y:    8  rightmost bits of instruction,   0 <= y <= 255   (FF hex)
z:    4  rightmost bits of instruction,   0 <= z <= 15    (F dec)
w:   Second word in instruction       -32768 <= w <= 65535
```

Registers

```
pc:   program counter register
sp:   stack pointer register
```

```
ac:     accumulator register
ct:     count register
cy:     carry register
bp:     base pointer register
ar:     absolute/relative register
temp:   designates a work register within the CPU
```

Note: An item followed by "12" in the instruction set
        descriptions denotes the 12 rightmost bits of that item.
        Main memory references (i.e., wherever "mem[...]" appears)
        use only the 12 rightmost of the address specified.

REFERENCES

Alfred V. Aho, Monica. S. Lam, Rava Sethi, Jeffrey. D. Ullman. *Compilers Principles, Techniques & Tools.* Pearson Education, Inc., 2007.

Keith D. Cooper, Linda Torczon. *Engineering a Compiler.* Morgan Kaufmann Publishers, 2004.

Tom Copland. Generating Parsers with JavaCC. Centennial Books, 2007.

Anthony J. Dos Reis. Assembly Language and Computer Architecture Using C++ and Java. Course Technology, 2004.

Anthony J. Dos Reis, *Introduction to Programming Using Java.* Jones and Bartlett, 2010.

David Galles. *Modern Compiler Design.* Scott/Jones, Inc., 2005.

Gerwin Klein. *Jflex User's Manual.* http://jflex.de/manual.html.

Peter Linz. *An Introduction to Formal Languages and Automata.* Jones and Bartlett Publishers, 2006.

Robert McNaughton. *Elementary Computability, Formal Languages, and Automata.* Prentice-Hall, 1982.

Webb Miller. *A Software Tools Sampler.* Prentice-Hall, 1987.

Theodore S. Norvell. *Java Tutorial.* http://www.engr.mun.ca/~theo/JavaCC-Tutorial.

Theodore S. Norvell. *JavaCC FAQ.* http://www.engr.mun.ca/~theo/JavaCC-FAQ.

Thomas W. Parsons. *Introduction to Compiler Construction.* W.H. Freeman, 1992.

Susan H. Rodger, Thomas W. Finley. *JFLAP An Interactive Formal Languages and Automata Package.* Jones and Bartlett Publishers, 2006.

Axel T. Schreiner, H. George Friedman, Jr. *Introduction to Compiler Construction with Unix.* Prentice-Hall, 1985.

Michael Sipser, *Introduction to the Theory of Computation,* Course Technology, 2006.

INDEX

*, 8,9, 93, 208-209, 613
+, 11, 93, 208-209, 613
?, 11, 93, 208-209, 613
→, 21
$\overset{*}{\to}$, 22
$\overset{+}{\to}$, 22
|, 6, 333, 613
∩, 6
~, 6
^, 116, 121
#, 121
$, 121

a assembler/linker 272-275, 315, 435-438
absolute address, 270
abstract syntax tree, 96- 97
ac register, 516
accept configuration, 122
accept state, 466
action, 216
advance operation, 121
algorithm, 476
alphabet, 1
ambiguous grammar, 54
    eliminating ambiguity, 56-59, 84-86
    parsing with, 160-163
anonymous token, 341
ArgsTokenMgr class, 129-132
assembler, 272-275
assembler directive, 438
assembly language, 265-285
associativity, 85, 90-92

attribute, 237
autoboxing, 133
automaton, 124

backtrack, 118
Backus-Naur form, 92-94, 216, 588
backslash-quote, 410-416
base address, 440
base register, 440
base regular expressions, 13, 484
binary search, 326
Bison, 587
bottom-up parsing, 89, 561-584
    with ambiguous grammars, 566-569
    with left recursive grammars, 565, 566
    with right recursive grammars, 565, 566
bp register, 440

CII, 553-558
calling a function, 439
caret line, 282
cascaded assignment statment, 388-391
central processing unit (CPU), 265-266
choice point, 362-367
Chomsky's hierarchy, 107-112
code generator, 4
    in S1, 293
compiler, 3
compiler-compiler, 332
compiler-interpreter, 548, 553-558
complement, 6
compound statement, 42, 43
concatenation, 7-9

constant folding, 535-537
construction rule, 13, 484
consume, 187, 251
context-free grammar, 19-105
context-free language, 23-24
context-sensitive grammar, 110, 111
context-sensitive language, 110
context-sensitive production, 107-110
control structures, 399-431
corner substitution, 159

dead nonterminal, 68-70
depth-first order, 51, 117, 157
derivation, 21-23
deterministic finite automaton, 466-468
  converting NFA to DFA, 478-479
  converting to a regular expression, 468-472
    converting to a regular grammar, 479-482
    definition, 466-467
    Java code, 472-474
    minimal DFA, 488-493
deterministic parser, 119-120
direct interior recursion, 30-31
direct left recursion, 30-31
direct right recursion, 30-31
disambiguating a grammar, 161
disjoint sets, 6
distinguishable states, 488
do-not-reduce rule, 569-570
do-while statement, 407-408
dw directive, 269

e program, 273-275, 316-318
early-as-possible rule, 295
entry directive, 284-285
empty set, 5
equivalent grammars, 26
ERROR token, 343-344
error recovery, 424-430
escape sequence, 410-415
essentially non-contracting grammar, 97-100
exponent notation, 7
expression, 83-89
extended regular expression, 14
extern directive, 436-438
external reference, 436

finite automaton, 465-495
FIRST set, 137-140, 163-165
FOLLOW set, 143, 163-165
full left context, 108
full right context, 108

getNextToken(), 239, 241

getNextChar(), 239, 241
getToken(), 313, 389
grep, 499

handle, 563
handle production, 563

I1, 549-552
if statement, 403-407
immediate instruction, 267
in-parts technique, 30
indirect recursion, 30-33
indistinguishable states, 227
infix notation, 227
inherited attribute, 237
inherently ambiguous, 59
instructions
  add, 272
  aout, 270
  asp, 439
  call, 437-439
  cmps, 459
  cora, 440
  din, 283-284
  div, 278
  dout, 268
  dupe, 389-391
  esba, 440
  halt, 268,
  ja, 400
  jnz, 400
  jz, 400
  ld, 515
  ldc, 516
  mult, 278
  neg, 392
  p, 266
  pc, 267-269
  pr, 440, 447
  pwc, 268
  reba, 442
  ret, 439
  rot, 289-291
  sout, 281
  st, 515
  stav, 275-280
  sub, 278
interpreter, 547-559
  handling control structures, 552-553
  advantages, 558-559
intersection, 6
item, 572

J1 computer, 265-266
J1 Software Package, 265

JavaCC, 331-378, 411-424, 429-430
  choice algorithm, 367-370
  choice points, 362-367
  error recover, 429-430
  handling backslash-quote, 411-415
  input file, 337-344
  regular expressions, 333-337
  semantic lookahead, 372
  syntactic lookahead, 371
  spanning lines, 419-422
  SPECIAL_TOKEN block, 422
  suppressing warning messages, 377-378
  universal block, 416-418
jflex, 612-618

kernel item, 573
Kleene closure, 9

l program, 457-458
L-attributed grammar, 236-238
label, 270-272
LALR parsing, 584
lambda closure, 477, 511
lambda production, 22
  eliminating, 60-64
  parsing, 152-153, 192-196
  determining selection set, 142-145
language, 2
language-preserving transformation
  eliminating lambda productions, 60-64
  eliminating unit productions, 64-66
  eliminating useless productions, 66-70
  recursion conversions, 71-75
  substitution, 52-54
language defined by a context-free grammar G,
  23-25
language over an alphabet, 2
left-right factoring, 158-160, 201-204
left and right contexts, 107-109
left factoring, 157-160, 199-204
leftmost derivation, 51, 52
lex, 587
lexer, 4
lexical 587, analyzer generator
lexical analyzer, 4
library, 457
linker, 436
linking, 435-438
LL(1) grammar, 137-165
LR(1) parsing, 579-584
logic error, 3
lookahead, 116, 119, 241
LOOKAHEAD directive, 362-366, 371-372
lookahead problem, 241

machine language, 3, 266-268
metasymbol, 25
minimal DFA, 488-493
mnemonic, 269

noncontracting grammar, 97
noncontracting production, 97
nondeterministic finite automata, 474-476
  converting to DFA, 478-479
  converting a regular expression to a NFA,
    484-488
  converting a regular grammar to a NFA,
    482-483
  definition, 474
  using as an algorithm, 508-513
nonleading terminal, 126
nonrepeating list, 44-45
nonterminal alphabet, 20
nonterminal, 20
null string, 6- 7, 76-77
nullable nonterminal, 59-60

object module, 436
one-or-more operator (+), 11, 93, 208-209,
  333, 613
one-way street, 57
opcode, 266
operand, 266
optimization, 529-531
  constant folding, 535-537
  peephole, 540-543
  register allocation, 537-539
  reusing temps, 532-535
  using ldc, 531-532
options block, 338, 345-347

PAIRED, 15, 31-32, 34, 37-38, 495
PAIRED4, 38
parse, 115
parse table, 124
parse tree, 49-50
parser, 4
parser generator, 52, 331
Pascal, 195
pass in a compiler, 4
pattern matching, 508
pc register, 265
peephole optimization, 540-543
positive closure, 11
postfix notation, 227
precedence, 12, 84, 90-92
prefix notation, 227
production, 20-21
proper subset, 6
public directive, 437-438

pumping property of regular languages, 493-495

pumping property of context-free languages, 101-105

pure interpreter, 548

pushdown automaton, 124, 183

question mark operator, 11

R1, 517-526

R1a, 531-532

R1b, 531-532

R1c, 531-532

R1d, 531-532

R1e, 531-532

range checking, 408-410

readInt statement, 393-395

recursion, 71-76

   doing things backwards, 210-211

   interesting case, 257-261

   tail, 204-208

recursive-descent parsing, 185-211

recursive-descent translation, 215-261

reusing temporary variables, 532-535

reduce-order principle, 567

reduce/reduce conflict, 579

register, 265

register allocation, 537-539

register directive, 516

register instruction set, 516

register-oriented architecture, 515-516

regular expression, 13-16

   extended, 14

   grammar, 503

   JavaCC, 333-337

   limitations, 15

   jflex, 613

   actions. 344-348

regular grammar, 35-38

regular expression compiler, 499-503

regular language, 14, 36

reject configuration, 124

reject state, 466

relative address, 440

returning from a function, 403

right linear grammar, 35-36

rightmost derivation, 51-52

right recursion, 90

righty, 150-152

S1, 289-324

   specifications, 289-305

   translation grammar, 300-301

S1j, 348-358

S1y, 606-612

S2, 318-324

   specifications, 320-324

   translation grammar, 322-324

S3, 383-396

   specification, 396

S4, 430-431

   specification, 430-431

S5, 435-458

   specifications, 458

   translation grammar, 447-457

S6, 458-460

   specifications, 458-460

s-code, 554

s-machine, 554

scanner, 4

selection set, 139

semantic analyzer, 96

semantic lookahead, 372

semantic rule, 3

sentential form, 23

separate assembly, 435-438

set, 4-7

set-builder notation, 5

shift/reduce conflict. 577-578

SKIP block, 339

SLR(1) parsing, 570-576

SLR(1) language,

source language, 3

source program, 3

sp register, 265

span lines, 418-422

SPECIAL_TOKEN, block, 422-424

stack-parser generator, 171

stack instruction set, 268, 621-624

stack parser, 120-134

   table-driven, 171-182

start-up code, 436

start state, 466

start symbol, 20

state, 466

string, 2, 281-283

subset, 6

subset algorithm, 478-479

substitution, 52-54

symbol table, 292

symbolic address, 270

syntactic lookahead, 371-372

syntax-directed translation, 215

syntax diagram, 94-95

syntax error, 3

syntax rule,

synthesized attribute, 237

table-driven stack parser, 171-183

target language, 3

target program, 3
temp variable, 521
terminal alphabet, 20
terminal string, 20
terminal, 20
three-address code, 96-97
token, 3
TOKEN block, 339-341
TOKEN_MGR_DECLS block,
token chain,
    creating, 251-253
    using, 373-377
token manager, 3, 238-253
    for S2, 318
    for regular expressions, 501-503
token manager generator, 331
token trace, 253
    controlling from command line, 395
    generating, 313, 319
tokenizer, 4
top-down parsing, 89, 115-134
total alphabet, 20
transition, 466
translation grammar, 215
    for prefix expressions, 253-257
trap state, 467

Tripled, 33, 44, 105
Turing machine, 112

unary minus, 391-393
unary plus, 391-393
uniform stack parser, 172-175
union, 6
unit production, 64-66
    eliminating,
universal block, 416-418
universal set, 5
unreachable nonterminal, 66-67
unrestricted grammar, 11-112
useless nonterminal, 66-70

whatever-follows-left-follows-rightmost rule,
    145
while statement, 399-403
word, 266
word size, 266

yacc, 587-612

zero-or-more operator (*), 8-9, 93, 208-209,
    613
zero-or-one operator(?), 11, 93, 208-209, 613